Praise for Stephen W. Sears and *Gettysburg*

"Definitive . . . *Gettysburg* confirms [Sears's] reputation as a master story-teller." —*Los Angeles Times*

"A vivid, panoramic overview of the remarkable Union victory."
—*New York Times Book Review*

"*Gettysburg* has all the hallmarks of Sears's classic campaign studies: impressive research, beautiful writing, and sound judgments. This excellent book is destined to become the standard single-volume treatment of Gettysburg." —George C. Rable, author of *Fredericksburg! Fredericksburg!*

"A milestone . . . The best one-volume history of Gettysburg ever. The book brings to life every major aspect of this complex battle. It is the perfect book to read before a pilgrimage to the battlefield."
—*Baltimore Sun*

"An authoritative work of impressive scholarship . . . A dramatic story . . . Sears is one of the best historians of the period writing today . . . It surely is the best one-volume account available."
—*Nashville Tennessean*

"Impressively comprehensive . . . [Sears] offers remarkable detail to illuminate the significance of every action, however minute, then blends the fragments into a highly readable whole." —*Dallas Morning News*

"Captivating . . . provocative." —*Army*

"[An] ultimately rewarding campaign of a book."
—*St. Louis Post-Dispatch*

"Distinctly the best . . . Distinguished by thorough research and vivid, graceful prose."
—Robert K. Krick, author of
The Smoothbore Volley That Doomed the Confederacy

"Stephen Sears's *Gettysburg* will heighten his already high reputation as one of the very finest Civil War historians."
— **Albert Castel, author of**
Decision in the West: The Atlanta Campaign of 1864

"Sears is a master of presenting clear accounts of complex battle action, astute critiques of the successes and failures of commanders, and sound analyses of the strategic background." — *Providence Journal*

"Gracefully written . . . Any serious student of the Civil War will want to keep this authoritative volume close at hand." — *BookPage*

"A deliberate, perceptive assessment . . . The book's strength is the consistent and striking characterizations of many generals and commanding officers involved in the battle." — *Library Journal*

"A fine study, detailed and challenging, that complements such popular accounts of the battle as Bruce Catton's *Glory Road* and Shelby Foote's *The Stars in Their Courses*." — *Kirkus Reviews*

"Sears leaves no stone unturned in his reconstruction of the battle . . . Readers thrilled by the minute details of battlefield maneuvers will be thoroughly engaged." — *Booklist*

"As always, Sears writes beautifully, and his work is a pleasure to read."
— *Choice*

"An outstanding battle study . . . Absolutely indispensable."
— *Publishers Weekly*

BOOKS BY STEPHEN W. SEARS

The Century Collection of Civil War Art

Hometown U.S.A.

The Automobile in America

Landscape Turned Red: The Battle of Antietam

George B. McClellan: The Young Napoleon

The Civil War Papers of George B. McClellan: Selected Correspondence, 1860–1865

To the Gates of Richmond: The Peninsula Campaign

For Country, Cause & Leader: The Civil War Journal of Charles B. Haydon

Chancellorsville

Mr. Dunn Browne's Experiences in the Army: The Civil War Letters of Samuel W. Fiske

Controversies & Commanders: Dispatches from the Army of the Potomac

On Campaign with the Army of the Potomac: The Civil War Journal of Theodore Ayrault Dodge

Gettysburg

A Harvest of Death, Gettysburg, July 1863

Gettysburg

Stephen W. Sears

A Mariner Book

HOUGHTON MIFFLIN COMPANY   *Boston / New York*

First Mariner Books edition 2004

Copyright © 2003 by Stephen W. Sears
all rights reserved

Visit our Web site: www.hmhco.com

Library of Congress Cataloging-in-Publication Data

Sears, Stephen W.
Gettysburg / Stephen W. Sears.
p. cm.
Includes bibliographical references and index.
ISBN 0-395-86761-4
ISBN 0-618-48538-4 (pbk.)
ISBN 978-0-618-48538-3 (pbk.)
1. Gettysburg, Battle of, Gettysburg, Pa., 1863. I. Title.
E475.53.S43 2003
973.7'349—dc21   2002191259
Printed in the United States of America

Book design by David Ford

Maps by George Skoch

22 2022
4500842101

For Sally, in loving memory

Contents

Maps

Maps by George Skoch

Introduction

CAPTAIN SAMUEL FISKE, 14th Connecticut, soldier-correspondent for a New England newspaper, seated himself in the shade of an oak tree on a Pennsylvania hilltop and prepared "to task my descriptive powers" to report the fighting he expected would open at any moment. It was midafternoon, July 2, 1863. The enemy, wrote Fiske, "are arrogant and think they can easily conquer us with anything like equal numbers. We hope that in this faith he will remain, and give us final and decisive battle here. . . ."

Just a day earlier, in the Confederate camps a mile or so to the west, a foreign visitor, Lieutenant Colonel Arthur J. L. Fremantle of Her Majesty's Coldstream Guards, had observed in the Rebel army that same arrogant attitude. In his journal Fremantle made note that "the universal feeling in the army was one of profound contempt for an enemy whom they have beaten so constantly. . . ."

What happened in the three days of Gettysburg, July 1–3, 1863, was in some measure a result of that arrogance. To be sure, there was good reason for Robert E. Lee and the Army of Northern Virginia to be contemptuous of the Yankees. At Fredericksburg the previous December they had beaten them easily, and two months ago at Chancellorsville they had beaten them again, less easily this time but against longer odds. General Lee marched into Pennsylvania in the confident expectation of winning a third battle — but now in the enemy's country and with the promise of a considerably more decisive outcome.

The Confederacy was greatly in need of such a victory in that early summer of 1863. Vicksburg was besieged and almost certainly beyond saving, thereby endangering the entire Confederate position in the western theater. Lee gained Richmond's approval for the Pennsylvania expedition not in any expectation of changing matters at Vicksburg, but rather with the hope of offsetting disaster there by a compensating victory in the East — particularly a victory of real consequence won in the Northern heartland. The stakes were therefore high indeed.

Lee's Pennsylvania gambit, of course, failed, and failed dramatically, and the Army of Northern Virginia had to beat a hasty retreat back across the Potomac. For General Lee, Gettysburg was a defining defeat, and in the fourteen decades since 1863 much effort has been expended to try and explain it. For the most part Lee succeeded in shielding himself and his wartime actions (as the poet Stephen Vincent Benét put it) "From all the picklocks of biographers." Yet at Gettysburg Lee's actions were uniquely uncharacteristic of him and they spoke volumes. *Why* he did what he did can therefore be deciphered.

With so much attention paid to the losers, and for so long, it is easy to lose sight of the victors. When General Pickett was asked to explain the failure of his charge, he famously remarked, "I think the Union army had something to do with it." George Gordon Meade and the men of the Army of the Potomac came to Gettysburg without contempt for their opponents, and as a consequence they never deceived themselves about the impending battle.

General Meade's accomplishments on the Gettysburg battlefield were remarkable, all the more so considering that July 1 was his fourth day of army command. As it happened, Meade fought the battle defensively just as he intended (if not in the place he intended). His fighting men were as remarkable as he was. At Gettysburg, wrote Captain Fiske on July 4, "the dear old brave, unfortunate Army of the Potomac has redeemed its reputation and covered itself with glory. . . ."

Gettysburg proved to be both the largest battle fought during the war and the costliest. The two armies between them lost more than 57,000 men during the Pennsylvania campaign, including some 9,600 dead. Repelling the Confederates' offensive and stripping the initiative from General Lee were the immediate consequences. The longer-term effects would not be so easily seen or felt; still, Gettysburg marked the turning point of the war in the East. As Winston Churchill said of El Alamein, another turning point in another war, "Now this is not the end. It is not even the beginning of the end. But it is, perhaps, the end of the beginning."

GETTYSBURG

1   *We Should Assume the Aggressive*

JOHN BEAUCHAMP JONES, the observant, gossipy clerk in the War De-partment in Richmond, took note in his diary under date of May 15, 1863, that General Lee had come down from his headquarters on the Rappahannock and was conferring at the Department. "Lee looked thin-ner, and a little pale," Jones wrote. "Subsequently he and the Secretary of War were long closeted with the President." (That same day another Richmond insider, President Davis's aide William Preston Johnston, was writing more optimistically, "Genl Lee is here and looking splendidly & hopeful.")[1]

However he may have looked to these observers, it was certainly a time of strain for Robert E. Lee. For some weeks during the spring he had been troubled by ill health (the first signs of angina, as it proved), and hardly a week had passed since he directed the brutal slugging match with the Yankees around Chancellorsville. Although in the end the enemy had re-treated back across the Rappahannock, it had to be accounted the costli-est of victories. Lee first estimated his casualties at 10,000, but in fact the final toll would come to nearly 13,500, with the count of Confederate killed actually exceeding that of the enemy. This was the next thing to a Pyrrhic victory. Chancellorsville's costliest single casualty, of course, was Stonewall Jackson. "It is a terrible loss," Lee confessed to his son Custis. "I do not know how to replace him." On May 12 Richmond had paid its last respects to "this great and good soldier," and this very day Stonewall was being laid to rest in Lexington. Yet the tides of war do not wait, and General Lee had come to the capital to try and shape their future course.[2]

For the Southern Confederacy these were days of rapidly accelerating crisis, and seen in retrospect this Richmond strategy conference of May 15, 1863, easily qualifies as a pivotal moment in Confederate history. Yet the record of what was discussed and decided that day by General Lee, President Davis, and Secretary of War James A. Seddon is entirely blank. No minutes or notes have survived. Only in clerk Jones's brief diary entry are the participants even identified. Nevertheless, from recollections and from correspondence of the three men before and after the conference, it is possible to infer their probable agenda and to piece together what must have been the gist of their arguments and their agreements — and their decisions. Their decisions were major ones.[3]

It was the Vicksburg conundrum that triggered this May 15 conference. The Federals had been nibbling away at the Mississippi citadel since winter, and by mid-April Mississippi's governor, John J. Pettus, was telling Richmond, "the crisis in our affairs in my opinion is now upon us." As April turned to May, dispatches from the Confederate generals in the West became ever more ominous in tone. In a sudden and startling move, the Yankee general there, U. S. Grant, had landed his army on the east bank of the Mississippi below Vicksburg and was reported marching inland, straight toward the state capital of Jackson. On May 12 John C. Pemberton, commanding the Vicksburg garrison, telegraphed President Davis, "with my limited force I will do all I can to meet him. . . . The enemy largely outnumbers me. . . ." Pemberton offered little comfort the next day: "My forces are very inadequate. . . . Enemy continues to reenforce heavily."

Grant's march toward Jackson threatened to drive a wedge between Pemberton in Vicksburg and the force that Joseph E. Johnston was cobbling together to go to Pemberton's support. On May 9 Johnston had been put in overall charge of operations against the Federal invaders of Mississippi, and by the 13th Johnston had grim news to report. He had hurried ahead to Jackson, he said, but the enemy moved too fast and had already cut off his communication with Vicksburg. "I am too late" was his terse verdict.[4]

Thus the highly unsettling state of the war in Mississippi as it was known to President Davis and Secretary Seddon as they prepared to sit down with General Lee to try and find some resolution to the crisis. To be sure, the Vicksburg question had been agitating Confederate war councils since December, when the Yankees opened their campaign there to clear the Mississippi and cut off the westernmost states of the Confederacy. At the same time, a second Federal army, under William Rosecrans, threatened Chattanooga and central Tennessee. For the moment, Braxton Bragg's Army of Tennessee had achieved a standoff with Rosecrans. Bragg, however, could scarcely afford to send much help to threatened Vicksburg. The defenders of the western Confederacy were stretched very close to the breaking point.

Early in 1863, a "western concentration bloc" within the high councils of command had posed the argument for restoring the military balance in the West by dispatching reinforcements from the East. Most influential in this bloc were Secretary of War Seddon, Senator Louis T. Wigfall of Texas, and Generals Joe Johnston, P.G.T. Beauregard, and one of Lee's own lieutenants, James Longstreet. It was Longstreet, in fact, who had been the first to offer a specific plan to rejuvenate affairs in the West.

In February, responding to a Federal threat, Lee had detached Longstreet from the Army of Northern Virginia and sent him with two of his four First Corps divisions to operate in southeastern Virginia. Taking fresh perspective from his new assignment, casting his eye across the strategic landscape, Longstreet proposed that the First Corps, or at the very least those two divisions he had with him, be sent west. It was his thought to combine these troops, plus others from Joe Johnston's western command, with Bragg's army in central Tennessee for an offensive against Rosecrans. Once Rosecrans was disposed of, the victorious Army of Tennessee would march west and erase Grant's threat to Vicksburg. All the while, explained Longstreet rather airily, Lee would assume a defensive posture and hold the Rappahannock line with just Jackson's Second Corps.[5]

General Lee was unimpressed by this reasoning. He thought it likely that come spring the Federal Army of the Potomac would open an offensive on the Rappahannock, and he had no illusions about trying to hold that front with only half his army. Should the enemy not move against him, he said, he intended to seize the initiative himself and maneuver to the north — in which event he would of course need all his troops. In any case, Lee believed that shifting troops all across the Confederacy would achieve nothing but a logistical nightmare. As he expressed it to Secretary Seddon, "it is not so easy for us to change troops from one department to another as it is for the enemy, and if we rely upon that method we may always be too late."[6]

Longstreet was not discouraged by rejection. After Chancellorsville — from which battle he was absent, there having not been time enough to bring up his two divisions to join Lee in repelling the Federals — he stopped off in Richmond on his way back to the army to talk strategy with Secretary Seddon. In view of the abruptly worsening prospects at Vicksburg, Longstreet modified his earlier western proposal somewhat. As before, the best course would be to send one or both of the divisions with him — commanded by George Pickett and John Bell Hood — to trigger an offensive against Rosecrans in Tennessee. But after victory there, he said, a march northward through Kentucky to threaten the Northern heartland would be the quickest way to pull Grant away from Vicksburg.

More or less the same plan was already familiar to Seddon as the work of General Beauregard, who from his post defending Charleston enjoyed exercising his fondness for Napoleonic grand designs. Emboldened by these two prominent supporters of a western strategy, and anxious to do something — anything — about the rapidly deteriorating situation in Mississippi, Secretary Seddon telegraphed Lee on May 9 with a specific proposal of his own. Pickett's First Corps division was just then in the vicinity of Richmond; would General Lee approve of its being sent with all speed to join Pemberton in the defense of Vicksburg?[7]

Lee's response was prompt, sharply to the point, and (for him) even blunt. He telegraphed Seddon that the proposition "is hazardous, and it becomes a question between Virginia and the Mississippi." He added, revealing a certain mistrust of Pemberton's abilities, "The distance and the uncertainty of the employment of the troops are unfavorable." Lee followed his telegram with a letter elaborating his arguments. He pointed out that it would be several weeks before Pickett's division could even reach Vicksburg, by which time either the contest there would already be settled or "the climate in June will force the enemy to retire." (This belief — misguided, as it turned out — that Grant's Yankees could not tolerate the lower Mississippi Valley in summer was widespread in the South.) Lee then repeated his tactful but pointed prediction that Pickett's division, if it ever did get there, would be misused by General Pemberton: "The uncertainty of its arrival and the uncertainty of its application cause me to doubt the policy of sending it."

But Lee's most telling argument was framed as a virtual ultimatum. Should any troops be detached from his army — indeed, if he did not actually receive reinforcements — "we may be obliged to withdraw into the defenses around Richmond." He pointed to an intelligence nugget he had mined from a careless Washington newspaper correspondent to the effect that the Army of the Potomac, on the eve of Chancellorsville, had counted an "aggregate force" of more than 159,000 men. "You can, therefore, see the odds against us and decide whether the line of Virginia is more in danger than the line of the Mississippi." When Mr. Davis was shown Lee's response, he endorsed it, "The answer of Gen. Lee was such

Robert E. Lee was photographed by Julian Vanerson in
Richmond in 1863. (Library of Congress)

as I should have anticipated, and in which I concur." Pickett's division
was not going to Vicksburg.[8]

YET THAT HARDLY marked the end of the debate. On the contrary,
Secretary Seddon's proposition for Pickett initiated a week-long series
of strategy discussions climaxed by Lee's summons to the high-level conference in Richmond on May 15. To prepare for the Richmond conference, Lee called Longstreet to the army's Rappahannock headquarters at
Fredericksburg, and over three days (May 11–13) the two of them intensely examined grand strategy and the future course of the Army of
Northern Virginia.

With the death of Stonewall Jackson, Lieutenant General James Longstreet was not only Lee's senior lieutenant but by default his senior adviser. The nature of their relationship in this period would be much obscured and badly distorted by Longstreet's self-serving postwar recollections. The truth of the matter, once those writings by "Old Pete" are taken with the proper discount — and once the fulminations of Longstreet's enemies who inspired those writings are discounted as well — is that on these May days the two generals reached full and cordial agreement about what the Army of Northern Virginia should do next. The evidence of their agreement comes from Old Pete himself.[9]

On May 13, at the conclusion of these discussions, Longstreet wrote his ally Senator Wigfall to explain the strategic questions of the moment and what he and Lee had agreed upon in the way of answers. A second Longstreet letter, written in 1873 to General Lafayette McLaws, covers the same ground with a candor and a scrupulousness too often absent in the recollections dating from Longstreet's later years.[10]

In their discussions the two generals pondered the army's past record and future prospects. In nearly a full year commanding the Army of Northern Virginia, Lee had fought five major battles or campaigns. By any measure, his record was dazzling. Still, in the context of the Confederacy's eventual survival, it was a record (as Longstreet phrased it) of "fruitless victories; . . . even victories such as these were consuming us, and would eventually destroy us. . . ."

On the Virginia Peninsula, in the summer of 1862, Lee had driven George McClellan away from the gates of Richmond, only to see the Federals reach a safe haven at Harrison's Landing on the James. At Second Manassas in August John Pope became Lee's victim, but Pope's beaten army managed to escape without further damage into the defenses of Washington. Sharpsburg, on September 17, could perhaps be claimed by Lee as a narrow tactical victory, but his army was too weakened, and McClellan's Federals too numerous, to continue the fighting to a showdown. Against Ambrose Burnside at Fredericksburg in December, and then against Joe Hooker at Chancellorsville in May, Lee won signal victories. But both times a larger victory eluded him when the enemy escaped back across the Rappahannock. Lee was heard to say that Chancellorsville depressed him even more than Fredericksburg had: "Our loss was severe, and again we had gained not an inch of ground and the enemy could not be pursued." What he wanted in future was battle on his terms, on ground of his choosing, with no barriers to a final outcome. For that he had formed a plan.[11]

Longstreet brought up the matter of Vicksburg and the dispatching of reinforcements to the western theater. Lee reiterated his objection to putting any of his men directly into Vicksburg under Pemberton's command. In writing of this to Senator Wigfall, Longstreet was surely reflecting Lee's blunt opinion when he remarked, "Grant seems to be a fighting man and seems to be determined to fight. Pemberton seems not to be a fighting man." Should Pemberton fail to take the battle to Grant but instead allow himself and his garrison to be penned up in Vicksburg, Longstreet went on, "the fewer the troops he has the better." Should Richmond decide to *order* Lee to send troops from Virginia, however, the proper course would be to give them to Bragg or Joe Johnston for an invasion of Kentucky. Only in that event was Grant likely to be drawn away from Vicksburg.

This latter western strategy was of course what Longstreet had recently been advocating with such fervor, but now Old Pete underwent an abrupt change of heart. This seems to have been entirely by Lee's persuasion. "When I agreed with the Secy & yourself about sending troops west," Longstreet confessed to Wigfall, "I was under the impression that we would be obliged to remain on the defensive here." Now, he continued, there "is a fair prospect of forward movement. That being the case we can spare nothing from this army to re-enforce in the West." Indeed, he called on Wigfall to support the sending of any available reinforcements directly to General Lee.

James Longstreet, in short, was made a convert to a new faith. What Lee confided to him was a plan to march north through Maryland and into Pennsylvania, and Old Pete declared himself enthusiastically in favor of the idea. "If we could cross the Potomac with one hundred & fifty thousand men," he speculated to Senator Wigfall, it should at least bring Lincoln to the bargaining table; "either destroy the Yankees or bring them to terms." He closed his letter with the observation that in a day or two Lee would be in Richmond "to settle matters. . . . I shall ask him to take a memorandum of all points and settle upon something at once."[12]

"We should assume the aggressive," Lee had written Mr. Davis just a month earlier. He meant by that, in modern military terminology, seizing the strategic initiative. This idea was at the very core of Robert E. Lee's generalship. It became his watchword the moment he first took command of the Army of Northern Virginia, back in June 1862. He recognized then — and it was even more obvious now, a year later — the stark reality that in the ever more straitened Confederacy his army would never achieve parity with the enemy's army. On campaign he would always be the underdog. Therefore he must assume the strategic aggressive whenever he could, and by marching and maneuver disrupt the enemy's plans, keep him off balance, offset his numbers by dominating the choice of battlefield. It must be Lee's drum the enemy marched to.

Taking the strategic aggressive on campaign did not necessarily imply an equal tactical aggressive when the chosen battlefield was reached. Indeed, in the best execution of the idea, it would mean just the opposite — marching and maneuvering so aggressively on campaign that Lee might accept battle or not, as he chose, with his opponent forced to give battle — to attack — at a time and in a place of Lee's choosing. According to Longstreet, this was precisely his and Lee's "train of thought and mutual understanding" for the proposed Pennsylvania campaign. "The ruling ideas of the campaign may be briefly stated thus," Longstreet summed up. "Under no circumstances were we to give battle, but exhaust our skill in trying to force the enemy to do so in a position of our own choosing."[13]

There was of course nothing unique or even novel about the "ruling ideas" of this strategic and tactical plan. It was exactly what *any* field general always hoped and dreamed of achieving — to maneuver the enemy into attacking him in circumstances and on defensive ground of his own selection. Already twice in this war Lee (with Longstreet's crucial participation) had come close to achieving the ideal. Second Manassas was fought defensively on ground chosen by the Confederates, and won by a breakthrough counterattack against the enemy's flank. It was marred only by the Federals' escape into the nearby Washington fortifications. At Fredericksburg, allowed by the bumbling Ambrose Burnside to defend a virtually impregnable position, Lee's army inflicted almost three times the casualties it suffered. Yet the defeated Burnside was able to retreat back across the Rappahannock without further harm. Next time, on the Federals' home ground in Pennsylvania, there should be opportunity for maneuver and for a greater and perhaps decisive victory.

In his later writings, flailing against the snares of those who would label him scapegoat for the campaign, Longstreet implied that Lee *promised* him he would fight tactically only a defensive battle in Pennsylvania. "Upon this understanding my assent was given . . . ," said Old Pete loftily. That of course was nonsense. No commanding general is obliged to promise a subordinate any future action, particularly anything like this that would tie his hands. Lee said as much when asked about it after the war. He "had never made any such promise, and had never thought of doing any such thing," was his reply, and he termed the idea "absurd."

So it was. A younger and more rational Longstreet, in May 1863, was confident that General Lee had heard him out and that they were in full agreement on the right and proper course — to (ideally) maneuver the Yankees into committing another Fredericksburg on any disputed ground in Pennsylvania. Longstreet even volunteered his First Corps to handle the defense of that ground (as he had at Fredericksburg), leaving Lee and the rest of the army free to fall upon the Army of the Potomac and destroy it.[14]

WHETHER OR NOT General Lee took "a memorandum of all points" with him to Richmond, as Longstreet suggested, he surely went well prepared to argue his case. On May 14 he boarded the Richmond, Fredericksburg & Potomac's afternoon train to the capital, and on Friday the 15th presented himself at the War Department in the old Virginia Mechanics Institute building on Franklin Street to confer on future strategy with President Davis and Secretary of War Seddon.

Like General Lee, the president was suffering poor health that spring, and for much of the past week he had been too ill to leave the Confederate White House. It was a measure of the importance of the meeting that he willed himself to attend at all. Davis looked pale and drawn, and in the days following he would have to return to his sickbed. The strain of the crisis marked Seddon as well. A few days earlier, clerk Jones had described the war secretary as "gaunt and emaciated. . . . He looks like a dead man galvanized into muscular animation."

Secretary Seddon, however, was both determined and dedicated, and it may be assumed he came to this conference with Vicksburg still very much on his mind. Even though the decision had already been made not to add Pickett's division directly to Vicksburg's defenders, the situation in Mississippi remained the Confederacy's overriding crisis of the moment. James Seddon had not given up the thought of assistance of some sort to try and save Vicksburg from the Yankees. Jefferson Davis would have been at the least a sympathetic listener; Mississippi was his native state.

"Hour of trial is upon us" was the latest stark message from Mississippi's Governor Pettus. "We look to you for assistance. Let it be speedy." At the same time, the editors of the *Jackson Mississippian* petitioned Richmond with the claim that "three-fourths in the army and out" were doubtful of General Pemberton's abilities and even of his loyalty. (It was widely noticed that Pemberton had been born and raised in Pennsylvania.) However unjust it might seem, they said, they wanted the gen-

9

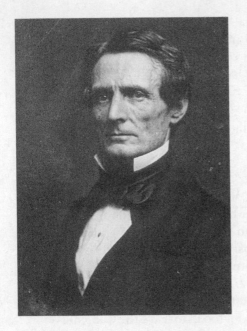

President Jefferson Davis, left, and his able secretary of war, James A. Seddon. (Chicago Historical Society–Museum of the Confederacy)

eral immediately replaced. "Send us a man we all can trust," pleaded the editors, and they nominated either General Beauregard or General Longstreet for the post. Mr. Davis had replied, "Your dispatch is the more painful because there is no remedy. Time does not permit the changes you propose if there was no other reason. . . ."[15]

As for the immediate military situation in the West, no news had reached Richmond more recent than Pemberton's complaints about being outnumbered and Joe Johnston's admission that the enemy had cut off his effort to reach Vicksburg with a relief column. The only reinforcements then on their way from the East were three brigades — some 7,700 men — that Secretary Seddon had wrangled out of General Beauregard in Charleston. Seddon, then, would probably have focused any such discussion at this War Department conference on the earlier plan to reinforce Bragg's Army of Tennessee with troops from Lee's army so as to take the offensive in central Tennessee, and from there to strike through Kentucky. The hope thereby was to force Grant to turn to meet this threat to the Northern heartland.

A month earlier, General Lee had addressed just this proposal from the western concentration bloc, stating the basic difficulty with any such reinforcement scheme. "I believe the enemy in every department outnumbers us," he had written, "and it is difficult to say from which troops can with safety be spared." He certainly did not see how the Army of Northern Virginia could safely spare any troops. As he had been reporting almost daily to Richmond ever since Chancellorsville, all his intelligence evidence suggested that the Army of the Potomac was being reinforced. As recently as May 11, Lee's count of these reinforcements had reached 48,000. This promised to make good the Federals' Chancellorsville losses and then some. "It would seem, therefore," Lee had explained to Davis, "that Virginia is to be the theater of action, and this army, if possible, ought to be strengthened."

Thus the simple, convincing argument, presumably laid out in his typically quiet, authoritative way by the Confederacy's most successful general: Any attempt to turn back the tide at Vicksburg as Seddon was proposing was bound to put Lee's army in Virginia at unacceptable risk. Possibly Lee clinched his argument with some variation on what he had said to Seddon back on May 10: "You can, therefore, see the odds against us and decide whether the line of Virginia is more in danger than the line of the Mississippi."

Robert E. Lee was not by nature a pessimist, however, and he must surely have offered Davis and Seddon some words of counsel on the Vicksburg dilemma. He had done so before. General Johnston, he had said in April, should "concentrate the troops in his own department" and then promptly "take the aggressive." As Lee saw it, it was essential in Mississippi (just as it was in Virginia) to seize the strategic initiative and thereby baffle the designs of the enemy. Act first, before the enemy could act. Unfortunately, it appeared that Joe Johnston had not taken this advice (or could not). Now it looked as if he and Pemberton, separately, would have to play out their dangerous game with the cards each had been dealt.[16]

Armchair critics would come to call Lee's position on Vicksburg parochial. His strategic focus, it was said, bore solely on the Virginia theater, at the expense of the failing Confederate war in the West. Yet at this strategy conference in mid-May of 1863 Lee could scarcely have taken any other stance. His intelligence sources told of his opponent, Joe Hooker, being heavily reinforced. If that pointed to a renewed Federal campaign, as seemed likely, it could be met with no better odds than before, which had been bad enough. The return of Longstreet's two divisions to the Rappahannock front did little more than make up the army's

Chancellorsville losses. Robert E. Lee was right. The choice for President Davis was Virginia or Mississippi, and just then there were simply no troops to spare in Virginia. It was in truth a Hobson's choice.[17]

Turn to the Virginia front, however, and Lee believed there was a meaningful choice to be made. In effect, he offered an antidote to the sickly prognosis for the West. In laying out for Davis and Seddon his plan to march north, Lee would not have been unveiling something new and unexpected. Back in April, before Hooker launched his Chancellorsville offensive, Lee had announced a May 1 deadline for an offensive of his own — into Union territory. "The readiest method of relieving pressure upon Gen. Johnston," he had pointed out to Seddon in a reference to the western theater, ". . . would be for this army to cross into Maryland." As a preliminary, he had ordered strong raiding parties into the Shenandoah Valley to disrupt Federal communications and to stockpile supplies for the army's planned advance. At the same time, substantial supplies to support the movement were being gathered by Longstreet in southeastern Virginia. The operation there took on the markings of a giant victualing expedition, and collected enough bacon and corn to feed the army for two months. As it happened, Hooker's attack had forestalled these preparations, but a foundation was laid. Now Lee proposed to build on it.[18]

IF IT IS NOT possible to list the precise arguments Lee may have used that day to gain approval for his Pennsylvania campaign, it is possible, through his dispatches and recollections, to record his thinking on the subject.

It had become General Lee's basic premise that his army should not — indeed could not — remain much longer on the Rappahannock. In the first place, it was not a good setting for yet another battle. At Chancellorsville, even in losing, Hooker had certainly improved on Burnside's effort of the previous December, and Lee had to wonder if he could fight off a third attempt. "To have lain at Fredericksburg," he would later say, "would have allowed them time to collect force and initiate a new campaign on the old plan." Even if he managed to repel a new effort, there was no promise of a decisive outcome. The Yankees would simply pull back across the river again and be out of reach.

In the second place, his men in their Rappahannock camps were hungry. They had been hungry there since the first of the year, and it appeared they were going to be hungry for some time to come if they remained there. In the Army of Northern Virginia the only occasion for full stomachs thus far in 1863 had been immediately after Chancellorsville, when they feasted on the contents of thousands of captured or abandoned Yankee knapsacks. Even now Lucius Northrop, the Confederacy's peevish commissary-general of subsistence, was drafting yet another rationing edict — a quarter of a pound of bacon daily for garrison troops, a third of a pound for those in camp in the field, raised to half a pound only when on active campaign. This was to be in force, Northrop said, "until the new bacon comes in" in the fall.

For the Army of Northern Virginia, the paltry rationing imposed by Richmond was made all the worse by a tenuous supply line. The decrepit Richmond, Fredericksburg & Potomac was not up to the task of supplying an army on the Rappahannock. This had nearly left Lee in dire straits at Chancellorsville. He was forced to accept battle there short 20,000 men, including Longstreet's two divisions absent on their victualing duty in southeastern Virginia. It was not an experience he intended to repeat. The most expedient way to solve this particular problem, he decided, was to live off the enemy's country. Lee was going to requisition the burdened barns and smokehouses of Pennsylvania to feed his army.[19]

There were two additional, probable factors behind Lee's determination to march north that he would not have mentioned to Davis and Seddon that day. They were private thoughts pertaining to his own soldierly judgments, thoughts he did not directly articulate but which surely colored his thinking. One had to do with Lee's previous invasion of enemy country, in September 1862. He had intended then, as he intended now, to seek a favorable battleground in Pennsylvania. But McClellan had trumped him, forcing a battle at Sharpsburg in Maryland before Lee was ready for it. Lee had liked to think he understood his timid opponent, and this abrupt resolution of McClellan's seemed totally out of character. Over the winter, said his aide Charles Marshall, "Gen. Lee frequently expressed his inability to understand the sudden change in McClellan's tactics."

Then, just this spring, Lee had finally learned the truth of the matter. He read in Northern newspapers of McClellan testifying to a congressional committee that "we found the original order issued to General D. H. Hill by direction of General Lee, which gave the orders of march for their whole army, and developed their intentions." To Lee's mind that must have explained a great deal. He had not been wrong in his calculations for that campaign after all. It was Fate or simply sheer misfortune, in the form of the infamous Lost Order, that had checked his plans at Sharpsburg. He might now march forth across the Potomac with renewed confidence in his military judgment. That was essential. There was sure to be great risk in thus marching into enemy country, and the general commanding would require a full measure of self-confidence to carry it off.[20]

The second factor was connected to the first. General Lee always formed his designs with the opposing general very much in mind. In September 1862 he had led his invading army into Maryland with the failings of George McClellan in his thoughts. At Chancellorsville he had beaten "Fighting Joe" Hooker, whom he privately referred to contemptuously as "Mr. F. J. Hooker," and now was looking forward to beating him again. Lee believed there was every chance that Hooker was demoralized by his recent defeat and would not be at his best in a second meeting. Hooker's army, too, would likely be suffering from demoralization. Nearly 6,000 Yankee soldiers had surrendered at Chancellorsville, hardly a sign of high morale.

Lee's insight into the Army of the Potomac was sharpened by his reading in the Northern papers of numerous regiments of two-year men and thousands of nine-month short-termers being mustered out that spring. It was said these losses would be made good by the newly instituted conscription in the North. However that might be, Lee expected all this to produce a good deal of confusion in the Federal ranks in the coming weeks, and he wanted to take advantage of it. In short, the Army of the Potomac, and its commander, looked just then to be fair game, another good reason for assuming the aggressive.[21]

To General Lee, then, the choice on this 15th of May was plain and the case unequivocal. He could not properly subsist his army on the Rappahannock line, and he had no wish to fight another battle there. The army needed to move. He had already made it plain to Secretary Seddon, in opposing sending Pickett to Vicksburg, that if his army was weakened — indeed, if it was not strengthened — he would probably have to fall back into the Richmond defenses. To do so (as he no doubt now pointed out) would be to surrender the strategic initiative and submit to slow death by siege. The options were clear, Lee would say: to "stand a siege, which must ultimately have ended in surrender, or to invade Pennsylvania." To go on the aggressive, to cross the Potomac and march on Pennsylvania, opened up all manner of possibilities.

First of all, it would pull the Army of the Potomac out of its fortified lines and disarrange all its plans for a summer offensive in Virginia. That alone would justify a march north. At the same time, it would free Lee of the defensive strictures of the Rappahannock line and allow him to maneuver at will. Once across the Potomac hungry Rebels could feast in a land of plenty, and the ravaged fields and farms of Virginia would have an opportunity for renewal.

In the larger scheme of things, Northern morale and will were sure to be shaken by the prospect of a Confederate army — a winning Confederate army — marching into its heartland. "If successful this year," Lee had predicted to his wife on April 19, "next fall there will be a great change in public opinion at the North. The Republicans will be destroyed & I think the friends of peace will become so strong as that the next administration will go in on that basis." A successful campaign in Pennsylvania — even the army's simply remaining there for some length of time — ought to give voice to the Northern peace movement. And a success there might even impress the European powers sufficiently to push them toward intervention or at least mediation.

However he made the case, nothing in Lee's correspondence or recollections suggests that he raised any hopes among his listeners that by marching into Pennsylvania he would pry Grant loose from Vicksburg. The argument that time and distance precluded the Confederates from sending reinforcements to Vicksburg that spring surely applied in the reverse direction to the Federals. In any case, it was too much to expect that the threat of a Confederate invasion of the North would paralyze Yankee efforts on every other war front. It was possible that an invasion would prevent the Yankees sending (as Lee put it) "troops designed to operate against other parts of the country," but that was the most that could be hoped for.[22]

On the other hand, the implications of a Confederate victory in Pennsylvania were well worth contemplating. Grant's taking of Vicksburg would be offset, indeed would pale by comparison. On the Southern home front a Lee victory, said an observer, would be "a slogan to arouse the impatient populace to new endeavors. . . ." To Richmond it was beginning to seem that the war might be lost in a year in the West, yet perhaps it could still be won in a day in the East. Should Lee gain another Fredericksburg or Chancellorsville on some battleground in Pennsylvania, especially if it was the more decisive battle he had long been seeking, the war would take on a whole new balance.

It cannot be imagined, during this War Department conference, that President Davis, Secretary Seddon, and General Lee had the slightest doubt that sending the army north across the Potomac would result in anything less than a major battle. Despite the talk of hungry troops, this was never designed as merely a massive victualing expedition. Nor was there any thought of an invasion to conquer and occupy territory north of the Mason-Dixon Line — to append Pennsylvania to the Confederacy. The conferees had to be aware that just as surely as a Southern army would rise to the defense of Virginia, a Northern army would fight an invasion of Pennsylvania. If the Army of Northern Virginia made a campaign in the North, there could be no avoiding a battle there.

To be sure, in the hindsight atmosphere of his reports and his postwar comments, General Lee was circumspect on this point. Still, it is unmistakable that from the first he intended the operation to end in a battle. In his reports he spoke of a march north offering "a fair opportunity to strike a blow" at the opposing army; and, again, he mentioned the "valuable results" that would follow "a decided advantage gained over the enemy in Maryland or Pennsylvania. . . ."

In a conversation in 1868 Lee was quoted as saying that "he did not intend to give general battle in Pennsylvania if he could avoid it." This was a matter of evasive semantics. In Lee's lexicon, to *give* battle was to seek it out deliberately and to attack. To *accept* battle (to accept "a fair opportunity"), however — which significantly Lee did not exclude in describing his plan — was electing to fight if conditions were favorable, or if by maneuver could be made favorable. This was precisely "the ruling ideas of the campaign" that he and Longstreet had discussed at length and agreed upon just before the Richmond conference. At the time of the decision-making Lee stated his objective with perfect clarity. On May 25, calling upon D. H. Hill for reinforcements, Lee wrote, "They are very essential to aid in the effort to turn back the tide of war that is now pressing South." Only battle could satisfy an objective so grand.[23]

In writing to his wife on April 19 about prospects for the coming campaigning season, Lee displayed a long view of affairs, looking toward breaking down the Republican administration in Washington. He did not suggest achieving this by one great war-ending battle of annihilation, a modern-day Cannae. His army was, after all, ever fated to be the smaller of the two armies. More realistically, Lee seems to have projected repeated morale-shattering victories that would eventually sap Northerners' support for the war. Gaining a third successive victory, of whatever dimension, over the Army of the Potomac, this time on Northern soil, should go a long way toward that goal. That was clearly a risk worth taking. As Lee himself argued, according to the record of a postwar conversation, "He knew oftentimes that he was playing a very bold game, but it was the only *possible* one."[24]

Some two weeks after the Richmond conference, President Davis wrote a letter to Lee that has been interpreted by some to show the president less than wholehearted in his support, and indeed that he was not even aware of Lee's intentions for the campaign. "I had never fairly comprehended your views and purposes . . . ," Davis wrote, "and now have to regret that I did not earlier know all that you had communicated to others." In fact, as is readily apparent from the context of this remark, and from their other letters exchanged in this period, Davis was not speaking of the proposed Pennsylvania campaign at all, but rather of the ongoing difficulty Lee was having with D. H. Hill over the matter of reinforcements.

While no directive was issued by Davis or Seddon formally approving the Pennsylvania campaign as Lee had outlined it on May 15, there cannot be the slightest doubt of their approval. Both Davis and Seddon fully agreed with Lee on its necessity. In that same letter, for example, Davis pledged to relieve Lee of any concern for Richmond's safety "while you are moving towards the north and west." Secretary Seddon, the earlier advocate of a western strategy, assured the general, "I concur entirely in your views of the importance of aggressive movements by your army. . . ." Lee could therefore return to his Rappahannock headquarters confident of Richmond's support. On Sunday, May 17, he set about the task of readying his army to march north.

What was debated and decided at the War Department that 15th of May held the promise of reshaping the very direction of the war. In one sense, the conference revealed how the crisis in Mississippi had passed well beyond Richmond's reach. The drama there seemed likely to play out without any further intervention from the Confederate capital. On the other hand, General Lee was persuasive in his argument that in the Virginia theater the road to opportunity pointed north, and that the way was open. By recapturing the strategic initiative he had surrendered after Sharpsburg, he proposed to take the war right into the Yankee heartland. At the least, a success in Pennsylvania would offset any failure at Vicksburg. At the most, a great victory on enemy soil might put peace within Richmond's reach. James Seddon said it well: Such a movement by the Army of Northern Virginia "is indispensable to our safety and independence."[25]

2   *High Command in Turmoil*

ON THE 13th of May 1863 — one day before General Lee set off for Richmond to discuss high strategy with President Davis — Fighting Joe Hooker was summoned from Falmouth on the Rappahannock to Washington to see *his* president. In Hooker's case, as in Lee's, the topic for discussion was what to do next with the army he commanded. In striking contrast to Lee, however, Joe Hooker soon discovered that his very role as general commanding was under attack.

President Lincoln's summons came in reaction to Hooker's latest planning paper, sent in earlier that day. "I know that you are impatient, and I know that I am," Hooker had written, "but my impatience must not be indulged at the expense of dearest interests." After an extended and generally gloomy discussion of the state of his army, and the presumed state of Lee's, he announced, "I hope to be able to commence my movement to-morrow, but this must not be spoken of to any one." Lincoln must have been taken aback by this offhand declaration of renewed warfare, for he promptly telegraphed, "please come up and see me this evening."

Hooker left no account of that evening's meeting at the White House, but the letter Lincoln wrote him the next day suggests a for-the-record summary of their discussion. He had earlier "had an impression," the president began, that a prompt resumption of the battle might catch the enemy "deranged in position" as a result of the Chancellorsville fighting. "That idea has now passed away. . . . It does not now appear probable to me that you can gain any thing by an early renewal of the attempt to cross the Rappahannock." Of course, he went on, if General Hooker believed he could "renew the attack successfully, I do not mean to restrain you." But until such time, the president would be content simply to see the enemy kept at bay "and out of other mischief" while the Army of the Potomac was gotten in good order again. In recognizing that his general was acting more dutiful than enthusiastic about renewing the offensive, Lincoln had concluded not to push the matter.

Thus even as General Lee was preparing his argument to Mr. Davis that by all accounts the enemy was readying a new offensive against him, Mr. Lincoln told General Hooker to put aside all thoughts of taking the offensive any time soon. In his letter to Hooker the president revealed an important reason for the postponement: "I must tell you that I have some painful intimations that some of your corps and Division Commanders are not giving you their entire confidence. This would be ruinous, if true. . . ."[1]

This bombshell must have surprised General Hooker as he read it, but on reflection he could hardly express himself shocked at evidence of a generals' revolt within his own army. After all, it was not that long since he himself had done his best to undermine the previous general commanding. The other conspirators who plotted Ambrose Burnside's downfall back in January had operated apart from Hooker, and with the goal of seeing General McClellan returned to power. Instead they got Joe Hooker. The chief ringleaders of the Burnside coup had been banished from the Potomac army, but others had risen to take their places. Now that defeat at Chancellorsville had left Hooker suddenly vulnerable, he became the target of these discontented lieutenants.[2]

They had wasted not a moment taking aim. As early as May 7, with the beaten army scarcely back in its camps around Falmouth and with President Lincoln and General-in-Chief Henry W. Halleck on the scene to appraise the defeat, the conspirators set to work. General Halleck, who had no use for Hooker to begin with, called the corps commanders into council and learned, according to Darius Couch, of "great dissatisfaction among the higher officers at the management of Chancellorsville." Henry W. Slocum, Twelfth Corps, went among his fellow corps commanders proposing a coup — petition the president then and there to dismiss Hooker and put George Gordon Meade, commander of the Fifth Corps, in his place.

It is not clear whether Slocum had a full co-conspirator in the Second Corps' General Couch, or if Couch was plotting independently. In any event, both Slocum and Couch required Meade's acquiescence for their scheming to have any real weight. Meade, however, balked at the idea. As he explained to his wife, "I told both these gentlemen I would not join in any movement against Hooker. . . ." Without Meade's agreement to stand for Hooker's place, the ringleaders lacked the stomach to make their case to the president. Rather lamely, Couch, Slocum, and John Sedgwick, all corps commanders senior to Meade on the major generals' list, assured Meade they would be pleased to serve under him as army commander should that time ever come.[3]

Joe Hooker now proceeded to play right into the conspirators' hands. Hooker's primary problem as a general had always been his runaway tongue, and in the aftermath of Chancellorsville he talked his way into the bad graces of practically all his senior lieutenants. He started off by dictating an ornate general order showering congratulations on the army for its achievements in the late battle. "If it has not accomplished all that was expected, the reasons are well known to the army," he said. That left his men scratching their heads in puzzlement. What in fact no one in the Army of the Potomac could understand was why they had failed to win at Chancellorsville, and especially why they had retreated back across the river when the struggle still seemed in the balance. Hooker's explanation was not much help: "In withdrawing from the south bank of the Rappahannock before delivering a general battle to our adversaries, the army has given renewed evidence of its confidence in itself and its fidelity to the principles it represents."[4]

Hooker might have left the matter there without much lasting damage — after all, he was hardly the first general in this war to employ bombast to paper over a defeat — but he then let it be known just who was responsible for the failure to accomplish "all that was expected" at Chancellorsville. The general commanding was heard to lay blame squarely upon three of the army's eight corps commanders — on Oliver Otis Howard, for allowing his Eleventh Corps to be routed in Stonewall Jackson's surprise attack on May 2; on John Sedgwick, for mismanaging command of the army's left wing during the battle; and on George Stoneman, head of the cavalry corps, for utterly failing to carry out his assignment to destroy Lee's railroad supply line.

There was in fact considerable truth to these charges — Howard *was* negligent, Sedgwick sluggish, Stoneman incompetent — but at the moment that was not widely recognized or admitted by anyone but Hooker. In any event, this outspoken and public attack on three of their own only caused the officer corps to close ranks and the dissidents to stiffen their resolve. Hooker, by leaks to the press, also sought to dilute his responsibility for the retreat, serving to further irritate his subordinates. "I see the papers attribute Hooker's withdrawal to the weak councils of his corps commanders," Meade angrily wrote his wife on May 10. "This is a base calumny."

So it was that the officer corps' nearly unanimous verdict finding General Hooker solely guilty for Chancellorsville stemmed in good measure from the general commanding's ill-judged and intemperate finger-pointing. But it was also these generals' convenient way of glossing over the serious command failings within their own ranks. They also ignored, or at least misunderstood, one of the major factors in the defeat. On May 3, in the midst of the heaviest fighting of the campaign, Hooker was felled and severely concussed by a Rebel cannon shot that hit the Chancellor house and shattered a porch pillar against which he was leaning. Although it was a hidden wound rather than an obvious one, the concussion rendered Hooker incapable of acting rationally throughout this pivotal day of the battle. Lincoln's tart comment accurately gauged the matter. "If Hooker had been killed by the shot which knocked over the pillar that stunned him," the president observed, "we should have been successful." The dissident officers were not so perceptive; indeed the more malicious among them attributed the general's comatose condition on May 3 to liquor.

George Meade, fairer-minded than most, was nevertheless convinced that "these last operations have shaken the confidence of the army in Hooker's judgment, particularly among the superior officers." War correspondent George Smalley, sent by the *New York Tribune* to Falmouth to investigate Hooker and the state of the army, confirmed Meade's opinion. Smalley, according to Captain Henry Abbott of the Second Corps, "stated the other day at Gen. Couch's table that he had asked the opinion of every corps commander in the army, & with one exception, they all stated in the most unequivocal manner, that they had lost all confidence in Fighting Joe." That one exception was the Third Corps' Daniel Sickles, a longtime ally of Hooker's — now perhaps his only ally.[5]

Among the clutch of concerned visitors that descended on the Falmouth camps in these days were three prominent senators, Benjamin Wade, Zachariah Chandler, and Henry Wilson. Wilson headed the Senate's Committee on Military Affairs, and Wade and Chandler were leaders of the Joint Committee on the Conduct of the War, a body notorious among Potomac army generals for its partisan prying into military matters. While the visit of Republicans Wade and Chandler was not official — the joint committee was then in recess — they put their investigative noses to the ground. What they came away with was what they had come to find. Their favorite Joe Hooker was not at fault for Chancellorsville ("I have full confidence in Joe Hooker both as to his courage & ability as a commander," Senator Chandler intoned); the responsibility for the reverse lay instead with certain of his generals. This finding was soon leaked to the press, providing further evidence, in the minds of the plotters, of the baneful (Republican) political influences that overlay the Army of the Potomac.[6]

Before leaving Washington to return to his Falmouth headquarters, Hooker had discovered what was behind the president's warning to him that certain of his lieutenants "are not giving you their entire confidence." Governor Andrew G. Curtin of Pennsylvania, yet another of those who hurried to Falmouth after Chancellorsville to appraise the army's condition, had called on the two most prominent Pennsylvanians in the high command, corps commanders George Meade and John Reynolds. "In the familiarity of private conversation," Meade recalled, he spoke frankly to the governor of what he believed were Hooker's mistakes during the late battle. Reynolds apparently delivered a similar message. Curtin, who was something of an alarmist, rushed to the White House to report that both Meade and Reynolds "had lost all confidence" in army commander Hooker.[7]

Hooker picked this up in the capital from an acquaintance of Curtin's, and back in Falmouth on May 15 he summoned Meade for an explanation. It was a stormy session. Rumors of the attempted command coup of May 7 must have reached Hooker's ears — the story was already all over Washington — and no doubt he was in a testy mood. Meade tried to explain that what he said to Curtin was during the course of a private conversation, which the governor had had no warrant to repeat. In any event, he said, every opinion he expressed to Curtin he had previously expressed directly to Hooker, as Hooker well knew, during the course of the Chancellorsville fighting. Therefore the general commanding had no cause "to complain of my expressing my views to others."

If General Hooker, in Meade's phrase, "expressed himself satisfied" with that explanation, it was a resolution reached only after the most heated debate. According to Alexander S. Webb of the Fifth Corps staff, Meade's volcanic temper got the best of him and he became so mad that he "damned Hooker very freely." At that Webb hastily left the tent so as not to become the witness required for court-martial charges. Eventually the two generals cooled off and parted without further fireworks, but permanent damage had been done. Afterward, relating the incident to a colleague, Meade was heard to say feelingly, "God help us all." Within a matter of days he was writing his wife, "I am sorry to tell you I am at open war with Hooker" — an admission by the general who Fighting Joe had recently assured the president was his best corps commander.[8]

Shortly after this contretemps, *Tribune* correspondent Smalley approached Meade "to lay certain matters before him." During Smalley's round of visits to the various corps headquarters, the chief dissidents — including at least Couch, Slocum, and Sedgwick — had prevailed upon him as a civilian and a neutral to present their case to Meade for allowing his name to be put up for the command. The correspondent, as he put it, was to "lay before him what my friends declared to be the wish of the army, or of a great part of the army." The moment the drift of the conversation became clear, Meade interrupted to say, "I don't know that I ought to listen to you." Smalley said he was not there as a negotiator but only to tell the general "what others thought." At that he was allowed to continue. "From beginning to end, General Meade listened with an impassive face . . . ," Smalley reported. "He never asked a question. He never made a comment. When I had finished I had not the least notion what impression my narrative had made on him." But simply by agreeing to hear his visitor out, Meade revealed how strained his relationship with the general commanding had become.[9]

Hooker responded disingenuously to the president's letter of warning, saying he had no idea of the identity of his disaffected lieutenants, and certainly he did not want any of his officers to think he suspected them of disloyalty. He preferred to leave it up to the president to investigate the matter. Officers who applied to him for permission to go to Washington would be urged to call at the White House. As he later testified, "I desired the President himself to ascertain their feelings . . . and he could then learn their views for his own information."

Secretary of the Treasury Salmon P. Chase, Joe Hooker's staunchest friend in the Cabinet, warned the general that it was a mistake "to have the Chiefs of Corps come up here to tell their several stories. . . ." Naturally each would say how much better the battle would have gone "if his counsel or his ideas had been followed." Chase preached that there must be no disaffected within the army's high command; weed them out, he urged; make new generals "of the best captains or lieutenants." Hooker disagreed. Although a veteran intriguer himself, he had never operated in the shadows. He saw no merit in conducting a witch-hunt among his lieutenants, as Burnside had vainly attempted in his last days of command. (Burnside's first candidate for dismissal had been Joe Hooker.) He thought it best to force the disaffected into the open. Make them voice their opinions and take their stands in front of their commander-in-chief.[10]

By Hooker's account, most of his corps commanders did indeed visit the capital over the next two weeks or so, although he claimed he never learned the results of any interviews with the president. But the message these generals delivered was clear enough. "No one whose opinion is worth anything has now any confidence in General Hooker," division

Major General Joseph Hooker and his staff, photographed at Falmouth in June 1863. Seated from left: chief commissary Henry F. Clark, chief of artillery Henry J. Hunt, quartermaster Rufus Ingalls, Hooker, chief of staff Daniel Butterfield. (U.S. Army Military History Institute)

commander John Gibbon wrote on May 25, "and the President has been told so. . . ." Darius Couch was one of these White House visitors, and he told Lincoln he would serve no longer under Hooker and submitted his application for transfer. Couch was the most senior of the corps commanders, Hooker's second-in-command at Chancellorsville, and the president sounded him out about his availability to command the army should it come to that. Couch excused himself by claiming his health was too fragile for the responsibility, but he took the opportunity to push George Meade for the post.

Other soundings were taken by the administration, more indirect and informal. John Sedgwick, another of the senior major generals, was one of those discussed for the army command, as he was well aware. "I think I could have had it if I had said the word," Sedgwick later wrote his sister, "but nothing could induce me to take it." Winfield Scott Hancock, a well-thought-of division commander in the Second Corps, was also given a look. He wrote his wife soon after Chancellorsville that he had been approached "in connection with the command of the Army of the

Potomac." Like Sedgwick, however, Hancock thought there were too many strings tied to the position. "I do not belong to that class of generals whom the Republicans care to bolster up. I should be sacrificed," he declared.

To be sure, General Hooker was not entirely friendless during all this infighting. The *New York Herald* reported on May 16 that Dan Sickles, the high-powered New York politico in command of the Third Corps, "has been closeted for two hours today" with the president, who was no doubt treated to a recital of Joe Hooker's military virtues by the loyal Sickles. But in truth, Hooker's best friend just then was Mr. Lincoln, who genuinely liked the general and admired his fighting skills, and who appreciated how solidly Hooker had reconstructed morale in the Army of the Potomac since taking over its command in January. A *Herald* correspondent, asking about Hooker's tenure, reported Lincoln's response that, having tried General McClellan "a number of times, he saw no reason why he should not try General Hooker twice." In any case, the president did not want to be perceived as so arbitrary that he had to continue changing generals after every battle.[11]

That perception had begun to haunt the administration, for thus far in the war it exactly described the Army of the Potomac's fortunes. Following that first and particularly inglorious defeat at Manassas in July 1861, Irvin McDowell was sacked in favor of George McClellan. In the summer of 1862, after the collapse of McClellan's Peninsula campaign, the army was taken from Little Mac division by division and handed over to John Pope. Pope's sad destiny after the next battle, at Second Manassas, was to watch the army handed back to McClellan. The terrible fight at Sharpsburg on Antietam Creek in September was a strategic standoff favoring the Union, but that did not save McClellan from dismissal. Burnside's brief tenure as army commander was sealed by the Fredericksburg disaster in December 1862. Now yet another defeat, Chancellorsville, threatened yet another general. Joe Hooker found himself being pushed toward oblivion from behind, by insurgents within his own officer corps.

It proved impossible to keep this high-command turmoil under wraps, and every day seemed to generate a new rumor about Hooker's fate. Samuel P. Heintzelman, commanding the Washington defenses, was ever alert to the latest gossip about the high command. "All sorts of rumors of changes in the command of the Army of the Potomac, and who shall command it," he recorded in his diary on May 15. Two days later he heard the capital's newsboys giving voice to the latest unfounded rumor as they cried, "General Hooker removed!" On the 18th, Marsena Patrick, the army's provost marshal, observed in *his* diary that "Hooker stock, in Washington, is rather low at present."[12]

At the core of General Hooker's command problems, after Chancellorsville, was his lack of a constituency among his chief lieutenants. The only generals who owed their corps postings to Hooker were Dan Sickles of the Third Corps, Otis Howard of the Eleventh, and George Stoneman of the cavalry, and after publicly criticizing Howard and Stoneman for their Chancellorsville failings Hooker lost whatever good will they might have retained. The others had climbed the ladder of command under General McClellan. Couch of the Second Corps and Slocum of the Twelfth were the earliest avowed advocates of Meade for the army command. Sedgwick of the Sixth Corps, already leaning toward the Meade camp, took his place there after what was described as "a stormy scene" with Hooker over Sedgwick's role at Chancellorsville. John Reynolds of the First Corps was the least vocal concerning the various controversies, but in time he too would take his stand behind Meade. And now Meade's professed neutrality toward Hooker was compromised by mutual antipathy. Of the eight, then, only Dan Sickles remained a loyal supporter of the general commanding.

Joe Hooker's inability to keep his mouth shut contributed greatly to the mess he was in. He might have ridden out the storm by quietly accepting responsibility for his defeat, but that was not his way, and it lost him respect as well as friends. At the same time, the intrigues hatched by his lieutenants were in blatant violation of military order and indeed subject to court-martial under the Articles of War. All in all, it was an ugly situation without precedent in a Northern army, posing the gravest threat not only to Hooker's ability to lead but to the very heart of the military command structure. Lincoln's warning to his general — "This would be ruinous, if true" — proved to be only too true.[13]

MORALE AMONG THOSE of lesser rank in the Army of the Potomac was far less compromised by the Chancellorsville defeat than was true of the generals. It had been a hard campaign to follow and it was hard to understand why it ended as it did, and that bred at least a certain frustration among the fighting men. Their initial reaction was well expressed by a Pennsylvania lieutenant, Francis Donaldson. "The men are morose, sullen, dissatisfied, disappointed, and mortified," Donaldson wrote his brother on May 14. "We are a good deal discouraged because we feel that we should not have lost the battle. I don't see how we can hope to succeed if we are not better handled."

Even so, Donaldson detected a new resiliency in the Falmouth camps: "But at the same time it must be confessed we are a remarkable army. I doubt very much if any other could have sustained two such tremendous disasters as Fredericksburg and Chancellorsville and held together as we are doing. Why, do you know that not withstanding our discouragements we are now fast recovering and could make a big fight today if we had someone to inspire us with confidence?" Captain Stephen Weld, First Corps, was similarly impressed by the basic spirit in the ranks. "This Army of the Potomac is truly a wonderful army," he told his family. "They have something of the English bull-dog in them. You can whip them time and again, but the next fight they go into, they are in good spirits, and as full of pluck as ever. . . . Some day or other we shall have our turn."

This attitude reflected a major change from the Yankee soldiers' abyssal demoralization following the Fredericksburg slaughter in December. In the weeks after that battle embittered men deserted by the thousands. By the end of January one man in ten on the roles of the Potomac army was listed as a deserter. The whole structure of military discipline was breaking down. On January 24 General Carl Schurz warned President Lincoln that he should "not be surprised when you see this great army melt away with frightful rapidity." Chancellorsville, however, triggered nothing like that mass exit of fighting men. Instead there was a calm (or at least resigned) acceptance of the defeat and a looking forward rather than back.

Lieutenant Donaldson pointed to another major difference between then and now. At Chancellorsville, unlike Fredericksburg, the Army of the Potomac had inflicted severe loss on the Rebels. "The enemy must have been badly crippled or else they would have followed up their success," he concluded, a view that was echoed in many home letters. There was general agreement that they had given as good as they got. "I think such getting whipped, on our part, will soon use up the Confederacy," Lieutenant Edward Ketchum of the 120th New York observed. "Their loss must have been fearful; for they came up, time after time, right in front of our batteries, closed en masse, . . . when our guns, double-shotted with grape, would pile them in heaps, and send them back, utterly cut to pieces. . . ."[14]

Still another factor softening the humiliation of defeat was the presence of a handy scapegoat on which to heap the blame. Stonewall Jackson's surprise assault on May 2 caught the Eleventh Corps entirely unsuspecting and facing in the wrong direction. The corps contained large numbers of Germans or men of German descent, known scornfully as Dutchmen by the nativist element in the army, and when they confronted the avalanche of screaming, charging Rebels the poor Dutchmen broke and ran. "But the Corps — I grant our Corps lost the day — and sorry enough I am to admit it," wrote a New England Yankee in the Eleventh. "But for the Corps we might have been successful in our movements." A great many men in the Army of the Potomac agreed with him.

The attitude of the troops toward their commanding general was mixed. Some letter writers, reflecting the views of the officer corps (and of the newspapers), attacked Hooker for letting himself be outgeneraled at Chancellorsville by Lee and Jackson. Others derided him for the address he had issued in the middle of the campaign that brashly predicted victory. "I should think Hooker would feel rather *small* after bragging so much," remarked Captain William Folwell of the engineers. "The only reasons I know for our repulse are, that Joe Hooker was out-generaled and our soldiers, *some* of them, beaten by the superior daring and skill of the rebels."

Yet there remained in this army a strain of genuine liking for Fighting Joe that outlasted his defeat. He was well known for taking care of his men, and well remembered for cleaning up the messes of the Burnside regime, for making sure everyone was fed and clothed and sheltered as they were supposed to be. Hooker had worked hard in the three months before Chancellorsville to restore the soldiers' pride in themselves, with a result evident in the resilient spirit they displayed after the lost battle. Connecticut soldier John Willard, writing home on May 15, insisted that "Gen. Hooker has the confidence of the troops. The Army feel that he will do his duty and that in the hour of the greatest danger he will do all in his power, even by his presence, to protect it, and help us out." (Willard added, however, in a reference to Hooker's raffish reputation, "I wish he was a man of prayer.")[15]

By all appearances, then, the rank and file in the Army of the Potomac had not had their morale shattered at Chancellorsville, and seemed ready and willing to resume campaigning within a reasonable time — although, to be sure, this time with the hope that they would be better handled. The army's officer corps, however, was considerably demoralized and in virtual revolt. It made no secret of its fervent desire to be rid of the general commanding, and in this objective it had an important ally in Washington in the person of General-in-Chief Halleck. For the moment, with all quiet on the Rappahannock, Joe Hooker still retained Mr. Lincoln's confidence, but it remained to be seen how long that would last if the quiet was shattered.

IN HIS RELUCTANT planning for a renewed offensive, sent to the president on May 13, General Hooker had pointed to an especially thorny problem — the need for what he termed a "partial reorganization" of the Army of the Potomac. This was necessary because of an ongoing, massive, and unavoidable reduction in his forces. During the next two months the Potomac army would have to come to terms with the mustering out of no fewer than fifty-three infantry regiments, 30,500 men. This came to better than 27 percent of the foot soldiers that had made the Chancellorsville fight.[16]

In the first weeks of the war, two Northern states, New York and Maine, had signed up volunteer regiments for two years of service rather than the three-year standard in other states. Spring 1863 saw these two-year men — thirty-one regiments of New Yorkers and two regiments from Maine — scheduled for mustering out. At the same time, 16,700 short-termers — nine-months' men from Pennsylvania and New Jersey, enlisted for service during the Peninsula–Second Manassas crisis times in August and September of 1862 — were also preparing to start for home. "The dull monotony of camp life," Corporal James Latta entered in his diary on May 24, was enlivened by "the occasional distant shouts of troops whose terms of enlistment has expired and may be heard day after day." According to General Sedgwick, every day, day after day, a thousand men were leaving the army.[17]

In mid-May, as Hooker and the president discussed the pros and cons of renewing the offensive on the Rappahannock, Hooker observed that his former numerical superiority over the enemy was shrinking alarmingly. "My marching force of infantry is cut down to about 80,000 . . . ," he explained on May 13. This reflected both the casualties of Chancellorsville and the tidal wave of departing men whose time was up, and the downward spiral of the numbers was not finished. No fewer than twenty-five regiments were due to be mustered out during June. Even an immediate advance would still leave troops of dubious motivation in the ranks. As General Sedgwick had observed of the same situation before Chancellorsville, "No troops with but a few days to leave are going to risk much in a fight." Unless it was reinforced, the Army of the Potomac, on July 1, would have nearly 48,000 fewer men than it had had on May 1.

Artist Edwin Forbes sketched a trainload of mustered-out Yankee soldiers heading for home on May 20, 1863. (Library of Congress)

These departures produced serious gaps in the army's organization. In the First Division of the First Corps, for example, an entire brigade, five regiments of nine-months' men, was slated for mustering out, and a second brigade in the division would lose three of its four regiments. The Second Corps saw nine regiments depart, resulting in the loss of a brigade and a general pruning. The Third Corps was reduced from three divisions to two as a result of its Chancellorsville losses and losing men whose time was up. Meade's Fifth Corps was hardest hit, losing thirteen regiments of short-termers and two-year men. Meade had to break up one of his divisions as a result, losing its commander, Andrew A. Humphreys, to another corps. "I am very sorry to lose Humphreys," Meade told his wife. "He is a most valuable officer, besides being an associate of the most agreeable character."[18]

Hooker requested reinforcements to make good at least some of these losses, but that only produced a steady diet of haggling with General Halleck. Of cordial cooperation between general-in-chief and general commanding there was none. The enmity between the two men dated back to their days in the old army in California, and when he assumed command of the Army of the Potomac in January, Hooker had made but a single stipulation — that he not have to deal with Halleck, but only with the president. He told Lincoln that neither he nor his army "expected justice" at Halleck's hands. This awkward arrangement had worked well enough, so far as Hooker was concerned, while he was re-

General-in-Chief Henry W. Halleck schemed to displace Hooker as
head of the Army of the Potomac. (National Archives)

forming and reinvigorating the Potomac army and planning his Chancellorsville campaign. Now, however, stigmatized by defeat and with few
allies, Joe Hooker had lost that upper hand.

Henry Halleck was a master of bureaucratic subterfuge and circuitous
paper-shuffling, talents he displayed when asked by Secretary of War
Edwin M. Stanton what replacements the Department of Washington
might furnish to the depleted Army of the Potomac. After numerous
paragraphs of hedging and cautionary foreboding, Halleck's answer was
. . . not a man could be spared. There was, to be sure, a "movable force" of
8,600 men attached to the Washington garrison, but in the general-in-

chief's opinion, no matter which direction General Hooker might move (or, indeed, which direction General Lee might move), this force must stay where it was. After all, should it go on active service, "we should then have no movable force to throw upon any point which should be seriously threatened." In due course, there would be reinforcements for the Army of the Potomac, but not all in time to be put to use, and none in time for Hooker's benefit. In the meanwhile, General Halleck quietly laid his snares for an unwary Fighting Joe.[19]

ONE OF THE MAJOR reforms of the Hooker regime had been the consolidation of the cavalry into a single corps. This belatedly matched the way the Confederates operated their cavalry, but more important, it gave the Yankee horse soldiers for the first time a unified strategic and tactical command. In the organization of the army's artillery, however, Hooker had gone in exactly the opposite direction. Brigadier General Henry J. Hunt, the Potomac army's outspoken, highly skilled chief of artillery, had argued for grouping batteries into brigades under centralized control for better flexibility on the battlefield. On the eve of the Chancellorsville campaign Hooker elected to decentralize instead. He reduced Hunt to a mere artillery adviser and scattered tactical control of the batteries among the army's twenty infantry-division commanders.

The system proved disastrous on the Chancellorsville battlefield. Time and again the Federal artillery, superior in numbers and materiel, found itself outclassed by the better-organized Rebel gunners. In the midst of the fighting Colonel Charles Wainwright, chief of artillery for the First Corps, complained to Hooker that the artillery was being managed as "badly as it well can. Batteries are being ordered in every direction, blocking up the roads; and no one seems to know where to go."[20]

Within a week of the battle, while not acknowledging his mistake, Hooker quietly initiated a sweeping reform of the artillery. He called on Hunt for a new organizational scheme. Special Orders No. 128, dated May 12, removed the batteries from the divisions, regrouped them, and attached them to the army corps. The seven infantry corps would now each have one brigade of artillery. The Sixth Corps' artillery brigade contained eight batteries, the Twelfth Corps' brigade, four; the other five corps' brigades had five batteries each. The cavalry corps had two artillery brigades. The artillery reserve's five brigades contained a total of twenty-one batteries. Hunt put his best veteran artillerymen in charge of these brigades, and their deployment was in the hands of Hunt and the corps commanders. Looking back on this long-overdue reform, a Federal artillerist remarked, "If what was thus done as a restorative had previously been done as a preventative, the probabilities are that Chancellorsville would have had another and a very different ending." Now that Henry Hunt again had something to say about it, the next campaign ought to see the Yankee artillery used to its full potential.[21]

The artillery might finally be in good hands, but the state of health of the cavalry was diminished and its leadership uncertain. Hooker was unrelenting in his anger at cavalry commander George Stoneman for his dismal performance at Chancellorsville, and he granted Stoneman's request for medical leave with unseemly haste. The general commanding let it be known, in appointing Alfred Pleasonton to temporary command of the cavalry corps, that he intended the change to be permanent. And so it was. Stoneman was shuffled off to a desk job in Washington, and Pleasonton became the Army of the Potomac's new cavalry chief.

General Pleasonton was something of a dandy, with waxed mustaches and a rakish straw hat and a sly look. Originally a protégé of General McClellan's, he had a gift for shameless self-promotion. As one of his colonels observed, "it is the universal opinion that Pleasonton's own reputation and Pleasonton's late promotions are bolstered up by systematic lying." Pleasonton appeared willing enough to engage the enemy, but he had never revealed the slightest talent for intelligence-gathering, one of the major functions of the cavalry arm. Indeed, when it came to hearing of enemy forces, Alfred Pleasonton had a tin ear. Hooker promoted him on the basis of seniority and, in hindsight, regretted it.

The soldier Hooker later said he wished he had made head of the cavalry was John Buford, whose commission postdated Pleasonton's by eleven days. Buford advanced to Pleasonton's old place as head of the cavalry's First Division. He was unassuming and entirely competent, experienced as leader of the brigade of regulars and skilled at intelligence-gathering. The Second Division was under David McMurtrie Gregg, a trooper seemingly cut from the same bolt as Buford — able, reliable, imperturbable, in battle conspicuously taking the time to light up his meerschaum to calm his men. In due course a reinforcing Third Division would go to Judson Kilpatrick, who was not in the least like Buford or Gregg. Kilpatrick was all flamboyance and burning ambition. He was mindlessly reckless with the lives of his men, and their nickname for him — "Kill-Cavalry" — was not intended as a compliment.

By the time May turned to June, the cavalry corps had been recruited to some 10,200 men. Continuing his reorganization on the march, Pleasonton would advance youthful new faces — Elon Farnsworth, Wesley Merritt, George Armstrong Custer — to the command of brigades. The cavalry leadership was now apparently willing to take to heart Hooker's earlier challenge to Stoneman: "Let your watchword be fight, and let all your orders be fight, fight, fight!"[22]

The commanders of the Army of the Potomac's infantry were likewise a mixture of the good and the indifferent, with at the moment the upper echelons of command generally united in their mistrust of Joe Hooker. At Chancellorsville, on the whole, the army's foot soldiers had not gotten the leadership they deserved, and General Hooker had good reason to view certain of his lieutenants with a mistrust of his own.

The First Corps' John F. Reynolds was an exception. Reynolds had not seen a great deal of battle-leading — he missed most of the Seven Days' fighting as a prisoner in Richmond, for example, and during the Antietam campaign he was seized upon by Governor Curtin to drill the Pennsylvania militia. But Reynolds was universally respected for his high character and sterling generalship, and in the coming campaign Hooker would lean heavily on his command skills.

Reynolds's three division commanders were not, on the record, regarded as overly distinguished. James S. Wadsworth was a political general of the Republican stripe, earnest in his patriotism but lacking a background of military skills. John C. Robinson, an old regular whose flowing beard lent him the look of a biblical prophet, had seen considerable fighting but was yet to be tested as a division commander. The Third Division was led by Abner Doubleday, another old regular. Doubleday's wartime career had been marked at every turn by abundant caution. Probably of most concern to Reynolds was the inexperience and lack of command continuity among his brigade commanders. The First Corps contained some first-rate troops — among them the celebrated Iron Brigade of westerners and the equally celebrated Bucktails of Pennsylvania — but the test would be in directing them. In due course the corps would gain the services of a rookie brigade of nine-month Vermonters, plucked out of the Washington defenses to fill the gap left by the earlier departure of nine-month and two-year men.

The gallant old Second Corps was awarded a new commander in the aftermath of Chancellorsville. When colorless, cautious Darius Couch refused any longer to serve under Joe Hooker, Winfield Scott Hancock, anything but colorless and cautious, was advanced from division to corps command. "Hancock the Superb" — the encomium had been applied by General McClellan during the Peninsula campaign — gave every evidence of being born to high command. As Lieutenant Frank

Haskell, a Second Corps staff man, observed of him, "I think if he were in citizens clothes, and should give commands in the army to those who did not know him, he would be likely to be obeyed at once, and without any question as to his right to command."

The Second Corps divisions were led by generals with ratings of good to excellent. Taking Hancock's place at the head of the First Division was John C. Caldwell, not a professional soldier but well enough self-taught that Hancock advanced him without hesitation. John Gibbon led the Second Division, and he was as good as any in the Potomac army. "A tower of strength he is," an admirer would say of Gibbon, "cool as a steel knife, always. . . ." The Third Division had been commanded at Chancellorsville by William H. French, but at the end of June French would be put on special assignment. His replacement was Alexander Hays, fierce and combative and usually found leading from the firing line.

The high rating for divisional commanders extended well into the ranks of the Second Corps' chiefs of brigade. Such brigade commanders as Edward Cross, Patrick Kelly (of the famous Irish Brigade), John Brooke, Samuel Zook, Norman Hall, Alexander Webb, and Samuel Carroll would make the Second Corps in this campaign the best led in the army. During the campaign the Second would be reinforced by a green brigade from the Washington garrison to partially make up for its nine mustered-out regiments.[23]

General Hooker's sole loyalist, Dan Sickles, commanded the Third Corps, marking him as the highest-placed political general in the Army of the Potomac. Sickles was all noise and notoriety. In 1859, as a Tammany Hall congressman from New York, he had murdered his wife's lover and then won acquittal in a lurid trial. With the coming of war, employing far more politicking than generalship, Sickles rose rapidly from recruiting a regiment to commanding a corps. As head of the Third Corps at Chancellorsville he blundered pugnaciously about the battlefield. "A 'Sickles' would beat Napoleon in winning glory not earned," growled fellow general Alpheus Williams. "He is a hero without an heroic deed! Literally made by scribblers." As a corps commander Dan Sickles was operating at a level far beyond his talents, and most everyone recognized it but Dan Sickles.

The Third Corps had been severely battered at Chancellorsville, with two of its three divisional commanders losing their lives there. A major reorganization was required. The Third Division was folded into the other two, and Andrew A. Humphreys brought over from the Fifth Corps to fill the vacant divisional post. The Fifth Corps' loss was the Third's gain. General Humphreys was a thoroughly professional officer who got things done, when necessary by means of a spectacular command of profanity. He was an advocate of leadership by example. At Fredericksburg, ordered to conduct an attack, he turned to his staff and, in his blandest manner, remarked, "Gentlemen, I shall lead this charge. I presume, of course, you will wish to ride with me."

The First Division provided the corps with a touch of continuity. David Bell Birney had led a brigade there since the early days of the Peninsula fighting, and succeeded to the divisional command after the fabled Phil Kearny was killed at Chantilly, during the Second Manassas campaign. A prominent lawyer in Philadelphia before the war, Birney brought intense study and close observation to the art of command. He also had an affinity for intrigue, and was among the leaders of the army's anti-Hooker cabal. Birney's three brigade commanders, Charles Graham, Hobart Ward, and Régis de Trobriand, promised sound leadership. However, Andrew Humphreys, new to his division, would be leading two (of three) officers entirely new to their brigades.[24]

General Meade's Fifth Corps, too, required a thorough reorganization as a consequence of the loss of two-year and short-term men. One-third of the regiments in the First Division and three-quarters of those in the Third Division had to be mustered out; the latter division was broken up and its General Humphreys shifted to Sickles's corps. When the First Division's Charles Griffin went on sick leave after Chancellorsville his place was taken by James Barnes, the senior brigadier. Barnes was sixty-one and lacking in both combat and command experience, and it was hoped that the veteran Griffin would return before Barnes was tested in battle. Of the division's three brigade commanders, all new, Colonel Strong Vincent was considered the most promising. The Second Division was George Sykes's, and included the brigade of regulars that Sykes had long commanded. Sykes was a slight, methodical, unimposing career army man whose nickname, "Tardy George," dated back to his West Point days. He might not inspire, but once on the battlefield he was known to be reliable. Sykes's regulars were led by colonels of limited combat experience; his single brigade of volunteers was headed by former artillerist Stephen Weed, a highly regarded protégé of Henry Hunt's.[25]

In February 1863 the division of Pennsylvania Reserves, which had fought in the Fifth Corps on the Peninsula and then in the First Corps during later campaigns, was posted to Washington for rest and recuperation. On June 25, with a new campaign heating up, the Reserves were finally dispatched to reinforce the thinly manned Fifth Corps. Even then, however, General-in-Chief Halleck held back from General Hooker one of the division's three brigades.

The Sixth Corps was the largest in the Army of the Potomac, and "Uncle John" Sedgwick was beloved as no other general. "From the commander to the lowest private he had no enemy in this army," a staff officer wrote. Sedgwick always took good care of his men, and on a battlefield he was a stalwart figure, leading by example. Yet the finer arts of command escaped him. A simple direct order satisfied John Sedgwick; a discretionary order perplexed him. Leading his First Division was Horatio G. Wright, an engineering officer newly appointed to both the corps and the Potomac army and therefore an unknown quantity. The other two divisions were led by Albion P. Howe and John Newton, as careful and conservative as Uncle John himself. Most of the heads of brigade were as safely competent as their superiors. The Sixth Corps' high command was not the place for carrying out daring battlefield designs.

Before Chancellorsville a newly formed Light Division, five regiments and a battery, had been attached to the Sixth Corps. Designed to travel light and move fast, it was meant to be a sort of fire brigade for battlefield emergencies. As employed at Chancellorsville, however, the Light Division was made the spearhead of a frontal assault and badly mauled. In the subsequent restructuring triggered by the expiration of enlistments, the Light Division was disbanded and its regiments distributed to fill gaps in the corps. Between casualties and the mustering out, the Sixth Corps would go on campaign in June with almost 8,000 fewer men than it had in April.[26]

The Eleventh Corps was the foster child of the Army of the Potomac — the foster child that no one wanted. It was assigned from John Pope's short-lived Army of Virginia, and Chancellorsville was its first battle with the Potomac army. "The spirit of this corps is broken, and something must be done to revive it," warned divisional commander Carl Schurz after the Chancellorsville debacle. There was little chance that a revival would be generated by the corps commander, Otis Howard. Howard was no better fitted to lead an army corps than was Dan Sickles, and one of his lacks was a commanding presence. As Colonel Charles Wainwright put it, "there is some doubt as to his having snap enough to manage the Germans, who require to be ruled with a rod of iron."[27]

The Eleventh's three division commanders formed a study in contrasts, but each in his way was well enough suited to his post. Brigadier

General Francis Channing Barlow, twenty-eight, graduate of Harvard (first in his class) and a lawyer, was a self-taught officer of resolute battlefield courage who was capable of ruling the Germans in his division with a rod of iron if anyone could. The same could be said of Adolph von Steinwehr, Prussian-trained and well respected by his men. Carl Schurz, an influential leader of the German-American community, had made himself an energetic student of the trade of soldiering. Of the corps' six brigades, four had commanders of experience, and two (both in von Steinwehr's division) were led by newcomers. Only one regiment of two-year men was scheduled to be mustered out, but its Chancellorsville losses left the Eleventh Corps sadly understrength.

The Twelfth Corps was another refugee from the Army of Virginia, but it had fought hard and well at Antietam and Chancellorsville and never had to share the stigma of the outcast Eleventh Corps. The corps commander, Henry Slocum, was a battle-scarred veteran — he had fought at First Manassas and was wounded there — who in generalship was much like John Sedgwick: competent, careful, cautious, and entirely without military imagination. There was a bitter, peevish streak in him that seemed to power his hatred of Hooker. (Hooker blamed this on Slocum's "digestive apparatus being out of repair.") Slocum's First Division was led by Alpheus S. Williams, the most experienced and one of the best divisional commanders in the army. In the reshuffling necessitated by the expiration of enlistments, Williams had one recast brigade under a brand-new commander, a veteran brigade under the battle-tested Thomas H. Ruger, and a third brigade of Maryland garrison troops that would join during the campaign.

Slocum's other divisional commander, John W. Geary, was a fearless giant of a man who led by example and had already been wounded three times in this war (and five times in the Mexican War). His three brigades had strong, experienced commanders in Charles Candy, Thomas L. Kane, and George Sears Greene. The Twelfth Corps would be fated to next go into battle with fewer than 10,000 men, but with leadership as good as any in the army.[28]

JOE HOOKER NEVER offered any detail on his ideas for resuming the offensive on the Rappahannock front after the Chancellorsville defeat. He would say only that next time he wanted to arrange matters so that he had "elbow-room" for maneuvering — no more trying to fight in the heavily wooded Wilderness region south of the river — and that instead of dividing the army into scattered independent commands as he had at Chancellorsville, he would keep all his forces "within my personal supervision." Clearly in the late battle he had lost as much confidence in his lieutenants as they had in him. As the spring campaigning season slipped away, however, it became evident that General Hooker was perfectly content to let the initiative fall into his opponent's hands.[29]

That his opponent intended to pounce on that initiative did not escape the notice of the Federals' sharp-eyed intelligence service. The Bureau of Military Information was another of Joe Hooker's innovations, and as important a one as any. Colonel George H. Sharpe, head of the B.M.I., reported to headquarters that the Confederate army was under marching orders, "and an order from General Lee was very lately read to the troops announcing a campaign of long marches & hard fighting in a part of the country where they would have no railroad transportation." That could mean nothing else but a march north.

The intelligence came from a deserter, Colonel Sharpe explained, and was confirmed by his own spies and supported by a broad hint from the *Richmond Examiner* of May 22. Speaking of the discouraging reports from Vicksburg, the *Examiner* offered the prediction that happenings in that quarter "will soon be eclipsed by greater events elsewhere. Within the next fortnight the campaign of 1863 will be pretty well decided. The most important movement of the war will probably be made in that time." With this fresh intelligence in hand, General Hooker and his chief of staff, Daniel Butterfield, went up to Washington on the evening of May 25 for what was termed "a kind of Council of War" at the White House.[30]

It appears that this council was attended only by the president, Generals Hooker and Butterfield, and Secretary of War Stanton. Not in attendance was General-in-Chief Halleck, who soon afterward again made complaint that Hooker never told him anything; clearly general-in-chief and general commanding remained at swords' points. The agenda of the White House meeting is not known, but with Hooker bearing news from the B.M.I. of a projected advance by the enemy, his primary concern just then had to be reinforcements. Hooker had earlier pursued intelligence about troops reportedly transferred to Lee from Charleston, and surely he was in Washington to seek reinforcements of his own to match what the Rebels were doing. This, he surely pointed out, was quite apart from the need to replace the troops being mustered out in their thousands day by day.

Nothing concrete came out of the discussion. Hooker's sole accomplishment was a promise by Secretary Stanton to send him a copy of the manpower analysis for the Department of Washington prepared a week earlier by General Halleck. No doubt Hooker threw up his hands when he read Halleck's smugly reasoned conclusion: "Under these circumstances, I think it my duty to urge the retention of the present force in Washington or its vicinity." While in Washington Hooker also met with his sole Cabinet ally, Treasury Secretary Chase, to talk about how to handle the army's discordant high command. Little good news came out of that discussion either, and the general commanding returned to his Falmouth headquarters little wiser than when he left. He did take back with him Secretary Stanton's injunction, "Command whatever service I can render you," but that rang of an empty promise.[31]

Apparently there was nothing about this White House meeting that convinced the president that General Hooker had regained the confidence of his lieutenants. That disappointment, and word that the Rebel army was stirring, persuaded Mr. Lincoln that he must seriously consider making a command change before the next battle. Shortly thereafter, Major General John F. Reynolds was summoned to Washington and offered the command of the Army of the Potomac.

Previously, when Lincoln had sounded out the most senior of Hooker's generals, Darius Couch, on this subject, he phrased it hypothetically; Couch took himself out of the running, citing poor health. Indirect soundings, through intermediaries, were then made to another of the Potomac army's senior generals, John Sedgwick, and to Winfield Hancock; neither expressed interest in the command. One notch below Sedgwick on the seniority list was John Reynolds, and now that it was Reynolds's turn the president decided on a more direct approach. At the White House, on June 2, the commander-in-chief spoke straight out to Reynolds about heading the army.

The previous January, during the last generals' revolt, against Ambrose Burnside, John Reynolds had unburdened himself in a private letter about the critical problem he saw in the high command. "If we do not get some one soon who can command an army without consulting 'Stanton and Halleck' at Washington," he wrote, "I do not know what will become of this Army." That was still a widely held view within the army's old guard, and reflected General McClellan's corrosive legacy. Repeatedly, to any of his generals who would listen, McClellan had blamed all the troubles of his troubled regime on "interference" from Washington — on Secretary Stanton for putting radical Republican schemes ahead of what was best for the army, on General Halleck for forcing his foolish, outdated military notions on those who would lead on the battlefield. Everyone in Washington, said McClellan (he included the president and congressional investigators in his indictment), was guilty of selfishly playing politics with the Army of the Potomac.

Reynolds's response to the president was that (as he later phrased it) he "was unwilling to take Burnside's and Hooker's leavings." He wanted assurances there would be no more interference from Washington in the running of the army. Whether he had thought it through or not, what John Reynolds was in fact insisting on, before he would take the command, was the suspension of the network of civilian control over the military. He was calling for an end to "interference" from the president, the commander-in-chief and his ultimate superior officer; from Secretary of War Stanton, the army's chief civilian overseer; even from General Halleck, his immediate superior officer. There is no record of the form Lincoln's reaction took, but obviously he did not — could not — accept such a bargain. In that case, said Reynolds, he could not accept the command.

During the conversation Reynolds seems to have spoken bluntly of Joe Hooker's shortcomings, and to have promoted General Meade (next on the seniority list) for head of the army. Yet there must have been something disturbing enough about Reynolds's expressed attitude toward the command that it hardened Lincoln's own attitude on the subject. These various generals were going out of their way to condemn Hooker as unfit, yet not one of them would step up to take his place. Rather than continuing this discouraging search through the seniority list, the president determined, at least for the time being, to stay with Joe Hooker. Reynolds quoted Lincoln as saying he "was not disposed to throw away a gun because it missed fire once; that he would pick the lock and try it again." The word was soon around the capital that the president had resolved to "re-try" General Hooker.

Ten days later Reynolds would relate this episode to Meade, but only after recasting it. As he now told it, he learned from a Washington acquaintance that he was being considered for the army command, and had marched straight to the White House to tell the president he did not want it and would not take it. Such a preemptive performance would have required a good deal more gall than John Reynolds was known to possess. Clearly he told it this way to spare his friend Meade from being backed into a corner — from having to set parallel conditions for accepting the command — if (as Reynolds expected) it was offered him. Later, after there was no need for such subterfuge, Reynolds explained to his artillery chief, Colonel Wainwright, that he had indeed been summoned to Washington and offered the army command, and refused it because he would have been under the same constraints as Burnside and Hooker. (In reporting this conversation in his diary, Wainwright added that he learned Reynolds had recommended Meade for the post.) Reynolds confided much the same story to his aide Stephen Weld: that he had been called in and offered, and had refused, the army command.[32]

Here then was the Army of the Potomac, once again defeated, in the midst of an organizational turmoil, by all reports on the eve of a new campaign, commanded by a general who nearly all his lieutenants regarded as unfit. And here was the president, deeply disturbed by this dissension and disloyalty in the officer corps, who could not seem to find a qualified general who actually wanted to lead that army. It was obvious to Lincoln that should he dismiss Joe Hooker now, he would have to order rather than ask another general to take his place. That was not a happy prospect. He had gone on record as supporting Hooker; to dismiss him would be a further sign of dissension and weakness within the administration. The president could only wait and watch — and hope that General Lee gave him time enough to resolve the dilemma somehow.

3   The Risk of Action

IT WAS May 18, 1863, the day after General Lee returned to Fredericksburg from the Richmond strategy conference, and Brigadier General Dorsey Pender sensed change in the air. "We have nothing in the world new," he wrote his wife, "but all feel that something is brewing and that Gen. Lee is not going to wait all the time for them to come to him." Pender's prediction rang true. Over the next two weeks, as Lee shaped his plans for the Pennsylvania campaign, change was the order of the day in the Confederate camps.

Lee made the army's high command his first priority. Stonewall Jackson's death necessitated a new commander for the Second Corps, and Lee seized on that requirement to alter the basic makeup of the Army of Northern Virginia. "I have for the past year felt that the corps of this army were too large for one commander," he wrote President Davis on May 20. Each corps "when in fighting condition," he said, contained some 30,000 troops, too many for one general to manage in battle, especially in wooded country. "They are always beyond the range of his vision, & frequently beyond his reach." To remedy this evil, he proposed revamping the two-corps army into a three-corps army.

This meant two new corps commanders, and Lee presented the president with his selections — for the Second Corps, Richard Stoddert Ewell, "an honest, brave soldier, who has always done his duty well"; and for the new Third Corps, Ambrose Powell Hill, who "upon the whole is the best soldier of his grade with me." Both men should be promoted to lieutenant general, said Lee, to rank alongside James Longstreet, the First Corps' commander. He went on to say that Richard H. Anderson and John B. Hood, both "capital officers," would make good corps commanders "if necessary" — that is to say, with proper deference, should Mr. Davis not approve General Lee's first choices. Both president and general knew full well that this was not going to happen. If Robert E. Lee, the Confederacy's most successful general, wanted Dick Ewell and Powell Hill as two of his three chief lieutenants, he would have them.[1]

Richard S. Ewell led the Confederate Second Corps in Stonewall Jackson's place. (Cook Collection, Valentine Museum)

There was one question about Dick Ewell — was he fit enough for field duty? Ewell had lost his left leg in the Second Manassas campaign the previous August, and his recuperation progressed slowly. He had not served in the nine months since, and was only now growing accustomed to his wooden leg. But when he reported for duty at Fredericksburg on May 29, newly minted a lieutenant general, he appeared in good enough health. General Ewell, wrote Sandie Pendleton of the Second Corps staff, "seems quite pleased to get back into the field. He manages his leg very well & walks only with a stick, & mounts his horse quite easily from the ground." Ewell's spirits were enlivened by the presence of his bride of three days, the former Lizinka Campbell Brown, widow. "Old Bald Head," well known for his eccentricities, lived up to his reputation by introducing Lizinka to his army colleagues as "my wife, Mrs. Brown."

Ewell was the natural choice for the Second Corps, for he had been Jackson's most trusted divisional commander, especially during the renowned Shenandoah Valley campaign of 1862. Indeed, it was said to have been Jackson's deathbed wish that Ewell succeed him. Old Bald Head had proven himself a sound battlefield tactician and a good manager of troops. Like all of Jackson's lieutenants, however, Ewell had always operated on a tight rein held in the iron grip of the secretive Stonewall. In the coming campaign he would have to prove himself anew in the more expansive role of corps commander. In the army it was generally agreed that while Jackson was irreplaceable, Dick Ewell was the best suited to manage the corps' painful transition from old to new. "Our old confidence in Jackson," wrote Colonel Clement Evans of the 31st Georgia, "has found a new birth in our faith in Ewell. Always a favorite with his division, he is now the idol of his corps."[2]

"He fights his troops well, and takes good care of them." So General Lee summed up A. P. Hill after Sharpsburg, and it would have been hard to ask much more of a divisional commander. Yet there were contradictions to Hill. For all his oft-proven fighting prowess, he was sometimes careless on a battlefield. At Second Manassas and at Fredericksburg his defensive postings were poor and nearly proved very costly. He had a strong affinity with his men, but often prickly dealings with his superiors, and was notorious for contretemps with both Longstreet and Jackson; presumably now, with Lee his only superior, that problem would abate. And, finally, Hill was prey to a mysterious ailment, which was liable to strike him during active service. (This has since been diagnosed as prostatitis, stemming from a youthful indiscretion of Hill's during his West Point years.) Like Dick Ewell, Powell Hill would be required to prove, on campaign, that he was up to the burdens and responsibilities of corps command.[3]

As Lee reorganized it, the army was to have three corps of three divisions each. Previously, there were eight infantry divisions, divided equally between Longstreet's First Corps and Jackson's Second. Now, Lee took Richard H. Anderson's division from the First Corps and Powell Hill's Light Division from the Second to form two-thirds of the new Third Corps. Hill's third division — the army's new ninth infantry division — would be a patchwork. Two brigades were plucked out of the

Ambrose Powell Hill commanded the Army of Northern Virginia's
Third Corps. (Cook Collection, Valentine Museum)

oversized Light Division and combined with two brigades of reinforcements to be brought up from North Carolina. This new division would
require a major general to command it, and another was needed to replace A. P. Hill as head of the Light Division.

To ease the transition for the troops being shuffled and reshuffled to
form the new corps, Lee proposed brigadiers from Hill's old division
for the two posts. Dorsey Pender, who had sensed the change brewing in
the Rappahannock camps, became one of the first beneficiaries of that
change. He was advanced from command of a brigade in the Light Divi-

sion to head of the division itself, as a major general — at twenty-nine, the youngest of that rank in the army. Lee praised Pender as a "most gallant" officer, and added, "I fear the effect upon the men of passing him over in favour of another not so identified with them." A. P. Hill's ringing endorsement of Pender as his successor sealed the bargain.

Henry Heth, commander of one of the two Light Division brigades slated for the Third Corps' new division, was promoted to major general and chief of the division. "Harry" Heth was a close friend of A. P. Hill's and something of a protégé of General Lee's, who in February had brought him into the Light Division from the western theater. Although Chancellorsville was only his first battle with the Army of Northern Virginia, Heth enjoyed General Lee's full confidence to manage the new division. "I have a high estimate of Genl. Heth," Lee assured the president. The makeup of Heth's division, however, soon became entangled in the highly volatile subject of reinforcements for the Army of Northern Virginia.[4]

GENERAL LEE SUPERVISED considerably more than just the Army (and Department) of Northern Virginia. He was responsible as well for operations throughout the Department of Virginia and North Carolina, focusing particularly on the possible enemy approaches to Richmond and on the defense of North Carolina's coastal region. Early in 1863, in response to a barrage of Federal threats to these areas, Lee had dispatched two brigades of his North Carolina troops, under Robert Ransom and John R. Cooke, to their native state. They were followed south shortly thereafter by Hood's and Pickett's divisions, under Longstreet. This cut in strength of 18,600 men left Lee to face Hooker's attacks at Chancellorsville with only 65,000 men of all arms. The battle's casualties came to 13,500. Thus simply to return the Army of Northern Virginia to its numbers at the beginning of the year would require 32,100 men.[5]

The first effort to meet this shortfall was imaginative, to say the least. On May 7, the day after the Chancellorsville fighting ended, a tired General Lee sent a somewhat rambling proposal to the president "to increase the strength of the Army." It was his thought to collect reinforcements from the various military departments to the south, where they were likely to be inactive that summer. It would be better, he wrote, "to order Gen. Beauregard on with all the forces which can be spared, and to put him in command here, than to keep them there inactive and this army inefficient from paucity of numbers. . . ." A month later Lee returned to the subject. He repeated to Davis that excess troops should be culled from these coastal areas, and "it would be well for Gen. Beauregard with the force made available . . . to be sent to reinforce Johnston in the West or be ordered to reinforce this army." Lee must have also discussed his idea with Longstreet, for on June 3 Old Pete explained to a colleague a plan current in the army to "let Beauregard come here with a Corps. We want everybody here that we can get. . . ."

Assigning Pierre Gustave Toutant Beauregard to this scheme was an inspired choice. Lee counted on the fact that Beauregard was as well known to the Yankees as any general in the South. He had commanded the opening guns at Fort Sumter and won the field at First Manassas. He had led an army in the western theater. More than once in 1862 a nervous General McClellan had invoked the shade of Beauregard and his army sweeping out of the west to fall on him. As recently as April, in command at Charleston, Beauregard had driven off a fleet of Union ironclads, inflicting grievous damage. To form a corps under the celebrated "Great Creole" to operate in northern Virginia in connection with the Army of Northern Virginia, so Lee believed, would alarm the Yankees as nothing else could. For whatever reason, however, Lee did not sufficiently pursue this idea with Mr. Davis or Secretary Seddon, and in time he would have cause to regret his oversight.[6]

In the meantime, preparing his army to march north and persuaded that the threats to southeastern Virginia and eastern North Carolina had abated, Lee called for the various pieces of his army to be returned to him. This move ran him squarely up against Major General Daniel Harvey Hill.

In 1861 and 1862 D. H. Hill had served as a superb combat general in the Army of Northern Virginia, but he was so contrary and cross-grained an individual that when in January 1863 Governor Zebulon Vance of North Carolina called for native son Hill to lead the defenders of his state against the Yankee invaders, General Lee raised no objection. By spring, thanks to the infusion of troops from Lee's army, the situation in North Carolina was stabilized. Then, during the Chancellorsville crisis, Hood's and Pickett's divisions were ordered back to the Rappahannock, and soon thereafter Lee sought the return of his other absent brigades. Harvey Hill began to grow very nervous.

In addition to their foothold at the tip of the Virginia Peninsula, from which they might threaten Richmond, the Federals held Norfolk and Suffolk in southeastern Virginia and various points along the North Carolina coastline, from all of which they might target objectives in General

Hill's bailiwick. Hill's intelligence on the Federals was sketchy at best, and unaware that he comfortably outnumbered the enemy, he found it easy to become alarmed at his prospects. He insisted that his forces were inadequate and spread too thin, and he determined to at least hold on to the best of them — which happened to be the veteran brigades sent to him from Lee's army. What followed was an unseemly tug of war between an increasingly willful Harvey Hill and an increasingly angry Robert E. Lee.

Hill first proposed a simple exchange — untested but fully recruited brigades from his command traded for veteran but depleted brigades from Lee's. Lee was disapproving. Such a scheme, he pointed out to Hill, would mean "taking away tried troops under experienced officers & replacing them with fresh men & uninstructed commanders. I should therefore have more to feed but less to depend on." In fact, there would be one such exchange — Junius Daniel's largely untried North Carolina brigade for Alfred Colquitt's Georgia brigade that had been bloodied at Chancellorsville, but Lee probably agreed to the trade as a convenient way to rid himself of the inept Colquitt. An essential point of difference remained: Lee was far less alarmed about the Federals' threat than was Hill, arguing that the enemy was actually reducing his forces along the Atlantic seaboard. "It is of course our best policy to do the same & to endeavor to repel his advance into Virginia," he observed.

So far as General Lee was concerned, the central issue here was the return of four brigades he regarded as merely on loan to Hill. These contained some of the best fighting men in his army, commanded by four of his best generals — Robert Ransom and John R. Cooke, whose brigades were sent to North Carolina in January, and Montgomery Corse and Micah Jenkins, whose brigades had been attached to Pickett's division when it went south but had since been detached for Hill's purposes. In due course, enduring what he surely regarded as the cruelest of blows, General Lee would find himself crossing the Potomac without a single one of these brigades. And not long afterward, General George Pickett would find himself confronting the challenge of his life . . . and lacking two of his best brigades.

How this transpired is a tale of misjudgment and misapprehension. General Lee might simply have ordered his subordinate D. H. Hill to return the four brigades and make the best defense he could with his own troops. As Lee read the intelligence, no great risk was involved. He told Hill he thought "the season has passed for making any movement in

North Carolina more than raids of devastation or attempts to retain there our troops in idleness. I hope you will be able to frustrate & punish all such efforts." But rather than issue direct orders, Lee was strangely indecisive in the matter. He sent Hill discretionary orders — every man not required to suppress such raids "I desire you to send to me & rely upon your good judgment to proportion the means to the object in view." Considering Hill's nervous state of mind, this polite instruction fairly begged to be evaded, and it was.[7]

Over the next days and weeks telegrams and letters flew back and forth between Fredericksburg and Goldsboro and Richmond. Troops were started this way and that and then back. President Davis and Secretary Seddon tried to judge and to mediate and to calm. At one point an alarmed Mr. Davis telegraphed Lee that "if last information be correct" from Goldsboro, to release Lee's brigades now "is to abandon the country to the enemy." A coldly angry General Lee replied with a stinging review of his dealings with General Hill: "He declined to act and requested positive orders. I gave such orders as I could at this distance. Now he objects. I cannot operate in this manner." Yet instead of taking a stand, he continued on his indecisive course. He asked to be relieved of command of the Department of Virginia and North Carolina, and thus all supervision over Hill, and suggested that the president issue "such orders to be given him as your judgment dictates." In a long, conciliatory letter the president tried to smooth his general's feathers, suggesting that rather than limiting his sphere of command "it would be better for you to control all the operations of the Atlantic slope. . . ."[8]

It was finally determined that the two brigades Lee required to fill out Harry Heth's new division in the new Third Corps would indeed come from D. H. Hill's command. But they would not be any of those Lee had sought. One was a brigade of North Carolina troops with no appreciable experience, led by Johnston Pettigrew, who was returning to the field after being wounded and captured on the Peninsula. The second brigade comprised one North Carolina and three Mississippi regiments with at least some combat experience, led by a nephew of President Davis, Joseph R. Davis, who had no command experience at all.

There was a moment late in May when it appeared that two of the brigades Lee sought might actually be released to join him on campaign, but then Federal movements on the Peninsula — tentative movements, as it turned out — so alarmed Richmond that they were recalled. So it happened that the veteran brigades of Ransom, Cooke, Corse, and Jenkins did not march with General Lee on his expedition north of the Potomac. Since the first of the year Lee had lost these four superior brigades and was now gaining but two considerably less than superior ones in return.

The Federal command on the Atlantic coast supplied the irony in the case. Never known for its initiative, it had managed more by accident than by design to (in Lee's words) "retain there our troops in idleness." Harvey Hill expressed no regrets for his mulishness and no sympathy for what Lee was seeking to accomplish. "Genl. Lee is venturing upon a very hazardous movement," he told his wife; "and one that must be fruitless, if not disastrous."

However badly this affair of reinforcements was handled, it was in the end a commentary on the severe manpower strains rending the Confederacy. "I readily perceive the disadvantage of standing still," President Davis wrote Lee on May 31, "and sorely regret that I can not give you the means which would make it quite safe to attempt all that we desire."[9]

"I AGREE WITH YOU also in believing that our Army would be invincible if it could be properly organized and officered," General Lee wrote on May 21, replying to a letter from John B. Hood, one of his divisional commanders. "There never were such men in an Army before. But there is the difficulty — proper commanders — where can they be obtained?" In his orders for the army's reorganization, issued May 30, Lee had to be concerned that his new choices for proper commanders would be worthy of the men they led.[10]

The First Corps was the least of his concerns, and the least affected by the reorganization. Longstreet was solid and capable and dependable, always an anchor on which to rely in a battlefield storm. Lafayette McLaws, square-built and burly, displayed many of Longstreet's qualities, and his division was an experienced one. None of McLaws's brigadiers — Joseph Kershaw, William Barksdale, Paul Semmes, and William Wofford — was a professional soldier, but each had made himself into a first-rate officer and combat leader.

In an army of notable fighters, Hood and his division were unsurpassed in the heat of combat. On a battlefield Hood was a magnetic figure to his men, and his fights at Gaines's Mill on the Peninsula and at Sharpsburg were pivotal actions in those battles. The Texas Brigade, once Hood's and now under the martial Jerome Bonaparte Robertson, and the Alabamians of Evander Law had fought side by side since the Peninsula campaign. The other two brigades in Hood's division were equally war-like Georgians, under Henry "Old Rock" Benning and George "Tige" Anderson, with fighting records also dating back to the Peninsula.

Neither Hood's division nor Longstreet's third division, under George Pickett, had been at Chancellorsville, and Pickett himself was something of a latecomer to battle-leading. Wounded at Gaines's Mill, he had not seen any sustained action since, and the Pennsylvania campaign would mark his first serious test in divisional command. He was a protégé of Longstreet's, and celebrated for the dashing figure he cut. "Long ringlets flowed loosely over his shoulders, trimmed and highly perfumed," wrote a Longstreet staff man of Pickett; "his beard likewise was curling and giving out the scents of Araby."[11]

The two brigades detached for D. H. Hill's benefit left Pickett with but three brigades, all of Virginians. His brigadiers were strikingly varied. Lewis Armistead was a brusque, crusty veteran of the old army, where after twenty-two years he had reached the rank of captain. Richard Brooke Garnett, a West Pointer who served in California with Armistead before the war, had incurred the wrath (unjustly) of Stonewall Jackson while leading the Stonewall Brigade, and now was consumed by the need to regain his honor. The third brigadier, James Kemper, was of the species political general — he had been speaker in the Virginia legislature — but with a grounding in military affairs that had made him a quick study and an able leader.

In contrast to the First Corps, the Second had to absorb and adjust to many changes after Chancellorsville. The new corps commander, Dick Ewell, appeared to have the confidence of everyone in the corps — everyone except perhaps himself. Ewell would write that he was "provoked excessively with myself at times at my depression of spirits & dismal way of looking at every thing, present & future & may be next day considering the same things as all 'Couleur de rose.'" The appointment seems to have caused General Lee some unease. In a postwar conversation, Lee said he had been aware of a certain "want of decision" that sometimes affected Ewell, and that before the Pennsylvania campaign he "talked long and earnestly with him" about it.[12]

Ewell's old division had been led since his wounding at Second Manassas by Jubal Early, widely acknowledged to be the most ill-tempered officer in the Army of Northern Virginia. Stooped by rheumatism and careless of appearances, Early was snarling and aggressive on the battlefield and off. General Lee called him "my bad old man" and trusted him with independent commands, but how Early might fare under Ewell's direction rather than Jackson's was less clear. Early's four brigades were led by an uncertain mix of officers. Harry Hays was fully up to the challenge of managing his rough-hewn brigade of "Louisiana Tigers," and John B. Gordon had earned the devotion of his Georgians. Before a charge Gordon assured them, "I ask you to go no farther than I am willing to lead!" and he was as good as his word. But there were questions about Early's other two brigades. Robert Hoke had gone down with a wound at Chancellorsville, and his brigade was now in the hands of Isaac Avery, a colonel exercising his first high command. Sixty-five-year-old William "Extra Billy" Smith — his sobriquet came from the extra fees he had collected as a mail contractor during Andrew Jackson's administration — was a former governor (and now governor-elect) of Virginia and the oldest general in the army. In commanding a brigade Extra Billy was straining the limits of his martial abilities.[13]

Robert Rodes had risen from captaining the company of "Warrior Guards" in Alabama in 1861 to earning the equivalent of a battlefield promotion to major general for the fight he made at Chancellorsville. A graduate of the Virginia Military Institute — he was the only non–West Pointer among Lee's division commanders — Rodes had the visage of a Viking warrior and was considered one of the rising stars in the army. His brigade leaders were, like Early's, a mixed lot. George Doles and Stephen Dodson Ramseur were highly rated leaders who most recently had spearheaded Jackson's flank attack at Chancellorsville. Alfred Iverson, however, was embroiled in bitter turmoil with his North Carolinians, and Edward O'Neal, a lawyer and politician in civilian life, had brought not a shred of military experience when he joined up — and it showed at Chancellorsville in his first brigade command. Rodes's fifth brigade was Junius Daniel's, brought up from North Carolina in trade for Alfred Colquitt's brigade. Daniel's men were inexperienced, but there were almost 2,200 of them, and Daniel himself was a West Pointer with considerably more leadership promise than the departed Colquitt.

Ewell's third division, once Stonewall Jackson's old division, underwent a complete change in its high command as a consequence of Chancellorsville. Raleigh Colston had led it poorly there, and Lee took the unusual step (for him) of unceremoniously relieving him. Colston's replacement was Edward Johnson, known as "Allegheny" for the mountains in western Virginia he had defended early in the war, and to distinguish him from the three other General Johnsons in Confederate service. He had been wounded in the Valley campaign, where he attracted the attention of Jackson, who bid for his services when he would be fit for duty.

That proved only in time for the Pennsylvania campaign. Allegheny was rough-edged and something less than a gentleman, and it was a question how he would take to the new command — his first in a year — and especially to four new heads of brigade.

The Stonewall Brigade mourned its commander, E. F. Paxton, killed at Chancellorsville, but his replacement was the quite capable James A. Walker. George H. Steuart took over the brigade of Edward Warren, wounded at Chancellorsville. "Maryland" Steuart he was called, a hard-bitten regular who Lee hoped would bring harmony to a bickering brigade made up of Marylanders, Virginians, and North Carolinians. The division's Louisiana brigade had also seen its general, Francis Nicholls, wounded in the late battle; the senior colonel, Jesse M. Williams, replaced him.

The case of the fourth brigade was a curious one. In the last three battles its commander, John R. Jones, had avoided combat in suspect fashion. The brigade was demoralized, and he was quietly but firmly removed . . . and replaced by another John Jones. John M. Jones, a West Pointer, had served thus far only in staff positions, presumably because of a drinking problem; he had been known since his Academy days as "Rum" Jones. Apparently he had gained the edge on his problem, for in proposing him for the brigade assignment Lee told President Davis that should Jones "fail in his duty he will instantly resign." John M. Jones had much to prove, to the army and to himself.[14]

A. P. Hill was a familiar figure to a large part of the new Third Corps, for at its heart was the Light Division he had first commanded on the Peninsula. Four of the Light Division brigades were designated a division and put in the charge of Dorsey Pender. Hill wrote enthusiastically that Pender "has the best drilled and disciplined Brigade in the Division, and more than all, possesses the unbounded confidence of the Division." Pender's old brigade went to Alfred Scales, a one-time member of the U.S. House of Representatives who in 1861 enlisted as a private and had risen through the brigade ranks. The proud South Carolina brigade was now under Colonel Abner Perrin, in place of the wounded Samuel McGowan. As an example of the army's shrinking leadership pool, it was at Chancellorsville that Perrin first led even a regiment in battle. Pender's other two brigades, however, had experienced and able generals in James H. Lane and Edward L. Thomas.[15]

Harry Heth's new infantry division, the army's ninth, had only one tested brigade leader — the combative James Jay Archer, who brought his Alabamians and Tennesseans over from the Light Division. The other

Light Division brigade, formerly Heth's, was now under plodding, uninspiring Colonel John Brockenbrough. Filling out the new division were the two untested brigades from North Carolina, under Johnston Pettigrew and Joe Davis, the president's nephew.

Richard H. Anderson, brought over from Longstreet's corps, led the third of Powell Hill's divisions. Dick Anderson was a thorough and much-respected professional. He had managed efficiently at Chancellorsville without Longstreet's presence, and was well regarded by General Lee. Four of his five brigades were led by competent but very different officers. The calmly efficient Cadmus Wilcox was resentful at being passed over for higher command (and rightly so), but it did not mark his generalship. Another solid veteran, Ambrose Ransom "Rans" Wright, lacked for color as well except when it came to writing his highly dramatized reports. William Mahone's feistiness and belligerency seemed designed to compensate for his diminutive figure. When news that he had taken a flesh wound at Second Manassas reached his wife, she knew it had to be serious, she said, "for William has no flesh whatever." Handsome Carnot Posey, invariably known as the "dashing Mississippian," had his first chance at brigade-leading at Chancellorsville and did well, winning the respect of his hard-to-please Mississippians. Anderson's fifth brigade, three small Florida regiments that totaled fewer than 800 men, was under the temporary leadership of Colonel David Lang, making his command debut.[16]

Unlike the Federals, the Confederate artillerists undertook no wholesale changes after Chancellorsville. Only a limited reshuffling was required in Lee's reorganization. One artillery battalion was assigned to each of the nine divisions, and the army's artillery reserve was broken up, replaced by a two-battalion reserve for each corps. To fit this pattern required the formation of just one additional battalion. The major personnel change was a new title for the army's senior artillerist, the bumbling William Nelson Pendleton. Rather than head the (now nonexistent) artillery reserve, Pendleton was given the more or less advisory title General in Chief of Artillery. His impatient subordinates hoped that would sever him from any combat role. Yet one much-needed reform remained out of reach. Throughout the Pennsylvania campaign some of the most skilled artillerists of the Civil War would find themselves loading often inferior guns with frequently shoddy ammunition.[17]

"I hardly think it necessary to state to your Excellency," General Lee wrote President Davis just after Chancellorsville, "that unless we can increase the Cavalry attached to this army we shall constantly be subjected

Allen C. Redwood, a staff officer in the 55th Virginia infantry, titled this drawing *Confederate Types*. (Century Collection)

to aggressive expeditions of the enemy similar to those experienced in the last ten days." His reference was to the Yankee cavalry raiders who had penetrated to the very outskirts of Richmond. The alarm was vastly greater than the damage, but changes followed swiftly. For the Pennsylvania campaign Lee would have double the cavalry force previously attached to his army.

At Chancellorsville J.E.B. Stuart's cavalry division had operated with but two brigades — those of Fitzhugh Lee, the commanding general's nephew, and W.H.F. "Rooney" Lee, the commanding general's son. The third brigade, under Wade Hampton, had like Hood's and Pickett's infantry been stationed south due to the food and forage shortages on the Rappahannock. Hampton was now back with the army, and in Hampton and the two Lees Jeb Stuart had three expert generals of cavalry. The commanding general then began to scour all the nearby commands to raise more troopers, with results that appeared somewhat problematical.

He was able to obtain from D. H. Hill, without the slightest protest, a small brigade under Beverly Robertson; Hill had characterized Robertson's command as "wonderfully inefficient." From southwestern Virginia came Albert Jenkins's brigade, very rough and unschooled by Stuart's standards. Jenkins was a Virginia planter-lawyer-politician who had rushed to the colors in 1861 and who was picking up his military education on the job. William E. Jones brought 1,700 troopers from the Shenandoah Valley. "Grumble" Jones was famously sour of disposition but trained at West Point, and therefore was of value in managing a brigade. He and Jeb Stuart struck sparks, however, not a promising sign. Lastly, there was the large brigade under John D. Imboden, from western Virginia. Imboden was a lawyer-politician who started his service in 1861 by organizing the Virginia Partisan Rangers, and his brigade retained much of that partisan flavor. Its forte was freewheeling detached service. These additions would give Stuart 12,400 troopers, fully half of whom would require very careful handling in order to realize whatever worth they might have.[18]

By the time he was prepared to cross the Potomac, General Lee could count under his command some 80,000 men of all arms — 67,600 infantry and artillery and 12,400 cavalry. It would be the largest army he had commanded since the opening of the Seven Days' Battles in June 1862; then his total force came to 92,400. On the Peninsula Lee had been within 13,500 men of achieving parity with the enemy. Marching into Pennsylvania a year later, he would fall short of parity by some 32,700 men.[19]

Questions were bound to be raised among thoughtful observers about the leadership in this new-formed Army of Northern Virginia. Chief among them, of course, involved the ultimate effects of Stonewall Jackson's death. How much of the leadership vacuum would be taken up by Dick Ewell and Powell Hill? How would Longstreet handle his new position as Lee's senior lieutenant? Could the army's new patchwork ninth division be shaped into an effective fighting force while on the march? Could the new additions to the cavalry be managed?

There were, to be sure, several brigades under uncertain leadership, yet some of these were just as uncertain before Chancellorsville as after. And without a doubt there were gains. Allegheny Johnson was manifestly an improvement on Raleigh Colston, for example, and the army was better off without John R. Jones and Alfred Colquitt. On balance, at the divisional and brigade levels the army was about as strong in leadership as before. Any challenges in the coming campaign would more probably be felt at the corps level.

ALL THROUGH MAY and into June the news reaching Richmond from Mississippi grew progressively worse. It was reported that General Pemberton finally had marched out of Vicksburg to challenge Grant's army in the field, only to be beaten badly twice. Pemberton's troops fled back into the Vicksburg lines with the Yankees hard on their heels. Grant soon ringed the city, reestablished his communications, and opened siege operations. Joe Johnston with his relief force watched from afar and called for more reinforcements. At first President Davis was optimistic, writing Lee that "Pemberton is stoutly defending the entrenchments at Vicksburg, and Johnston has an army out side, which I suppose will be able to raise the siege." A few days later, however, his optimism had faded. "Genl. Johnston did not, as you thought advisable, attack Grant promptly," he told Lee, "and I fear the result. . . ." As early as June 15 Johnston would end the suspense. "I consider saving Vicksburg hopeless," he telegraphed Richmond.[20]

Lee was meanwhile hastening his preparations for the march. While he saw no possibility of saving Vicksburg by his own operations, there was the strong possibility of countering or neutralizing the evil effects of its loss. He explained the case to Secretary Seddon: "As far as I can judge there is nothing to be gained by this army remaining quietly on the defensive. . . ." He spoke of the risk of "taking the aggressive" against the large Federal army entrenched on the other side of the Rappahannock. "Unless it can be drawn out in a position to be assailed," Lee said, it would in its own time renew the offensive and likely push the Army of Northern Virginia back into the Richmond defenses. "This may be the result in any event, still I think it is worth a trial to prevent such a catastrophe." He put the matter in a nutshell: "There is always hazard in military movements, but we must decide between the positive loss of inactivity and the risk of action."

General Lee set June 3 as the starting date for the Pennsylvania campaign. "I recall the morning vividly," wrote First Corps artillerist Porter Alexander. "A beautiful bright June day, & about 11 A.M. a courier from Longstreet's headqrs. brought the order. Although it was only to march to Culpeper C. H. we knew that it meant another great battle with the enemy's army. . . ."[21]

4   Armies on the March

FOR THE PAST ten days, as May turned to June, rumors had been flying through the Army of Northern Virginia about where the army was
bound. Since it was considered highly unlikely that General Lee would
retreat or withdraw after a victory, the consensus opinion was an advance north. Not a few speculated that Pennsylvania was the target. "I
am no convert to the invasion theory with an army no larger than ours,"
Captain Charles M. Blackford of Longstreet's staff wrote his father, "but
still I have so much confidence in Gen. Lee that I am satisfied with his
plans be they what they may." Blackford's was a view widely echoed. As
Porter Alexander remembered those June days, "nothing gave me much
concern so long as I knew that Gen. Lee was in command. I am sure there
can never have been an army with more supreme confidence in its commander than that army had in Gen. Lee. We looked forward to victory
under him as confidently as to successive sunrises."[1]

One of the fine arts of the military craft is disengaging one's army
from a guarding army without striking sparks and igniting a battle. Initially, Lee's task was made easier by the fact that the Rappahannock
firmly separated the two forces, and by the Wilderness region west of
Fredericksburg that concealed his opening moves. Lafayette McLaws's
division of Longstreet's corps was first to move, from its position behind
Fredericksburg. In the event, McLaws's troops setting the pace on the
bright morning of Wednesday, June 3, 1863, formally marked the start of
the Pennsylvania campaign. Precisely one month later the campaign
would reach its climax.

Lee set the assembly point for his march of invasion at Culpeper, some
30 miles northwest of Fredericksburg. Culpeper, a court house village
on the Orange & Alexandria Railroad, was a dozen miles south of the
Rappahannock and, most notably, well beyond the right flank of Joe
Hooker's army. On the afternoon of June 3, John B. Hood's division, also
from Longstreet's First Corps, was ordered to Culpeper from its posting
to the south on the Rapidan. For the moment, Longstreet's third divi-

sion, under George Pickett, remained well to the south at Hanover Junction, as a guardian for Richmond.

Over the next two days, Dick Ewell's three divisions joined the march to Culpeper. Lee's design now became clear: to shift two-thirds of his army to the northwest and past Hooker's flank, while A. P. Hill's Third Corps remained entrenched at Fredericksburg to observe Hooker and perhaps fix him in place long enough for the rest of the army to gain several marches on the Federals. Mr. Davis expressed his worry that Lee "could not get away" from the Rappahannock without being attacked, but Lee seemed confident he could do just that and then move swiftly north to threaten Washington. That, he thought, should engage the Federals' full attention and distract them from any thought of making a dash at Richmond. Once he was in a position to menace the enemy's capital, Lee said, "there was no need of further fears about their moving on Richmond."[2]

Joe Hooker's intelligence sources were vigilant, and hints of Confederate activity across the river soon reached Army of the Potomac headquarters. As early as June 4 Colonel George Sharpe of the Bureau of Military Information was reporting, "There is a considerable movement of the enemy. Their camps are disappearing at some points." Hooker reacted quickly. He had a pair of pontoon bridges thrown across the Rappahannock just downstream from Fredericksburg, and ordered a division of Sedgwick's Sixth Corps across as a reconnaissance in force "to learn, if possible, what the enemy are about." After skirmishing for a time with A. P. Hill's troops, Sedgwick reported that he could not advance 200 yards without bringing on a battle. The enemy was strongly posted, he said, and "I am satisfied that it is not safe to mass the troops on this side." General Lee, as a precaution, had halted the march of Ewell's corps, but when the Federal interlopers showed no signs of aggression, he sent Ewell on his way.[3]

For several days, too, intelligence had been accumulating of Jeb Stuart's cavalry massing around Culpeper in preparation, so the stories went, for a major raid of some sort. The raid rumor was actually planted by the Rebels to distract from their infantry movements, but in any event it suited Hooker perfectly as offering an opportunity for a fight.

Ever since taking command of the Potomac army in January, Joe Hooker had sought to inject some backbone into the cavalry. In March he had ordered the troopers under General Stoneman to "attack and rout or destroy" Fitz Lee's cavalry brigade in the vicinity of Kelly's Ford on the Rappahannock. Although Stoneman failed to press his battle to a conclu-

Union artillery shells Rebel positions across the Rappahannock on June 5 as the Sixth Corps prepares to cross the river to make a reconnaissance in force. Drawing by Alfred Waud. (Library of Congress)

sion, his men at least had demonstrated their mettle as fighters, and morale went up. Hooker now determined to repeat the experiment. If Stuart intended making mischief with one of his raids, he told the president, it was his "great desire to 'bust it up' before it got fairly under way." He would send all the cavalry against Stuart, stiffened by about 3,000 infantry.[4]

Hooker meanwhile was trying to divine Lee's intentions. He telegraphed Lincoln on June 5 that Confederate infantry appeared ready to move up the Rappahannock "with a view to the execution of a movement similar to that of Lee's last year" — that is, to cross the upper Potomac into Maryland, as Lee had done in September 1862 — or "to throw his army between mine and Washington. . . ." If Lee did indeed intend to move north, he was known to be holding back a substantial force south of the Rappahannock around Fredericksburg. "After giving the subject my best reflection," said Hooker, "I am of opinion that it is my duty to pitch into his rear." Whatever else this might achieve, Hooker was confident that it would check the enemy's offensive plans.

Lincoln replied that he was turning Hooker's telegram over to General Halleck for a proper professional military response, but then he went on to offer his own view of the case — an astute view, couched in one of his vivid frontiersman's metaphors. Should Lee move north, leaving behind a force at Fredericksburg, "tempting you to fall upon it," he warned his general not to take the bait. "In one word, I would not take any risk of being entangled upon the river, like an ox jumped half over a fence, and liable to be torn by dogs, front and rear, without a fair chance to gore one way or kick the other. If Lee would come to my side of the river, I would keep on the same side & fight him. . . ."

General Halleck expressed the same opinion, if less colorfully. If Lee was in fact marching toward the northwest, Hooker ought to be on his flank and in position to cut him in two. "Would it not be more advantageous to fight his movable column first, instead of first attacking his intrenchments, with your own forces separated by the Rappahannock?" asked the general-in-chief. He also warned of Washington's vulnerability to the enemy's main force should the Army of the Potomac lag too far behind. Hooker subsided, contenting himself with his reconnaissance in force at Fredericksburg and with pressing his attack against Stuart's cavalry at Culpeper.[5]

ALL THIS TIME Jeb Stuart was preening himself in pleased expectation of leading the largest cavalry force the Confederacy had ever assembled. By the May 31 returns, Stuart at the moment had under his command five brigades of cavalry and six batteries of horse artillery, 10,292 officers and men all told. He scheduled a grand review of his mounted legions for June 5. Guests, most of them female, were invited from Culpeper and surrounding counties. Special trains carrying the visitors pulled into Brandy Station on the Orange & Alexandria, close by Stuart's headquarters, and on the evening of June 4 there was a grand ball in celebration of the grand review. According to a newspaper account, that evening Culpeper's court house was a "gay and dazzling scene, illuminated by floods of light from numerous chandeliers," and the gallant cavaliers and their ladies partook of "revelry by night."

The grand review on June 5 was surely the proudest day of Jeb Stuart's thirty years. As he led a cavalcade of resplendent staff officers to the reviewing stand, trumpeters heralded his coming and women and girls strewed his path with flowers. Before the awed spectators the assembled cavalry brigades stretched a mile and a half. After Stuart and his entourage galloped past the line in review, the troopers in their turn saluted

James Ewell Brown Stuart, the preeminent Confederate cavalier.
(Cook Collection, Valentine Museum)

the reviewing stand in columns of squadrons. In performing a second "march past," the squadrons started off at a trot, then spurred to a gallop. Drawing sabers and breaking into the Rebel yell, the troopers rushed toward the horse artillery drawn up in battery. The gunners responded defiantly, firing blank charges. Amidst this tumult of cannon fire and thundering hooves, a number of ladies swooned into their escorts' arms. In the evening there was an outdoor ball, lit by soft moonlight and bright bonfires. "It was a brilliant day," wrote Major Henry B. McClellan of the cavalry staff, "and the thirst for the 'pomp and circumstance' of war was fully satisfied."

Stuart's only disappointment was the absence of General Lee, who was involved in getting Dick Ewell's corps started on its march west from Fredericksburg. Nothing daunted, Stuart scheduled a second grand review, for June 8. Absent civilian spectators, this was less the spectacle of June 5 and more a strictly military exercise. The general commanding would not strain horseflesh or waste gunpowder, so this time there was no mock charge against the guns. Nevertheless, with 10,000 horsemen going through their reviewing evolutions, there was spectacle enough. "It was a splendid sight," General Lee wrote his wife. "The men & horses looked well. . . . Stuart was in all his glory."[6]

Orders for the next day called on General Stuart to lead his cavalry division across the Rappahannock to screen the northward march of the infantry. That night, still aglow from the splendor of the review, Stuart allowed his various commands to scatter widely across the landscape so they might conveniently reach the river crossings in parallel columns the next morning, June 9. He made his headquarters bivouac on Fleetwood Hill, an eminence overlooking Brandy Station. If Jeb Stuart gave any thought at all to the enemy that night, he probably focused on just where north of the river he might first encounter the Yankee cavalry.

At that moment the Yankee cavalry was just barely north of the Rappahannock — quietly massing in great force opposite Beverly Ford and Kelly's Ford so as to cross the river in the early hours of the morning of June 9 and carry out Joe Hooker's crisp orders "to disperse and destroy" the Rebel cavalry reported to be "assembled in the vicinity of Culpeper. . . ."[7]

The task Hooker had assigned to Alfred Pleasonton was a straightforward one. His was neither an intelligence-gathering mission nor a reconnaissance in force, like Sedgwick's at Fredericksburg. Instead he was simply to smash up Stuart's cavalry before it could make any mischief, thereby testing the fighting spirit of the Federal cavalry and its new commander. The right wing of the assault, crossing the Rappahannock at Beverly Ford, was under John Buford, with his own division, the cavalry's reserve brigade, and a reinforcing brigade of infantry. The left wing, crossing at Kelly's Ford six miles downstream, was commanded by David Gregg. Gregg had his own division and the division of Alfred Duffié, plus an infantry brigade. The whole force came to some 7,900 cavalry and 3,000 infantry. The two wings were to join at Brandy Station on the railroad — a march of four miles for Buford and eight for Gregg — and then strike out together the six miles to Culpeper and the reported bivouac of

Alfred Pleasonton challenged Stuart's cavalry at Brandy
Station. (Library of Congress)

the Rebel cavalry. General Pleasonton set the starting time for the crossing at "earliest dawn," 4:30 A.M. — earlier by a good margin than the
time Stuart had set for *his* river crossing that morning.

As it happened, only half of Pleasonton's force followed the timetable,
which left the whole operation seriously out of balance. At Kelly's Ford
the division of Colonel Duffié was slated to lead the march and act as a
flank guard at Stevensburg, south of Brandy Station, to intercept any
Confederate reinforcements drawn to the battle. But Duffié was misdirected and did not reach the crossing site until after 6:00 A.M. Gregg's division, which was intended to link up with Buford at Brandy Station at

an early hour, could not complete its river crossing until 9 o'clock. By that time, the Battle of Brandy Station was already four hours old, and was being fought on the Federal side only by John Buford's forces.[8]

By 5:00 A.M. Buford's right wing, spearheaded by Benjamin "Grimes" Davis's brigade, had rushed through streaming white mist obscuring Beverly Ford to seize the crossing with hardly a shot fired. The surprised pickets, a company of 6th Virginia cavalrymen, sent off couriers to raise the alarm and fell back firing before the enemy advance. Their nearest cavalry support was the Virginia brigade of William "Grumble" Jones, encamped at St. James Church some two miles distant. Between the church and the ford were four batteries of Stuart's horse artillery, casually posted for the planned march north that day and entirely unsupported but for the company of the 6th Virginia on picket duty — which just then was heading for the rear. In a letter home, artillerist Charles Phelps reported that "about daylight the Yanks drove in our Picket stationed at Beverly's Ford on the Rappahannock and came near surprising us in bed. . . . They charged up to our camp and killed & wounded several horses before we could get out."

That they got out at all was thanks, first, to Captain James Hart, who managed to drag one gun of his South Carolina battery into the roadway and open on the charging Yankee cavalry with canister. Behind this covering fire the rest of the guns were hitched up and started for the rear. At the same time a ragtag body of Rebel troopers, pressed to the front by Grumble Jones to rescue the batteries, rode headlong at the head of the Federal column. These troopers, from the 6th and 7th Virginia, many of them half dressed and some even riding bareback, set back the enemy long enough for the horse artillery to make good its escape and establish a gun line on a ridge near St. James Church. The Federal drive was further disrupted when Grimes Davis, fighting at the head of his brigade, was shot through the head and killed.[9]

Thus far the battle was one of mutual surprise — the Confederates startled by the unexpected Federal offensive, the Federals startled to encounter major opposition so far in advance of the Confederate cavalry encampment they had supposed was at Culpeper. Both sides scrambled to reinforce the spreading fight at St. James Church.

From his headquarters at Fleetwood Hill Jeb Stuart sent couriers flying in every direction — to Beverly Robertson to cover the lower Rappahannock fords, to Fitz Lee's brigade eight miles in the rear to come to the front, to Rooney Lee to support Grumble Jones on the left, to Wade Hampton near Stevensburg to come up and tie into Jones's line on the right. General Buford, seeing the Confederate line swelling into a broad arc in front of him, widened his own line to the left by bringing Thomas Devin's brigade to the front, and his reserve brigade (U.S. regulars and the 6th Pennsylvania) to support the right and center. Buford posted the brigade of his supporting infantry in the woods to the rear to act as an anchor if his line should waver at any point.

This maneuvering along the St. James Church battle lines was accompanied by a succession of charges and countercharges across a half-mile of open field, with much close-in cavalry fighting, both mounted and dismounted. The Confederates in particular made skillful use of sharpshooters to harass the Yankee flanks. "I had a fine opportunity of witnessing some fine cavalry fighting," wrote the Southern horse artillerist Charles Phelps. "Our men charged them into the woods but were met by two brigades of infantry and had to fall back. Then the Yanks charged our cavalry. . . . I thought at one time I was gone, the fighting being so general that we could not use our pieces."

The Yankee countercharge Lieutenant Phelps described was launched by the 6th Pennsylvania, supported by the 6th U.S. regulars. "Never rode troopers more gallantly . . . ," admitted Captain Hart, whose South Carolina battery was a target of the assault, "as under a fire of shell and shrapnel, and finally of canister, they dashed up to the very muzzles, then through and beyond our guns, passing between Hampton's left and Jones' right. Here they were simultaneously attacked from both flanks, and the survivors driven back." The 6th regulars lost 67 men in the charge, a quarter of their attacking force. The 6th Pennsylvania reported one-third of its men unhorsed by the "terrible fire of rifle shot in front and of grape and canister from the enemy's battery on our left." General Buford would credit the bold attack with stabilizing his left, and indeed the two sides appeared so stunned by the melee that an uneasy calm fell across this sector of the field.[10]

Jeb Stuart was on the scene of the St. James Church fighting now, and during the lull several of his youthful staff members scrambled into a big cherry tree to feast on the ripe fruit, pitching what they didn't eat down to Stuart and his generals. Without warning a Federal shell came screaming through the tree, splintering branches and sending the cherry pickers all plunging to the ground in unseemly haste. Stuart roared with laughter, recalled one of the staff, and called out, "What's the matter, boys, cherries getting sour?"

He was still in good humor when a courier reached him from Grumble Jones, relaying a warning from Beverly Robertson's pickets that Federal cavalry was on the march from the Kelly's Ford crossing. "Tell General Jones to attend to the Yankees in his front, and I'll watch the flanks," Stuart told the courier. Grumble Jones, who had little use for Stuart to begin with, was irritated by the cavalier tone of this response. "So he thinks they ain't coming, does he?" Jones snapped. "Well, let him alone; he'll damned soon see for himself."

And so he did. Shortly before noon, a breathless courier reined up with a message from Stuart's adjutant, Major Henry McClellan, at cavalry headquarters on Fleetwood Hill. The courier announced that a Federal column was just then approaching Brandy Station — squarely in the rear of the Confederate battle line at St. James Church. Stuart's first reaction was disbelief. "Ride back there," he ordered one of his officers, "and see what this foolishness is all about!" Just as the man was starting back, a second courier rushed up. "General," he shouted, "the Yankees are at Brandy!" Frank Robertson of the staff long remembered the moment. "The only time in my fourteen months service with Gen. Stuart," he wrote, "that he seemed *rattled* was when Frank Deane, one of his couriers, dashed up and told him the Yankees were at Brandy Station. This was startling indeed. . . ."[11]

Major McClellan, manning headquarters alone, with but a few couriers on call, had been utterly astonished to see a long column of enemy cavalry approaching "within cannon shot" of the station and of Fleetwood Hill, the dominant high ground in the area. McClellan could not understand how the Federals had evaded Beverly Robertson's brigade, which Stuart had earlier charged with guarding the downriver crossings, especially Kelly's Ford. General Robertson, it seemed, was exceedingly literal-minded. As ordered, he had posted his command, some 1,500 men, on the direct route from Kelly's Ford to Brandy Station. When the Federals took a more roundabout route, Robertson duly reported that fact . . . and stayed right where he was while two divisions of Yankee cavalry marched past without the least hindrance.

This was David Gregg's left wing of the operation, finally across Kelly's Ford and pushing ahead fast, anxiously hearing the din of battle from the direction of Buford's right wing. Alfred Duffié's division went on ahead toward Stevensburg to seal off the southern flank; Gregg's division, led by the brigade of Sir Percy Wyndham, turned up the road leading to Brandy Station. Sir Percy was easily the gaudiest figure in the Federal cavalry. A British soldier of fortune who had been knighted for his service with Garibaldi, he sported spectacular waxed mustaches and a phalanx of medals from various European armies.

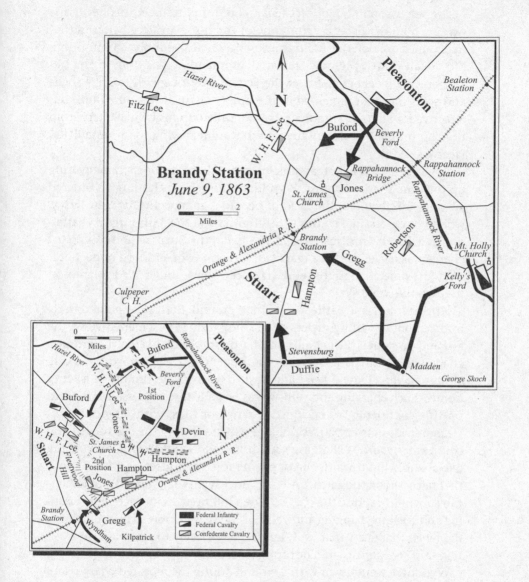

Brandy Station
June 9, 1863

0   2
Miles

Hazel River

Fitz Lee

W. H. F. Lee

N

Pleasonton

Bealeton
Station

Buford

Beverly
Ford

Rappahannock
Station

St. James
Church

Jones

Rappahannock
Bridge

Rappahannock River

Orange & Alexandria R. R.

Brandy
Station

Gregg

Robertson

Mt. Holly
Church

Culpeper
C. H.

Stuart

Hampton

Kelly's
Ford

Stevensburg

Duffie

Madden

George Skoch

0   1
Miles

Hazel River

Buford

W. H. F. Lee

Buford

Beverly
Ford

1st
Position

Pleasonton

Rappahannock River

W. H. F. Lee

Jones

Devin

St. James
Church

Hampton

N

Stuart

Fleetwood
Hill

2nd
Position

Hampton

Jones

Orange & Alexandria R. R.

Brandy
Station

Gregg

Wyndham

Kilpatrick

■ Federal Infantry
▨ Federal Cavalry
▨ Confederate Cavalry

69

The sole weapon Major McClellan could find to meet this new crisis was a 6-pounder howitzer from one of the horse artillery batteries that had pulled out of the fight at the church to resupply ammunition. McClellan posted the howitzer in a commanding position on the hill and opened a deliberate fire at the Federal advance with the few shells and solid shot that remained in the limber chest. It was pure bluff, but effective for all that. Wyndham halted, called up his own artillery from the rear for counterbattery fire, and began deploying for an assault on Fleetwood Hill.

Once again, at the last possible moment, Rebel troopers came pelting up to blunt a Federal thrust. Wyndham himself was leading an ordered advance up the hill at the head of his old regiment, the 1st New Jersey, when he was assailed by the 12th Virginia and the 35th Virginia battalion that had been dispatched at the gallop by Stuart. The hasty Rebel charge was ragged and disorganized, something of a forlorn hope, but it won just time enough for reinforcing regiments under Wade Hampton to reach the scene.[12]

It became a classic battle for the high ground. Both sides poured in reinforcements. Swirling melees of slashing, firing horsemen covered the hill and its slopes; dust clouds and battle smoke blanketed the ground, challenging gunners to separate foe from friend, or even to fire at all. Walter Taylor, General Lee's adjutant, described the tumult in a letter home: "Such charging and yelling was never before witnessed and heard on this continent. We occupied a range of hills, with large tracts of cleared fields in every direction, and whichever way the eye turned you could see squadrons charging squadrons, and whole regiments rushing like a whirlwind towards the opposing force and meeting with a shock that fairly shook the earth." A New York cavalryman named Noble Preston sought to capture the chaos: "Then followed an indescribable clashing and slashing, banging and yelling. . . . We were now so mixed up with the rebels that every man was fighting desperately to maintain the position until assistance could be brought forward."

Wyndham went down with a wound during the repeated charges and countercharges. David Gregg, normally the soul of calm reserve in battle, was caught up in the moment and led one of the assaults himself. "As they neared the enemy General Gregg showed an enthusiasm that I had never noticed before," one of his men wrote. "He started his horse on a gallop . . . swinging his gauntlets over his head and hurrahing. . . ." A wild charge by 1st New Jersey troopers carried them right in among the guns of William McGregor's Virginia battery, one of whose gunners remembered the scene with amazement: "One of our men captured a prisoner with his sponge staff. Another one with a trail hand spike captured another prisoner. The writer had no weapon, tried to capture one with words only, but he heeded me not. Why did he not shoot me down, as I stood on the ground, looking at him, at a distance of a few feet only?"[13]

Gregg's second brigade was led by the reckless Judson Kilpatrick, who proceeded to live up to his nickname, "Kill-Cavalry." When he ordered two New York regiments to the charge, they were quickly broken one after the other and sent flying, leaving Kilpatrick "wild with excitement." Rushing up to his remaining regiment, the 1st Maine, he shouted to its colonel, Calvin Douty, "what can you do with your regiment?"

"I can drive the rebels to Hell, sir!" came the prompt reply, and the Maine troopers made a valiant effort to honor their colonel's pledge. They gained the crest of Fleetwood Hill and sliced right through two of Wade Hampton's regiments that had just put the New Yorkers to rout. The 1st Maine simply kept going, for over a mile, but from flank and rear the Rebels closed in and soon isolated it. At one point these Down East Yankees came near the Barbour house, where Generals Lee and Ewell and their staffs were watching the battle. "General Ewell," mapmaker Jed Hotchkiss remarked in his diary, "said we could gather into the house and defend it to the last." No such last-ditch effort become necessary. Douty's regiment, what was left of it, turned aside and finally managed to circle around and escape to the Federal lines.[14]

The fruitless charge of the 1st Maine marked General Gregg's last best effort. Gregg had no reserves left, three of his guns had already been overrun, and it did not appear that either of the divisions of Buford or Duffié was about to join him to carry on the battle for Fleetwood Hill. It was midafternoon now, and by all appearances Jeb Stuart's headquarters was secure and this latest crisis had been averted.

The hasty dispatch of forces by Grumble Jones and Wade Hampton from St. James Church to defend Fleetwood Hill seemed at first to promise new life for John Buford's stalled operation. It was not to be so, however. Rooney Lee's Virginians and North Carolinians took up good defensive positions and continued to block the Federal advance. Fighting in this sector during much of the day was more like an infantry than a cavalry engagement, with both sides often fighting dismounted. Indeed, it was here that the Federal supporting infantry got into the action, when a company each from the 2nd Massachusetts and 3rd Wisconsin flushed sharpshooting Rebel troopers out from behind a stone wall. In one final burst of charge and countercharge, Rooney Lee received a severe saber gash in the leg before finally driving back the enemy.

At Stevensburg, at the southern end of the sprawling battlefield, Colonel Calbraith Butler and the 200 men of his 2nd South Carolina managed to stymie an entire Yankee cavalry division. Initially the Federals here rode roughshod right over the 4th Virginia. "We drove them through the thick woods," wrote William Rawle Brooke of the 3rd Pennsylvania, "and it was a regular steeple chase, through ditches, over fences, through underbrush, getting our hands, faces, clothes torn. . . ." The South Carolinians were made of sterner stuff, however, and Colonel Duffié — who like Beverly Robertson on the Confederate side did not seem inclined to march to the sound of the guns elsewhere on the field — made only halfhearted efforts to brush away Butler's troopers. Colonel Butler's stand would cost him his right foot, shot off by a cannonball, but he prevented some 1,900 Yankees from joining the fight for Fleetwood Hill.[15]

Almost from the first clash of arms that day, General Pleasonton had cast his dispatches in pessimistic language. The enemy was found sooner than expected, at Brandy Station, and in great force — "Prisoners report that Stuart has 30,000 cavalry here" — and the fighting was severe and he had lost heavily. "They were aware of our movement, and were prepared," he insisted. Hooker responded that if Pleasonton could make no headway against the enemy cavalry, he should break off and return. By midday it was evident that the two wings could not unite, and in midafternoon Pleasonton issued orders to Buford and Gregg to pull back to the Rappahannock crossings.

Jeb Stuart was content to see the Yankees go. General Lee had told him during the fighting that the incursion was apparently a reconnaissance "to determine our force and position," which he had no intention of revealing, and he told Stuart not to expose his men too much. In any event, the presence of the Federal infantry made a cavalry pursuit highly risky. So it was that by 9:00 P.M. the Yankees had completed their recrossing unmolested. The Battle of Brandy Station had lasted some sixteen hours and was, everyone there agreed, the largest cavalry fight of the war thus far — a distinction it would in fact maintain through 1865.[16]

While Brandy Station certainly qualified as a battle spectacle, it was tactically inconclusive and produced no immediate strategic effect on either army. Lee's march north was neither hampered nor unduly delayed.

Alfred Pleasonton had quite failed to carry out his orders to "disperse and destroy" the Rebel cavalry, and the effort cost him considerably more casualties than he inflicted. Federal losses came to 866, with almost 45 percent marked as missing. Confederate casualties were 523. Stuart had managed the fighting skillfully enough, but the fact remained that he had been inexcusably surprised. Furthermore, he was exceedingly fortunate that the Yankees' delay at Kelly's Ford allowed him to fight Buford first and then Gregg, rather than facing the two simultaneously, attacking from front and rear.[17]

Pleasonton, characteristically, set about transmuting his role at Brandy Station from lead into gold. As he would later tell it in various quarters, instead of launching an attack to break up Stuart's cavalry, his Rappahannock crossing was actually a reconnaissance in force to find out what the enemy was planning. Then, during the fighting, he claimed to have captured the camp of the Rebel horse artillery "with important papers," after which he "seized Stuart's headquarters with all its documents." All this, along with a sighting of a trainload of Confederate infantry, was evidence enough for General Pleasonton to claim he discovered Lee's plan for invading Pennsylvania. All this, in fact, was fiction. The few fragments of intelligence gleaned from this day-long battle were already known to the Bureau of Military Information, and the Federals grasped no more of Lee's plan on June 10 than they had on June 8.[18]

Jeb Stuart, characteristically, claimed victory. He congratulated his men on a "glorious day." A strong force of the enemy "tested your mettle and found it proof-steel. . . . An act of rashness on his part was severely punished by rout and the loss of his artillery." The Southern press, however, took a rather different view of Brandy Station. An "ugly surprise" was how the *Charleston Mercury* characterized it, and the *Richmond Enquirer* concluded that "Gen. Stuart has suffered no little in public estimation by the late enterprises of the enemy." The *Richmond Examiner* spoke of the "puffed up cavalry" of the Army of Northern Virginia suffering the "consequences of negligence and bad management." Stuart was more prideful than most, and this public criticism stung him. General Dorsey Pender wrote his wife, "I suppose it is all right that Stuart should get all the blame, for when anything handsome is done he gets all the credit," but surely Stuart himself did not view the matter that philosophically.[19]

The surprise was the subject of comment by infantrymen. Major Henry McDaniel, whose 11th Georgia had to round up cavalry stragglers, explained to his wife that "Our boys have the heartiest contempt for Cavalrymen and never let slip an opportunity of taunting them with

73

their dread of battle. They do well enough in raids, frightening women and children, flirting with the ladies, and plundering the farmers," he noted, but the real fighting was left to "the ragged, barefoot infantry."

The most significant consequence of Brandy Station was its effect on the Federal cavalry arm. The astute Confederate observer of cavalry matters, Major Henry McClellan, looked back on Brandy Station and observed that "it *made* the Federal cavalry. Up to that time confessedly inferior to the Southern horsemen, they gained on this day that confidence in themselves and in their commanders which enabled them to contest so fiercely the subsequent battle-fields. . . ." A trooper in the 3rd Pennsylvania put it more simply: "the Cavalry begins to hold up its head."[20]

ON WEDNESDAY AFTERNOON, June 10, as scheduled, Dick Ewell's Second Corps stepped off for the Shenandoah Valley. It was Lee's plan for Ewell to clear the Valley route to the Potomac, followed by Longstreet marching east of the Blue Ridge to screen Ewell and to mystify the enemy (or in Lee's phrase, "with the view of creating embarrassment as to our plans"). In due course, depending upon the Federal response to these moves, Powell Hill's Third Corps would follow by way of the Valley.

From Culpeper Ewell followed a route well to the west, avoiding contact with the Yankee cavalry picketing the Rappahannock. "We found the grass, clover and timothy, perfectly luxuriant, a great change from the bare fields of Fredericksburg," Jed Hotchkiss noted in his diary. "The men marched well." On the 12th, Robert Rodes's lead division passed through Chester Gap in the Blue Ridge and descended into the Shenandoah. One of Rodes's men, Louis Leon, recorded their march as 56 miles in fifty-two hours, not unusually testing for the veterans of Jackson's foot cavalry. "We marched through Front Royal," Private Leon wrote, "where the ladies treated us very good."

That evening the cavalry brigade of Albert Jenkins, ordered over from southwestern Virginia, joined the column, and General Ewell gathered his lieutenants to plan their Valley campaign. Lee selected Ewell to lead the operation primarily because he had played a major role in Jackson's victorious Valley campaign of 1862. Furthermore, the bulk of Stonewall's old Valley army was now under Ewell in the Second Corps, and very much attuned to reconquering the Shenandoah. The Federals were known to be holding the lower Valley with large garrisons at Winchester and Harper's Ferry, and with lesser garrisons at Berryville and Martinsburg. It was Dick Ewell's task to clear away the enemy forces in his path and open the passage to the upper Potomac for a crossing into Maryland.

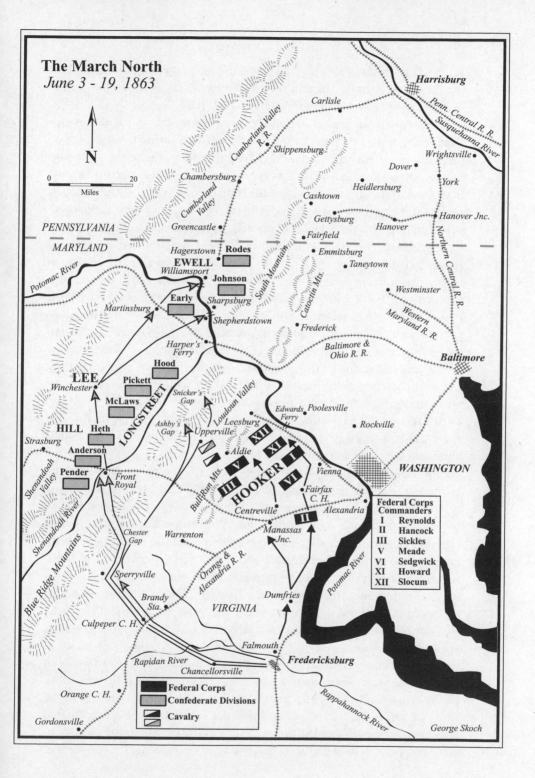

The March North
June 3 - 19, 1863

N

0 ____ 20
Miles

Harrisburg

Penn. Central R. R.

Susquehanna River

Carlisle

Cumberland Valley R. R.

Shippensburg

Wrightsville

Dover

Chambersburg

Heidlersburg

York

Cumberland Valley

Cashtown

Greencastle

Gettysburg   Hanover   Hanover Jnc.

Fairfield

PENNSYLVANIA

MARYLAND

Hagerstown   Rodes

Emmitsburg

Northern Central R. R.

EWELL   Taneytown

Williamsport

Johnson   Westminster

Potomac River

Early   Sharpsburg   Western Maryland R. R.

Martinsburg   Shepherdstown

Frederick   Baltimore

Harper's Ferry   Baltimore & Ohio R. R.

Hood

Pickett

LEE   McLaws   Snicker's Gap   Edwards Ferry   Poolesville

Winchester   Loudoun Valley

Ashby's Gap   Leesburg   Rockville

HILL   Heth   Upperville   XII

Strasburg   Aldie   XI

Anderson   V   WASHINGTON

Pender   Front Royal   III   HOOKER   I

Vienna

Shenandoah Valley   Centreville   Fairfax C. H.   Federal Corps Commanders

Chester Gap   Alexandria   I   Reynolds

Warrenton   II   VI   Sedgwick

Manassas Jnc.   II   Hancock

III   Sickles

Orange & Alexandria R. R.   V   Meade

Sperryville   VI   Sedgwick

Dumfries   XI   Howard

Brandy Sta.   XII   Slocum

Culpeper C. H.   VIRGINIA   Potomac River

Rapidan River   Falmouth

Chancellorsville   Fredericksburg

Orange C. H.   Federal Corps

Confederate Divisions

Gordonsville   Cavalry   Rappahannock River   George Skoch

Blue Ridge Mountains

With 23,000 men of all arms, Ewell's concern was whether the Yankees would get away before he could catch any of them — and whether the Army of the Potomac might interfere in the chase.[21]

The previous September, when General Lee set off on his first incursion north of the Potomac, he made a point of assuming the role of military statesman. He proposed to Mr. Davis that they couple the army's offensive into Maryland with a peace overture to Washington. Let the world understand, said the general, that in this war the Confederacy sought not conquest but only independence. "Such a proposition, coming from us at this time, could in no way be regarded as suing for peace," he explained. Quite the contrary, for "being made when it is in our power to inflict injury upon our adversary," it would actually give teeth to the claim for independence. Shrewdly, Lee pointed out that should Lincoln and his Republican administration reject the peace overture, they would have to accept the onus of prolonging the war "for purposes of their own." Northerners going to the polls that fall, he said, could easily see who was responsible for the continued fighting.

Nothing had come of this proposal, for just ten days after offering it Lee and the army were back in Virginia following the bloodletting at Sharpsburg. Now it was nine months later, and as Ewell led the vanguard of this second incursion toward the Potomac, General Lee again donned the mantle of military statesman. This time, however, he went beyond shrewdness and became positively Machiavellian.

In a letter to President Davis dated June 10, Lee pointed to what he termed "the rising peace party of the North" — and how it was being viewed in the South. He warned that the Confederacy dare not neglect any "honorable means of dividing and weakening our enemies," especially since it was becoming only too evident that the disparity of forces between the two sides was steadily growing. Southerners must not "conceal from ourselves that our resources in men are constantly diminishing," and therefore they could not afford to "abstain from measures or expressions that tend to discourage any party whose purpose is peace."

What troubled Lee was the hostility of Southern writers and public speakers, as expressed in the newspapers, toward "friends of peace at the North" who were linking an end to the fighting with restoration of the Union. Such parties should be encouraged by the Southern press, not spurned, said Lee. He opposed drawing "nice distinctions" between those declaring for "peace unconditionally and those who advocate it as a means of restoring the Union. . . ." Should the belief among Northerners "that peace will bring back the Union become general," he pointed out, "the war would no longer be supported, and that after all is what we are interested in bringing about." Divide first and then conquer was General Lee's objective, and that end justified any means: "When peace is proposed to us it will be time enough to discuss its terms. . . ."

President Davis's response to Lee's letter has not survived, but apparently he concurred with Lee's thinking. "I have received today your letter of the 19th," Lee wrote him, "and am much gratified by your views in relation to the peace party at the North." Even should they be unable to promote this "pacific feeling," said Lee, "our course ought to be so shaped as not to discourage it." As it happened, just then Mr. Davis had in hand a possible means to expand on Lee's ideas and to talk peace with the enemy.

From Georgia Alexander H. Stephens, the Confederacy's vice president, had written Davis volunteering to initiate talks with Washington to revive the lagging prisoner-exchange cartel. Stephens added the significant point that such a high-level meeting might offer the opportunity to discuss "on *any point*" in regard to the war, and thereby "to turn attention to a general adjustment. . . ." On June 18 Davis wired Stephens to come to Richmond immediately. It was the president's thought to attach the vice president to Lee's invading army as a sort of minister plenipotentiary. Indeed Mr. Davis could visualize thereby conquering a peace — the glorious moment when Lee's army, having vanquished the foe on some Pennsylvania battlefield, would require the services of a peace commissioner.[22]

The first dispatches from the Shenandoah must have nourished the president's hopes. The Federal commander at Winchester, Major General Robert H. Milroy, was a military amateur with a chip on his shoulder. He had little tolerance for professional soldiers, and in fact little tolerance for almost everyone. General Milroy, said one of his men, "was of the extremely nervous, excitable kind. He was generally out of patience with something or other, and when in such a mood it seemed difficult for him to treat one civilly." For the past six months Milroy had been considerably more than uncivil to the citizens of Winchester, who considered his regime there tyrannical and intolerable. President Davis charged him with outlawry, and Dick Ewell and his men were eager to execute sentence on this Yankee vandal.[23]

The intelligence that the Rebels were on the move had been slow to reach Washington, and watered down on arrival. Finally, at what would prove to be the eleventh hour, General-in-Chief Halleck telegraphed Milroy's superior, Major General Robert Schenck, that Winchester "should" be evacuated. When he was shown this dispatch, the belligerent Milroy fired back that he could hold Winchester "against any force the rebels can afford to bring against me." ("I deemed it impossible," Milroy said later, that any of Lee's main force could have slipped away from the Army of the Potomac's grasp.) Schenck, a politician turned general, took Halleck's "should" to be discretionary, and told Milroy, "Be ready for movement, but await further orders." At last, from Halleck, came peremptory orders to pull everything back to Harper's Ferry. Mr. Lincoln, following these exchanges at the War Department telegraph office, was sharply direct with Schenck: "Get General Milroy from Winchester to Harper's Ferry if possible. He will be gobbled up, if he remains, if he is not already past salvation."[24]

The president's prediction came all too true, and all too soon. On June 13, just one day after crossing into the Valley, Ewell had his forces pressing in close on Milroy. The divisions of Jubal Early and Allegheny Johnson were directed against the Winchester garrison. Robert Rodes's division, with Jenkins's cavalry, swung off to the right to sweep up the Berryville garrison, 10 miles east of Winchester, and then to push rapidly down the Valley for Martinsburg. Milroy had some 6,900 men to defend his Winchester fortifications, with another 1,800 at Berryville, and he had no suspicion that the Confederates he was skirmishing with on the outskirts of town were anything more than cavalry raiders.

The primary defenses of Winchester were three forts on high ground north and west of the town, armed with two dozen cannon. After a reconnoiter, Ewell concluded that taking these forts might be more of a test than he had expected. As one of his men put it, "we all began to feel as if we had caught the elephant, but could not tell what to do with it." On the other hand, Ewell was pleased that the Yankees had not run but stayed to fight. Jubal Early pointed out some higher ground to the west, a ridgeline that dominated one of the forts. He proposed a concealed flanking march to seize this ridge as an artillery platform from which to assail the fort. Ewell approved the scheme. On Sunday, the 14th, Early set off on his eight-mile flank march with three brigades of infantry and seven batteries of artillery. Ewell meanwhile occupied the Federals' attention with a series of noisy demonstrations south of the town.[25]

It was 5:00 P.M. by the time Early was ready to signal his surprise assault. Twenty guns, concealed below the crest of the ridge, were quickly run up into firing position and opened in unison. The fort's startled defenders tried to return fire but their battery was overwhelmed by the

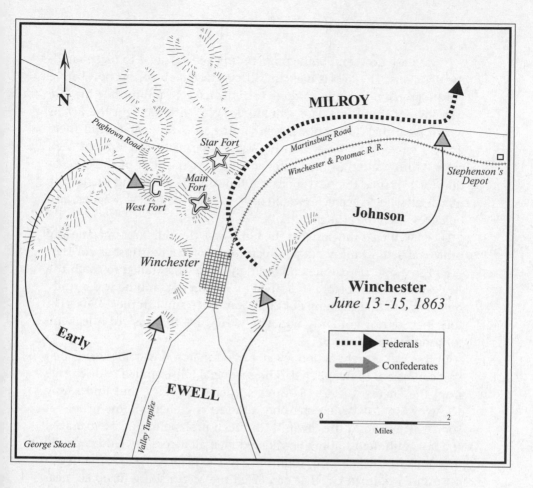

Winchester
June 13 -15, 1863

Federals
Confederates

George Skoch

storm of shells. Harry Hays, whose brigade of Louisiana Tigers was poised to rush forward, recorded the fire as so accurate that "scarcely a head was discovered above the ramparts." As the barrage lifted, the Tigers raised the Rebel yell and charged into the fort.

Watching all this through his field glasses, Dick Ewell could hardly contain himself. "Hurrah for the Louisiana boys!" he cried. "There's Early! I hope the old fellow won't be hurt." Just then Ewell was staggered by a spent bullet striking him in the chest. His surgeon, Dr. Hunter McGuire, diagnosed the injury as a bad bruise, and tried to get the general to lie down under cover by taking his crutches. But Ewell would have none of it, and he was soon stumping about again and cheering on the troops. The course of the fighting could be easily measured as more and more Yankees were seen to break out of the back of the fort and flee for their lives. Hays's triumphant men turned two of the captured cannon on the fugitives to speed them on their way.[26]

It was dark now, and both commanding generals had to make rapid-fire decisions. The Rebels had cut Milroy's telegraph connection before Washington's peremptory orders to retreat reached him, but his fate was obvious should he dare wait any longer. With daylight the Rebels would soon make Winchester's remaining forts untenable. And there was no longer any doubt that he was facing major elements of Lee's army. Milroy called in his lieutenants and set the start of the evacuation for 1:00 A.M. the next morning, June 15. To speed and silence the march, all wheeled vehicles would have to be left behind — wagons, ambulances, even the artillery.

Dick Ewell read the portents the same way. He could not imagine any other course for Milroy but a retreat north toward Martinsburg or Harper's Ferry, and he planned accordingly. Rodes had failed to catch the Berryville garrison before it escaped to Winchester, and he was already on his way to Martinsburg. But Ewell wanted to ambush the Federals before their retreat got fairly under way. He gave that task to Allegheny Johnson and his division.

In this war a night action, even a night march, invariably generated vast confusion. In the pitch darkness General Johnson had to disengage from the enemy, collect his three scattered brigades, and find a way to swing around Winchester and intersect the enemy's line of retreat somewhere beyond the town. With much profane urging he managed the task, although trailing bewildered men all across the landscape. By 4 o'clock in the morning Johnson had the beginnings of an ambush set up in a railroad cut that paralleled the Martinsburg turnpike, near Stephenson's Depot. Suddenly, in the dark road, Milroy's advance guard stumbled into the flash and crash of gunfire and the battle was on.

General Milroy had grimly determined "to cut our way out," and without hesitation he hurled his troops against the ambush line. It was a close-run, wild fight in the smoky darkness. Allegheny Johnson was outnumbered until his trailing brigade finally reached the battlefield, and for a time all that held his wavering line together was the fire of Captain William Dement's 1st Maryland battery. On the Federal side, the lack of artillery was demoralizing to the outgunned foot soldiers. It was hard to tell foe from friend in the dimness, and at one point a confused 18th Connecticut poured fire into the backs of the 87th Pennsylvania. "Darkness concealed the truth," reported the mortified Connecticut colonel.

It was first light when Milroy broke off the assaults and gave the order for everyone to get away as best he could. Not relishing being taken captive by what he had termed "the rebel fiends," General Milroy was the first to leave. With that the already badly shaken Federal command collapsed. Men went off in every direction, and scores and then hundreds began to throw down their arms. Allegheny Johnson boasted he personally captured thirty Yankees "with his opera glass."[27]

This Second Battle of Winchester — the first had been won by Stonewall Jackson in May 1862 — was a Confederate victory of resounding proportions. Milroy lost 443 men killed and wounded, and no fewer than 4,000 prisoners. The total, 4,443, was something over half his force. The fleeing survivors would thereafter be known as "Milroy's weary boys." Winchester yielded up 300 loaded wagons and some 300 horses, substantial quartermaster and commissary stores, and 23 pieces of artillery, with 5 more cannon taken by Rodes at Martinsburg. The 17 highly prized 3-inch rifles among the captures quickly replaced outmoded smoothbores in Ewell's corps artillery. All this had been achieved at the cost of just 269 casualties — 47 killed, 219 wounded, 3 missing.[28]

On only the third day after entering the Shenandoah, Dick Ewell had completely cleared away the enemy facing him in the Valley, with immense captures, and opened the passage to the Potomac and Maryland. Rodes had seized Martinsburg and he and Jenkins's cavalry were already across the river. The few Federals left in the Valley were huddled defensively at Harper's Ferry. The Army of Northern Virginia was greatly impressed. As Captain Charles Blackford put it, "Ewell won his right to Jackson's mantle at Jackson's game on Jackson's ground. This success will give the corps more confidence in Ewell."

The next day, June 16, there was a ceremony in the main fort at Winchester, now renamed Fort Jackson. The ladies of Winchester had stitched together a makeshift Confederate flag, made from two U.S. flags, and it was run up the flagpole to the accompaniment of a 13-gun salute. The ladies then raised three cheers for General Ewell. Ewell thanked them for the honor, and said mischievously, "now call on General Early for a speech." Quickly came the cry, "Speech from General Early!" Jubal Early, a confirmed bachelor and a notorious misogynist, was equal to the occasion. "Ladies," he said, with a tip of his hat, "I never could find courage to address *one* of you — of course I can't speak to a hundred."

The troops feasted on captured Yankee commissary stores and sutlers' stocks and looked forward to more such easy conquests. The one regret was the escape of the vandal Milroy. There was much relief among the citizens of Winchester, who regarded themselves as literally liberated. A Virginia gentlewoman and longtime resident wrote a friend, "You may imagine the happiness of the people here to be relieved from the arrogant Tyranny of those wretches. . . ."[29]

MILROY'S WEARY BOYS pushed waves of rumor and panic ahead of them as they stumbled into Harper's Ferry and on into Maryland and even Pennsylvania. The Rebels, they cried, were right on their heels. Newspapers in Baltimore, Philadelphia, Harrisburg, and Pittsburgh picked up these cries and raised the alarm. Pennsylvania's Governor Curtin beseeched the president to call out the militia. On June 15, in Washington, Secretary of the Navy Gideon Welles entered in his diary, "Something of a panic pervades the city this evening. Singular rumors of Rebel advances into Maryland. It is said they have reached Hagerstown, and some of them have penetrated as far as Chambersburg."[30]

Soon enough these rumors acquired a certain weight when a small party of Albert Jenkins's Virginia cavalrymen slipped across the Pennsylvania line and briefly occupied Chambersburg. The roads became choked with dusty columns of refugees, many of them runaway slaves and free blacks trying to evade these outriders of slavery. Those who did not flee quickly enough were ridden down and rounded up by Jenkins's troopers. Some fifty blacks were formed into a coffle and marched south to be sold into bondage. Albert Jenkins's men are best described as irregulars, and they seem to have undertaken these lucrative captures for their own accounts. There is no evidence that the practice was officially sanctioned, but numerous Confederate officers obviously looked the other way. Nor did the practice end with this Chambersburg episode.[31]

A railroad executive named Ambrose Thompson bought into the general panic and became the first (of many) to demand that Mr. Lincoln call up General McClellan to lead an army of home guards against the invaders. The magic of Little Mac's name, Thompson claimed, would rally 50,000 men to the colors within twenty-four hours.

In official Washington, at least, there was relief when it was found that some of this panic had been self-generated. Word came, wrote Secretary Welles, "that the stragglers and baggage-trains of Milroy had run away in a fright, and squads of them, on different roads, had alarmed each other, and each fled in terror with all speed to Harrisburg." This revelation left the president, Welles noted, "delighted and in excellent spirits."

Taking the longer view as was his habit, the president had some reason to be in excellent spirits. On May 24 General Grant had telegraphed, "The enemy are now undoubtedly in our grasp. The fall of Vicksburg and the capture of most of the garrison can only be a question of time," and nothing in Grant's dispatches since had suggested a lesser eventual outcome. Now it appeared certain that General Lee had taken the offensive in some fashion or another, and in that Mr. Lincoln saw opportunity beckoning should the Confederate army venture out of Virginia. All eyes turned to Joe Hooker and the Army of the Potomac.[32]

For General Hooker, however, discovering where this enemy offensive might be headed was proving uncommonly complicated. As Daniel Butterfield, his chief of staff, put it, "We cannot go boggling round until we know what we are going after." The Bureau of Military Information found it inherently more difficult to track and evaluate the Rebel army on the move than when it was encamped. The enemy's security was tighter, and it was hard to infiltrate spies into marching columns. To further complicate matters, when Pleasonton's cavalry picked up prisoners or deserters, it usually neglected to turn them over to the skilled B.M.I. interrogators, thereby losing much useful intelligence. The Federal troopers, in fact, were generally inept at intelligence-gathering, and proved unable to penetrate Jeb Stuart's cavalry screen for a direct look at the Army of Northern Virginia. General Pleasonton himself was easily misled. For some days, for example, he insisted that Lee's target was Pittsburgh, far to the west; citizens there frantically threw up barricades in the streets.[33]

Should it indeed be Lee's intention to march north on either a raid or an invasion, Hooker had told the president on June 10, and if he were permitted "to operate from my own judgment," he would seize this opportunity to strike at Richmond — "the most speedy and certain mode of giving the rebellion a mortal blow." According to Hooker's information, hardly more than a provost guard now defended the Confederate capital. He argued that in case Lee should attempt a counterstroke against Washington, the garrison there could hold the fortifications long enough for "all the disposable part" of his army to "be thrown to any threatened point north of the Potomac at short notice. . . ."

It was an intriguing proposal, and if executed with the sort of imaginative planning that Hooker had employed in the opening of his Chancellorsville campaign, it would almost certainly have forced Lee to cancel his Pennsylvania incursion. President Davis was as sensitive about Richmond's safety as President Lincoln was about Washington's; surely Davis would summon Lee to the rescue the moment a Yankee army appeared before the gates of Richmond. As it happened, however, it was the sensitivity about Washington that decided the question. Within ninety minutes of receiving Hooker's telegram, the president quashed the idea.

"I would not go South of the Rappahannock, upon Lee's moving North of it," the commander-in-chief told his general. "I think *Lee's* Army, and not *Richmond,* is your true objective point." He then delivered a crisp directive: "If he comes toward the Upper Potomac, follow on his flank, and on the inside track, shortening your lines, whilst he lengthens his. Fight him when opportunity offers. If he stays where he is, fret him, and fret him." When it came to his concurring with the president's views, General-in-Chief Halleck said simply, "I do so fully." Consequently, on June 11, Joe Hooker put the Army of the Potomac on alert to march. Robert E. Lee had thrown down the gauntlet . . . and it was Abraham Lincoln who picked it up.[34]

Yet essential questions remained. March where? Where were the three main elements of the Army of Northern Virginia (the B.M.I. had discovered Lee's new three-corps organization), and where was each bound? Answers now reached the B.M.I. from an exceptional discovery, a bright young contraband from Culpeper named Charley Wright, who had been a servant in Lee's army and who displayed a remarkable knowledge of its units and their whereabouts. On June 12 intelligence officer Captain John McEntee could report with confidence that Ewell and Longstreet had marched through Culpeper; that Ewell had set off for the Shenandoah, with Longstreet to follow; and that A. P. Hill was still at Fredericksburg. "I think statement reliable," said McEntee. Here finally was firm enough evidence to act on, and on Saturday, June 13, Joe Hooker started the Army of the Potomac in pursuit. It was a more than timely move, and it actually stole a march on the Rebels — not until the 15th would Longstreet start from Culpeper and Hill start from Fredericksburg.

Lieutenant Colonel Rufus Dawes, commanding the 6th Wisconsin, explained to his fiancée that should the Rebels "envelop themselves around our right the inevitable 'apron string' will probably draw us back to old Bull Run. This Army seems to bear pretty much the same relation to the city of Washington that I do to you." His was an apt observation. It was made clear to General Hooker that whatever else he did, he must always commit the Army of the Potomac to the care and protection of the capital.[35]

The concealing topography of the region greatly favored Lee's offensive operations. Three parallel ranges, running north by northeast, slanted through central Virginia to the Potomac, crossing the narrow waist of Maryland and extending into Pennsylvania. The Blue Ridge and the westernmost of the three ranges, the Alleghenies, framed the Shenandoah Valley. To the east, between the Blue Ridge and the Bull

Run Mountains, lay the Loudoun Valley. Key to the safe passage of armies through these valleys was control of the various passes or gaps in the ranges. Securely holding the gaps in the Blue Ridge, for example, would turn the Shenandoah Valley into a veritable "covered way" to the Potomac, at which point a Rebel army might continue northward into Maryland and Pennsylvania, still sheltered by the mountains, or turn eastward to threaten Washington and Baltimore. In August 1862, in the Second Manassas campaign, Lee had employed the Loudoun Valley to advance his forces, sending Jackson's corps and then Longstreet's through Thoroughfare Gap in the Bull Run Mountains to fall on Pope's army at Manassas Junction, outside Washington. Now, in June 1863, Lee was planning to use both the Shenandoah and Loudoun valleys to conceal his forces and confound his enemies.

General Hooker, for his part, would be following what Mr. Lincoln termed the inside track, marching due north from Falmouth, keeping his army always between the Rebels and Washington. The movement required shifting the Army of the Potomac's supply line from Aquia Landing on the Potomac to the Orange & Alexandria Railroad running out of Alexandria, close by the capital. For the opening of the march Hooker split his forces into two major columns. The westernmost column was to aim initially for Manassas Junction, to secure the army's left flank and to block any sudden advance by Lee on Washington by way of Thoroughfare Gap. The second column, after withdrawing the bridgehead across the Rappahannock, would march in parallel to the east, acting as a rear guard and protecting against a sweep around the army's right. Headquarters would travel with this easternmost column — the Second, Sixth, and Twelfth corps, and the reserve artillery. Hooker's choice of a commander for the other column reflected his continuing problems with the officer corps.

Following Chancellorsville, Hooker had named George Meade as his ablest corps commander. But now, a month later, he and Meade were hardly on speaking terms. Furthermore, Hooker had certainly learned of Meade being put forward as his successor by the dissident corps commanders. So he chose instead John Reynolds to manage this wing of the army — First, Third, Fifth, and Eleventh corps, along with Pleasonton's cavalry. Hooker also surely knew of Reynolds being summoned to the White House on June 2, and could easily guess why. Since ten days later he remained general commanding, Hooker must have concluded that Reynolds was without ambition for the post and could be trusted with this important independent command. However that may be, Hooker would express himself as entirely satisfied with his choice. Speaking afterward of Reynolds's role in the campaign, he was generous in his praise: "I never had an officer under me acquit himself so handsomely."[36]

It was not yet certain just how far north the point of the Rebel advance might have reached, and the order went to Reynolds to make forced marches to reach Manassas as quickly as possible. The June weather had turned very hot and very dry, and the march was grueling. Colonel Charles Wainwright, the First Corps' chief of artillery, thought he would suffocate passing through one stretch of particularly dense woodland. "The sides of the road were lined with men, who had dropped from exhaustion," he noted in his diary. "There must have been near a thousand of them, many of whom had fainted entirely away. The surgeons had their hands full. . . ." From close by Manassas on Monday, June 15, Colonel Dawes of the 6th Wisconsin wrote of the ordeal to his fiancée: "We marched Sunday morning and all day Sunday and all night, and until the middle of the afternoon to-day, when we reached this point, tired, sore, sleepy, hungry, dusty, and dirty as pigs. . . . Our army is in a great hurry for something."[37]

WITH THE CAMPAIGN against General Lee now under way, Joe Hooker found himself, at the same time, at war against General-in-Chief Henry Halleck. The stake in their behind-the-scenes battle was nothing less than Hooker's continued command of the Army of the Potomac, and both men knew it.

Hooker's first designs for countering Lee's offensive — striking at the rearmost third of the Confederate army still at Fredericksburg, or marching on Richmond to pressure Lee to turn back — had been rejected by the president, but, Hooker suspected, mostly on the advice of the general-in-chief. Halleck sensed that confidence in Hooker's generalship had slackened enough that now was his opportunity to erase Hooker's special arrangement with the president whereby Lincoln dealt with the Army of the Potomac ("ran the machine himself," as Halleck phrased it) without reference to the general-in-chief. Halleck's mistrust of Hooker ran deep, and he set as his goal, using whatever means came to hand, to maneuver Hooker out of the command. Three issues dominated Hooker's relations with Washington in these critical mid-June days, and General Halleck left his mark on Fighting Joe in each of them.

The first issue was manpower. Since April the Potomac army had been steadily losing men by the thousands due to expiration of the nine-month and two-year enlistments. During June, twenty-five more regiments were scheduled to be mustered out. By July 1, unless reinforced, the Army of the Potomac would be down to 89,200 men of all arms present for duty. If nothing was done about this, Hooker projected that in the campaign ahead he would be outnumbered — cavalryman Pleasonton estimated each of the three Confederate corps at 30,000, plus some 10,000 cavalry. There seem to have been no B.M.I. estimates of Confederate strength for this period, to act as a corrective for Pleasonton's overcounting, but Hooker could hardly be blamed for expressing his frustration so long as Halleck refused to strengthen the Potomac army from any of the other commands.[38]

The second issue between general and general-in-chief was the question of unified command. At the first signs of a Confederate offensive, Hooker had spoken of "the necessity of having one commander for all of the troops whose operations can have an influence on those of Lee's army." Any march northward by the enemy was bound to affect General Heintzelman's Department of Washington and General Schenck's Middle Department (of which Milroy's division was a part) in addition to the Army of the Potomac, and a unified command, even if only temporary, had the force of logic. "I trust that I may not be considered in the way to this arrangement," said Hooker modestly, but by suggesting it he clearly expected it. (Ironically, when taking the army command in January, Hooker had applauded making the Washington command a separate department.) Halleck's reply sidestepped around the issue without touching it. Department heads would be directed "to forward military information" to General Hooker, and any movement of their troops "you may suggest" would be ordered — "if deemed practical." General Halleck very rarely deemed a Joe Hooker suggestion practical.[39]

The third issue involved the exercise of command. "Your army is entirely free to operate as you desire against Lee's army, so long as you keep his main army from Washington," Halleck assured Hooker, but with each new report from the beleaguered Federal forces in the Shenandoah, Washington pressed Hooker to take immediate action. The president's advice was general and strikingly put. "If the head of Lee's army is at Martinsburg and the tail of it on the Plank road between Fredericksburg and Chancellorsville," he telegraphed Hooker on June 14, "the animal must be very slim somewhere. Could you not break him?" Halleck took that generality and made it into specifics. He urged that any Confederate raiding force be pursued, and he insisted that Hooker do something to save Harper's Ferry from capture. In short order Harper's Ferry became a bone of contention between the two men — and the issue Halleck was looking for to bring down Joe Hooker.

General Hooker grew petulant. All his plans for meeting the enemy threat had been rejected, he told a colleague, and he could detect little evidence of support from any direction. Henceforth he would act only on direct orders from Washington, taking no responsibility for the consequences. Giving President Lincoln his view on how best to meet Lee's threat, he added, "I do not know that my opinion as to the duty of this army in the case is wanted." He began another dispatch with the disclaimer, "Please accept my suggestions in regard to what should be done in the spirit with which they were given." Whether intended or not, Fighting Joe Hooker began to radiate an impression of indecisiveness. Gideon Welles, after a talk with the president one evening, entered in his diary, "I came away from the War Department painfully impressed. After recent events, Hooker cannot have the confidence which is essential to the success, and which is all-important to the commander in the field."

On the morning of June 16, while the Confederates were taking the salutes of the citizens of liberated Winchester, General Hooker unburdened himself. "You have long been aware, Mr. President," he telegraphed, "that I have not enjoyed the confidence of the major-general commanding the army, and I can assure you so long as this continues we may look in vain for success, especially as future operations will require our relations to be more dependent upon each other than heretofore."[40]

Joe Hooker was surely expecting too much if he thought this declaration would result in Halleck's dismissal as general-in-chief. What he apparently intended by it was to force a showdown, an acknowledgment by the president that their special arrangement for cutting General Halleck out of the Potomac army's decision-making process was still in force. Or perhaps Hooker was just going on record, building a case in the event he needed to defend his tenure as general commanding. However that may be, he challenged his commander-in-chief — a challenge the president could not and did not ignore.

Lincoln sought first to reason with his troubled general. Taking the same friendly but candid tone that marked all his correspondence with Hooker, he composed a letter marked "private" and had it hand-delivered to the army's new field headquarters at Fairfax Station, outside Washington. He explained, in regard to General Halleck, "You do not lack his confidence in any degree to do you any harm," which may or may not have reassured General Hooker. The president then appealed for understanding at this critical time: "If you and he would use the same frankness to one another, and to me, that I use to both of you, there would be no difficulty. I need and must have the professional skill of both, and yet these suspicions tend to deprive me of both." Finally, he spoke of what he saw as a rare opportunity: "As it looks to me, Lee's now returning toward Harper's Ferry gives you back the chance that I thought McClellan lost last fall. . . . Now, all I ask is that you will be in such mood that we can get into our action the best cordial judgement of yourself and General Halleck, with my poor mite added. . . ."

Late that June 16 evening, after reading an exchange of less than enlightening telegrams between Halleck and Hooker over the defense of Harper's Ferry, Lincoln determined to lay down the law. "To remove all misunderstanding," he telegraphed Hooker, "I now place you in the strict military relation to Gen. Halleck, of a commander of one of the armies, to the General-in-Chief of all the armies. . . . I shall direct him to give you orders, and you to obey them."

Possibly the president's letter of earlier in the day softened the blow somewhat, yet Fighting Joe Hooker could hardly doubt he had now lost his private war with the general-in-chief, and that his days as general commanding might well be numbered.[41]

5   *Into the Enemy's Country*

ON JUNE 15, 1863, in Washington, Elizabeth Blair Lee wrote her navy-officer husband, "Yesterday there was a panic in town made by the ambulance trains — which were so large & enough to affright the people. . . ." In past months the sight of a grim procession of army ambulances, lumbering across the Long Bridge from Alexandria or up from the steamer wharves on the Potomac, bound for the capital's military hospitals, signaled some great battle. This time, however, the alarm proved false. These were the sick from the Army of the Potomac, evacuated from Aquia Landing when the base there was closed. "That army is in motion," Mrs. Lee concluded her letter, "& it is a race between Hooker and Lee, the first having the inside circle. . . ."[1]

Official Washington was already reacting to the race. To better administer the defense of Pennsylvania, Secretary of War Stanton established the military Department of the Susquehanna, covering roughly the eastern two-thirds of the state. To head the new department Stanton appointed one of the chief dissidents in the Potomac army, Darius Couch, whose distaste for Joe Hooker was so strong that he had surrendered command of the Second Corps. On June 11 General Couch established headquarters at Harrisburg and looked around for something and someone to command. All he could find, for the moment, were several out-of-work, out-of-favor generals and a small company of elderly veterans of the War of 1812, the sole responders to Pennsylvania governor Andrew Curtin's appeal for latter-day minutemen to defend "our own homes, firesides, and property from devastation."

June 15 saw the president issue a proclamation summoning 100,000 militia to meet the threat of a Confederate invasion. Pennsylvania was called upon for 50,000 men, Ohio for 30,000, Maryland for 10,000, and the new state of West Virginia for 10,000. The term of federal service was to be six months "unless sooner discharged." It was soon evident, particularly in Pennsylvania, that the minuteman tradition had not been passed down from the Revolutionary War generation.

THE ENEMY
IS APPROACHING!

I MUST RELY UPON THE PEOPLE FOR THE

DEFENCE of the STATE!

AND HAVE Called THE MILITIA for that PURPOSE!

A. G. CURTIN, Governor of Pennsylvania.

THE TERM OF SERVICE WILL ONLY BE WHILE THE DANGER OF THE STATE IS IMMINENT.

APPLY AT

FALSTAFF HOTEL, N.W. cor. 6th & Jayne

Capt. JOHN McCORMACK.

J. CARTER, 1st Lieut.

Pennsylvania Governor Andrew Curtin's call for militia to meet
Lee's invasion. (American Antiquarian Society)

The essential problem in Pennsylvania was the lack of a standing militia organization. There was no one at hand to answer Lincoln's call promptly except a token force in Philadelphia — an infantry unit called the Philadelphia Grays, two artillery batteries, and two troops of cavalry. After much pushing and pulling and paper-shuffling in Harrisburg and Washington, some 8,000 Pennsylvania "emergency men" were mustered in time to confront the Confederate invasion. As defenders of their home place, they were embarrassingly outnumbered by the 12,000 militiamen generously dispatched by New York in answer to the president's appeal. The New Yorkers reached Harrisburg even before the contingent from Philadelphia. But from wherever they came, these were at best Sunday soldiers, no match for Lee's veterans, and they knew it. As General Couch admitted, his home guardsmen in their camps seemed more interested in going home than anything else.[2]

The Cabinet meeting on June 16 was thinly attended, which irritated Navy Secretary Welles. In this time of crisis, he thought, all should be present "for general consultation." Earlier in the day Welles had been to the War Department for news, and came away frustrated and empty of any expert commentary. General-in-Chief Halleck, he complained, "sits, and smokes, and swears, and scratches his arm and shakes it, but exhibits no mental capacity or intelligence. Is obfusticated, muddy, uncertain, stupid as to what is doing or to be done." At the meeting Treasury Secretary Chase, Joe Hooker's one ally in the Cabinet, urged a demonstration be launched against Richmond if the Rebels should indeed come north, but (wrote Welles) "the President gave it no countenance." Welles added that no suggestions of this kind ever came from General Halleck. There was the distinct impression that everything now lay in the hands of the Army of the Potomac.

As if to emphasize that point, as soon as Hooker advanced his headquarters to Fairfax Station, west of the capital, Secretary Chase visited the general to appraise his morale and that of the army. He was impressed by both. As Welles recorded his impressions, Chase found that "The troops are in good spirits and excellent condition as is Hooker himself. He commends Hooker as in every respect all that we could wish." Welles still had grave doubts about Joe Hooker, but for the moment at least he was encouraged by this. He had earlier noted that Mr. Lincoln "has a personal liking for Hooker, and clings to him when others give way."[3]

One of the arguments made by General Lee for invading the enemy's territory was the encouragement it should give those he called "friends of peace at the North." These were the peace Democrats — termed Copperheads for what Republican Unionists described as their poisonous views — and they had grown increasingly vocal since the Federal defeats at Fredericksburg and Chancellorsville. Those battles had taken place below the Mason-Dixon Line, however, and among Northerners there was some question about how the Copperheads would react to an invading Confederate army in their midst — and certainly doubts about how their peace message would be received should it be backed by enemy bayonets. An observant New Yorker, George Templeton Strong, noted in his diary on June 17, "Unless rebeldom gain some great decisive success, this move of Lee's is likely to do good by bothering and silencing our nasty peace-democracy." General Hooker made the same point, rather more forcefully. He called Lee's move "an act of desperation. . . . It will kill copperheadism in the North."[4]

In these mid-June days, as he set his army in motion to keep pace with Lee's, Joe Hooker began to formulate a campaign plan of his own. He explained to the president that if Lee chose to cross the Potomac "to make an invasion, . . . it is not in my power to prevent it." Although he alerted General Reynolds to be prepared to attack the extended enemy column "if opportunity offers," Hooker did not relish fighting a general battle in the Shenandoah or in the constricted areas of the Blue Ridge. "If they are moving toward Maryland," he told Lincoln, "I can better fight them there than make a running fight." In fact, although he did not choose to mention it to his superiors, Hooker was eager for Lee to cross from Maryland into Pennsylvania.

Colonel Sharpe of the Bureau of Military Information, in a private letter, said it was the current view at Hooker's headquarters that if Lee headed toward Pennsylvania, "we propose to let him go, and when we get behind him we would like to know how many men he will take back." Hooker's chief of staff, Dan Butterfield, later recalled a conversation about this time with the general commanding on the same subject. The administration in Washington, Hooker said, was "finding great fault with me" for not preventing Lee from crossing the Potomac. "Why, I would lay the bridges for him" to ensure that he did cross, he said. In that event, "if Lee escapes with his army the country are entitled to and should have my head for a football."

In his recollection Butterfield then has Hooker pointing to the vicinity of the town of Gettysburg on a map of Pennsylvania and saying, "we will fight the battle here." Possibly at this point hindsight colored Butterfield's remembrance. Nevertheless, it is clear enough that the impression of irresolution in Hooker's dispatches to Washington in these days, stemming from his intramural battle with General Halleck, was an illusion. When he later described his campaign plan in testimony to a congressional committee, Hooker spoke of cutting in behind Lee's army in Pennsylvania and severing his communications. "For this reason," he said, "I felt that it was for me to say when and where I should fight him. I felt that I could choose my position and compel him to attack me." That, of course, was exactly the plan of maneuver Lee and Longstreet had agreed to pursue once the Army of Northern Virginia crossed the Potomac into Yankee territory.[5]

However confident in his mind Joe Hooker may have been of his own course, he quite failed to convince Washington of that fact. Nor — perhaps his biggest mistake — did he take his restless and discontented lieutenants into his confidence. Marsena Patrick, the army's provost marshal, surely typified the majority view within the officer corps. General Hooker, Patrick entered in his diary on June 17, "acts like a man without a plan and is entirely at a loss what to do, or how to match the enemy, or counteract his movements. Whatever he does is the result of impulse. . . ." The general commanding, he summed up, was merely a Mr. Micawber, "'waiting for something to turn up.' . . ."[6]

BY JUNE 15, General Lee could feel confident that his plan was on course and his predictions were on track. By now it was evident that Hooker's army was quitting the Rappahannock line and shifting northward, no doubt in response to Dick Ewell's eruption into the Shenandoah Valley. As Lee had anticipated, the mere threat of a move toward Washington was drawing Hooker to the defense of the capital — and away from a countermove against Richmond. Having thus successfully disengaged from the enemy army without any entanglement, the next step was to consolidate his own army and thereby increase the pressure on the Yankees.

Powell Hill had already started his Third Corps west from Fredericksburg, bound for Culpeper. On the evening of the 15th Lee gave James Longstreet his marching orders. First reports from Ewell at Winchester were highly favorable, Lee told his lieutenant, and it was time for the First Corps to support the movement. Rather than following Ewell directly into the Shenandoah, however, Longstreet was directed to march northward along the eastern face of the Blue Ridge. This ought to confuse the Federals about where the army was bound, Lee thought, and at the same time screen Ewell's corps already in the Valley as well as Hill's corps marching toward the Valley along Ewell's track. Jeb Stuart's cavalry would in its turn screen Longstreet in the Loudoun Valley, guarding the gaps in the Bull Run Mountains to the east. In due course, as Hill closed up on Ewell at the Potomac, Longstreet would cross into the Shenandoah to act as the army's rear guard. Then, with Ewell in the van, the Army of Northern Virginia would drive on through Maryland and into Pennsylvania.[7]

In marked contrast to Joe Hooker, Robert E. Lee enjoyed harmonious relations with his masters in Richmond and with his subordinates in the army. Yet Lee and Hooker were alike in one respect — the frustration both were feeling just then over the matter of reinforcements. As he started his march north, Lee was optimistic that he would finally regain at least one of George Pickett's two brigades earlier expropriated by D. H. Hill. But, once again, it was not to be. A new spasm of Federal activity on the Virginia Peninsula so alarmed Richmond that Montgomery Corse's brigade was held back to guard the capital. When Pickett came up from Hanover Junction, it was with but three of his original five brigades, making his the weakest division in Longstreet's First Corps. At the same time, and for the same reason, Lee's hopes were dashed that another First Corps brigade, John R. Cooke's, would be returned to him.

He was even denied a reinforcement in effigy. General Lee's inspired thought of bringing P.G.T. Beauregard north from Charleston to command a mini-army of Richmond's defenders or perhaps merely a mystery army — an army in effigy — in northern Virginia, while Lee's army maneuvered in Pennsylvania, deserved a better fate than it met. "His presence," Lee remarked of General Beauregard, "would give magnitude to even a small demonstration, and tend greatly to perplex and confound the enemy. . . . The good effects of beginning to assemble an army at Culpeper C. H. would I think, soon become apparent. . . ." Those good effects, Lee thought, might include drawing Federal forces away from the Pennsylvania front to protect Washington from the Great Creole.

Lee had first raised the Beauregard matter with Mr. Davis back on May 7, and he brought it up again with the president a month later. But he did not submit his scheme as a concrete proposal until June 23, although then he pursued it vigorously. But this more than two-week delay sapped the idea of its promise. Perhaps it foundered on Mr. Davis's personal antipathy toward Beauregard. Or perhaps in those weeks Lee was lulled by the thought that he might obtain all the reinforcing brigades he had sought. In any event, Richmond seemed unable even to grasp the proposal at that late date, and did not, or could not, act on it. General Beauregard remained in Charleston, and the Confederates missed one of the more intriguing opportunities of the campaign.[8]

Lee, then, had finally to settle for boldly invading the North with an army of 80,000 men, just 15,000 more than he had had at Chancellorsville. And more than half that increase was in the cavalry, the arm of least use on the battlefield proper. Lee's infantry strength came to 61,500, an increase of only some 5,300 over his infantry count at Chancellorsville.[9]

The mood of the men of the Army of Northern Virginia was buoyant when they realized they were to march north and take the war to the Yankees. For too long the fighting and the destruction had scarred only the states of the Confederacy; now Northerners would feel the lash of civil war. And evident among a good many of Lee's soldiers was a spirit of vengeance. Sometimes it was a personal vengeance. A Mississippi private who learned his home place had suffered at the hands of Federal raiders told his mother, "I can fight so much Harder since I have got a gruge against them it is my Honest wish that my Rifle may Draw tears from many a Northern Mother and Sighs from Many a Father before this thing is over." Men who had witnessed depredations by the Army of the Potomac — the pillage visited on Fredericksburg at the time of the battle there in December was the worst example — spoke of retaliation. A Georgian in Hood's division wanted the army to "take horses; burn houses; and commit every depredation possible upon the men of the North. . . . I certainly love to live to kill the base usurping vandals."

There was as well a spirit within the army seeking potential retribution for the undeniably worsening news from Vicksburg. The Federal ring around the city had now become a stranglehold. Joe Johnston insisted he was too weak to hazard an attack to relieve the garrison. "Without some great blunder of the enemy . . . ," he said, he considered the situation in Mississippi hopeless. "The news from Vicksburg is so meager and unsatisfactory that it carries much uneasiness," General Lafayette McLaws wrote his wife. "Its fall would be so discouraging and its successful defense so inspiring that everything concerning it, is looked for with the greatest anxiety."[10]

Before entering what he called "the enemy's country," General Lee issued General Orders No. 72, which prohibited the plundering of private property and specified rules for requisitioning supplies. It was Lee's intention that his army live off the enemy's country in every respect, paying market prices — in, of course, Confederate currency or vouchers. There was a certain vagueness about these prohibitions, however, requiring Solomonic judgments on the part of hungry and footsore (and vengeful) Rebel soldiers. Therefore, said one, "they paid no attention to any order of the kind, and took everything they could lay their hands on in the eating line." At the time, to a Pennsylvania farmer or storekeeper, it was a matter of outright confiscation; anyone paid in Confederate currency or vouchers would recoup his losses only if the South should win the war. To Confederate eyes, of course, it was perfectly legal confiscation. Bemused Northerners noticed that Lee's army transported its grossly depreciated currency in flour barrels.

Taliaferro Simpson of the 3rd South Carolina explained to his home folks that "most of the soldiers seem to harbor a terrific spirit of revenge and steal and pillage. . . ." As for the prohibitions, "the soldiers paid no more attention to them than they would to the cries of a screech owl. . . . The brigadiers and colonels made no attempt to enforce Lee's general orders. And Lee himself seemed to disregard entirely the soldiers' open acts of disobedience." Confirming the officers' attitude is a letter by Clement Evans, colonel of the 31st Georgia. "The rascals are afraid we are going to overrun Pennsylvania," Colonel Evans wrote his wife. "That would indeed be glorious, if we could ravage that state making her desolate like Virginia. It would be just punishment."[11]

"YOU MAY DEPEND upon it," General Hooker told Mr. Lincoln on June 16, "we can never discover the whereabouts of the enemy, or divine his intentions, so long as he fills the country with a cloud of cavalry. We must break through that to find him." This reflected ill upon Alfred Pleasonton and the cavalry. Thus far the Yankee troopers had learned little beyond rumor of the enemy's whereabouts, and Pleasonton's contribution to the intelligence picture consisted largely of wild guesses. General-in-Chief Halleck rendered a tart verdict: "The information sent here by General Pleasonton is very unsatisfactory." Brusque orders went out to cavalry headquarters. General Hooker, Pleasonton was told, "relies upon you with your cavalry force to give him information of where the enemy is, his force, and his movements. . . . Drive in pickets, if necessary, and get us information. It is better that we should lose men than to be without knowledge of the enemy, as we now seem to be."[12]

Pleasonton was quick enough to act on these orders, but he continued befuddled about the task of intelligence-gathering. He simply set out, on June 17, to pick a fight with the first Rebel cavalry he found in the Loudoun Valley. Near the village of Aldie, in Aldie's Gap in the Bull Run Mountains, the Federals got all the fight they could handle.

From Aldie two turnpikes ran westward across the Loudoun Valley to Ashby's and Snicker's gaps in the Blue Ridge, necessary vantage points for any Federal efforts to locate Lee's army. To prevent that, Jeb Stuart had Fitz Lee's brigade — just then commanded by Colonel Thomas Munford — guarding the two highways just west of Aldie. With his characteristic brashness, Judson Kilpatrick sent the four regiments of his brigade charging headlong against the Rebel blocking forces. But Kill-Cavalry launched his attacks piecemeal, just as he had at Brandy Station, and with similar results. There was some very sharp cavalry fighting done that afternoon, but at the end of the day Munford still controlled the two important roads.

The ordeal of the 1st Massachusetts troopers exemplified Kilpatrick's management of the Aldie battle. The regiment was fed into the action one squadron after another, and each ran a gauntlet of saber-swinging Rebel horsemen and a line of sharpshooters sheltered behind a stone wall. "My poor men were just slaughtered and all we could do was to stand still and be shot down," wrote Captain Charles Francis Adams, Jr., grandson and great-grandson of presidents. "The men fell right and left, and the horses were shot through and through. . . . I was ordered to dismount my men to fight on foot . . . and in a second the rebs were riding yelling and slashing among us." The 1st Massachusetts lost 77 dead and wounded — the greatest battle toll of any Union cavalry regiment during the Pennsylvania campaign — and another 90 men captured. By day's end the Federals had lost 305 men at Aldie, against the Confederates' 119. In his report Colonel Munford remarked, "I do not hesitate to say that I have never seen as many Yankees killed in the same space of ground in any fight. . . ."[13]

In General Pleasonton's sole effort at reconnaissance that day, the 1st Rhode Island passed through Thoroughfare Gap, a dozen miles south of Aldie Gap, and ranged northward through the Loudoun Valley. Colonel Alfred Duffié, demoted to regimental command after Brandy Station, led the Rhode Islanders to Middleburg, west of Aldie, and nearly swept up Jeb Stuart and his headquarters. As Stuart's adjutant phrased it, general and staff "were compelled to make a retreat more rapid than was consistent with dignity and comfort." That was the high point of Duffié's expedition, however. That night he barricaded himself in Middleburg and called on Pleasonton for help, but his plea was ignored. By the next day his regiment had been systematically cut up and captured nearly *en masse;* just 61 of the 275 Rhode Island troopers made it back to Union lines.

General Lee had dispatched Longstreet's First Corps into the Loudoun Valley in part to confuse the Yankees about Confederate intentions. It turned out to be a wasted ruse. On June 18, with Longstreet's foot soldiers spread all along the eastern base of the Blue Ridge, General Pleasonton informed headquarters, "From all the information I can gather, there is no force of consequence of the enemy's infantry this side of the Blue

Ridge." Chief of Staff Dan Butterfield fired back, "The general says your orders are to find out where the enemy is, if you have to lose men to do it."[14]

On the 18th Pleasonton sent several parties probing toward the Blue Ridge, but none could get past the screening Rebel cavalry. Stuart was in the comfortable position of knowing exactly what the Federals were about. John Singleton Mosby, the partisan leader who held sway throughout this part of Virginia — widely known as "Mosby's Confederacy" — had captured a pair of Union officers carrying dispatches for Pleasonton. From these it was clear the Federals were largely in the dark about Lee's movements. "The advance of the infantry," one dispatch read, "is suspended until further information of the enemy's movements." To preserve this advantage, Stuart determined to keep his cavalry screen in the Loudoun Valley intact by using defensive tactics.

The next day, June 19, Pleasonton adopted another straight-ahead drive on the Aldie pattern, this time against Middleburg, five miles to the west on the road leading to Ashby's Gap in the Blue Ridge. The affair at Middleburg proved a virtual repeat of the standoff at Aldie. Stuart took position on a low ridge west of the town and fended off charge after charge. At one point a squadron of the 10th New York, under Major John Kemper, rode into an ambush in a narrow defile in the woods, with dismounted Rebel troopers behind a stone wall firing point-blank into the New Yorkers as they charged past. The survivors ran up against Stuart's reserves, turned back, and to escape had to run the gauntlet a second time. Eighty men began the charge; five returned. "Don't go into those woods," a shaken Major Kemper told a fellow squadron leader. "It is a slaughter pen."

As the Federal pressure continued, Stuart broke off the action and pulled back to the next ridgeline. The two sides rested and licked their wounds. The next day Pleasonton reported to headquarters, "We cannot force the gaps of the Blue Ridge in the presence of a superior force."[15]

On June 21, a Sunday, Pleasonton launched his most ambitious effort yet to crack Stuart's cavalry screen. The scene of this latest attempt was Upperville, a village only some four miles from Ashby's Gap in the Blue Ridge. Thus far in these Loudoun Valley cavalry fights Stuart had made effective use of defensive skirmish lines of dismounted troopers, most of them sharpshooters, posted behind stone walls and other obstructions and supported by batteries from his horse artillery. He massed his mounted units behind these deadly barricades, poised to counterattack. At Upperville General Pleasonton countered with a new tactic of his own

Alfred Waud sketched dismounted 1st Maine troopers skirmishing with Rebel cavalry in the Loudoun Valley on June 19. (Library of Congress)

— clearing away these defensive thickets not with cavalry but with infantry.

Pleasonton borrowed from Hooker an entire Fifth Corps infantry division, although that day the cavalryman would use just a single brigade, under Colonel Strong Vincent. On Sunday morning the Yankee infantrymen — 20th Maine, 16th Michigan, 44th New York, 83rd Pennsylvania — led the way in dislodging the Rebel troopers from their defensive skirmish lines. Lieutenant William Fuller's Battery C, 3rd United States, took on Captain James Hart's defending South Carolina battery and bested it, blowing up a limber chest and so damaging one of Hart's English Blakely rifles that it had to be abandoned. Stuart would make sad note that this was the first piece his horse artillery had ever lost to the enemy.

With the first line of defense breached, David Gregg's Yankee cavalry now engaged Wade Hampton's troopers. There were swirls of close-in clashes, fought desperately with carbines, pistols, and sabers amidst great clouds of dust. A fierce counterattack against Kilpatrick's brigade led personally by Hampton, "seemingly angered, looking a veritable god of war," emptied dozens of saddles. The Confederates parried successive blows and fell back to take up new defensive positions. A Fifth Corps infantry captain watching from high ground wrote that "the sight was magnificent — the sabres flashed in the sun light as the men mingled together and fought in a writhing mass, cutting and slashing each other. Riderless horses ran to and fro over the fields, many of them covered with the blood of their late riders."

As originally planned, John Buford's division was meanwhile supposed to turn the Confederates' northern flank, but that flank was not where it was said to be, and instead Buford joined in the general combat around Upperville. The Federals' General Gregg had his horse shot out from under him, and for a time Kill-Cavalry himself was surrounded and nearly captured. A charge by the 6th U.S. regulars, under a leader green and inexperienced, started off at the gallop far too soon and bogged down in exhaustion and had to turn back, to the hoots of friend and foe alike. As the light faded, Federal troopers approached Ashby's Gap, only to find it securely held by the enemy. Pleasonton pulled his cavalry corps back to Aldie for rest and refitting. "The road we charged was literally covered with blood," a man in the 1st Maine wrote, "and to see the dead piled up was perfectly horrid."[16]

The intense cavalry fighting in the Loudoun Valley had indeed been costly. All told, over a five-day span, the Federals lost 883 men and the Confederates 510, reflecting the aggressive moves of Pleasonton and the defensive tactics of Stuart. Stuart had denied the Yankees any look at Lee's main body, but from deserters Pleasonton was finally able to deduce that Longstreet's corps had been in the Loudoun Valley but now had passed through the Blue Ridge gaps into the Shenandoah. Ewell's corps had gone toward Winchester the previous week, Pleasonton reported, "and another corps (A. P. Hill's, I think) is to move with Longstreet into Maryland. Such is the information given by the negroes here." This intelligence might be somewhat speculative, but at least it appeared logical. It made sense that General Lee would conceal his whole army in the Shenandoah. What was still not at all clear, however, was whether the Confederates would continue on northward into Maryland and Pennsylvania or suddenly turn eastward toward Washington or Baltimore. Until Joe Hooker could get an answer to that question, he must hold his army below the Potomac to protect the capital.[17]

DURING THESE HOT June days that saw Jeb Stuart fend off the Yankees, General Lee carefully maneuvered his forces behind the cavalry screen, building up for the thrust into Pennsylvania. By June 19 Dick Ewell's three divisions were marking time on or just across the Potomac — Early at Shepherdstown on the river, Rodes at Hagerstown and Allegheny Johnson at Sharpsburg, in Maryland. Longstreet's corps crossed

In an unfinished drawing by newspaper artist Edwin Forbes, Yankee cavalry, right, charges Stuart's command near Upperville on June 21. Ashby's Gap is in the left distance. (Library of Congress)

the Blue Ridge into the Shenandoah by way of Ashby's and Snicker's gaps, sealing off both passes in support of Stuart. Powell Hill's Third Corps meanwhile pushed down the Valley to fall in behind Ewell. Lee opened headquarters at Berryville in the Valley to supervise. "The General seemed yesterday in fine spirits . . . ," General Dorsey Pender wrote of Lee on the 23rd. "It is stated on all sides that Hooker has a small army and that very much demoralized. The General says he wants to meet him as soon as possible and crush him and then if Vicksburg and Port Hudson do their part, our prospects for peace are very fine."

Matters had advanced well enough by June 22, the day after the cavalry fight at Upperville, that Lee started the Second Corps into Pennsylvania. Ewell's primary function would be to collect supplies for the army, and while he did so Lee intended to occupy Hooker's attention — "should we be able to detain General Hooker's army from following you," he explained to Ewell, "you would be able to accomplish as much,

unmolested, as the whole army could perform with General Hooker in its front." Ewell was to advance his three divisions fan-wise toward the Susquehanna. They would cross the Pennsylvania line, marching in parallel columns, and enter the Cumberland Valley, the extension of the Shenandoah Valley. Throughout they would be shielded on the east by South Mountain, the extension of Virginia's Blue Ridge. Rodes and Johnson would continue north by east through Greencastle and Chambersburg and Carlisle toward Harrisburg, the state capital. "If Harrisburg comes within your means," Ewell was told, "capture it." Early's division would be assigned to turn off through South Mountain in a more easterly direction to Gettysburg and on to York.[18]

It was thought that for this scheme to work required Stuart's cavalry guarding and screening the eastern flank of Ewell's columns at every turn. Lee and Stuart puzzled out the best way to accomplish that task. The major puzzle was the lack of information on the enemy. Pleasonton's aggressive tactics had tied Stuart down, preventing him from doing what he did best — gathering intelligence on the Yankee army. Just then the sole intelligence gatherer was the partisan John Mosby. The Potomac army headquarters dispatches Mosby had captured located only two of the seven Federal corps, and only as of June 17. Colonel Mosby crept about in his private Confederacy and on his return suggested to Stuart that the cavalry corps, rather than marching northward alongside the rest of the army, instead swing eastward through or entirely around the Yankees, cross the Potomac to the east of them, and form up on Ewell's right in Pennsylvania.

Jeb Stuart had gained renown for twice riding around McClellan's army, once during the Peninsula campaign and again after Sharpsburg, and surely this proposal to ride around Joe Hooker's army had great appeal for him. For one thing, it ought to create havoc in the Army of the Potomac's rear areas, cutting its communications with Washington. For another, it ought to confuse the Federals as to Lee's intentions. And, perhaps not incidentally, it ought to restore the shine to a reputation tarnished by the Brandy Station surprise.

According to Mosby, it would be easy enough to do. "I had located each corps and reported it to Stuart," Mosby later wrote. "They were so widely separated that it was easy for a column of cavalry to pass between them. No corps was nearer than ten miles to another corps." Mosby's confidence was seriously misplaced; he had probably observed the camps of only two or three of the Federal corps, those closest to the Bull Run Mountains. And by the time it could be acted on, Mosby's freshest intelligence would be some forty-eight hours old.

Stuart met with Lee and Longstreet on June 18 at Paris, a village just east of Ashby's Gap, to discuss the cavalry's coming role, and at this meeting he apparently introduced the thought of riding around Hooker as one of the options. On the 22nd Lee sent Stuart his orders, in outline — should the enemy be found to be moving northward, the cavalry was to move into Maryland with intent to form on Ewell's right. Stuart was to guard Ewell's column, gather intelligence on the enemy, "and collect all the supplies you can for the use of the army." This directive was delivered by way of Longstreet, who wrote Lee that he was forwarding it to Stuart "with the suggestion that he pass by the enemy's rear if he thinks that he may get through." That Lee knew of and approved of this idea of riding around Hooker's army was evident in Longstreet's covering letter to Stuart. The general commanding, Longstreet wrote, "speaks of your leaving, via Hopewell Gap" — a pass in the Bull Run Mountains just south of Aldie Gap — "and passing by the rear of the enemy."

The next day Lee sent Stuart a second directive, an apparent but rather confusing attempt to clarify the cavalryman's options. If Hooker's army "remains inactive," Stuart was told to leave two brigades to watch the

Blue Ridge passes and "withdraw the three others" as planned. But should Hooker "not appear to be moving northward," Stuart must pull back through the Blue Ridge and accompany the main body of the army down the Valley to the Potomac crossing at Shepherdstown.

Although this June 23 directive has mystified observers ever since that day — what difference was there between remaining inactive and not moving? — it does not seem to have mystified Jeb Stuart. He simply followed the directions in the next paragraph: "You will, however, be able to judge whether you can pass around their army without hinderance, doing them all the damage you can, and cross the river east of the mountains. In either case, after crossing the river, you must move on and feel the right of Ewell's troops, collecting information, provisions, &c."

At 1 o'clock on the morning of Thursday, June 25, at the head of the brigades of Wade Hampton, Fitz Lee, and John Chambliss (commanding in place of the wounded Rooney Lee), Jeb Stuart set off for Pennsylvania. Events over the next eight days would demonstrate that, whatever else occurred, Stuart faithfully carried out General Lee's orders. He rode around the enemy's army (although not without hindrance) and confused it and broke its communications, he gathered military intelligence, he collected ample supplies, and he tried his best to "feel the right" of Ewell's corps. In doing all this he also rode into a torrent of controversy.[19]

The question going to the heart of Stuart's "ride around Hooker" is why it was undertaken at all. Longstreet, on June 22, noted that if Stuart's cavalry should cross the Potomac along with the rest of the army — that is, passing from the Shenandoah Valley into the Cumberland Valley — it would "disclose our plans." That seems the flimsiest of answers. If the gaps in the Blue Ridge continued to be securely held (as Lee's orders specified), surely the Yankees would continue to be mystified as to Confederate intentions. In any event, by Lee's design he *needed* to have the enemy follow him if he was to shift the seat of war into Northern territory; it was merely a matter of timing. Fast-moving cavalry, starting promptly, could easily catch up with Ewell's infantry by this direct route through the Valley — half the distance of the more easterly, roundabout route. Should there be the threat of congestion at the Shepherdstown Potomac crossing, a short detour would take the cavalry to Williamsport, one of Ewell's earlier crossing points.

Perhaps the true answer to this question is inherent in Dorsey Pender's remark in his June 23 letter — "It is stated on all sides that Hooker has a small army and that very much demoralized. The General says he wants to meet him as soon as possible. . . ." General Lee's contempt for Fighting

Joe Hooker ("Mr. F. J. Hooker"), and for Hooker's army, had only been reinforced by Chancellorsville; Lee never grasped how much Dame Fortune had shaped his victory on that battlefield. Jeb Stuart had no doubts at all that he could ride around or even through the hapless Yankees to achieve all General Lee wanted of him, to a harvest of glory, and Lee fully subscribed to his attitude. The very concept of Stuart's expedition was fueled by overconfidence and misjudgment at the highest command level. As soldier-historian Porter Alexander judged the matter, "We took unnecessary risk, which was bad war, & the only bad war, too, I think, in all our tactics."[20]

The first day of Stuart's march, June 25, brought numerous and sobering surprises. The unexpected presence of Yankee infantry forced the troopers to detour through the more southerly Glasscock Gap in the Bull Run Mountains. Then they encountered the marching infantry of the Federal Second Corps. Efforts to knock a gap in the column with the horse artillery failed. Scouting during the day to the south and east revealed one road after another filled with marching Yankees. Stuart fell back to the mountains for the night.

Lee's orders stipulated that Stuart pass around the enemy without hindrance; surely here were hindrances enough to send him back to the main army. Stuart only became more determined; contempt for the enemy overcame reason. On the 26th he looped farther south by east until at last he found a clear path toward Fairfax Court House, Joe Hooker's recent headquarters. In forty-eight hours Stuart had covered but 35 miles. Twice he sent dispatches to Lee reporting that the Federals were on the march. Neither courier got through. So far as the Army of Northern Virginia was concerned, Stuart's cavalry had entered a total eclipse.

At 3:00 A.M. on June 28 Stuart's 5,000 horse soldiers completed a difficult crossing of the Potomac at Rowser's Ford, 8 miles from Rockville, Maryland. They had managed to pass by the rear of the Federal army, but it had consumed seventy-four hours, and their appointed rendezvous with Ewell's corps in Pennsylvania lay 70 miles to the north. Meanwhile, during those seventy-four hours, the campaign had changed dramatically.[21]

THE CONFEDERATE INFANTRY'S crossings of the Potomac, at Shepherdstown and Williamsport, were occasions for celebration and symbolic observances. Bands played "The Bonnie Blue Flag" and "Dixie" and especially (and repeatedly) "Maryland, My Maryland." The Rebel yell echoed from shore to shore. Randolph Shotwell of Pickett's division watched the columns splashing through the waist-deep waters, with "colonels on horseback, flags fluttering, and the forest of bright bayonets glistening in the afternoon sun. . . ." When General George "Maryland" Steuart reached the far shore, he dismounted and kissed the ground of his native state. This inspired another chorus of "Maryland, My Maryland." During General Lee's passage of the Potomac, a steady rain failed to deter a band from saluting him with "Dixie." Lee was greeted as Maryland's deliverer by a delegation of local ladies, who attempted to adorn Traveller with an enormous wreath. The horse balked, however, and it was agreed that one of the general's aides would carry the wreath henceforth.[22]

Lieutenant Colonel Arthur James Lyon Fremantle, Her Majesty's Coldstream Guards, in America to observe the hostilities, had attached himself to the Army of Northern Virginia for the march north. Colonel Fremantle was struck by the confidence he found among all ranks. In his diary he recorded a conversation with two Louisiana officers: "At no period of the war, they say, have the men been so well equipped, so well clothed, so eager for a fight, or so confident of success. . . ." As to their equipment, Fremantle remarked on the large number of wagons and cannon in every column he encountered that bore U.S. markings. It appeared that the Rebel army depended upon Washington as much as Richmond for its transport and artillery. And he questioned how well clothed the men were. Hood's division of Longstreet's First Corps, he noted, was composed in part "of Texans, Alabamians, and Arkansians, and they certainly are a queer lot to look at. They carry less than any other troops; many of them have only got an old piece of carpet or rug as baggage; many have discarded their shoes in the mud; all are ragged and dirty, but full of good-humour and confidence in themselves and in their general, Hood."

In an interview with Longstreet, the general explained to Fremantle that the army intended to live entirely off the enemy's country, but no more than that: "Whilst speaking of entering upon the enemy's soil, he said to me, that although it might be fair, in just retaliation, *to apply the torch*, yet that doing so would demoralize the army and ruin its now excellent discipline." It proved quite true that the Confederates did not apply the torch to Pennsylvania, except in the case of certain military targets, nor did they leave a trail of deadly mayhem. Yet they laid a very heavy hand on the inhabitants — a far heavier hand, in matters of officially sanctioned confiscation, than anything the Army of the Potomac had inflicted during any campaign in Virginia.[23]

Dick Ewell, playing the role of commissary for the expedition, performed efficiently and with all required promptness. On the morning of Monday, June 22, Robert Rodes's Second Corps division, with Albert Jenkins's cavalry in the van, led the historic march across the Maryland-Pennsylvania border into the enemy's country. The brief dash of Jenkins's cavalry into Chambersburg on the 15th had served to tip off the inhabitants as to Confederate intentions, and local merchants and bankers and farmers had rushed to hide their goods and valuables or to send them off to safer places. Still, when the Second Corps crossed into Pennsylvania a week later, there remained more than plenty to gather up in that bounteous land.

Greencastle was the first Pennsylvania town called upon for tribute. The requisition list included 120 pistols, 100 saddles and bridles, 1,000 pounds of leather, 2,000 pounds of lead, 200 currycombs, 12 boxes of tin, and such foodstuffs as onions, potatoes, radishes, and sauerkraut. The town council threw up its hands at these demands, after which the Confederates simply collected all they found or were offered and marched on. That proved to be the pattern among the main Rebel army units — they seized whatever they could of their tribute demands, but without resort to violence. The majority of the reported depredations were committed by less disciplined cavalrymen.

The outraged *Lancaster Daily Express* was not inclined to draw fine distinctions among these exemplars of Southern chivalry. By its way of thinking, "If highway robberies, profanity, vulgarity, filthiness and general meanness are the requisite qualifications for constituting a high-toned gentleman then indeed may the southern soldiers claim the appellation."

When a final tally was made of foodstuffs collected by the Rebel army over the course of two weeks in Maryland and Pennsylvania, it approximated 6,700 barrels of flour, 7,900 bushels of wheat, 5,200 cattle, 1,000 hogs, 2,400 sheep, and more than 51,000 pounds of cured meat. No count seems to have been made of horses seized, but they were a favorite target and totaled well into the thousands. These figures for the most part covered only booty gathered by officially designated foraging parties. An uncountable volume of good things to eat must be credited to an uncountable number of Rebel soldiers foraging on their own accounts.[24]

Southern soldiers writing of the Pennsylvania campaign filled their letters with admiring descriptions of the bounty they found in barns and smokehouses and kitchen larders; many of these men had never eaten so well in their lives. If this kept up, said General Ewell, "we will all get fat here." Mississippian Edward Burruss wrote of McLaws's division camping near Chambersburg, "where we lived on the very fat of the land — milk, butter, eggs, chickens, turkeys, apple butter, pear butter, cheese, honey, fresh pork, mutton & every other imaginable thing that was good to eat." Georgian Joseph Hilton assured his sweetheart that he and his comrades "have inflicted serious injury upon the corpulent Dutch farmers of that loyal state in the destruction of bee gums, fowls, eggs, butter, cherries, green apples, cider and apple butter. It will take at least three seasons to replenish the stock, besides playing sad havoc with their horses and cattle." As Captain Benjamin Farinholt, 53rd Virginia, wrote his wife, with satisfaction, "Our Army will not cost the Confederacy a great deal as long as we remain in Pa."

After crossing into Pennsylvania, the men got into the habit of marching up to the front doors of farmhouses and townhouses and asking, with rifles in hand but politely enough, for something to eat. Cowed householders almost invariably accommodated the enemy. One of Harry Hays's Louisiana Tigers discovered a particular source of their fright. As a housewife was preparing him a meal, she asked him his regiment. Seventh Louisiana, he replied, at which she collapsed in a faint. It seemed that the raucous 35th Virginia cavalry battalion, known as the "Comanches," had earlier ridden through the town exclaiming that "the Louisiana Tigers would kill, burn and destroy everything and everybody in the country." This was an extreme example of a widespread impression. In Greencastle, wrote North Carolinian Louis Leon, "We got the ear of one or two ladies, and after proving to them that we were not wild animals or thieves, they gave us what we wanted. . . ."[25]

This area of south-central Pennsylvania was largely settled by Germans, frugal, skilled farmers with enormous barns and intensively cultivated fields who (as a 7th Virginia soldier put it) "will do anything to save property or their hides." During these crisis weeks they did not, on the whole, act the part of staunch Unionists. Colonel Fremantle considered them unpatriotic, in contrast to those in the Southern states he had recently visited. These Pennsylvania Germans, Fremantle wrote, "openly state that they don't care which side wins, provided they are left alone."

That indifference was not limited to the invaded areas of Pennsylvania. Businessman George Fahnestock found a similar attitude in Philadelphia. "Thousands of able bodied young fellows are ever parading the streets, but no enlistments go with spirit," Fahnestock entered in his diary on June 27. "These chaps can lounge and dress, swinging canes, or twirling moustaches, but they have no patriotism in their souls." This

Edwin Forbes pictured Baltimore citizens barricading their streets on June 28 to repel Rebel cavalry raiders. (Library of Congress)

apathy was in sharp contrast to the patriotic spirit Philadelphia had displayed nine months earlier when Lee first marched north. Now, as his second invasion pushed across the Mason-Dixon Line, militia recruiting continued to lag. War-weariness had taken its hold on the Keystone State. Just that spring the Democratic majority in the General Assembly had condemned Lincoln's running of the war and called for restoring the Union through a constitutional convention. It appeared that General Lee had little to fear from any popular uprising in Pennsylvania.[26]

What Lee's invasion did trigger was a tidal wave of refugees flooding toward the Susquehanna and Harrisburg. Merchants bearing their goods, bankers carrying their deposits, farmers driving their stock, free blacks evading Rebel slave-catchers, families fleeing the imagined horrors of military occupation — all rushed to the capital from southern Pennsylvania. Not to be outdone, there was a simultaneous exodus farther northward by Harrisburg's citizens.

The city's railroad stations, reported Charles Coffin of the *Boston Journal,* "were crowded with an excited people — men, women, and children — with trunks, boxes, bundles; packages tied up in bed-blankets and

110

quilts; mountains of luggage — tumbling it into the cars, rushing here and there in a frantic manner; shouting, screaming, as if the Rebels were about to dash into the town and lay it in ashes. . . . There was a steady stream of teams thundering across the bridge; farmers from the Cumberland valley, with their household furniture piled upon the great wagons . . . ; bedding, tables, chairs, their wives and children perched on the top; kettles and pails dangling underneath. . . ." At a second Susquehanna bridge a massive traffic jam formed while the bridgekeeper insisted on collecting the regular toll. It took the intervention of General Couch to persuade the bridge company to waive the tolls in the emergency.

Another witness to the chaotic scene in Harrisburg was a touring pianist named Louis Gottschalk. "The panic increases," Gottschalk wrote. "It is no longer a flight — it is a flood. . . . Carriages, carts, chariots, indeed all the vehicles in the city have been put into requisition. The poor are moving in wheel-barrows. A trader has attached to his omnibus, already full, a long line of carts, trucks, buggies, whose owners probably had no horses. . . . The confusion is at its height. Cattle bellowing, frightened mules, prancing horses, the noisy crowd, the whistling locomotives, the blinding dust, the burning sun."[27]

The pursuit and capture of blacks, initiated by Jenkins's cavalry in Chambersburg, continued as the Army of Northern Virginia crossed the Pennsylvania line. In Mercersburg, for example, Professor Philip Schaff recorded in his diary that "public and private houses were ransacked, horses, cows, sheep, and provisions stolen day by day without mercy, negroes captured and carried back into slavery (even such as I know to have been born and raised on free soil), and many other outrages committed. . . ." Dr. Schaff attributed these captures to the partisan bands of John H. McNeill and John S. Mosby and the cavalry irregulars under John D. Imboden. In one instance, it is recorded that a dozen blacks were swept up in one of Mosby's forays into Pennsylvania.

Slave-catching was practiced by Confederate infantry as well. William S. Christian, colonel of the 55th Virginia in Harry Heth's division of the Third Corps, wrote his wife from Greenwood on June 28, "We took a lot of negroes yesterday. I was offered my choice but as I could not get them back home I would not take them." Colonel Christian went on to say, "In fact, my humanity revolted at taking the poor devils away from their homes," and he turned them loose. Such gestures were apparently not widespread. Slave-catching, whether or not it was officially sanctioned, was without question widely and officially tolerated. Three days later, Longstreet's adjutant, in a dispatch to General Pickett, made note that

"The captured contrabands had better be brought along with you for further disposition." The number of free or fugitive blacks condemned to slavery during these weeks can only be estimated, but widespread testimony suggests that it was in the hundreds. Of various ugly incidents stemming from Lee's Pennsylvania invasion, this was surely the ugliest.[28]

On June 22, just beyond Greencastle, Robert Rodes was briefly alarmed by a rumor that General McClellan was approaching at the head of a 40,000-man army of home guards. The reality was a brush with a scouting Union cavalry company, a brush that cost Corporal William F. Rihl his life. Rihl, a Pennsylvanian, was the first to die defending his state against invasion.[29]

By the 25th Dick Ewell had his three divisions at or near Chambersburg, and he called his lieutenants together to plan their marches over the next days. By its location, Chambersburg served as a strategic keynote in Robert E. Lee's invasion scheme. At the heart of the bountiful Cumberland Valley, 15 miles north of the Maryland border, sheltered from Federal forces by South Mountain to the east, Chambersburg became the jumping-off point for the advance of Ewell's Second Corps and the rendezvous point for Longstreet's First Corps and A. P. Hill's Third.

At their meeting, Ewell instructed Rodes, followed by Allegheny Johnson, to continue north by east down the Cumberland Valley, by way of Shippensburg and Carlisle, toward Harrisburg and the Susquehanna. Ewell himself would travel with this column. Jubal Early's division was to turn due east, cross South Mountain by the Cashtown Gap, and, passing through Gettysburg and York, reach the Susquehanna at Wrightsville, 25 miles downstream from Harrisburg. Early's task was to cut the North Central Railroad at York, then burn the Columbia Bridge over the Susquehanna at Wrightsville, thus severing Hooker's rail links with Harrisburg. His work of destruction finished, Early would rejoin Ewell at Carlisle to plan for the next move, against Harrisburg. Already Imboden's cavalry had torn up the Baltimore & Ohio; occupying Harrisburg would add the Pennsylvania Central's main line to the list of destroyed Yankee railroads.[30]

Jubal Early, "Old Jube," fierce-minded and cantankerous, quickly set the tone for his march. At South Mountain he came upon the Caledonia Iron Works, the property of abolitionist Congressman Thaddeus Stevens. The works superintendent tried to convince General Early that Stevens only kept the unprofitable furnace and rolling mill and forge open as employment for the local working poor. "That is not the way Yankees do business," Early scoffed, and ordered the place burned to the ground.

He did so, he later wrote, because Congressman Stevens "had been advocating the most vindictive measures of confiscation and devastation" against the South.[31]

On the afternoon of June 26 the veteran 35th Virginia cavalry battalion, the Comanches, leading Early's column into Gettysburg, skirmished briefly with the 26th Pennsylvania militia. Recognizing how greatly they were overmatched, the raw militiamen promptly fled the scene. "The officers were running around waving their swords, shouting and swearing, but no one dreamed of obeying them," a militiaman wrote; "the men . . . were falling in behind the fences, and others streaking off over the fields." During the subsequent pursuit, twenty-year-old Corporal George W. Sandoe, of the local Adams County cavalry, was shot down and killed, becoming the first Federal soldier to die at Gettysburg.

Several citizens, hoping to pacify the Comanches, unwisely offered them liquor. Professor Michael Jacobs of Pennsylvania College recorded the consequence: "The advance guard of the enemy, consisting of 180 to 200 cavalry, rode into Gettysburg at 3¼ P.M., shouting and yelling like so many savages from the wilds of the Rocky Mountains; firing their pistols, not caring whether they killed or maimed man, woman, or child. . . ." General Early now rode into the town to levy his tribute — 7,000 pounds of bacon, 1,200 pounds of sugar, 1,000 pounds of salt, 600 pounds of coffee, 60 barrels of flour, 10 barrels of onions, 10 barrels of whiskey, 1,000 pairs of shoes, and 500 hats; or, alternatively, $5,000 in cash. The town fathers, pleading poverty, opened the stores to the invaders, but few of their demands could be met. "Some horses were stolen, some cellars were broken open and robbed, but so far as could be done, the officers controlled their men, and all those in and around the streets behaved well," a Gettysburg woman wrote. The following morning, after paroling their militia prisoners, the Rebels set off eastward on the turnpike to York.[32]

The invaders' entry into York was peaceful and indeed novel. Brigadier General William "Extra Billy" Smith, sixty-five years old, at heart more politician than soldier, directed the column to halt in the town square. Extra Billy had served five terms in Congress and one term as governor of Virginia, and he could not resist an opportunity to address a crowd, whatever its sympathies might be. "My friends," he began with good cheer, "how do you like this way of coming back into the Union?" He went on to explain that he and his fellow soldiers had felt the need of a summer outing, "and thought we would take it at the North." They might be conquerors, he said — "this part of Pennsylvania is ours today; we've got it, we hold it, we can destroy it, or do what we please with it" —

but they were also Christian gentlemen and would act accordingly. "You are quite welcome to remain here and to make yourselves entirely at home — so long as you behave yourselves pleasantly and agreeably as you are doing now. Are we not a fine set of fellows?"

With his honeyed words he had the crowd in the palm of his hand, only to be interrupted by a querulous, impatient Jubal Early. Old Jube forced his way through the onlookers to confront Extra Billy and snarled, "General Smith, what the devil are you about? Stopping the head of this column in this cursed town!" Not the least taken aback, Extra Billy replied, "Having a little fun, General, which is good for all of us, and at the same time teaching these people something that will be good for them and won't do us any harm."

Old Jube was not inclined toward a little fun, and he proceeded to levy a sizable tribute on York's town fathers. Among his demands were 28,000 pounds of baked bread, 3,500 pounds of sugar, 1,650 pounds of coffee, 32,000 pounds of beef or 21,000 pounds of bacon, 2,000 pairs of shoes, and no less than $100,000 in cash. If these demands were not met, he announced, he would turn his men loose to sack the town. York complied to a considerable extent, although it could furnish only 1,500 pairs of shoes and just $28,000. Early was sufficiently mollified to let the town stand.

Captain William Seymour of Harry Hays's Louisiana brigade marveled at how far these Pennsylvanians would go to conceal their animals. "Horses were found in bedrooms, parlours, lofts of barns and other out of the way places," Seymour wrote. One day his brigade quartermaster was interrogating the owner of a large and finely furnished house when he heard a neigh from the next room. "The Major quietly opened the door and there in an elegant parlour, comfortably stalled in close proximity to a costly rosewood piano, stood a noble looking horse. . . ." The quartermaster led his prize from its "novel stable," paying for it in Confederate currency that was all but worthless to the owner.

General Early had thus far found so little opposition to his march that he determined to capture, rather than destroy, the Columbia Bridge over the Susquehanna at Wrightsville. His thought was to use the bridge as entry for capturing Harrisburg, and he assigned the task to John B. Gordon's brigade of Georgians. In late afternoon of June 28 Gordon came in sight of Wrightsville, only to find the town barricaded and the mile-long bridge guarded by entrenchments, apparently fully manned. In expectation of stampeding the militia defenders, Gordon opened on the town with his artillery. His two most effective guns were 20-pounder

Parrott rifles seized from Milroy in Winchester two weeks earlier. To the quiet satisfaction of many townsmen, one of the shells heavily damaged the rooms of the Sons of Temperance Association.

Among the defenders in the entrenchments was a local company of free blacks — volunteers protecting their homes — and one of these men was killed in the bombardment, the sole death in the fight for the Columbia Bridge. The shelling soon had the desired effect, and the militiamen scrambled back across the bridge. Gordon's men rushed forward, but the Federals had carefully prepared the bridge for destruction, and it was soon spectacularly ablaze. "The scene was magnificent . . . ," a newspaper reported. "The moon was bright, and the blue clouds afforded the best contrast possible to the red glare of the conflagration. The light in the heavens must have been seen for many miles." When the fire threatened to spread into Wrightsville, Gordon's troops joined the townspeople in bringing it under control. The next day the citizenry with great relief watched the Rebels march away.[33]

In the meantime, Dick Ewell had marched northward from Chambersburg at a leisurely pace with Rodes's and Johnson's divisions. At each town he laid tribute. In Shippensburg, for example, the womenfolk were conscripted through the night to bake the required numbers of breads, pies, and cakes, to be delivered to the Rebel troops in the town square. General Ewell wrote his new wife that the march reminded him of the war with Mexico. "It is like a renewal of Mexican times to enter a captured town," he told her. "The people look as sour as vinegar & I have no doubt would gladly send us all to kingdom come if they could." On June 27 a diarist in the village of Newville noted, "The cavalry are raiding our corn cribs tonight." The next day she wrote, "An exciting Sabbath. Johnny Reb left this morning with almost 300 cattle."

On Saturday, the 27th, a deputation of leading citizens of Carlisle met Ewell's outriders under a flag of truce and surrendered the town, giving assurances that all the militia units had departed for safer quarters. Fifteen-year-old James Sullivan, peeking from a second-story window, watched the first Rebel troopers enter Carlisle: "Big men, wearing broad-brimmed hats, and mounted on good horses, they had a picturesque air of confidence and readiness for action. Their carbines were carried butt resting at the knee and barrel pointed upright." Soon afterward the infantry marched in singing "Dixie."

General Ewell made his headquarters at Carlisle Barracks, the army post where he had been stationed as a second lieutenant of dragoons twenty years before. The post flagpole soon bore a Confederate ban-

ner, and speeches were offered by several of the generals. "Quite an ani-
mating scene," Jed Hotchkiss, the staff cartographer, noted in his diary.
On General Lee's orders, Ewell refrained from burning the army barracks, but instead scoured them of their military accouterments. He then
turned his attention to planning the capture of Harrisburg.[34]

That Saturday, June 27, the day after Ewell set out from Chambersburg
for the Susquehanna, Robert E. Lee rode into Chambersburg in company
with A. P. Hill and the Third Corps. Longstreet's First Corps was a short
march behind. General Lee established headquarters outside town in a
pleasant grove called Messersmith's Woods, on the Chambersburg Pike
leading to Gettysburg. Lee, along with two-thirds of his army, would
pause three days at Chambersburg while events quite beyond his reach
strikingly reshaped the campaign.[35]

In one change of plan, the Army of Northern Virginia would not be
carrying with it a minister plenipotentiary to negotiate peace terms with
the Yankees on some northern battlefield. Confederate Vice President
Alexander Stephens had reached Richmond from Georgia on June 26,
to discover to his horror that the diplomatic scheme he had proposed
for discussing "a general adjustment" with Washington had been trans-
posed by President Davis into something very different. Stephens balked
at Davis's idea of sending him to join Lee's army — even if he could catch
up with it in Pennsylvania — where he would be expected to parley with
the enemy. Stephens eventually agreed to shifting the parley site to the
Virginia Peninsula. From there, on July 4, he requested a meeting with
the Lincoln administration. But by then any Confederate initiative for
negotiating a peace had been overtaken by events. President Lincoln refused to meet with him, and Alexander Stephens returned home empty-
handed and disillusioned.[36]

On June 25 Lee had written to Mr. Davis, calling once again for any
available reinforcements, and returning to his scheme for either a real or
an effigy army to be assembled under General Beauregard to threaten
Washington. He explained that he had abandoned his communications
with Virginia, and would live off the enemy's country. He set as his most
modest goal drawing Hooker's army north across the Potomac, "embar-
rassing their plan of campaign in a measure, if I can do nothing more and
have to return." The truth of the matter, however, was that General Lee,
as he had from the first, fully anticipated fighting a battle north of the
Potomac.

At Dick Ewell's headquarters on the evening of the next day, the 26th,

Jed Hotchkiss closed his daily diary entry by noting, "Gen. Lee wrote to Gen. Ewell that he thought the battle would come off near Fredericks City or Gettysburg." Although this dispatch to Ewell is not on record to elaborate the point, it is clear enough from Hotchkiss's notation that General Lee believed he still controlled the initiative in the campaign, and, most important, that he still would be able to dictate where any battle was fought. That was certainly his mood when he greeted General Hood at the Messersmith's Woods headquarters: "Ah! General, the enemy is a long time finding us; if he does not succeed soon, we must go in search of him."

In projecting one probable battle site as Frederick, Maryland, some two days' march south of his present position at Chambersburg, Lee took it for granted that the Federal army had not yet crossed the Potomac and was still in Virginia, guarding Washington. According to the last intelligence, dated June 23, Hooker "was prepared to cross the Potomac" and had a pontoon bridge across the river at Edwards Ferry, near Leesburg, Virginia. Yet nothing about any actual Potomac crossing by the enemy had been reported by Jeb Stuart. Surely, Lee believed, such intelligence could not have escaped his ever vigilant cavalryman. Talking to General Isaac Trimble at this time, Lee explained that when the enemy finally did come up, "probably through Frederick," he would throw what he described as "an overwhelming force on their advance," then follow up that initial success by driving one corps back upon another to gain the victory. Lee told General Trimble, as he had told Dick Ewell, that one probable site for the coming battle was the Pennsylvania town of Gettysburg.[37]

ON MONDAY, June 22, the day after the big cavalry fight at Upperville — and the day Dick Ewell started his raiding columns across Maryland into Pennsylvania — the Army of the Potomac was massed to protect Washington and poised to push across the Potomac on command. Solid intelligence about the Rebel army was at last beginning to come in. The decision to start Jeb Stuart on his "ride around Hooker" would prove a boon to Federal intelligence-gathering. Without Stuart's tight cavalry screen, Lee's hidden army became visible. To be sure, Stuart had left two cavalry brigades, under Beverly Robertson and Grumble Jones, with the army, but Lee put them to guarding the Blue Ridge gaps rather than furnishing security during the army's advance. Albert Jenkins's troopers, out front with Ewell's corps, were too busy raiding Pennsylvania barns and smokehouses to perform cavalry functions. The same was true of John Imboden's irregulars, foraging and slave-catching on the western flank of Lee's advance.

As a consequence, information began to funnel into General Hooker's headquarters from no fewer than fifteen organized intelligence-gathering groups. The Potomac army's Bureau of Military Information ran several spying operations, as did General Couch in Harrisburg. The Signal Corps established observation posts. The railroads in the region directed scouting parties that reported over the lines' telegraph facilities. On-the-scene scouting parties, such as that of David McConaughy, a leading citizen of Gettysburg, supplied eyewitness testimony. Gradually the hazy picture of the invading army began to clear.

The B.M.I.'s Sergeant Milton Cline, for example, used the cavalry fight at Aldie to slip his espionage party behind enemy lines. They slipped back during the Upperville battle to report on the location of Longstreet's divisions and to confirm that A. P. Hill was also in the Valley. The passage of Jubal Early's division through Gettysburg and on toward York was detailed by David McConaughy and his citizen-scouts. The arrival of Ewell's outriders in Chambersburg and Carlisle, and their requisitions, was promptly passed on to Couch's headquarters in Harrisburg. By all reports, it was evident that Ewell's corps, as soon as it crossed into Pennsylvania, was embarking on a giant raiding expedition. Of immediate concern was the exact whereabouts and intentions of the remaining two-thirds of the Rebel army — the corps of Longstreet and Hill. Would they follow Ewell into Pennsylvania, or would they await his return to the Potomac with his booty and then strike eastward toward Washington or Baltimore?[38]

On June 24 the answer came from the B.M.I.'s third-in-command, John Babcock, posted at Frederick in Maryland. The "main body" of Lee's army was crossing the Potomac at Shepherdstown, he reported, and "large bodies of troops can be seen" from vantage points in Maryland. Ewell's corps had passed that way two days earlier and was now in Pennsylvania. Babcock closed by saying, "All of which may be considered as reliable." In a second telegram that day, he confirmed from additional "reliable sources" that "Longstreet and A. P. Hill are crossing rapidly." Equally important, no Rebel forces had been sighted in the direction of Frederick and the South Mountain passes, indicating that the Army of Northern Virginia was marching not eastward but northward toward Pennsylvania. Fighting Joe Hooker now had the intelligence he needed. That night orders went out for the Army of the Potomac to begin crossing the Potomac at Edwards Ferry the next day, Thursday, June 25.

In a curious twist, this intelligence put Longstreet's corps marching ahead of A. P. Hill's, when just the reverse was true. But the solid central fact, on the authority of one of the B.M.I.'s best officers, was undeniable — the two-thirds of the Confederate army not previously fully accounted for was in fact crossing, or about to cross, the Potomac and marching on northward. As it happened, the whole of Hooker's army would be across the river some hours before the whole of Lee's. Joe Hooker still held the inside track.[39]

On the 23rd Hooker had made a flying visit to Washington to confer with the War Department and the president. There is no record of what was discussed, but surely it included the subject of reinforcements. General-in-Chief Halleck was then in Baltimore, forestalling an opportunity for the two men to sort out their differences, had they been so inclined. It appears that neither Hooker nor the president gained much from their meeting that day. Mr. Lincoln appeared afterward at a Cabinet meeting, and Gideon Welles noted in his diary, "His countenance was sad and careworn, and impressed me painfully." According to another Cabinet member, Montgomery Blair, the president remarked that he had dismissed McClellan the previous fall because he let Lee "get the better of him in the race to Richmond." Now Lincoln seemed to have it in mind that if Hooker was beaten in the present race, he "would make short work of him." The president's confidence in his general was clearly waning. In another conversation, Welles quoted Lincoln as saying that General Hooker "may commit the same fault as McClellan and lose his chance." Still, he tried to be hopeful: "We shall soon see, but it appears to me he can't help but win."

The next day Hooker sent his chief of staff, Dan Butterfield, to Washington and Baltimore to pin down just what reinforcements the Potomac army might expect from the garrisons there. The latest intelligence, now arriving from observers in Hagerstown, through which most of the Rebel army was passing, put Lee's infantry strength at 91,000. This was not an unreasonable surmise, considering all the reports of Rebel reinforcements coming up from Richmond and the Carolinas since Chancellorsville, and all the difficulty of confirming the accuracy of those reports. (Soon enough the B.M.I. would have more clearly defined reports from Hagerstown, producing a more realistic figure of 80,000 for Lee's army.) The count of the Potomac army, reflecting the two-year and nine-month regiments so far sent home, was down to some 90,000.

Halleck agreed to surrender but four brigades of replacements from the Department of Washington — two brigades of Pennsylvania Reserves on loan from the Army of the Potomac, a small brigade of New Yorkers, and a Vermont brigade of nine-month men, 8,400 troops all told — but only after he judged the immediate threat to the capital was past. Not until June 25, when Lee was seen to be crossing the Potomac, did these troops set out to try and catch up with the Potomac army. Butterfield could obtain no further troops in Washington, and just one small brigade in Baltimore. How much easier "for your plans and purposes," he told Hooker, had all the departmental forces likely to confront Lee's army been "concentrated under one commander."[40]

There remained the nagging issue of Harper's Ferry. Hooker was now determined to gain the 10,000-man garrison there for the manpower edge he felt he had to have. As he later put it, "with all the additions I could receive" the two armies would be essentially equal in strength. He might go on to win the coming battle, but to prevent his opponent from escaping afterward "required, in my judgment, a little superiority of one over the other."

Hooker formulated a plan for using these Harper's Ferry troops. On June 25 he ordered the garrison commander, William French, to prepare "to march at a moment's notice." Henry Slocum's Twelfth Corps would move up the Potomac, combine with French's force, cut Lee's communications by destroying his Potomac bridges, and finally take up a blocking position in the rear of the Rebel army. Should Lee turn back to strike at Slocum's blocking force, John Reynolds, advancing to Middletown in Maryland with the First, Third, and Eleventh corps, would be in position to launch a flank attack.

Orders went out to French and Slocum and Reynolds, yet Hooker told Washington nothing of his plan. This had to be deliberate. He had decided to challenge General Halleck over the question of exercising command as he believed the situation warranted; or, as he later put it, the question was whether the army was "to be maneuvered from Washington." His was a bold and aggressive plan, and certainly one easy enough to justify. Instead, on the evening of June 26, he telegraphed Halleck and asked, "Is there any reason Maryland Heights" — the main defensive position overlooking Harper's Ferry — "should not be abandoned. . . ." He said nothing of how he intended to use the garrison, only that he would go to Harper's Ferry the next day to inspect the place. He reminded Halleck that he "must have every available man to use on the field."[41]

Halleck replied sharply on the morning of the 27th. Harper's Ferry had always been regarded as an important point; much labor and expense had been expended on the works there: "I cannot approve their abandonment, except in case of absolute necessity."

Hooker promptly accelerated his challenge — and the stakes. He and chief engineer Gouverneur Warren were now at Harper's Ferry and had inspected the position, and both realized what a liability it had become. "I strongly urged the abandonment of Harper's Ferry," Warren recalled, "and this was so apparent to both of us that my views were only a confirmation of his." Hooker responded to Halleck that the garrison at Harper's Ferry was "of no earthly account there." There was nothing worth defending; the enemy would never take possession of the fortifications. The troops should be marched to where they could be of service. "Now they are but a bait for the rebels, should they return." He closed by asking that his telegram "may be presented to the Secretary of War and His Excellency the President" for a decision.

With the telegraph battle thus joined, Hooker proceeded with his plan. He ordered the cavalry to push northward to Gettysburg, his predicted point of possible collision, "to see what they can of the movements of the enemy." The assignment would go to John Buford's division. Hooker handed march instructions to General French. Because this superseded his standing orders, French telegraphed the general-in-chief for confirmation. Halleck had not yet received Hooker's morning telegram calling for the case to be laid before Lincoln and Stanton, and his response fully displayed his contempt for the Potomac army commander. "Pay no attention to General Hooker's orders," he told French.

This was not only an insult but a calculated one, for Halleck well knew that French would have to show this countermanding order to Hooker. As Halleck hoped, Joe Hooker — perhaps impulsively — treated it as the last straw. Without waiting for the president to respond to his earlier dispatch — without realizing that Lincoln had not even seen that dispatch — Hooker dashed off a brief telegram to the general-in-chief. His instructions required him to cover Harper's Ferry, he began. "I beg to be understood, respectfully but firmly, that I am unable to comply with this condition with the means at my disposal, and earnestly request that I may at once be relieved from the position I occupy." Halleck's reply was bland: "Your dispatch has been duly referred for Executive action."[42]

Mr. Lincoln seems to have conferred with no one except Halleck and to have hesitated not at all in accepting Hooker's resignation. At a Cabinet meeting the next day, Gideon Welles recorded Lincoln's sparse comments on the matter: "The President said he had, for several days as the

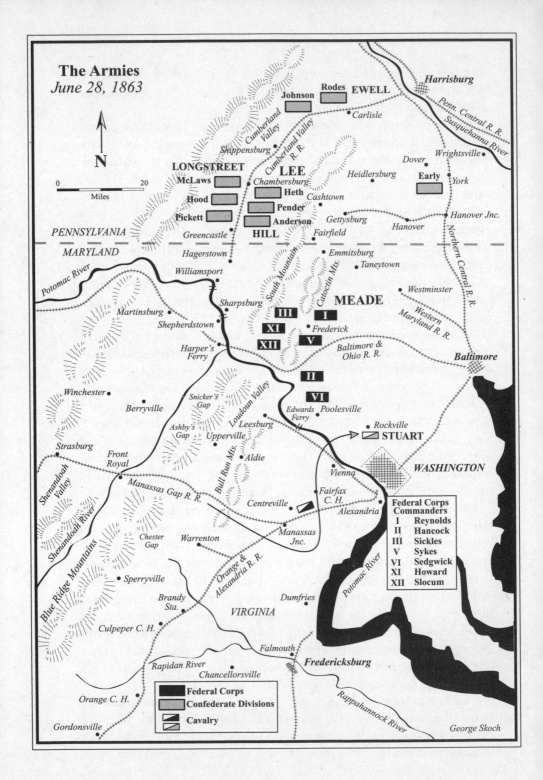

The Armies
June 28, 1863

N

0   20
Miles

EWELL

Johnson   Rodes

Harrisburg

Penn. Central R. R.

Carlisle

Cumberland Valley

Shippensburg

Cumberland Valley R. R.

Susquehanna River

Dover   Wrightsville

Heidlersburg

LONGSTREET

McLaws

Hood

Pickett

LEE

Chambersburg

Heth

Pender

Anderson

HILL

Cashtown

Gettysburg

Fairfield

Early

York

Hanover

Hanover Jnc.

Northern Central R. R.

PENNSYLVANIA

MARYLAND

Greencastle

Hagerstown

Emmitsburg

Taneytown

Potomac River

Williamsport

South Mountain

Catoctin Mts.

Westminster

Western Maryland R. R.

Martinsburg

Sharpsburg

Shepherdstown

III   I

XI

XII   V

MEADE

Frederick

Baltimore & Ohio R. R.

Baltimore

Harper's Ferry

Winchester

Berryville

Snicker's Gap

Loudoun Valley

II

VI

Edwards Ferry   Poolesville

Rockville

STUART

Ashby's Gap

Upperville

Leesburg

WASHINGTON

Strasburg

Front Royal

Aldie

Vienna

Shenandoah Valley

Manassas Gap R. R.

Bull Run Mts.

Centreville

Fairfax C. H.

Alexandria

Shenandoah River

Chester Gap

Warrenton

Manassas Jnc.

Federal Corps Commanders
I   Reynolds
II   Hancock
III   Sickles
V   Syles
VI   Sedgwick
XI   Howard
XII   Slocum

Blue Ridge Mountains

Sperryville

Brandy Sta.

Orange & Alexandria R. R.

Dumfries

Potomac River

VIRGINIA

Culpeper C. H.

Orange C. H.

Gordonsville

Rapidan River

Chancellorsville

Falmouth

Fredericksburg

Rappahannock River

Federal Corps
Confederate Divisions
Cavalry

George Skoch

conflict became imminent, observed in Hooker the same failings that were witnessed in McClellan after the Battle of Antietam — a want of alacrity to obey and a greedy call for more troops which could not and ought not to be taken from other points." When Halleck opposed him on abandoning Harper's Ferry, said the president, "Hooker had taken umbrage at the refusal, or at all events had thought it best to give up the command." Lincoln did not mention the lack of confidence in Hooker displayed by his lieutenants, but it surely weighed heavily in his decision.

Nor did Lincoln hesitate about naming a successor. The Potomac army's chief officers had left no doubt they wanted George Meade for the post, and in any event four other eligible generals had already turned it down. That evening General Orders No. 194 was drawn up, relieving General Hooker as commander of the Army of the Potomac and appointing General Meade in his place.

That night a special train sped James Hardie, of the army's adjutant-general's office, through Maryland to Frederick, and at 3 o'clock on the morning of Sunday, June 28, Hardie awakened General Meade at his Fifth Corps headquarters outside town. "At first," Meade would tell his wife, "I thought that it was either to relieve or arrest me, and promptly replied to him, that my conscience was clear. . . ." After reading the orders Hardie had brought, Meade stifled his misgivings and (he told his wife) "as a soldier, I had nothing to do but accept and exert my utmost abilities to command success. This, so help me God, I will do. . . ."

At daybreak Meade and Hardie rode to the camp of the general commanding. Hooker had learned of Hardie's arrival and surmised his mission, and was dressed in full uniform to meet them. He and Meade conferred in the headquarters tent for some time. In due course Meade, looking grave, emerged and found his son, an aide-de-camp, waiting for him. With "a familiar twinkle of the eye, denoting the anticipation of surprise at information to be imparted," he announced, "Well, George, I am in command of the Army of the Potomac."[43]

SUNDAY, JUNE 28, proved to be a day of surpassing importance to the commander of the Army of Northern Virginia as well. At 10 o'clock that night, at Longstreet's headquarters near Chambersburg, the provost guard brought in a dusty, scruffy-looking man in civilian clothes who insisted on seeing the general. Longstreet's chief of staff, Moxley Sorrel, recognized the visitor as Old Pete's favorite spy, Henry Thomas Harrison. In his memoirs Sorrel would describe Harrison as "altogether an extraordinary character." Longstreet had first used his services in the Suffolk campaign in April, at which time he appeared with a letter of introduction from Secretary of War Seddon. In the first week of June Longstreet had called in Harrison, filled his pockets with gold, and sent him to Washington to find out all the intelligence he could about the Federal army and to report back by the end of the month.

The story Harrison told was a revelation. Rather than still being massed below the Potomac in Virginia as the Confederate high command assumed, Hooker's army had begun crossing the river three days earlier and was now well up into Maryland. Harrison gave an accounting for five of the seven Federal corps — three at Frederick, two between Frederick and South Mountain. Old Pete, "immediately on fire at such news," as Sorrel put it, sent the spy in the care of aide John Fairfax to General Lee. At first Lee was suspicious of the unlikely figure and dubious about talking to him. He told Major Fairfax he did not know what to do: "I cannot hear from General Stuart, the eye of the army. What do you think of Harrison?" Fairfax replied that he did not think much of spies, "but General Longstreet thinks a good deal of Harrison." Lee finally agreed to see the man, and heard him out "with great composure and minuteness."[44]

General Lee was certainly not taken aback by the news that the Yankees had crossed the Potomac — it was after all his intent that they should follow him into the enemy's country — but what was startling and deeply disturbing was only now hearing about it, three days after the event. If the spy Harrison was right that Hooker started his army across the Potomac on June 25, by all rights Lee should have learned about it no later than the 26th. Never before had Jeb Stuart let him down, and the lapse was unsettling.

Even now he had no idea where Stuart was, nor any idea of the whereabouts of the enemy's forces beyond what Longstreet's spy had just told him — information that was already twenty-four hours old — nor, in fact, any idea of how to remedy this intelligence-gathering void. The unpleasant truth was that Mr. F. J. Hooker had stolen a forty-eight-hour march on him. As a consequence, before midnight that Sunday a headquarters courier went pounding down the road north of Chambersburg bearing urgent orders to pull together the scattered elements of the Army of Northern Virginia.[45]

6   High Stakes in Pennsylvania

ON JUNE 25, three days before Major Hardie handed him his appointment as commanding general of the Army of the Potomac, George Gordon Meade discussed that very possibility in an introspective letter to his wife. The army command had been in Meade's thoughts since early May, when the generals plotting Hooker's overthrow sought Meade's blessing for their scheme to promote him as Hooker's successor. Mrs. Meade, the general noted, seemed still to have visions of his being placed in the command, but he thought by now it had all blown over. "It is folly to think I stand any chance upon mere merit alone," he explained. He lacked the necessary friends, "political or others," to advance his case. Still, he was proud enough of his mere merits to elucidate them.

For one thing, he said, no one could accuse him of being "an unprincipled intriguer, who had risen by criticising and defaming my predecessors and superiors." Nor could he be called incompetent, for "so far as I have been tried I have been singularly successful." And certainly none could say "I had never been under fire, because it is notorious no general officer, not even Fighting Joe himself, has been in more battles, or more exposed, than my record evidences." The one thing that could be said, "and I am willing to admit the justice of the argument, is that it remains to be seen whether I have the capacity to handle successfully a large army." However that might be, he would not indulge "in any dreams of ambition," but simply await events and do his duty. He closed his letter by gently chiding his wife: "I think *your* ambition is being roused and that you are beginning to be bitten with the dazzling prospect of having for a husband a commanding general of the army. How is this?"[1]

George Meade's self-analysis was as perceptive and practical as the man himself. A career soldier, age forty-seven, he had a drab professorial look about him and as a figure of command was utterly lacking in color. But he was sharp-minded and quick-tempered. As one of his staff remarked, "I don't know any thin old gentleman, with a hooked nose and cold blue eye, who, when he is wrathy, exercises less of Christian charity

George Gordon Meade was the sixth and last general to lead
the Army of the Potomac. (Library of Congress)

than my well-beloved Chief!" On the battlefield Meade was conscientious and energetic and led from the front. He had been twice wounded
at Glendale on the Peninsula, and he came away from Fredericksburg
with two bullet holes in his hat. He was hardly known outside the Fifth
Corps, and less than well known there. But of surpassing importance was
the respect he enjoyed among the army's general officers. Their lack of

respect for Joe Hooker all but destroyed that general's usefulness; their pledged confidence in George Meade was the strongest card in his command hand.[2]

"I was delighted, on the road, to hear that Gen. Meade was in command of the army," General John Gibbon wrote home. ". . . I now feel my confidence restored and believe we shall whip these fellows." That confident tone was reflected all through the officer corps. Alpheus Williams, commanding a division in the Twelfth Corps, "rejoiced at the change of commanders. . . . Now with a gentleman and a soldier in command I have renewed confidence that we shall at least do enough to preserve our honor and the safety of the Republic." At headquarters that June 28, wrote Provost Marshal Marsena Patrick, "Of course this has caused great commotion, but as yet I have heard no regret."

Beyond any doubt, by his miscalculations and intemperate talk and his too mistrustful attitude toward his lieutenants, Joe Hooker alienated his fellow generals and helped precipitate his own downfall. Yet at the same time, these fellow generals plotted within a climate of military disloyalty they themselves had created, beginning in the Burnside regime and reaching fruition in the Hooker regime. The generals' revolt critically wounded Hooker in the eyes of Mr. Lincoln, and Henry Halleck then provided the excuse to push Fighting Joe over the edge. Now, their wish granted, the dissidents had little option except to serve one of their own with absolute fealty.

At 6 o'clock on the evening of that eventful Sunday, Joe Hooker made his farewells to the army in which he had fought for two years and which he had led for five months. "Hooker feels his removal very much," wrote the First Corps artillerist Charles Wainwright, especially on the eve of a battle "in which he might wipe off the opprobrium attached to him for his last." But Wainwright thought Hooker's farewell order to the army, which described his successor as a brave and accomplished soldier, was excellent, "the most modest of all his productions." As reported by Charles Coffin of the *Boston Journal,* the principal officers at headquarters were drawn up in line. General Hooker "shook hands with each officer, laboring in vain to stifle his emotion. The tears rolled down his cheeks. The officers were deeply affected." Hooker said he had hoped to lead them to victory, but "the power above him had ordered otherwise. He spoke in high terms of General Meade." Marsena Patrick tried to sum up the moment in his diary: "He leaves few friends behind him, altho' personally, he is the most agreeable commander I have yet served under. . . ."[3]

The reaction among the rank and file was muted. The troops were not suffering the kind of crisis in morale that had caused Hooker to be welcomed and Burnside condemned after Fredericksburg. Indeed it was Joe Hooker's legacy that now the army was well managed and its morale restored. This was the fifth command change in the Army of the Potomac within the past year, and the response of many was a resigned shrug at the mysterious ways of Washington. "Again a change in the face of the enemy & yet the government ask us to believe that they know what they are about!" exclaimed Captain Charles Francis Adams, Jr. According to T. C. Grey of the *New York Tribune*, "The relieving of Hooker is received with a kind of apathetic indifference by the army, although many are loud in denouncing the act *at this particular time*." There were regrets, however, for Joe Hooker was remembered by many as the soldier's friend. A man in the 1st Minnesota entered in his diary on June 28, "The intelligence that 'Fighting Joe' is superceded by Gen. Meade falls on us 'like a wet blanket.'"[4]

The colorless Meade was a virtual stranger, little more than a name to troops outside the Fifth Corps. "Few of our men knew him by sight," Rufus Dawes of the 6th Wisconsin remembered. "He was sometimes seen riding by the marching columns of troops at a fast trot, his hat brim turned down and a poncho over his shoulders." Meade had marched his corps hard to reach Maryland, and the change of command caught some of his men out of sorts. "'Old Four Eye,' as General Meade is termed by the men, appears to be a man universally despised in the Corps," Captain Francis Donaldson observed. "He certainly cares very little for the rank and file, and curses loud and deep are hurled at him, (for obeying instructions, as he must be doing), in marching us so tremendously." In the end, there was considerably more excitement about the change of command in Washington than in the army. In the capital, the *Cincinnati Gazette*'s correspondent wrote, "the crowds talked over the strange affair in all its phases; a thousand false stories were put in circulation . . . , darkening the very air."[5]

Along with the order for Meade to take command of the Potomac army came a letter of instruction from the general-in-chief. Halleck assured Meade he would "not be hampered by any minute instructions from these headquarters. Your army is free to act as you may deem proper. . . ." Meade was reminded, however, that the Army of the Potomac was the covering force for Washington and Baltimore as well as the operational force confronting the Rebel invaders. Should General Lee move against either city, "it is expected that you will either anticipate him or arrive with him so as to give him battle." Meade was also authorized to appoint or remove officers without regard to seniority, an important power to wield during the heat of a campaign.

Now that he had succeeded in maneuvering Joe Hooker out of the army command, Halleck was prompt to remove the restraints he had used to tie Hooker's hands. The new commanding general was told that "All forces within the sphere of your operations will be held subject to your orders," and Halleck pointedly included a specific: "Harper's Ferry and its garrison are under your direct orders." Having used any means to justify the end, Henry Halleck preened himself on a job well done. Had Hooker remained in command, he assured U. S. Grant, "he would have lost the army and the capital."[6]

Meade's first task that crowded Sunday was to learn where the enemy was and where the elements of his own army were — he had earlier complained of Hooker's habit of keeping his corps commanders in the dark. His early-morning conference with his predecessor included a briefing by Dan Butterfield, and afterward Meade decided, until "I can post myself up," to continue the massing of the army at Frederick. Hooker's plan had been to cross into Pennsylvania in pursuit of the enemy and let events there dictate his course. For the moment, that would be Meade's course as well. "I can only now say," he telegraphed Halleck that morning, "that it appears to me I must move toward the Susquehanna, keeping Washington and Baltimore well covered. . . ."

The picture of Lee's army was clarified that day by a remarkable piece of intelligence, dating from June 27, from citizen-spies in Hagerstown. As Colonel Sharpe of the Bureau of Military Information summarized it, a careful count of the Rebel army passing through Hagerstown "could not make them over 80,000," with 275 pieces of artillery. There was much reinforcing detail about enemy units that had passed through the town and where they were bound. In forwarding this report to Washington, Meade made note that the intelligence it contained "is confirmed by information gathered from various other sources regarded as reliable." This picture of the enemy was accepted, at least for the moment, by Potomac army headquarters. In point of fact, except for Stuart's absent cavalry, it was a remarkably accurate picture. The actual count of Lee's army ready for battle would come to 80,000, with 283 guns.[7]

Meade hurried through various administrative tasks on day one of his new command. He tried first to obtain a chief of staff of his choice. Seth

Williams, the army's adjutant general, and Gouverneur Warren, its chief engineer, each pleaded too much work in their departments to take on the burdens of a new job. Andrew Humphreys wanted to keep his divisional command in the Third Corps. Consequently Meade retained Dan Butterfield in the post. Butterfield was an able staff administrator who knew where every unit in the army was to be found, and he made the command transition a smooth one. Although Butterfield was suspect in many eyes as a Hooker partisan, and in due course would become an avowed enemy of Meade's, while in his service as chief of staff he served loyally. Meade was himself an able administrator, and between the two of them they maneuvered the army with considerable efficiency. Other key department heads, such as artillery chief Henry Hunt and quartermaster Rufus Ingalls, also remained in their posts.

General Meade even approved a hasty cavalry reorganization. Hooker had managed to wrest the cavalry division of Julius Stahel away from the Department of Washington, and Alfred Pleasonton then managed to wrest the divisional command away from Stahel and give it to Judson Kilpatrick. At the same time, Meade agreed to Pleasonton's stratagem of jump-promoting three youthful captains, Elon Farnsworth, Wesley Merritt, and George Armstrong Custer, to be brigadier generals and commanders of brigades in the newly revamped cavalry. The strength of the cavalry corps was now some 15,000.[8]

From Washington that day came a disturbing report that Confederate cavalry had been sighted across the Potomac not far from Washington in at least two-brigade strength. Then came worse — Rebel troopers said to be under Jeb Stuart had pounced on a 150-wagon supply train near Rockville, Maryland, bound for the Army of the Potomac. Washington lacked cavalry to meet this threat, and Meade quickly dispatched two cavalry brigades and a battery "to proceed at once in search and pursuit." The news generated flickers of panic in the capital. Stuart himself, so it was reported, told one of his wagon-train prisoners at Rockville that were it not for his jaded horses "he would have marched down the 7th Street Road — took Abe & Cabinet prisoners. . . ." In recording this, Elizabeth Blair Lee remarked, "For the life of me I cannot see that he would have failed had he tried it."

Enemy cavalry between the Potomac army and Washington posed an obvious threat to Meade's communications and his supply line, and indeed for a time the Rebels knocked out the telegraphic links between the army and the capital. They also damaged the Chesapeake & Ohio Canal, and tore up the Baltimore & Ohio rail line leading to Frederick, but the resourceful railroader Herman Haupt soon had a new supply line in operation over the Western Maryland Railroad from Baltimore to Westminster.[9]

By day's end that Sunday, General Meade had marching orders in the hands of all his commanders. Starting at 4:00 A.M. the next day, June 29, the Army of the Potomac would press northward from the Frederick area in a fan-shaped advance toward the Pennsylvania line. The first day's objectives stretched from Emmitsburg on the west through Taneytown to Westminster on the east, a span of 20 miles. That line, Meade thought, ought to confront the Rebels on any course they might take toward Baltimore or Washington from their reported positions in Pennsylvania. "Our new commander is determined not to let the grass grow under his feet," artillerist Wainwright entered approvingly in his diary on the 29th, "and his dispositions would indicate that he has some pretty certain ideas as to where Lee is, and what he ought to do himself."[10]

JEB STUART'S REMARK on June 28 that but for his jaded mounts he might have dashed into Washington and captured the president and his Cabinet was a typical bit of Stuart bravado. To be sure, just then the capital's defenses were undermanned, but Stuart had no way of knowing that and he had to respect the ring of forts and their garrisons. In his report he spoke of surprise lost and the hazards of a night attack, and consequently he determined "to proceed directly north." Washington was not in the danger it imagined.

In any case, the Confederate raiders found much to distract them in Maryland. "Pushed on to Rockville," wrote the cavalryman-novelist John Esten Cooke, "where a female seminary was fairly running over, at doors and windows, with pretty girls, in fresh nice dresses — it was Sunday — low necks, bare arms and other pleasing devices, waving, . . . laughing, exclaiming and wild with joy. . . ." The report of an approaching Yankee wagon train wrenched the troopers back to duty. "Scene magnificent," Cooke noted when they charged the train. "Wagons smashing, crashing, rumbling, burning — the mules crazy, the drivers 'crazy mad.'" When it was over Stuart found himself with 125 intact U.S. army wagons, all brand-new, complete with full harness and fresh teams, loaded mostly with fodder. He decided the train would be a godsend to Confederate quartermasters, and took his prize along. The wagon train, when added to the damaged Chesapeake & Ohio Canal, the sev-

A drawing by Adalbert Volck pictures Jeb Stuart, center, and his raiders with horses captured in Pennsylvania. (Library of Congress)

ered telegraph lines, the torn-up Baltimore & Ohio tracks, was proof how effectively Stuart was carrying out key provisions in General Lee's orders for the raid.

But with all these tasks Stuart had fallen further and further behind schedule, and the captured train continually held him up. Not until the morning of June 30 did he cross into Pennsylvania. Even then the entire Yankee army was on his left, squarely between his column and Lee's. He had no communication with Lee or Ewell and no intelligence even on where to find Ewell — and as he approached Hanover he discovered a column of Yankee cavalry across his path. It was now the sixth day of the expedition, and it was evident that his "ride around Hooker," conceived in such heady optimism, had become a nightmare.[11]

At Chambersburg, meanwhile, with the Federal army discovered to be much closer than he had supposed, and with only the spy Harrison's report to go on, General Lee had to make rapid calculations. His first orders, sent by courier to Ewell the night of June 28, called for the army to reassemble at Chambersburg. Then by morning Lee had second thoughts. Harrison's report put two Federal infantry corps approaching South Mountain, and that was a matter of concern. The army might live comfortably off the enemy's country as to food and forage, but Lee needed the option of a supply line back to Virginia for at least ammunition resupply. With Ewell having cleared the Shenandoah, Lee thought if need be a cavalry escort ought to be sufficient to bring a wagon train safely through the Shenandoah and Cumberland valleys. That route was also required more immediately to carry off the booty being collected in Pennsylvania. However, should those two Federal corps in Harrison's report proceed west through the South Mountain passes and into the Cumberland Valley, they would effectively intercept Lee's communications with Virginia.

That in fact was exactly what Joe Hooker had had in mind for the Twelfth Corps and the Harper's Ferry garrison, but Hooker's idea was set aside along with his army command. Instead Meade was massing the Army of the Potomac to the east at Frederick, well away from South Mountain, and issuing orders to march from there north into Pennsylvania. Lee lacked any way to learn of this move by his opponent — "In the absence of the cavalry, it was impossible to ascertain his intentions," he would say in his report. So he determined to counter the perceived threat to his communications with a threat of his own. He would shift his army out of the Cumberland Valley and move it east of the South Mountain range, thereby posing an apparent threat to Baltimore and Washington. To protect these cities the Federal army would surely have to collect itself and follow his lead. Unspoken but inherent in Lee's decision to retain the initiative and to unite his army east of the mountains was his deliberate challenge to the enemy — ideally, of course, on a battlefield of his own choosing.

So it happened — thanks to an intelligence drought and a consequent miscalculation — that the two armies were set to marching on a collision course. The Army of the Potomac's intelligence chief, Colonel George Sharpe, fixed the stakes for the contest when he wrote that day, "I hope our friends understand that in the great game that is now being played, everything in the way of advantage depends upon which side gets the best information."[12]

EARLIER ON JUNE 28, before the arrival of the spy Harrison at his camp, General Lee had ordered a concerted movement across the Susquehanna and against Harrisburg. Dick Ewell was to lead the way, supported by Longstreet's corps. A. P. Hill would follow in Jubal Early's tracks toward York, cooperating with Ewell "as circumstances might require." Their objective was to seize the Pennsylvania capital and complete the destruction of the railroad network supplying Baltimore and Washington and the Federal armies.

Lee's dispatch sent that night canceled the Harrisburg movement, and his revised orders, written in the morning, reached Ewell at Carlisle late in the day on June 29. Rather than returning south by west through the Cumberland Valley to Chambersburg, as first ordered, Ewell was now to march due south "in the direction of Gettysburg, via Heidlersburg. . . ." Rodes's division would follow this route, and Early, countermarching westward from York, would intersect his line of march. Allegheny Johnson's division, in response to the earlier order, had already left that afternoon on the road to Chambersburg. Instead of recalling him, Ewell told Johnson to turn off eastward below Shippensburg and cross South Mountain at the Cashtown Gap.

All this made Old Bald Head most unhappy. He had carefully worked out his plan for taking Harrisburg, and in fact earlier in the day Jenkins's cavalry had shelled the enemy works there. According to Jed Hotchkiss, "The General was quite testy and hard to please, because disappointed, and had every one flying around." There was disappointment in the ranks as well. A man in Maryland Steuart's brigade recalled the "ill-concealed dissatisfaction" of the men, who "found the movement to be, as they supposed, one of retreat." But obedient soldier that he was, Dick Ewell had Rodes's troops on the road south at first light on Tuesday, June 30.

While Ewell was prompt enough responding to these new orders, General Lee had not communicated any particular sense of crisis to the case, and the Second Corps' march proceeded at the usual pace. At Papertown Ewell found time to tour the Kempton & Mullen paper mill, which, he discovered, supplied military forms of various sorts to the Union army. The Confederacy being perpetually short of such items, Ewell announced to the mill owner that he was making a $5,000 purchase. He had his quartermaster load up the wagons with a generous selection of boxed forms, after which he presented the hapless owner with a Confederate government voucher — worth about as much as the form it was written on.

Allegheny Johnson also made a brief stop on his way south. His column encountered a party of Pennsylvania militiamen that Jubal Early had captured, then paroled and sent on their way home. Johnson halted the column, looked the scared militiamen over, and ordered them to take off their shoes. That was inhumane, someone said. Nonsense, said Allegheny. They were on their way home, and his troops needed those shoes far more than they did, "as he had work for his men to do."[13]

At the same time, General Lee started the rest of his army eastward

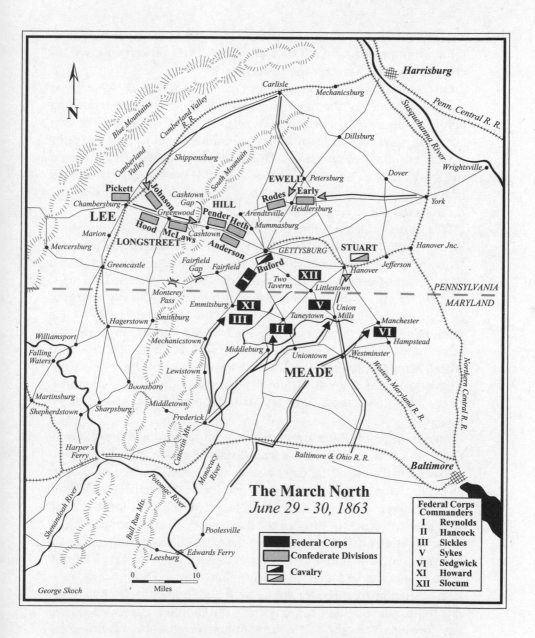

The March North
June 29 - 30, 1863

Federal Corps			
Federal Corps	
Confederate Divisions	
Cavalry	

Federal Corps Commanders

I	Reynolds
II	Hancock
III	Sickles
V	Sykes
VI	Sedgwick
XI	Howard
XII	Slocum

George Skoch

0   10
Miles

from Chambersburg and across South Mountain for the rendezvous with
Ewell. A. P. Hill's Third Corps led the way on the 29th, Harry Heth's division gaining Cashtown, east of the mountains, by day's end. Eight miles
ahead to the southeast, reached by the Chambersburg Pike, was Gettysburg. At the hub of a network of good roads, nearly equidistant from

Carlisle and Chambersburg, Gettysburg looked on the map to be a natural assembly point for Lee's divided forces. Hill's other two divisions camped that night short of the Cashtown Gap.

On Tuesday, the 30th, Longstreet's First Corps followed Hill as far as Greenwood, west of the mountains, with Pickett's division remaining behind to secure Chambersburg. Pickett's infantry was doing the cavalry's job, made necessary by Stuart's continued absence. For the same reason, Evander Law's brigade of Hood's division was detached to guard the army's right at the village of New Guilford. Having some two-thirds of his army crowded onto the Chambersburg Pike, and in considerable disorder, did not seem to bother General Lee.

First Corps artillerist Porter Alexander remembered the Chambersburg Pike being quite muddy that day from recent rains, and therefore the infantry marched in the fields alongside the road. Alexander took note of a Pennsylvania-German farmer in visible distress as he watched the Rebel soldiers tramp a path in his wheat and pump his well dry trying to fill their canteens and track mud all over his front porch. "De well is done pump dry!" the farmer exclaimed to Alexander. "And just look at dis porch vere dey been! And see dere vere dey trampled down dat wheat! Mine Gott! Mine Gott! I'se heard of de horrors of war before but I never see what dey was till now!" Alexander admitted this sounded "like a made up anecdote, but it is verbatim & literatim as I saw & heard it myself."[14]

The sharp point of the army's advance on June 30 was the village of Cashtown, where Harry Heth's lead division had camped. Heth determined to make use of the day by sending a foraging party eight miles ahead to Gettysburg, to "search the town for army supplies (shoes especially), and return the same day." He selected for the task Johnston Pettigrew, whose North Carolina brigade had been pried away from D. H. Hill to fill out Heth's new division. While the expedition was undertaken on Heth's initiative — rumor had it that in Gettysburg there was a plentiful stock of shoes to be found, something much needed by his division — he had strict instructions for Pettigrew. It was thought only Sunday-soldier militiamen might be in Gettysburg, but should Pettigrew encounter any "organized troops" of the Army of the Potomac, he was not to engage them. As Pettigrew's aide, Lieutenant Louis Young, remembered it, "The orders to him were peremptory, not to precipitate a fight." Harry Heth was here surely expressing standing orders for the day from higher authority — from corps commander A. P. Hill, perhaps from General Lee himself — for just then there were no other troops within supporting distance of Heth's division.

Pettigrew dutifully set off that morning with three regiments and a wagon train to carry off the shoes and the supplies. As the expedition approached Gettysburg, he was warned by what Lieutenant Young described as "General Longstreet's spy" (apparently the enterprising Harrison), and also by a local Confederate sympathizer, that Federal cavalry in force was approaching the town. Pettigrew halted and sent back to General Heth for further orders. Heth's reply repeated his earlier instructions, and expressed doubt there was anything more than home guards in Gettysburg.

Johnston Pettigrew was not a professional soldier and he had had only limited command experience before being severely wounded on the Peninsula, but he was highly intelligent and fully confident that he knew real enemy cavalry when he saw it. These Yankee troopers were in plain sight now and by-the-book aggressively probing toward his advanced skirmishers. Obeying his orders not to precipitate a fight, Pettigrew withdrew and marched empty-handed back to Cashtown.

While Pettigrew was making his report that evening to General Heth, corps commander A. P. Hill rode up. Perhaps because Pettigrew was a self-taught soldier and not well known to either general, they both cast doubt on his story. As Heth remembered the conversation, Hill insisted that any cavalry seen in Gettysburg was nothing more than what he termed a detachment of observation: "I am just from General Lee, and the information he has from his scouts corroborates what I have received from mine — that is, the enemy is still at Middleburg and have not yet struck their tents." Middleburg was 20 miles to the south, in Maryland. An exasperated Pettigrew called in Lieutenant Young, who had served under Hill and was known to him, in the hope that Young's report "might have some weight with him." Young testified that all the movements of the Yankee cavalry he had observed "were undoubtedly those of well-trained troops and not those of a home guard."

Powell Hill remained emphatic in his disbelief, but with a bravura flourish said that he hoped the Potomac army *was* up, "as this was the place he wanted it to be." In his report, Hill said that he forwarded Pettigrew's Gettysburg sightings — or his own version of them — to General Lee, and also to Dick Ewell, and announced "that I intended to advance the next morning and discover what was in my front." At Cashtown that night Harry Heth said he still wanted to get those shoes he believed to be in Gettysburg, and did General Hill have any objections? "None in the world," said Hill.[15]

At Greenwood the night of June 30, Lee made his headquarters camp near Longstreet's, and Porter Alexander took the opportunity to pay a visit to friends on the commanding general's staff. "I recall the conversation as unusually careless & jolly," Alexander wrote, with no one expressing any premonition of fighting to come. He remembered writing to his wife from Greenwood and "telling her that of course we would have to have a battle before very long, but, as yet, there was no prospect of it." General Dorsey Pender, commanding a division in Hill's corps, had much the same feeling. He wrote his wife, "Everything seems to be going on finely. We might get to Phila. without a fight, I believe, if we should choose to go. . . . Confidence and good spirits seem to possess everyone."[16]

The British observer Colonel Fremantle was traveling with Longstreet's headquarters, and in the Greenwood camp on the 30th he recorded in his journal important news of the enemy: "In the evening General Longstreet told me that he had just received intelligence that Hooker had been disrated, and that Meade was appointed in his place." Fremantle went on to note Longstreet's reaction: "Of course he knew both of them in the old army, and he says that Meade is an honorable and respectable man, though not, perhaps, as bold as Hooker."

There is no contemporaneous record of Lee's reaction to this news. Some years later Armistead Long of his staff recalled the general mentioning the difficulties Meade would face in taking command at this advanced stage of the campaign: "He was therefore rather satisfied than otherwise by the change." It is more probable that, at least privately, General Lee was disappointed at missing the opportunity to face Mr. F. J. Hooker a second time.[17]

In a postwar conversation Lee said he had hoped to maintain his army in the Cumberland Valley through the summer, although he anticipated he would have to give battle before returning to Virginia in the fall. Yet here it was not even July and battle was very likely on the horizon. Still, Lee cannot have been greatly surprised that the Yankees would make a fight for their home ground. Indeed he had good reason to welcome the battle now rather than later. A Federal army demoralized by recent defeat, disorganized by expired enlistments, and perhaps bewildered by this change of commanders ought to be better game than an army reinvigorated by time and training.

Robert E. Lee's problem on that June 30, as he pondered events in his

Greenwood camp, was that he had only the most general idea of the whereabouts of the enemy's forces. This did not bode well for his plan to wage a campaign of maneuver and to fight only on his own terms and only on his chosen ground. The answer seemed to be to mark time while continuing the concentration of his forces. That evening he sent a courier to meet Dick Ewell at Heidlersburg with orders for the next day "to proceed to Cashtown or Gettysburg, as circumstances might dictate." His receipt of Powell Hill's dispatch describing Pettigrew's sortie, and Hill's own intention of advancing to Gettysburg on July 1 "to discover what was in my front," merely caused Lee to make Ewell's orders discretionary.

The other burning question on Lee's mind was the whereabouts of Jeb Stuart. It had been the assumption, when Lee approved the plan for the cavalry raid, that Stuart would be across the Potomac and in contact with Ewell's corps within three or at most four days — that is, by June 27 or 28. Lee had further assumed that during their separation the always resourceful Stuart would get word to him of any changes in the Federal dispositions. But there had been no word. The Federals had crossed the Potomac and advanced dangerously near before being discovered. The sole notice of Stuart had arrived just the day before, the 29th. A Second Corps' staff man, James Power Smith, on his way from Richmond to join Ewell, told Lee that as of June 27 Stuart and his cavalry were still back in Virginia. According to Lieutenant Smith, "The General was evidently surprised and disturbed" by this report.[18]

Stuart and Lee had taken care, in planning the "ride around Hooker," not to leave the army without a force of cavalry during the anticipated three or four days of Stuart's absence. The brigades of Beverly Robertson and Grumble Jones — 2,700 troopers, with Robertson, the senior officer, in command — were carefully instructed in their assignments by Stuart. He made Robertson responsible for guarding Ashby's and Snicker's gaps in the Blue Ridge against Yankee intruders, and, among other things, Robertson was "to watch the enemy. . . . Be always on the alert; let nothing escape your observation. . . ." Should he see the Federals moving "beyond your reach," he was told, he too should move, staying on the right and rear of Lee's infantry.

Thus far in the war Beverly Robertson had not been a general to inspire confidence. In North Carolina D. H. Hill, otherwise stubbornly opposed to sending reinforcements to General Lee, gave up Robertson and his brigade without a murmur. At Brandy Station Robertson performed poorly, displaying a conspicuous lack of initiative. Longstreet had urged Stuart to leave the able and aggressive Wade Hampton with the army instead of Robertson, but Stuart elected to take his best and most trusted generals with him on the raid. He seems to have reasoned that Robertson would probably not have to fight, but only guard the Blue Ridge gaps and observe and report on the enemy — standard roles for any trained cavalryman. In any event, Grumble Jones was considered an excellent outpost officer, and on this occasion ought to set an example for Robertson.

As it happened, however, Robertson (and Jones) simply stayed in their mountain gaps day after day, gazing across a Loudoun Valley landscape empty of Yankees. All during this time Lee's headquarters was in frequent touch with Robertson, but if he was asked for intelligence on the enemy it is not on the record; certainly he delivered none. The entire Army of the Potomac crossed the Potomac without Beverly Robertson being the wiser. On June 29, when he realized Stuart was not going to be rejoining the army any time soon, General Lee called Robertson out of the Shenandoah. Even then Robertson moved sluggishly, and reported with his command only on July 3, far too late for any good purpose. "General Robertson was an excellent man in camp to train troops," cavalryman William Blackford summed up, "but in the field, in the presence of the enemy, he lost all self-possession, and was perfectly unreliable."

John S. Mosby, who might have helped to fill this intelligence void, had lost touch with Stuart soon after the cavalry raid began. Lacking an assignment, Mosby drifted off to the west. Operating out of the Shenandoah Valley, he and his partisans raided into Pennsylvania and collected booty.[19]

General Lee had been strangely passive (or perhaps supremely self-confident) ever since entering Pennsylvania, particularly in this matter of keeping track of the opposing army. Over the past year he had become totally dependent on Stuart to deliver intelligence on the Yankees, or to arrange for its delivery. Now, at this critical moment, Stuart was not there. "It was the absence of Stuart himself that he felt so keenly," Major Henry McClellan wrote of Lee. ". . . It seemed as if his cavalry were concentrated in one person, and from him alone could information be expected." Should any delay or mischance befall Stuart's bold scheme — surely distinct possibilities — Lee had no contingency plan, no one else on whom he could or would rely. The partisan Mosby was ignored. Beverly Robertson was well known as a weak reed, yet neither Lee nor anyone else at headquarters seems to have made any effort to find out what he and Grumble Jones were actually doing while Stuart was absent. This is all the more surprising since, as early as June 23, Lee knew the Federals had a pontoon bridge across the Potomac and were poised to cross. Earlier Joe Hooker had been accused by one of his generals of being a Mr. Micawber, "waiting for something to turn up." During this last week of June General Lee seemed to better fit the characterization.

Stuart's now much-delayed march around the Federal army had left Lee not only without timely notice of the Yankees' passage of the Potomac, but also without intelligence on the march routes of their various corps since then. By the same token, Lee was entirely in the dark as to the terrain and features of any likely battlegrounds. Had Stuart remained with the army on its march north, or had he linked up with Ewell on schedule in Pennsylvania, he would currently be in position to reconnoiter most of the ground between the converging armies.

Thus all that Lee could assume on this last day of June, from his map and from what the spy Harrison had told him, was that the Army of the Potomac, reported by Harrison to be at Frederick in Maryland, was now probably one or two days' march closer to the forthcoming concentration of his own army in the Cashtown-Gettysburg area. "A scout reports Meade's whole army marching this way," Lee would complain to a staff man, "but that is all I know about his position." Fast approaching a probable collision with the enemy, Lee was figuratively blindfolded.[20]

IF GENERAL LEE'S intelligence on the Army of the Potomac was sparse, the bag of intelligence on the Army of Northern Virginia was filled to overflowing. Without Jeb Stuart's cavalry patrolling between the two armies, much important information on Lee's forces was collected without hindrance by the Federals' wide-ranging intelligence network. The location and movements of A. P. Hill's and Longstreet's corps soon became known to Meade, thanks to the efforts of such citizen-spies as David McConaughy's group in Gettysburg and similar agents in Chambersburg. "The General directs me to thank you . . . ," the B.M.I.'s Colonel Sharpe wrote McConaughy on June 29. "You have grasped the information so well in its directness & minuteness, that it is very valuable."

The one important disruption Stuart achieved — perhaps the one real accomplishment of his raid — was to cut off Meade's telegraphic connections with Washington during the 29th and part of the 30th. Most of the intelligence gathered on Ewell's Second Corps, especially during its stay in Carlisle and York, was promptly funneled to General Couch in Harrisburg, who transmitted it by telegraph to Washington for retransmission to the Army of the Potomac. Much information of this sort was directed to Harrisburg by observant Northern Central and Pennsylvania

Central railroad agents. When on June 30, in response to Lee's order, Ewell started the divisions of Johnson and Rodes south from Carlisle, and had Jubal Early countermarch from York, reports of these departures were not long in reaching Couch. But with Stuart's troopers tearing down the wires in Maryland, word of these key changes in the enemy's dispositions did not reach Meade until he had already made significant decisions about where to march his army.[21]

General-in-Chief Halleck's June 27 instructions gave Meade two not necessarily complementary objectives: to protect Washington and Baltimore while at the same time operating "against the invading forces of the rebels." Should Lee strike boldly for Baltimore, say, Meade's decision would be obvious. But should Lee position his forces in an arc from Chambersburg in the Cumberland Valley to Harrisburg and beyond on the Susquehanna (as it appeared he was doing), Meade's decision became complicated. Should he mass his army and march challengingly toward Lee's center, he risked leaving Baltimore uncovered and having his flanks turned, especially his eastern flank. Jubal Early's division reported at York certainly appeared to be a threat to Baltimore, less than 50 miles to the south.

George Meade was by nature a careful, cautious general, yet the moment called for boldness and decisiveness . . . which he clearly understood. Here he was, newly appointed to the command and abruptly so, leading a recently twice-beaten army of possibly doubtful morale, confronting a recently twice-victorious army led by a daring opponent. Meade refused to be intimidated. "We are marching as fast as we can to relieve Harrisburg," he wrote Mrs. Meade on June 29, "but have to keep a sharp lookout that the rebels don't turn around us and get at Washington and Baltimore in our rear. . . . I am going straight at them, and will settle this thing one way or the other. The men are in good spirits; we have been reinforced so as to have equal numbers with the enemy, and with God's blessing I hope to be successful. Good-by!"[22]

With two of the three Rebel corps reliably reported to be advancing eastward between Chambersburg and Gettysburg, Meade in response pointed the main weight of the Army of the Potomac in the direction of Gettysburg. He retained Joe Hooker's innovation of giving John Reynolds the advance in command of the army's left wing — now consisting of Reynolds's own First Corps, Dan Sickles's Third Corps, and Otis Howard's Eleventh Corps. Slocum's Twelfth and Hancock's Second Corps formed a second tier behind Reynolds. But needing to guard against having his flank turned on the east, Meade ordered the Fifth Corps, now under George Sykes, and John Sedgwick's Sixth Corps, largest in the army, to shift eastward to Union Mills and Manchester in Maryland. Had Stuart not severed the army's telegraph connections with Washington, Meade would have learned of Ewell's and Early's countermarches southward soon after they began, and redirected Sykes and Sedgwick accordingly. So it happened that on June 30 something over a quarter of the Potomac army's infantry strength was marching obliquely away from what seemed a likely confrontation at Gettysburg.[23]

As June ended and the two great armies steadily closed on each other, their intelligence needs changed from the strategic to the tactical. Here again the Federals maintained their decisive edge in the intelligence war. Tactical field intelligence was primarily a function of cavalry, of which at the moment Lee had none and Meade had the better part of a corps.

As one of his last acts, Joe Hooker had ordered his cavalry to reconnoiter Gettysburg, and in due course the task was assigned to John Buford. In cavalryman Buford General Meade had probably the best intelligence gatherer in the Potomac army. At 11 o'clock on the morning of June 30 Buford rode into Gettysburg with two brigades of his cavalry division. His orders from headquarters were to "cover and protect the front, and communicate all information of the enemy rapidly and surely." Buford reported the townspeople in Gettysburg "in a terrible state of excitement on account of the enemy's advance upon this place."

Buford hurried troopers out west of the town to investigate this enemy force — it was Johnston Pettigrew's North Carolina brigade — but it withdrew before they could get an identification. By day's end, however, Buford had gathered identifications aplenty. From the reports of the scouting parties he sent out in all directions, and with the assistance of Colonel Sharpe's B.M.I. men riding with the troopers, an increasingly clear picture began forming of the Confederate army closing in on Gettysburg.

As Buford reported in a 10:30 P.M. dispatch to wing commander Reynolds, whose three infantry corps were closest to the scene, A. P. Hill's corps — its divisions correctly identified as commanded by Heth, Pender, and Anderson — was "massed just back of Cashtown, about nine miles from this place." Rebel infantry pickets on the Chambersburg Pike west of town were within sight of Buford's own picket line. "Longstreet, from all I can learn, is still behind Hill." To the north of Gettysburg, near Heidlersburg, a Confederate courier had been captured that day and was full of talk. He told of Ewell's corps coming south from Carlisle, with Rodes's division "being at Petersburg in advance." Buford added, "I have many rumors and reports of the enemy advancing upon me from toward York." Buford sent the same intelligence to Pleasonton, who passed it to General Meade at Taneytown.

Buford's report could be accepted as reliable not only because it was the work of the respected Buford, but because it confirmed and expanded on the picture of the enemy carefully assembled over recent days by Colonel Sharpe's B.M.I. intelligence network. The one uncertainty in the picture was the exact location of Ewell's corps, but Buford's findings strongly suggested a threat was building from north of Gettysburg as well as from the west.

The problem with this excellent collation of intelligence was the impossibility of everyone concerned receiving it in timely fashion. Gettysburg was some 14 miles by road from army headquarters at Taneytown. Buford's courier delivered the dispatch to General Reynolds around midnight of June 30, but it was morning before Meade saw it. The army commander had, in the meantime, sent out marching orders for July 1. The objectives for the day included: "First Corps to Gettysburg; Eleventh Corps to Gettysburg (or supporting distance). . . ."[24]

ON THE LAST DAY of June New Englander Samuel Fiske, a soldier-correspondent in the Second Corps, wrote to the *Springfield Republican* from Uniontown, Maryland, about what lay ahead for the oft-maligned Army of the Potomac: "We of the unfortunate 'grand army,' to be sure, haven't much reason to make large promises; but we are going to put ourselves again in the way of the butternuts, and have great hopes of retrieving, on our own ground, our ill fortune in the last two engagements, and, by another and still more successful Antietam conflict, deserve well of our country." Captain Fiske looked back, and then ahead: "Our troops are making tremendous marches some of these days just past; and, if the enemy is anywhere, we shall be likely to find him and feel of him pretty soon."

"Tremendous marches" was not an exaggeration. Abner Small of the 16th Maine, in Reynolds's First Corps, recorded that his regiment set out from Middletown in Maryland at 7:30 Sunday evening, June 28, and reached Frederick at 3:00 A.M. Monday morning. "We left at five o'clock, and marched through Lewistown, Catoctin Furnace, and Mechanicstown to Emmitsburg, arriving at Emmitsburg at a quarter to six Monday evening." Small calculated that to be 36 miles in just over twenty-two hours, "with a two-hour stop!"

On June 29 the Second Corps, delayed initially by a misdirected order,

Bugler Charles W. Reed, 9th Massachusetts battery, did this sketch of Union troops on the march to Pennsylvania. (Library of Congress)

was pushed by the hard-driving Winfield Scott Hancock 32 miles in eighteen hours. High humidity and bursts of drenching rain added to the misery. In trying to make up for the lost time that day, General Hancock resorted to forced marching. One of his men defined the term: "To see men fall from exhaustion, clothes wet, faces and teeth black with dust, lips parched, eyes sunken, feet blistered, and then driven on at the point of the bayonet. This is a forced march." Pennsylvanian Francis Donaldson remarked that all this "extreme haste" to reach what he called the "rebellious" might gratify the high command, but it was "extremely ruffling to the temper of us dough bellies as we poor infantrymen are called by those chicken thieves, the cavalry. . . ."[25]

For the most part, however, the army's first marches under its new commander were highly organized and efficiently managed. Start times and routes were carefully plotted by Dan Butterfield and the headquarters staff. Where terrain permitted, artillery and supply trains were doubled up in the roadway and the troops marched in the fields on either side. Pioneer parties in advance removed obstructions and bridged streams. General Meade watched over all this with a cold and demanding eye. After Sickles's Third Corps had made only 12 miles by 6:00 P.M. on June 29, and with his trains holding up other troops behind, headquarters dealt a rebuke to General Sickles. "The commanding general noticed with regret the very slow movement of your corps yesterday," it began. There followed a listing of Sickles's various failings during the march, which "was far from meeting the expectation of the commanding general. . . ." Dan Sickles, political general, was no favorite of professional soldier Meade to begin with, and this reprimand suggested further conflicts to come.[26]

In general, the troops marched in good enough spirits. In part this was simply a matter of leaving northern Virginia, where they had been campaigning since the previous fall. "We have marched through some of the most beautiful country I ever saw," the 6th Wisconsin's Rufus Dawes wrote on June 30. "It is very refreshing to get out of the brown desert of Virginia into this land of thrift and beauty." Morale took a further leap upward as a consequence of their welcome from the citizenry of Maryland and Pennsylvania. Major Alexander Biddle, commanding the 121st Pennsylvania in Reynolds's corps, wrote his wife on the 29th, "In all the towns people came out and waved handkerchiefs and showed very cheering signs of friendship." In Frederick the welcome got out of hand after the provost guard neglected to close down the taverns. The next day's march witnessed any number of hung-over stragglers.

Virtually every diarist and letter writer in the army commented on the friendliness of the inhabitants they met north of the Potomac, in contrast to what they had encountered over the past months in Virginia. The First Corps crossed the Pennsylvania line on June 30, and Lyman Holford of the 6th Wisconsin noted in his diary, "The people here turn out in holiday attire, wave flags, give us bread and butter, and water and in every way show their good will toward us." Diarist Charles Wainwright, commanding the First Corps' artillery, took note of this as well, but he also noticed citizens who did not let their Unionist feelings interfere with the profit motive. "The people along the road sell everything, and at very high prices," Wainwright grumbled; "fifty cents for a large loaf of bread, worth, say, twenty; fifteen to twenty-five cents for a canteen, three pints, of skimmed milk; how much for pies I do not know, but they were in great demand. . . ." But he admitted that this was by no means the universal practice. Many of the people "will not sell, but give all they can; and we are cheered through all the villages by good wishes and pleasant smiles."

This welcome was particularly exhilarating to the men in the sixty-seven Pennsylvania regiments posted to the Army of the Potomac. When the 12th Pennsylvania Reserves, just now joining the Potomac army as a reinforcement from the Department of Washington, crossed the Mason-Dixon Line into their home state, E. D. Burdick entered in his diary: "The Col. halted us at the time and the boys gave 3 cheers for old Pa. and we vowed never to leave the State until we had driven the rebels out . . . or perish in the attempt; this is how we feel to-day." Burdick added, "we all felt enthused and showed our determination by increasing our speed."[27]

Once the army had crossed the Potomac into Northern territory, headquarters issued stringent general orders warning the troops to be on their best behavior. As Major John Nevin, commanding the 93rd Pennsylvania, put it, the new regulation meant "total abstinence from pillage and 'takings' as we are now in friendly country." The 93rd was a veteran outfit, accustomed to taking what was necessary for its camping comfort, and by its interpretation of the new regulation, no one should be *caught* taking the needed items. On June 29, after a march of 24 miles, the regiment approached its campground for the night, and as was their custom the men snatched up the rails of the nearest roadside fence for their supper fires. Thus burdened, they unsuspectingly marched past the tent of an officer who happened to be none other than Major General John Sedgwick, commander of the Sixth Corps.

Uncle John Sedgwick, aroused by this blatant violation of the new regulation, personally collared poor Major Nevin and ordered him to halt his command and return every one of the fence rails to its rightful place. Not satisfied with this, the wrathful Sedgwick then rounded on brigade commander Frank Wheaton. "General Wheaton!" Nevin heard him yell, "what do you mean by allowing your men, in direct disobedience of the Order . . . , etc. etc." In the end, Nevin explained, "enough of the rails were carried back to make a show, but I'm afraid that the majority of them were slyly dropped into the long grass, the moment the men knew what was wrong. I *know* our chaplain and our surgeon each dropped one."

A circular from army headquarters on June 30 included instructions to issue the men three days' rations and sixty rounds of ammunition. With that announcement veterans knew that fighting was surely on the horizon — perhaps even around the next bend in the road. The banter stopped and the columns marched in an eerie quiet. A man in the 27th Indiana watched a division pass by silently, with "no warning whatever of their approach, until their head of column filed around a turn in the road. . . . In regular formation, a knot of mounted officers in front and rear of each regiment, the men in perfect ranks, in files of four, line officers and file closers on either side, all were reaching out in long, rapid steps. Regiment after regiment fairly glided by, with no word spoken, that could be heard a rod away."[28]

As further preparation for battle, General Meade issued on the 30th a call to his commanding officers to "address their troops, explaining to them briefly the immense issues involved in the struggle." As Meade phrased it, "the army has fought well heretofore; it is believed that it will fight more desperately and bravely than ever if it is addressed in fitting terms." Delivering addresses to the troops was an Army of the Potomac tradition begun by General McClellan, but the effort by honest, uninspiring George Meade was not quite up to the rhetorical flourishes of the Young Napoleon. Meade's language was stilted (failure "will leave us no such welcome as the swelling of millions of hearts with pride and joy at our success would give to every soldier of this army"), but he added a riveting closing sentence: "Corps and other commanders are authorized to order the instant death of any soldier who fails in his duty at this hour."[29]

While Meade with his address sought to imitate the morale-boosting technique of General McClellan, in Washington Mr. Lincoln was laying the shade of McClellan to rest. In recent days there had been much talk in the press and the army and among the public aimed at bringing back the Young Napoleon to lead the fight against the invaders. Colonel Wainwright wrote on June 29 that many of the troops believed Meade was in command only temporarily, "until McClellan can be sent for." Governor Joel Parker of New Jersey urged the president to appoint McClellan head of either the Army of the Potomac or the militia forces in Pennsylvania. "If either appointment be made, the people would rise *en masse.*" The *New York Herald,* the country's largest newspaper, beat its drum loudly for McClellan. Pennsylvania editor Alexander K. McClure telegraphed, "to call McClellan to a command here would be the best thing that could be done."

Lincoln was diplomatic with Governor Parker about "the difficulties and involvements of replacing Gen. McClellan in command," but he was more direct with editor McClure. "Do we gain anything by opening one leak to stop another?" he asked McClure. "Do we gain anything by quieting one clamor, merely to open another, and probably a larger one?" These were anxious days for the president, but at least he was certain that George McClellan was not the answer to any of his problems. Indeed he continued to argue that this was a time of great military promise. As he told Governor Parker, "I really think the attitude of the enemies' army in Pennsylvania, presents us the best opportunity we have had since the war began."[30]

At his headquarters at Taneytown in Maryland, General Meade was pondering that opportunity. He needed first to compare the strength of his own army with the latest estimate for the enemy. The earlier estimate for Lee, based on counts of his forces that passed through Hagerstown, had been 80,000 infantry and 275 guns, and lacked a figure for cavalry. Now that was superseded. From counts made of the Rebels in Chambersburg, Carlisle, and other towns, the new figures came to 92,000 infantry, 270 guns, and 6,000 to 8,000 cavalry — a total in round numbers of 100,000 men. This was compiled from eyewitness reports — admittedly for the most part made by nonmilitary observers — and was accepted by Colonel Sharpe's B.M.I. in lieu of anything better. It represented in fact about a 20 percent overcount. But a Confederate army 100,000 strong was the figure General Meade used in making his battle plans.

In laying out this latest count of the enemy army, Meade hastened to add, "Our numbers ought to equal it. . . ." He went on to say that when General French's command arrived from Harper's Ferry, he expected the count of his forces, "if not too much weakened by straggling and fatigue," to exceed that of the enemy. As Meade calculated it that morning of July 1, then, the Army of the Potomac should field almost 105,000 men against Lee.[31]

Meade's advantage was greater than he realized. The returns for June 30, being compiled as he wrote, gave him something over 104,000 men — without counting French's troops, who never got closer than Frederick, Maryland. There were in addition reinforcements that had reached the army, or were about to reach it, but did not make it into the June 30 returns. All told, Meade would have under his command in time to fight a total of 112,700 men "present for duty." Nevertheless, he would fight his battle with the understanding that his forces only slightly exceeded the enemy's.[32]

GENERAL MEADE'S NEXT STEP was to plot a battle plan. By June 30 — his third day of command — intelligence sources had unveiled a picture of the enemy clear enough for him to shape a plan of action. Word was not yet in of the hurried recall of Ewell's corps from the Susquehanna, but still Meade was satisfied he had achieved his first goal. "The general believes," his circular announced, "he has relieved Harrisburg and Philadelphia, and now desires to look to his own army, and assume position for offensive or defensive, as occasion requires. . . ."

It was evident now that two-thirds of the Confederate army was advancing, at an undetermined pace, from Chambersburg across South

Mountain's Cashtown Gap in the direction of Gettysburg. Meade's first instructions therefore went to John Reynolds, commanding the army's left wing and closest to the enemy force. In a dispatch sent at 11:30 A.M. on the 30th, Meade observed that it was not yet known if Lee was at Cashtown Gap for the purpose of blocking a Federal advance or using it as a springboard for his own advance. But with Buford's cavalry scouting from Gettysburg and Reynolds's infantry between Emmitsburg and Gettysburg, there should be sufficient warning. Should the Rebels move against him, Reynolds was instructed to fall back to Emmitsburg, where Meade would reinforce him with nearby corps. Indeed, if in Reynolds's judgment Emmitsburg offered a strong defensive position, he was authorized to fall back without waiting either for the enemy or for further orders.

This withdrawal scheme for Reynolds was a first step in General Meade's larger plan — to force Lee to battle, but if at all possible to fight that battle defensively on ground of his own choosing. He had already chosen that ground. His engineer's eye was attracted to the high ground of Parr's Ridge in Maryland, just south of his Taneytown headquarters. The ridge overlooked a small tributary of the Monocacy River called Pipe Creek, and was nicely positioned to cover his own supply line while blocking the direct route to Baltimore. Meade ordered a circular drawn up that fully explained this Pipe Creek plan to his corps commanders. In the event that "the enemy assume the offensive, and attack, it is his intention, after holding them in check sufficiently long, . . . to withdraw the army from its present position. . . ." There was much detail on routes to be taken and the positioning of supply trains and march discipline. In the middle of the lengthy document was a one-sentence disclaimer, in small print as it were: "Developments may cause the commanding general to assume the offensive from his present position." Twenty paragraphs for defense, one sentence for offense.

It was Meade's intention that the Pipe Creek circular be in his generals' hands before day's end that Tuesday, the 30th, but Dan Butterfield and the headquarters staff did not finish the paperwork and the delivery before Wednesday, July 1. By then events were overtaking General Meade's best-laid plan. This left him in high temper. According to an eyewitness, Stephen M. Weld of the First Corps staff, Meade "roundly damned" his chief of staff "for his slowness in getting out orders." Meade said he "had arranged for a plan of battle, and it had taken so long to get the orders out that now it was all useless." The general commanding, Captain Weld noted, was "very much disturbed indeed."

If the Pipe Creek circular was a dead letter even as it was being issued, it did clearly reveal its author's state of mind toward his new command and how he intended to use it. George Meade was far too tough-minded a general to be intimidated simply by the prospect of meeting Robert E. Lee in battle. But Meade very much wanted the Army of the Potomac — after its two consecutive defeats, after all the high-command upheavals of the Hooker regime — to be able to fight defensively when it came time to fight. He wanted to force the other man to give battle, to do the attacking. Had he known it, this was precisely General Lee's intention for the Pennsylvania campaign. Ironically, of the two generals, it was Meade who had the only opportunity to attempt such a plan — and he missed only by the narrowest of margins.[33]

That night of June 30 John Reynolds made camp at Moritz's tavern, across the Pennsylvania line at Marsh Creek on the Emmitsburg Road, some five miles from Gettysburg. With him were his three First Corps divisions. Also under his command were Howard's Eleventh Corps, posted that night to the south at Emmitsburg, and behind Howard, Sickles's Third Corps. Reynolds passed the evening with Otis Howard, who remembered making "cheerful conversation on ordinary topics during the meal," and then for several hours the two of them reviewed the latest dispatches and discussed the fluid situation. The burden of all this intelligence, Howard wrote, "forced the conclusion upon us that Lee's infantry and artillery in great force were in our neighborhood." Howard felt Reynolds was depressed by the uncertainty pressing in on him.

In writing a reply to Meade's dispatch of earlier that day, giving him the option of falling back on Emmitsburg in the face of enemy attack, Reynolds explained that if the Rebels should occupy Gettysburg and then move against him, he proposed defending a line behind Middle Creek just north of Emmitsburg. There was reason to believe, he said, "that the main force of the enemy is in the vicinity of Cashtown, or debouching from the Cumberland Valley above it." Reynolds soon saw this confirmed, along with a good deal of ominous detail, in John Buford's 10:30 P.M. intelligence report from Gettysburg that reached him around midnight. When he finally lay down for a few hours' sleep on the floor of Moritz's tavern, General Reynolds had not yet received his marching orders from army headquarters, which told him, on the 1st of July, to take his First Corps to Gettysburg.[34]

General Meade, too, ended this last day of June in a state of some unease. He had undertaken several initiatives that day more on intuition than on hard facts. He knew much about the divided condition of his

Major General John F. Reynolds of the First Corps commanded the
Army of the Potomac's left wing. (National Archives)

opponent's army, yet he lacked up-to-the-minute information on the exact whereabouts of all those various elements. At Taneytown he was 14
miles from what surely was soon to be a point of some confrontation, at
Gettysburg, and the distance made fresh information all the harder to
come by. Yet he must maintain a central location amidst his own divided
forces. In any event, Taneytown was the best place from which to direct
the assembling of his proposed defensive line behind Pipe Creek. "I continue well," he wrote his wife that evening, "but much oppressed with a
sense of responsibility and the magnitude of the great interests entrusted

to me. . . . Pray for me and beseech our heavenly Father to permit me to be an instrument to save my country and advance a just cause."[35]

That evening of June 30 in his camp at Greenwood, on the Chambersburg Pike west of the Cashtown Gap, General Lee's serene self-confidence had to be at least somewhat inwardly eroded by the continuing mystery of Stuart and the cavalry. In response to the spy Harrison's revelations, Lee had done all he could for the time being. He had called Dick Ewell back to the army, and sent for Beverly Robertson's cavalry, although those troopers had too far to come to offer much immediate hope of lifting the intelligence blackout. Just that evening he told Powell Hill that his scouts — whoever they might now be — had put the entire Federal army still in camp in Middleburg, Maryland, 10 miles below the Pennsylvania line. From the lack of urgency in his marching orders, Lee apparently accepted that as fact. General Hill had said tomorrow he would take a second, longer look at whatever Yankees Johnston Pettigrew thought he had seen in Gettysburg that morning. That too General Lee seemed to accept with equanimity.[36]

For Jeb Stuart June 30 was the worst of days. At Hanover, 30 miles to the east of Lee's Greenwood camp, he engaged in what William Blackford called "a hot affair" against Judson Kilpatrick's Yankee troopers. At nightfall Stuart at last managed to disengage from the Federals and, by detouring ever farther to the east, sought to make contact with Jubal Early's infantry somewhere in the vicinity of York. It was a terrible all-night march, with men and horses pushed to the edge of exhaustion and beyond. Dawn brought them no reward. Without a hint of where Ewell's corps might have gone, Stuart set his course northwest, toward Carlisle.[37]

In Gettysburg during that last night of June, John Buford called together his officers to brief them on what to expect the next day and to post them for the fighting he anticipated. Brigade commander Tom Devin expressed confidence that his men would handle anything thrown at them over the next twenty-four hours. "No, you won't," answered grim-faced Buford. "They will attack you in the morning and they will come booming — skirmishers three deep. You will have to fight like the devil to hold your own until supports arrive."[38]

7   A Meeting Engagement

GETTYSBURG, PENNSYLVANIA, could boast of a true founding father, by name James Gettys, who laid out the town in the 1780s and nurtured its early growth. Incorporated in 1806, the seat of Adams County, Gettysburg by 1863 enjoyed a comfortable prosperity. The majority of the buildings where its 2,400 residents lived or worked or traded were of brick, and there were two institutions of higher learning, the Pennsylvania College and the Lutheran Theological Seminary. It was a market town that listed its leading businesses as carriage-making and blacksmithing. But none of this was enough to mark Gettysburg on history's calendar. What was shortly to burn its name into the national consciousness was a simple fact of geography. Like another rural market town, Sharpsburg, down in Maryland, Gettysburg was a place where the roads came together.[1]

Angling into the town from the west was the Chambersburg Pike, the axis of advance for two corps of Lee's army; it became, leaving town toward the east, the York Pike. Trisecting the northern quadrants west to east were roads from Mummasburg, Carlisle, and Harrisburg, over which Ewell's corps was advancing. The roads entering town through the southeastern quadrant, over which the Federals advanced, were (from east to south) the Hanover Road, the Baltimore Pike, and the Taneytown and Emmitsburg roads. Running south by west was the Hagerstown Road. Ten roads altogether, entering from all points of the compass. For anyone traveling (or marching) through south-central Pennsylvania, it was hard to avoid Gettysburg.

John C. Ropes, the future Civil War historian who carefully inspected Gettysburg in the fall of 1863, described it as lying at the center of "a beautiful basin surrounded some ten to twenty miles off by mountains of say 500 to 1000 feet in height. . . . There is a great deal of open country. The hills are not sharp, bold, well-defined hills, at least these are rare, but long rather low table lands, with meadows and pasture grounds between." To Ropes it seemed to resemble an English countryside, with woodlands "composed of fine tall trees."

Ropes's long low tablelands lay off to the west, forming a series of modest north-south ridgelines. The first, three-quarters of a mile from town, was Seminary Ridge, well wooded, taking its name from the Lutheran Theological Seminary that was situated in a pleasant grove just south of the Chambersburg Pike. Next came McPherson's Ridge, some half-mile farther west. Generally open and rolling, with patches of woods, it merged north of the pike into more sharply featured Oak Ridge. The most westerly of these three ridgelines, Herr's Ridge, was the most pronounced, lying some two miles from Gettysburg. Running north of and paralleling the Chambersburg Pike was the roadbed of an unfinished, abandoned railroad line, its course marked by grading and by excavated cuts through the ridgelines.

Immediately south of Gettysburg the topography was considerably more striking. As John Ropes put it, "Round Top Hill is quite an anomaly, and looks as if dropped down from New England." This distinctive and soon-to-be-famous topography actually contained what could be regarded as four anomalies for that region. Jutting up at the northern end of the formation likened in shape to a giant fishhook were rugged Culp's Hill and Cemetery Hill, three-quarters and one-half mile respectively from Gettysburg. From Evergreen Cemetery atop 100-foot-high Cemetery Hill the terrain sloped southward and downward forming Cemetery Ridge — the mile-and-a-half shank of the fishhook — to reach almost ground level. At this point, rising up abruptly to form the fishhook's eye, were the two other anomalies, Little Round Top and the taller Round Top. Militarily speaking, in addition to its road network, Gettysburg offered the sort of high ground much sought after by generals.[2]

Just then the one Union general who knew the most about Gettysburg — and also knew the most about the Confederates' immediate proximity to Gettysburg — was John Buford. As such, Buford was the only general in either army to be certain beyond any doubt that the next day, Wednesday, July 1, 1863, was going to bring fighting down upon Gettysburg.

Ever since he and his troopers rode into the town late on the morning of June 30, cavalryman Buford had been carefully reconnoitering the nearby terrain and pondering the reports of his scouts. It became evident that A. P. Hill's corps was on his immediate front to the west, at Cashtown, and that perhaps Ewell's corps was not too distant to the

Above: Gettysburg, looking eastward from Seminary Ridge along the axis of the Hagerstown Road. Below: The Chambersburg Pike, looking westward toward Seminary Ridge. The Lutheran Seminary is at left, the railroad cut at right. (Gettysburg National Military Park)

north. As yet Buford had precious little guidance from headquarters. At day's end on June 30 his operative orders were still those from cavalry chief Pleasonton, on the 29th, to "cover and protect the front" at Gettysburg.

John Buford was a hard man and a hard fighter, and with Pleasonton's instructions in mind he determined not to give up the town without a fight. At the least, he could promise a vigorous delaying action by his horse soldiers. At the most, should Reynolds or Meade choose to support him with infantry, there was the promise of a battle. General Buford's experienced soldier's eye told him if it came to that, Gettysburg would not be a bad place to make a fight.

He commanded some 2,950 troopers, in two brigades, with which to make whatever kind of fight there was to be. Buford planned a defense in depth, fighting his men dismounted, using the series of ridgelines west of Gettysburg to hamper and delay the Rebel infantry he was certain would "come booming" down the Chambersburg Pike in the morning. That night, to gain early warning, he set picket outposts three miles and more from town in a wide arc from the Hagerstown Road on the southwest to the Harrisburg Road on the northeast. His outermost posts on the Chambersburg Pike reported seeing the campfires of Rebel picket posts opposite them. Buford's troopers slept that night on their arms.

The troopers had been warmly welcomed on the 30th by the citizens of Gettysburg. As their column trotted through the streets there was much cheering and handkerchief-waving and singing of patriotic songs. A trooper in the 8th Illinois wrote that "some brought out baskets of eatables which caused our ranks to be broken for a moment in spite of our prompt officers, . . . but their only chance was to join us heart and hand until said baskets were empty." That evening the particularly fortunate among them were invited into private homes for hearty suppers. But at first light on July 1, as the troopers took their posts with a "blood red sunrise" at their backs, it was all business again.[3]

Buford's signal officer, Lieutenant Aaron Jerome, remembered the general cautioning his lookouts to "watch everything," to watch for campfires at night and for dust clouds in the morning. "He seemed anxious, more so than I ever saw him," Jerome remarked. At about first light on July 1 Buford's anxiety was somewhat lessened by the arrival of a dispatch from army headquarters. It was General Meade's circular with the orders of march for July 1. Buford read — no doubt with relief — that Reynolds's First Corps had orders to march to Gettysburg that morning, and that Howard's Eleventh Corps was to follow to at least a supporting position. With that, Buford's decision of yesterday to offer a fight for Gettysburg took on real weight, although to be sure a final decision on that score would now depend on Major General Reynolds. "By daylight on July 1," Buford wrote laconically, "I had gained positive information of the enemy's position and movements, and my arrangements were made for entertaining him until General Reynolds could reach the scene."[4]

Like Buford, John Reynolds went to sleep on the night of June 30 lacking any orders for the next day. His orders only reached him at Moritz's tavern at 4:00 A.M. on July 1, by way of his aide William Riddle, just back from headquarters at Taneytown. After being awakened, Reynolds had Major Riddle read the orders to him three times, apparently to be certain he was not missing something. Meade's circular specified each corps' march destination for the day, and directed the cavalry to advance "well out in all directions" to give notice of the enemy. As he listened, it was clear enough that on July 1 Reynolds was to march the First Corps to Gettysburg, with the Eleventh Corps in close support. What was not made clear was what he was supposed to do when he got there.

Since nothing in Meade's circular spoke of further details or explanations to come, Reynolds treated the assignment as a routine short march of five or six miles to reach Gettysburg. But being a conscientious soldier, and knowing from Buford the likely proximity of the enemy, he determined to waste not a moment. Normal routine called for rotating the divisions' order of march, to even out the choices of campgrounds and to make sure no one ate more dust than necessary. James Wadsworth's division had led yesterday's march and was camped in the most advanced position. Today, to save time getting under way, Reynolds canceled the usual rotation and told Wadsworth to take the lead once again. Issuing a flurry of orders as left wing commander, Reynolds had Abner Doubleday bring up the rest of the First Corps, ordered Otis Howard with his Eleventh Corps to come along behind the First, and directed Dan Sickles to move the Third Corps up through Emmitsburg.

It was 8:00 A.M. when Wadsworth's men set off along the Emmitsburg Road for Gettysburg. General Reynolds rode with the advance. Colonel Charles Wainwright, First Corps artillery chief, entered in his diary, "I rode on ahead to learn what I could as to the prospects of a fight. I saw General Reynolds, who said that he did not expect any: that we were only moving up so as to be within supporting distance to Buford, who was to push out farther." Thus John Reynolds's expectations for a quiet day.[5]

General Meade fully intended to better inform Reynolds with a dispatch supplementing his circular's bare-bones order to march to Gettysburg. Morning on July 1 finally brought him General Couch's reports of Ewell's pullback from Harrisburg and turn to the south, probably to reunite with Lee. As apparent confirmation, Meade now had Buford's intelligence from Gettysburg. Consequently, thanks to the well-organized Federal intelligence network, the general commanding knew a great deal about the Confederate army and where it was and where it was headed that morning of July 1.

Yet, as it happened, this advantage did not allow Meade to dictate the choice of giving or accepting battle. These reports came too late to bridge the time gap between the intelligence-gathering and its delivery. Meade's July 1 supplementary dispatch never reached Reynolds. Like the Pipe Creek circular, this effort by General Meade to shape and manage the anticipated battle became moot, overtaken by events.

This aborted dispatch of Meade's reveals a general struggling to gain a grip on his new command and to evaluate his men and their prospects. Thus far, he wrote — July 1 started his fourth day of command — he had had "with the position of affairs . . . no time to learn the condition of the army as to *morale*. . . ." Should the enemy be concentrating "in front of Gettysburg or to the left of it," he knew nothing of the nature of the country there and whether it was best suited to offense or defense. The commanding general "cannot decide whether it is his best policy to move to attack" until he knew more of the enemy. That he hoped to learn during the course of the day. Consequently, General Meade was depending on General Reynolds on the scene to form an opinion of the case, and "would like to have your views."

George Meade and John Reynolds enjoyed a longtime friendship marked by shared respect and mutual trust. On the day of Meade's appointment, Reynolds had called on him to offer his support, and the two discussed events at length. Having inherited Reynolds as left wing commander of one-third of the army, Meade reappointed him to that position without a second thought. For his part, Reynolds knew Meade well enough to sense the breadth of that role. Even though Reynolds never saw Meade's July 1 dispatch seeking his views, as wing commander in this situation he understood he was entrusted to act on the scene at Gettysburg in Meade's stead — to exercise the responsibility for fighting, if it came to that, or withdrawing to another line. It was not in John Reynolds's character to shun such responsibility. Just a month before, he had been offered command of the Army of the Potomac, and he refused it not because of any doubt of his own abilities. Now, at this time and in this place, he would act for the army commander.[6]

It was nearly 9 o'clock that morning and the advance of Wadsworth's division had closed to within three miles of Gettysburg when from the west came the growing muttering sound of gunfire. At that moment a horseman came pelting up to the column from the direction of the town. Reynolds rode out to meet him. Breathlessly the man presented the compliments of General Buford and handed Reynolds a note from the cavalryman. It announced that Rebels in force were advancing along the Chambersburg Pike toward Gettysburg. His cavalry, said Buford, was fully engaged. "Immediately," wrote a staff man, "General Reynolds went into the town on a fast gallop. . . ."[7]

WHEN DICK EWELL reached Heidlersburg on the evening of June 30 he found the message from General Lee directing him to march his two divisions the next day to either Cashtown or Gettysburg, "as circumstances might dictate." There was also a note from A. P. Hill saying his corps was at Cashtown. Ewell talked this over with his generals, trying to puzzle out what the circumstances actually dictated he should do. Old Bald Head probably had never seen a single discretionary order while serving under Stonewall Jackson, and this one apparently bothered him. He was heard to grumble that General Lee needed someone on his staff who could write an intelligible order. He finally determined he would move westerly toward Hill at Cashtown, but by routes that would allow him to turn south toward Gettysburg — as circumstances might dictate. As the circumstances unfolded, it developed that Dick Ewell handled his first discretionary order very well indeed.[8]

This order of Lee's for Ewell to join the rest of the army on July 1 at either Cashtown or Gettysburg was surely written with Harry Heth's planned expedition to Gettysburg in mind. Should Heth occupy Gettysburg, gaining a new concentration point for the army — or should he run into trouble there — either circumstance would direct Ewell to the scene. However that might be, Lee took it for granted that his generals understood that their instructions for June 30 to not bring on a general battle were still in force for July 1 as well. Lee wanted his entire army within easy reach before he went looking for a fight.

However, nothing in the record suggests that Lee reminded A. P. Hill (or Harry Heth) of this caution. Nor, apparently, did Lee make any response to Hill's Tuesday evening dispatch announcing his intention "to

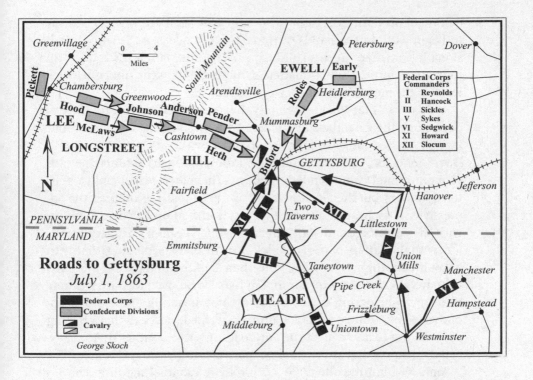

Roads to Gettysburg
July 1, 1863

Federal Corps
Confederate Divisions
Cavalry

George Skoch

Federal Corps
Commanders
I   Reynolds
II Hancock
III Sickles
V   Sykes
VI Sedgwick
XI Howard
XII Slocum

advance the next morning and discover what was in my front." By thus leaving the opening moves on July 1 entirely to the discretion of his two new corps commanders, General Lee once again displayed a strangely passive frame of mind. He evidently saw no reason for concern. As he emphasized in a postwar conversation, he "did not know the Federal army was at Gettysburg, *could not believe it. . . .*"

Discretion, however, was not characteristic of the aggressive Powell Hill. Lacking any cavalry, his would have to be an all-infantry reconnaissance. Instead of directing Heth to mount a simple reconnoiter, with just enough force behind it to brush aside the home guards he was expected to encounter, Hill put two-thirds of his corps — two full divisions, some 13,500 infantrymen, supported by two battalions of artillery — on the road to Gettysburg that morning. It was too large a force for a reconnaissance mission . . . and too large a force to back away from any Yankee challenge.

Moreover, corps commander Hill would not be riding with the advance to make any decisions his aggressiveness might require. Describing himself to Colonel Fremantle as "very unwell," Hill remained behind in his Cashtown camp. This left the expedition, vaguely defined to begin with, in the hands of Harry Heth, the least experienced divisional commander in the Third Corps. The one significant action Hill took that morning was a matter of routine — he sent notice to Dick Ewell of the impending advance on Gettysburg.[9]

At 5:00 A.M. that Wednesday, July 1, General Heth set off for Gettysburg along the Chambersburg Pike. At the head of the column he put James J. Archer's brigade, followed in order by the brigades of Joseph R. Davis, Johnston Pettigrew, and John Brockenbrough. Behind them, in support, came Dorsey Pender's division. The march began amidst scattered showers, but then it cleared and warmed rapidly, promising the oppressive, sultry heat of a typical Pennsylvania summer's day. Right up with the advance guard was William "Willie" Pegram's artillery battalion, with the battery of the Fredericksburg Artillery leading. Expecting to encounter nothing more dangerous than Yankee militia, Heth intended to scatter them with a cannon shot or two. "We moved forward leisurely smoking and chatting as we rode along, not dreaming of the proximity of the enemy," one of Pegram's gunners recalled. Harry Heth, in talking after the war to an Army of the Potomac officer, said rather rhetorically, "I did not know that any of your people were north of the Potomac."[10]

Some few minutes after 7:00 A.M. brought a mutual sighting. The advanced picket post of the 8th Illinois cavalry spotted a dust cloud over the Chambersburg Pike just west of Marsh Creek. The Yankee horse soldiers were spotted in their turn by Colonel Birkett D. Fry's 13th Alabama, marching at the point of the Confederate advance. Colonel Fry ordered the colors uncased and shook out a skirmish line. Lieutenant Marcellus E. Jones, 8th Illinois, after passing back word of the enemy's approach, gathered matters in his own hands. As one of his men described the scene, Lieutenant Jones "took Serg't Shafer's carbine, rested it across a fence-rail and fired at the commanding officer as the column of rebel infantry came across the Marsh Creek bridge. . . ."

Thus the storied first shot of the Battle of Gettysburg. It would be remembered so faithfully by Lieutenant Jones and his comrades that twenty-three years later they returned to the spot and erected a memorial marker, suitably inscribed with the heading, "First Shot at Gettysburg, July 1, 1863, 7:30 A.M." To be sure, the first shot found no target and triggered only a scattering of picket-line firing. As the Rebel skirmishers pushed forward, gunners of the Fredericksburg Artillery opened fire with a 3-inch rifle in the expectation of seeing the Yankee militiamen turn and run. But no one turned and ran. Nor did they after eight or ten more rounds from Pegram's guns. General Heth soon enough realized that he was in for more than he — or General Hill or General Lee — had bargained for that morning.[11]

Heth saw his task, nevertheless, as straightforward: "Archer and Davis were now directed to advance, the object being to feel the enemy; to make a forced reconnaissance. . . ." At first sighting, the Federals were made out to be a cavalry picket, but as the horsemen slowly gave way they appeared to be replaced by infantry skirmishers. This was a deception by design. The picket line troopers had dismounted, with every fourth man designated as horse holder, and formed an advanced skirmish line spread out along Herr's Ridge. As Lieutenant Amasa Dana, 8th Illinois, put it, "Scattering my men to the left and right at intervals of thirty feet and behind posts and rail fences . . . we gave the enemy the benefit of long range practice."

Buford's design for a defense in depth was to make it a fight for time. He intended his main line of resistance to be McPherson's Ridge — William Gamble's brigade would hold the line south of the Chambersburg Pike and Tom Devin's brigade north of it — but not before he resisted the enemy's initial advance steadily and stubbornly and well forward. He had to force the Confederate infantry to take the time, under fire, to deploy in full line of battle.

The 550 troopers on Buford's advanced skirmish line poured out so rapid a fire that cavalryman Dana claimed, with pardonable exaggeration, that it "induced the belief of four times the number actually present." The cavalry's breech-loading carbines, with a faster rate of fire than an infantryman's rifle, contributed to this impression, and the guns of Lieutenant John H. Calif's horse artillery added to the din. General Heth had wanted to keep his troops advancing apace in column along the Chambersburg Pike, clearing the way with just a skirmish line, but the Yankee cavalry's stiff resistance ended that hope. Heth was forced to halt the column and deploy Archer's and Davis's brigades, an exercise that consumed some 90 minutes.[12]

It was about 9 o'clock when the Confederates in full battle array started forward against Herr's Ridge. James J. Archer's Alabamians and Tennesseans were on the right, south of the Chambersburg Pike. Joe Davis's Mississippians and North Carolinians were on the left, north of the pike. Their line of battle, some 2,900 strong, was almost a mile wide. The line of Yankee troopers, essentially a reinforced picket line, had done its job well and gained General Buford a good two hours and more, but now it was time to go. Slowly, turning back to fire, the troopers drifted down

On July 1 Henry Heth, left, led his Confederate division against Union cavalry-man John Buford. (Valentine Museum–National Archives)

the slope of Herr's Ridge, splashed across Willoughby Run, and joined the cavalry's main line on McPherson's Ridge.

From the crest of Herr's Ridge, Harry Heth now surveyed the scene before him and came to a momentous decision. He phrased the moment in his report: "it became evident that there were infantry, cavalry, and artillery in and around the town." This was what he had been sent to Gettysburg that morning by corps commander Hill to find out — what enemy lay in front of them. If General Heth's analysis of the enemy before him was something less than accurate — just then he was confronted not by infantry but by two dismounted cavalry brigades and a battery of horse artillery — the error was understandable. These Yankees surely *acted* like infantry. But what had to be evident beyond any doubt — from the presence of the artillery, if nothing else — was that this was the Army of the Potomac. Furthermore, it was an Army of the Potomac showing no signs of backing away.

In the spirit of General Lee's orders — the instructions to Heth on June 30 not to bring on a general engagement may or may not have been repeated to him on July 1 (the record is ambiguous), but certainly they had

164

not been rescinded — General Heth should have broken off the action at this convenient stopping point and withdrawn to Cashtown to report his findings. Alternatively, he might have held the good high ground on Herr's Ridge and sent back to A. P. Hill for consultation and further orders. Instead, he ordered Archer and Davis "to move forward and occupy the town."

This was a reckless act, in no way justified by Heth's claim in his report that at the moment "I was ignorant what force was at or near Gettysburg. . . ." In fact he knew there was force in front of him, he saw that it intended to dispute his advance, and as a mere division commander on a reconnoitering mission he was bound to report his findings to a superior before he charged headlong into battle (or as he later put it, with unintended irony, "*stumbled* into this fight"). In so doing, Harry Heth committed to his half share of responsibility for bringing on the Battle of Gettysburg.

At about the same time, less than a mile to the east, John Reynolds was committing to his own half share of responsibility for the battle. General Reynolds had at least been delegated the authority for making such a decision.[13]

DURING THESE EARLY-MORNING hours of July 1, from the cupola of the Lutheran Theological Seminary on Seminary Ridge, Federal signalman Aaron Jerome tracked the expanding fight in front of him, and in turn with his strong glass anxiously scanned to the southeast for Reynolds's corps. At last, on the distant Emmitsburg Road, he sighted a column of troops. Jerome promptly reported his sighting to General Buford, who knew from his returned courier that this had to be the First Corps. With that, at a few minutes after 10 o'clock, Buford wrote out a dispatch for General Meade. He announced that the Rebels were "driving my pickets and skirmishers very rapidly." He was certain the whole of A. P. Hill's corps was advancing on him from the west, and that from the direction of Heidlersburg to the north another "large force" was driving in his pickets. Help was on the way, however: "General Reynolds is advancing, and is within 3 miles of this point with his leading division."

After receiving Buford's earlier note on the march, Reynolds with several of his staff had left the infantry column and ridden hard for Gettysburg. Just before reaching the town, they encountered a fleeing, badly frightened civilian, who gasped out the news that the cavalry was in a fight. They galloped on into Gettysburg where, noted Reynolds's orderly Charles Veil, "there was considerable excitement," then hurried on out the Chambersburg Pike in search of Buford. They found him on McPherson's Ridge with his men. Buford explained the cavalry's dispositions and his defense-in-depth plan, and Colonel Gamble expressed the urgency, calling out to Reynolds, "Hurry up, General, hurry up! They are breaking our line!" According to Sergeant Veil, "The General ordered Genl. Buford to hold the enemies in check as long as possible, to keep them from getting into town. . . ."

To deliver a message of his own to Meade, Reynolds called on his aide Stephen Weld. Captain Weld was to say to the general commanding that "the enemy were coming on in strong force, and that he was afraid they would get the heights on the other side of the town before he could; that he would fight them all through the town, however, and keep them back as long as possible."

Weld was told to ride with all speed, to ride his horse to death if he had to, and he delivered the message to headquarters in Taneytown by about 11:30 A.M. This was ahead of Buford's courier, and Weld reported that General Meade "was very much disturbed indeed at the receipt of the news. He said, 'Good God! If the enemy get Gettysburg, we are lost!'" But when Weld went on to tell of Reynolds's promise to barricade the streets of the town and hold back the Confederates as long as he could, Meade exclaimed, "Good! that is just like Reynolds."[14]

After dispatching Weld on his mission, ordering Howard to advance the Eleventh Corps with all speed, and sending to Sickles to bring up the Third Corps from Emmitsburg, Reynolds spurred back through the town and out the Emmitsburg Road toward the head of the First Corps column. He had his aides tear down the roadside fences so that the men and guns could cut across the fields to bypass Gettysburg and reach the front more quickly. He showed not the slightest hesitation in committing the First Corps to battle.

John Reynolds's decision, for all its promptness, was surely made with calculation — and surely with more calculation than Harry Heth's decision. On the Emmitsburg Road Reynolds had passed close by the high ground south of Gettysburg and, like John Buford, took note of its defensive possibilities. He promised Meade he would "fight them all through the town" to hold that ground. A. P. Hill's whole corps might be advancing on Gettysburg along the Chambersburg Pike, as Buford believed, but by all appearances the Confederates were marching only on that single road and thus would not be able to push their forces to the front any faster than Reynolds could reach the battlefield with his First Corps divisions. Buford warned of a possible threat from the north as well, and

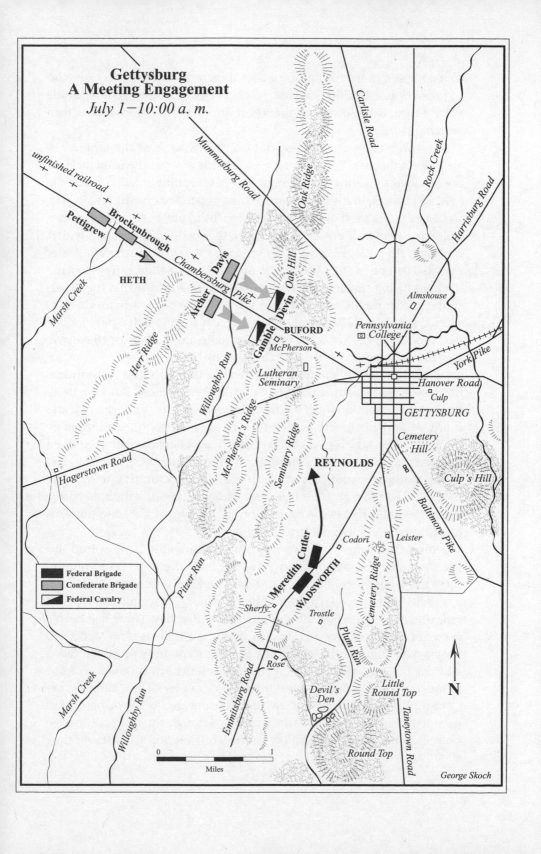

Gettysburg
A Meeting Engagement
July 1—10:00 a. m.

unfinished railroad

Pettigrew

Brockenbrough

Chambersburg Pike

Davis

HETH

Marsh Creek

Archer

Herr Ridge

Willoughby Run

Gamble

Devin

Oak Hill

Oak Ridge

Mummasburg Road

Carlisle Road

Rock Creek

Harrisburg Road

Almshouse

Pennsylvania
College

BUFORD

McPherson

Lutheran
Seminary

McPherson's Ridge

Seminary Ridge

Hagerstown Road

REYNOLDS

York Pike

Hanover Road

Culp

GETTYSBURG

Cemetery
Hill

Culp's Hill

Baltimore Pike

Pitzer Run

Meredith

Cutler

WADSWORTH

Codori

Leister

Cemetery Ridge

Sherfy

Trostle

Plum Run

Emmitsburg Road

Rose

Devil's
Den

Little
Round Top

Taneytown Road

Marsh Creek

Willoughby Run

Round Top

	Federal Brigade
	Confederate Brigade
	Federal Cavalry

0   1

Miles

N

George Skoch

that appeared to be the major risk. Yet there was the Eleventh Corps on the march, just behind the First, to counter that threat. And if Meade should second the decision, the Third and Twelfth corps were within marching range.

Certainly there was risk here, but on the evidence of the moment it was reasonable risk. Reynolds recognized this as what the military textbooks called a meeting engagement. Battle was unintended; neither side held an immediate advantage; everything depended on which side marshaled its forces most quickly and efficiently. In any event, General Reynolds as a matter of principle was more than willing to give battle that morning. All his aggressive instincts as a soldier were aroused. Abner Doubleday, one of the First Corps' division commanders, remembered Reynolds being "inflamed" a few days before on learning that the Rebels were plundering his native state. He was "in favor of striking them as soon as possible. He was really eager to get at them." Gettysburg looked like a good place to get at the enemy. John Reynolds, granted the discretion to act, accepted the risk and the responsibility.

Reynolds's most urgent need just then was to get his lead division, under James Wadsworth, to McPherson's Ridge to relieve Buford's hard-pressed troopers. Lysander Cutler's brigade — one Pennsylvania and four New York regiments — was at the head of the column, followed by Captain James A. Hall's 2nd Maine battery, and Reynolds directed them to march cross-lots with all speed. For a time he sat his big black charger at the roadside turnoff, an inspiriting figure directing traffic into the fields, letting the men see the general who was pointing them to battle. When Reynolds had everyone in motion, he spurred ahead to put Cutler's troops and Hall's guns into position personally.[15]

Behind them came Wadsworth's other brigade, the famous Iron Brigade, commanded by Solomon Meredith. Like the rest of the column, these five western regiments — 2nd, 6th, and 7th Wisconsin, 19th Indiana, 24th Michigan — had been marching along peacefully on this hot morning, with no expectation of any action that day. There had been a flutter of excitement in the ranks at the rumor that General McClellan was back in command of the army, but like most army rumors it faded quickly. The 6th Wisconsin's Lieutenant Colonel Rufus Dawes had just unfurled the colors and told his drum major to play "The Campbells are Coming," so as to "make a show" on entering Gettysburg, when shells were seen bursting west of the town. Soon enough the word was passed from General Meredith to follow Cutler's brigade and to waste no time about it.

On McPherson's Ridge Reynolds posted Hall's Maine battery between the Chambersburg Pike and the railroad cut north of the road. It was a dangerously exposed position, Reynolds admitted, but the crisis required it. With the separate sections of Calif's horse battery outgunned and forced to withdraw, Hall's six 3-inch rifles were all there was at the moment to challenge the Rebel artillery. Hall was told he must distract the enemy gunners so the infantry would not have to deploy under damaging artillery fire. Reynolds told Wadsworth to put in Cutler's infantry specifically to protect the battery, then rushed off to hurry the rest of the infantry deployment. In these critical minutes wing commander Reynolds was playing the role of a general of division, even of brigade.[16]

It would be reported, when Archer's Tennesseans and Alabamians suddenly confronted the Iron Brigade, that one of the Rebels grumbled, "There are those damned black-hatted fellows again! 'Taint no militia." Whether actually expressed, it must have been a common thought, for the black-hatted fellows were an all-too-familiar sight to the Army of Northern Virginia. These westerners, refugees from John Pope's Army of Virginia, had been taken in hand by John Gibbon and made into one of the best-known fighting outfits in the Potomac army. They had gained their sobriquet in the Antietam campaign and burnished it in all the fighting since, and liked to think they had earned their lofty status: First Brigade in the First Division in the First Corps. Gibbon outfitted them with distinctive Hardee hats: black tall-crowned regulars' headgear, adorned with a black ostrich feather and with one brim turned up and pinned with a brass eagle emblem. Their current brigadier, Solomon Meredith, was himself distinctive. A gaunt figure who stood six feet seven inches tall, Meredith was a veteran of many fields and known to his men as "Long Sol." Mr. Lincoln liked to point out that Meredith was the only Quaker general he had in his army.[17]

It was evident to both sides that a key to the McPherson's Ridge position was the five-acre woodlot adjacent to the McPherson farm buildings that would serve as a kind of redoubt for whichever side held it. Colonel Gamble's Yankee cavalrymen were being pressed back through the woods and fields under the rising pressure of Archer's skirmishers pushing across Willoughby Run and starting for the western slope of the ridge. The experienced Archer was dubious, however, telling General Heth he thought his brigade, with fewer than 1,200 men, was "light to risk so far in advance of support." Archer could detect very little of what might lie in wait in McPherson's Woods along the ridge, and the division's two supporting brigades, under Pettigrew and Brockenbrough, were actually not within supporting distance at all. Heth, far less experienced, was unconcerned and insistent, and ordered Archer to send his battle line forward.

At the same time, on the eastern face of McPherson's Ridge, John Reynolds was driving the Iron Brigade into action. "Forward men, forward for God's sake and drive those fellows out of those woods!" he shouted. The brigade was coming up to the ridgeline from the southeast on a slant. "Forward, into line!" came the command, then "Forward, double-quick!," the men running, pausing to load, then coming on again. The four leading Iron Brigade regiments, 1,450 men, reached the crest in an echelon formation, right to left, and collided with Archer's battle line in a sequence of violent, thunderous explosions.

Surprise was mutual, but Archer's Confederates got in the first volley. The 2nd Wisconsin, first on the scene on the Federal right, was staggered by what a regimental historian described as a "murderous volley." Perhaps seventy-five men went down, a quarter of the regiment. Lieutenant Colonel George Stevens was killed, then Colonel Lucius Fairchild was hit, his left arm so badly shattered that it would require amputation. Yet somehow the regiment gathered itself, returned fire, and continued its charge.[18]

On the crest of the ridge, after the 2nd Wisconsin had passed him, John Reynolds turned in his saddle to follow the advance of the rest of the brigade. "As he did so," his orderly Charles Veil explained, "a Minnie Ball struck him in the back of the neck, and he fell from his horse dead. . . . I have seen many men killed in action, but never saw a ball do its work so *instantly* as did the ball which struck General Reynolds. . . ." The fatal shot had most likely come from the 7th Tennessee, either in that first deadly volley or immediately afterward. Sergeant Veil and two other staff men carried the general to the rear, found an ambulance, and in due course escorted the body to Taneytown. The general Mr. Lincoln had wanted to command the Army of the Potomac, the general who had committed that army to battle at Gettysburg, was dead after hardly an hour on the scene. Abner Doubleday, senior divisional commander, was notified that he was now in command on the battlefield.[19]

The meeting engagement grew rapidly and spread, producing varying fortunes for both sides. The first misfortune would be General Archer's. He found his earlier fears borne out — he had walked into a virtual ambush, he had no support, and he had almost no time to get his brigade in hand. When it crossed Willoughby Run a gap had opened between the 7th and 14th Tennessee on the left and the 1st Tennessee and 13th Ala-

The death of Union Major General John F. Reynolds early in the fighting on July 1, as sketched by Alfred Waud. (Library of Congress)

bama on the right, and General Archer, now commanding dismounted, proved to be too immobile to maintain effective control over his diverging forces.

The momentum of the 2nd Wisconsin's initial charge, supported by the 7th Wisconsin now coming up on its left, sent the Tennesseans in front of them stumbling back toward Willoughby Run. To the south of McPherson's Woods was a large wheatfield, into which the 13th Alabama had advanced at an oblique angle. Alabama private W. H. Bird recalled, "all of the sudden a heavy line of battle rose up out of the wheat, and poured a volley into our ranks, . . . and they charged us, and we fell back to the ravine again." These were Yankees from the 19th Indiana, crossing the crest of McPherson's Ridge at exactly the place and at exactly the moment they were most needed. Finally it came the turn of the 24th Michigan, the fourth in this Iron Brigade echelon of advance. The 24th overlapped the Confederate line on the south, and its colonel, Henry A. Morrow, opportunely curled his men around the open flank and struck into the rear of the Alabamians. As Private Bird remembered the scene, "it seemed to me there were 20,000 Yanks down in among us hallooing surrender . . . and of course I had to surrender."

In the hot, still air a dense blanket of battle smoke hung low among the trees and in the valley between Herr's and McPherson's ridges, making it difficult to separate friend from foe; the battle flags visible above

171

the smoke clouds drew torrents of fire. The flag of the 14th Tennessee twice disappeared into the smoke, and twice it rose again. Archer's men from all across the field instinctively sought the cover of McPherson's Woods in which to make their escape. Before long they were tangled together without particular order or command, and the four Iron Brigade regiments swarmed into the melee. The 7th Tennessee's Lieutenant Colonel S. G. Shepard reported that Federals appeared "suddenly upon our right flank with a heavy force and opened upon us a cross-fire." Trapped Rebels by the score began to throw down their arms. Just across Willoughby Run the 2nd Wisconsin's Private Patrick Mahoney spotted a Confederate officer and rushed at him to make a personal capture. He found his prisoner to be none other than Brigadier General James J. Archer.

General Archer had brought some 1,200 men to Gettysburg that morning, and in perhaps an hour of fighting could count almost one-third of them dead, wounded, or captured and the rest in full retreat. Archer himself, exhausted and much ruffled, would be brought by a guard into General Doubleday's presence. The two were acquaintances from the old army, and Doubleday was cordial: "Good morning, Archer! How are you? I am glad to see you!" Ignoring the outstretched hand, Archer snapped, "Well, I am not glad to see you by a damn sight!"[20]

GOOD TRAINING, good tactical leadership, and good fortune had in short order gained the field south of the Chambersburg Pike for the Iron Brigade. But even as that assault was delivered, north of the pike the fortunes of war were exactly reversed. Here it was the Mississippians and North Carolinians of Davis's brigade who quickly gained the upper hand, threatening to overturn the Iron Brigade's gains even as they were being made.

Joseph R. Davis's brigade seemed an unlikely choice to play such a role. It had come up from North Carolina, from D. H. Hill's command, and not as General Lee's first choice for a reinforcement. Only two of its four regiments had any combat experience, and its brigadier was exercising his first combat command. Joe Davis, nephew of President Davis, had spent most of the war serving on his uncle's staff in Richmond; July 1 would mark his first day of on-the-job training. He had but three of his regiments with him, the veteran 11th Mississippi having been detached to guard the division's trains. Davis and better than two-thirds of his 1,700 men would be going to battle that morning for the first time.[21]

Davis's line advanced on a front a half-mile wide north of the Chambersburg Pike and also north of the unfinished railroad that paralleled the pike. The roadbed's embankments and excavated cuts served to cover the Confederates' right flank and also to shield them from the Federals' view. Consequently, the element of surprise favored the Rebels. In addition, the arrival of Lysander Cutler's Federal brigade was not as timely as that of the Iron Brigade farther south. Davis's three regiments — 55th North Carolina, 2nd Mississippi, and 42nd Mississippi — crossed the crest of McPherson's Ridge first and caught the Yankees before they were fully deployed.

Captain James Hall's 2nd Maine battery, positioned on the ridgeline just north of the pike, initially attracted the fire of Willie Pegram's several batteries, just as General Reynolds had intended. In a duel lasting a good half-hour, Hall would more than hold his own. Cutler's infantry column, some 1,550 men all told, was meanwhile being directed to support the guns — the two trailing regiments, 84th and 95th New York, to the left of the battery; and the three lead regiments, 76th and 147th New York and 56th Pennsylvania, to protect on the right or northern flank. Just then, for the moment at least, the McPherson farm, at the center of the battlefield where the 84th and 95th New York were posted, proved to be an oasis of calm and they had little shooting to do. The northern flank, however, would witness a thunderous and confusing and deadly melee. As General Davis put it with nice understatement, "The engagement soon became very warm."

What happened on this far northern flank was a mirror image of what was happening on the far southern flank, but with the positions reversed. The 42nd and 2nd Mississippi piled straight into the three Yankee regiments as they came slanting across a wheatfield attempting to deploy from column into line of battle. Seeing his advantage, Colonel John M. Stone drove his 2nd Mississippi, the one veteran regiment with Joe Davis that morning, straight at the confused Yankees. Stone went down with a wound, but Major John A. Blair took the command and kept the attack moving.

Captain Leander Woollard of the 42nd Mississippi recorded in his diary, "just as we were charging them we came to the top of a hill in a wheat field & beheld a *regiment* of the blue bellies immediately in front & not over 100 yards from me & just as they leveled their guns . . . I gave the command to 'lay down,' and a shower of balls passed over our heads. . . ." With Colonel Stone charging ahead on their left, Captain

Woollard wrote, the 42nd was urged to match his pace, and "with a shout — such as Southern enthusiasm alone can give . . . drove the line of enemy that confronted us down the hill."

The 55th North Carolina, on the far left of the Confederate battle line, considerably overlapped the 76th New York, the right-hand Federal regiment — just as the 24th Michigan was overlapping the 13th Alabama to the south, and with similar results. The North Carolinians, in their first battle and with their colonel, John K. Connally, eagerly taking the colors to lead them personally, wheeled around the Federals' flank and toward their rear. As flag bearer, Colonel Connally immediately became a target, and soon he was down with an arm wound severe enough to require amputation. How badly was he hurt, Major Alfred Belo asked him. Badly enough, Connally replied, but help was at hand. "Go on, and don't let the Mississippians get ahead of you!"

The fighting was at close range now, and the toll rose rapidly on both sides. Major Andrew J. Grover, commanding the hard-pressed 76th New York, tried to turn his line to meet the flanking assault of the North Carolinians and was killed in the attempt. General Cutler, who was with the New Yorkers and Pennsylvanians, was unstinting in his praise — they "fought as only brave men can fight, and held their ground until ordered to fall back. . . ." That order soon came from division commander Wadsworth. The two northernmost regiments retreated in considerable disorder to Seminary Ridge, where their surviving officers tried to rally them. In perhaps twenty minutes of fighting, much of that time caught in a crossfire, the 76th New York had 169 men killed and wounded, 45 percent of its numbers.[22]

General Wadsworth had intended that all three of the regiments on the northern flank should fall back, but his retreat order had no sooner reached the 147th New York's Lieutenant Colonel Francis C. Miller than Miller was severely wounded by a bullet in the throat and then was carried off by his runaway horse. The regiment fought on, oblivious of Wadsworth's order. Soon it was facing assault on two fronts — the 42nd Mississippi attacking from the west, the 2nd Mississippi and 55th North Carolina coming now from the north.

It was at this point in his so far victorious advance that Joe Davis began to lose control of his forces. Two of his regimental commanders had fallen, and in the excitement of the chase lesser officers were taking matters into their own hands. Companies were scattering in pursuit of the Yankees retreating toward Seminary Ridge, others were turning back to attack the beleaguered 147th New York, still others were aiming at Captain Hall's Maine battery just north of the Chambersburg Pike.

To infantrymen, there was no more tempting target than an exposed enemy battery. Captain Hall would write of his astonishment when abruptly a line of Rebel infantry "rose up on my *front and right,* at a distance of not more than *fifty yards,*" aiming a killing fire at his gunners and his battery horses. Hall managed to swing his center and right sections sharply right and open on his tormentors with double canister. This drove them back to the shelter of the roadbed embankment behind which they had approached unseen. But Hall knew he could not hold his position long in the absence of infantry support. What, he wondered in growing anger, had happened to Cutler's regiments supposed to be protecting him on the right?

In fact, beyond the obscuring battle smoke and unknown to Hall, the 147th New York was making the most desperate kind of stand to hold off the Rebels. Major George Harney, now in command, refused the right of his line to meet the attacks from the north. "We had been firing but a short time when I saw the right of our regiment suddenly swing back, then formed to the rail fence on our right and fired very rapidly," recalled Lieutenant J. V. Pierce. He added that the next thing he saw was the colors of the 56th Pennsylvania and 76th New York "away back to the rear in the edge of the woods." Now these Yankees were caught in an ever more destructive crossfire. "Balls whistled round our heads like hail," wrote Private Francis Pease. "The men very soon began to fall very fast and many wounded."

At last General Wadsworth realized the plight of the 147th and sent one of his staff to bring it off. When the staff man reached him with Wadsworth's order, Major Harney wasted no time in obeying. He called out a somewhat unmilitary but highly practical command: "In retreat, double-quick run!" The New Yorkers, every man for himself, headed for the rear. Sergeant William Wybourn picked up the fallen regimental colors and managed to carry them to safety despite being shot through the body. In perhaps a half-hour of fighting, the 147th New York saw better than three-quarters of its men killed, wounded, or captured. "We fight a little and run a little," General Cutler told the survivors. "There are no supports."[23]

The 147th's last stand bought time, just barely, for the 2nd Maine battery to escape isolation and capture, although at the moment Captain Hall was not aware of this sacrifice. Hall had concluded that if the position on McPherson's Ridge was proving too advanced for infantry, it was definitely too advanced for artillery, and he did not wait for orders to pull out. His word for the subsequent ordeal was "hellish." All the horses of the two guns of his right section were shot down; one of the guns was left, the other dragged off by hand. Hall withdrew his four remaining guns from the ridgeline by rolling them back down the slope by hand under cover of the smoke from their last shots, then limbering them at the bottom of the ridge. Getting them back through the fence at the pike one at a time was another ordeal, involving hand-to-hand combat between his gunners and Rebel skirmishers. Somehow Captain Hall got away with the loss of the one gun (which would later be retrieved), 28 battery horses killed, and 18 of his gunners wounded. When he encountered General Wadsworth he was still in a fury, and spoke with disgust of the "cowardly operation of the infantry forsaking my right."[24]

Victory could be as disorganizing and bewildering as defeat, and on this day that was true of Joe Davis's brigade. In its rout of Cutler's Yankees it had suffered heavy casualties, especially in officers, and the troops were exhausted and scattered and uncertain what they were to do next. They "were jumbled together without regard to regiment or company," admitted Major John Blair of the 2nd Mississippi. Davis and his staff were not experienced enough to get their troops in hand to meet a counterattack, and an order to retire was issued too late to be effective. Captain Woollard of the 42nd Mississippi would record in his diary that just when "we were feeling that the day at that point at least, was ours, lo — a cloud of blue coats, fresh & eager for the fray, confronted us. . . ."

That particular cloud of blue coats was the 6th Wisconsin infantry. General Doubleday had held the 6th out of the Iron Brigade's attack as a reserve in case of need; clearly, with Cutler's men fleeing toward Seminary Ridge, the need was now. One of Doubleday's staff reined up before Lieutenant Colonel Rufus Dawes and ordered him to move the 6th to the right and to "go like hell!" It was 750 yards to the Chambersburg Pike, wrote Dawes, and "I moved by a right flank on a run." As they neared the pike he could see Cutler's front collapsing, and he ordered the regiment to deploy and align on the roadside fence. Just then his horse was hit and he went sprawling. As he scrambled to his feet, "the men gave a hearty cheer." Thereafter Colonel Dawes fought his battle on foot, which proved a wise precaution.

Resting their rifles on the fence rails, the Wisconsin men opened a well-aimed, withering fire. "This fire took the enemy enfilade, and

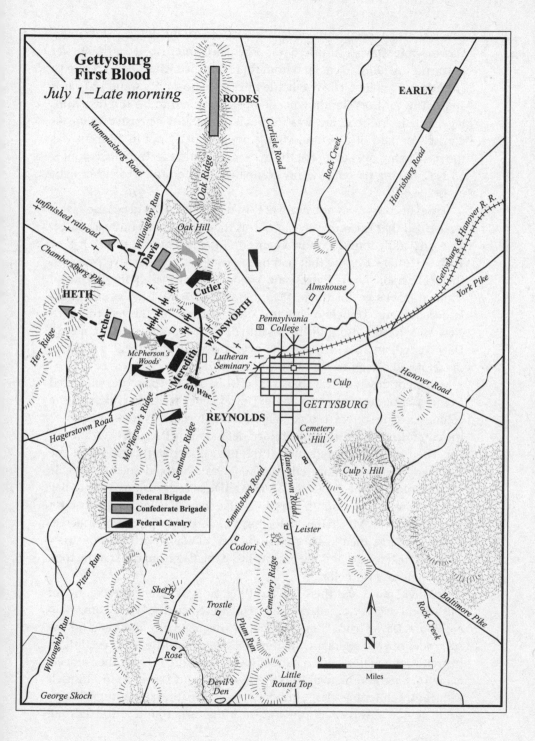

**Gettysburg
First Blood**

July 1—Late morning

RODES

EARLY

Mummasburg Road

Carlisle Road

Rock Creek

Harrisburg Road

Oak Ridge

Gettysburg & Hanover R. R.

unfinished railroad

Willoughby Run

Oak Hill

Davis

York Pike

Chambersburg Pike

Almshouse

HETH

Cutler

Herr Ridge

Archer

WADSWORTH

Pennsylvania
College

Hanover Road

McPherson's
Woods

Lutheran
Seminary

Culp

McPherson's Ridge

Meredith

GETTYSBURG

6th Wisc.

Hagerstown Road

REYNOLDS

Cemetery
Hill

Seminary Ridge

Culp's Hill

Emmitsburg Road

Taneytown Road

Federal Brigade
Confederate Brigade
Federal Cavalry

Pitzer Run

Leister

Codori

Cemetery Ridge

Sherfy

Rock Creek

Baltimore Pike

Willoughby Run

Trostle

Plum Run

N

Rose

0   1

Miles

Devil's
Den

Little
Round Top

George Skoch

checked his advance immediately and mixed up his line considerably," Dawes wrote. Davis's surprised troops recoiled and rushed for the shelter of the nearby railroad cut, and from there returned what Dawes termed a "murderous" volley. The two battle lines were now only some 125 yards apart. The Yankees standing in the open appeared to be at a disadvantage, but the railroad cut was to prove of dubious defensive value. As diarist Woollard of the 42nd Mississippi succinctly put it, "the cut was too deep to fire over except at the extreme left and the 2nd Mississippi & 55 N.C. having passed over my company were too thick to either fight or escape."[25]

Dawes of course was not aware of this, nor of the railroad cut itself, and he decided that the only way out of this stalemate was to order a charge. To his relief, he found reinforcements on his left. This was the 95th New York of Cutler's brigade that had been posted in comparative peace on the McPherson farm. Dawes saw Major Edward Pye of the 95th and shouted, "Let's go for them, Major!" and Pye waved his sword in acknowledgment. Unbeknownst to Dawes, farther on the left the 84th New York would also join the assault. "Forward double-quick charge!" Dawes cried, and his men climbed over the roadside fences ("a sure test of metal and discipline") and stormed the cut.

Men went down by the dozens, and wounded by the scores staggered to the rear, but there was no pause. Dawes kept shouting, "Align on the colors! Close up on the colors!" Then suddenly Yankees were lined up at the cut, firing down into the huddled defenders, yelling for their surrender. The right-hand companies of the 6th got across the mouth of the cut, ready to fire down its length. There was a bitter, desperate struggle for the colors of the 2nd Mississippi. Yankees "kept rushing for my flag and there were over a dozen shot down like sheep in their madly rush for the colors," the Mississippi color bearer, W. B. Murphy, remembered. Finally "a large man" — Corporal Francis A. Wallar, 6th Wisconsin — "made a rush for me and the flag. As I tore the flag from the staff he took hold of me and the color."

Colonel Dawes was there now, calling out, "Where is the colonel of this regiment?" A Confederate major answered coolly, "Here I am. Who are you?" Dawes said, "I am colonel of this regiment and demand the surrender of your regiment." Rather to Dawes's surprise, and certainly to his relief, the major calmly handed over his sword. Then other officers came forward and handed him their swords, and Dawes found himself awkwardly clutching a large bundle of weaponry until his adjutant came to his rescue. It was an abrupt and stunning turnaround to the fighting on the northern flank. A good many Confederates escaped out the other end of the cut, and Joe Davis collected these and the other survivors of his brigade on Herr's Ridge. By Dawes's count there were 232 prisoners taken in the railroad cut by his regiment, and he credited the 84th and 95th New York with further captures. General Wadsworth, watching the charge, exclaimed to his staff, "My God, the 6th has conquered them!"

But Rufus Dawes had many to mourn. A few days later he wrote his fiancée, "Our bravest and best are cold in the ground or suffering on beds of anguish. . . . One young man, Corporal James Kelly of Company 'B,' shot through the breast, came staggering up to me before he fell and opening his shirt to show the wound said 'Colonel, won't you write to my folks that I died a soldier.' Every man of our color guard was shot and several volunteer color bearers." Of the 420 men under Dawes's command that morning, nearly 200 were casualties.[26]

IT WAS NOON NOW, and there was a sudden hush in the hot, smoky fields and woods and on the ridges west of Gettysburg. Harry Heth's two broken brigades had fallen back to Herr's Ridge to regroup. They brought off their wounded, but their dead lay scattered in the wheat-fields and meadows and woodlots and along the railroad right-of-way. In due course Willie Pegram's guns began a desultory, defiant fire, and a picket line staked out its claim, but this time General Heth was going to await orders before doing anything further. In his report he would write, with careless irony, "The enemy had now been felt, and found to be in heavy force in and around Gettysburg."[27]

Heth's morning had been altogether careless. For his march on Gettysburg he gave no credence to Johnston Pettigrew's warning of his encounter the day before, and went prepared for nothing more menacing than a Yankee militia company or two. His idea of a reconnaissance was to go to battle to force the enemy to reveal his hand. Even when it was quickly evident he was facing not militia but the Army of the Potomac, Heth pushed ahead with an assault in violation of his orders — and a poorly supported assault in the bargain. To complete his catalog of command sins, in his tactics he ignored the well-founded warning of James Archer, his most experienced subordinate.

To be sure, it happened that General Heth was also the victim of sheer bad luck that morning. First he encountered the best cavalryman in the Yankee service, John Buford, and was thereupon much delayed. Then he was ambushed by perhaps the best fighting unit in the Army of the Potomac. The Iron Brigade was expertly led at every turn, and its men fought

179

The railroad cut on the July 1 battlefield, west of Gettysburg. Alfred Waud drew this scene of captured Confederates, after the morning's fighting, "from an officer's description." (Library of Congress)

so aggressively that they wrenched the initiative away from Archer's brigade in a matter of minutes. To cap off its triumphs, the Iron Brigade's 6th Wisconsin led the way to salvaging victory from imminent defeat on Cutler's front.

Yet among the victorious Federals there was little sense that the fighting was over for the day. The Johnnies had been sharply checked, but if the past year was any guide, veterans said, it was likely they would be back before long. The captains and their sergeants sorted out the companies and counted the men and tried to get ready. Canteens were filled and coffee boiled and knapsacks searched for hardtack. The wounded were taken back. A young Gettysburg boy would always remember that day: "On stretchers passing our front door were borne the bloody, mangled forms of tall Westerners, bearing on their black felt hats the red circular patch denoting their membership in the first division of the First Corps, many of them of the 'Iron Brigade.' . . ."

That more fighting was to come was certainly the view of General Doubleday, commanding on the field after Reynolds's death. Doubleday had been briefed early that morning by Reynolds on the latest intelligence, and was therefore aware that A. P. Hill's whole corps was somewhere off to the west along the Chambersburg Pike, and that there was thought to be an unknown force off to the north. Determined to carry on Buford's and Reynolds's plan to win time with a defense in depth, Doubleday ordered Wadsworth's two brigades to consolidate on McPherson's Ridge. The flanks were guarded by Buford's cavalry, Gamble's troopers on the left and Devin's on the right, north of Gettysburg.[28]

Abner Doubleday came to Gettysburg with the reputation of being a cautious, deliberate plodder, but during the morning's fighting, carrying on for Reynolds, he had his best command hours of the war. First he took the decision to hold back the 6th Wisconsin as a reserve, then the decision to commit the 6th at what proved to be just the right moment. Doubleday's exalted role was about to end, however. He would have to surrender command of the field and return to the First Corps as soon as his senior, Otis Howard of the Eleventh Corps, came on the scene.

First blood in this meeting engagement may have favored the Federals, but the issue promised to be decided finally by which side got the most fresh troops to the field. When Reynolds reached McPherson's Ridge that morning and had met with Buford, he issued rapid-fire orders. He sent off Captain Weld of his staff to deliver a status report to army commander Meade. Sickles was ordered up from Emmitsburg. But the top priority was to bring forward the men of the First and Eleventh corps "as fast as possible." He would see to the First Corps personally. As for the Eleventh Corps, Reynolds gave verbal instructions to Captain Daniel Hall, who had been sent ahead by Howard for orders. As one of his staff remembered it, Reynolds directed Howard to get his corps to Gettysburg with all speed, and he included "a direction to put a proper reserve of Infantry and Artillery on Cemetery Hill. . . ." That was to secure the high ground south of Gettysburg that Reynolds had just told General Meade he would hold, if he had to fight street by street through Gettysburg to do it.

General Howard, receiving this message at the head of his column on the Emmitsburg Road, ordered his corps to speed up its march and then hurried ahead himself to Gettysburg. His first act, in obedience to Reynolds's order, was to reconnoiter Cemetery Hill. "This, Colonel, seems to be the military position," he told his chief of staff, Charles Asmussen. "Yes, General," Asmussen observed, "this is the only position." Both Buford and Reynolds had earlier recognized that fact; now Howard was committed to holding the high ground with the Eleventh Corps.[29]

Apparently deciding his task was to remain behind to secure the rear area until further orders, Howard sent aides to report his arrival to Reynolds and then went searching for the best place from which to view the battlefield. He eventually found it in Gettysburg itself. Atop the three-story Fahnestock Brothers dry-goods store on Baltimore Street was a sort of observation deck, and citizens guided Howard to this vantage point. "I was delighted with the open view," Howard wrote. "With maps and field glasses we examined the apparent battlefield." He had not been there long — Howard noted the time as 11:30 A.M. — when one of General Reynolds's staff called up to him that the general had been killed and that he was ranking officer on the field. "My heart was heavy and the situation was grave indeed! but surely I did not hesitate a moment," Howard recalled. "God helping us, we will stay here till the army comes. I assumed the command of the field. . . ."[30]

8   The God of Battles Smiles South

AS JAMES LONGSTREET remembered it, General Lee set out that Wednesday morning "in his usual cheerful spirits." Clearly Lee had anticipated July 1 would be a day of little event, for the night before he made camp with the rearmost elements of the army, at Greenwood, west of the Cashtown Gap. As had become his habit, his headquarters tents were pitched close by those of Longstreet. For the day's march he asked Old Pete to ride with him. A short march was planned, just to Cashtown, eight miles to the east across South Mountain. Cashtown and perhaps Gettysburg ("as circumstances might dictate") were to be the assembly area for the army. According to Colonel Charles Marshall of the headquarters staff, the pace of the army that day would be "very deliberate."

It was also to be a day for straightening out the army's tangled order of battle. Each of the three corps was short one division. Richard Anderson's division of A. P. Hill's Third Corps was started early so as to catch up with the rest of the corps in the advance. Longstreet's First Corps was set to follow Anderson along the Chambersburg Pike. Lee sent for Imboden's brigade of irregular cavalry to occupy Chambersburg and relieve Pickett's division, so that Pickett might rejoin the First Corps the next day. That would give Longstreet all his troops except one brigade of Hood's division that, for want of a cavalry screen, was at New Guilford guarding the army's southern flank. Shortly after the march from Greenwood started, Allegheny Johnson's division, which had marched apart from Ewell, escorting the Second Corps trains, cut into the Chambersburg Pike from the northwest. Lee had Longstreet halt to let Johnson go ahead so that he might reunite with Ewell's other two divisions coming down from the north. According to plan then, by the 2nd of July the Army of Northern Virginia ought to be properly organized and suitably massed to meet the Federals — as soon as Jeb Stuart reported on where the Federals were to be found.[1]

At midmorning, as Lee and Longstreet rode together across the crest of the Cashtown Gap, they could hear faintly from the east the rumble of artillery fire. This might be coming from Powell Hill's advance, or from Dick Ewell's advance, or even from the long-absent Stuart, but no one really knew what it signified. Nor did any courier reach the party with an explanation. (In campaigns past, Jeb Stuart always had the explanation, often before Lee asked for it.) As staff man Armistead Long recalled, "This caused Lee some little uneasiness." After a time uneasiness turned to impatience, and leaving Longstreet to direct the First Corps' march, Lee hurried ahead to Cashtown and A. P. Hill's headquarters.

Hill was wan and weak and just out of his sickbed, but already concerned enough about the artillery fire that he was preparing to ride out to the advance. He told Lee his only information was a dispatch from Harry Heth, sent early in the day, saying he had encountered Yankee cavalry in front of Gettysburg. No doubt there was an awkward moment when Hill explained to Lee that to reconnoiter Gettysburg he had sent two full divisions and two battalions of artillery, but he sought to reassure the commanding general by affirming that Heth had been instructed not to bring on a general engagement. Nevertheless, the volume of fire was disturbing, and Hill rode off eastward to find out about it.[2]

Deciding he should not be thought of as looking over his subordinate's shoulder, Lee waited at Cashtown while Hill acted on the matter. At noon, his patience waning, Lee called in Dick Anderson, of Hill's corps, to discuss the situation. Anderson would remember the commanding general being "very much disturbed and depressed." What seemed to disturb Lee the most was not having Stuart on the scene. "In the absence of reports from him," Lee said, "I am in ignorance as to what we have in front of us here." It might be the whole Federal army; it might be only a detachment. "If it is the whole Federal force," Lee said, "we must fight a battle here."

Shortly afterward, Major Campbell Brown of the Second Corps staff found Lee and delivered a message from Dick Ewell. At 9 o'clock that morning, Ewell reported, he had received A. P. Hill's notice that he was advancing on Gettysburg. Ewell had immediately redirected Rodes's and Early's divisions, then marching in the direction of Cashtown, to roads leading south toward Gettysburg. He acted in response to Lee's discretionary order of the day before to direct the Second Corps to either place, according to circumstances.

After he had reported this "change in our movement," Brown recalled, General Lee "asked me with a peculiar searching, almost querulous, impatience which I never saw in him before, . . . whether Genl. Ewell had heard anything from Genl. Jeb Stuart. . . ." When Brown replied in the negative, Lee was uncharacteristically blunt, saying he "had heard nothing from or of him for three days, and that Genl. Stuart had not complied with his instructions." Instead of keeping in constant communication, Lee complained, "he has gone off clear around Genl. Meade's army and I see by a Northern paper that he is near Washington. A scout reports Meade's whole army marching this way, but that is all I know about his position." Major Brown was greatly surprised by this outburst, this departure from Lee's "habitual reserve." Looking back on the episode, he wrote, "I now appreciate that he was really uneasy & irritated by Stuart's conduct. . . ."

His irritation at Stuart and the report of Ewell's change of direction seem to have crystallized Lee's thinking. He determined to ride ahead to take control of what every minute was sounding more and more like a battlefield. He ordered Anderson to follow with his division. He instructed Major Brown to tell Ewell to make every effort to get in touch with Stuart, and he delivered an emphatic order to the commander of the Second Corps. "General Lee," Brown wrote, "then impressed on me *very strongly* that a general engagement was to be avoided until the arrival of the rest of the army."[3]

AT HIS HEADQUARTERS at Taneytown, 14 miles south of Gettysburg, George Gordon Meade began that 1st of July much better informed about the whereabouts of the enemy's army than did Robert E. Lee. Early that morning Meade finally received intelligence from Harrisburg — relayed to him from Washington over the newly repaired telegraph circuit — that Ewell's force threatening the Pennsylvania capital had turned back, presumably to unite with Lee's main force. He had intelligence from cavalryman Buford in Gettysburg that placed A. P. Hill's corps at Cashtown, pointing eastward, with Longstreet's corps behind Hill — to which Buford added, "Rumor says Ewell is coming over the mountains from Carlisle." At midday Meade telegraphed General-in-Chief Halleck, "The news proves my advance has answered its purpose. I shall not advance any, but prepare to receive an attack in case Lee makes one. A battle-field is being selected to the rear. . . ."[4]

Official Washington was watching events in Pennsylvania intently, hanging on General Meade's every telegraphed word. "This is an anxious day," Treasury Secretary Chase entered in his diary on July 1. "Meade's army seems to be drawing right to the rebel positions. Is he not too far to the right? May not Lee turn his left and so get between him and Washington? These are questions much discussed. Gen. Halleck and the

President both seem uneasy." Chase had obviously been listening when Halleck fussed at Meade, "Do not let him draw you too far to the east." Navy Secretary Gideon Welles also sought the latest news at the War Department, and was convinced that the general-in-chief was entirely too cautious in his directions to Meade and the Army of the Potomac. Like the president, Welles regarded Lee's invasion as a great opportunity — and feared the opportunity might not be seized. "Halleck's prayers and efforts, especially his prayers, are to keep the Rebels back," Welles wrote, " — drive them back across the 'frontiers' instead of intercepting and annihilating them." Still, Welles had hopes for the new general commanding: "Meade will I trust keep closer to them than some others have done."[5]

Gettysburg was too distant for the sound of the guns to carry as far as Taneytown, so Meade only learned of the fighting there at about 11:30 A.M., from Reynolds's hard-riding aide Stephen Weld. Meade cannot have been overly surprised by the news, considering the intelligence he had already received on the enemy's movements, but it left him in a quandary. He was not, on July 1, any more prepared or anxious to fight at Gettysburg than was Lee. On the contrary, Meade's favored plan for the day was to mount a defense of his chosen ground behind Pipe Creek, just below the Pennsylvania-Maryland line.

Earlier that morning Winfield Scott Hancock had brought his Second Corps to Taneytown as ordered, and upon reporting to headquarters he received a briefing from Meade on the plan. The two men shared friendship as well as mutual respect, and Meade seemed eager (unlike Joe Hooker) to share his thinking with his lieutenants. As Meade remembered their conversation, he expressed his willingness "to fight in front if practical; if not, then to the rear, or to the right or the left, as circumstances might require." Hancock remembered the general commanding expressing a definite preference about where he wanted to fight: "He said he had made up his mind to fight a battle on what was known as Pipe Creek . . . , which presented more favorable features than any other position he could see." It was what Meade termed a "contingent plan." The essential contingency was for Reynolds with the First and Eleventh corps to "hold the enemy in check sufficiently long" at or near Gettysburg to bait the Rebels into following as he fell back on the rest of the army at Pipe Creek. In expectation of this sequence, Meade had spent the morning refining the plan for Slocum and Sedgwick, his senior generals.

Meade's high hopes began to erode with the arrival of Captain Weld and his report that Reynolds was committing his forces to try and beat the enemy to the high ground at Gettysburg, "and keep them back as long as possible." From what Weld said of Reynolds's stated determination to fight street by street through the town, Meade concluded that Reynolds had not received the Pipe Creek circular, nor even the explanatory dispatch asking him simply to evaluate the scene when he reached Gettysburg. The Pipe Creek plan appeared in jeopardy, and Weld heard the general curse Chief of Staff Butterfield for not sending out the orders sooner. After making all the arrangements for a plan of battle, Meade said bitterly, "now it was all useless." Everything lay in the hands of his chief lieutenant on the spot — the right man for the job, certainly, but as it happened, acting without the latest guidance from the general commanding.[6]

Here was a moment for decision, and General Meade was less than decisive in meeting it. In the verbal message delivered by Captain Weld, Reynolds implied but could not state unequivocally that he wanted to stake the army to a stand at Gettysburg — that, after all, should be General Meade's decision — but Meade misinterpreted Reynolds's intent. For lack of any later instructions, Reynolds (so Meade believed) must be acting on *yesterday's* instructions — that is, should the Confederates gain Gettysburg before he did, or in spite of him, he was to fall back to Emmitsburg. Meade's immediate concern with this was Reynolds's route of withdrawal. If he fell back by the Emmitsburg Road rather than by the Taneytown Road, as called for in the Pipe Creek plan, it would leave a gap in the middle of the Army of the Potomac for the Rebels to exploit. Meade therefore ordered Hancock to advance the Second Corps some way up the Taneytown Road to fill the gap.

During all this, General Meade made no provision for a quite different contingency — that Gettysburg would be the battlefield of choice or chance. If that was indeed the case, Reynolds and his forces on the scene, confronting what was understood to be two-thirds of the Rebel army, could greatly profit from immediate reinforcement. Before noon that day, for example, the Third Corps had arrived north of Emmitsburg, some eight miles from Gettysburg. The Twelfth Corps had marched to Two Taverns, on the Baltimore Pike, only five miles distant. If ordered immediately, one or both corps could reach the battlefield by midafternoon. Meade, however, was reading John Reynolds as fighting only a temporary holding action at Gettysburg — and Reynolds's death precluded any clarification.

Meade did make one effort at least to harass the enemy closing on Gettysburg by telegraphing General Couch in Harrisburg "to throw a force in Ewell's rear" as the Rebel column marched southward. Since Couch had only militia under his command, this was easier asked than accomplished. Couch dutifully sent some of his Sunday soldiers across the Susquehanna toward Carlisle, where they tangled with Albert Jenkins's cavalry. "Just now," Couch admitted, "things do not look well."[7]

Meade's hopes for fighting a battle on ground of his own choosing were further eroded by the first report, delivered about 1:00 P.M., that John Reynolds was dead or severely wounded and that Otis Howard was in command on the field. Howard was no more likely to have received the Pipe Creek circular than had Reynolds, and in any event Meade did not think highly enough of Howard to want him making such fundamental decisions as where the army would give battle.

Still, Meade clung stubbornly to the tatters of hope that remained. At the same time that General Lee was riding toward the battlefield to take personal command, General Meade elected to remain where he was, at Taneytown, 14 miles from the fighting. Here he would be better poised to manage a stand on the Pipe Creek line should it come to that. In the meantime, he would continue commanding by proxy. He rode over to Hancock's headquarters with a letter to that general ordering him to Gettysburg, and authorizing him to decide whether and where the army should fight.

Lieutenant Colonel Charles Morgan, Hancock's chief of staff, recorded that in the conversation, "General Meade's attention was called to the fact that General Howard, commanding the Eleventh Corps, was senior to General Hancock, to which he replied, in effect, that he could not help it; that he knew General Hancock, but did not know General Howard so well, and at this crisis he must have a man he knew and could trust." If Hancock thought the ground and the position at Gettysburg "a better one on which to fight a battle," he should so advise the general commanding, "and he will order all the troops up." Furthermore, having just finished reviewing the whole strategic and tactical situation with Hancock, Meade was satisfied that he had picked not only the best man for the job, but the best informed one as well. By 1:30 P.M. Hancock was off for Gettysburg.

In selecting Hancock to take Reynolds's place in command on the field, Meade was exercising the special appointment powers granted him by General-in-Chief Halleck under authority of Secretary of War Stanton ("You are authorized . . . to appoint to command as you may deem expedient"). At this time and in this place, seniority could be and would be trumped by perceived ability, and George Meade did not hesitate to act on that basis. Indeed, in the same letter that put Hancock in field command, Meade ordered John Gibbon, not the senior among Hancock's divisional commanders, to take over the Second Corps. And by day's end, Meade would name John Newton, a division commander in the Sixth Corps, to head the First Corps rather than Abner Doubleday, the corps' senior officer.[8]

OLIVER OTIS HOWARD was a West Pointer who lacked both a martial bearing and a warrior's inspiration. While his personal courage was never in question — he had lost his right arm leading his brigade at Seven Pines on the Peninsula — he often appeared more interested in religious orthodoxy and abolitionism than in generalship. He had pressed a claim of seniority with Hooker to wrangle command of the Eleventh Corps, but at Chancellorsville his negligence exposed the corps to Stonewall Jackson's merciless flank attack. Two months later morale was still a tender issue in the Eleventh Corps, and the men's contempt for Howard was best expressed in their nickname for him, "Old Prayer Book." In this new campaign what the Eleventh Corps needed to resurrect itself was driving, hands-on leadership . . . precisely what Otis Howard was ill equipped to provide.

By Howard's watch it was 11:30 A.M. when he learned of Reynolds's death and that he was, by seniority, commander on the field. Beyond Reynolds's earlier instruction to him to hold the high ground of Cemetery Hill south of the town, Howard had little to go on regarding a plan for the fighting. Several of Reynolds's staff had gone to escort the general's body to the rear, and were not available to explain what orders he had given and what dispatches he had sent. Still, it seemed apparent to Howard that he ought to follow Reynolds's lead and attempt (as he later phrased it) "to hold Gettysburg, . . . to hold this strategic position till the army came up."

It was approaching noon now and except for the sporadic artillery duel west of the town, there was a tense but continuing lull in the fighting. To the west, Rebel troops could be seen massing along the Chambersburg Pike in front of Wadsworth's First Corps division. By report from Buford's troopers posted on the right flank, Rebels in some force were closing in from the north. This midday pause was clearly a time for incisive decision-making. General Howard's response was indecision. If it was indeed his intention to hold the strategic position at Gettysburg "till the army came up," he was grievously hesitant about calling for the reinforcements vitally needed to do so.

It was not until 1:00 P.M. that Howard sent messages to the nearest supporting troops — Sickles's Third Corps and Slocum's Twelfth — and then it was merely to "inform" them that "Ewell's corps is advancing from York" and that the left wing of the Potomac army was "engaged with A. P. Hill's corps." He said nothing of Reynolds's death, nothing about any intent to fight for Gettysburg, nothing about needing help. After second thoughts that required another half-hour, Howard finally sent appeals for support to Sickles and to Slocum. Taking into account the delivery time for these messages, it would be well after 3 o'clock before any response to his appeal could even be considered.

And only at 2 o'clock, two and a half hours after he took the command, did Howard get around to reporting to General Meade. He briefly explained that he was posting his forces west and north of the town, that he was facing both Hill's and Ewell's corps, and that he had "ordered General Sickles to push forward." He said nothing to Meade about any determination to hold at Gettysburg until the rest of the army came up, nothing about the therefore urgent requirement to reinforce the First and Eleventh corps, nothing about his request to Slocum for assistance. Blunt John Buford sent a status report of his own that afternoon. General Reynolds had been killed, he told cavalry chief Pleasonton, and "In my opinion, there seems to be no directing person." He added a stark postscript: "We need help now."[9]

Curiously, it was the one nonprofessional soldier in the quartet of Meade, Howard, Slocum, and Sickles who displayed the one spark of soldierly initiative in this situation. That morning, passing through Emmitsburg, Dan Sickles had sent an aide ahead to find General Reynolds for fresh orders. The aide returned with Reynolds's battlefield injunction, delivered just before he was killed — "Tell General Sickles I think he had better come up." In the interim, however, Sickles had been handed Meade's Pipe Creek circular that ordered the Third Corps to hold Emmitsburg to guard the army's western flank. Sickles was in a dilemma. Two days before, Meade had berated him for not carrying out a marching order; now he had an order from his immediate superior that directly conflicted with an order from the army commander.

Sickles temporized by sending again to Reynolds for clarification, but the arrival of Howard's call for help, and word that Reynolds was dead, spurred him to a decision. Leaving two brigades at Emmitsburg to satisfy Meade's order, he marched for Gettysburg with his other four. When this was reported to Meade, who was still clinging to his Pipe Creek plan, he sent to Sickles to "hold on" at Emmitsburg "as it is a point not to be abandoned excepting in an extremity." Receiving this dispatch en route, Sickles regarded it as overtaken by events and continued his march.[10]

As it happened, Dan Sickles's action came too late to affect events at Gettysburg that day, but at least he showed the initiative to (in effect) march to the sound of the guns. Henry Slocum, for much of the day only five miles from the battlefield, did a good deal less than that. At Two Taverns on the Baltimore Pike, which Slocum's Twelfth Corps reached in midmorning, the sound of the fighting was quite distinct. "The cannonading became more and more furious," a Wisconsin soldier remembered, ". . . until in the distance it sounded like one continual roll of thunder." There was no doubt, wrote Edmund Brown, 27th Indiana, "that musketry firing was mixed with that of the artillery." Corporal Brown and his comrades were perplexed as their peaceful stay at Two Taverns stretched well into the afternoon.

General Slocum was an unassertive, exceedingly careful, by-the-book officer. He had no orders from headquarters to advance beyond Two Taverns, nor did he possess initiative enough to promptly send a staff man ahead to find out about those sounds of battle, or to go himself, nor was he moved to respond to Howard's plea for reinforcements. After all, General Howard had no authority to give General Slocum orders. In due course, when it was finally clarified for him that a battle was actually in progress, Slocum did march his corps for Gettysburg . . . and started far too late to change anything. Major Charles H. Howard, General Howard's brother and aide-de-camp, remarked in exasperation that on July 1 General Slocum demonstrated "the fitness of his name *Slow come.*"

So it happened that through much of that hot July afternoon, when the fighting resumed at Gettysburg in greater force than before, there was a decided misconnection between the Yankee generals on the battlefield and the Yankee generals in the rest of the Army of the Potomac. As a consequence, all the infantry fighting on the Federal side that day would be done solely by the First Corps and the Eleventh Corps.[11]

While these ranking generals haltingly tried to puzzle out what was going on and what if anything they ought to do about it, the troops called up earlier by General Reynolds were arriving to fill out the thin Union battle lines west of Gettysburg. During the midday lull the rest of the First Corps, the divisions of John C. Robinson and Thomas A. Rowley — Rowley was taking Doubleday's place — reached the scene first and took their places alongside Wadsworth's bloodied division. Doubleday posted Rowley's two brigades, under Chapman Biddle and Roy Stone, on

McPherson's Ridge to the left and right respectively of Meredith's Iron Brigade. Cutler's brigade north of the Chambersburg Pike was reinforced by Henry Baxter's and Gabriel Paul's brigades of Robinson's division. Colonel Wainwright brought up the other four First Corps batteries in support.

The left and center of this line continued facing west in expectation of a renewed assault by A. P. Hill's corps. On the right, north of the Chambersburg Pike, the expectation of Ewell's approach caused the line to turn to face north by west. One important First Corps reinforcement, however, would not reach the field in time. General-in-Chief Halleck's manipulations to unseat Joe Hooker had included holding back Hooker's reinforcements, and consequently the brigade of Vermonters under George Stannard, assigned to the First Corps from the Department of Washington, had been started north too late to join the fighting that day. The four brigades of Rowley's and Robinson's divisions that did reach the battlefield comprised some 7,700 effectives. The First Corps, including Wadsworth's battered division, would thus confront the enemy that afternoon with fewer than 10,000 men.

The Eleventh Corps was now coming on the field as well. Like the First, the Eleventh contained six brigades in three divisions, but it remained sadly understrength after its Chancellorsville debacle, and on this day would bring fewer than 8,700 men to Gettysburg. Barlow's and Schurz's divisions, marching on parallel roads, arrived by 1 o'clock and were directed by Howard to march on through Gettysburg and out to the fields north of the town. Schurz assumed field command of the corps. The third division, von Steinwehr's, arrived about 2 o'clock and was posted as a general reserve on Cemetery Hill, where Howard had established his headquarters. With von Steinwehr in reserve were two of the corps' five batteries.

General Howard probably had only an approximate idea of the strength of the First Corps, but he was certainly aware of the depleted condition of his own corps. Yet here he was posting some 5,200 infantry and three batteries in the fields to the north of Gettysburg to do prospective battle with what by all accounts was Ewell's Confederate corps. And Howard knew this *was* Ewell, having reviewed the latest intelligence with Reynolds the evening before and with Buford after arriving on the field. It was understood that Ewell represented one-third of Lee's army. The Eleventh Corps represented one-seventh — a small one-seventh, as it were — of Meade's army. The case could therefore be made that Otis Howard's failure to call immediately and aggressively for reinforcements was negligence on a level with his failings at Chancellorsville. He may well have intended, as he later said, to "hold until at least Slocum and Sickles . . . could reach the field," but the wait would be longer than it had to be and proved costly beyond all expectations.[12]

The brigade was the basic unit of maneuver in these armies, and in the Gettysburg campaign Union and Confederate brigades were, on average, virtually identical in size. Confederate divisions, however, were substantially larger, and therefore in this July 1 contest the Rebels held a considerable manpower edge. West of Gettysburg, for example, the divisions of Heth and Pender each contained four brigades, while the Federal First Corps divisions of Wadsworth, Rowley, and Robinson opposing them contained but two brigades each, leaving the Yankees outnumbered eight brigades to six. On the developing northern front the disparity was even greater. Dick Ewell's two divisions, under Rodes and Early, had five and four brigades respectively, while the three Eleventh Corps divisions under Schurz, Barlow, and von Steinwehr had only two brigades each — a commanding Confederate edge of nine to six; and with von Steinwehr in reserve, the edge on the field was actually nine to four. The failings of Howard to promptly ask for reinforcements (and of Meade to promptly order them) would greatly imperil the Army of the Potomac on this first day of July.

General Howard was as slow to appraise the prospective battlefield as he was to call for reinforcements to defend it. According to Doubleday, it was not until 2 o'clock or after that Howard rode out to McPherson's Ridge to inspect the First Corps' position. Buford had picked this ridgeline that morning as part of his defense-in-depth scheme to inflict maximum delay on the Rebels advancing from the west. Reynolds had put Wadsworth's infantry there for the same purpose, and to relieve Buford's beleaguered troopers. Now, four hours later, much had changed. Ewell was reported approaching from the north, making the McPherson's Ridge position suddenly and exceedingly vulnerable to being turned. Tactical wisdom called for pulling the First Corps back to more easily defended Seminary Ridge, and doing so during the midday calm. That in turn would give the Eleventh Corps a shorter and more compact line to defend against Ewell north of the town.

If such tactical wisdom occurred to Howard, it was but a belated thought. The hour was late, the enemy was threatening, and Howard kept Doubleday in place on McPherson's Ridge, merely telling him (as Doubleday remembered it) to retreat in case he was "forced back." Few elements of the military art are more difficult than conducting an orderly withdrawal while under attack (something Otis Howard in particular should have remembered from Chancellorsville). In the event, the First Corps stayed where it was, the two thin Eleventh Corps divisions manned a widely extended line facing north — and a recipe for military disaster was fixed in place.[13]

DICK EWELL, riding with Robert Rodes's division, had reached the village of Middletown on their morning's march toward Cashtown when A. P. Hill's courier found him and reported that Hill was embarked on an expedition to Gettysburg. Ewell promptly turned Rodes south onto the Carlisle Road toward Gettysburg, and sent orders to Jubal Early to turn his division toward the same objective by way of the Harrisburg Road to the east. When they had closed to within about four miles of Gettysburg, Ewell and Rodes were surprised to hear sounds of battle. They hurried ahead to investigate. From an eminence called Oak Hill they looked upon a scene to warm any general's heart. As Rodes put it, "I could strike the force of the enemy with which General Hill's troops were engaged upon the flank, and . . . whenever we struck the enemy we could engage him with the advantage in ground."

James Thompson of the 6th Alabama, Rodes's division, would remember the view from atop Oak Hill as extraordinary. Rank upon rank of A. P. Hill's troops were plainly seen "away to our right across broad fields of ripe wheat. . . ." Thompson described it as "the only time during the war that we were in a position to get such a view of contending forces. It seemed like some grand panorama with the sounds of conflict added."[14]

The god of battles appeared to be smiling upon the Confederacy. Beginning the day knowing virtually nothing about the Federals' whereabouts, the two wings of the Army of Northern Virginia had stumbled blindly into positions to smite the Yankees in front and flank simultaneously. It was as if they had planned it that way.

To press the advantage, Rodes directed his division to leave the road and advance along the wooded crest of Oak Ridge, which would not only give him the high ground but ought to conceal his approach as well. With five brigades his was the largest division in the army, although somewhat uneven in leadership. Dodson Ramseur and George Doles were skilled enough brigadiers, but Junius Daniel, up from North Carolina with his new brigade, would be experiencing his first command test in Lee's army. Alfred Iverson displayed a singular discordance with his men, and Edward O'Neal thus far had demonstrated minimal command skills; O'Neal was heading Rodes's old brigade over Rodes's pro-

On July 1 the Union's O. O. Howard, left, faced attack by Robert Rodes. (Library of Congress–U.S. Army Military History Institute)

tests. To get into line of battle as quickly as possible, Rodes had to post his brigades according to their order of march — a decision that in the end would cost him much of his initial advantage.

Rodes's haste was made necessary by a rapidly changing battlefront. Tom Devin's cavalry pickets, alerted by Federal intelligence, were posted north of Gettysburg specifically to look for Ewell's approach, and they sounded the alarm in timely fashion. In the uneasy calm following the repulse of Heth's morning attacks from the west, Doubleday ordered Henry Baxter's brigade from Robinson's newly arrived First Corps division to move up to protect the corps' northern flank. Howard gave the same mission to the Eleventh Corps divisions of Schurz and Barlow as they arrived. Rodes and Ewell, during the time it took to deploy the troops for battle, found themselves surveying a new military chessboard. Surprise would not be a deciding factor in the contest after all.[15]

Perhaps remembering how deliberately his mentor, Stonewall Jackson, had posted his forces before striking the Union flank at Chancellorsville, Rodes held off the launch of his own flank attack until everyone, reserves as well as front line, got into place. Meanwhile, to initiate the new battleground, he brought forward two batteries to Oak Hill and opened on the Yankee infantry north of the Chambersburg Pike. Two of Colonel Wainwright's batteries responded. Then Harry Heth's guns to the west chimed in. In the midst of this artillery duel, Major Campbell Brown arrived back from his mission to General Lee and found Ewell helping to post Rodes's guns. Brown reported the army commander's orders: a general engagement "was to be avoided until the arrival of the rest of the army."

Now it was Dick Ewell's turn to face a moment of decision, and he acted with Jackson-like decisiveness. Rodes held the high ground and was deploying for battle. His guns were already engaged with those of the enemy. To the west, Powell Hill had apparently already been heavily engaged. To the east, long columns of Yankee infantry were emerging from Gettysburg and approaching Oak Hill, very possibly to strike at Rodes's flank. "It was too late to avoid an engagement without abandoning the position already taken up," Ewell would write in his report, "and I determined to push the attack vigorously."[16]

It was 1:30 P.M. now, and about a mile and a quarter southwest of Oak Hill, on a rise of ground called Belmont Ridge alongside the Chambersburg Pike, General Lee joined Powell Hill to observe fighting he had not anticipated, and did not want, erupt before his eyes in a barrage of flame and smoke and thunderous noise. So far as he could see, it was as yet only an artillery battle — Ewell's guns on the high ground to the northeast and Harry Heth's guns on the Chambersburg Pike dueling with the Yankee batteries in front of Gettysburg. Perhaps he might yet gain control of events.

Just then Harry Heth rode up. Still smarting from his morning's defeat and anxious to redeem himself, he addressed Lee: General Ewell was on the enemy's flank; was it not time to put his division, reinforced now by Pender's, back into the fight? Lee's response was brief and pointed and no doubt intended as a reproof to both Heth and Hill. "I do not wish to bring on a general engagement today," he said; "Longstreet is not up." Lee sent Heth back to his division, and continued watching and waiting to see what Dick Ewell was going to do in response to his earlier instructions.

During this noisy hiatus General Lee received another messenger — Andrew Venable of the cavalry, at last bringing word from the long absent Jeb Stuart. Major Venable had set out that morning from Dover, a village well to the east, near York, and had ridden some 30 miles in search of the army. This was Lee's first direct communication with Stuart in a week. General Stuart, Venable explained, was then on his way to Carlisle on the trail of Ewell's corps. Lee sent Venable hurrying back to Stuart with orders to bring the cavalry to Gettysburg "at once." It would be midnight before Venable could reach Carlisle, which promised the arrival of the cavalry late in the day on July 2 at the earliest. Whatever decisions General Lee might make, he would not have the benefit of any cavalry intelligence or reconnaissance or screening for at least the next twenty-four hours.[17]

DESPITE LEE'S (and Meade's) best intentions, the battle at Gettysburg was taking on a life of its own. That morning A. P. Hill had sent in a reconnoitering force too strong to back away from a challenge. Then John Reynolds defiantly threw down a challenge. Now Dick Ewell saw a glittering, now-or-never opportunity squarely before him. Determined to seize the opportunity — and to strike before he himself was struck — Ewell ordered Rodes to the attack.

Rodes designed his assault with a wary eye to his left, where the Yankees were seen to be bringing troops through Gettysburg and toward Oak Hill. He determined to attack on a two-brigade front, sending in O'Neal's and Iverson's men simultaneously, then following up with Daniel's brigade in echelon on the right. George Dole's brigade was posted well off to the left, to defend against the enemy forces approaching from Gettysburg until such time as Jubal Early's division arrived from the north to secure Rodes's exposed flank. Dodson Ramseur's brigade would act as a reserve, and Thomas Carter's battalion would furnish the artillery support. Rodes's tactical plan was a sound one, but in execution his offensive was bungled right at the start. As it happened, setting off at 2:30 P.M., this largest of the divisions in the Army of Northern Virginia launched its decisive attack against the enemy's flank with barely a thousand men.

Colonel Edward O'Neal's talents, it appeared, were more those of the politician he had been than the warrior he aspired to be. Instead of calculating his advance and coordinating it with Iverson's brigade, he rushed in his Alabama brigade entirely on its own. Furthermore, he attacked with only three of his five regiments. Rodes himself had detached the 5th Alabama to help secure the division's exposed left flank. Then O'Neal apparently could not grasp the meaning of an order that the 3rd Alabama should align with the brigade on its right, and he simply left it behind. To complete his malfeasance, he remained safely in the rear rather than personally directing the assault, as was expected of any officer in Robert E. Lee's army. O'Neal's colonels became confused, missed their target, and struck the strongest part of the Yankee line head-on.[18]

That Yankee line comprised six veteran and very tough Massachusetts, Pennsylvania, and New York regiments led by a brigadier general who was perhaps even tougher than his men. Henry Baxter was a miller and storekeeper from Michigan who had joined the war as a captain in the 7th Michigan. He rose to command of the regiment and along the way was badly wounded first in the Peninsula campaign, then again at Antietam, then a third time at Fredericksburg. He had only gained his star in March, and his command was newly reconstituted, one brigade out of two, in the army's May reorganization. Still, Baxter was firmly in charge and had his men well primed for battle.

During the tense midday pause, with the enemy's intentions not yet clear, General Robinson posted Baxter's brigade to guard the First Corps' flank by facing half to the west and half to the north. Baxter assumed a shallow inverted V-formation along the Mummasburg Road slanting diagonally across the formative battlefield. On their approach march Baxter's Yankees had been screened by woods, and as a consequence O'Neal's misdirected Alabamians came on them suddenly and unexpectedly. "Our presence proved a surprise," a man in the 88th Pennsylvania observed dryly. In his report General Rodes rendered a succinct verdict: O'Neal's three regiments — 6th, 12th, 26th Alabama — "moved with alacrity (but not in accordance with my orders as to direction) and in confusion into the action."

The action was as fierce as it was confusing. The three Federal regiments that met the main weight of the attack — 88th and 90th Pennsylvania and 12th Massachusetts — had some protection from a roadside fence and a stone wall, on which the men rested their rifles for a steady aim. They also had help from the newly arriving Eleventh Corps. The 45th New York of Schurz's division, coming up from the right, poured a flanking fire into the Rebels in what would be remembered as a moment of sweet revenge. The 45th had been one of the first regiments routed by Rodes's men during Stonewall Jackson's Chancellorsville assault. Another payback was delivered by Hubert Dilger's Battery I, 1st Ohio Light Artillery, Eleventh Corps. Captain Dilger had conducted a memorable fighting retreat against Jackson at Chancellorsville, which for all its gallantry was still a retreat, and he welcomed this second chance at the enemy. Dilger's six well-handled Napoleons delivered canister against the Rebel infantrymen and counterbattery fire against their supporting artillery. Captain R.C.M. Page's Virginia battery was decimated by this fire, losing 4 gunners dead, 26 wounded, and 17 battery horses.

O'Neal's brigade, without Iverson advancing on its right, found itself quite alone. Captain Robert Park of the 12th Alabama recorded in his diary that the "balls were falling thick and fast around us, and whizzing past and often striking some one near." Then Park himself was down with a wound. "It was a wonder, a miracle, I was not afterward shot a half dozen times," he wrote. Although it seemed an eternity to those in the heat of the fighting, O'Neal's brigade was broken and driven into retreat in less than thirty minutes. The attack, Rodes reported angrily, "was repulsed quickly, and with loss."[19]

There would be no rest for Baxter's victorious Yankees. A second Confederate battle line was seen advancing from Oak Hill, starting from west of where O'Neal's Alabama brigade had started earlier, apparently aiming for the gap between Baxter's brigade and Cutler's, of Wadsworth's division. General Robinson had Baxter "close this interval" by shifting his regiments left so they now faced northwest and were lined up behind a stone fence. Baxter told the men to lie down and ordered the flags down as well, so that from the Confederate perspective there would be nothing to see upon crossing a low ridgeline but a stone fence on the far border of an open grassy meadow.

It was a perfectly designed ambush, but it required a blunder on the enemy's part to be fully successful. Brigadier General Alfred Iverson supplied the blunder, and worse. Like O'Neal, Iverson chose to stay behind rather than personally direct his advance. Then he sent his brigade — 5th, 12th, 20th, and 23rd North Carolina, some 1,350 men in all — into battle without any advance reconnaissance and without skirmishers in the lead. As the historian of the 23rd North Carolina would phrase it, bitterly, "unwarned, unled as a brigade, went forward Iverson's deserted band to its doom."[20]

Iverson's battle line, well closed up, colors all aligned, moving with parade-ground precision, came slanting across farmer John Forney's field at an oblique angle to the stone fence. Aiming for a woodlot beyond the end of Baxter's line, it presented as much flank as front to its unseen foe. Abruptly, as the range closed to less than 100 yards, the Yankee line rose up and with a shout delivered the most killing volley anyone on the field that day had ever witnessed. Men went down by dozens, by scores, quite literally in windrows. It was like a farmer harvesting grain with long swings of a scythe. Lieutenant George Bullock, 23rd North Carolina, would say that in all his war service, from the Peninsula to Appomattox, that field that afternoon at Gettysburg was the only one "where the blood ran like a branch. And that too, on the hot, parched ground."

There was a swale running across the field in front of the stone fence,

An anonymous primitive artist titled his painting *Attack on Seminary Ridge*. The neatly aligned Federal troops storm the Rebels at left rear. (Karolik Collection, Museum of Fine Arts, Boston)

and the Tar Heels ducked down into it for whatever cover it provided from the deadly fire. "I believe every man who stood up was either killed or wounded," a man in the 20th North Carolina recalled. It must have seemed that way. The 12th North Carolina, on the extreme left of the formation and farthest from the stone fence, escaped the worst of the ambush; even so, the 12th lost more than a third of its men. Iverson's desperate men in the swale could not advance, and dared not expose themselves in the open trying to retreat. On the other side of the field Lysander Cutler's Yankees, bloodied in the morning's fight, moved up to strike the front and left of the beleaguered Rebel brigade.

Here and there men began to wave hats or handkerchiefs in token of surrender. Henry Baxter, taking in the situation, shouted, "Up boys, and give them steel!" His Yankees leaped over the stone fence and dashed toward the swale. General Baxter was right with them. In the face of their bayonets Rebels all across the field threw down their rifles. When there was time for a count, it was found that 322 in Iverson's brigade had surrendered. Almost twice that many had been killed or wounded. Three battle flags were taken by Baxter's men. Two-thirds of Iverson's brigade had become casualties in these few minutes of slaughter. The 23rd North Carolina would count but 34 men in its ranks; it lost 89 percent of those it took into battle that afternoon.

The next day Confederate artillerist Henry Berkeley examined the field of Iverson's disaster. "This morning on getting up," Berkeley entered in his diary, "I saw a sight which was perfectly sickening and heart-rendering in the extreme. . . . There were, in a few feet of us, by actual count, seventy-nine (79) North Carolinians laying dead in a straight line. I stood on their right and looked down their line. It was perfectly dressed. Three had fallen to the front, the rest had fallen backward; yet the feet of all these dead men were in a perfectly straight line. Great God!"

Earlier, the repulse of Archer's and Davis's brigades on the Chambersburg Pike had produced an impasse and an extended pause. Now, however, despite the disasters to O'Neal and Iverson, the fighting on the Mummasburg Road would rush on after only the briefest of pauses. Dick Ewell had the Second Corps fully committed to battle. Daniel's brigade was already advancing to Iverson's relief, and Ramseur's and Doles's were moving into O'Neal's vacated spot. And to the east, the outriders of Jubal Early's division were on the field.

Iverson's brigade was wrecked beyond any further use, and Iverson himself was thrust into limbo. There would be rumors of cowardice and drunkenness, and while proof of such charges was lacking, it was evident that his men would no longer tolerate him in command. The mortally wounded Colonel Daniel Christie of the 23rd North Carolina told his surviving men that while he might not live to command them again, he would see to it that "the imbecile Iverson never should." Nor did he, and three months later Alfred Iverson was transferred out of the Army of Northern Virginia. Edward O'Neal too was permanently tarnished as brigade commander. Lee pocketed O'Neal's promotion to brigadier general, confining him thereafter to regimental command.[21]

As soon as it was evident that Ewell was fully engaged, an impatient Harry Heth rode back to Belmont Ridge to find Generals Lee and Hill. Heth reported the enemy withdrawing troops from his front to defend against Ewell — this would have been John Robinson's brigades — and once again he asked permission to attack.

Lee realized now there could be no turning back from a battle of some dimension or another at Gettysburg. Apparently Ewell had been too deeply committed to break off by the time he received Lee's injunction that "a general engagement was to be avoided." Although still in the dark about how much of Meade's army he might have to face that day, Lee was quick to seize the opportunity that chance was offering him. Seldom had he been presented an opening like this to strike the enemy's front and flank simultaneously. "Wait awhile and I will send you word when to go in," he told Heth. Heth hurried back to his division on the Chambersburg Pike and, he wrote, "very soon an aide came to me with orders to attack."

Four days before, talking to General Isaac Trimble, Lee had speculated about his hopes for engaging the enemy in circumstances eerily similar to what was happening on this 1st of July. At the time, he had predicted the Federal army would come up through Frederick into Pennsylvania strung out and exhausted by hard marching. He would then strike its advance with "an overwhelming force," crush it, drive one corps back upon another, and "create a panic and virtually destroy the army." Now, today, it was learned from prisoners that Heth had encountered the First Corps, the advance of the Army of the Potomac. Suddenly Lee found himself in the position to crush this advance, driving one Yankee corps back upon another. Furthermore, Lee had predicted to Trimble (and also to Dick Ewell) that such an encounter might take place at Gettysburg. There were two important differences between prediction and reality, however. This clash of armies on July 1 was by chance rather than by Lee's choice; and Lee lacked any knowledge of the Federals beyond their advance guard.[22]

The 88th Pennsylvania's Lieutenant George Grant made note of a sudden quiet along the Mummasburg Road following the repulse of O'Neal's and Iverson's brigades, but he sensed "it was only the calm preceding the storm." However brief the lull, Henry Baxter used it to pull his brigade out of the line before the Rebels renewed their attack. It was 3:00 P.M. now, and after almost two hours of fighting his men were down to their last few cartridges. General Robinson moved up Gabriel Paul's brigade to take Baxter's place. Paul would be facing long odds — Ramseur's and Daniel's and Doles's fresh brigades bent on regaining the impetus of Robert Rodes's stalled offensive.

Paul's brigade, assuming the same shallow V-formation as had Baxter's, facing west and north, contended initially with Dodson Ramseur's North Carolinians. Paul's brigade was very much a geographic mix — 16th Maine, 13th Massachusetts, 107th Pennsylvania, 94th and 104th

New York — and Paul was new to its command, but it made a steadfast, stubborn fight. Early on, General Paul was shot in the face and blinded, and before the afternoon's fighting was done, three more officers pressed into command of the brigade would fall wounded. Stretches of fences and stone walls changed hands after sharp local attacks and counterattacks. Major Abner Small of the 16th Maine captured the moment: "I remember the still trees in the heat, and the bullets whistling over us, and the stone wall bristling with muskets, and the line of our men, sweating and grimy, firing and loading and firing again, and here a man suddenly lying still, and there another rising all bloody and cursing and starting for the surgeon."

Paul's brigade formed the angular link between the First Corps facing west and the Eleventh Corps facing north, and it clung fiercely to that critical position despite Dodson Ramseur's best efforts. Only when their flanks were threatened by Rodes's remaining uncommitted forces, the brigades of Daniel and Doles, would Paul's Yankees have to face the prospect of retreat or being cut off.[23]

THE FIRST THREAT to Paul's left or western flank would come from Daniel's North Carolina brigade. Junius Daniel was a West Pointer, a big man with a powerful voice and a pronounced martial bearing who had last commanded his brigade in the Department of North Carolina and who on this day was making his combat-command debut in Lee's army. The men of his brigade, the largest in Rodes's division, had very limited battle experience, but they were well drilled and Daniel had them well in hand. Initially he had to divert two of his regiments to the rescue of Iverson's bungled attack, and they sparred with Baxter's and then Paul's Yankees. With only the 32nd and 45th North Carolina and the 2nd North Carolina battalion, Daniel then attempted to break the First Corps line to the south and west along the Chambersburg Pike. Like every other Rebel attacker that day, he was greeted by a sudden and deadly fire.

The defenders here were from Thomas Rowley's (formerly Doubleday's) First Corps division — Roy Stone's brigade of Pennsylvanians that Stone had christened the "Bucktail Brigade." Stone had been an officer with the original Bucktails, the 13th Pennsylvania Reserves, skilled hunters who advertised their marksmanship by pinning the tails of bucks to their caps, and he so named and so decorated his new brigade to enhance morale. At the moment that morale was being tested by a crossfire laid on the brigade from north and west by the Rebel artillerists. Colonel Stone devised a ruse. He had the colors of the 149th Pennsylvania shifted some fifty yards to the left front of the brigade. The enemy gunners obligingly shifted their aim to this new target. This proved to be a trial for the 149th's color guard, but a considerable relief to the rest of the brigade.[24]

As he awaited the advance of the enemy's infantry, Colonel Langhorne Wister of the 150th Pennsylvania, Stone's brigade, was startled to see a civilian approach him on the firing line and announce that he wanted to join the fight. He was an incongruous figure, grizzled, well advanced in years, wearing a long linen duster and a high-crowned felt hat and carrying a flintlock musket, a powder horn, and a pocketful of bullets. This proved to be John Burns, age sixty-nine, veteran (noncombat) of the War of 1812, former constable of the borough of Gettysburg, regarded by his fellow citizens as cantankerous and something of a town character. Colonel Wister decided the man was serious but that this was too exposed a place for him. He sent him off to the left, to McPherson's Woods, where he would have cover and be shaded from the midday sun. John Burns went on to make his fight that afternoon with the Iron Brigade — "I pitched in with them Wisconsin fellers," he would say — blazing away from behind a tree until he was nicked by three bullets and concluded his fighting career. He was noticed in General Doubleday's report, would meet Mr. Lincoln, and in the years left to him would be lionized as the "Old Patriot" of Gettysburg.[25]

July 1 marked the first major battlefield trial for both Stone's Pennsylvanians and Daniel's North Carolinians. Both met the trial with the flinty resolve of veterans. Daniel's first assault was severely undermanned and was soon thrown back by the Bucktails, assisted by Colonel Wainwright's guns. Some of the Rebels ducked into the railroad cut north of the pike, and, as Harry Heth's men had discovered that morning, found it a dubious shelter. Lieutenant James Stewart's Battery B, 4th U.S., had the angle to fire down the length of the cut, helping to turn it into what one of Daniel's staff called "that horrible hole." As Lieutenant Stewart reported it, "meeting with such a storm of lead and iron, they broke and ran over the rising ground entirely out of sight." The 149th Pennsylvania, in pursuit, chased off the last of the Rebels and took up a position along the north rim of the cut.

In a booming voice General Daniel rallied his scattered troops and collected his other two regiments and renewed the assault at full strength against Stone's brigade. During this second attack, the railroad cut between the two battle lines once again became a deadly no man's land.

While the cut seemed to offer an inviting shelter from cannon fire and musketry, it was only really useful defensively at either end, where it was shallow enough to serve as a trench. For most of its length through McPherson's Ridge the sides of the cut were high and steep, forming a trap rather than a refuge. The 149th Pennsylvania, for example, defended the cut to good effect for a time — its lieutenant colonel reported opening a murderous fire at the advancing Rebels at a range of precisely twenty-two paces — but when finally forced back it lost some 30 men captured who could not climb out to the rear fast enough. The Southerners, in their turn, could not hold the line of the railroad either, and fell back to their starting point. During this exchange Colonel Stone was badly wounded and captured, and his successor, Colonel Wister of the 150th Pennsylvania, was shot in the face. The Bucktails girded for the next assault under the command of Colonel Edmund Dana of the 143rd Pennsylvania.[26]

By now, as if two extended powder trains had been lit, the afternoon battle was expanding explosively out from its center, erupting across an ever wider front. Even as Paul's and Stone's brigades, under their replacement commanders, clung stubbornly to their positions at the hinge connecting the Federal northern and western battle lines, the extremities of those lines came under attack and began to crumble.

Abner Doubleday, whatever his shifting official status, had sole responsibility for the First Corps from first to last on July 1. General Howard, on his one visit to McPherson's Ridge, merely told Doubleday to hold on as long as he could and then retreat. Not long afterward, watching the massive buildup of A. P. Hill's forces to the west, Doubleday sent his adjutant E. P. Halstead to Howard to say that unless he had the support of von Steinwehr's Eleventh Corps division, then in reserve on Cemetery Hill, his corps would be sacrificed. If support was not forthcoming, Doubleday wanted permission to retire to the better defensive position on Seminary Ridge while he "was still able to do so in good order."

Howard refused him both von Steinwehr and the withdrawal order. When Major Halstead pointed out a column of enemy troops about to overlap the First Corps' flank, Howard snapped, "Those are nothing but rail fences, sir!" To prove it he had a staff man focus his glasses on the spot, only to be told, "General, those are long lines of the enemy!" Howard looked, said Halstead, "the picture of despair," but with the stubbornness of the small-minded he still would not approve a pullback to Seminary Ridge. He did say, "you may find Buford and use him," but since Colonel Gamble's troopers already guarded Doubleday's left, it was an empty gesture. The First Corps would have to stand, or fall, on McPherson's Ridge.[27]

Colonel Charles Wainwright, the First Corps' chief of artillery, had finished posting his guns and was studying the scene to the west with growing concern. He would write in his diary that as he watched, "a long column of rebels came out of the wood a mile or so in our front, and filed off to our left. This was soon joined by another column, which when they faced into line formed a second line for them. They marched along quietly and with confidence, but swiftly. I watched them from the battery, and am confident that when they advanced they outflanked us at least half a mile on our left."

This July 1 fighting marked the first test of the Potomac army's new artillery command system — batteries grouped in brigades, one brigade per infantry corps, to be directed only by the corps commander and his artillery chief — and Wainwright found it working somewhat raggedly. Divisional commander Wadsworth, for example, as ardent as he was inexperienced and undisciplined, kept ordering batteries right up to the firing line without furnishing the infantry support vital to their survival. When Wainwright wasn't quietly repositioning his guns, a colonel working around a brigadier general, he was having to cope with the strange doings of another brigadier, Thomas Rowley. Put in command of the Third Division when Doubleday took over the First Corps, General Rowley rushed around in a highly agitated state, throwing out bewildering orders right and left. Wainwright was convinced the man was drunk. At one point Rowley had men of Chapman Biddle's brigade posted squarely in front of the battery it was supposed to be supporting. As it was, Wainwright concluded that the prospects for holding McPherson's Ridge were slight, "even had our Third Division commanders had any idea what to do with their men, which they had not."[28]

The columns of Rebel troops Wainwright saw deploying for battle were the last two uncommitted brigades of Harry Heth's division, commanded by John Brockenbrough and Johnston Pettigrew. It was Pettigrew's brigade that overlapped the Federal left — four Tar Heel regiments up from the Department of North Carolina, almost 2,600 strong and the largest brigade in the army, most of them facing their first serious combat this day. Awaiting them on the flank was Chapman Biddle's brigade. Undermanned to begin with, Colonel Biddle had just seen his largest regiment, the 151st Pennsylvania, pulled back to Seminary Ridge to act as the First Corps' sole reserve. Biddle's position was an unpromising one, entirely in the open and with no terrain feature on which to anchor a defense. At the point of contact on the far Federal left, then, the 1,120 men of the 47th and 52nd North Carolina confronted the 886 men of the 121st and 142nd Pennsylvania and the 80th New York.

"The order rang along the line, 'Fire, fire,' and we all discharged our guns and commenced to load and fire at will . . . ," remembered Yankee Private Edwin Gearhart. "The enemy were not getting close but still they came." They came close most quickly against the left-hand regiment, the 121st Pennsylvania. Major Alexander Biddle, cousin of the brigade commander, tried to refuse the 121st's line to face the attackers curling around his flank, but he ran out of both men and time. As the faces of the Rebels in line of battle appeared over the crest of the ridgeline, Biddle wrote, "we fired effectually into them, and, soon after, received a crushing fire from their right, under which our ranks were broken and became massed together as we endeavored to change front. . . ."

Brigade commander Chapman Biddle rode right into this tangle, waving the national colors in a bold attempt to rally his wavering men. Then his horse was killed and his scalp was creased by a bullet and the flag went down and was lost, and, as Major Biddle put it, "it was soon evident the position was no longer ours." One of the retreating men admitted that the speed made by the 121st Pennsylvania in reaching Seminary Ridge "was remarkable, perhaps the best on record." In recognizing the bravery of Colonel Biddle, the historian of the 47th North Carolina noted that it was with "openly expressed pleasure our men heard he was not killed."

The collapse of Biddle's flank regiment doomed the next regiments in line, the 80th New York and the 142nd Pennsylvania, leaving first one and then the other open to simultaneous attack from front and flank. Both regiments attempted that most difficult of feats, a fighting withdrawal, starting back toward Seminary Ridge at a measured pace, turning frequently to fire at their tormentors. "Someone yelled retreat . . . ," Private Gearhart of the 142nd Pennsylvania recalled. "Our line kept falling back slowly firing as it went, but, the enemy giving us a heavy volley at pretty close range, we broke." As he tried to stem the tide, the 142nd's Colonel Robert Cummins went down with a severe wound, and the party of his men carrying him to the rear was shot to pieces until just one man was left. Wounded himself, unable to carry his burden any farther, he rescued the dying officer's sword and bade him a tearful Godspeed.[29]

With the Iron Brigade in McPherson's Woods already fiercely engaged against Brockenbrough's Virginians and Pettigrew's other two North

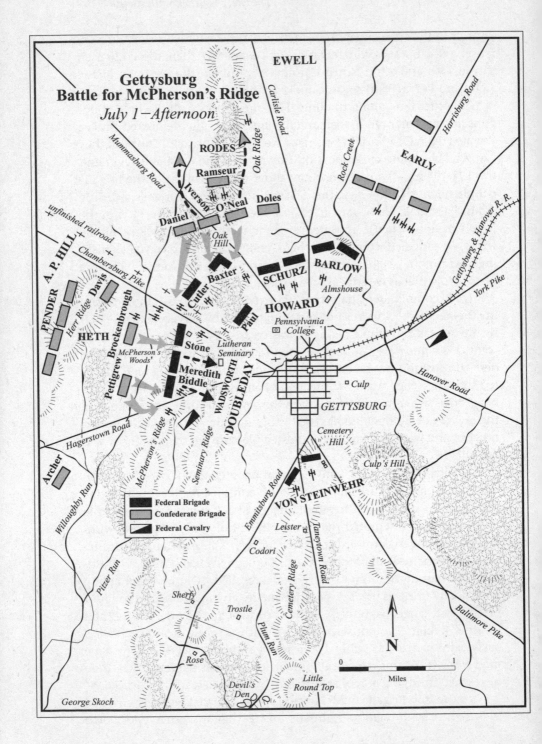

Gettysburg
Battle for McPherson's Ridge
July 1–Afternoon

EWELL

RODES

Ramseur

Iverson

O'Neal

Doles

Daniel

Oak Hill

EARLY

Oak Ridge

Carlisle Road

Mummasburg Road

unfinished railroad

Chambersburg Pike

PENDER

A. P. HILL

Herr Ridge

Davis

HETH

Brockenbrough

Pettigrew

McPherson's
Woods'

Baxter

Cutler

SCHURZ

BARLOW

Paul

Almshouse

HOWARD

Pennsylvania
College

Stone

Lutheran
Seminary

Rock Creek

Harrisburg Road

Gettysburg & Hanover R. R.

York Pike

Meredith
Biddle

WADSWORTH

DOUBLEDAY

Culp

GETTYSBURG

Hanover Road

Hagerstown Road

McPherson's Ridge

Seminary Ridge

Archer

Cemetery
Hill

Culp's Hill

Federal Brigade
Confederate Brigade
Federal Cavalry

Emmitsburg Road

VON STEINWEHR

Leister

Taneytown Road

Codori

Cemetery Ridge

Pitzer Run

Willoughby Run

Sherfy

Trostle

Plum Run

Baltimore Pike

N

0   1

Miles

Rose

Devil's
Den

Little
Round Top

George Skoch

208

Carolina regiments, it was essential that Doubleday somehow shore up his swiftly eroding left flank. His only reserve was the 151st Pennsylvania, on Seminary Ridge. He ordered it forward to try and seal off the threat to the Iron Brigade's flank. The 151st was one of only two nine-month Pennsylvania regiments still in the Army of the Potomac, and was due to go home before the end of July. With the exception of a brief skirmish at Chancellorsville, it had never before been on a battlefield.

When the 151st arrived on the field, its commander, Lieutenant Colonel George F. McFarland, said that he had "cautioned the men against excitement and firing at random. . . ." When in due course they went into action, he "did not order them to fire a regular volley, but each man to fire as he saw an enemy on which to take a steady aim." That was a good deal to expect of untried troops, but his Pennsylvanians coolly met the challenge and, McFarland reported with satisfaction, "many of the enemy were brought low."

The First Corps' battlefront on McPherson's Ridge was narrowed now to less than a thousand yards, from the Chambersburg Pike south through McPherson's Woods and into a grassy field beyond. Near the pike the 150th Pennsylvania from Stone's brigade faced west and helped drive off the initial assaults of two of Brockenbrough's regiments. The Iron Brigade in the center turned McPherson's Woods into a citadel against Brockenbrough's Virginians and Pettigrew's North Carolinians. Having already broken Biddle's brigade, Pettigrew could now focus entirely on the Iron Brigade — and on the late-arriving 151st Pennsylvania. "The fighting was terrible," wrote the 26th North Carolina's Major John T. Jones; " — our men advancing, the enemy stubbornly resisting, until the two lines were pouring volleys into each other at a distance not greater than 20 paces."

"It was a very hot day and I was in a hot place," Corporal Nathan Cooper of the 151st Pennsylvania wrote to his wife of this struggle. "My gun got so hot I could scarcely hold to it. The bullets was thick as hail. . . . I was just as cool and composed as I ever was butchering hogs. The men were falling every second but I paid no attention to them. I could not help them."

The Iron Brigade's left-hand regiment, the 19th Indiana, was forced to fight at the edge of McPherson's Woods facing south as well as west. The fire from the south, delivered mostly by the 11th North Carolina, was particularly destructive. According to the 19th's Lieutenant Colonel William W. Dudley, its effect was literally annihilating: "The line was held as long as there were men left to hold it." When they saw the 151st Penn-

Allen Redwood of the 55th Virginia, Brockenbrough's brigade, depicted his regiment doing battle with the Iron Brigade at the McPherson barn during the afternoon of July 1. (Century Collection)

sylvania come up from the rear, the Hoosiers thought it was their much-needed relief and pulled back through the woods. Fully half of them had been killed or wounded.[30]

Grudgingly, step by step, the Iron Brigade was now pressed back toward Seminary Ridge. Its commander, Long Sol Meredith, went down with a head wound and was additionally injured when his riddled horse fell on him. The most savage and relentless of the fighting here involved the 24th Michigan against the 26th North Carolina. "I have taken part in many hotly contested fights," Lieutenant Louis Young of General Pettigrew's staff would write, "but this, I think, was the deadliest of them all. . . ." The battle lines here closed to within forty yards, then twenty yards. The slaughter was mutual and assured. The 26th North Carolina's Company F entered the fight with ninety-one officers and men, and at the close all ninety-one were dead or wounded. The 26th witnessed fourteen of its color bearers shot down, including the regimental commander, Colonel Henry K. Burgwyn, fatally wounded by a bullet through his chest. The 24th Michigan had nine color bearers hit, including *its* commander, Colonel Henry A. Morrow, wounded in the head and captured. The only man of the Michigan color guard still alive at the end of the day was badly wounded.

In the midst of this maelstrom, a bullet struck Harry Heth in the head. All that saved him, he would later say, was his hat. It was a new felt hat he had picked up in Cashtown, the band of which his aide had stuffed with tightly folded paper to make it fit properly. It was this reinforcement, said General Heth, that deflected the bullet enough that it only cracked his skull instead of killing him.

Finally the repeated anvil blows from front and flank became too great for the heavily outnumbered Yankees, and General Doubleday passed the word to the First Corps to fall back to Seminary Ridge. The struggle for McPherson's Ridge was over at last. Colonel Brockenbrough, discouraged by his initial rebuffs, had failed to press ahead with his Virginia brigade, leaving Johnston Pettigrew's North Carolinians to bear the burden of the Confederate assault. Both Pettigrew and his Tar Heels were new to sustained combat; both he and they proved more than equal to the test. But the cost was staggering. The brigade lost more than a thousand men. The 26th North Carolina had gone into battle with 840 men — it was the largest regiment in the Confederate army — and that night would count but 216 men still standing. The battered and bloodied Yankees stood defiantly on Seminary Ridge, but to dislodge them would now require Dorsey Pender's fresh division.[31]

AS THE STRUGGLE for McPherson's Ridge grew in intensity and violence, at the opposite end of the battlefield Dick Ewell's Rebels were exerting a comparable crushing pressure on the Eleventh Corps. In parallel to what was happening to their western front, the Federals' northern front was overlapped and crumpled by fresh enemy troops.

Major General Oliver Otis Howard entered the Gettysburg campaign believing that both he and his Eleventh Corps had a burden to bear and much to prove. Howard had been mortified when Jackson routed the Eleventh Corps at Chancellorsville. "I wanted to die . . . ," he insisted. "That night . . . I sought death everywhere I could find an excuse to go on the field." Three days later when Hooker called his generals together to debate continuing the campaign or retreating, Howard voted to stay and fight; his corps, he said, was responsible for the crisis, and he sought its redemption. Now, on this afternoon of July 1, Howard appeared still to be seeking that redemption. Once again, as at Chancellorsville, the Eleventh Corps formed the extreme right of the army, and in his stubborn refusal to fall back to better defensive positions, on either front, Howard had the look of a general out to prove that whatever the cost, this time the men under his command would stand their ground and fight.[32]

Carl Schurz, moved up to command of the two Eleventh Corps divisions in the field by Howard's elevation to the overall command, faced a simple but daunting problem. On the ground he was required to defend there were in his four small brigades too few men to deploy in standard line of battle. Furthermore, the ground north of Gettysburg was, militarily speaking, largely featureless — something over a square mile of farm fields, open and flat and without cover. Finally, Schurz faced a particular problem at the extreme right of the line, where Francis Barlow had advanced his division several hundred yards ahead of the neighboring division in order to seize the only elevation on the field, a modest hillock called Blocher's Knoll.

The logic of the moment behind Barlow's taking of Blocher's Knoll was to prevent the Rebel troops then visible to the north — George Doles's brigade, of Rodes's division — from occupying it and using it as an artillery platform. Barlow insisted he acted "as directed," a claim General Howard in his memoirs confirmed. Carl Schurz in *his* memoirs said that Barlow must have misunderstood his orders. However that may be, Schurz's own division (now under Alexander Schimmelfennig) was thereby stretched and thinned in places to little more than a one-rank-deep skirmish line in order to connect with Barlow. Schurz sent an aide pelting back to Cemetery Hill to plead with Howard for all or part of von Steinwehr's division from the reserve, but it was soon evident that the enemy was not going to grant time for reinforcements to arrive.[33]

Sweeping along the Harrisburg Road toward this cobbled-together line was Jubal Early's division, deployed in a three-brigade-wide battle front that was almost a mile across — and overlapped the Union line by almost half a mile. Here again, the god of battles was smiling south this day. When Ewell's order came that morning to turn south toward Gettysburg, Early happened to be positioned to take the Harrisburg Road, which slanted across the prospective battlefield at exactly the right angle to turn the Eleventh Corps' flank. Like Robert Rodes before him, "Old Jube" announced his presence with an artillery barrage, delivered against the enemy flank by Hilary Jones's battalion. Jones quickly established superiority over Barlow's guns. Early then pitched John B. Gordon's brigade of Georgians straight at Blocher's Knoll.

It was Early's thought to fix the Federal defenders in place with Gordon's frontal attack, then swing around their exposed flank with the brigades of Harry Hays and Isaac Avery. At the same time, to Early's right, Doles's Georgians would open an assault in tandem with Gordon's Georgians. John B. Gordon was a self-taught soldier with a talent for inspiring his men and personally dominating a battlefield. This day he rode a splendid black stallion captured from the Yankees at Winchester. Ordering the charge, Gordon on his warhorse was just behind the battle line, "right in among the slanting barrels and bayonets . . . ," wrote artillerist Robert Stiles, "standing in his stirrups, bareheaded, hat in hand, arms extended, and, in a voice like a trumpet, exhorting his men. It was superb; absolutely thrilling."

The immediate object of Gordon's charge was Colonel Leopold von Gilsa's brigade posted on Blocher's Knoll, and to von Gilsa's three undermanned, largely German regiments — barely 900 men all told — it must have seemed a nightmare revisited. Only two months before, two of these regiments had been the initial target of Stonewall Jackson's Chancellorsville attack, and if this day's attack was less of a surprise than the earlier one, it was no less unnerving. The Georgians splashed across Rock Creek and came straight up the hill at them, hallooing the Rebel yell.

The men of the 54th and 68th New York stood and fought as long as they could, but that was not long and they were overwhelmed and forced back. This in turn left the supporting 153rd Pennsylvania to absorb the full weight of Gordon's attack. The 153rd, with the 151st the only nine-month Pennsylvania regiments still with the army, was looking forward to going home on July 24. It had been mauled by Jackson at Chancellorsville, losing 85 men there, and now it was to lose another 211 at Gettysburg — a stiff price for a short-term "emergency" regiment to have to pay. Private Reuben Ruch, himself wounded, recalled the 153rd's dead: "They were piled in every shape, some on their backs, some on their faces, and others turned and twisted in every imaginable shape."[34]

Francis Channing Barlow was cast from the same mold as his opponent, John Brown Gordon — a self-taught volunteer whose rise through the ranks was fueled by gritty determination in leading men in battle. Barlow had been given his Eleventh Corps command in May for the purpose of inserting backbone into the division that had paced the rout at

Chancellorsville, but today he was sorely disappointed with the result of his efforts. "We ought to have held the place easily," he wrote home a few days later of Blocher's Knoll, "for I had my entire force at the very point where the attack was made. But the enemies skirmishers had hardly attacked us before my men began to run. No fight at all was made." Barlow afterward elaborated on the point: "But these Dutch won't fight. Their officers say so & they say so themselves & they ruin all with whom they come in contact." Spurring his horse into the melee to try and form a second line, Barlow took a bullet in the side. He dismounted and attempted to walk off the field — "Everybody was then running to the rear & the enemy were approaching rapidly," he explained — but he collapsed from shock and loss of blood. Moments later, riding with the advance, Gordon came on Barlow, identified him as an officer probably by his shoulder straps, and in a nice gesture ordered him carried to the rear for medical attention.

One of Gordon's Rebels was more generous in his judgment of the Germans than was Barlow. "They then began to retreat in fine order, shooting at us as they retreated," wrote G. W. Nichols of the 61st Georgia. "They were harder to drive than we had ever known them before." However that may be, however much of a fight it put up initially, von Gilsa's brigade when it broke was not to be stopped. Von Gilsa did his best, riding in among the fleeing men, shouting at them to rally and delivering mighty oaths in German.

Their collapse left Barlow's second brigade, under Adelbert Ames, in a critical position. Already assaulted in front by Doles's brigade, it was now taken in the flank by Gordon's. Ames sought to stem the flood by counterattacking with his 75th Ohio and 17th Connecticut, but the enemy's crossfire of artillery and musketry stopped them in their tracks. The 17th Connecticut was further demoralized when its commander was decapitated by a shell from one of Hilary Jones's guns. Ames joined von Gilsa in disordered retreat. The case was summed up by Colonel Andrew L. Harris of the 75th Ohio: "The pressure soon became so great and the fire of the enemy so hot and deadly that it was evident our brigade and in fact the division could not long hold its ground." In perhaps twenty minutes of intense combat, Blocher's Knoll fell to the Confederates, and the entire right of the Eleventh Corps' line was gone with it.

Among the Union dead from this fight for Blocher's Knoll was nineteen-year-old Lieutenant Bayard Wilkeson, commanding Battery G, 4th U.S. Artillery. Young Wilkeson was the son of correspondent Samuel Wilkeson, covering the campaign for the *New York Times*. Three days

Lieutenant Bayard Wilkeson, center, was mortally wounded directing his Union battery in the defense of Blocher's Knoll, on the Federal right, on July 1. Drawing by Alfred Waud. (Historic New Orleans Collection)

later Sam Wilkeson began his story for the *Times*, "Who can write the history of a battle whose eyes are immovably fastened upon a central figure of transcendingly absorbing interest — the dead body of an oldest born son, crushed by a shell in a position where a battery should never have been sent, and abandoned to death in a building where surgeons dared not to stay?"[35]

Now the Eleventh's other division, under General Schimmelfennig, attempted to take up the struggle. Colonel Wladimir Krzyzanowski's brigade, advancing across the open fields in compact marching formation, was bracketed by a deadly crossfire from Rodes's and Early's batteries. An Ohio captain remembered how "their shells plunged through our solid squares, making terrible havoc." Then, as they deployed, Doles's infantry took them under fire. Captain Theodore Dodge, 119th New York, watched the two battle lines exchanging volleys hardly 100 yards apart: "Every five or six seconds some poor fellow would throw up his arms with an 'Ugh!' and drop. . . . Another would drop flat on his face, or his back, without a sound; another would break down, and fall together in a heap. . . . One brave boy near me, I remember, shot in the leg, sat there loading and firing with as much regularity and coolness as if untouched, now and then shouting to some comrade in front of him to make room for his shot. . . ."

This battle-line stalemate was shortly broken by what was becoming a pattern for Federal defeat on this Wednesday afternoon. Krzyzanowski's brigade was chipped away, one regiment after another, by Early's troops angling in against its flank. It fell back in confusion toward the town. Schimmelfennig launched a last-ditch counterattack, using the 157th New York from his last uncommitted brigade, Colonel George von Amsberg's. It was a disaster. Doles's Georgians pounced on the New Yorkers from three directions. "The men were falling rapidly," wrote the 157th's Colonel Philip Brown, "and the enemy's line was taking the form of a giant semi-circle . . . , concentrating the fire of their whole brigade upon my rapidly diminishing numbers." By the time Colonel Brown could finally extract his regiment from the trap, it had suffered 307 casualties — 75 percent of its numbers.

In the midst of this action, General Doles's horse suddenly bolted — straight for the Federal line. The general's best efforts to rein him in were unavailing, and at the last moment he threw himself off. Fortunately he landed in a field of tall wheat and escaped the enemy's notice. Remarkably, both horse and badly shaken general made it back safely to the Confederate lines.

From the start, confronting the well-positioned and well-led Confederate assaults, the Eleventh Corps' defense was confused and incoherent. Early was able to break through the Federal lines initially without even using the flanking brigades of Hays and Avery. Gordon and Doles, although outnumbered overall, brought greater numbers and superior tactics to bear at each point of contact with the enemy. There would be no redemption for the poor Dutchmen of the Eleventh Corps.[36]

General Howard sent Schurz a battery and one of the two infantry brigades from von Steinwehr's reserve force, under Colonel Charles Coster, but the move was too late and only added to the casualty list. Hays's and Avery's brigades swarmed around the flank of Coster's hastily formed battle line just north of the town. As the Rebels bore down on him, recalled the 154th New York's Private Charles McKay, "It seemed as though

they had a battle flag every few rods, which would indicate that their formation was in solid column," and he added, "Our fire did good execution. . . ." Coster's brigade did win some valuable time for Schurz's retiring columns, but soon enough it too was joining the retreat. "We shot
them down, bayoneted them & captured more prisoners than we had
men," reported Lieutenant Joseph Jackson of the 8th Louisiana. Coster
had led some 800 men to the battlefield; 313 of them left it as prisoners.
Two of the four guns of the reinforcing battery were captured as well.

About this time Dick Ewell was hurrying to Early's front to follow the
action there when a shell fragment killed his horse and he was thrown violently to the ground. Staff men helped him up and found him another
horse, and he rode on, not injured beyond a shaking up.

The Eleventh Corps' collapse was complete by 4 o'clock. It had taken
the Rebels no more than an hour. The toll would come to some 3,200
men (1,400 of them prisoners), about half the force General Schurz was
able to get to the firing line that afternoon. The losses in Gordon's and
Doles's brigades did not exceed 750.[37]

ON SEMINARY RIDGE, meanwhile, Colonel Charles Wainwright was
massing his guns for a last-ditch defense of the Federals' western flank.
An order had reached him from General Howard's headquarters that
Cemetery Hill was to be held "at all hazards." The German aide who
delivered the message spoke broken English, however, and Wainwright
knew nothing of any cemetery, and he assumed that what was meant
was the Lutheran Seminary's hill. That in any case was where his batteries were, and he grimly prepared to do battle, at all hazards, to the bitter end.

This renewed contest on the First Corps' front matched Wainwright's
guns, supported by the infantry of the Iron Brigade and Biddle's and
Stone's brigades, what little was left of them, against two fresh Confederate brigades from Dorsey Pender's division. A. P. Hill had brought Pender
along that morning as a support for Harry Heth, and now that Heth had
exhausted his division driving the Yankees off McPherson's Ridge, it became Pender's task to drive them off Seminary Ridge. Pender chose Alfred Scales's North Carolinians and Abner Perrin's South Carolinians for
the job. Perrin's brigade, overlapping the Federals' left flank, had the key
position in the attack. Abner Perrin had been a company captain at
Fredericksburg, a regimental commander at Chancellorsville, and was
now leading a brigade for the first time. Alfred Scales, too, was a first-time
brigade commander.

As these First Corps Yankees had demonstrated throughout this day of battle, they were extremely stubborn about giving up ground, whatever the odds against them. Centering their line in the grove around the Lutheran Seminary building, they took cover behind a stone wall and some rough fence-rail breastworks and opened a blistering fire on the advancing Carolinians. Wainwright had massed eighteen guns on a front only 200 yards wide, and they laid down a devastating barrage. One section commander of Battery B, 1st Pennsylvania Light, had an oblique angle on the attackers, Wainwright wrote, and "His round shot, together with the canister poured in from all the other guns, was cutting great gaps in the front line of the enemy." Colonel William Robinson of the 7th Wisconsin found a stark simile for the slaughter: "When they were within easy range, the order was given, and their ranks went down like grass before the scythe. . . ." In Scales's brigade the general was wounded by a shell fragment, and in his five regiments every field officer but one was killed or wounded. Scales launched his attack that afternoon with 1,350 men. That evening barely 500 answered roll call.[38]

With Scales's brigade stunned into paralysis, the burden of the attack fell on Perrin's brigade. It too was greeted ferociously. The color bearers of all four regiments were killed almost immediately. A man in Company K, 14th South Carolina, recalled the scene: "At the charge bayonets, the enemy was behind a rock fence and we could hear their officers distinctly encouraging their men to hold their fire until the command to fire was given. They obeyed their command implicitly and rose to their feet, took as deliberate aim as if they were on dress parade, and to show you how accurate their aim was, 34 out of our 39 men fell at the first fire of the enemy."

As his brigade wavered, Colonel Perrin rode out ahead of the line and redirected the assault more toward the Union flank. He had detected a gap in the Union line — some 50 yards, between Chapman Biddle's left-hand regiment, the 121st Pennsylvania, and Colonel Gamble's flank guard of cavalrymen — and drove straight for it. Perrin himself led the charge. "Filled with admiration for such courage as defied the whole fire of the enemy," wrote J.F.J. Caldwell of the 1st South Carolina, ". . . the brigade followed, with a shout that was itself half a victory."[39]

The fate of the Federals' McPherson's Ridge line was now exactly repeated on Seminary Ridge. Lacking the men to extend its battle line southward far enough to match the enemy's line, Biddle's brigade unraveled, regiment by regiment, under Perrin's deadly flanking fire. This in turn imperiled the rest of the First Corps line. The 6th Wisconsin's Rufus

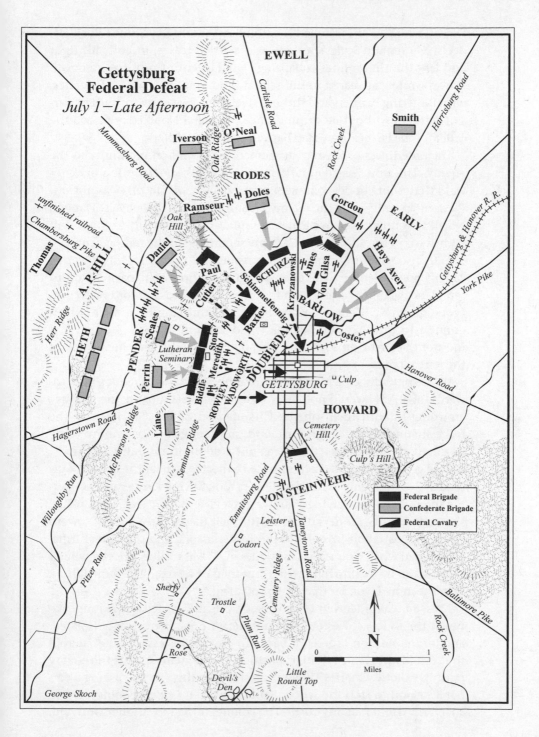

Gettysburg Federal Defeat

July 1—Late Afternoon

EWELL

Carlisle Road

Harrisburg Road

Smith

Mummasburg Road

Iverson   O'Neal

Oak Ridge

RODES

Doles

Gordon   EARLY

Ramseur

Oak Hill

Gettysburg & Hanover R. R.

unfinished railroad

Chambersburg Pike

Thomas

A. P. HILL

Daniel

Paul

SCHURZ

Hays Avery

Cutter

Schimmelfennig

Krzyzanowski

Ames

Von Gilsa

York Pike

Herr Ridge

HETH

Scales

PENDER

Perrin

Lutheran Seminary

Stone

Meredith

Baxter

BARLOW

Coster

Hagerstown Road

McPherson's Ridge

Willoughby Run

Biddle

ROWLEY

WADSWORTH

DOUBLEDAY

GETTYSBURG

Culp

Hanover Road

Lane

Seminary Ridge

HOWARD

Cemetery Hill

Culp's Hill

Emmitsburg Road

VON STEINWEHR

Pitzer Run

Leister

Federal Brigade

Confederate Brigade

Federal Cavalry

Codori

Cemetery Ridge

Taneytown Road

Baltimore Pike

Sherfy

Trostle

Plum Run

N

Rock Creek

Rose

Devil's Den

Little Round Top

0   Miles   1

George Skoch

Dawes, who had just watched the Iron Brigade and Roy Stone's Bucktails decisively repulse Scales's assault, was startled to see, to both his right and left, the Union lines collapsing. The Eleventh Corps to the north, Dawes wrote, "appeared in full retreat, and long lines of Confederates, with fluttering banners and shining steel, were sweeping forward in pursuit of them without let or hindrance." General Doubleday passed the order for the First Corps to fall back to Cemetery Hill.

The orderliness of the retreat seemed to depend on proximity to the enemy. The Iron Brigade and Stone's Bucktails generally fell back toward Gettysburg under some semblance of control, but this was not easily done in units with the enemy closing right on their heels. Daniel's North Carolinians renewed their assault, and Lieutenant Colonel William Lewis of the 43rd North Carolina reported, "At the railroad cut, 400 or 500 prisoners surrendered to the brigade. . . ." The 121st Pennsylvania, caught point-blank by the enemy's flanking fire, went back "without semblance of order," every man for himself. Nor did the word reach everyone promptly. Colonel Wainwright, still thinking he must hold his gunners to their task on Seminary Ridge "at all hazards," discovered most of the First Corps infantry already gone by the time he learned of the retreat order.

Wainwright directed his batteries to limber up "and move at a walk towards town." He would not allow them to trot lest it panic the infantry crowding in with them on the Chambersburg Pike. "As I sat on the hill watching my pieces file past, and cautioning each one not to trot," he entered in his diary, "there was not a doubt in my mind but that I should go to Richmond. Each minute I expected to hear the order to surrender. . . ." Suddenly Rebel skirmishers took the road under fire, scattering the infantry and giving Wainwright a clear path. "Trot! Gallop!" he shouted, and his gunners dashed with their pieces three abreast toward safety. His battalion loss would be three caissons and one 3-inch rifle, abandoned when its team was shot down. "I was terribly grieved when I heard about it," Wainwright wrote, but then he added, "The more I think of it, the more I wonder that we got off at all."[40]

These retreat orders left Gabriel Paul's brigade, posted at the hinge between the Federals' western and northern fronts, increasingly isolated, and John Robinson ordered it back. To buy the necessary time, he told the 16th Maine it must hold its position as rear guard against the enemy pursuit. Colonel Charles Tilden protested that this was like asking a corporal's guard to stop the whole Rebel army, but General Robinson was adamant: "Hold it at any cost!" The colonel turned to his men and said,

"You know what that means," and back they went to their stone wall by the Mummasburg Road. "We got there just as a flag and a line of battle showed up across the way," Major Abner Small wrote; "we heard distinctly the commands of a rebel officer directing his men to fire; and a volley crashed. . . . Our line blazed away in reply, and the rebel flag went down, and the officer pitched headlong in the stubble."

The attackers were Dodson Ramseur's North Carolinians, from Robert Rodes's division, and they were far too numerous to be held back for long. When Colonel Tilden saw nothing but butternut to both left and right as well as in front, he concluded the 16th Maine had done its job and ordered a retreat. When the Yankees reached the infamous railroad cut they found themselves trapped in a crossfire and it became every man for himself. The 16th Maine went into battle on July 1 with 298 men; that night Major Small counted 35 survivors.[41]

IT WAS AFTER 4 o'clock now, and the focus of the day's sprawling contest shrank abruptly to the streets of Gettysburg. The men of the Eleventh Corps had to pass through the town to reach the promised safety of Cemetery Hill directly to the south, and as they rushed into the narrow, crowded streets whatever order they might have retained was largely lost. A Union surgeon watching their flight wrote in his journal, "Away went guns and knapsacks, and they fled for dear life, forming a funnel shaped tail, extending to the town. . . . I did not see an officer attempt to rally or check them in their headlong retreat." Captain Frederick Winkler of Krzyzanowski's brigade was appalled by the scene: "It seemed so awful to march back through those same streets whipped and beaten. It was the most humiliating step I ever took."

General Early turned his division's pursuit over to Hays's Louisianians and Avery's North Carolinians, and they came rushing into Gettysburg from the north right on the heels of the Eleventh Corps. On Stratton Street there was a bloody hand-to-hand struggle for the flag of the 154th New York, and although 172 of the New Yorkers would be captured this day, their flag was saved. Before long the First Corps began to join the exodus, multiplying the noise and the chaos — and the bloodshed — in the streets. No one at headquarters had thought to designate withdrawal routes for the two corps, compounding the confusion. On High Street there was another battle for Union colors, this time those of the 150th Pennsylvania; and this time the Yankee soldiers could not save their flag. It would in due course be presented to President Jefferson Davis.

Abner Perrin's South Carolinians entered the town from the west behind the First Corps. Sergeant John Leach, 1st South Carolina, would remember that as they hurried into Gettysburg they saw, visible down the cross streets, solid columns of Federals marching on parallel streets both north and south of them; "why we were not all captured has been a mystery to me," he wrote.[42]

Gettysburg's citizens were in a turmoil. Since morning a growing flood of wounded men had been brought into public buildings and dozens of private homes. Refugees — including every free black who had not already left — crowded the roads south and east of town. Those who stayed sought whatever shelter they could find, including the vault of the Gettysburg Bank. Now, in late afternoon, the war surged right into the heart of town. Stray shells plunged through roofs, canister and rifle fire rattled off storefronts. The streets were crowded with disheveled, running Union soldiers. "No one can imagine in what extreme fright we were in when our men began to retreat," Sarah Broadhead entered in her diary. An officer rode up to one family helping the wounded and shouted, "All you good people go down into your cellar or you will be killed!" Soon Rebel soldiers were on the scene too, and there was fighting in the streets. "We watched through the cellar windows," Liberty Hollinger remembered, "and Oh, what horror filled our breasts as we gazed upon their bayonets and heard the deafening roar of musketry. Yes, we were really in the midst of an awful reality."

Gettysburg was a closely built-up town, with narrow lanes and alleyways and lots enclosed by board fences, and fugitive soldiers trying to evade capture were likely to run themselves into traps. One such was Brigadier General Alexander Schimmelfennig. Schimmelfennig had been bringing up the rear of his command, trying to prod it into an orderly retreat, when in the confusion he became separated and found himself in a dead-end alley with shouting Rebels close behind. The general was in casual military dress, his rank not apparent, and when he scaled a high fence and dropped into the kitchen garden of the Henry Garlach family, his would-be captors did not bother chasing him. Discovering that there were Confederates on every side, the general concealed himself behind a woodpile. There he elected to wait out the battle, nourished by bread and water slipped to him by Mrs. Garlach.[43]

As bad as this Gettysburg scene was for the Federals that afternoon, it could have been even worse. The exceedingly high cost of the fighting for McPherson's Ridge and Seminary Ridge blinded A. P. Hill to a bright opportunity to seal the day's victory. In the brigades of James Lane, then lightly skirmishing with the Yankee cavalry, and Edward Thomas, which had yet to fire a shot, Dorsey Pender had 3,000 fresh troops with which he might have blocked the southern exits from Gettysburg. A prompt advance of only a mile by such a force would surely have swept up most of the First Corps' survivors, and perhaps a number of Eleventh Corps stragglers as well. But Lane and Thomas were not called out, leaving the pursuit to two of Abner Perrin's bloodied and exhausted South Carolina regiments.

The 1st South Carolina would triumphantly raise its flag in Gettysburg's town square, but by then most of the Yankees were gone. "If we had any support at all," Perrin later insisted, "we could have taken every piece of artillery they had and thousands of prisoners." General Hill displayed a surprisingly cautious turn of mind: ". . . my own two divisions exhausted by some six hours' hard fighting, prudence led me to be content with what had been gained, and not push forward troops exhausted and necessarily disordered, probably to encounter fresh troops of the enemy."[44]

When he finally gained Cemetery Hill with the few survivors of the 16th Maine, Major Abner Small encountered a welcome sight: "Directing the placing of troops where we turned up was Hancock, whose imperious and defiant bearing heartened us all." "Imperious and defiant" nicely summed up Major General Winfield Scott Hancock that afternoon. The head of the Second Corps, dispatched by General Meade to assume overall command at Gettysburg, arrived on Cemetery Hill between 4:00 and 4:30, about the same time as the battered First and Eleventh corps, and he quickly made his presence felt. Winfield Hancock on horseback made a splendid martial figure, with his great booming voice and his command of profanity and his knack for inspiring troops to fight.

Hancock came on Orland Smith's brigade of von Steinwehr's division — the sole infantry reserve on Cemetery Hill — in its posting overlooking Gettysburg, and Colonel Smith long remembered their brief conversation. "My corps is on the way but will not be here in time," Hancock told him. "This position should be held at all hazards. Now, Colonel, can you hold it?" "I think I can," Smith replied. Hancock said again, more sternly, "Will you hold it?" This time he got the answer he wanted: "I will!" Colonel Smith concluded his account, "And we did."[45]

Riding up to Howard's headquarters, Hancock saluted and said he had been instructed by General Meade to take command on the field. Somewhat flustered, Howard protested that he was the senior officer. "I am aware of that, General," Hancock said, "but I have written orders in my pocket from General Meade which I will show you if you wish to see them." Howard seems to have taken his demotion with the best grace possible under the circumstances — there was little else he could do — and Carl Schurz, for one, was complimentary: "Howard, in spite of his heart-sore, cooperated so loyally with Hancock that it would have been hard to tell which of the two was the commander and which the subordinate."

For the most part, Howard set out to rally the Eleventh Corps and post it for defense, and Hancock did the same for the First Corps. Hancock, however, made it abundantly clear that he was in charge. When he ordered Doubleday to send a force to hold Culp's Hill, on the right of the forming Union position, Doubleday objected that his men were fought out and short of ammunition. "General," said Hancock sharply, "I want you to understand that I am in command here. Send every man you have." The Iron Brigade was soon on its way to Culp's Hill.

Beyond the immediate need to hold Cemetery Hill and to infuse fresh fighting spirit into the two beaten corps, Hancock's instructions required him to cast his vote on the selection of a battlefield. "I think this the strongest position by nature upon which to fight a battle that I ever saw," he observed, and when Howard agreed, Hancock made it official: "Very well, sir, I select this as the battle-field." Gouverneur Warren, chief engineer of the Army of the Potomac, went over the ground with Hancock and concurred: "we came to the conclusion that . . . it would be the best place for the army to fight on if the army was attacked." Hancock reported this finding to General Meade in a 5:25 P.M. dispatch — "we can fight here," he reported, "as the ground appears not unfavorable with good troops." The battle that had begun so haphazardly that day at Gettysburg would continue at Gettysburg — if the Federals had anything to say about it.[46]

General Howard also reported to the general commanding, in the same uninformative manner as his earlier dispatches. In summarizing the day's fighting, he reversed the order of the culminating events ("The First Corps fell back, when outflanked on its left, to a stronger position, when the Eleventh Corps was ordered back, also to a stronger position.") and offered scarcely a hint of the dimensions of the defeat. Howard went even further in blackening the First Corps' fighting record for the day — in truth incomparably superior to that of Howard's own Eleventh Corps — by twisting the facts for Hancock's benefit. Dutifully Hancock reported to Meade, "Howard says that Doubleday's command gave way." As a consequence, that evening General Meade reached into the Sixth Corps to find a general, John Newton, to replace Doubleday as head of the First Corps. Abner Doubleday never forgave Howard (and Meade) for this "unfounded accusation" against him and against the First Corps.[47]

After he had given all the orders he could, and seen all of the Cemetery Hill position he could, Winfield Hancock sat on a stone wall with Carl Schurz and watched and waited anxiously for the enemy's next move. Around them the Federal defenses had fallen slowly but steadily into place. The core of the infantry defense was the intact 1,600-man brigade of Orland Smith, Eleventh Corps, posted there all afternoon in reserve. Around Smith's brigade were arranged the broken pieces of the First and Eleventh corps. According to estimates by Generals Doubleday and Howard, there remained perhaps 7,000 men from the two corps. Regiments fell into line behind their flags with sadly diminished numbers. The 13th Massachusetts counted 99 men ready for action; the 121st Pennsylvania, 80; the 25th Ohio, 60; the 2nd Wisconsin, 45; the 24th Michigan, 27. (One of the 2nd Wisconsin's killed in the retreat was Irishman Pat Maloney, who had personally captured General Archer that morning.) More threatening in appearance were the ranks of cannon. First Corps artillery chief Charles Wainwright and the Eleventh Corps' Thomas Osborn had twenty guns covering the western front toward Seminary Ridge and twenty-three to the north overlooking the town.

From their vantage point Hancock and Schurz scanned to the west and the north with their glasses, searching for signs of impending attack. Schurz, the self-taught soldier, would remember his nervousness, and was relieved to see that the warrior Hancock seemed nervous too. Rebel troops were sighted moving from place to place, especially in and about the town, but they could not detect any massing for an assault. Slowly the minutes passed and the hours and then it was dusk and still there was no enemy movement, and the two generals began to relax. Hancock said he was sure now that with the Twelfth Corps soon to be in place they would be able to hold Cemetery Hill. For whatever was to come, the Union would have the high ground.

Finally it was dark and there was a full moon, and General Schurz would long remember the scene. "We of the Eleventh Corps," he wrote, "occupying the cemetery, lay down, wrapt in cloaks, with the troops among the grave stones. There was profound stillness in the graveyard, broken by no sound but the breathing of the men and here and there the tramp of a horse's foot; and sullen rumblings mysteriously floating on the air from a distance all around."[48]

9 *We May As Well Fight It Out Here*

THE SILENT NIGHT of the 1st of July was a blessing for the Army of the Potomac, and indeed (as it proved) a blessing for the Union cause. In the battle that day that neither side expected or willed, the Federals had been soundly beaten. Yet it was not, in the end, a battle to the finish. Why it was not reveals a tale of misapprehension and misjudgment on the part of the high command of the Army of Northern Virginia.

At Chancellorsville, during the long hours in the saddle on his famous flanking march of May 2, Stonewall Jackson had been in a rare reflective mood. The problem for the Confederacy's undermanned armies, he observed to one of his cavalry officers, was the lack of reserves to exploit their successes. "We have always had to put in all our forces, and *never* had enough at the *time* most needed," Jackson insisted. Now, late on a hot July afternoon two months later, Jackson's successor, Dick Ewell, was casting about for the reserves to exploit the latest Confederate success.[1]

It was getting on toward 5 o'clock when Second Corps commander Ewell rode into Gettysburg's town square behind his victorious troops. He found a tumultuous scene — Confederate infantrymen from various commands milling about, mounted officers rushing to and fro, Union prisoners by the hundreds being herded to the rear. Ewell called his generals together to discuss their next move. Amidst the elation of victory was urgency to complete the day's success. Still, Ewell's last order from General Lee had been to not provoke a general battle, which with his guns already firing he had felt obliged to ignore. Now fresh guidance from the general commanding would have been welcome.

Ewell first called the roll of his own reserves. He had just been informed that his absent third division, Allegheny Johnson's, was advancing over the Chambersburg Pike and was about an hour's march away. When Robert Rodes was asked about *his* division, he was not optimistic. Rodes reported his command had suffered 2,500 casualties that afternoon, mostly in its bitter fight with the Union First Corps, and was much exhausted and disordered. As he later phrased it, to expect him to attack, unaided, the "formidable line of infantry and artillery immediately in my front . . . would have been absurd." Jubal Early's division, on the other hand, had suffered a good deal less in its assault on the Eleventh Corps, and Old Jube urged (as *he* later phrased it) "an immediate advance upon the enemy, before he could recover from his evident dismay and confusion."

Ewell rode with Early out Baltimore Street toward Cemetery Hill to see about such an advance. Yankee sharpshooters in buildings at the foot of the hill sent them ducking for cover, but they soon found a protected spot from which to study what an assault might encounter. Victory produces about as much disorder as defeat, and there had not been time enough to regroup Hays's Louisianians and Avery's North Carolinians to set them right on the heels of the retreating Yankees. Now the prospect was daunting. They could see a number of batteries in place on Cemetery Hill — in due course, if they counted them, forty-three cannon in all — supported by lines of infantry, facing north toward the town and west toward A. P. Hill's corps. It was quickly apparent that mounting an assault on Cemetery Hill would require a major effort.

To advance in column through Gettysburg's narrow streets and deploy under the muzzles of those guns would invite a slaughter. Instead they would have to swing the troops around either or both sides of the town, and even then they would need support to mount at the least a diversion. Worse, Ewell could see no good locations for artillery with which to beat down the Federals' fire. Early could muster but three brigades for an attack, Rodes's help was questionable, and it was bound to be a race against darkness. Nevertheless, Dick Ewell was willing to make the effort — provided he could get help from Powell Hill.

Ewell told Early and Rodes to get their troops ready, and turned to Lieutenant James Power Smith, who had just come from General Lee, and asked him to find the general again. "Please tell him what Generals Early and Rodes wish to say," said Ewell. The two told Smith to say that it was their "earnest desire" to advance against Cemetery Hill "provided they were supported by troops on their right." No sooner had Lieutenant Smith left to find Lee than Walter Taylor of Lee's staff appeared with a message for General Ewell. Lee's instructions were "to carry the hill occupied by the enemy, if he found it practicable, but to avoid a general engagement until the arrival of the other divisions of the army. . . ." Here was another of Lee's discretionary orders — and one with a seeming contradiction. The decision was left entirely in Ewell's hands, and he was urged to start a fight but not to start a battle.[2]

While Ewell attempted to parse the commanding general's latest wishes, a new complication arose. Early's fourth brigade, under "Extra Billy" Smith, had been held back to guard the division's flank and rear. Now came an excited Lieutenant Frederick Smith, Extra Billy's son and aide, with a report that his father had sighted a heavy enemy column approaching from the northeast along the York Pike. Campbell Brown of the corps staff heard Early say to Ewell, "General, I don't much believe in this, but prefer to suspend my movements until I can send & inquire into it." He inquired by sending Gordon's brigade out the York Pike, thereby reducing his available force for a move against Cemetery Hill to just two brigades, Hays's and Avery's.

Ewell agreed to this diversion because a sighting like Smith's could not be ignored. Due to the dearth of Confederate intelligence-gathering, and in the absence of Stuart's cavalry screen, the Yankees might surprise by approaching Gettysburg from practically any point of the compass. Ewell took the threat seriously enough to ride out the York Pike with Early and Rodes to set the matter straight. All they could see was a distant line of Smith's pickets. No one seems to have asked General Smith exactly what it was that alarmed him (one of his men thought it might have been a far-off line of fence posts that deceived Extra Billy's sixty-five-year-old eyes), but in any event, Ewell left both Smith's and Gordon's brigades on guard in the army's rear.

James Power Smith, meanwhile, had ridden west and found Generals Lee and Longstreet on Seminary Ridge studying the enemy's position. Smith delivered his message: General Ewell would move against Cemetery Hill if supported by troops from Lee's side of the field. Lee inquired of Longstreet and was told that the closest First Corps division was six miles distant. (Longstreet was, said Smith, "indefinite and noncommittal.") With that, Lee instructed the lieutenant to tell General Ewell that "he regretted that his people were not up to support him on the right, but he wished him to take the Cemetery hill if it were possible; and that he would ride over and see him very soon."

If Lieutenant Smith's recollection of this meeting is accurate — his is the only account — Lee's statement was curiously incomplete. Longstreet's First Corps, to be sure, was "not up," but Powell Hill's entire Third Corps was already there at the front. Hill might be chary about calling on Heth's and Pender's divisions after their bloody struggle with the Yankee First Corps, but the corps' artillery was comparatively undamaged and available for further use. And Richard Anderson's 7,100-man division was certainly available. When Lee rode toward the nascent battlefield from Cashtown, he had told Anderson to follow. By Anderson's recollection, a message came to halt and bivouac behind the front. Hearing the sounds of battle, Anderson rode ahead to find Lee to be certain the message was correct. It was indeed correct, Lee told him. Anderson's division was the only uncommitted Third Corps unit, and "a reserve, in case of disaster, was necessary."[3]

Clearly, General Lee had not yet decided, despite the favorable outcome of the day's fighting, whether Gettysburg was to be the scene of his showdown battle on Northern soil. Lee was also revealing his dependence on James Longstreet — "my old war-horse," as he had said affectionately of Longstreet at Sharpsburg. He appeared reluctant to either initiate or accept battle without having the First Corps and its trustworthy commander at hand. Finally, his injunction to Dick Ewell to take Cemetery Hill "if it were possible" — but using only his own men — demonstrated anew Lee's day-long uneasiness concerning this unwanted confrontation with an unknown fraction of General Meade's army.

Even before Lieutenant Smith delivered Lee's rejection of Ewell's request for help, Ewell had begun to shift his attention to a secondary but possibly more promising objective, the "high peak" some 800 yards to the east of Cemetery Hill known as Culp's Hill. If he could occupy this high ground, Ewell would command Cemetery Hill and perhaps force its evacuation almost without a fight. He sent two staff officers, Thomas Turner and Robert Early, to reconnoiter Culp's Hill. Should they find it free of Yankees, he could use Allegheny Johnson's division, whose arrival was promised at any moment, to occupy it. Storming Cemetery Hill and its guns would no longer be an issue, and Ewell would be honoring Lee's wish to avoid a general battle.

Lieutenants Turner and Early climbed to the crest of the hill and found no Yankees anywhere — except those clearly visible to the west on Cemetery Hill. From Culp's Hill, they reported, the enemy's position could be rendered untenable. It so happened that either the two lieutenants did not discover the Iron Brigade, ordered over to Culp's Hill by General Hancock, because of the thick tree cover, or they reached the scene just before the Yankees did. In any event, their reconnaissance produced yet another miscalculation by the Confederate high command.

Allegheny Johnson had by now reached Gettysburg, but his division had not, and he was in an ill temper about it. His four brigades had marched some 25 miles that day, he said, and were held up along the Chambersburg Pike by a lumbering wagon train — no doubt one of A. P.

Hill's trains — and contrary to his earlier promise they would not be up for another hour. The delay meant an arrival time of sunset or later. Mulling over this latest complication, Ewell was struck by a new thought: occupy Culp's Hill immediately by using Jubal Early's two brigades already on the scene, Hays's and Avery's. Johnson's troops when they arrived could move into Early's line on the Gettysburg front.

But Old Jube — his earlier belligerence evaporating — bristled at the thought. His command, he said, "had been doing all the hard marching and fighting and was not in condition to make the move." Johnson for his part did not appreciate the implied invidious comparison with his command, and the two generals exchanged sharp words. Dick Ewell now made his first real mistake of the day. Instead of ordering the immediate occupation of the (supposedly) unoccupied Culp's Hill, he humored Early and let his men stand down, and assigned the task to Johnson's division whenever it might arrive.

Ewell's decision had momentous consequences. To be sure, just then Hays's Louisianians and Avery's North Carolinians would have been forced to make a fight for the (in fact) occupied Culp's Hill, but with some 2,400 men to confront the few hundred weary survivors of the Iron Brigade, and with as much as two hours of daylight to work with, and with Johnson's reinforcements soon at hand to secure the hill, the outcome would seem assured.[4]

Allegheny Johnson's division made its way through the battlefield and into Gettysburg along the roadbed of the abandoned railroad, its last brigade not arriving until after sunset. Ewell sent the division around to the east toward Culp's Hill, assigning Lieutenants Turner and Early as guides. His orders to Johnson were strangely tentative. Johnson was to take Culp's Hill — if he found it unoccupied. Soon afterward Ewell was visited by General Lee, became preoccupied with matters of larger strategy, and absent-mindedly left the matter of Culp's Hill entirely in the hands of General Johnson.

Rodes and Early were present with Ewell at the generals' conference, convened in an arbor behind a house on the outskirts of town, and Early left the only record of what was discussed there. Early's recollection is freighted with self-importance and special pleading, but at least in outline probably reflects the subjects that were discussed. General Lee, who had not met with Ewell since the start of the campaign, inquired about the overall state of the Second Corps as well as its condition after the day's fighting. What was not discussed, apparently, was any assault that evening on Cemetery Hill; Lee accepted the fact that Ewell had not found it practicable. What the commanding general did want to know was whether it would be practicable the next day. "Can't you, with your corps, attack on this flank at daylight tomorrow?" Early quoted Lee as asking.

Early cast himself in the lead role at finding fault with this idea. The terrain was against it, the enemy was in force there, the result "might be doubtful." Even if successful, "it would inevitably be at very great loss." Ewell and Rodes added their own arguments against such an offensive, which led Lee to ask if the Second Corps might be at risk where it was. Might it be better to "draw you around towards my right," said Lee, before the enemy broke through the corps' extended line? There came a chorus of objections to this idea as well. After winning such a dramatic victory that day, it was said the troops would be demoralized by having to pull back from their conquests. There were the wounded to consider, and the booty collected from the Yankees. General Lee was assured that the enemy would encounter great troubles launching an attack from the heights of Cemetery Hill; "we could repulse any force he could send against us," Early proclaimed.

So it was left, rather hazily, that the Second Corps would remain in and around Gettysburg, facing south, confronting the Yankee line on the heights. Although Early in his account did not mention it, Ewell surely told Lee of his proposed occupation of Culp's Hill, and how that ought to dominate the enemy's position on Cemetery Hill. The main thrust on July 2, Lee suggested, would be against the Federal left, with Ewell to deliver a diversion against the Federal right — with the option (wrote Early) of making the diversion "a real attack on discovering any disorder or symptoms of giving way on the enemy's part. . . ."[5]

After Lee left to return to Seminary Ridge, Ewell and his staff relaxed and reflected on a good day's work. Ordnance chief William Allan remembered that "everybody was in fine spirits. After all we had gained a great victory. . . ." Ewell's adjutant, Sandie Pendleton, remarked with particular satisfaction that "we finished the 11th Federal corps which we had beaten at Chancellorsville." This pleasant interlude was interrupted by the arrival of Colonel Charles Marshall of the headquarters staff with a message from General Lee. The general commanding, on second thought, had decided to evacuate Gettysburg, and to swing the Second Corps back around to join the rest of the army on the right. This announcement stunned Ewell. After discussing it with Rodes and Early, he determined to ride back with Colonel Marshall to argue the case with Lee personally.

General Lee took the stone house of the widow Mary Thompson, on the Chambersburg Pike, as his headquarters. (Library of Congress)

Lee and his lieutenant talked for an hour, and Ewell must have been persuasive. His chief argument was that with Allegheny Johnson's division occupying Culp's Hill, he could drive the Federals off their Cemetery Hill citadel with comparative ease. That ought to immeasurably aid any offensive on the right. This argument — perhaps combined with Ewell's newly evident aggressive attitude — caused Lee to change his mind once again and allow the Second Corps to stay where it was.

It was after midnight when Ewell returned to his headquarters outside

Gettysburg, and he immediately sent Lieutenant Turner to check on Johnson's occupation of Culp's Hill — something he had neglected to do before he rode off to meet with Lee. Turner's report gave Dick Ewell his second major shock of the night. General Johnson, as it happened, had not gotten around to carrying out Ewell's order of some five hours earlier to take Culp's Hill, should it prove to be unoccupied. Reminded now to do so, Johnson sent out a reconnoitering party "with orders to report as to the position of the enemy. . . ." Near the crest of the hill, in the darkness, the party met a sharp fire, suffered several casualties, and beat a hasty retreat. (This ambush was the work of the 7th Indiana, one of Lysander Cutler's First Corps regiments that had spent the day in the rear guarding trains. It reached the field that evening and was rushed over to Culp's Hill to extend the Iron Brigade's line.)

If this was not bad news enough, on its return to Confederate ground the reconnoitering party captured a Union courier bearing a dispatch written at 12:30 A.M. by General Sykes, commander of the Fifth Corps, to General Slocum, commander of the Twelfth Corps. It revealed that the Fifth Corps was just four miles east of Gettysburg and would resume its advance at 4:00 A.M., while the courier's presence on the outskirts of Gettysburg suggested that the Twelfth Corps was already on the scene.

Lieutenant Turner delivered this captured dispatch to Ewell, along with Johnson's report of his belated reconnaissance and his request for further orders regarding Culp's Hill. Whatever might have been, whatever chance there was to seize Culp's Hill with little bloodshed, was gone now. The chance to shift the Second Corps to a new position was gone as well. "Day was now breaking," wrote Ewell in his report, "and it was too late for any change of place."[6]

In the postwar years much would be made of the Confederates' failure to follow up their July 1 victory by promptly driving the Federals out of their Cemetery Hill sanctuary. Dick Ewell was most often found guilty in these old-soldier skirmishes. Ewell's crime, it seems, was that he was not Stonewall Jackson. Yet absent any help from Hill's corps — a decision entirely General Lee's — it is highly doubtful if even Stonewall could have conquered Cemetery Hill on July 1. That was Porter Alexander's informed opinion. "This delay has been sometimes criticised," Alexander wrote. "I think any attack we could have made that afternoon would have failed." Campbell Brown of Ewell's staff put the case nicely when he wrote, "The discovery that this lost us the battle is one of those frequently-recurring but tardy strokes of military genius of which one hears long after. . . ."

The Confederates' failure to even attempt to seize Culp's Hill that evening or night, however, finds General Ewell guilty of inattention at the least. He appeared not to credit the Federals with the wit to see how important Culp's Hill was to their defensive position, and consequently did not order Early's brigades to take it when the taking was good. In regard to Allegheny Johnson's misadventure, Major Brown remarked, "I know that Gen'l Ewell held him not altogether free from blame in the matter. . . ." Yet Ewell, by failing to sufficiently impress Johnson with the importance of his task, and then failing to monitor his progress (or lack of it), was hardly free of blame himself. In this instance, Dick Ewell seems to have misplaced that touch of Stonewall Jackson decisiveness he had displayed earlier in the day.[7]

ROBERT E. LEE spent the evening of July 1 engrossed in hours-long deliberations with his lieutenants, trying to decide on his course. When not meeting with Ewell to negotiate the Second Corps' next actions, he was consulting with Hill or Longstreet. Old Pete was singularly unimpressed with the prospects before them, and as Lee's senior lieutenant and self-appointed senior adviser he did not hesitate to express himself on the subject. Longstreet's idea of the perfect battle was Fredericksburg, where, firmly established on the high ground, he had shot the attacking Federals to pieces. Now, as he stood on Seminary Ridge studying the high ground opposite him with his field glasses, he could envision a Fredericksburg in reverse.

Longstreet chose an oblique approach to the commanding general. "We could not call the enemy to position better suited to our plans," he observed. "All that we have to do is to file around his left and secure good ground between him and his capital." His remark was an unspoken reference to the "understanding" he believed the two of them had reached back in Virginia — that in Pennsylvania they would combine offensive strategy with defensive tactics — and he assumed Lee would surely agree with those "ruling ideas of the campaign."

But Lee did not agree. He said, with a show of impatience, "If the enemy is there tomorrow, we must attack him." Longstreet's reply was prompt and more pointed than he perhaps intended: "If he is there, it will be because he is anxious that we should attack him — a good reason, in my judgment, for not doing so."

Longstreet's blunt rejoinder was a measure of his dismay. In a postwar letter to General Lafayette McLaws, he explained how he and Lee had reached their understanding, so he thought, about giving or accepting

James Longstreet, Lee's senior adviser, opposed Lee's tactics at
Gettysburg. (Cook Collection, Valentine Museum)

battle in Pennsylvania. "You will now understand my surprise at finding
all of our previously arranged plans so unexpectedly changed," he wrote,
"and why I might wish and hope, to get the Gen. to consider of our former arrangements."

By Longstreet's description, he and the commanding general had an
extended discussion on the subject, interrupted only by Lee's visit to
Ewell's headquarters. Longstreet seems first to have suggested a wide
turning maneuver by the whole army. The march would be southward
and then a turn to the east to get between Meade and Washington,
thereby forcing Meade to do the attacking to regain his supply line and
defend his capital. Such a march route might pass through Fairfield,

southwest of Gettysburg, then swing eastward, perhaps on the roads through Emmitsburg and Taneytown. (Indeed, the ideal position in which to invite a Federal attack might be the Pipe Creek line that General Meade had earlier chosen for *his* ideal battlefield.)

Any maneuver of this kind could only take place behind a cavalry screen, of course, and Lee no doubt explained that he finally had word from Stuart, and that the cavalry would not be rejoining the army for perhaps twenty-four hours. The Federals would have to be scouted to fix their position, another function of cavalry. The army might remain in place for those twenty-four hours, waiting for Stuart, but Lee was intent on challenging Meade in detail, before all the Yankee forces reached the scene. With that, Old Pete suggested a less radical movement, one that was more tactical than strategic — still a swing around the enemy's left, but closer in, on or near the present battlefield. As he later put it, "I thought that we should move around to his left, that we might threaten it if we intended to maneuvre, or attack it if we determined upon a battle."

General Lee did not reject Longstreet's schemes out of hand, and he certainly had them in mind when he sent Colonel Marshall to Ewell with orders to evacuate Gettysburg and bring the Second Corps around to the army's right. Campbell Brown recorded Lee's caution to Ewell that night that he should not become too entangled with the enemy: "I have not decided to fight here — and may probably draw off by my right flank . . . so as to get between the enemy & Washington & Baltimore — & force them to attack us in position." In the end, however, it was Ewell's strenuous objections to evacuating Gettysburg, and his assurances about occupying Culp's Hill, that caused Lee to change his mind again and to leave the Second Corps where it was.[8]

When Longstreet returned to his camp that evening, he was of the belief that Lee may have made up his mind to attack the next day, but was "confident that he had not yet determined as to when the attack should be made." In fact no attack orders for July 2 were issued by Lee that night; all planning was left to the next day. Longstreet did issue orders, however, to Pickett's division at Chambersburg and to Evander Law's brigade of Hood's division, at New Guilford, to march immediately for Gettysburg.

That evening Old Pete did not share the general euphoria in many Confederate camps over the results of the day's fighting. Writing to the general after the war, Dr. Dorsey Cullen, the First Corps' medical director, recalled how Longstreet did not take the "same cheerful view of it that I did; and presently you remarked, that it would have been better had we not fought than to have left undone what we did." The enemy had taken a posting, Longstreet said, "that it would take the whole army to drive them from, and then at a great sacrifice." In conversation with British Colonel Fremantle, Longstreet even suggested that the Federals' position at Gettysburg had "greater advantages" than the position the Confederates had occupied at Fredericksburg.[9]

In his campaign reports, Lee did not even list Longstreet's proposals for a turning movement among his options that Wednesday evening. Instead he gave two rather lame reasons for deciding to pursue the battle on July 2. Should he attempt to pull back to or through South Mountain, he said, withdrawing the army's "extensive trains would have been difficult and dangerous." Remaining where they were to await an attack was no better — foraging in the countryside "in the presence of the enemy" would be risky, due especially to the parties of local militia. Surely General Lee and his veteran army had nothing to fear from Pennsylvania's Sunday soldiers, especially when he could call on Imboden's troopers back at Chambersburg and, shortly, Stuart's entire cavalry division. And surely the trains could withdraw safely in any direction with the entire Army of Northern Virginia to shield them.

If Lee gave thought to standing on the defensive right where he was, forcing the decision-making onto Meade's shoulders, he left no hint of it beyond the faint excuse of a supply problem. In fact, on July 2, supplies were not a problem. Confederate foraging parties had at hand at least a week's supply of food, with the potential of much more to be collected, under the cavalry's protection, in untouched Fulton and Cumberland counties to the west. Nor, according to the astute engineer's eye of Porter Alexander, was there a problem with Seminary Ridge as a defensive line. "It was not such a really *wonderful* position as the enemy happened to fall into," Alexander admitted, "but it was no bad one." And he added, "it could never have been successfully assaulted." Alexander concluded that in the end, committed to this great invasion of the enemy's country, General Lee was simply too audacious for such a conservative tactic.

By Longstreet's recollection, Lee was not his usual self that evening of July 1: "He seemed under a subdued excitement, which occasionally took possession of him when 'the hunt was up,' and threatened his superb equipoise. The sharp battle fought by Hill and Ewell on that day had given him a taste of victory." Other observers traveling with the army had their own thoughts about what was different about Robert E. Lee after he reached Gettysburg. "Lee was not at his ease, but was riding to and fro, . . . making anxious enquiries here and there, and looking care-worn," recalled the Prussian military observer Justus Scheibert. The London *Times* correspondent Francis Lawley found General Lee "more anxious and ruffled than I had ever seen him before, though it required close observation to detect it."

The fact of the matter seems to be that Robert E. Lee was deeply angered. At midday, talking to General Anderson and to Ewell's aide Campbell Brown, he had made no effort to conceal his anger at Jeb Stuart for failing to obey instructions. Lee was surely displeased with Harry Heth for disobeying *his* instructions, to not bring on a general engagement, and equally displeased with corps commander Powell Hill for letting it happen. Under questioning, Dick Ewell (along with his lieutenants) had displayed, first, strong reluctance to move against the enemy's right, then strong reluctance to shift forces around to the enemy's left as Lee proposed. Longstreet was being stubbornly and outspokenly contrary to the whole plan of battle. Lee was without Jeb Stuart's eyes, on which he had grown utterly dependent. He was entangled in a battle he had not wanted in a place he knew little about against a foe he could not describe. It was not any wonder that he seemed "anxious and ruffled."[10]

Although this was General Lee's sixth campaign in his one year of command, it was his first experience with recalcitrant subordinates. He seemed deeply troubled by this unexpected development, and initially uncertain how to handle it. To be sure, previous battles had not always gone just as they were planned — battles seldom do — but never before had his battlefield planning or his decisions been questioned or challenged. Stuart's absence (and his silence) bordered on insubordination. Ewell and his generals appeared to have nothing positive in the way of ideas for the Second Corps after the July 1 fighting, yet they were uniformly negative toward Lee's ideas. Longstreet was persistent in seeking a basic change in Lee's scheme for the fighting, a change as fundamental as switching from offensive to defensive. It is not clear what, or even if, Lee may have argued in return, but it is obvious that he finally dug in his heels. In order to assert his authority, he would not — increasingly he could not — alter his plan.

Beyond anything else, Lee determined to keep the initiative. Throughout this Pennsylvania expedition he had considered it essential to make the Federals march to his drum, to be always in position to give or accept battle on his own terms. With the smaller army — his was always the smaller army — keeping the initiative was critical, yet Stuart's continued absence severely limited Lee's powers in this respect. The 1st of July was an example. The advance that morning — infantry forced to do the cavalry's job — had stumbled into an encounter that Harry Heth was unwilling or unable to back out of. Ewell's fortuitous arrival on the field turned the encounter into a battle and the battle into a victory. At the end of the day the initiative remained in Lee's hands, but he believed he had to act promptly to hold on to it.

Time, he believed, was the other key factor. From prisoners it was clear that the Federals who fought at Gettysburg on July 1 were Buford's cavalry division and the First and Eleventh corps of infantry. The dispatch captured by Allegheny Johnson's reconnaissance party was put in Lee's hands, revealing that the Twelfth Corps was already on or near the field and the Fifth Corps would be there shortly. That left three Federal infantry corps to be accounted for. Lee could calculate that by dawn on the 2nd, General Meade would have had as much as eighteen hours' notice of the fighting at Gettysburg. If Meade elected to make a stand there, he would surely have the rest of his army on the march. If Lee was to attack with any advantage — his entire army against some fraction of Meade's — he could not afford to wait for Stuart or anyone else. "A battle had, therefore, become in a measure unavoidable," Lee would explain in his report, "and the success already gained gave hope of a favorable issue."

It was Longstreet, in a letter written a month later, who confirmed how pivotal the factor of time was to Lee's decision. Events at Gettysburg, Longstreet wrote his friend Senator Wigfall, were "due I think to our being under the impression that the enemy had not been able to get all his forces up. Being under this impression Gen. Lee thought it best to attack at once."[11]

Colonel Fremantle spent that Wednesday evening at Longstreet's headquarters, and was struck by the attitude of the general's staff. "The Staff officers spoke of the battle as a certainty," Fremantle entered in his journal, "and the universal feeling in the army was one of profound contempt for an enemy whom they have beaten so constantly, and under so many disadvantages." Longstreet's staff officers, to be sure, had witnessed none of the fighting on the 1st of July, while those who had witnessed it may not have shared their contempt for the foe. Powell Hill, in fact, had remarked to Fremantle of the July 1 battle "that the Yankees fought with a determination unusual to them."

The divisions of Harry Heth and Dorsey Pender could attest to that. Between them they could count almost 4,000 casualties. Two of Heth's brigades, Archer's and Davis's, had been routed, and it was only the superior weight of Pender's division that had finally pushed the Yankee First

239

Corps off Seminary Ridge. Robert Rodes of Ewell's corps also had cause to be respectful, having launched four brigades against those First Corps Yankees, seen two of them smashed back, and suffered in the bargain some 2,300 casualties. If the battle was resumed on July 2 — if there was a Day Two at Gettysburg — it promised, from these experiences, to be no less fierce and costly.[12]

GEORGE GORDON MEADE spent a tense afternoon on July 1 at army headquarters in Taneytown awaiting word from Gettysburg. His newly appointed field commander, Winfield Scott Hancock, sent back a situation report about 4:30, shortly after reaching Gettysburg, but by that time Meade had already determined on his course. Dispatches received earlier from Howard and relayed through Dan Sickles firmly identified two Confederate corps, Hill's and Ewell's, as fighting at Gettysburg, and that was enough for Meade. He put his Pipe Creek plan aside and crisply made his decision — he would make his fight at Gettysburg. Indeed, in a mirror image of Lee's plan, Meade hoped the next day to mass the whole of the Army of the Potomac at Gettysburg to attack some fraction of the enemy's army. "A. P. Hill and Ewell are certainly concentrating," Meade telegraphed General-in-Chief Halleck at 6 o'clock that evening; "Longstreet's whereabouts I do not know. If he is not up to-morrow, I hope with the force I have concentrated to defeat Hill and Ewell; at any rate, I see no other course than to hazard a general battle."[13]

Meade went about assembling his army swiftly but carefully. His orders to Dan Sickles of the Third Corps and to John Gibbon, temporarily commanding Hancock's Second Corps, were designed to continue to guard the army's left, between Emmitsburg and Gettysburg, against being turned — the very move Longstreet was then urging on Lee. The march orders for Sykes's Fifth Corps and Slocum's Twelfth were confirmed. Two brigades from the artillery reserve were sent forward. Meade's greatest concern was bringing up John Sedgwick's Sixth Corps in time. It was the largest of the army's corps and one of the most reliable, and it was the farthest away. On July 1 Sedgwick was at Manchester, well to the southeast in Maryland, and his orders to march to Gettysburg did not reach him until 8 o'clock that night; he had the vanguard of his corps on the road within the hour. He had 35 miles to march.

Winfield Hancock, when he had done all he could for the night at Gettysburg, rode back to headquarters at Taneytown to report to the general commanding. Hancock's dispatches and now his personal report served to ratify Meade's decision to take his stand at Gettysburg. Finally, with everyone and everything well started, General Meade himself set out for Gettysburg.[14]

Henry Slocum's Twelfth Corps, the closest reinforcement to Gettysburg when the fighting started that morning, had only begun reaching the scene about 5:30 P.M., thanks to its belated start. General Slocum, the senior among the corps commanders, continued acting the pinched army bureaucrat. He had paid no attention to the pleas for help from his junior, Howard, nor had he displayed soldierly initiative by hurrying to the sound of the guns; he was waiting instead for orders from headquarters. At 4 o'clock, with the battle falling to pieces around him, General Howard sent his brother Charles to urge Slocum to speed his troops and to come himself to Cemetery Hill. Major Howard recorded Slocum's response: "In fact refused to come up in person saying he would not assume the responsibility of that day's fighting and of those two corps." General Slocum was not going to dirty his uniform cleaning up other generals' messes. Another of Howard's aides, also getting no response from Slocum, said he considered the general's conduct on that occasion "anything but honorable, soldierly or patriotic."

In due course Slocum had to accept temporary command of the field — Hancock turned it over to him and told him it was by Meade's order — but by then the messes were cleaned up and everything had been done that needed doing, and Slocum's duties were mostly placing newly arriving troops. These were coming in a rush. Among the first were odd regiments of the Eleventh Corps released from special duties, and the First Corps' 7th Indiana that was hurried over to Culp's Hill. The 2,000-man Vermont brigade under George Stannard, fresh from the Department of Washington, was a welcome reinforcement for Rowley's First Corps division.

The two divisions of Slocum's Twelfth Corps arrived by different routes to the left and right of Cemetery Hill. John Geary's division marched up the Baltimore Pike and formed along Cemetery Ridge, extending the army's line southward. Alpheus Williams's division swung off to the right on a country road and made for what Williams described as "a high, bald hill," seeking to get there before the Rebels, "who, it was reported to me, were advancing in that direction in heavy column." General Williams was just ordering the storming of this high ground — Benner's Hill, a thousand yards northeast of Culp's Hill — when a messenger from Slocum reached him and explained that the army had been driven back from Gettysburg and that he was in danger of being cut off. Williams recalled his troops and bivouacked in safety along the Baltimore Pike. "I put out strong pickets in all directions, as it was dark and I literally knew nothing of the topography or geography of the country," he wrote, ". . . rolled myself in an india-rubber poncho and slept most splendidly until daylight."[15]

It was dusk when Dan Sickles and the first elements of his Third Corps reached Gettysburg. To satisfy Meade's earlier directive, Sickles had left one brigade from each of his two divisions to hold Emmitsburg, and the first to arrive on the battlefield were troops of David Birney's division. They had made a wearing but uneventful march over the Emmitsburg Road and were posted on Cemetery Ridge. The march of the other Third Corps division, under Andrew Humphreys, proved to be something of an adventure.

To avoid crowding on the Emmitsburg Road, Sickles had directed Humphreys north by west to strike the Hagerstown Road between Fairfield and Gettysburg, and proceed to the battlefield from there. During the march, however, there came several warnings that any troops they might encounter on their left would be Confederate. Reaching a fork in the road, and with those warnings in mind, Humphreys thought discretion the better part of valor and they should take the right fork leading back to the Emmitsburg Road. In charge of the march was Lieutenant Colonel Julius Haydon of Sickles's staff, who according to one of Humphreys's colonels was "more noted for froth and foam than for common sense." Haydon insisted they follow Sickles's directions to proceed via the left fork to the Black Horse Tavern on the Hagerstown Road.

Humphreys obeyed but with reservations, and as they approached the tavern in the darkness he had the column halted in "perfect silence" and went ahead on foot with a small party to reconnoiter. He returned and announced that the place was full of Rebels. In well-ordered haste and "majestic silence" he had the column reversed and they made their way back to Union ground. It was 2 o'clock in the morning when they finally reached their place on Cemetery Ridge. Humphreys's disgust had not evaporated when he wrote a friend a month later, "You see how things were managed in the Third Corps!"[16]

In the small hours of the morning on July 2 General Meade and his party reined up at the gatehouse of Evergreen Cemetery, on Cemetery Hill, after a wearying ride from Taneytown. Corps commanders Slocum, Howard, and Sickles and chief engineer Gouverneur Warren were there to greet him. He asked their opinion about the ground the army was de-

The gateway to Evergreen Cemetery, on Cemetery Hill, photographed four days after the battle by Timothy O'Sullivan. (Library of Congress)

fending. There was general agreement that it was good ground. "I am glad to hear you say so," Meade remarked, "for it is too late to leave it."

Carl Schurz saw Meade a few hours later as he was inspecting the Cemetery Hill positions. The general commanding, Schurz thought, looked haggard and careworn and tired; apparently he had not slept that night. "There was nothing in his appearance or his bearing . . . that might have made the hearts of the soldiers warm up to him, . . . nothing of pose, nothing stagey, about him. His mind was evidently absorbed by a hard problem. But this simple, cold, serious soldier with his business-like air did inspire confidence." The curious who crowded around, Schurz wrote, "turned away, not enthusiastic, but clearly satisfied." In answer to Schurz's question about the forces available, Meade said, "in the course of the day I expect to have about 95,000 — enough I guess, for this business." Then, with a sweeping glance across the field, he added, "Well, we may as well fight it out here just as well as anywhere else."[17]

PRIVATE ISAAC TAYLOR, 1st Minnesota, John Gibbon's division, entered in his diary for July 2, 1863, "Arroused at 3 A.M. & ordered to pack up & at 4 A.M. move towards the battle field where we arrive at 5-40 A.M. Order from Gen. Gibbon read to us in which he says this is to be the great battle of the war & that any soldier leaving the ranks without leave will be instantly put to death." The Army of the Potomac was on notice as to where its duty lay.[18]

One of General Meade's first tasks was to reckon the cost of the previous day's fighting. The First Corps was in ruins. It had taken just over 9,000 men into action on July 1, and lost some 5,600 of them — more than 62 percent. Included in this toll were some 2,000 missing or captured, a consequence of the chaotic last minutes of the retreat from Seminary Ridge to Cemetery Hill. Corps commander John Reynolds was dead, and of the six brigade commanders, three were wounded, one was wounded and captured, and one, Thomas Rowley, was in arrest for being drunk. (Rowley would be tried by court-martial and found guilty, reinstated by Secretary of War Stanton, and finally resign from the service.) In what lay ahead, Stannard's newly arrived Vermont brigade would have a role to play, as would Colonel Wainwright's artillery and some of General Wadsworth's men on Culp's Hill, but for the rest of the First Corps, after Wednesday's epic stand, it seemed that no more could be asked. It was put on reserve status.

The Eleventh Corps was not granted such relief, and had not earned it. The Eleventh put five of its six brigades, 7,000 men, into a mere hour's action that Wednesday afternoon and lost 3,200 of them. Almost half that number were prisoners. In its fight north of Gettysburg the corps had made a better stand than at Chancellorsville, certainly, but nevertheless it was again roundly defeated. It suffered four-plus casualties for every one it inflicted. Poor morale hastened and deepened its defeat, and the rest of the army continued to scorn the poor Dutchmen. Even Major Charles Howard, the general's brother and aide, admitted privately that Barlow's division "did not fight *very well* the first day." The corps lost division commander Barlow, wounded and a prisoner, and brigade commander Schimmelfennig, missing and presumed captured. That evening General Howard resumed command of the Eleventh Corps, posted in the main line on Cemetery Hill.

In view of the Confederates' advantage in men and position, the day's outcome was predictable, yet the final retreat to Cemetery Hill need not have been so disorderly and costly. The problem started at the top, where Otis Howard failed to rise to his emergency command. Howard was tardy in making the case for a stand at Gettysburg, and inflexible in directing the defenses there. The generalship in the First Corps, on the other hand, was expert. Abner Doubleday, although unappreciated, ably rose to the occasion, as did divisional commanders James Wadsworth and John Robinson. The Third Division's officers worked around the drunken Rowley and rendered him harmless. At the brigade level, Solomon Meredith, Lysander Cutler, Henry Baxter, Chapman Biddle, and Roy Stone all excelled. The Iron Brigade's fight on July 1 would be remembered as a true epic — but an epic the brigade never recovered from.

In the case of the Eleventh Corps, it had been posted on such poor defensive ground that its officers, however able they may have been, were helpless to meet the Rebels' relentless flanking attacks. As one of the Eleventh's company commanders put it, "We officers redoubled our exertions, shouted, waved our swords, swore, struck the men most inclined to give way, went to almost every extreme, but with no avail. . . . There was no disguising the fact that we were fairly driven off the field."[19]

Before the first streaks of dawn on Thursday, July 2, General Meade, with a party including Howard, artillery chief Henry Hunt, and engineer William H. Paine, set out to survey the battlefield that John Reynolds had left as his legacy. The vista was ominous, with campfires of the enemy visible to the west, to the north, and to the northeast. From Cemetery Hill they rode southward along the length of Cemetery Ridge — the long shank of the fishhook — as far as the dip in the ridge at the base of Little Round Top. The party then circled back around to the east and north, crossing the Taneytown Road and the Baltimore Pike, inspecting Culp's Hill and the ground on the army's right, and finally returning to Cemetery Hill. Henry Hunt made note of positions for his batteries, and on Captain Paine's sketch of the ground Meade indicated the positions he wanted for the infantry. He also approved the selection of army headquarters, a little white farmhouse on the east slope of Cemetery Ridge, just south of Cemetery Hill, that belonged to the widow Lydia Leister.

Meade told Hunt that ideally he would have preferred defending a straighter line along a ridge about a half-mile to the east, behind Rock Creek, anchored on an eminence called Wolf's Hill. As Hunt explained it to his artillerists, "it had been determined to hold our present position, but if driven from it we should then take up the other." Meade also took the precaution of having his chief of staff, Dan Butterfield, draw up a contingency plan for an orderly retreat should the battle finally go against them.

With daylight, General Meade's primary concern, naturally enough, was for the front immediately facing Ewell's corps in and around Gettysburg. A brisk exchange of picket-line firing at dawn heightened his concern. (One of the killed in this exchange, close by Culp's Hill, was Private Wesley Culp, 2nd Virginia, Stonewall Brigade, of the family Culp of Gettysburg.) The Eleventh Corps, with plentiful artillery, was established on Cemetery Hill, but the position on Culp's Hill needed strengthening. Meade chose Slocum's Twelfth Corps for that purpose. John Geary's division, which the night before had occupied the far left of the Union position, at Little Round Top, was now called all the way over to the far right. By about 6:00 A.M. Geary's two brigades were taking position next to Wadsworth of the First Corps, extending the line from the west slope of Culp's Hill and across the crest, facing to the east. Next came Alpheus Williams's division, carrying the line — the barb of the fishhook — down the south slope of Culp's Hill to Rock Creek. At 8:00 A.M. General Williams greeted Henry Lockwood's brigade, just sent up from Baltimore as a reinforcement for the Twelfth Corps. Slocum's men took advantage of the wooded, rocky terrain to throw up breastworks and turn Culp's Hill into a citadel.

Meade concluded that since Lee appeared to be concentrating here, so must he concentrate as well. He called up the two brigades Dan Sickles had left the day before at Emmitsburg, and brought forward the Second Corps from its guarding position on the Taneytown Road to the south. The Second Corps, with Hancock back in command, was posted at the center of the line on Cemetery Ridge, tied to the Eleventh Corps on its right. Sickles was told to post his Third Corps on Hancock's left, taking the place of Geary's division that had been called to Culp's Hill, and to extend the line to Little Round Top. Henry Hunt posted his five brigades of the reserve artillery centrally behind the front.

George Sykes's Fifth Corps, meanwhile, was arriving on the ground after a brutal two days' march. The Fifth Corps, along with the Sixth, had formed the right wing of the Federal advance, and late on June 30 it reached Union Mills, Maryland, after 23 hard miles. On the 1st of July orders called for only a 12-mile advance to Hanover in Pennsylvania. The men were peacefully bivouacked at Hanover late in the afternoon when word came of the fighting at Gettysburg. Sykes put them on the road again for an additional 8 miles, halting at midnight. By 4:00 A.M. on the 2nd they were on the road again, for the final 4 miles to Gettysburg. Meade posted the tired Fifth Corps in reserve behind the center of the line.

Samuel Crawford's Pennsylvania Reserves, another of the Department of Washington reinforcements that General-in-Chief Halleck had belatedly released to Meade, had been marching frantically to catch up to the army. After an all-night march on June 30, the two brigades of Reserves covered 25 more miles on July 1. On the morning of the 2nd they marched the last 10 miles and took their posting as the Third Division of the Fifth Corps.[20]

Thus by noon that Thursday, Meade had all of the Army of the Potomac gathered on the battlefield, with all of his reinforcements, except "Uncle John" Sedgwick's Sixth Corps. The big Sixth contained about one-fifth of the army's infantry, and Meade regarded it as his ultimate equalizer against Lee's legions. His orders, reaching Sedgwick on the evening of July 1, were to hasten to Gettysburg by forced marches. "Tell General Sedgwick," Meade instructed the courier, "that I expect to put him in on the right, and hope he will be up in time to decide the victory for us." Sedgwick had the last of his corps on the road from Manchester, in Maryland, by 10 o'clock that night. It proved fortunate for the men of the Sixth that July 1 had been a day of rest after days of arduous marching, for now Uncle John would demand of them nineteen hours of almost continuous marching.

Meade's first thought had been to bring the Sixth Corps to army headquarters at Taneytown and on to Gettysburg from there, but after he learned the dimensions of the fighting on the 1st, he had Sedgwick change his route to the more direct Baltimore Pike. This required a certain amount of backtracking in the darkness which, as the historian of the 5th Maine put it, "caused much strong language." Men remembered the night march as a strange and eerie experience. James L. Bowen, 37th Massachusetts, wrote that "the step which has been light becomes heavy and mechanical, and the soldiers are transformed into mere machines, to plod on as steadily as possible all the interminable night, . . . the men as they walk are like those moving in a dream." In Horatio Wright's division, inspiration was furnished by a band that struck up "John Brown's Body." Soon marchers in great numbers were singing, and choruses of the stirring battle hymn echoed across the dark and silent countryside. "Whoever was responsible for it, had a happy inspiration," wrote a man in the 5th Wisconsin. "It helped the men wonderfully."

At daybreak on July 2 there was a brief halt, and some men had time to boil coffee; most did not. Then the march resumed. The blazing sun

The Union corps of George Sykes, left, and John Sedgwick were the last to reach the field, on July 2. (Library of Congress–National Archives)

weighed cruelly on the marchers. As Robert Orr of the 61st Pennsylvania described it, "Toward noon the radiating heat could be observed in waves, like colorless clouds, floating from the earth and mingling with the fine dust created by the moving columns." In the village of Littlestown citizens put out buckets of cold water on the horse blocks along the road, and the marchers dipped in their tin cups as they passed. Almost every house bore a flag, almost every citizen raised a cheer. In the afternoon, half a dozen miles from Gettysburg, there was another brief rest, and then the final push to the battlefield. By 5 o'clock the Sixth Corps was filing across Rock Creek, 35 miles and nineteen hours from its starting point. As shells burst above the trees and "the familiar roar of battle" was heard, Uncle John's veterans quickened their step.[21]

From first light onward, General Meade had been alert for an attack against some point in his lines. Of particular concern was an assault aimed at his extreme right, curling around the ground south of Culp's Hill and driving into the army's rear. Should the Rebels get astride the Baltimore Pike they would cut Meade's direct access to his base at Westminster, in Maryland. Westminster was the terminus of the Western Maryland Railroad, a dilapidated little road that the Union's railroad genius, Herman Haupt, was just then in the process of resurrecting to supply the army. To forestall any threat to the right, in midmorning Meade asked Slocum and chief engineer Warren to survey the ground there for a spoiling attack of his own. Both recommended against it because (said

Warren) "of the character of the ground." Meade's mind was soon eased by the arrival of the Fifth Corps as a reserve in this area, and the anticipated arrival of the Sixth Corps during the afternoon. With that he elected to stand on the defensive for the rest of the day.

"I have to-day," Meade telegraphed General-in-Chief Halleck at 3 o'clock, "up to this hour, awaited the attack of the enemy, I having a strong position for defensive. I am not determined, as yet, on attacking him till his position is more developed. He has been moving on both my flanks, apparently, but it is difficult to tell exactly his movements. . . . If not attacked, and I can get any positive information on the position of the enemy which will justify me in so doing, I shall attack." This promise of aggression was for Washington's benefit. General Meade, in just his fifth day of army command, in a "strong position for defensive," was more than willing to see Robert E. Lee do the attacking.[22]

Early that morning, John Buford had applied to cavalry chief Pleasonton for relief. He said his troopers, just then guarding the army's left, had fought the day before and were tired and lacked food and forage and their mounts were worn. All this was true enough, yet Pleasonton was greatly exaggerating matters when he testified that he agreed to the request because Buford's command had been "severely handled" on July 1. Buford's two brigades had actually lost only about 125 men — just over 4 percent — and their situation on July 2 was hardly an emergency.

Meade raised no objection to Pleasonton's sending Buford back for rest and refitting, assuming that as a matter of course his place would be taken by another cavalry detachment. He failed to query Pleasonton on this latter point, however, and Pleasonton witlessly ordered Buford's two brigades to Westminster without sending anyone forward to take their place. For the rest of that Thursday the Federals' southern flank was unscreened and unguarded and unscouted. When he found it out, this left General Meade "exceedingly annoyed." It left Dan Sickles exceedingly nervous.[23]

Among all the corps commanders, Sickles found himself defending the least defensible ground in the Union line. His assigned section was roughly the southernmost third of Cemetery Ridge, extending from Hancock's Second Corps position southward to Little Round Top. At the point where the ridge reached the shoulder of Little Round Top it was virtually no longer a ridge; for some 100 yards the advantage of high ground was lost. Nevertheless, this was the ground General Meade had inspected at dawn and had ordered the Third Corps to occupy. Dan Sickles, being a political rather than a professional general, seemed to believe corps-commander rank entitled him to considerable flexibility in obeying orders. In midmorning, when Captain George Meade, the commanding general's son and aide, inspected the Third Corps' position at his father's order, he was told that General Sickles (who was resting after a sleepless night) had not yet deployed his corps because he was in doubt about where he should put it.

When this message was carried back to headquarters, General Meade, "in his quick, sharp way when annoyed," told Captain Meade to go back and tell Sickles that "he is to go into position on the left of the Second Corps, that his right is to rest on General Hancock's left, and that he is to occupy the general line held by General Geary the night before and also to say to him that it is of the utmost importance that his troops should be in position as soon as possible." Nothing could be clearer, thought General Meade, and he turned to other pressing matters.

But to General Sickles it was not clear. At about 11 A.M. Sickles rode to headquarters at the Leister house to complain about his poor position. He may also have told Meade about the cavalry departing from the army's left. In any event, once again Meade repeated his instructions, apparently (so far as the record shows) keeping his temper in check. He even pointed at Little Round Top as the very visible anchor for Sickles's line. Beyond requesting a staff officer to assist him in posting his guns, Sickles did not reveal the scheme he was concocting. Meade remembered him saying, "there was in the neighborhood of where his corps was some very good ground for artillery." Sickles also asked if he was authorized to post his corps in a manner he "should deem the most suitable." Meade replied, "Certainly, within the limits of the general instructions I have given to you; any ground within those limits you choose to occupy I leave to you." For Dan Sickles, with his elastic notions of military practices and procedures, that was all he needed to hear.[24]

Meade gave him artillery chief Henry Hunt to help post the Third Corps guns. Instead of returning southward along the crest of Cemetery Ridge, Sickles led Hunt along the Emmitsburg Road, which slanted in from the southwest through the shallow valley between Cemetery and Seminary ridges. Alongside the road, atop a modest ridge, was Joseph Sherfy's peach orchard, and it was here that Sickles said he wanted to post his corps. It was some 1,500 yards west of the line on Cemetery Ridge that Meade had ordered the Third Corps to hold.

Sickles pointed out that this was comparatively higher ground than a portion of what Meade had assigned him on lower Cemetery Ridge, and therefore it was important to prevent the enemy from occupying it. It

Henry W. Slocum, left, and Daniel E. Sickles led the Union Twelfth and Third Corps, respectively. (National Archives–Library of Congress)

had superior artillery positions. With Buford's cavalry gone, Sickles felt better able to keep track of the enemy from this forward line. All that might be true, said Hunt, but in advancing the Third Corps into Mr. Sherfy's peach orchard — soon to become *the* Peach Orchard — Sickles would be climbing out onto a limb. The position formed a salient, liable to attack from both flanks. Worst of all, Sickles did not have enough troops to man this extended line — it was twice the length of his assigned Cemetery Ridge line — and still connect with Hancock on the right and with Little Round Top on the left.

Hunt's was the voice of military experience and training, but the cocksure, decidedly untrained Sickles paid scant attention. He asked if Hunt would authorize his advancing the Third Corps as he had described. "Not on my authority," said Hunt; "I will report to General Meade for his instructions." Before Hunt left, he cautioned Sickles to reconnoiter the woods beyond the Emmitsburg Road — Pitzer's Woods — before he did anything else.

Sickles at least accepted that advice. Four companies of the 1st U.S. Sharpshooters soon crossed the Emmitsburg Road into Pitzer's Woods to flush out any Rebels they might find. They encountered enemy pickets and pushed them back, then stumbled into a fierce firefight with a goodly body of infantry. Back came the sharpshooters in haste, to report to General Sickles that there were numerous Rebels immediately west of the Peach Orchard.

Dan Sickles took this to mean that the Peach Orchard line he coveted was about to be occupied by the enemy. At 2:00 P.M., without authorization from Meade, without even informing Meade, he ordered the Third Corps forward. The divisions of Andrew Humphreys and David Birney soon occupied the Peach Orchard and the ground to the south of it.

In the Second Corps line on Cemetery Ridge, Generals Hancock and Gibbon watched in astonishment as Humphreys's division on their left advanced "in beautiful style" some three-quarters of a mile westward toward the Emmitsburg Road. "We could not conceive what it meant," John Gibbon later wrote, "as we had heard of no orders for an advance and did not understand the meaning of making this break in our line." In the heat of the moment, their reaction was rather more outspoken. As the Third Corps advanced, reported a witness, "Gibbon & Hancock both exclaimed, what in hell can that man Sickles be doing!"[25]

It was just about this time that Captain Samuel Fiske, Hays's division, Second Corps, sat down in a shady spot on Cemetery Ridge to write one of his soldier's letters to the *Springfield Republican* back in Massachusetts. "I am sitting here under a noble oak," Fiske began, "in a splendid central position, all ready to describe a battle to you, but somehow it hangs fire." Fiske went on to tell of the random outbursts of picket-line firing he had been watching in the valley between the lines, where the two armies brushed against each other and struck sparks. "Very likely," Fiske concluded, "the butternuts will burst out upon us about sundown, after the old Jackson style, with the heaviest kind of an attack, which will give all of us as much battle as we can wish for. . . ."[26]

THE CONFEDERATE HIGH COMMAND had gotten an early start that morning. At 4:00 A.M. General Lee set his day's battle plan in motion by sending a reconnaissance party to investigate the Federals' left flank. Captain Samuel R. Johnston, an engineer officer on Lee's staff, and Major John J. Clarke, an engineer of Longstreet's, were told (as Johnston remembered it) "to reconnoiter along the enemy's left and return as soon as possible." Lee was no more specific than that, nor did he need to be, said Johnston; it was understood "that he wanted me to consider every contingency." In this instance, Lee would have profited by being more specific, for Johnston and Clarke carried out one of the strangest reconnaissances of the war.

According to Captain Johnston's recollection (Major Clarke, so the record shows, never wrote a word about the expedition), the party rode from Lee's headquarters near the Chambersburg Pike southward behind Seminary Ridge to a crossing of Willoughby Run, then eastward toward the Peach Orchard, then south again along Seminary Ridge and across the Emmitsburg Road, "and got up on the slopes of round top, where I had a commanding view. . . ." They then continued southward "along the base of round top" and beyond that high ground for a distance before turning back. On recrossing the Emmitsburg Road, they waited in hiding until a small Federal cavalry patrol passed up the road toward Gettysburg before they returned to army headquarters.

Those three or four troopers, Captain Johnston reported, were the only Yankees they saw on their entire three-hour reconnoiter. He traced his route on a map for General Lee, Johnston recalled, and "When I got to the extreme right of our reconnaissance on the Little Round Top, General Lee turned and looking at me, said, 'Did you get there?' I assured him that I did."

In point of fact, if Johnston's party went where he told Lee it went, there was no way it could have failed to see or hear at least some trace of the better part of two Yankee infantry corps and two brigades of Yankee cavalry. Little Round Top was occupied by two regiments of Geary's Twelfth Corps division until well after daylight on July 2, before they departed for Culp's Hill. That night and early morning the scattered elements of Sickles's Third Corps were either camped immediately north and west of Little Round Top or were marching past it on the Emmitsburg Road. At the same time, the Second Corps was passing behind both Round Tops to its position on Cemetery Ridge. John Buford's troopers patrolled south of the Round Tops all night and morning before leaving the field just before noon. None of these units had orders to operate silently; if not seen, they could surely be heard. All of them had pickets well out and on alert for Rebels.

The answer to the mystery seems to be that Johnston either did not go as far as to climb Little Round Top and, in his recollections, embellished his role rather than confess his failings; or that he unwittingly went somewhere else. If, for example, he took his "commanding view" from heavily wooded Round Top — which was actually the far left of the perceived Federal position he was told to investigate — it was easily possible he would not have seen or heard any Yankees. But however it happened, his reconnoiter produced utterly false intelligence on the Union position.[27]

In addition to Johnston's mission, Lee sent Charles Venable of his staff to Dick Ewell to plot action against the Union right. Lee's initial message delivered to Ewell was to delay any move by Allegheny Johnson until the sound of Longstreet's guns was heard on the opposite flank. Other reconnaissance missions, toward the Federal left, were undertaken by artillery chief William Pendleton and staff aide Armistead Long, but neither produced the seemingly assured results reported by Samuel Johnston.[28]

That morning, while awaiting Johnston's report, General Lee met with a succession of his lieutenants in a shaded eminence on Seminary Ridge near the Lutheran Seminary building. Foreign observers gathered there too to watch the prospective battle — British Colonel Fremantle, Prussian Captain Justus Scheibert, Austrian Captain FitzGerald Ross ("very Scotch as to name," noted staff officer Moxley Sorrel, "but Austrian to the core"), and London *Times* correspondent Francis Lawley. Fremantle and Scheibert climbed into the crotch of a big oak tree to better observe the action. "Just below us," Fremantle wrote, "were seated Generals Lee, Hill, Longstreet, and Hood, in consultation — the two latter assisting their deliberations by the truly American custom of *whittling* sticks."

Longstreet had been first to join the general commanding, at daylight, and he once again took up his argument against assuming the offensive that day. He pressed on Lee his idea of a turning movement that would position the army between General Meade and his capital and force Meade to do the attacking. "He seemed resolved, however," Longstreet later wrote, "and we discussed the probable results."

That mild summation papered over what was by now a seething disagreement between the general commanding and his senior lieutenant. Moxley Sorrel, Old Pete's chief of staff, perceptively captured the moment. The lieutenant general, Sorrel wrote, "did not want to fight on the ground or on the plan adopted by the General-in-Chief. As Longstreet was not to be made willing and Lee refused to change or could not change, the former failed to conceal some anger. There was apparent apathy in his movements. They lacked the fire and point of his usual bearing on the battlefield."[29]

As he waited expectantly for intelligence on the enemy, General Lee paced along the ridge, pausing at intervals to inspect with his binoculars the lines across the way on Cemetery Ridge. When John B. Hood reported his First Corps division had reached the field, Lee remarked to him, "The enemy is here, and if we do not whip him, he will whip us."

The focus of his evolving plan was clearly a flanking attack spearheaded by Longstreet's First Corps. "The General is a little nervous this morning," Longstreet explained to Hood; "he wishes me to attack; I do not wish to do so without Pickett. I never like to go into battle with one boot off." Hood noticed that Lee "seemed full of hope, yet at times, buried in deep thought."

Lee's deep thought crystallized upon Captain Johnston's return from his reconnoiter. Lee was sitting on a log in conversation with Longstreet and A. P. Hill when Johnston rode up and was invited to report. Whatever the actual phrasing of his report — only Johnston's suspect recollection is on record — he left the indelible impression that the Yankees' left flank was exposed, in the air, without an anchor, susceptible to being rolled up. This immediately roused memories of Chancellorsville and another unsuspecting Yankee flank in the air. No sooner had Johnston confirmed the target's vulnerability than Lee turned to Longstreet and said, "I think you had better move on."[30]

Presently Lafayette McLaws arrived with the second of Longstreet's divisions. General Lee now took a startling and quite uncharacteristic action. It had been his habit, since taking command of the Army of Northern Virginia, to follow a strict battlefield protocol: He would deliver an overall tactical plan to his lieutenants, then leave it to them to carry out its specific workings. Now, as Longstreet paced back and forth within earshot, Lee called McLaws to him and proceeded to lay out exactly where he was to go and exactly what he was to do in the forthcoming offensive. This intrusion into Longstreet's prerogatives was Lee's deliberate signal to his reluctant lieutenant that he was in no temper to brook further disputation and was thereby taking full direction of the offensive.

Lee marked a position on the map perpendicular to the Emmitsburg Road, south of the Peach Orchard, from which to open an oblique attack against the enemy's Cemetery Ridge line. "I wish you to get there if possible without being seen by the enemy," he told McLaws. "Can you do it?" McLaws said he saw nothing to prevent his doing it, but wanted to take a skirmish party and reconnoiter. Lee told him that Captain Johnston of his staff had already reconnoitered the area, to which McLaws said, in that case he would go with Johnston to see for himself. At this, Longstreet stepped in and said, "No, sir, I do not wish you to leave your division." Pointing to the map, Longstreet told McLaws to take a position parallel to the Emmitsburg Road.

"No, General," said Lee firmly, "I wish it placed just perpendicular to that." McLaws repeated his request to reconnoiter with Johnston, but (wrote McLaws) "General Longstreet again forbade it." Lee said nothing further, and McLaws returned to his division to prepare for the march. "General Longstreet appeared as if he was irritated and annoyed," McLaws wrote, "but the cause I did not ask."

McLaws's account of this episode might suggest that Lee thought the enemy's line was actually posted that morning as far forward as the ridge along which the Emmitsburg Road ran, and by positioning McLaws's division perpendicular to it he believed an attack along the road's axis would strike the Yankees squarely in the flank. Yet from Lee's vantage point on Seminary Ridge the actual Federal line on Cemetery Ridge could be plainly seen; what could not be seen from there, however, was how far south along the lower portion of Cemetery Ridge it extended. Captain Johnston's report seemed to settle that question. By posting McLaws in a concealing position on the Emmitsburg Road, Lee was simply indicating the northerly thrust of his design for assaulting the exposed enemy flank on Cemetery Ridge.

In addition to the divisions of McLaws and Hood, Lee told Powell Hill that he wanted Dick Anderson's fresh division from the Third Corps to join the assault on the Federal left. Anderson's position would be to the left of Longstreet's two divisions, to attack toward the center of the enemy's Cemetery Ridge line and assist in rolling it up. Of necessity, Anderson would have to be in position first, so that McLaws could form on him. His division was back on Herr's Ridge to the west, and it was noon by the time it was brought forward and started into position.[31]

In the meantime, Lee rode over to consult with Dick Ewell at his headquarters outside Gettysburg. Ewell had already toured his lines that morning with Major Venable of Lee's staff, pointing out the difficulty of mounting a major attack from the Gettysburg front. Once again Lee broached the possibility of shifting the Second Corps around to the right to shorten the Confederate lines and add weight to an offensive there. And once again Ewell persuaded the general commanding to leave his corps where it was.

General Lee surely recognized that Ewell's position north and northeast of Gettysburg, curling as it did nearly all the way around the hook of the Federals' fishhook, was a poor one tactically. It greatly extended the army's lines, and confronted the most defensible part of the Federal lines. Indeed, having failed to seize Culp's Hill, the Second Corps' potential was now largely being wasted in this position. Nevertheless, on this 2nd of July, in his unaccustomed misalliance with his subordinates, Lee yielded to Ewell's views . . . and overrode Longstreet's.

It was left that as soon as he heard Longstreet's guns, Ewell would move against Cemetery and Culp's hills — at the least to prevent the enemy from reinforcing his threatened flank, at the most to convert the threat into the capture of one or both these pieces of high ground. According to Jed Hotchkiss, Lee was "not, in my opinion, very sanguine of its success."[32]

Lee returned to Seminary Ridge at 11 o'clock and announced his decision on Ewell's role. Longstreet took this to be the commanding general's official go-ahead for the movement. Lee was said to be exasperated that his lieutenant had not earlier begun his preparations for the march. On the other hand, having made plain by his orders to McLaws that he was assuming tactical command of the operation, Lee had not issued any earlier start-up order.

However that might be, Longstreet had not been entirely idle. He put Porter Alexander in charge of the corps artillery, and told him to investigate the elevated ground at the Peach Orchard for his guns and the best route to get them there. Alexander was especially cautioned to stay out of sight of the Yankee flag-signal station now visible on Little Round Top. He set out along the route of the Johnston reconnoitering party. At what Alexander described as "a high bare place" in full view of the Yankee signal station, he turned off and led his battalion cross-lots "through fields & hollows" and back to where the road was again concealed from view. He parked his guns along Willoughby Run and awaited the infantry.

Longstreet's second step was to petition General Lee to await the arrival of Law's brigade of Hood's division. Old Pete had been told there was not time enough to wait for Pickett's division, but he was stubborn about wanting Hood to have a full division for the assault. He was also stubborn about not starting his march until it was certain that Law would get there. Lee agreed to wait. The delay was only some 40 minutes, for Law set a remarkably fast pace. Having started out from New Guilford at 3 o'clock that morning, his men marched 24 miles in some nine hours. It was noontime when Law's brigade reached Gettysburg, and within the hour Longstreet set his divisions in motion.[33]

At just about this time, after General Lee's field headquarters on Seminary Ridge had emptied out and was quiet, Lee received yet another of his lieutenants, the long-lost Jeb Stuart. Early that morning Stuart had left his cavalry column on the road from Carlisle and ridden alone on ahead to Gettysburg. No one witnessed his meeting with Lee (or at least no one, including Lee and Stuart, left a record of it), but the report making the rounds in the army was that Lee's greeting was abrupt and frosty.

As soldier-historian Porter Alexander put it, "although Lee said only, 'Well, General, you are here at last,' his manner implied rebuke, and it was so understood by Stuart." Stuart seems to have confided his chastisement to his aide Henry McClellan, who regarded the incident as painful beyond description. The commanding general ordered the cavalry, when it would finally arrive, to support Ewell on the army's left.[34]

By Lee's orders, McLaws's four brigades led Longstreet's flanking column, followed by Hood's four — 14,500 infantry all told, plus three battalions of artillery. From their starting point on Herr's Ridge to the Emmitsburg Road and the Peach Orchard was some four miles by the intended route. The intended route, however, soon produced unintended consequences.

Captain Johnston was designated by Lee to guide the column because (as McLaws put it) "he alone of all of them had reconnoitered, and . . . every step taken was under his direction. . . ." Longstreet, classifying himself on this march as a supernumerary, rode with Hood's trailing division. The first part of the march, from Herr's Ridge southward to the crossing of the Hagerstown Road at Black Horse Tavern, was uneventful. Then, just beyond the tavern, they reached the "high bare place" Porter Alexander had encountered earlier. The guide Johnston must have been taken aback, for when he rode through here in the early morning there had been no signal station on Little Round Top. Now wigwagging signalmen's flags were clearly visible, and to cross the open hilltop would unmask the column before it had gone a third of its way.

McLaws and Johnston went off on a search for an alternate route. The tracks where Alexander's batteries had turned off cross-lots to avoid the hilltop were plainly seen, but no one in the infantry column knew anything about them. Alexander himself, on an errand to the rear, happened on the scene, saw the halted column, and pointed out the solution to the impasse. Unfortunately, at the moment no one in authority was present to take the decision; no regimental colonel was about to assume the responsibility of directing the First Corps off into the fields and hollows. Alexander rode on, shaking his head.

In due course, McLaws and Johnston returned and then Longstreet rode up from the rear to find the reason for the holdup. He rode with McLaws to the crest of the hill to reconnoiter. "Why, this won't do," Longstreet snapped. "Is there no way to avoid it?" All he could see to do, said McLaws, was to countermarch and try another route. Grudgingly, Longstreet agreed. Brigadier Joseph Kershaw was watching all this, and

The divisions of John B. Hood, left, and Lafayette McLaws attacked the Union left on July 2. (Valentine Museum–Museum of the Confederacy)

reported, with polite restraint, "Very soon those gentlemen returned, both manifesting considerable irritation, as I thought."

(It was just here that what Moxley Sorrel termed his chief's "apparent apathy" may have affected the march. On another day, Longstreet would likely have resolved an impasse like this decisively — finding out about Alexander's detour, say, then following his tracks with the confidence that if Alexander's guns went this way, then the rest of the corps' guns, infantry, and wagons could as well. But Old Pete did not step up to reclaim the lead he believed Lee had expropriated.)

The quickest way to countermarch was simply to about-face the troops, but McLaws had been assigned specifically by General Lee to lead the column into attack position and he felt obliged to hold that place. Much time passed as the column doubled back on itself. Eventually the marchers returned nearly to their starting point, turned northeasterly on the Hagerstown Road, then by way of country tracks and farm lanes wound their way along Willoughby Run and back to the road leading to

Seminary Ridge and the Peach Orchard. (With fine irony, this detour produced a deception. Federal signalmen sighted the marchers at the point
where they were momentarily heading away from the battlefield. The
Little Round Top signal station warned, "A heavy column of enemy's infantry, about 10,000 strong, is moving from opposite our extreme left toward our right.")[35]

At last, approaching 3:00 P.M., the column came in sight of its objective — and was startled to find it swarming with Yankees. General
McLaws, writing to his wife a few days later, recorded the moment: "The
intention was to get in rear of the enemy who were supposed to be stationed principally in rear of Gettysburg or near it. The report being that
the enemy had but two regiments of infantry and one battery at the
Peach orchard. On arriving at the vicinity of the Orchard, the enemy
were discovered in greater force than was supposed. . . ."

From this, it is evident that further intelligence on the Federals in
the Peach Orchard must have reached the column during the march,
but while superior to what Captain Johnston had furnished, it still fell
far short of reality. Obviously new orders were needed. In the meantime, Kershaw's lead brigade deployed, essentially as a matter of self-
defense, paralleling the Emmitsburg Road and fronting the Peach Orchard. "The view presented astonished me," McLaws wrote, "as the
enemy was massed in my front, and extended to my right and left as far
as I could see." He reported the new conditions at the front to Longstreet
in the rear, then posted the rest of his division. Barksdale's brigade went
to Kershaw's left, connecting with Cadmus Wilcox's brigade of Anderson's division in Pitzer's Woods. (It was Wilcox who had tangled earlier
with Sickles's 1st U.S. Sharpshooters.) McLaws positioned Wofford's and
Semmes's brigades in a second line in immediate support of Kershaw and
Barksdale.

Twice aides had ridden up to McLaws with Longstreet's queries as to
why the attack did not open as planned. A third order was peremptory,
and McLaws shrugged and replied that he would go forward within five
minutes. Moments later a courier dashed up with orders to hold up his
assault. Longstreet said that now Hood's division would take the lead —
on the right. With General Lee's concurrence or at his bidding — impatient at all the delays on the misbegotten march, Lee had ridden forward
to join Longstreet — the day's battle plan was being altered at the last
possible moment. Learning of the need for a new plan, Longstreet with
Lee's approval ordered Hood to double his men past McLaws's division

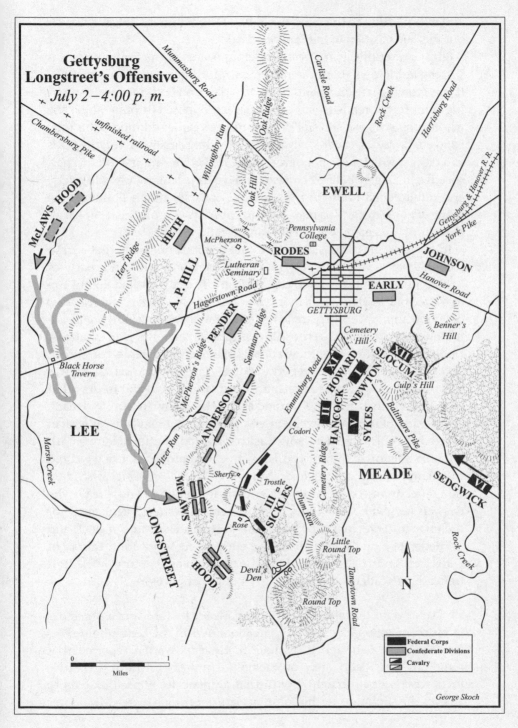

Gettysburg
Longstreet's Offensive
July 2 – 4:00 p.m.

Mummasburg Road

Chambersburg Pike

unfinished railroad

Willoughby Run

Carlisle Road

Rock Creek

Harrisburg Road

Oak Ridge

Oak Hill

McLAWS HOOD

HETH

Herr Ridge

McPherson

A. P. HILL

Lutheran Seminary

Hagerstown Road

EWELL

Pennsylvania College

RODES

Gettysburg & Hanover R. R.

York Pike

JOHNSON

Hanover Road

EARLY

GETTYSBURG

Benner's Hill

McPherson's Ridge

PENDER

Seminary Ridge

Black Horse Tavern

ANDERSON

Pitzer Run

Cemetery Hill

XI
HOWARD

SLOCUM XII

NEWTON

Culp's Hill

LEE

Marsh Creek

II
HANCOCK

V
SYKES

Codori

Baltimore Pike

MEADE

McLAWS

Sherfy

Cemetery Ridge

Trostle

III
SICKLES

Plum Run

SEDGWICK VI

Rock Creek

LONGSTREET

Rose

HOOD

Devil's Den

Little Round Top

Round Top

Taneytown Road

N

0   1
Miles

| | Federal Corps |
| Confederate Divisions |
| Cavalry |

George Skoch

261

and take position to the right, or south, along Seminary Ridge, to search out the true position of the Yankees' flank.

Shortly after this, Longstreet himself appeared at the front and began sniping at McLaws about the placement of his guns and other matters. It was growing late on an altogether bad day, and both men were suffering from frayed tempers. James Longstreet, opposed in principle to the whole offensive, was still smarting from Lee's earlier dilution of his role. Lafayette McLaws, caught between two feuding superiors, regarded this as a day on which just about everything had gone wrong. From his perspective he largely blamed Longstreet. Five days later he was still angry, and unburdened himself to his wife. "I consider him a humbug," he wrote of Longstreet, "— a man of small capacity, very obstinate, not at all chivalrous, exceedingly conceited, and totally selfish."

In his new role as attack leader, General Hood concluded that a fresh reconnaissance would be very much in order, and sent out a party of trusted Texas scouts to investigate his front. They discovered Round Top to be free of the enemy and, more importantly, that the Federal rear, east of Round Top, was entirely undefended. Hood then sent a flurry of pleading messages to Longstreet to allow him to change the plan of attack. Hood captured the gist of these appeals in a postwar letter to Longstreet: "I considered it my duty to report to you at once my opinion, that it was unwise to attack up the Emmitsburg road, as ordered, and to urge that you allow me to turn Round Top and attack the enemy in flank and rear."

This kind of turning movement was exactly what Old Pete earlier had urged on Lee. The problem now was that instead of undertaking it with a sizable fraction of the army, as Longstreet had proposed, Hood wanted to attempt it with his single division — and with only McLaws's division, already in contact with the enemy, for support. And already the day was far gone. Three times Hood sought Longstreet's agreement for the change. Three times he was denied. It was close to 4 o'clock and Confederate batteries had already opened when Major John Fairfax of Longstreet's staff delivered to Hood the final and peremptory order: "It is General Lee's order — the time is up — attack at once!"[36]

AT 3 O'CLOCK that afternoon, General Meade had convened a meeting of his corps commanders at army headquarters in the Leister house. Before there could be much discussion, General Warren reported that something was badly awry on Sickles's Third Corps' front — matters there were "not all straight." With that, Dan Sickles himself rode up to answer the summons to the commanders' meeting. George Meade was not one to tolerate fools gladly, and already his patience was paper-thin after Sickles's repeated puzzlements and complaints about the position assigned him. "I never saw General Meade so angry if I may so call it," remembered engineer William Paine. "He ordered General Sickles to retire his line to the position he had been instructed to take. This was done in a few sharp words." Meade told Sickles he was not even to dismount; he must return to his command immediately, and Meade said he would follow presently. Before he left to see to the Third Corps' front, Meade instructed General Sykes to shift his Fifth Corps from its reserve position toward the left with all speed, "and hold it at all hazards."

Some months later, when the historian John C. Ropes sat down with General Meade to review with him the Gettysburg campaign, he took careful notes as Meade reported his encounter with Dan Sickles that afternoon of July 2. Even at that late date Meade had barely cooled on the subject. "Afterwards he rode down to the line," Ropes wrote, "and to his utter surprise after passing the Second Corps, found a gap. He met Sickles and asked him where the devil his troops were. 'Out here, sir,' says Sickles, and pointed to positions half or three-quarters of a mile in advance. Meade asked him what the devil they were out there for, to which Sickles replied that he thought they would better protect Round Top than they would here."

Meade's temper was now on the boil as he rode out to inspect the Third Corps' new line from a vantage point behind the Peach Orchard. He cut short Sickles's explanation that he had merely acted within the scope of Meade's earlier instructions. Pointing to the ground where they sat their horses, Meade said, "General Sickles, this is neutral ground, our guns command it, as well as the enemy's. The very reason you cannot hold it applies to them." Sickles asked if he should pull his divisions back to their original line. He might try, Meade said, but delivered a warning: "You cannot hold this position, but the enemy will not let you get away without a fight. . . ."

He was prophetic. As if on cue, Confederate artillery abruptly opened on the Third Corps' new position. Should he go ahead with the withdrawal, Sickles asked, shouting over the shellfire. "I wish to God you could," said Meade, "but the enemy won't let you!"[37]

10   *A Simile of Hell Broke Loose*

AS GENERAL LEE had carefully explained it to Lafayette McLaws that Thursday morning, McLaws's division would spearhead the attack up the Emmitsburg Road, striking obliquely into the Federals' exposed and vulnerable left flank on Cemetery Ridge. In successive support *en echelon* would come Hood's division and then Dick Anderson's Third Corps division, rolling up the Yankee line from south to north. All this would take place on open, easily traversed ground. At the same time, Dick Ewell would launch a diversion (and perhaps something more) against the other Federal flank. This battle plan rested on two givens — that scout Samuel Johnston had spied not a single Yankee soldier from his vantage point on Little Round Top that morning; and that therefore General Meade lacked either the troops or the intellect to anchor his left flank properly.

On July 2, however, nothing was as it seemed. Captain Johnston had bungled his morning's reconnoiter, and General Meade would soon prove himself a worthy opponent indeed. On the other hand, Dan Sickles's adventuring that afternoon turned Meade's assumptions, as well as Lee's, upside down.

By thrusting his Third Corps out ahead of the Cemetery Ridge line as far as the Peach Orchard and the Emmitsburg Road, Sickles not only forced Lee to modify his battle plan at the last moment, but also brought into play a very different military landscape. Lee's prospective battlefield was extended southward some three-quarters of a mile. Hood deployed his four brigades, newly designated as the outflanking division, along Seminary Ridge facing due east, toward Round Top and Little Round Top. The half-mile or so of terrain between Hood and the two heights contained what military cartographers euphemistically termed "broken ground."

A small stream, Plum Run, winds through this broken ground along the base of the two Round Tops, with their stony heights forming the eastern face of little Plum Run valley. The valley's western face is framed largely by Houck's Ridge, a modest spur slanting off Cemetery Ridge. At the southern end of Houck's Ridge is another of the geological anomalies of the region, a ten-acre tangle of enormous granite boulders and slabs known as Devil's Den, so called for an eerie cave or den deep among its jumbled rocks. The balance of the ground between the Round Tops and the Emmitsburg Road was in 1863 a checkerboard of fields, woodlots, and orchards, set off by fences, many of them of stone. It was the worst kind of terrain in which to maneuver troops and manage a battle.

David Birney's division formed the left half of Sickles's salient. Birney's three brigades were angled back from the Peach Orchard in an irregular, misshapen line — Charles Graham's brigade on the right, at the Orchard, Régis de Trobriand's in the center, and Hobart Ward's on the left. Ward's brigade was stretched thinly across farmer John Rose's woodlot to reach as far as Devil's Den. At the literal end of the line — the extreme left of the Army of the Potomac — was Captain James E. Smith's New York 4th Independent Battery, posted on Houck's Ridge overlooking Devil's Den. General Birney's division had just over 5,000 men that day, considerably too few to properly cover the ground assigned him by Sickles's reckless action.[1]

General Hood hastily arranged his assault plan on a two-brigade front — Evander Law's and Jerome Robertson's brigades leading, Henry L. Benning's and George T. Anderson's brigades in immediate support. Hood's was a crack division. John Bell Hood was perhaps the most highly regarded fighting general in the Army of Northern Virginia. His troops had performed outstandingly at Gaines's Mill on the Peninsula and at Sharpsburg in Maryland, to note just two of their battles, and Hood led them by inspiration and from up front. On this 2nd of July Hood's mission was essentially what Lee originally intended for McLaws — to smother the enemy's flank and start to roll it up. Once that process was begun, McLaws and then Dick Anderson would take up the task. Hood determined to strike the newly found Federal left with Robertson's brigade directly, while Law on the right swung across Round Top and Little Round Top to turn the Federals' flank.

The battle opened with a violent artillery barrage. Along Seminary Ridge to the west of the Emmitsburg Road, Porter Alexander had posted a powerful line of guns — four of his own batteries from the First Corps reserve and four of McLaws's batteries under Henry Cabell, thirty-six pieces all told — and directed them at Sickles's salient just 400 to 600

Newspaper artist Edwin Forbes based this painting on his battlefield sketches. Longstreet's Confederates advance toward Little Round Top, left, and Round Top on the afternoon of July 2. (Library of Congress)

yards away. At that range, wrote Alexander, "I thought that if ever I could overwhelm & crush them I would do it now." But this was not the ill-managed Yankee artillery of Chancellorsville; Henry Hunt had done his work well. "They really surprised me," Alexander admitted, "both with the number of guns they developed, & the way they stuck to them."

Evander Law's Alabama brigade waited out the Federals' strong return

fire with perhaps more patience than Robertson's Texas brigade, for it had already put in a full day's work — its 24-mile march that morning from New Guilford — and welcomed the pause. Longstreet too was taking advantage of the moment, carefully studying the task before him. A Texan saw Old Pete behind Alexander's gun line, "sitting his horse like an iron man with his spyglass to his eye. . . . Limbs of trees fell and crashed around him, yet he sat as unmoved as a statue." Longstreet was all business now. Argument was cast aside, battle was joined, and he was very much in charge. Four o'clock came and the infantry moved out. In Law's brigade it was "Shoulder arms! Right shoulder; shift arms! Forward;

guide center; march!" Hood personally sent the Texas brigade, his old command, into battle with more verve: "Fix bayonets, my brave Texans! Forward and take those heights!"

There were nine regiments in Hood's two lead brigades, and before long, due to the broken ground and the fierce Yankee fire — and to unclear directives — they started diverging from their appointed paths. A man in the 4th Texas remembered the charge being made "not at an orderly double-quick, but in a wild, frantic and desperate run, yelling, screaming and shouting; over ditches, up and down hill, bursting through garden fences and shrubbery. . . ."

Three of Law's Alabama regiments advanced straight east toward Round Top, and two of Robertson's, under orders to conform to Law's movements, stayed alongside them on their left. W. C. Ward of the 4th Alabama recalled hearing "charges of canister passing over us with the noise of partridges in flight," and a comrade calling out, "Come on boys; come on! The 5th Texas will get there before the 4th! Come on boys; come on!" Robertson's other two regiments farther on the left, 1st Texas and 3rd Arkansas, slanted off on their own to attack Ward's brigade and Smith's battery north of Devil's Den. Further entangling the tactical picture, Law's two right-hand regiments, to avoid being elbowed out of the fight, turned northward up Plum Run valley behind the rest of their brigade and launched an attack of their own at Devil's Den.

General Hood was up front, poised to untangle all of this or at least to manage it, when suddenly a shell exploded over his head and a fragment slashed into his left arm. It was a severe wound — he would lose the use of the arm — and he was carried off the field. There was some delay in notifying General Law to take the division command, and when he did, Law proved less decisive than Hood had promised to be. As a consequence, the striking power of this crack division would be divided and diluted over the course of the fighting.[2]

The Federal high command was galvanized by the attack. "All was astir now on our crest," noted Frank Haskell of General Gibbon's staff. "Generals and their Staffs were galloping hither and thither." Artillery chief Henry Hunt, exercising his newly designated command role, ordered up Lieutenant Colonel Freeman McGilvery's five batteries from the artillery reserve to support Sickles, and Hunt himself rode to the far left to see to James Smith's battery above Devil's Den. Smith's position was awkward and exposed and only large enough for four of his six Parrott rifles; one section had to be posted 150 yards to the rear. The guns would likely come under a crossfire from both artillery and infantry, and Hunt remarked to Captain Smith that he would probably lose his battery before the day was done. When he went off in search of infantry support for Smith, General Hunt had to force his way through a herd of the locals' cattle maddened and stampeded by the shellfire. In so doing, recalled Hunt, "I had my most trying experience of that battle-field."

Army commander Meade, before riding off to see Sickles's folly for himself, had taken two critical, rapid-fire decisions. First, he ordered Sykes's Fifth Corps, two miles to the rear and his only infantry reserve, to march to the left with all speed and at all hazards to reinforce the now vulnerable Third Corps. Second, he dispatched chief engineer Gouverneur Warren to Little Round Top to check on what force Sickles had assigned to guard that vitally important piece of high ground. Then, after confronting Sickles and taking the measure of the impending crisis there, Meade was informed of something else to worry about — the sustained crash of artillery fire from the north. That suggested the possibility of a second Confederate assault, this one against Cemetery and Culp's hills. This new enemy barrage, on the other hand, might just be (as Colonel Wainwright observed) "a mere divertissement." In any event, Meade had already committed his reserves to the left. At least for the time being, the right would have to fend for itself.[3]

Gouverneur Warren and his aides spurred up the rocky slopes of Little Round Top to the flag-signal station on the crest, and were stunned to find there no Federal soldiers at all except for the handful of signalmen. Not only had Dan Sickles disobeyed orders about positioning his battle line, he had also disobeyed Meade's specific instruction to anchor his line on Little Round Top. It was further apparent, from what the signalmen had seen and from Warren's own observations, that Confederate attackers were less than a mile away and moving toward the heights even as they watched. That discovery, Warren later wrote, "was intensely thrilling to my feelings and almost appalling." Earlier in the day he had written his wife, "we are now all in line of battle before the enemy in a position where we cannot be *beaten* but fear being turned." Now that fear was upon him. To General Warren it was instantly clear that if Rebel infantry and artillery seized Little Round Top, they would utterly dominate the Potomac army's position on Cemetery Ridge.

Warren hurriedly dispatched an aide to Meade with a call for troops to meet the crisis. Then, seeking even quicker action, he sent Lieutenant Ranald Mackenzie of his staff to find Sickles and have him order one of his nearby brigades to the crest — in effect, to tell Sickles to do what he should have done in the first place. Dan Sickles, however, was under hot

Alfred Waud's sketch of Union engineer
Gouverneur Warren at the Little Round Top
signal station. (Library of Congress)

enemy fire and beginning to realize the dimensions of his folly. According to Mackenzie, Sickles "refused to do so, stating that his whole command was necessary to defend his front, or words to that effect."

Lieutenant Mackenzie spurred back to Cemetery Ridge to look for other troops he might commandeer, and came upon Major General Sykes, leading his Fifth Corps to the front on Meade's orders, and just then on a personal reconnoiter to see where to place his men. George Sykes, stolid, not known for enterprise, in only his fifth day of corps command, promptly rose to the occasion (as had Abner Doubleday on July 1). Without hesitation, without clearing the matter with headquarters, Sykes sent a courier to the commander of his lead division, James Barnes, with orders to answer Warren's call.

In a second stroke of good fortune, Sykes's courier, in his search for Barnes, encountered Colonel Strong Vincent, commanding the Fifth Corps' lead brigade. "Captain, what are your orders?" Vincent demanded of the courier. He needed to find General Barnes, said the courier. "What are your orders?" Vincent repeated. "Give me your orders." The captain answered, "General Sykes told me to direct General Barnes to send one of his brigades to occupy that hill yonder," pointing to Little Round Top.

"I will take the responsibility of taking my brigade there," said Vincent. As the corps' lead brigade, Vincent's was the logical choice for this task, but in sensing the crisis and bypassing the chain of command, Strong Vincent, too, rose to the occasion. His variegated brigade — 20th Maine, 83rd Pennsylvania, 44th New York, 16th Michigan — was soon scrambling up the rocky face of Little Round Top.[4]

MINUTE BY MINUTE the Confederate high command was forced to revise its already altered attack plan. While the 1st Texas and 3rd Arkansas of Robertson's brigade, and the 44th and 48th Alabama of Law's brigade, smashed at the Federal defenders of Devil's Den, General Law steered the remaining five regiments of Hood's lead brigades straight toward the Round Tops.

As Law's advance against the heights took shape, it divided into two distinct columns. The two right-hand regiments, 15th and 47th Alabama, under the 15th's Colonel William C. Oates, labored up the steep, heavily wooded slopes of Round Top, crossed its crest, then headed down its north face to the low saddle connecting Round Top with Little Round Top. Colonel Oates's instructions were to locate "the left of the Union line, to turn it and do all the damage I could. . . ." Meanwhile, to his left, the 4th Alabama and 4th and 5th Texas followed a shorter curving course across the western shoulder of Round Top before taking aim at Little Round Top. At first the primary obstacles were the rugged terrain, the late-afternoon heat, and extreme fatigue, especially among Law's men, already tired from a full day's worth of marching. "My men had to climb up, catching to the bushes and crawling over the immense boulders," said Colonel Oates. To this point opposition was limited to a few score Yankee sharpshooter skirmishers, but that was about to change.

As these Rebels labored across the slopes of Round Top, they could see and hear the fighting already raging off to their left in the area of Devil's Den. Hobart Ward's defending brigade there — nearly 2,200 men in six regiments and two companies of sharpshooters — was the largest in the Third Corps. These were veteran troops under a veteran commander. Ward had the 4th Maine and 124th New York posted to support Smith's battery on the far left, with the rest of the brigade formed to the north along Houck's Ridge.

The fighting here was begun by the 3rd Arkansas and 1st Texas, Robert-

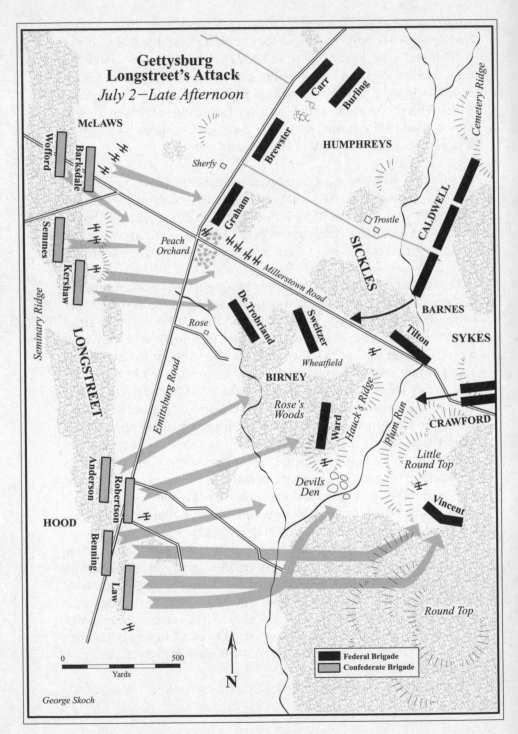

Gettysburg
Longstreet's Attack
July 2—Late Afternoon

McLAWS

Wofford

Barksdale

Seminary Ridge

Semmes

Kershaw

LONGSTREET

HOOD

Anderson

Robertson

Benning

Law

Sherfy

Peach Orchard

Rose

Emmitsburg Road

De Trobriand

Sweitzer

Wheatfield

BIRNEY

Rose's Woods

Ward

Hauck's Ridge

Devils Den

Millerstown Road

Graham

Brewster

Carr

Burling

HUMPHREYS

Trostle

SICKLES

CALDWELL

Cemetery Ridge

BARNES

Tilton

SYKES

CRAWFORD

Plum Run

Little Round Top

Vincent

Round Top

0   500
Yards

N

Federal Brigade
Confederate Brigade

George Skoch

272

son's two regiments that had the shortest way to go to reach the Yankees. Shrilling the Rebel yell, they stormed into Rose's Woods and collided with Ward's line on Houck's Ridge. Sickles's troops had lacked the time, and apparently the inclination, to throw up breastworks, and except for the natural cover of terrain it was a stand-up fight. "For an hour and upward, these two regiments maintained one of the hottest contests, against five or six times their number, that I have witnessed," wrote General Robertson with pardonable exaggeration. In fact, the initial Yankee fire was delivered by three regiments — 86th New York, 20th Indiana, and 99th Pennsylvania, with some flanking fire from one of de Trobriand's regiments to the north. So great was the din that the 3rd Arkansas' Colonel Van Manning had to take his men by the shoulders and turn them to meet this flanking fire.

Casualties rose rapidly in this slugging match. In less than 30 minutes of fighting the 20th Indiana lost more than half its men. Its colonel was killed and lieutenant colonel wounded. The 86th New York lost its commander wounded. On the Confederate side, the 3rd Arkansas' Colonel Manning fell wounded, one of 182 casualties in his command that afternoon. According to General Robertson, "as fast as we would break one line of the enemy, another fresh one would present itself. . . ."[5]

Pressure on the stalled Texans and Arkansans was relieved somewhat by Evander Law's two right-hand orphaned regiments, 44th and 48th Alabama, that threatened to turn the Federals' flank by pushing up Plum Run valley. The Alabamians' target was Smith's battery and the 4th Maine and 124th New York defending it. Soon enough General Ward had to call the 99th Pennsylvania from his far right to brace his threatened left. Captain Smith, his stock of case shot exhausted, called out to his gunners, "Give them shell! Give them solid shot! Damn them, give them anything!"

As the Rebel battle lines crept closer, the 124th New York's Colonel Van Horne Ellis and his major, James Cromwell, determined that their best hope lay in a counterattack. Ellis and Cromwell mounted and took their places for the charge. To a staff man who urged them to lead on foot, Colonel Ellis said only, "The men must see us today." At the cry of "Charge!" from Major Cromwell, the New Yorkers rushed down the west face of Houck's Ridge at the double-quick. The 1st Texas reeled back some 200 yards under the surprise onslaught. "The conflict at this point defied description," wrote an officer of the 124th. "Roaring cannon, crashing rifles, screeching shots, bursting shells, hissing bullets, cheers, shouts,

Artist Waud made this quick sketch of the July 2 fighting at Devil's Den on the Union left. The view is looking west. (Library of Congress)

shrieks and groans. . . ." Suddenly behind the wavering Rebel line there was revealed through the battle smoke an unwavering second line that "poured into us a terrible fire which seemed in an instant to bring down a quarter of our numbers." Major Cromwell tumbled dead off his horse, shot through the chest. Then Colonel Ellis was down, shot through the head. The 124th New York, leaderless and spent, staggered back to its starting point. Command fell to Captain Charles Weygant, who counted barely a hundred men to defend their original line.[6]

This second Confederate line was the Georgia brigade of Henry Benning, advancing in support of Hood's first line of attack. Benning, a former justice of the Georgia Supreme Court, was an imposing figure and a fighter of renown, known to his men as "Old Rock." He was not one for battlefield oratory, simply going into action with the announcement, "Give them hell, boys — give them hell!"

Old Rock had detected the gap between the two wings of the initial Confederate assault on the Devil's Den area, and after repelling the 124th New York's counterattack, he quickly moved up to fill it. Alongside him, in answer to an urgent summons from General Robertson, was the last of Hood's forces — George "Tige" Anderson's Georgia brigade. Advancing on Benning's left through Rose's Woods, Anderson smashed up against Régis de Trobriand's Yankee line.

De Trobriand had already given up one regiment to hard-pressed Hobart Ward, but he mustered strength enough to counter this new threat. The Rebels, he wrote his daughter, "converged on me like an avalanche, but we piled all the dead and wounded men in our front." During the attack, the 17th Maine got into a fierce head-to-head struggle with the 11th Georgia over possession of a stone wall along the northern edge of Rose's Woods. Finally, wrote one of the Mainers, the enemy "received such a scorching fire at short range that he thought better of the enterprise. . . ." Repelled in his initial assault, Tige Anderson pulled back to regroup for a second attempt. While he was reorganizing his troops, however, Anderson was hit in the right leg and carried out of the battle.[7]

Captain Smith's New York battery was now under relentless pressure. Alabamians were coming at his guns from the left, Georgians from the center, Texans from the right. He turned to the battered 124th New York, crying "For God's sake, men, don't let them take my guns away from me!" But the New Yorkers were too busy trying to keep from being taken themselves. Among the battery's other defenders, losses in the 4th Maine were approaching 50 percent, in the 99th Pennsylvania, 40 percent. One of Smith's four front-line pieces had earlier been damaged and withdrawn, and now he doubted he would have time to get the other three away safely if he stopped firing. In the end he had to abandon all three of the Parrott rifles, taking with him the friction primers and other firing tools so the guns could not be turned against him. (The 1st Texas claimed capture of the guns, which the next day were put in order and turned against the Yankees.)

General Birney was desperately scraping up help for Ward's brigade. From the neighboring brigade, de Trobriand's, he borrowed the 40th New York, and from Andrew Humphreys's division on the corps' right, the 6th New Jersey. The 40th New York, known as the "Mozart Regiment" for its link to New York City's Mozart Hall political machine, was surely the most oddly composed regiment in the Army of the Potomac. In the heady days of patriotism in 1861 it had accepted four companies of Massachusetts men, and since then it had merged with or been assigned segments of no fewer than five New York regiments. Somehow Colonel Thomas W. Egan had melded these disparate pieces into a whole with high morale. "I immediately ordered my men to charge," Egan wrote proudly, "when with great alacrity they pushed forward at a double-quick. . . ."

The 40th New York plunged into Plum Run valley to try and block that path to Ward's flank. Then commenced a bitter fight with Benning's Georgians and Law's Alabamians in rocky, broken ground on the verge of Plum Run that soldiers would remember as the "Slaughter Pen." Finally, threatened with being outflanked, the 40th fell back and scrambled out of range. Its retreat was covered by the other new arrival, the 6th New Jersey. Colonel Egan wrote that in this fight he sustained "the loss of many of my bravest and most faithful men. . . ." That proved to be more than a third of his numbers.

The struggle in Devil's Den and the Slaughter Pen and throughout this boulder-strewn landscape was often highly personal and like nothing either army had experienced before. "Each side wanted the protection of those rocks," wrote a private in the 3rd Arkansas. "One in particular. It was very large, about four or five feet high. I saw smoke coming from behind that one and made a run for it, swerving to the right, with my gun ready. I cried, 'Hands up,' they dropped their guns and came out from behind the rock. There were six of them. One said, 'Young man, where is your troops?' I told them I was it, and showed them to the rear. . . ."

By now Hood's division had secured the Devil's Den area and a lodgment on Houck's Ridge. It had been, a Texan insisted, "one of the wildest, fiercest struggles of the war." A Yankee with a literary bent was reminded of the warring din of Milton's fiends in Pandemonium. Hobart Ward's brigade and Smith's battery were driven from the field, and new forces from both armies were already joining battle on new fronts. The weight of the fighting was shifting northward to Mr. Rose's fields and woodlot and to Mr. Sherfy's orchard and, at the same time, to the stony slopes of Little Round Top.[8]

COLONEL STRONG VINCENT, commanding Third Brigade, First Division, Fifth Corps, was Harvard class of 1859 and a lawyer rather than a professional soldier, yet he possessed all the right soldierly instincts. After volunteering his brigade in response to General Sykes's order to occupy Little Round Top, he spurred on ahead up the east face of the hill to find the best place to post his men. Vincent, unaware that General Warren was at the signal station on the crest, was acting entirely on his own. (Nor would Warren witness the arrival of Vincent's brigade.) From what Vincent could see and hear, the threat would come from Round Top to the south and from the area of the fighting to the west, at Devil's Den. Facing south, he discovered a projecting spur and a rough, stony shelf

Above: Confederate dead of Hood's division at the base of Round Top, by James Gibson. Below: Alexander Gardner photographed the scene at the Slaughter Pen soon after the battle. (Library of Congress)

that slanted westerly across the hillside that he thought ought to serve nicely as a defensive line.

His brigade was meanwhile hurrying up the slope following Vincent's track. An occasional enemy shell, aimed at the signal station, arced over the crest and exploded in the treetops or against the rocky hillside. Riding alongside Colonel Joshua L. Chamberlain of the 20th Maine were his two brothers. "Boys," Chamberlain said, "I don't like this. Another such shot might make it hard for mother." He sent them off on separate duties. As the troops came up, Colonel Vincent rushed them into position. He put the 20th Maine on the left, then in succession, forming an ascending curve around toward the west face of the hill, the 83rd Pennsylvania, 44th New York, and 16th Michigan — some 1,350 men all told. Vincent made sure Colonel Chamberlain understood that the 20th Maine's station was now the extreme left flank of the Army of the Potomac: "You understand! Hold this ground at all costs!" "At all costs" meant no retreat, under any circumstances.[9]

Strong Vincent's soldierly sense of urgency was prophetic. Hardly were his men in place and his skirmishers edging out front than Rebels in force were sighted among the trees on the saddle between Round Top and Little Round Top. Surprise was mutual. First to appear were the three regiments of Hood's (now Law's) loosely conceived right wing that had taken the shorter route across the shoulder of Round Top. This right wing was loosely commanded as well as loosely conceived. Of the three lead regiments, two (4th and 5th Texas) were from the brigade of Jerome Robertson, who was himself a half-mile away leading the fight against Birney's division. The third regiment was the 4th Alabama, of Law's brigade. Evander Law, who might otherwise have exercised unified command over the right wing, was instead in the rear commanding the division in place of the wounded Hood. In the ensuing struggle, then, these three regiments would be fought separately by their colonels, which task was further complicated when the two Texas colonels fell wounded early on. Meanwhile, to the farthest right, considerably delayed by their climb over the crest of Round Top, would come two more of Law's regiments, the 15th and 47th Alabama. These were under the charge of Colonel Oates, 15th Alabama, and Oates would make his fight independently of everyone else.

Private Elisha Coan of the 20th Maine described the battleground: "Our regt was formed in an open level space comparatively free from rocks and bushes, but in our front was a slight descent fringed by ledges of rock. . . . Beyond this line of ledge and other rocks . . . the eye could not penetrate on account of the dense foliage of bushes." In their opening assault, the Texans and Alabamians emerged from this cover to strike at the Federal center, the 44th New York, then slid progressively right, against the 83rd Pennsylvania and the 20th Maine. "It did not seem to me that it was *very* severe at first," Colonel Chamberlain recalled. "The fire was hot, but we gave them as good as they sent, and the Rebels did not so much attempt at that period of the fight to force our line, as to cut us up by their fire." As Private Coan remembered it, "Soon scattering musketry was heard in our front. Then the bullets began to clip twigs and cut the branches over our heads, and leaves began to fall actively at our feet. Every moment the bullets struck lower and lower until they began to take effect in our ranks. Then our line burst into flames, and the crash of musketry became constant."[10]

The 4th Texas made its first attack inspirited by the Rebel yell, but after they were driven back the Texans did not waste breath in further yelling. There was little coordination in this or subsequent advances; at one point the 5th Texas in the center found itself out front all alone while its neighboring regiments fell back under their own orders. After two raggedly conducted assaults were repelled, the attackers proceeded more slowly and carefully, using the cover of rocks and trees, stressing marksmanship. Casualties grew heavy on both sides. "Every tree, rock and stump that gave any protection from the rain of Minié balls that were poured down upon us from the crest above us, was soon appropriated," wrote Texan Val Giles. "John Griffith and myself pre-empted a moss-covered old boulder about the size of a 500-pound cotton bale."

Colonel Oates's two regiments now joined the fight, focusing on the Union left manned by the 20th Maine. His opening assault was met, Oates remembered, by "the most destructive fire I ever saw." His line "wavered like a man trying to walk against a strong wind." In Colonel Chamberlain's phrasing, "They pushed up to within a dozen yards of us before the terrible effectiveness of our fire compelled them to break and take shelter." Using his 15th Alabama primarily, Oates now began to work around to the west, past the Federals' far flank. To counter this threat, Chamberlain stretched and thinned his line until it was only a single rank deep, and refused his left at a sharp angle. At the same time, the Texans at the other end of the battle line pressed hard against Colonel Vincent's right-flank regiment, the 16th Michigan. In isolation from the rest of the battlefield, the fight for Little Round Top settled into a bitter, grinding battle of attrition among the rocks and ledges and trees, with both flanks of the Yankee line coming under growing pressure.[11]

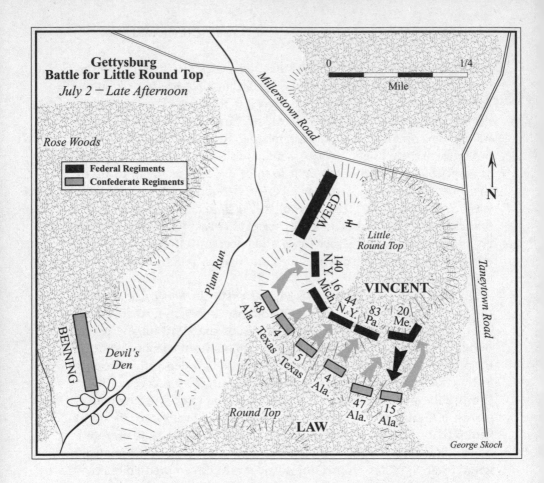

Gettysburg
Battle for Little Round Top
July 2 — Late Afternoon

Rose Woods

■ Federal Regiments
■ Confederate Regiments

0   1/4
Mile

N

Millerstown Road

WEED

Little Round Top

VINCENT

140 N.Y.

16 Mich.

44 N.Y.

83 Pa.

20 Me.

48 Ala.

4 Texas

5 Texas

4 Ala.

47 Ala.

15 Ala.

Plum Run

BENNING

Devil's Den

Round Top

LAW

Taneytown Road

George Skoch

In the midst of this struggle, General Warren at the signal station on the crest was welcoming Charles Hazlett's Battery D, 5th United States Artillery. Like Colonel Vincent, Hazlett was a very opportune arrival. As Augustus Martin's Fifth Corps artillery brigade approached the field, Captain Martin and Lieutenant Hazlett, whose battery was leading, searched for gun positions to support Sickles. Little Round Top appeared to command the area where the Third Corps was fighting, and Martin told Hazlett to post his battery there. Ordering the guns to follow, Hazlett rode up the hill to reconnoiter and there encountered General Warren. The hilltop was rough and space for artillery was limited. "It was no place for efficient artillery fire, both of us knew that," said Warren. "I told him so." "Never mind that," said Hazlett; simply the sound of his guns would encourage the troops fighting below. In any event, he pointed out, "my battery is of no use if this hill is lost."

It was a terrific struggle for drivers and teams to haul the guns up the stony hillside. The first section had to be manhandled the last few yards into firing position, with General Warren himself pitching in to help. When the guns opened, the sound heartened both the troops fighting below and Vincent's men fighting on the south face of the hill. Hazlett's battery soon drew return enemy fire, and Warren narrowly escaped serious injury when a bullet nicked his throat.

Strong Vincent's battle line was not in Warren's line of sight from the crest, but by now Warren could hear the fighting there and see the battle smoke and had learned enough to realize that reinforcements were needed for that front as well as to support Hazlett's guns. He determined to find them himself. With his aide Washington Roebling, Warren hastened down the hill to commandeer the first troops he could find.

By a nice happenstance, the first infantry Warren encountered was from his old Fifth Corps brigade, now under Stephen H. Weed. Weed had ridden on ahead to place the troops, and Colonel Patrick O'Rorke, 140th New York, was at the head of the column. Warren galloped up to him and shouted, "Paddy, give me a regiment!" O'Rorke explained that General Weed was up ahead and they were ordered to follow him, but Warren cut him off: "Never mind that, Paddy! Bring them up on the double-quick — don't stop for aligning! I'll take the responsibility!" This was, after all, his old commander speaking, and Paddy O'Rorke promptly marched his 140th New York up the hill, guided by Lieutenant Roebling. In due course, the rest of Weed's brigade would follow.

General Warren, believing now he had done all he could at Little Round Top, rode off to report to General Meade. Gouverneur Warren would in time be acclaimed the savior of Little Round Top, and indeed he alone was responsible for recognizing the crisis there, for Vincent's brigade being sent up the hill, and for commandeering the 140th New York and the rest of Weed's brigade as reinforcements. Yet at that moment Strong Vincent's men had their backs literally against the mountain wall, and the issue of Little Round Top remained very much in the balance.[12]

EARLIER, AT 4 O'CLOCK, artillery chief Henry Hunt's well-trained ear detected, over the roar of the gun duel raging in front of him on the Third Corps' front, the opening of a second gun duel off to the north. Hunt rushed to the scene like a shepherd to his flock. Atop Cemetery Hill he made a rapid appraisal. From Seminary Ridge to the northwest and from Benner's Hill to the northeast, the Rebels had Cemetery Hill in an artillery crossfire. Hunt saw that his own well-sited batteries were returning the fire at least shot for shot, and after observing matters for a time, he could detect no sign of an impending infantry assault. Henry Hunt's confidence in his artillery was absolute. "As soon as I saw that it would lead to nothing serious," he wrote dismissively, "I returned direct to the Peach Orchard. . . ."

Dick Ewell had ordered this artillery assault in response to Lee's directive "to make a simultaneous demonstration upon the enemy's right, to be converted into a real attack should opportunity offer." This vague, indefinite instruction reflected both Lee's and Ewell's general discouragement with the Second Corps' position. Artillery placement was a particularly thorny problem. Neither Seminary Ridge nor Benner's Hill offered real advantages, but they were the best sites available. The three batteries from the corps reserve battalion posted on Seminary Ridge were 1,700 to 2,600 yards from Cemetery Hill, too distant for very accurate shooting. Benner's Hill at 1,500 yards was within better range, but it was some 40 feet lower than Cemetery Hill and without any natural cover for the guns and their caissons and teams.

At least Ewell had his best artillerist on Benner's Hill. Nineteen-year-old Joseph W. Latimer, the "Boy Major," had learned artillery tactics from Professor Thomas J. Jackson at the Virginia Military Institute. He had risen rapidly and impressed everyone, and today he was leading Allegheny Johnson's artillery battalion in place of the wounded Snowden Andrews. Major Latimer quickly ranged fourteen pieces across a wheatfield on the crest of Benner's Hill and opened fire on the Yankees. In immediate support were six long-range 20-pounder Parrott rifles, and from Seminary Ridge a dozen more pieces added their fire.

Charles Wainwright, the First Corps artillery chief, had twenty-five guns on Cemetery Hill aimed toward Benner's Hill, supported by ten Eleventh Corps guns as well as a battery on Culp's Hill. There were thirty-three Yankee guns to counter fire from Seminary Ridge. Colonel Wainwright was unknowingly complimenting Latimer when he wrote in his journal, "their fire was the most accurate I have ever seen on the part of their artillery. . . ." (Charles Wainwright had been observing Confederate artillery fire since the Peninsula campaign.) He witnessed one shot that struck a line of infantry lying down behind a stone wall: "Taking the line lengthways, it literally ploughed up two or three yards of men, killing and wounding a dozen or more." Lieutenant James Gardner, Battery B, 1st Pennsylvania Light, recorded the effects of the Confederate crossfire: "The shots of the enemy came thick and fast, bursting, crushing, and ploughing, a mighty storm of iron hail, a most determined and terrible effort of the enemy to cripple and destroy the guns upon the hill."[13]

When all the Federal batteries were ranged in and firing, however, the pressure on Latimer's batteries became unbearable. A man in the 1st Maryland Battery put it starkly: "Benner's Hill was simply a hell infernal." It is recorded that in one battery, one piece was disabled, two caissons blown up, and twenty-five horses killed. The Rebels scored their share of spectacular hits as well. A direct hit on a caisson in Battery B, 4th U.S., blew the three ammunition chests sky-high. The frantic team "started on a run toward the town" before it was finally halted. "The men ran after them and brought them back; every hair was burnt off the tails and manes of the wheel horses." The drivers' injuries were minor. But later that afternoon one of Battery B's limber chests was exploded, killing two men and two horses.

After two tumultuous hours and more than 1,100 rounds fired, Major Latimer confessed to General Johnson that he could no longer hold his posting on Benner's Hill. He was told to evacuate all but four guns, which would be used to support the infantry. Not long afterward, directing this remaining battery, the Boy Major was grievously wounded by a shell fragment; he died a month later. Joseph Latimer's "soldierly qualities," Dick Ewell would say, "had impressed me as deeply as those of any officer in my command."

The cannonade that cost Latimer his life and his battalion 10 dead and 40 wounded gained virtually nothing of consequence. As a demonstration it quite failed to distract the Federals, with General Meade continuing to reinforce at will against Longstreet's offensive. It also quite failed to uncover any obvious "opportunity" for a "real attack" against the Federal right. As for softening up the defenses preliminary to such an attack, it achieved even less. Major Thomas Osborn, chief of artillery for the Eleventh Corps, insisted that "no impression was made on the artillery beyond the loss of a very few men killed and wounded, a few horses killed, and a caisson or two blown up. The batteries were in no way crippled or the men demoralized." Over on the far left the battle raged on. Here on the right the defeated Confederate batteries ceased their fire. For the infantry behind the batteries the minutes dragged by in silence. If Dick Ewell intended to convert his demonstration "into a real attack," he was being very slow about it.[14]

LONGSTREET'S SPRAWLING OFFENSIVE began now to expand northward like a prairie wildfire, fueled by fresh troops from both armies. While the guns dueled on Benner's Hill and Cemetery Hill, while the struggle on Little Round Top rushed toward a climax, a new battleground opened on the John Rose farm. Mr. Rose's farmstead fronted on the Emmitsburg Road and covered much of the ground eastward to Plum Run and northward to the Millerstown Road, an east-west track intersecting the Emmitsburg Road at the Peach Orchard. Rose's house and barn were substantial structures of stone — General Kershaw would remember being startled by the loud clatter of Yankee canister against their stone walls — and his woodlot covered some 40 acres. Between Rose's Woods and the Millerstown Road lay Mr. Rose's 20-acre wheatfield, fated this day (like Mr. Sherfy's peach orchard) to earn capitalization as *the* Wheatfield.

General Longstreet had gauged the progress of Hood's offensive, and when he saw it reaching its limits — and saw the enemy fully committing to Hood's front — he determined to send in McLaws's division. "I was waiting General Longstreet's will," said McLaws. Like Hood, McLaws had deployed on Seminary Ridge on a two-brigade front, Kershaw's and Barksdale's brigades in the front line, Semmes's and Wofford's brigades in immediate support. To continue the offensive *en echelon,* Kershaw on the right would go in first, with Semmes following behind him.

There was a prearranged signal for this. McLaws's artillery chief, Henry Cabell, was to pause in his cannonade, fire three guns in rapid succession, pause again, then resume steady firing. With that, Joseph Kershaw's South Carolinians stepped forward "with great steadiness and precision. . . ." Longstreet himself rode along with the battle line as far as the Emmitsburg Road. As Kershaw remembered it, "The directions were 'to dress to the right and wheel to the left.' This was the language." This involved an advance eastward through the Rose farm, conforming to Tige Anderson's brigade renewing its advance on the right, then a wheel left to face north — there to confront a line of Yankee guns in battery along the Millerstown Road. In a letter to his wife, Colonel David Aiken, 7th South Carolina, summed up what happened next: "We fought for half hour or more, and drove the enemy for half a mile perhaps, and during my experience I have never seen so much damage done both parties in so short a space of time."[15]

The Federal defenders in Rose's Woods fringing the Wheatfield included de Trobriand's thinned brigade and, in support, on a modest outcropping called with descriptive simplicity Stony Hill, two newly arrived Fifth Corps brigades. Artillery support here was furnished by the six Napoleons of Captain George Winslow's Battery D, 1st New York Light, posted along the northern edge of the Wheatfield. Régis de Trobriand was by birth a French aristocrat and by aptitude a member of the New

York literati. In 1861 he had taken up soldiering, becoming colonel of the 55th New York, the Gardes Lafayette. Today was his first battle in brigade command. Having already fought off one assault by Tige Anderson's Georgians, de Trobriand was depending now on the support of James Barnes's Fifth Corps division in the persons of William Tilton and Jacob Sweitzer and their brigades.

Henry Hunt had ordered up five batteries from the army's artillery reserve to brace the Third Corps' wavering line, positioning them on the Millerstown Road near the Peach Orchard. Kershaw's advance first took him across the front of these guns — catching their heavy fire as he did so — before (according to the plan) he wheeled left with his three left-hand regiments and stormed them. All was proceeding according to plan, and the Yankee gunners had ceased firing and were preparing to pull back before they were overrun, when the unthinkable happened. Private John Coxe, 2nd South Carolina, would never forget the moment: "But just then — and, ah me! to think of it makes my blood curdle even now, nearly fifty years afterwards — the insane order was given to 'right flank.'"

Someone — it was never determined who — had misunderstood Kershaw's orders or his intent and with this false order aborted the attack. The three regiments obediently wheeled right. Before the mistake could be corrected, the Yankee gunners returned to their pieces and mercilessly shelled the suddenly vulnerable column passing close in front of them. "Hundreds of the bravest and best men of Carolina fell, victims of this fatal blunder," Kershaw lamented.[16]

While his left wing staggered back and tried to regroup, Kershaw's three right-hand regiments — 3rd, 7th, and 15th South Carolina — drove straight ahead under General Kershaw's direction. William Tilton's Fifth Corps brigade was struck first. A man in the 22nd Massachusetts watched the Rebel line as it approached Rose's Run in front of the Stony Hill position: "Across the run, the indistinct form of masses of men, presenting the usual dirty, greyish, irregular line, were dimly visible and moving up with defiant yells, while here and there the cross-barred Confederate battle flags were plainly to be seen. Nearer and nearer came the charging masses." With a roar the battle lines engaged. Private John Smith, 118th Pennsylvania, wrote his wife that "the rebs came down the hill in front of us in droves and we opened fire on them very lively. . . . They were so thick that you could shut your eyes and fire and could hit them, and they jumped behind every tree and stump for cover. . . ."

To Kershaw's right, Tige Anderson's Georgians now made their second charge at de Trobriand's brigade and at its newly arrived support, Jacob Sweitzer's Fifth Corps brigade. As they had earlier, de Trobriand's men met the Georgians' attack and brought it to a standstill. "I had never seen any men fight with equal obstinacy," Colonel de Trobriand wrote proudly. Colonel Sweitzer was equally proud of his Second Brigade. "We had an elegant position and unless they had flanked us I think the old Second could have held it against considerable odds 'till the cows came home,'" he claimed. On the far left of the line the 17th Maine continued clinging stubbornly to its stone wall. The Mainers broke up an outflanking attempt, wrote one of their officers, "leaving us more at peace than at any previous time." He remembered the sense of relief being overwhelming: "We were simply hilarious." Then the unthinkable happened again, this time to the Yankees.[17]

Brigadier General James Barnes, commanding First Division, Fifth Corps, was on the field now and issuing orders without notice to General Birney and without paying attention to de Trobriand or his circumstances. The sixty-one-year-old Barnes, filling in for Charles Griffin, absent on sick leave, brought no real combat-command experience to the job. Apparently unnerved by Kershaw's threatening move toward the right of the Federal line holding the Wheatfield, Barnes ordered Tilton's brigade to change front to the right and fall back beyond the Millerstown Road. Colonel Sweitzer was likewise directed to "fall back in good order." In taking his decision Barnes neither consulted anyone nor notified de Trobriand.

Colonel de Trobriand had expressed himself much encouraged by the arrival of the two Fifth Corps brigades. Then, he wrote, "I saw these troops rise up and fall back hurriedly at the command of their officers." He galloped up to the nearest officer and demanded, "Where are you going?" "We do not know," replied the officer. "Who has given you orders to retire?" de Trobriand persisted. "We do not know," came the reply. That settled matters, de Trobriand wrote: "Our position was no longer tenable." He had no choice but to fall back as well. The Wheatfield was abandoned.

Before many minutes, Rebel riflemen were as close as a hundred yards to both flanks of Winslow's Battery D, 1st New York Light, along the northern border of the Wheatfield, picking off horses and gunners. Captain Winslow's infantry support had run out of ammunition and withdrawn, and he began the difficult task of pulling back as well. "I withdrew my guns, one at a time, from the left," he reported matter-of-factly, "keeping up the fire of remaining pieces until the last withdrew." It was

Joseph Kershaw's South Carolinians at the right advance against Captain George Winslow's Third Corps battery. Artist Waud lightly sketched Winslow's infantry support in the foreground. (Library of Congress)

anything but a matter-of-fact accomplishment. One gun, its entire team shot down, was gotten off hooked to the caisson's limber and hauled by two stray horses collected from James Smith's routed New York battery. Captain Winslow would count ten men wounded and eight missing.

Longstreet's attack had now driven a wedge deep into Meade's flank. Devil's Den, Rose's Woods, and the Wheatfield were all in Rebel hands. The whole left half of Sickles's salient was broken in, and the rest of the Third Corps appeared to be facing the same fate.[18]

EARLY ON, as the folly of Sickles's salient became evident, General Meade had ordered Hancock's Second Corps, at the center of the Cemetery Ridge line, to furnish support as needed for the Third Corps. General Hancock assigned the task to his leftmost division, under John C. Caldwell, but as Caldwell approached the battleground he found Barnes's Fifth Corps division already on the scene. His orders being contingent,

Caldwell returned to his place in the Second Corps line. But within an hour the situation had worsened enough for Meade to repeat the order, although this time he phrased it as support for the Fifth Corps. Apparently General Meade wanted George Sykes giving directions rather than Dan Sickles. Hancock read the order and said briskly, "Caldwell, you get your division ready."

Heading Caldwell's column of march was the brigade of Colonel Edward E. Cross. Colonel Cross went about pre-battle preparations in his usual forthright fashion — "Boys, you know what's before you," he told his troops. "Give 'em hell!" — but personally he had a premonition. Typically before going into battle Cross tied a red bandanna around his head; today it was a black bandanna. As they prepared to march, General Hancock rode up to wish the men of his old division well. "Colonel Cross," said Hancock, "this day will bring you a star." "No, general," Cross replied, "this is my last battle."

Caldwell's division set off with Cross in the lead, followed by the brigades of Patrick Kelly, John R. Brooke, and Samuel K. Zook. As they neared the fighting, one of Sickles's aides, Major Henry Tremain, came galloping up to the tail of the column and collared Zook. There was an emergency, said Tremain; no time to find higher authority; would General Zook bring his troops right away? Tell me General Sickles's order, said Zook, "I will obey it." Said Tremain, "General Sickles's order, General, is that you file your brigade to the right and move into action here." Zook promptly did so. Unbeknownst to General Caldwell, his command was reduced by one quarter.[19]

In its original position on Cemetery Ridge, Caldwell's division had been arrayed in "columns of regiments by brigades" — that is, in each brigade the regiments were stacked one behind the other facing west, each regiment in its double line (front rank, rear rank) of battle. Caldwell had elected the fastest way to move south toward the battlefield by left-facing each regiment and marching one brigade after another "closed en masse." In this unusual but expedient formation they reached the Millerstown Road in a mere 20 minutes, where one of Sykes's staff found Caldwell and concluded a hasty briefing with the warning, "The enemy is breaking in directly on your right — strike him quick!" That injunction, at the moment, was the extent of the Federals' battle plan.

For Cross's leading brigade to deploy to the right to meet this threat, and to do so on the instant, produced a drillmaster's nightmare. Cross ordered "By the right flank — march!" and his four regiments quickly spaced themselves out along the Millerstown Road. Cross then ordered

"Left face!" to confront the enemy — and everything became backward. What had been each regiment's front rank when it was ordered off Cemetery Ridge was now the rear rank, and each rear rank was in front. Right and left companies were reversed. Officers and file-closers were out ahead instead of behind the regiment; the colors were at the rear. "Of course there was instant confusion," wrote Lieutenant Charles Hale, 5th New Hampshire. A Yankee in the 61st New York observed wryly, "To have fronted would have presented our *backs* to the Rebels, and that was not the side we had been accustomed to present to them." Kelly's and Brooke's following brigades also deployed "faced by the rear rank."

The most obvious misplacements were hastily put right — officers and file-closers pushed through to the rear, color guards pushed to the front — but for the rank and file drilled to react by rote in battle, there promised to be confusion trying to maneuver under fire. And they immediately came under fire.[20]

Colonel Cross led his brigade into the Wheatfield so rapidly that twenty Confederate skirmishers were scooped up. Midway across the field they engaged Tige Anderson's Georgians firing from the fringes of Rose's Woods. "The Rebs had their slight protection," wrote Charles Fuller of the 61st New York, "but we were in the open, without a thing better than wheat straw to catch a minnie bullet that weighed an ounce. Of course our men began to tumble." Cross and his officers dismounted to become lesser targets. Preparing for a charge, Cross went to the left to check the posting of his old regiment, the 5th New Hampshire, which was scrapping for the stone wall that the 17th Maine had earlier fought over. Before he could signal the attack, Cross was shot through the stomach by a Rebel marksman concealed behind a boulder. As the mortally wounded Cross was carried to the rear — he would live but six hours — Sergeant Charles Phelps patiently searched out his colonel's killer and shot him dead. (Within the hour, Sergeant Phelps too was down with a fatal wound.)[21]

Cross's brigade pressed on, supported now by Patrick Kelly's fabled Irish Brigade. The Irishmen — 63rd, 69th, and 88th New York, 28th Massachusetts, 116th Pennsylvania — whittled down by long and hard service to hardly 530 muskets, went in under their emerald flags on Cross's right. Farther to the right, Zook's brigade, put into the fight independently by Dan Sickles, struggled ahead through retreating Fifth Corps troops. "They called out 'Don't mind us, step anywhere; step on us,'" recalled one of Zook's men. "They enjoyed seeing us get between them and the enemy." Kelly's and Zook's brigades pushed into the northern

Wheatfield toward Stony Hill, where they engaged Joseph Kershaw's South Carolinians.

As Josiah Favill of Zook's brigade remembered it, "the firing became terrific and the slaughter frightful. We were enveloped in smoke and fire, not only in front, but on our left, and even at times on the right. . . . Our men fired promiscuously, steadily pressing forward, but the fighting was so mixed, rebel and union lines so close together, and in some places intermingled, that a clear idea of what was going on was not readily obtainable." General Zook had remained mounted during the advance, apparently to inspire his men, and that decision was the death of him. A conspicuous target, he was fatally wounded by a shot through the body. When his aide Lieutenant Favill reached his side, Zook grasped his hand and said, "It's all up with me, Favill." He would die the next day. Already two of Caldwell's four brigade commanders were out of the battle.[22]

Zook's and Kelly's brigades continued to push ahead vigorously toward Stony Hill, where they particularly threatened Kershaw's flank regiment, the 7th South Carolina. "They were handsomely received and entertained by this veteran regiment," Kershaw remarked, "which long kept them at bay. . . ." It was not long enough, however. Although the 7th refused its right to better meet the attack, it could not prevent the Yankees from pressing toward the gap between Kershaw's and Tige Anderson's brigades.

In Zook's brigade the heaviest firepower was delivered by the 140th Pennsylvania on the right, which with more than 500 men was larger than the brigade's other three regiments combined. The 140th's Colonel Richard Roberts paced behind his battle line, yelling "Steady, men! Fire low! Remember you are Pennsylvanians!" Such massed fire was brutally effective. Fighting to hold on to Stony Hill were the four Thomas brothers of Company K, 3rd South Carolina. By day's end Private Lewis P. Thomas was killed, Lieutenant William R. Thomas mortally wounded, and Private Thomas S. Thomas severely wounded. (A fifth Thomas brother had been killed at Second Manassas.) Only Corporal John A. Thomas survived unhurt to tell the tale.

Rose's Woods was the theater of action now, and it was a nasty place in which to fight. The ground was uneven and rocky, and in the still, hot air thick streamers of battle smoke hung low among the trees. Men crouched or even lay down to try and see their foes; by its muzzle flashes an enemy line became known. In this short-range fighting the Irish Brigade, equipped mostly with .69-caliber smoothbores firing buck-and-ball cartridges (three buckshot, one ball), had a decided advantage. Kelly's lines and Zook's soon became entangled in the smoke and, reported Major Peter Nelson of the 66th New York, "we were in a deplorable state of confusion." Straightening out the confusion in the heat of battle was made all the harder by the backwardly aligned formations.

With his advance stalled and under growing pressure, Kershaw rode quickly to the rear to find General Paul Semmes, whose brigade was assigned to follow him in support. Kershaw wanted Semmes's Georgians to fill the gap between his brigade and Tige Anderson's, and Semmes promised to do so. His brigade had hardly started forward, however, before Semmes was fatally wounded. Returning to the front, Kershaw realized he was becoming outgunned and would be unable to hold his position much longer. He ordered a measured withdrawal through the woods to better positions on the Rose farmstead. At about the same time, on the Union side of the lines, General Caldwell was committing his last brigade, under Colonel John Brooke, to the fight. It was Caldwell's thought for Brooke to relieve Cross's brigade, which had been first to engage and must now be nearly out of ammunition.[23]

Brooke pushed his men rapidly through the Wheatfield. When they came under the enemy's guns, he halted and ordered fire to be returned at will. According to Daniel Bingham, colonel of the 64th New York, "The men were firing as fast as they could load. The din was almost deafening. . . ." After a few minutes of this, Brooke ordered bayonets fixed for a charge. With help from some of Cross's regiments, Brooke's Yankees pushed right into Rose's Woods and swept Tige Anderson's brigade back through the trees. The Georgians were by now nearly fought out and low on ammunition, and this fresh tidal wave of Yankees was more than they could handle. At one point, when the advance seemed to falter as it came up against Semmes's fresh brigade, Colonel Brooke seized the flag of the 53rd Pennsylvania and led the charge personally.

Brooke's men finally checked up on the western edge of Rose's Woods. Their dramatic advance, combined with Kershaw's gradual but steady withdrawal to the Rose farm, marked the first sustained Federal gain in the afternoon's fighting. Colonel Brooke, with pardonable overstatement, summed up his attack: "Pressing forward, firing as we went, we drove back the first line of the enemy, capturing a great number, and then charging the second line, drove it from its almost impregnable position on a rocky crest." The Wheatfield and most of Rose's Woods were now regained, and thanks to the Second Corps, a good portion of the Third Corps' broken line appeared to be restored . . . for at least the moment.[24]

AT THE SAME TIME John Caldwell's counterattack was sweeping the Confederates out of the Wheatfield and through Rose's Woods, some three-quarters of a mile to the east the bitter struggle for Little Round Top was reaching its own dramatic finale. Both contestants here — the four regiments of Strong Vincent's Fifth Corps brigade and the six Texas and Alabama regiments from Law's and Robertson's brigades of Hood's division — had fought to the verge of mutual exhaustion. Lacking unified command, the Confederate attacks had been raggedly executed, grinding down the defenders, certainly, but failing so far to dislodge them.

The failure of their frontal attacks turned the Rebels toward the Yankee flanks, which began to appear vulnerable. On the Federal far left, William Oates's determined efforts to turn the 20th Maine had pushed the Mainers' line almost back on itself. Oates set about collecting his remaining strength for one final effort. On the Federal far right, meanwhile, the 4th Texas, joined now by the 48th Alabama, had discovered a soft spot.

Colonel Vincent's right-hand regiment, the 16th Michigan, was the smallest of the brigade's regiments to begin with, and then its two largest companies were deployed as skirmishers to tie the line to the defenders of Devil's Den. This detachment and the casualties suffered in the first Rebel assaults left the 16th Michigan manning its hillside perch with hardly 150 men. Now, as the Texans and Alabamians once again scrambled up the rocky slopes toward him, the 16th's Lieutenant Colonel Norval Welch became rattled and took a misstep. He later claimed that some higher authority — he thought General Sykes or Weed, although neither was then on the scene — called on the regiment to pull back up the hill to a more defensible spot, and one of his lieutenants, by an "entirely unwarrantable assumption of authority," ordered the colors back. Be that as it may, Welch and his color guard and a goodly number of his men left the battle line for safer ground to the rear. Oliver Norton, brigade bugler, subsequently found Colonel Welch with his regimental colors and "some forty or fifty of his men" well behind the lines.[25]

Strong Vincent saw the 16th Michigan's flag going back and the right of his line crumbling, and he rushed over to try and rally the remaining defenders and almost immediately was shot down with a mortal wound. Seeing the Yankee colors in retreat, the Rebels redoubled their efforts.

Already that afternoon Little Round Top had witnessed two miraculously timely arrivals, in the persons of Gouverneur Warren and Strong

Union defenders of Little Round Top on July 2: Colonel Joshua Chamberlain, left, 20th Maine, and his brigade commander, Colonel Strong Vincent. (National Archives–U.S. Army Military History Institute)

Vincent, and now it witnessed a third — Paddy O'Rorke, leading the 140th New York into the breach. Patrick H. O'Rorke, West Point '61, had ranked number one in the Academy's first Civil War graduating class and been marked highly promising. He took command of the new 140th New York in September 1862, and July 2 would be its (and his) first serious action. Following General Warren's directive, he led his regiment up the rocky east slope of Little Round Top with all speed and then traced the sounds of the fighting to the south crest. While his men hastily formed line of battle, he inspected the scene before him and recognized the crisis building on the right.

Returning to his troops, Paddy O'Rorke swung off his horse and waved his sword and shouted, "Down this way, boys!" and led the way to where what remained of the 16th Michigan was about to fall under the Rebels' rush. "It was about this time," wrote Sergeant James Campbell, "that Col. O'Rorke, cheering on his men and acting as he always does, like a brave and good man, fell, pierced through the neck by a Rebel bullet." His enraged men rushed past their fallen colonel and into the vacated line, meeting a storm of fire and delivering a storm of fire of their own. As for Colonel O'Rorke's killer, one of the first New Yorkers to reach the battle line wrote, "that was Johnny's last shot, for a number of Companies A and G fired instantly." It was said that this particular Johnny was hit, by actual count, seventeen times.

The 140th arrived at the last possible moment to seize and hold the endangered flank. As one of its men summed up, "We soon got our position, when we opened on them. They soon fell back, our boys being too much for them; but they did cut us down dreadfully while we were advancing." The 140th New York engaged some 450 men that afternoon, and in those brief moments a quarter of them were casualties. On the other side, the 4th Texas and 48th Alabama stumbled back down the stony slope for the final time that afternoon, having lost a quarter of their men and leaving at least the right of the Federal line secure.[26]

On the opposite flank the Little Round Top drama rushed toward another climax. Here the 20th Maine, like the 140th New York, was undergoing its first real test of battle. Colonel Oates grimly prepared one last all-or-nothing assault, and Colonel Chamberlain grimly pondered his diminished numbers and depleted ammunition. Oates's own manpower was considerably diminished. The 47th Alabama on his left was demoralized by the failed attacks and had lost its commander, lying badly wounded between the lines, and (wrote Oates) the leaderless men "broke and in confusion retreated back up the mountain." Oates would have to make his attack with just his own 15th Alabama.

He strode along his line, crying "Forward, men, to the ledge!" but in the smoke and the din of musketry he could not be easily seen or heard. He would have to lead by example: "I passed through the column waving my sword, rushed forward to the ledge, and was promptly followed by my entire command in splendid style." From one of his fallen men he paused to snatch up a rifle and fire off several shots of his own. The Alabamians managed to gain the ledge and there was a savage, often hand-to-hand struggle as they tried to hold it. As Chamberlain remembered the scene, "The edge of conflict swayed to and fro, with wild whirlpools and eddies. At times I saw around me more of the enemy than of my own men: gaps opening, swallowing, closing again with sharp convulsive energy. . . ." The 20th's company officers held their wavering line together by gripping their swords in both hands and pressing the blades flat against the men's backs. There was a desperate scramble for the 15th Alabama's flag, and it was saved, said Oates, only when Sergeant Pat

O'Connor "stove his bayonet through the head of the Yankee, who fell dead." At the peak of the action Colonel Oates witnessed his brother, Lieutenant John Oates, fall mortally wounded.

With clubbed muskets and in many cases their last shots — "In the midst of this," said Chamberlain, "our ammunition utterly failed" — the Mainers finally regained control of the ledge and forced Oates's exhausted Alabamians back down the slope. As Oates tried to rally his scattered troops, he sent for support to his left, to what was now the next Confederate regiment in line, the 4th Alabama. His aide soon returned to say that there was no sign of anyone on the left, except Yankees. At the same time, it was reported that musketry was coming at the Alabamians from the far right. Colonel Oates could see no alternative now but retreat. At his signal, he told his officers, "we would not try to retreat in order, but every one should run in the direction from whence we came. . . ." But before he could give the signal, the matter was wrenched out of his hands.[27]

Joshua Chamberlain also took a decision, one he (like William Oates) believed to be inevitable. His men around him were displaying empty cartridge boxes; his line, he thought, was thinned far beyond the point of holding off another charge. At the foot of the slope in front of him he saw the "hostile line now rallying in the low shrubbery for a new onset." All Chamberlain could think to do now to meet his orders to hold the position "at all costs" was to launch a charge of his own, to surprise and break up the Rebels before they could form for another attack.

Just then Lieutenant Holman Melcher, commanding Company F at the center of the line, came to Chamberlain with a plea to let him advance his company to rescue some wounded comrades trapped between the lines. "Yes, sir, in a moment!" said Chamberlain. "I am about to order a charge!" His order "Fix bayonets!" ran swiftly along the line. Lieutenant Melcher returned to his company and immediately led it forward, along with the regimental colors. With a shout the right half of the 20th Maine charged down the slope.

The order to charge had not reached the left wing before the right started forward, but Captain Ellis Spear, commanding on the left, saw the colors advancing and quickly seized the moment. "The left took up the shout and moved forward," Spear recalled; ". . . every man eager not to be left behind, the whole line flung itself down the slope through the fire and smoke upon the enemy." The effect was stunning, as explained by Private Elisha Coan of the 20th's color guard: "The rebel front line, amazed at the sudden movement, thinking we had been reinforced . . . throw down their arms and cry out 'don't fire! We surrender,' the rest fled in wild confusion."

To meet the earlier flanking assaults, the left of Chamberlain's line had been sharply refused until it was facing more east than south. The Confederates here, abruptly confronted by a rushing line of yelling Yankees, took the shortest route to safety, which was south toward Round Top. In its pursuit, then, Captain Spear's left wing executed a spectacular, entirely spontaneous right wheel that swept all before it. To complete the Confederates' discomfort, Captain Walter Morrill's Company B, sent out earlier by Chamberlain as a skirmish-line guard on the far left, saw Rebels fleeing straight across its front and unleashed a murderous fire. By the time Colonel Oates issued his retreat order, the retreat was in full swing. "When the signal was given," Oates admitted, "we ran like a herd of wild cattle."

The woods that covered the saddle between Little Round Top and Round Top now became a wild tumult of smoke and gunfire and running men — and fallen men. Corporal William Livermore of the Yankee color guard described the not often seen spectacle of fleeing Confederate soldiers: "Some threw down their arms and ran, but many rose up, begging to be spared. We did not stop but told them to go to the rear, and we went after the whipped and frightened rebels, taking them by scores. . . ." Colonel Chamberlain, right in the midst of this melee, suddenly came face to face with a defiant Rebel lieutenant who leveled his pistol at him and pulled the trigger. Somehow the shot went wide and Chamberlain knocked the pistol away with his sword and forced the man's surrender.[28]

Finally, well up the slopes of Round Top, the Confederates turned and made a stand and held back their pursuers. Chamberlain ordered recall. As his triumphant companies rejoined their colors they gave three cheers. The 20th Maine — and especially its colonel — had passed the test of battle with those colors flying. Chamberlain and Oates each lost about one-third of their numbers in this head-to-head struggle on the Potomac army's far-left flank. Chamberlain would claim the capture of 368 Rebels from various regiments, but by Confederate count the total of prisoners lost from the six regiments engaged at Little Round Top came to 218; there was surely miscounting on both sides.

As gallant and dramatic as were the exploits of the 20th Maine and its commander on July 2, they by themselves did not save Little Round Top for the Union. Colonel Oates, whose own conduct and that of his 15th Alabama was easily as gallant as that of the Mainers, spoke truthfully when he later admitted, "Had I succeeded in capturing Little Round Top isolated as I was I could not have held it ten minutes." Indeed it was Strong Vincent's entire brigade that won Little Round Top, a triumph then ensured by the arrival of Charles Hazlett's battery and Stephen Weed's Fifth Corps brigade, spearheaded by the 140th New York.[29]

The Union's Little Round Top victory was drenched in blood. Vincent's brigade and the 140th New York together suffered 485 casualties, or just over 27 percent of those engaged. Command casualties included Colonel Strong Vincent mortally wounded and Colonel Patrick O'Rorke of the 140th New York killed. Even as the victory was sealed there came two additional command casualties. Brigadier General Stephen H. Weed had hardly arrived on the hill with his brigade when a Confederate bullet felled him with a mortal wound. Weed was only recently transferred from the artillery to an infantry command, and *in extremis* he called for his friend, artillerist Charles Hazlett. As he bent close to hear Weed, Hazlett was shot in the head and fell across his friend's body. Speechless and insensible, Hazlett died within the hour. Stephen Weed was borne to the rear where his aide sought to comfort him. "General, I hope that you are not so very badly hurt," he said. Weed replied, "I'm as dead a man as Julius Caesar." And so he was.[30]

GENERAL CALDWELL, having watched in satisfaction as his Second Corps division retook the Wheatfield and swept the Rebels out of Rose's Woods, rode to the rear and made the rounds seeking reinforcements to secure his gains. He was explaining his need to General Romeyn Ayres, whose Fifth Corps division had just reached the field, when a concerned Lieutenant William Powell of Ayres's staff interrupted. "General," he said to Ayres, "you had better look out, the line in front is giving way." In what Powell would remember as a rather sharp manner, Caldwell turned to him and said, "That's not so, sir; those are my troops being relieved." Lieutenant Powell would not be put off. A few moments later he interrupted again: "General Ayres, you will have to look out for your command. I don't care what anyone says, those troops in front are running away." At that Caldwell looked again, and then without a word spurred away to see to this latest turn of the battle.[31]

Like previous turns that bloody afternoon, it was an injection of fresh troops that changed the course of the fighting. From McLaws's division Longstreet had committed the last of his forces, the brigades of William Barksdale and William Wofford. The fiery Barksdale had been champing at the bit. He was posted opposite the Peach Orchard and enduring enemy artillery fire, and when Longstreet came past he rushed up to him and said, "I wish you would let me go in, General; I would take that battery in five minutes!" "Wait a little," said Old Pete, "we are all going in presently."

The artillery contest here was prolonged and particularly intense. Porter Alexander, commanding Longstreet's artillery, had posted his battalion along Seminary Ridge only some 600 yards from the Federal positions, and at that range the effects were deadly. "I don't think there was ever in our war a hotter, harder, sharper artillery afternoon than this," Alexander later wrote. He estimated casualties in his six batteries on July 2 to be almost 100 men and more than 75 horses. The ordeal for infantry supporting the batteries was equally severe. When the Rebel guns ceased firing so that Barksdale's infantry might advance, there was actually a sense of relief among the Yankee infantrymen; at least now they could fire back.

One of the ideas behind attacking *en echelon* was to invite the enemy to commit his forces against each advance and so leave an easier path for the next advance in the line. So it happened now. Joseph Kershaw might complain about Barksdale not advancing in concert with him — "I have always believed that had he been shoulder to shoulder with me nothing could have stopped us," Kershaw later wrote — yet with Caldwell's Yankee division fully committed to stopping Kershaw, there was no reserve behind the first line of defenders to check Barksdale. And that first line of defenders was not up to its task.

The Peach Orchard, at the intersection of the Emmitsburg and Millerstown roads, formed the blunt point of Sickles's salient. The defenders here were the Pennsylvanians of Charles Graham's brigade, Birney's division. Graham's brigade mustered six regiments, but one of them was diverted to supporting artillery along the Millerstown Road, and a second one frittered away its ammunition on skirmishing duty and was sent to the rear. That left four regiments, barely a thousand men, to cover a front of some 500 yards from the Peach Orchard northward to the lane leading to the Abraham Trostle farm. At the center of this line were the six Napoleons of Battery E, 1st Rhode Island Light, with support on the left from a two-gun section of Captain James Thompson's Pennsylvania battery. Against this array now marched, in compact line of battle, the 1,600 Mississippians of Barksdale's brigade.

McLaws's aide G. B. Lamar watched General Barksdale: "He was in front of his brigade, hat off, and his long white hair reminded me of the 'white plume of Navarre.' I saw him as far as the eye could follow, still ahead of his men, leading them on." A man in the Union Second Corps was also watching: "We see the long gray lines come sweeping down upon Sickles' front, and mix with the battle smoke; now the same colors emerge from the bushes and orchards upon his right, and envelop his flank in the confusion of the conflict."[32]

Captain John Bucklyn's Rhode Island battery was the first target of Barksdale's assault. Captain Bucklyn's guns were posted along the Emmitsburg Road on the Sherfy farm, with one section in Mr. Sherfy's flower garden. "I fire slow and carefully," Bucklyn entered in his diary. "Men and horses fall around me. The rebel infantry advance to within 40 yards of me and give me a volley. . . . I limber up and move slowly to the rear. . . . I have got a case shot through my left shoulder and feel faint. My battery is torn and shattered and my brave boys have gone, never to return. Curse the rebels." Bucklyn would count his day's casualties as 30 men and 61 horses.

The 21st Mississippi, under the redoubtable Benjamin Humphreys, bore down hard against the critical point in Graham's line, his left, held by the 68th Pennsylvania in the Peach Orchard. The gap between Graham's brigade and de Trobriand's had plagued General Birney throughout the fight, and now it was firmly and finally exploited by the Rebels. The 68th's colonel, Andrew Tippin, faced the 21st Mississippi coming directly at him, the 17th Mississippi moving against his right flank, and he no doubt sighted in the distance Wofford's Georgia brigade bearing down on the gap on his left, and it all became too much to bear. "We held the position as long as it was possible to hold it," he would insist, and that was likely the truth — Colonel Tippin lost very close to half his regiment in those few minutes.

The Yankee batteries sited along the Millerstown Road and their supporting infantry now had to fall back or be swept up by Barksdale's Mississippians or Wofford's Georgians or by both. Leaving Wofford's brigade and his 21st Mississippi to continue eastward along the axis of the Millerstown Road, General Barksdale turned the rest of his brigade northward against Graham's remaining regiments. They tumbled like dominoes. The 57th Pennsylvania, for example, scattered among the Sherfy outbuildings, was unable to change front soon enough against the advancing Rebels. One of Colonel Peter Sides's officers pointed out their predicament, and Colonel Sides agreed: "Yes, I think we will go now." Even then it was too late, and the 57th Pennsylvania lost 115 men this day, half of them prisoners; Colonel Sides was among the wounded.

Graham's brigade went reeling back toward Cemetery Ridge, carrying

The brigades of Brigadier Generals Joseph Kershaw, left, and William Barksdale spearheaded the July 2 assaults by McLaws's Confederate division. (U.S. Army Military History Institute–Library of Congress)

General Graham along in the tide of fugitives. The general had two horses shot under him, then a shell fragment hit him, and finally a bullet struck him in the upper body. He managed to turn command over to Colonel Tippin of the 68th Pennsylvania, but refused any aid, and the last Tippin saw of him he was limping toward the rear. Before long, however, General Graham was overtaken by the 21st Mississippi and made a prisoner.

The 141st Pennsylvania, supporting a battery along the Millerstown Road, was the last of Graham's regiments to retreat, and it paid a terrible price for its stubborn resistance. Of the 209 men the 141st carried into battle, 149 became casualties. The entire color guard was lost, and it was Colonel Henry Madill who brought the colors off. With perhaps twenty of his men Madill was making his labored way across the Trostle farm when he encountered a frantic Dan Sickles. "Colonel!" Sickles cried, "for God's sake can't you hold on?" Colonel Madill pointed to the forlorn remnant of his regiment and said, "Where are my men?"[33]

General Sickles had tried to shore up his collapsing Third Corps front by shifting troops about to meet each new threat. He cannibalized

George Burling's brigade of Humphreys's division, for example, sending individual regiments here and there to try and fill gaps after they opened — always too little and too late — until poor Colonel Burling had no troops at all and wandered haplessly into Humphreys's headquarters. The thoroughly professional Andrew Humphreys was infuriated by what he took to be Sickles's amateurish actions. "Had my Division been left intact," he told his wife shortly after the battle, "I should have driven the enemy back, but this ruinous *habit* (it don't deserve the name of system) of putting troops in position & then drawing off its reserves & second line to help others, who if similarly disposed would need no such help, is disgusting."

As the Mississippians pushed toward Sickles's corps headquarters near the Trostle barn, general and staff set off for the rear. Just then a solid shot caught Sickles in the right leg and all but tore it off. He was placed on a stretcher and a tourniquet applied, then borne off to an aid station. Game to the end, Sickles puffed jauntily on a cigar as he was carried away. That evening his leg was amputated, and he was rushed to Washington for recuperation. (An officer in the Second Corps, commenting privately on Sickles, expressed the sense of relief common within the Potomac army's officer corps: "The loss of his leg is a great gain to us, whatever it may be to him.") The corps command was turned over to the senior general, David Birney, and General Meade called on Winfield Hancock for another brigade for the left. When Meade learned of Sickles's wounding, however, he put Hancock in charge of the Third Corps as well as the Second. For the first time this long afternoon, the Federal left wing would have one overall commander.[34]

Until Hancock could exercise that overall command, the Federals' left continued the fight largely without central direction. Before he was wounded, Sickles had dashed along his cracked and breaking lines like the little Dutch boy at the dike, seeking to commandeer help from any quarter. As the Fifth Corps brigades reached the field, General Sykes was ordered by Meade to keep his formations intact instead of handing them over piecemeal to the Third Corps; this afternoon more than ever George Meade had little reason to trust Dan Sickles. Sykes was prompt to dispatch two brigades, Vincent's and Weed's, to hold Little Round Top. As for Tilton's and Sweitzer's brigades and Romeyn Ayres's two brigades of regulars, Sykes seems to have intended them simply to act as a backup line of defense behind Sickles's salient, employing them on a wait-and-see basis that had no connection with Sickles himself.

John Caldwell, when he led his Second Corps division into the struggle for the Wheatfield, came closest to heading a unified command. Yet even then it was a matter of personal, time-consuming negotiations. After committing his last brigade, Brooke's, Caldwell sought the support of Sweitzer's brigade of the Fifth Corps. He rode up to Sweitzer "in haste" and explained that Brooke "was driving the enemy like hell over yonder in the woods," pointing beyond the Wheatfield, and that he needed Sweitzer's help. Sweitzer said he was willing but could act only on the orders of his superior, General Barnes. Caldwell then hurried off to find Barnes. The punctilious Barnes was agreeable to the request, but would not release Sweitzer without the formality of an exchange of orders and not until he had the troops drawn up and imparted a few "patriotic remarks" to them.

Caldwell was conducting a similar negotiation with General Ayres for the support of Ayres's two brigades of regulars when it was pointed out to him that it was his troops that were streaming out of Rose's Woods in hasty retreat. Caldwell could not at first believe the abrupt turn of events. After he had rushed off to find out what was going on, the veteran Ayres pointed out to his staff that there was no doubt about those troops being in flight. "A regiment does not shut up like a jack-knife and hide its colors," he explained, "without it is retreating."[35]

What triggered this retreat was Wofford's Georgia brigade. Advancing on Barksdale's right rear, it drove into the gap between the Peach Orchard and de Trobriand's old position at Stony Hill. The Georgians were an especially welcome sight to Kershaw's weary South Carolinians, trying to sort themselves out on the Rose farm. A 2nd South Carolina officer shouted to his men, "That's help for us!" and rallied them for a renewed advance.

William Wofford was a self-made, aggressive officer who on attack made himself highly visible. As his brigade passed through Alexander's gun line the artillerists raised "a thousand cheers," and a gunner watching Wofford wrote afterward, "Oh he was a grand sight, and my heart is full now while I write of it. . . ." Longstreet was there too, seeing the men into the fight, and as the Georgians strode past him they raised a cheer of their own. Old Pete's response was tart: "Cheer less, men, and fight more!"[36]

Wofford's brigade seemed to have a particularly chilling effect on the Yankee defenders. A man in the 57th New York, of Zook's brigade, watched apprehensively as "the Rebels in battalion front came from the opposite woods into the opening. They were marching steadily, with colors flying as though on dress parade, and guns at right-shoulder-shift.

They looked harmless, but the lingering boys did not care to make a closer acquaintance and hurried on. . . ." William Tilton's Fifth Corps brigade, likewise intimidated, turned and marched to the rear. Captain Francis Donaldson, of the 118th Pennsylvania, Tilton's brigade, noticed that "with dogged silence the men retired slowly and without apparent panic or hurry, for they were perfectly well satisfied of the impossibility of long holding their ground."

Wofford's advance, guiding along the Millerstown Road and picking up Kershaw's rallied men on the way, outflanked Caldwell's Second Corps brigades that had retaken the Wheatfield and Rose's Woods. John Brooke's brigade, for example, out ahead on the western edge of the woods, was suddenly confronted from three directions by belligerent Georgians — Tige Anderson's on the left, Paul Semmes's in front, William Wofford's on the right. Brooke had called on General Caldwell for help, but there was not time enough for any help to reach him. His retreat, said Brooke, was carried out in good order and "the whole command came off the field slowly," firing as it retired. His men recalled matters rather differently. The misaligned formations surely added confusion to the orders, and it was soon every man for himself. "We went back, if not as fast and noisy as we went in, still the most of us made fair time," Stephen Osborn of the 145th Pennsylvania recalled; "the Johnnies were close behind . . . and yelling like mad." General Brooke was wounded and only escaped with the aid of "a burly fellow under each arm."

Lieutenant Colonel Charles Morgan, chief of staff for the Second Corps, was shocked to see Caldwell's division "flying to the rear," seemingly without a shadow of organization. He discovered remnants of the Third Corps back as far as the Taneytown Road. "All attempts to form them or any of Caldwell's division within reach of the enemy's bullets was useless." Morgan's report of this incensed General Hancock, for Caldwell's division had previously been his own command. But after learning the manner in which Caldwell had been trapped, Hancock concluded that "no troops on the field had done better."[37]

That as many of Caldwell's men escaped as they did was due in part to Jacob Sweitzer's Fifth Corps brigade. Sweitzer had dutifully marched into the Wheatfield with orders to support Caldwell's advance, and ended up, at considerable cost, covering its retreat. Colonel Sweitzer soon found himself in a nasty crossfire coming from Rose's Woods and Stony Hill. "Colonel," said his flag bearer, "I'll be damned if I don't think we are faced the wrong way; the rebs are up there in the woods behind us, on the right." That observation was confirmed by the right-hand regiment, the 4th Michigan, which reported hearing the heavy tread of marching men fifty yards behind them. Sweitzer recorded another aide telling him "that we were surrounded and in a damned bad shape." Sweitzer refused his flanks, forming a salient, and directed a fighting withdrawal. At one point there was a savage hand-to-hand battle for the 4th Michigan's flag, a battle won by the 4th's Colonel Harrison Jeffords only at the cost of his life. Colonel Sweitzer's horse was killed and he took a bullet through his hat. When there was time for a count, he found he had lost 420 of the thousand men he led into the Wheatfield.

The collapse of Birney's Third Corps division, the repulse of Caldwell's Second Corps division, and the retreat of Barnes's Fifth Corps reinforcements now left just Romeyn Ayres's two small brigades of regulars in the Wheatfield. Seemingly energized by Wofford's bold advance, the Confederates swarmed into the Wheatfield from three directions — Wofford's brigade, Kershaw's, Semmes's, Tige Anderson's, even some from Old Rock Benning's brigade. With the exception of Kershaw's South Carolinians, they were all Georgians, and they scented victory and tore wildly into Ayres's regulars.[38]

Sergeant Frederick Coriette, 14th Infantry, had anticipated an order to charge, but instead it was "about face" and so "we were cut to pieces. . . . I would not have given one cent for my life, and was half mad." Rather than a hasty if disorderly retreat with every man for himself, the disciplined regulars were about-faced and marched to the rear "as if on drill." It made an admirable spectacle, but in their ordered ranks scores were fated to be shot in the back — or, as it was phrased, "they allow themselves to be decimated without flinching." The 11th Infantry, reported its commander bitterly, lost half its men "without inflicting the slightest damage upon the enemy."

The close pursuit was checked by the Fifth Corps' Battery L, 1st Ohio Light, firing double canister over (and through) the regulars into the ranks of the charging Georgians. A man in the 3rd Infantry survived this friendly fire only because "I saw the artillery men waving their hats to lie low. I got behind a boulder with a number of my men when the battery opened. . . ." How many of his comrades did not find shelter in time is not recorded.[39]

The sun was low in the west now, glowing dull red in the drifting smoke, and Longstreet, after two hours of fierce struggle, after committing all his forces, was across the Emmitsburg Road and in control of Devil's Den, Houck's Ridge, Rose's Woods, and the Wheatfield, and was driving northward beyond Trostle's lane toward Cemetery Ridge.

To keep pace, Porter Alexander initiated a charge of his own. In a spectacular rush, he limbered up his six batteries and drove them from their Seminary Ridge positions right onto the Emmitsburg Road ridgeline to furnish the infantry with close-in artillery support. His gunners were "in great spirits, cheering & straining every nerve to get forward in the least possible time. . . ." When fences blocked the guns' passage, the artillery's Major James Dearing commandeered a group of Union prisoners, waving his sword and shouting, "God damn you, pull down those fences!" In moments the fences "literally flew into the air." Colonel Alexander's pledge, as he directed his gunners and urged them on, was to "finish the whole war this afternoon."[40]

SOLDIER-CORRESPONDENT Captain Samuel Fiske, from his vantage point in the Second Corps' line on Cemetery Ridge, recorded his impressions as the battle rushed toward him: "The tremendous uproar of hundreds of cannon, the screeches and hisses of shells tearing through the air and bursting over our heads, and burying themselves in the earth at our feet, the sharp crack of musketry and whirring of bullets, the sulphurous canopy of smoke that soon darkened the air and made all things dim around us, the rapid movements of troops flying hither and thither to take up new positions, constituted altogether such a scene of excitement and confusion and grandeur and horror, as nothing but the simile of hell broke loose is at all adequate to describe."[41]

George Meade was watching this maelstrom intently, anticipating the needs of his generals, then acting decisively to meet them. At the first report of Sickles's deformed line, and even before Longstreet attacked, Meade had ordered Sykes's Fifth Corps to brace the left. When it became clear that Sickles required rescuing, Meade called on Hancock for a division, and Caldwell's was sent. Then, with Caldwell in retreat, Meade asked Hancock for an additional brigade, and for good measure assigned him Sickles's corps as well as his own. When Sedgwick reached the field in advance of his Sixth Corps, Meade greeted him and directed him to support the threatened left. Finally, he would reach out to General Slocum on the right at Culp's Hill for whatever could be spared of the Twelfth Corps, and even to the battered First Corps on Cemetery Hill. Meade was in the saddle most of this long afternoon and evening, taking many of these decisions based on what he saw personally, at one point riding close enough to the fighting that his horse was wounded.

In striking contrast, the Confederate high command — with the notable exception of James Longstreet — was virtually static throughout the battle. General Lee, after returning from Longstreet's column where he altered the direction of the opening attack, remained quietly at his field headquarters on Seminary Ridge. Colonel Fremantle, still perched in his oak-tree observation post, remarked on the fact that the commanding general seemed to be a spectator at his own battle. He reported Lee watching the fighting through his field glasses and sometimes consulting with General Hill or with Colonel Armistead Long of his staff. "But generally he sat quite alone on the stump of a tree."

To be sure, this was General Lee's nature and practice. As he told the Prussian observer Justus Scheibert, he made his plans as perfect as possible and brought his troops to the battlefield; "the rest must be done by my generals and their troops, trusting to Providence for the victory." Nevertheless, what could hardly have escaped Lee's notice, since it was squarely in front of him, was the faulty disposition of Dick Anderson's five brigades.[42]

Anderson's division, of A. P. Hill's Third Corps, was intended to supply the finishing blow in Longstreet's offensive. As Anderson understood his role, he would put his troops "in action by brigades as soon as those of General Longstreet's corps had progressed so far in their assault as to be connected to my right flank." Since Longstreet's line (Anderson further understood) would be attacking "nearly at right angles with mine," he expected that by the time Longstreet reached his right, the Yankees would be on the run northward, with Old Pete at their heels. Anderson would simply join in to roll up the enemy's line — adding momentum, as it were, to a victory march. One of his brigadiers described the assignment as "holding all the ground the enemy yielded." Therefore, at Hill's direction, or at least with Hill's approval, Anderson had his five brigades strung out in a row on a front a mile long, "covering" the enemy's front to almost opposite Cemetery Hill.

In writing thus in his report, Dick Anderson was reciting the original plan for the July 2 battle. But Lee had changed the plan even as the guns opened, and rather than attacking an exposed Federal flank and rolling it up northward, Longstreet's two divisions found themselves for the most part attacking straight ahead, due east, seeking to break the enemy line. They made their attacks in depth — Hood and McLaws each striking powerfully on a two-brigade front, each backed by two brigades. After two hours or so of fighting, this change of course surely became evident to Anderson and his superior, A. P. Hill. Yet neither made any change in Anderson's dispositions. Nor did General Lee intervene. In due course Anderson advanced on a wide front as originally planned, an attack that was all width and no depth. Anderson then compounded the misstep by putting only three of his five brigades fully into the fight.

If Dick Anderson did little that afternoon, Powell Hill did less. Hill on July 2 remains a shadowy figure, just as he was on July 1. His health must have improved, for he was seen in Colonel Fremantle's oak-tree observation post. What little is recorded of his activities places him with General Lee; nothing suggests he played an active role in the fighting; certainly he did nothing to direct or redirect Anderson's efforts. Since Hill had been with Lee during much of the previous day's action as well, it may be that he was simply feeling his way in his new corps commander's role, imitating Lee's hands-off style of management. Be that as it may, the Powell Hill of Light Division days would have been right up on the line directing his command.[43]

At the time, it would not have occurred to General Andrew Humphreys that there was the slightest flaw in the Confederates' tactics when they charged upon him and his division. As he explained to his wife, "the fire that we went through was hotter in artillery and as destructive as at Fredericksburg. It was for a time positively terrific. . . ." The smashing of Graham's brigade in the Peach Orchard completed the destruction of the left half of Sickles's salient, leaving Humphreys, commanding the right half, to face attack from two directions. From his left came Barksdale's triumphant Mississippians of McLaws's division. From his front came Cadmus Wilcox's yelling Alabamians of Anderson's division.

Humphreys was riven by conflicting missions. General Birney, initially taking over for Sickles, wanted him to anchor a new line tied to Little Round Top, and Humphreys tried to abide the order even as the enemy rendered it hopeless. He had only two brigades at hand, under Joseph Carr and William Brewster. His third brigade, his reserve, had been cannibalized by Sickles to plug gaps in the line, and now he had to cope with this new invasion of Rebels from the west. "Finally having driven back others, the enemy in my front advanced upon me," Humphreys summed up for his wife, "while those on my left having forced off our troops also gave their attention to me." He added, "I have lost very heavily."

"Now our time for action had come," Edmund Patterson, 9th Alabama, entered in his journal, ". . . and as Gen'l Wilcox rode along down the line giving orders to charge, cheer after cheer filled the air almost drowning the sound of shells that were bursting above and around us." The two batteries in Humphreys's line were driven back, one of them leaving four of its six guns when the teams were shot down. Andrew

Humphreys was old army, stubborn and disciplined and richly profane, and when he finally had to pull back, it was done slowly and with all deliberation. "Twenty times did I bring my men to a halt & face about," he told his wife, "myself & Harry and others of my staff forcing the men to it." John Gibbon of the Second Corps sent over two regiments to help cover the retreat, and Gibbon, veteran artillerist that he was, had his gunners lob solid shot over the heads of the retreating men into the ranks of their pursuers.

Not every Yankee retreated in such a controlled fashion. One of Gibbon's men remembered how Third Corps fugitives "came like a great billow, rushing with an irresistible force that no troops could check. . . . They swept over us, they stepped on or between the men and even tumbled over us. . . ." In due course what remained of Humphreys's two brigades reached a newly forming line on Cemetery Ridge. General Hancock saw them there, crowded around their tossing regimental flags, still defiant. Their losses came to 1,600 men, 45 percent of those engaged. The 11th Massachusetts lost eight color bearers. In the 11th New Jersey more than half the men were casualties, including the three senior officers, leaving a lieutenant in command; then he too was wounded.[44]

The retreat of Humphreys's division took with it the last infantry support for the gun line Freeman McGilvery had established along the Millerstown Road. Captain John Bigelow, 9th Massachusetts battery, remembered Colonel McGilvery riding up and telling him that Sickles's men had withdrawn, leaving his battery "alone on the field, without support of any kind; limber up and get out!" Bigelow's was the last of the four batteries to go. Their particular nemesis here was Benjamin Humphreys's 21st Mississippi, of Barksdale's brigade. When these Mississippians broke through the Peach Orchard, they bowled straight into the flank of the gun line, very nearly collecting Judson Clark's Battery B, New Jersey Light. One Mississippian crept close enough to yell out, "Halt, you Yankee sons of bitches! We want those guns!" Corporal Samuel Ennis yelled back, "Go to hell! We want to use them yet awhile." Clark got his guns away finally, losing twenty men and one caisson.[45]

Colonel Humphreys's Mississippians next set their sights on Bigelow's 9th Massachusetts battery. This was the 9th's first experience of battle, and now it was asked to carry out one of the more difficult artillery maneuvers — to "retire by prolonge firing." Captain Bigelow realized that the Rebels would quickly overrun his guns if he stopped firing long enough to limber up. Instead, the prolonge, or towing rope, was hooked between gun trail and limber, allowing the piece to be dragged away without undue delay. "I say my battery retired by prolonge," Bigelow later explained; "I should perhaps more properly say by the recoil of its guns, for the prolonges were only used to straighten the alignment. . . ." The six Napoleons went back more than 400 yards this way, blasting away at their pursuers with canister, bounding backward in spurts of recoil.

By the time it reached Mr. Trostle's farmyard, the 9th had gained enough ground that Bigelow ordered the guns properly limbered up. Then Colonel McGilvery reappeared, with a forbidding order. Freeman McGilvery was another of those Union officers who on this 2nd of July met each fresh crisis with fresh resolve. He was a rugged Mainer who had followed an odd route — sea captain to artillery captain — to reach his present station as Henry Hunt's lieutenant. McGilvery was stunned to find that behind the crumbling Third Corps line there was a quarter-mile or more of space on Cemetery Ridge containing nothing but stragglers. While he attempted to cobble together some sort of last-ditch artillery line to fill this void, McGilvery ordered the 9th Massachusetts battery to buy him the time. "I gave Captain Bigelow orders," he wrote, "to hold his position as long as possible at all hazards. . . ." In Bigelow's phrase, "In other words the sacrifice of the command was asked in order to save the line."

Bigelow posted his guns in Trostle's cramped farmyard, piling ammunition by each piece for quick firing, and loaded double canister for a fight to the death. The men of the 21st Mississippi obliged him. "When the enemy appeared breast high above the swell of ground, they were within 50 yards, and in close ranks," Bigelow reported. "They attacked furiously, but the battery men double shotted every gun and swept them back. Again and again they rallied. . . ." When the Yankees ran short of canister, they fired shell and case shot with fuzes cut short to explode at the muzzle.

The Mississippians would be thrown back, rally and re-form, and come on again from three directions through the billowing smoke, "yelling like demons." Finally they got in among the guns, and it was clubbed muskets against rammer staffs and handspikes. Colonel Humphreys saw "Lt. George Kempton . . . astraddle of a gun waving his sword and exclaiming 'Colonel, I claim this gun for Company L.' Lt. W. P. McNeily was astraddle of another, claiming it for Company E." Two of the six guns were gotten away. Captain Bigelow, hit twice, escaped with the aid

596

Bugler Charles Reed did this sketch of his 9th Massachusetts battery, commanded by Captain John Bigelow, under attack on July 2 by the 21st Mississippi of William Barksdale's brigade. (Library of Congress)

of his gallant bugler, Charles Reed. The 9th Massachusetts battery lost 28 men and 45 horses and four guns, but it won perhaps thirty minutes. That in the end proved to be enough.[46]

Some 300 yards east of the Trostle farm and across Plum Run, Colonel McGilvery used that time to patch together a new artillery line from all the bits and pieces of batteries he could commandeer. The cornerstone of his line was a fresh battery just up from the army's reserve, the 6th Maine Light. Around the Mainers' four Napoleons he corralled one gun here or

Bigelow's Massachusetts battery made its last stand near the Abraham Trostle barn, winning valuable time but losing four guns and forty-five battery horses. Photograph by Timothy O'Sullivan. (Library of Congress)

a section there from batteries of his own reserve battalion, from the Second and Fifth corps, from a battery he had no time even to identify. With canister serving as a substitute for infantry support, the line held, but barely.

Benjamin Humphreys's Mississippians still had one charge left, and it was enough to overrun Battery I, 5th United States, as it unlimbered and to seize its four guns. Colonel Humphreys could see no support of his own, however, and he had already lost a third of his men. "I now saw we had advanced too far to the front for safety," he explained, and reluctantly ordered his regiment back to the Trostle farm. The 21st Mississippi had made a remarkable run that afternoon. It broke up the left of the Yankees' Peach Orchard line and captured Brigadier General Graham, it broke up the Yankees' artillery line on the Millerstown Road, and it broke up two Yankee batteries and took eight of their pieces. Humphreys's only regret was that he had no means to carry off the captured guns.[47]

AS THE FIGHTING in the Wheatfield and Peach Orchard accelerated and became more threatening, and as there was as yet no sign of an infantry assault against his right, General Meade proceeded to borrow from the right to salvage the left. This simple transaction was compromised by the continued obtuseness of Henry Slocum. Early in the day, when a spoiling attack by Slocum's Twelfth Corps and Sykes's Fifth was briefly contemplated, General Slocum got it in his head that by seniority he was thereby (and thereafter) "right wing commander." This proved to be a thought no one at army headquarters shared. In any event, Slocum put Alpheus Williams in command of the Twelfth Corps, and Williams duly handed his division over to Thomas Ruger. General Sykes then took the Fifth Corps off to fight on its own, which left Slocum in command (so he believed) of the army's right wing, now consisting of . . . the Twelfth Corps.

There is no record of exactly what Meade asked of Slocum by way of reinforcements, but by the testimony of acting corps commander Williams it was a discretionary order — "to detach all I could spare, at least one division. . . ." That fits with Meade's actions that day regarding other frontline units, such as his calling on Hancock for a single Second Corps division to rescue Sickles. Williams dutifully marched Ruger's division off Culp's Hill and southward toward the fighting. As he left, he reminded Slocum of the necessity of retaining the Twelfth Corps' other division, John Geary's, in the Culp's Hill lines. But for reasons he did not share with anyone, General Slocum — perhaps practicing what he regarded as a wing commander's unbridled discretion — rejected the advice and ordered two brigades of Geary's division to follow Ruger. That left only George Sears Greene's brigade — some 1,400 men — on Culp's Hill to face what was known to be Dick Ewell's army corps.

A dozen years later, in response to criticism, Slocum claimed that in fact Meade had called on him for the *entire* Twelfth Corps; he was able to hold back Greene's brigade, he said, only by appealing to the general commanding. To be sure, by then General Meade was dead and the official record was silent on the matter, and Henry Slocum preferred not to be reminded of his serious misstep. On July 1 he had failed to exercise a commander's discretion to march to the sound of the guns; on July 2, it may be said, he overexercised that discretion. And as it happened,

Slocum's exercise went for naught — John Geary lost his way and his troops never reached the battleground.[48]

As Alpheus Williams led Ruger's division toward the sound of the guns, other Union reinforcements were also rushing to the battleground. Meade called on the First Corps on Cemetery Hill for help, and the first to march was George Stannard's Vermont brigade, newly arrived from the Washington defenses. Hancock sent for *his* Department of Washington newcomers, George Willard's brigade, to plug a gap in the line, and led it there himself. The last of the Fifth Corps' divisions, Samuel Crawford's Pennsylvania Reserves, was on the field, and Sedgwick's hard-marching Sixth Corps was arriving. The burning question was whether all this new strength would be in time to prevent Longstreet and Dick Anderson from punching right through the shattered Union defenses.

The final Confederate forces to be committed to the battle were from Anderson's division. Advancing quickly on Wilcox's left was David Lang's Florida brigade, smallest in the army — three regiments, engaging fewer than 750 men. It caught Andrew Humphreys's retreating Yankees in the flank and added greatly to their discomfort. Colonel Lang said he did not remember "the dead lying thicker than where the Yankee infantry attempted to make a stand in our front." Next in Anderson's line of battle came Ambrose Ransom "Rans" Wright's Georgia brigade. Thus four brigades — Barksdale's of McLaws's division, and those of Wilcox, Lang, and Wright of Anderson's division — were now driving in an extended line toward the large gap where Caldwell's division of the Second Corps had been pulled out to go to Sickles's aid. Confronting them was Winfield Scott Hancock and a very sketchy patchwork of men and guns, held together largely by the dominating force of General Hancock's personality.

Nor did Hancock's responsibility end there. He recognized he was being handed a dirty job when Meade put him in charge of Sickles's corps in addition to his own. John Gibbon, to whom Hancock turned over the Second Corps, heard Hancock muttering at the change. "I was not surprised," Gibbon wrote, "that he should utter some expressions of discontent at being compelled at such time to give up command of one corps in a sound condition to take command of another which, it was understood, had gone to pieces." The Third Corps' shattered front, plus the portion of the Second Corps' front from which Caldwell's division had been withdrawn, added up to perhaps a three-quarter-mile-wide gap that somehow had to be filled. The southern end of this gap — Little Round

Top, the Wheatfield, the Trostle farm — would be the preserve of the Fifth and Sixth corps. Some way or another, Hancock would have to fill up the rest of the hole.

"Hancock the Superb," General McClellan had called him on the Peninsula. On the 2nd of July he might have been called "Hancock the Magnificent." He was everywhere and saw everything and missed nothing. On this smoky, thunderously loud, immensely confusing battlefield, reinforcements often had no notion of where they were supposed to go. But Hancock knew. When Willard's brigade, the Second Corps' reserve, was sent off to the fighting, Hancock was there to lead it to where it was needed. Later, Captain Henry Abbott of Gibbon's division watched as Hancock rode by at the head of a body of First Corps reinforcements "in the handsomest manner. He led them forward on horseback, with his hat off. They cheered him & as soon as we saw him we sent up a tremendous cheer."

Lesser concerns caught Hancock's eye as well, and roused his temper. When he saw a battery charging right through a marching infantry column, he collared the battery commander and told him in no uncertain terms, "if I commanded this regiment I'd be God Damned if I would not charge bayonets on you!" And he set examples. Inspecting the 19th Maine's position, Hancock seized on Private George Durgin, on the far left of the formation, marched him out ahead a few dozen yards, and demanded in a loud voice, "Will you stay here?" Private Durgin realized he had little choice in the matter. "I'll stay here, General, till hell freezes over," he said. With a smile, Hancock ordered the 19th Maine to form on Private Durgin, and rode on.[49]

Dan Sickles's original push forward to the Peach Orchard had opened a half-mile gap between the Third and Second corps, further widened when Caldwell's division was ordered to the Wheatfield. John Gibbon stretched William Harrow's brigade in scattered fashion across this expanse in front of Cemetery Ridge. He posted the 15th Massachusetts and 82nd New York on the Nicholas Codori farm along the Emmitsburg Road, where they might cover Frederick Brown's Battery B, 1st Rhode Island. Farther to the south, Gulian Weir's Battery C, 5th U.S., was supported by the 19th Maine, and Evan Thomas's Battery C, 4th U.S., by the 1st Minnesota. It was a stopgap arrangement at best, and now David Lang's Floridians and Rans Wright's Georgians proceeded to tear into it piece by piece.

After pursuing Humphreys's men, the Floridians turned their attention to Lieutenant Weir's battery. They came on so fast and against such

Winfield Scott Hancock led the Union Second Corps in the defense of Cemetery Ridge on July 2. (Library of Congress)

light opposition that Weir soon ran out of canister, the artillerist's primary weapon against infantry. He limbered up but then was encouraged by the supporting fire of the 19th Maine and decided to try to stay and fight. But, wrote Weir, "The enemy were too close." In the end he managed to get only three of his six Napoleons away.

Meanwhile, on the Codori farm, the 15th Massachusetts and 82nd

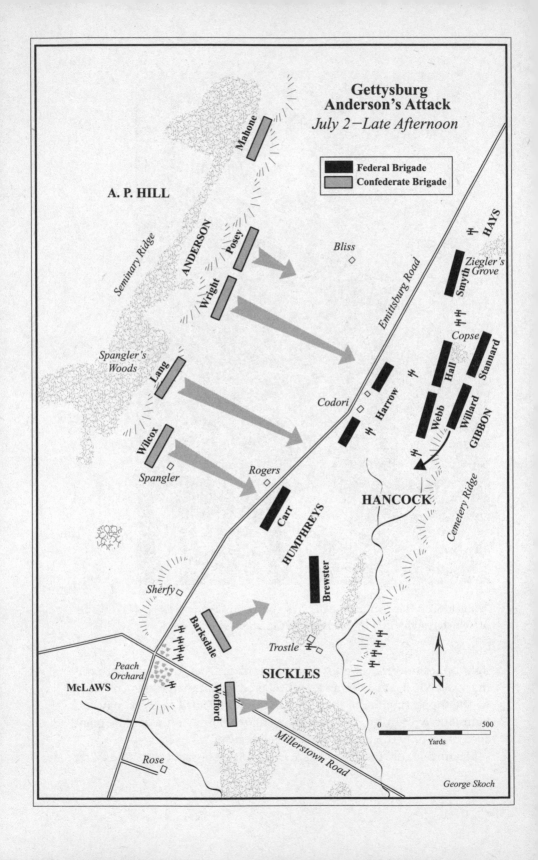

Gettysburg
Anderson's Attack
July 2 — Late Afternoon

Federal Brigade
Confederate Brigade

A. P. HILL

Mahone

ANDERSON

Posey

Bliss

Wright

HAYS

Ziegler's Grove

Smyth

Seminary Ridge

Spangler's Woods

Lang

Copse

Hall

Stannard

Codori

Harrow

Webb

Willard

GIBBON

Wilcox

Emittsburg Road

Spangler

Rogers

HANCOCK

Cemetery Ridge

Carr

HUMPHREYS

Brewster

Sherfy

Barksdale

Trostle

N

Peach
Orchard

McLAWS

Wofford

SICKLES

0   500
Yards

Rose

Millerstown Road

George Skoch

New York faced the massed charge of Rans Wright's Georgians. The Yankees here had piled up fence rails as a makeshift breastworks and, wrote one of them, "With a shout we sprang up on our knees and resting our muskets over the rails, we gave them one of the most destructive volleys I ever witnessed. . . . They hesitated, then reeled, they staggered and wavered slightly. . . ." But the Georgians recovered quickly. Overlapping the Federals' right, they killed the 15th Massachusetts' Colonel George H. Ward and the 82nd New York's Lieutenant Colonel James Huston, and both leaderless regiments soon "retired in some disorder. . . ."

The Georgians surged across the Emmitsburg Road and made straight for Lieutenant Brown's Rhode Island battery. A Federal infantryman overrun by the charge tried to surrender, but "they spoke not a word to me but passed over and on, every reb's eye seemed to be fixed on our artillery. . . ." Brown's gunners employed case shot, cutting their fuzes shorter with each firing, then switching to canister, then double canister. "And as our artillery fire cut down their men," wrote the battery's historian, "they would waver for a second, then close up and continue to advance, their battle flags fluttering in the breeze. . . ." Wright's men would not be denied, and swarmed into the battery. Lieutenant Brown got only three of his six guns off safely. The Georgians pushed on up Cemetery Ridge.[50]

General Wright had noticed that Carnot Posey's brigade on his left was not keeping pace, and he sent one of his aides back to Anderson to inform him of that fact. The aide returned with word that Posey's orders would be repeated to him, and that meanwhile Wright should press on. What orders Anderson actually sent to Posey is unclear, but certainly they proved ineffectual. For some hours Posey's Mississippians had been feuding with the Yankees over possession of William Bliss's farm buildings midway between the lines, and now they simply renewed the feud more forcefully, capturing Mr. Bliss's large brick barn, then settling down short of the Emmitsburg Road to snipe at the Federals at a distance. In their advance Wright's Georgians talked some men of the 48th Mississippi, Posey's right-hand regiment, into joining them ("Get up and fight!"), but that was the extent of the Mississippi brigade's role in the assault.

By far the oddest behavior, however, was William Mahone's. Mahone's Virginia brigade was the northernmost of Anderson's five brigades on Seminary Ridge, and supposedly he would advance with the rest of the division. When he did not, Anderson sent a staff officer to order him forward. Mahone refused; General Anderson, he said, had personally told him to remain where he was. But, said the staff man, "I am just from General Anderson and he orders you to advance." No, said stubborn Billy Mahone, he already had his orders from the general and he would stay put. And he did.

At no time during the fighting that day was Dick Anderson at the front to direct or correct affairs. He did nothing, for example, about Mahone's intransigence when it was reported to him. An angry Cadmus Wilcox would report that during the battle he sent his adjutant to General Anderson at his headquarters several hundred yards "back in the woods," where he found the general's horse tied to a tree "and all his staff lying on the ground (indifferent) as tho' nothing was going on. . . . I am quite certain that Gen'l. A. never saw a foot of the ground on which his three brigades fought on the 2nd July."[51]

EVEN AS RANS WRIGHT'S GEORGIANS strode toward a little copse of scrub oaks behind an angled stone wall on Cemetery Ridge — they would be credited (in retrospect) with reaching the "high-water mark" of General Lee's July 2 offensive — the tide of the battle was already turning slowly but irrevocably away from the Confederacy. It was near sunset now, and all along the torn, smoking battleground, from the copse of trees southward to Little Round Top, the Union was striking back with fresh troops.

When General Meade called on the Second Corps for an additional brigade for the embattled left, Hancock had turned to Alexander Hays's division, then in the quietest sector of the line. Hays, in turn, selected George L. Willard's brigade, posted in reserve. To Colonel Willard, Hays forthrightly announced, "Take your Brigade over there and knock the hell out of the rebs!"

Willard's brigade — 39th, 111th, 125th, and 126th New York — had something to prove on this 2nd of July. Back in September 1862, during the Maryland campaign, these New Yorkers had been swept up by Stonewall Jackson when he captured Harper's Ferry. The 126th New York was particularly humiliated when, barely three weeks in the army, it broke and ran trying to defend the post. "The Regiment," wrote one of its men, "panted to remove that stigma." The brigade was paroled after Harper's Ferry and then served in the Washington defenses; today would mark its first opportunity for redemption. Hancock overtook Willard's column as it marched to the battlefront and directed him to deploy behind Colonel McGilvery's patched-together artillery line.

After smashing through Graham's brigade at the Peach Orchard, William Barksdale had turned his Mississippians northward against Andrew Humphreys's division. With Wilcox's help, Barksdale forced Humphreys into retreat, and then pushed his men on into the widening gap in the Federal line. The Mississippi brigade had now advanced perhaps a mile from its starting point, overcoming everything in its path but losing heavily, and fierce Barksdale continued driving it forward. When his lieutenants urged him to pause and regroup, his answer was emphatic: "No! Crowd them — we have them on the run. Move your regiments!" Suddenly, from behind the ridgeline in their front there was a solid line of men rising "as if from the earth and . . . moving down upon them."

Hancock had pointed out to Colonel Willard this advancing Rebel line threatening McGilvery's guns behind Plum Run, and Willard issued the command "Forward!" and the brigade started down the slope. Someone called out, "Remember Harper's Ferry!" and hundreds took up the cry. It so happened that Barksdale's brigade had been at Harper's Ferry in 1862, and chased away the rookie 126th New York, so redemption could be sweeter than the New Yorkers realized. "Men fell at every step," wrote a captain in the 111th New York. "We officers were kept busy closing the ranks as they were depleted and pushing on, not heeding the storm of metal." The Mississippi regiments, disordered from their long advance, were not prepared to meet this hard-driving attack, and they fell back in confusion. General Barksdale rushed into the melee to rally his men and went down mortally wounded. He would die during the night, in a Union hospital. His opposite number, George Willard, died instantly when hit in the face by a shell fragment.

One regiment from each brigade, the 39th New York and the 21st Mississippi, staged a separate contest of their own. The Mississippians, captors of eight Yankee guns, were attempting to turn the cannon on their former owners when the New Yorkers rushed them and drove them off after a sharp fight. One of those leading the charge with rifle in hand was Lieutenant Samuel Peeples, a battery officer determined to reclaim his guns. In due course Willard's men had to pull back in the face of Porter Alexander's gun line at the Peach Orchard, but Barksdale's memorable charge was finally brought to a standstill. It cost Barksdale his life, and his brigade half its men. In his report General Hays recognized the redemption of Willard's New York brigade: "The history of this brigade's operations is written in blood," washing away the Harper's Ferry taint.[52]

Alpheus Williams was meanwhile leading Ruger's Twelfth Corps division up the east slope of Cemetery Ridge toward the sound of the guns. In elevating himself to wing commander, General Slocum had named

Williams acting head of the Twelfth Corps, but now Williams acted as a divisional commander in directly putting his men into the battle. He encountered evidence of heavy fighting and a good many stragglers and wounded, he wrote, "but nobody seemed to know where to go in, nor did any of them offer to go in with us." Then he came upon an old friend, Colonel McGilvery, who was delighted to see him and knew exactly where the infantry ought to go — to support his embattled gun line. Williams ordered in Henry Lockwood's brigade, which had reached the army only that morning from its posting at Baltimore. These newcomers occupied Mr. Trostle's woodlot and recaptured Captain Bigelow's four abandoned guns in the process. Williams deployed the rest of Ruger's troops to seal off the gap that had opened in front of McLaws's division.[53]

After putting in Willard's brigade, General Hancock was riding north on Cemetery Ridge behind Plum Run with a single aide when in the shadows and smoke he saw what he took to be some Third Corps troops in retreat. He hurried forward to rally them and in a moment the air around him was full of bullets, two of which wounded his aide. He ducked away and spurred back to seek something to plug this new break in the dike. All he found, alongside Evan Thomas's battery of regular artillery, was a single, not very large regiment. "My God!" he exclaimed. "Are these all the men we have here? What regiment is this?" "First Minnesota," answered Colonel William Colvill. In a fight Winfield Hancock was not one to waste words. Pointing to the flag of the enemy force that had fired on him, he barked, "Advance, Colonel, and take those colors!"

With that, said Colonel Colvill, "I immediately gave the order 'Forward double-quick,' and under a galling fire from the enemy, we advanced. . . ." The veterans of the 1st Minnesota, that state's one regiment in the Army of the Potomac, had fought at First Bull Run and in every campaign since and they knew a forlorn hope when they became one, yet they fixed bayonets and charged anyway. Their swift, bold move took the Rebels by surprise — these were Cadmus Wilcox's Alabamians — and sent them scrambling backward. "The first line broke in our front as we reached it, and rushed back through the second line, stopping the whole advance . . . ," wrote Lieutenant William Lochren; "they kept a respectful distance from our bayonets. . . ." The Alabamians soon recovered and opened a devastating return fire. The Yankees sought what cover they could in the thickets along Plum Run and in the stream bed itself. But the Rebel fire overlapped their line and losses mounted alarmingly. Colonel Colvill was an early casualty, and before long not a single field officer was left standing. Company captain Nathan Messick took the command.

The 1st Minnesota made its charge with only some 260 men, and Wilcox had a considerable advantage in manpower, but he sensed that his brigade had lost its momentum. He attempted no counterattack. Thomas's battery and other Federal guns were pounding the Alabamians, no support was forthcoming on either flank or from General Anderson, and they began taking fire from three directions. Seeing that he could neither go forward nor stay where he was, Wilcox ordered his men back. As their fire slackened, the Minnesotans, what few were left, fell back as well. They did not capture the Rebel flag as Hancock ordered, but they had plugged the gap long enough for reinforcements to arrive. The cost to the 1st Minnesota would be reckoned at 68 percent of those engaged, in hardly fifteen minutes of action. "I cannot speak too highly of this regiment and its commander in its attack . . . ," General Hancock would write.[54]

On the Federal left, where the day's fighting had started, substantial re-. inforcements (and the promise of more) were at last swinging the balance in the Union's favor. The Fifth Corps division of Samuel Crawford had reached the battlefield now, and General Crawford could hardly wait to throw it into the breach. His two brigades of Pennsylvania Reserves — General-in-Chief Halleck had retained the third brigade for Washington's defenses — were naturally expected to lead in the defense of their home state. General Sykes ordered one of Crawford's brigades to support the other Fifth Corps troops on Little Round Top. That left the brigade of William McCandless to contend with the Rebels who had reclaimed the Wheatfield and were pushing ahead to the marshy ground along Plum Run, hoping to cut off Little Round Top.

Crawford's troops could not enter the fight until Romeyn Ayres's regulars were off the field in front of them. Richard Auchmuty of the division staff watched the scene unfold: "Suddenly a sheet of fire swept the Regulars. . . . The rebels had flanked them. Up they rose, fell back a little way in good order, then broke and came in a disorderly mob back to our line, followed by the rebels, yelling like mad." McCandless and his officers steadied the ranks as the regulars came through, then Crawford ordered the troops forward. "We advanced a little and fired a volley," wrote Captain Auchmuty, "and then Crawford took a flag, and, followed by us all, rode out into the swamp. The brigade, only 1,400 strong, followed, cheering."

The flag the general took belonged to the 1st Reserves, whose flag bearer was resentful of this usurpation. As Crawford rode at the head of the brigade, leading it into the swirling battle, the 1st's flag bearer ran right alongside, clutching the general's pants leg. When he was satisfied the troops were advancing properly, Crawford surrendered the colors to their very determined rightful owner.

"Suddenly," wrote Auchmuty, "a cheer came from the hills behind us, now crowded on every rock and tree by the runaways, as spectators, and the troops in position. I then saw that the rebels were running. . . ." They were not in fact running. They were retreating on orders. Captain Auchmuty's mention of "the troops in position" referred to the massed advance units of the Sixth Corps that were now visible not only to him but, on the other side of the line, to James Longstreet as well.

It was dusk now and Longstreet had committed every man in his two divisions to the offensive — lacking George Pickett's division, he had not a single soldier in reserve to secure what had been gained. In contrast, it was apparent that the Federals had substantial forces lined up, just waiting to be committed to the battle. William Wofford and his officers were angry at the pullback order. They had not been attacked in their forward positions on the Millerstown Road and their confidence was strong. The fiery Wofford, it was reported, "shook his pistol" at Longstreet in protest. But Longstreet saw the harsh reality of the situation. "We felt at every step the heavy stroke of fresh troops . . . ," he later explained. "We received no support at all, and there was no evidence of co-operation on any side. To urge my men forward under these circumstances would have been madness, and I withdrew them in good order to the peach orchard. . . ."[55]

On the far left of the Confederates' mile-and-three-quarters-wide offensive, where Rans Wright was storming the center of the Cemetery Ridge line, the tide of battle also peaked. Wright's Georgians crossed the Emmitsburg Road, overran Brown's Rhode Island battery, advanced up the ridge, and collided violently with Alexander Webb's brigade of the Second Corps. "They came up in splendid order passed through one of my batteries and arrived within about 25 yards of me," General Webb told his wife, "when I opened fire with one regiment behind a fence." The regiment behind that stone fence was the 69th Pennsylvania, whose historian described what happened next: "still came on the mad Georgians until they reach point-blank range of our rifles. We met their charge with such a destroying fire that they were forced back in confusion." The moment he saw the enemy line begin to waver, Webb wrote,

The view on the evening of July 2 from Little Round Top, painted by Edwin Forbes from his battlefield sketch. The guns are those of Lieutenant Charles Hazlett's Battery D, 5th United States. (Library of Congress)

"I put in another regiment at a double-quick and gave them another volley. . . . In five minutes they ran. . . ."

Much to his disgust, Rans Wright found himself all alone in the middle of the Yankee line — what seemed the middle of the Yankee army. Lang's Floridians on his right were under attack themselves, and on *his* right Lang saw Wilcox fall back, and so in self-defense he fell back across the Emmitsburg Road. Carnot Posey's Mississippi brigade on the left was nowhere to be seen. Second Corps batteries were blasting canister into Wright's left flank, Webb's brigade was blocking his advance in front, and Andrew Humphreys's rallied command had opened fire on his right. The imaginative Wright entered in his report that "We were now complete masters of the field, having gained the key, as it were, of the enemy's whole line." All he lacked was support. Since that was not forthcoming, "with painful hearts we abandoned our captured guns, faced about, and prepared to cut our way through the closing lines in our rear."[56]

Nearby on Cemetery Ridge the 13th Vermont of Stannard's brigade, the first of the First Corps' reinforcements, reported for duty to General Hancock. The general, pointing to Lieutenant Weir's battery, said to Colonel Francis Randall, "The enemy are pressing me hard — they have just captured that battery yonder. . . . Can you retake it?" The 13th Vermont was a nine-month regiment, fresh from the Washington defenses, never in action before, but Colonel Randall was not cowed by a challenge. "I can, and damn quick too, if you will let me," he said. Hancock let him.

Randall was leading his Vermonters down the slope at the double-quick when his horse was hit and he was pinned by the fallen animal. "Go on boys," he yelled, "I'll be at your head as soon as I get out of this damned saddle." He was as good as his word. The 13th ran right over the surprised Rebel line and recaptured Weir's battery. General Hancock, following along behind, told the Vermonters to go on ahead and he would take care of the prisoners.[57]

General Meade was right on the battlefield as well. He and several of his staff, riding the lines on Cemetery Ridge, had reined up in the gap Rans Wright was striving to reach. Just then, amidst the drifting battle smoke and the din of musketry and cannon fire, they could see no Yankee troops to fill the void. "The general realizes the situation but too well," wrote Meade's son and aide. "He straightens himself in his stirrups, as do also the aides who now ride closer to him, bracing themselves up to meet the crisis. It is in the minds of those who follow him that he is going to throw himself into the breach. . . ." But just then someone cried out, "There they come, General!" Up rode John Newton, new commander of the First Corps, heading a column of reinforcements. Newton reported for orders and offered the commanding general his flask, and the two drank a toast even as an enemy shell spattered them with dirt. Waving his hat, General Meade called out, "Come on, gentlemen!" and led the troops into a blocking position.[58]

Soon afterward orders came to Alpheus Williams that matters were now safely in hand on Cemetery Ridge and that his Twelfth Corps division should return to Culp's Hill. As he rode northward in the dusk Williams came on General Meade and a gathering of his officers, and he learned that "we had successfully resisted all the Rebel attacks and had punished them severely. There was a pleasant gathering in an open field, and gratification and gratulation abounded."

It was perhaps at this gathering that Captain George Meade, the general's son, heard someone observe that affairs that day had seemed at one time to be pretty desperate. "Yes," said General Meade, "but it is all right now, it is all right now." His sentiment proved to be somewhat premature, yet that did not diminish the essential truth of it.[59]

11 Determined to Do or Die

BRIGADIER GENERAL George Sears Greene was sixty-two, the oldest Union general on the field. He had graduated second in West Point's class of 1823, taught engineering at the Academy, and in 1836 resigned and started a new, and distinguished, career as a civil engineer. He had served in field command since the spring of 1862. When his brigade arrived on Culp's Hill on the morning of July 2, Greene met with divisional commander John Geary to mark out their defensive line. General Geary said that personally he opposed building breastworks. After fighting behind breastworks, he said, the men became less than stalwart in the open field. But he would leave the matter to his brigadiers. "Pop" Greene thought Geary's theory absurd. Fighting behind breastworks as recently as Chancellorsville had not left *his* men timid, and by noon, under his expert engineer's eye, his brigade had erected an imposing defensive line. The rest of Geary's division followed Greene's example.

"Culp's Hill was covered with woods, so all the materials needful were at our disposal," wrote one of Greene's officers. "Right and left the men felled the trees, and blocked them up into a close log fence. Piles of cordwood which lay near were quickly appropriated. The sticks, set slanting on end against the outer face of the logs, made excellent battening." Rocks and dirt served as reinforcement, and felled trees blocked the approaches. At least part of the works included raised head-logs, enabling riflemen to fire with nearly complete protection. This irregular line of works faced eastward and extended from the crest of Culp's Hill to its base, near Rock Creek. At his brigade's right flank, halfway down the hill, engineer Greene constructed a traverse line at right angles to the main line to guard a difficult stretch of ground. Lieutenant Randolph McKim, on the staff of "Maryland" Steuart's Confederate brigade confronting this line, wrote of July 2, "Greatly did officers and men marvel as morning, noon, and afternoon passed in inaction — on our part, not on the enemy's, for, as we well knew, he was plying axe and pick and shovel. . . ."[1]

Dick Ewell had been told that Longstreet's offensive would commence at 4:00 P.M., and so he was prompt to open his artillery demonstration at that hour. As to the second half of General Lee's directive — the demonstration "to be converted into a real attack should opportunity offer" — Ewell seems to have defined "opportunity" by two factors. The first was signs of progress on Longstreet's front. Ewell sent staff members climbing into the cupola of the Catholic church in Gettysburg to view the fighting against the enemy's left, which by early evening, if sight and sound could be believed, appeared to be progressing well. The ultimate objective, to join with Longstreet's forces atop Cemetery Hill, seemed feasible. Second, since he and his lieutenants had assured Lee of the grave risks in assaulting Cemetery and Culp's hills in daylight, Ewell apparently welcomed concealing dusk as the opportune time for an attack. In any event, as his failed artillery bombardment sputtered out (and, unknown to him, as Longstreet's offensive sputtered out), and as the sun sank in the west, General Ewell ordered his infantry forward.

Here as elsewhere on the field that day, Confederate tactics called for an attack *en echelon.* First, Allegheny Johnson would strike Culp's Hill from the east. Once Johnson's assault was under way, Jubal Early would move his division against Cemetery Hill from the northeast, followed by Robert Rodes against Cemetery Hill from the northwest. Johnson started forward about 7 o'clock; sunset was due at 7:29. The operation would hardly be well along before it was full dark. The moon was one night past full, but how much illumination it might furnish in wooded areas and on a smoke-blanketed field was problematical.

Ewell's timing was unknowingly perfect. Five of the six Twelfth Corps brigades had been pulled out to meet Longstreet's offensive. Only Greene's 1,400-man brigade remained on Culp's Hill to confront Allegheny Johnson's division. Johnson made his attack with just three of his four brigades — the Stonewall Brigade was occupied with Yankee cavalry in the rear — or some 4,700 men. That kind of manpower edge would likely have been decisive elsewhere on the field that day, but against Pop Greene's providential and well-constructed breastworks the odds leveled out.

The moment the rest of the Twelfth Corps was ordered away, Greene had begun shifting and extending his five regiments to man at least some of the empty breastworks on his vulnerable right, toward the base of the hill. Much as Joshua Chamberlain had done with the 20th Maine on Little Round Top, Greene ended up with a much-thinned single-rank battle line without reserves. Then, the moment the enemy began its

Brigadier General George Sears Greene led his brigade in the defense of Culp's Hill on the evening of July 2. (National Archives)

advance, he called on the First and Eleventh corps to his left for help. In due course General Wadsworth, manning the north face of Culp's Hill, would send over three of his battle-worn First Corps regiments. From Cemetery Hill General Howard added four of his Eleventh Corps regiments. These reinforcements totaled only about 750 men, but they served Greene as a valuable reserve and as relief for units running low on ammunition.[2]

John M. Jones's brigade, on the right of Johnson's battle line, faced the most daunting prospect — a climb up the steepest part of Culp's Hill to reach the Yankee line on the crest. In the darkening evening Jones's Virginians scrambled up the rocky slope through the brush and trees, losing all alignment until, said T. R. Buckner of the 44th Virginia, "all was confusion and disorder." The appearance of the works on the heights above came as a shock. Captain Buckner described them, with some exaggeration, as "of a formidable character, and in some places they could scarcely be surmounted without scaling-ladders." According to the 42nd Virginia's Captain Jesse Richardson, his regiment "got within 30 paces of the enemy's works, driving all the enemy within them. Some of the men got nearer." Still, these charges must have been beaten off with comparative ease (wounding General Jones in the process), for losses in the 60th New York, which took the brunt of Jones's attack, were described as "very small, so perfect was our concealment." It might have been otherwise, wrote one of the 60th New York's officers: "Without breastworks our line would have been swept away in an instant by the hailstorm of bullets and the flood of men."

The Louisiana brigade under Colonel Jesse M. Williams, at the center of the Confederate attacking force, had very much the same experience as Jones's Virginians. The terrain was rugged, the night dark, the enemy works forbidding. Williams reported reaching a position some 100 yards from the Yankee line on the hill, and from there launching "several attempts to carry the works by assault . . . attended with more loss than success." The regiments defending the breastworks here, the 78th and 102nd New York, suffered but a handful of casualties during what Colonel Williams claimed was "an almost incessant fire for four hours. . . ."[3]

While Jones and Williams achieved nothing in their assaults, Maryland Steuart came a good deal closer to breaking the Culp's Hill line that evening. Steuart's advantages were twofold: The terrain near the base of Culp's Hill was considerably less forbidding, and Steuart's battle line was considerably longer than Greene's.

Maryland Steuart had been brought in by General Lee to harness a fractious brigade that contained three regiments from Virginia, two from North Carolina, and a Maryland battalion (a battalion in name but a regiment in size). Perhaps with state rivalries in mind, Steuart set up his attack line with the 10th, 23rd, and 37th Virginia regiments together on the left, separated from the 3rd North Carolina by the 1st Maryland battalion; the 1st North Carolina was in reserve. Like the rest of Johnson's division, Steuart's brigade had spent the day in concealment east of Rock Creek, so there was no advance reconnaissance of the Federal positions. Some delay was encountered crossing Rock Creek, deepened here by a milldam downstream, so that on this east face of Culp's Hill it was getting dark even before Steuart's men made contact with the Yankees.

Steuart's regiments on his right went up against the works manned by

Edwin Forbes's painting, based on his battlefield sketch, depicts the sturdy breastworks on the crest of Culp's Hill. (Library of Congress)

the Union flank regiments, the 149th and 137th New York, and made little progress. But the 137th, last in the line of Greene's regiments, was outflanked by both the 23rd and 10th Virginia, and that was a recipe for trouble.

The two Virginia regiments soon discovered that the enemy fire was coming from their right rather than from their front. Indeed, the 10th Virginia found itself peering into a line of empty breastworks, "which was carried with a shout," said its colonel. The Virginians promptly wheeled right and began firing into the unprotected flank of the 137th New York. "I ordered Company A, the right-flank company, to form at right angles with the breastworks and check the advance of the enemy . . . ," the 137th's Colonel David Ireland reported, "but being sorely pressed, they fell back. . . ." The New Yorkers were sorely pressed all the way back to the traverse line that Pop Greene had fortuitously erected facing south. Behind this they were able to make an equal fight against further Rebel advances. But the cost was high; that night Colonel Ireland lost almost a third of his men.

By this time it was full dark, and the battle fought by faint moonlight in the woods amidst clouds of choking smoke turned chaotic. Colonel Edward Warren, 10th Virginia, later tried to explain: "It was now dark and the regularity of our lines was not preserved and some confusion arose on account of our uncertainty as to the position of the enemy and of our forces, and great apprehension exhibited by officers and men lest we should fire into our friends." Exactly that happened. Lieutenant Randolph McKim of Steuart's staff brought up the 1st North Carolina from its reserve position to brace the assault, and as he placed the men he saw muzzle flashes from where he supposed the enemy to be. "Fire on them, boys; fire on them!" he cried. After several volleys a Confederate officer came rushing up to McKim shouting, "They are our own men!" So they were — the 1st North Carolina had fired into the 1st Maryland battalion. "I believe no injury resulted from my mistake," McKim wrote hopefully, but according to the 1st Maryland's historian, there were casualties from this friendly fire.[4]

The reinforcements rushed to General Greene had their share of adventures. The First Corps sent over Rufus Dawes's 6th Wisconsin, of the Iron Brigade, which Greene directed toward his threatened flank. In the darkness the 6th stumbled blindly right into a line of equally surprised Rebels, who, Dawes wrote, "rose up and fired a volley at us, and immediately retreated down the hill. This remarkable encounter did not last a minute. We lost two men, killed — both burned with the powder of the guns fired at them."

There was one adventure of a rather different sort. When he heard the eruption of firing from Culp's Hill, Winfield Hancock quickly deduced the threat it represented, and "without application or instructions" volunteered help from his Second Corps. One of the regiments sent was the 71st Pennsylvania. The 71st was welcomed by Captain Charles Horton of Greene's staff and put in next to the embattled 137th New York. The newcomers were subjected to a scattering of fire in the darkness — not very severe fire, according to Captain Horton — when to Horton's astonishment the Pennsylvanians abruptly "rose up and retreated in line, apparently without panic or disorder." Horton demanded an explanation from Colonel Richard P. Smith. Smith said without apology that he had ordered his regiment to retreat, "saying that he would not have his men murdered." The 71st Pennsylvania, wrote an angry Captain Horton, "thereupon marched to the rear to the sound of the enemy's guns." Colonel Smith would report fourteen casualties suffered during his brief stay on Culp's Hill that night, and his strange behavior apparently went unremarked — at least in the Second Corps.[5]

By now the five absent brigades of the Twelfth Corps were being recalled to Culp's Hill. "I returned toward my entrenchments after dark," wrote General Alpheus Williams, "and was met with the astounding intelligence that they were taken possession of by the Rebels in my absence!" There followed a series of sharp, exceedingly confusing encounters in the dark woods as the Yankees tried to reclaim their former positions and Maryland Steuart's Virginians tried to hold on to their gains.

The 2nd Massachusetts approached its old lines "crawling along cautiously and quietly" in the darkness when voices were heard ahead. Major Charles F. Morse advanced two scouts. "Boys, what regiment do you belong to?" one of the scouts called out. "Twenty-third" was the reply. "Twenty-third what?" asked the scout. "Twenty-third Virginia" was the response, suspicious now, and then, "Why, they are Yanks!" There was a brief tussle and one of the scouts was captured but the other one escaped to spread the alarm. The 2nd Massachusetts pulled back to safer ground.

General Williams saw no merit to these blind encounters. "I had had experience in trying to retake breastworks after dark," he wrote, "so I ordered all the brigades to occupy the open field in front of the woods, put out a strong picket line, and waited daylight for further operations." For his part, Allegheny Johnson had to rest content with the foothold Steuart's brigade had won in the unoccupied Yankee works. The brigades of John M. Jones and Jesse Williams were pulled back off Culp's Hill and they too waited for daylight and fresh orders.[6]

ON CEMETERY HILL Otis Howard was tracking the assault on Culp's Hill with some trepidation, for he suspected he would be the Rebels' next target and his confidence in the fighting men of his Eleventh Corps was not very high. Two months earlier, at Chancellorsville, the Eleventh Corps had collapsed under Stonewall Jackson's attack. Twenty-four hours earlier, under attack by Jackson's successor Dick Ewell, it collapsed again. General Howard, calling for help from other corps, admitted that he could not rely on his own men.

Howard had to be prepared for attack from two directions — from the northwest against Cemetery Hill proper, and from the northeast against that portion of the hill east of the Baltimore Pike, called East Cemetery Hill. The core of his defense, regardless of direction, was artillery. Facing northwest were some twenty-five guns, braced by the infantry of Carl Schurz's and Adolph von Steinwehr's divisions. It was from Schurz's division that Howard had sent reinforcements to Pop Greene on Culp's Hill. Positioned on the crest of East Cemetery Hill by Colonel Wainwright specifically to meet an infantry assault were four batteries, twenty-two guns. The infantry support here was Barlow's division, led now, after

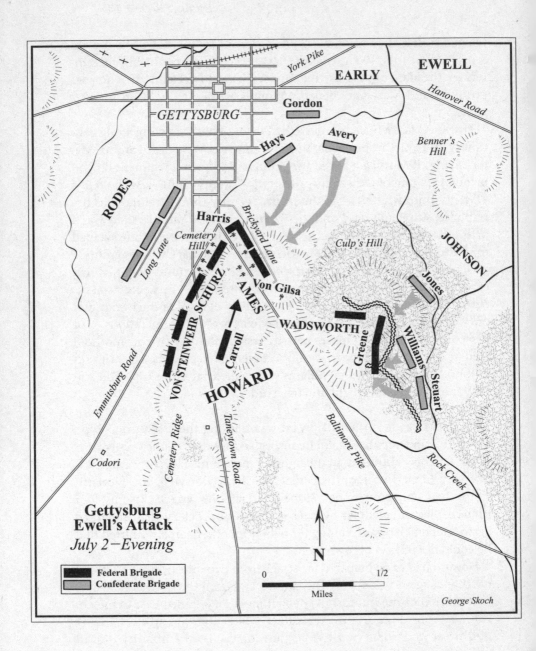

**Gettysburg
Ewell's Attack**

July 2—Evening

▇	Federal Brigade
▇	Confederate Brigade

0   1/2

Miles

George Skoch

Barlow's wounding and capture on July 1, by Adelbert Ames. Leopold von Gilsa and Andrew Harris led Ames's two brigades, both of which had been badly mauled on Wednesday. "You can now command your brigade easily with the voice, my dear Colonel," von Gilsa's aide told him; "this is all that is left." Ames estimated the strength of his division at 1,150 men after yesterday's battle; and after yesterday's battle, Ames, like Howard, had little confidence in those men.

It appeared to General Howard that the attack, when it came, would open against his East Cemetery Hill position, and he deployed his infantry some 120 yards out ahead of the guns. Along the base of the hill was a stone wall paralleling Brickyard Lane that ran southward out of Gettysburg, and Ames posted his troops behind this barrier. On the left, toward the town, the wall made a right-angle turn, and manning this angle was Colonel Harris's brigade — 25th, 75th, and 107th Ohio, and 17th Connecticut. Forming the right half of the battle line was Colonel von Gilsa's brigade — 41st, 54th, and 68th New York, and 153rd Pennsylvania. Extending von Gilsa's line was the 33rd Massachusetts from Orland Smith's brigade. Not engaged on July 1, the 33rd regiment's 490 men added an important reinforcement to Ames's defense.

Jubal Early marched his attacking force out of Gettysburg and deployed it east of town. "Just before dark," wrote Louisiana Captain William J. Seymour, "the solitary figure of old Gen. Early is seen emerging from one of the streets of the town and, riding slowly across the field in the direction of our position, the little puffs of dust that arise from around his horse's feet show that the Federal sharpshooters are paying him the compliment of special attention. Presently the old General reaches us and after inquiring whether we are ready, gives the order to charge."

Early arranged his assault on a two-brigade front — Harry Hays's Louisiana brigade and Isaac Avery's North Carolina brigade, with Hays in overall command. In support would be John Gordon's brigade. General Early left Extra Billy Smith out on the York Pike to guard the division's rear. Early understood (he later wrote) that this was to be a general attack, with Rodes's division advancing on his right — and with A. P. Hill advancing on Rodes's right. In writing thus, Early underscored yet another command failure in Hill's Third Corps. Dorsey Pender's division of the Third formed the link between Hill's and Ewell's corps. If Pender was scheduled to join the fighting on July 2, his division quite missed the signal. To be sure, Pender himself was wounded late that afternoon by a shell fragment (a wound that would prove mortal), but that did not excuse the lack of coordination between his division and Rodes's.[7]

The best view of the forming Rebel ranks was from Stevens's 5th Maine battery posted on a knoll at the far right of the Union line. "Look! Look at those men!" called out one of the gunners, pointing across the darkening fields to hundreds of dim figures climbing over fences and taking up a battle line. Lieutenant Edward Whittier, commanding in place of the wounded Greenleaf Stevens, ordered case shot for the six Napoleons and opened fire "by battery." According to a nearby infantryman, "suddenly, right over my head it seemed, there was a blaze, a crash and a roar as if a volcano had been let loose." Stevens's battery, being on the attackers' flank, would maintain a steady, deadly fire throughout the assault. As the battery's report put it, "enfiladed their lines, at a distance of 800 yards, with spherical case and shell, and later with solid shot and canister. . . ."

From their starting point outside Gettysburg, Early's forces had to make a giant wheel to their right to strike Ames's line on East Cemetery Hill. Harry Hays's five Louisiana regiments extended out from the pivot of the wheel. Isaac Avery's three North Carolina regiments, on the outer edge of the wheel, had the longer march. All the Yankee guns that would bear now opened fire. Captain Michael Wiedrich's Battery I, 1st New York Light, closest to the onrushing Louisianians, went to canister almost immediately. Before long all the batteries were firing canister, then double canister. When they ran out of canister they fired case shot without fuzes, the missiles exploding as they left the muzzles.

The guns sent great clouds of smoke roiling into the still air. In the growing dark a Twelfth Corps soldier returning to his lines saw a lurid glare lighting the sky ahead. "The smoke had settled down so thickly that the flashes of the artillery could only be seen glaring red as blood through it," he wrote. "The thick clouds settled down over the hills, fields, and woods like a pall, illuminated at times with the crimson fire of the artillery as it flashed and burned against the sky." He thought the scene, from a distance at least, was "magnificently grand."[8]

For the infantrymen of the Eleventh Corps crouched behind the stone wall at the base of East Cemetery Hill, the scene before them — wide lines of men in butternut advancing apace through the dusk and the smoke and the din — was terrifying rather than magnificent. "But on, still on, they came, moving steadily to the assault, soon the infantry opened fire, but they never faltered," recalled Colonel Harris in describing Hays's Louisianians. "They moved forward as steadily, amid this hail of shot shell and minnie ball, as though they were on parade. . . ." Hays's

The Confederate assault on East Cemetery Hill on the evening of July 2, sketched by Alfred Waud. The view looks westerly past Stevens's Maine battery toward the cemetery gateway. (Library of Congress)

brigade was best known as the Louisiana Tigers, a name synonymous in the Confederate army with hard fighting and high living. Now, whooping the Rebel yell, the Tigers stormed the stone wall with intent to seize the batteries on the hill behind.

Just before the shooting started, General Ames had moved the 17th Connecticut from the center of Harris's line over to the right, to better tie in with von Gilsa's brigade. This left a gap, which Harris hastily tried to cover by stretching out his nearby regiments, the 25th and 75th Ohio, to fill the space. "This left my line very thin and weak," he said. Now every man "could get to the stone wall . . . and have all the elbow room he wanted." The Tigers pushed straight for this thinned line.

"Our orders were to shoot low," wrote Ohioan Frederick Nussbaum, "and we mowed the Tigers down as they came up the hill." Such shooting inflicted grievous losses, but the Louisianians resolutely closed up and continued on toward the wall. The closer they came the more they evaded the artillery fire, for a number of the Yankee guns could not depress their barrels enough to sweep the slope directly in front of them. Lieutenant Joseph Jackson, 8th Louisiana, described how "We 'fotched up' at a stone fence behind which mr. yank had posted himself and he did not want to leave. But with bayonets & clubbed guns we drove them back." It had become so dark now, Lieutenant Jackson added, that no one could tell "whether we were shooting our own men or not."

The two left-hand Federal regiments, 107th and 25th Ohio, were overwhelmed by this rush and stumbled back up the hill toward Captain Wiedrich's New York battery. The Tigers, "yelling like demons," were right on their heels. Angry artillerist Charles Wainwright entered in his diary that the Eleventh Corps' German infantry "ran away almost to a man." Yet he had to admit that Wiedrich's cannoneers, also German, "fought splendidly," making a hand-to-hand defense of their battery. There was wild, savage fighting among the guns. A Confederate flag bearer leaped on one of the guns to claim its capture and was instantly killed. Another man seized the flag and "with a wild shout" took the first man's place, and then he was shot down. A third man, already wounded, climbed up on the gun with the flag and "waved it over his head with a cheer." He soon went down in a hail of bullets. Wiedrich's cannoneers meanwhile stood their ground, smashing at the Rebels with rammers and handspikes. One of them was seen to tear the rifle right out of a Tiger's hands and run him through with the bayonet. "This would show," Wainwright concluded, "that the Germans have got fight in them." Whatever fault there was, he thought, must be with their officers.

General Schurz, over on the west side of Cemetery Hill, saw and heard the commotion, commandeered two nearby regiments, and led them at the double-quick through streams of panicked stragglers to the fighting. In Wiedrich's battery, Schurz wrote, "we found an indescribable scene of melee. . . ." The Ohioans chased back earlier from the stone wall had rallied by the guns and were continuing the fight; indeed, the 107th Ohio captured the flag of the 8th Louisiana. The arrival of what Harry Hays described as "heavy masses" of Federal infantry now persuaded him to recall the Tigers. By Schurz's description, "Our infantry made a vigorous rush upon the invaders, and after a short but very spirited hand-to-hand scuffle, tumbled them down the embankment."[9]

Isaac Avery was leading the North Carolinians in place of Robert Hoke, wounded at Chancellorsville, and Colonel Avery apparently thought it would make a better impression on his new command if he led the advance on horseback, as he had on July 1. On this day, however, he was barely halfway to the target when he was hit in the neck by a bullet and knocked off his horse. Sensing the wound was mortal, Avery scrawled a last thought in a note to his second-in-command: "Major: Tell my father I died with my face to the enemy."

The North Carolinians surged past their fallen leader. Bracing to meet them on the right of the line was the 33rd Massachusetts, whose colonel, Adin Underwood, watched a Rebel regiment — it was the 57th North Carolina — striding toward him through a storm of artillery fire: "The gaps close bravely up and still they advance. Canister cannot check them." The range narrowed and behind the wall Colonel Underwood ordered the 33rd to engage: "My regiment opened a severe musketry fire on them, which caused gaps in their line and made it stagger back a little. It soon rallied and bravely came within a few feet of our wall. . . ." Stevens's Maine battery was less than 200 yards from the Rebels' flank, point-blank range, firing double canister. The enemy's line, Underwood reported, "which was almost on to us — their colors nearly within reach — was broken and finally driven back, leaving great heaps of dead and wounded just in front of us."

Farther to the left, the Confederates found a tender spot. Von Gilsa's four regiments had been roughly handled at Chancellorsville, and then again the day before north of Gettysburg. Now they were being thrust into the cauldron for a third time. For many of them their stay in this new battle line would be comparatively brief. Two adjacent regiments, 54th and 68th New York, were the first to break and retreat up the hill. A portion of the 41st New York, anchored to the 33rd Massachusetts, stayed and fought, but its left-hand companies joined in the retreat. On the other side of the break, the 17th Connecticut and the 153rd Pennsylvania also stood and made a fight of it. A nine-month regiment, the 153rd had seen its first action at Chancellorsville and its second on July 1, and now it was facing yet another charge by the Rebels' Second Corps. The 153rd's historian described the action at the wall as pure melee: "clubs, knives, stones, fists — anything calculated to inflict death or pain was resorted to." Still, a second gap was now torn in the Federal line, and a second battery became a battle scene.[10]

This was Battery F–G, 1st Pennsylvania Light, Captain R. Bruce Ricketts. After the experiences of July 2, Captain Ricketts (like Colonel Wainwright) would wax opinionated about the Dutchmen of the Eleventh Corps. "As soon as the charge commenced," Ricketts wrote, "they, although they had a stone-wall in their front, commenced running in the greatest confusion to the rear, hardly a shot was fired, certainly not a volley, and so panic stricken were they that several ran into the canister

Jubal A. Early directed the July 2 attack on East Cemetery Hill.
(Cook Collection, Valentine Museum)

fire of my guns and were knocked over." No doubt Ricketts's view was colored by the fact that his battery suffered twenty casualties that evening — casualties he would always regard as unnecessary.

After Henry Hunt visited Cemetery Hill during the late-afternoon artillery duel, he returned to the artillery reserve and selected Ricketts and his six 3-inch rifles to send to Colonel Wainwright to relieve whichever of his batteries most needed relief. Wainwright posted Ricketts in the center of the East Cemetery Hill gun line and told him, "this is the key to our position, . . . and must be held and in case you are charged here, you will not limber up under any circumstances, but fight your battery as long as you can." That, as it happened, was precisely what Ricketts did. In his pocket diary he left a succinct description of his evening's work: "My battery charged by Gen. Early's division just at dusk — punished them terribly with our canister — They took my left gun, spiked it, killed six men, wounded 11 and took 3 prisoners. The boys fought them hand to hand with pistols, handspikes and rammers."

During this struggle a Rebel lieutenant tried to seize the battery's guidon, only to be shot by its guardian, Private James H. Riggin. Private Riggin in his turn was mortally wounded as he sought to carry off the guidon to safer ground. A Confederate who picked up the fallen banner was soon struggling for it with one of the gunnery sergeants. Then Lieutenant Charles Brockway stepped in. Having no weapon, Brockway smashed the Confederate in the head with a rock, and the sergeant finished off the interloper with his clubbed musket. That, finally, secured the battery's guidon. All the while this was taking place in the battery's left section, on the right Captain Ricketts was keeping the rest of his guns firing.[11]

At the same time that he volunteered support for Pop Greene on Culp's Hill, said Winfield Hancock, "I heard the crack of musketry on Howard's front. . . . Recognizing the importance to the whole army of holding the threatened positions, I directed General Gibbon to send a brigade instantly to Genl. Howard's assistance. . . ." As with all of Hancock's decisions that 2nd of July, this one was fortuitous. The brigade sent was Samuel S. Carroll's, and Colonel Carroll was a soldier who did not waste time.

"We started for this point on the double-quick," reported J. L. Dickelman of the 4th Ohio, "which soon became a dead run, many of our men throwing away their knapsacks and blankets in order to keep up with the mad dash." They rushed through Evergreen Cemetery and past its gatehouse, and when Carroll was told that Rebels were in Ricketts's battery ahead, he quickly formed up for a charge. Colonel Carroll possessed what was called a clarion voice, and now he was easily heard all across East Cemetery Hill: "Halt! Front face! Charge bayonets! Forward, double-quick! March! Give them hell!"

The Confederate attack had peaked and was starting to ebb when Carroll's brigade made its dramatic entrance, yet it supplied the final and necessary push. Through Ricketts's battery it went, the 14th Indiana in the lead, and chased Avery's and Hays's men down the hill and across the stone wall and Brickyard Lane and into the fields beyond. By now it was too dark to see anything ahead, and Carroll ordered his men to cease firing. According to Sergeant Dickelman, Carroll's brigade always remembered July 2, 1863, as a "never-to-be-forgotten day."

It struck Carroll that his brigade was out ahead of everyone else, and he called for the Eleventh Corps to form a connection with his troops. Word

Alfred Waud drew the July 2 night assault by the Louisiana Tigers on a Union battery on East Cemetery Hill. (Library of Congress)

came back that General Ames would like Colonel Carroll and his men to stay where they were, for Ames had no confidence in any of his own men to hold that advanced line. Colonel Carroll had a blunt reply for General Ames: "Damn a man who has no confidence in his troops!" Corps commander Howard held the same view as Ames. When he tried to send a force from the Eleventh Corps to reinforce Carroll's brigade, Howard could not find a single officer who would carry out the order. Why did he not have them shot, Colonel Wainwright asked. "I should have to shoot all the way down," Howard replied; "they are all alike."[12]

Harry Hays, in common with most generals whose attacks have failed, laid the blame on a lack of support. On this occasion he was quite right. With matters hanging in the balance on East Cemetery Hill, Hays had sent to Gordon's brigade to hurry forward to support the toehold he had won. He was told that Gordon had no orders to advance. With that, said Hays, "my only course was to withdraw my command," and he returned his troops to their starting point.

Jubal Early had already concluded that to send Gordon forward "would have been a useless sacrifice," and for having to make that decision he blamed Robert Rodes. Rodes, for his part, asserted that an attack on the right by his division "would be a useless sacrifice of life." Rodes went on to suggest — which Dick Ewell confirmed — that the real blame lay farther to the right, with Powell Hill and Dorsey Pender's division and

340

their failure to attack. As General Early later explained, in reference to this contretemps, "an army in battle array is like a complicated machine," requiring perfect coordination or "all the parts are powerless or are thrown out of joint."[13]

There was nothing wrong with General Rodes's resolution. In fact, it was he who that afternoon thought the enemy on Cemetery Hill was astir and suggested to Early a joint attack "just at dark." But Robert Rodes was new to divisional command, and he seems to have greatly underestimated how long it would take to move his five brigades out of Gettysburg's narrow streets and deploy them west of the town for an assault. By the time they were in position, Early's assault was over. Even after this misjudgment, Rodes might have gone ahead but for the advice of his two most reliable brigadiers, Dodson Ramseur and George Doles. Ramseur edged forward to reconnoiter Cemetery Hill in the moonlight and saw two ranks of infantry behind stone walls, and artillery "in position to pour upon our lines direct, cross, and enfilade fires." When Doles concurred with Ramseur in this report, Rodes canceled the attack. To be sure, those two ranks of infantry were Dutchmen of the shaky Eleventh Corps, but General Rodes had no way of knowing that.

In taking his decision, Rodes was no doubt influenced by the lack of any signs of life in Pender's division to his right. James H. Lane, who succeeded to the divisional command after Pender's wounding, said his only orders were to cooperate "if a favorable opportunity presented." When Ewell suggested that such an opportunity was now present, he received no reply. On July 2, it seemed, no one in A. P. Hill's corps was *ordered* to do anything. Yet privately Dick Ewell, as reported by his aide Campbell Brown, mainly attributed the evening's defeat to "Rodes' failure to co-operate. For this Ewell always thought Rodes fairly censurable. . . . Ewell & Early both thought Rodes had been too slow."[14]

It was late, after 10:30, when the moonlit hills and fields marking the Gettysburg battleground fell mostly silent except for the occasional crack of a picket's rifle and that ever present undertone of every battlefield, the moans and cries of the wounded. Soon visible from Devil's Den all the way around to Culp's Hill were the bobbing lanterns of the stretcher bearers searching for casualties. By unspoken mutual agreement the opposing pickets left these samaritans to their work.

AT 8 O'CLOCK that Thursday evening, General Meade reported on the day's fighting to General-in-Chief Halleck in Washington. "The enemy attacked me about 4 P.M. this day," he began, "and, after one of the severest contests of the war, was repulsed at all points." After noting casualties, especially in the officer corps, Meade sketched out his plans: "I shall remain in my present position to-morrow, but am not prepared to say, until better advised of the condition of the army, whether my operations will be of an offensive or defensive character."

Within the hour, to advise him on the critical matter of the condition of the enemy's army, Meade summoned to headquarters Colonel George Sharpe, of the Bureau of Military Information. In the cramped front room of the Leister house, Sharpe found General Meade seated at a small table and, on a rough cot in the corner, Generals Hancock and Slocum. Hancock sat at the foot of the cot and Slocum was stretched out on it. A note from the B.M.I. had come to Meade in late afternoon reading, "Prisoners have been taken today, and last evening, from every brigade in Lee's Army excepting the four brigades of Picketts Division." Meade asked Sharpe for any further intelligence that might elaborate on that earlier finding. Sharpe excused himself and consulted with his aide John Babcock and soon returned to headquarters to find the three generals in the same tableau.

Sharpe explained that some 1,300 prisoners were under guard by the provost marshal, and that interrogation of them under Babcock's direction had identified nearly 100 Confederate regiments in action on Wednesday and Thursday. On the B.M.I.'s carefully charted order of battle for the Army of Northern Virginia, not one of those regiments belonged to Pickett. Sharpe was assertive: "Pickett's division has come up and is now in bivouac, and will be ready to go into action fresh tomorrow morning." At that, Hancock turned to Meade, raised his fist, and said emphatically, "General, we have got them nicked!"

Hancock had good reason for his confidence. From Sharpe's report it was now clear that Lee had already committed his entire army, except for Pickett's division, to the battle — and had been, in Meade's phrase, "repulsed at all points." Lee had only Pickett to enhance a further attack (and Pickett had, in fact, three brigades rather than four as credited by the B.M.I.). The Army of the Potomac had Sedgwick's big Sixth Corps to enhance its defense (or its offense). With this vital intelligence in hand, General Meade determined to call his lieutenants into council to discuss the army's course for the next day.[15]

The gathering, as John Gibbon noted, "was at first very informal and in the shape of a conversation. . . ." The room was small, not more than twelve by twelve feet, stuffy and thick with cigar smoke, lit by a single candle. Howard was the last to arrive, after the Cemetery Hill position was secured, raising the total of generals present to twelve — Meade; John Newton, new commander of the First Corps; Hancock, wing commander on the left; Gibbon of the Second Corps; David Birney of the Third Corps, replacing the wounded Sickles; Sykes of the Fifth Corps; Sedgwick of the Sixth; Howard of the Eleventh; Alpheus Williams of the Twelfth; Slocum, self-appointed right-wing commander; Chief of Staff Butterfield; and chief engineer Warren. Seeing Slocum already there, Williams asked Meade if he should leave, but was directed to stay. Thus the Twelfth Corps, like the Second, was doubly represented. Gouverneur Warren, exhausted from his long day's labors, lay down in a corner and slept through the proceedings.

The first need was to evaluate the condition of the army, and each general in turn recounted the day's fighting on his front and the state of his troops. Birney said the Third Corps was "used up" and not in good condition to fight after Thursday's ordeal. Each was asked how many men he could put in the field the next day. The total came to 58,000 infantry. Newton, who had only just arrived on the field with the Sixth Corps, was quoted by Gibbon as saying, "this was no place to fight a battle in." Newton was well respected as an engineer, and his remark set off some discussion. His point, as he later described it, was that there was danger that Lee would turn the army's left and get between it and its supplies — "and ought to do so." He recalled, Newton wrote, "taking the ground that Lee was not fool enough to attack us in front after two days' fighting which had ended in consolidating us into a position immensely strong." At the same time, it was pointed out that pulling back to prevent the left from being turned — back to the Pipe Creek line, say — would be a highly dangerous maneuver to attempt in the immediate presence of the enemy. Hancock said he was "puzzled about the practicability of retiring."

There was also discussion about supplies. In the recent days of maneuvering the army had outrun its supply line, with the closest depot at Westminster, in Maryland. "We had but one single day's rations for the army," Alpheus Williams wrote. "Many corps had not even one." It was hoped that with the beef cattle and flour on hand, he added, "we could eke out a few half-fed days." But supplies remained a worrisome problem.

Through all this discussion, which went on for some time — and which was accompanied by the last of the cannonading from Cemetery Hill — General Meade said little beyond an occasional comment, but seemed to be listening for the tenor of his lieutenants' thinking about the next day. He had, after all, already told Washington he would "re-

General Meade's council of generals at his headquarters on the evening of July 2, as an artist imagined it. Meade, standing, faces a gesturing Winfield Scott Hancock. (U.S. Army Military History Institute)

main in my present position to-morrow. . . ." He seems to have decided that their thinking should be on record, for in due course, when Butterfield suggested formulating questions for a vote, in the manner of a council, Meade agreed.

With the commanding general's concurrence, Butterfield posed three questions:

> "1. Under existing circumstances is it advisable for this army to remain in its present position or to retire to another nearer its base of supplies?
> 2. It being determined to remain in present position, should the army attack or wait the attack of the enemy?
> 3. If we wait attack, how long?"

Answers were solicited from the nine generals of corps rank in reverse order of seniority. John Gibbon therefore went first. In consideration of Newton's view about the army's lines, Gibbon voted (as Butterfield recorded it), on the first question, to "correct position of the army but would not retreat." Williams, Birney, Sykes, Howard, and Sedgwick voted simply, "stay." Slocum said, "Stay and fight it out." Hancock wanted to "rectify" the position, but only "without moving to give up the field." Newton used the same phrasing as Gibbon, and Gibbon wrote that "we had some playful sparring as to whether he agreed with me or I with him." The vote was unanimous that the army should stay where it was, whether "correcting" its lines or not.

On the second question, of attacking or awaiting attack, the vote to await attack was also unanimous. Some were emphatic. "By all means not attack," said Newton. "In no condition to attack," said Gibbon. Hancock offered the only qualification: "No attack unless our communications are cut."

On question three, on how long to wait for Lee's attack, there was more variation of opinion, apparently in part because of the supply question. Answers ranged from one day, to "until Lee moved" (Gibbon), to if not attacked, "attack them" (Howard). But again, the overall result was unanimity. General Meade now had a clear sense of his generals' thinking. "I recollect there was great good feeling amongst the Corps Commanders at their agreeing so unanimously," Gibbon wrote, "and Gen. Meade announced, in a decided manner, 'Such then is the decision.'"

John Gibbon, in command of the Second Corps at the center of the line on Cemetery Ridge, concluded his account of the evening's council by recording a conversation he had with Meade at about midnight, just as they adjourned. There was no question the council had favored acting on the defensive, "awaiting the action of Lee," and in reference to this, wrote Gibbon, "Meade said to me, 'If Lee attacks tomorrow, it will be *in your front.*' I asked him why he thought so and he replied, 'Because he has made attacks on both our flanks and failed and if he concludes to try it again, it will be on our centre.' I expressed a hope that he would and told Gen. Meade with confidence that if he did, we would defeat him."

Privately Meade expressed his own confidence. Early next morning he took a moment to write a hurried note to his wife: "Dearest love, All well and going on well with the Army. We had a great fight yesterday, the enemy attacking & we completely repulsing them — both armies shattered. . . . Army in fine spirits & every one determined to do or die."[16]

A DOZEN YEARS after the war, analyzing the Confederates' Day Two fighting, Lee's aide Walter Taylor concluded that "The whole affair was disjointed. There was an utter absence of accord in the movements of the several commands, and no decisive result attended the operations. . . ." General Lee seems to have held the same opinion — a visitor to army headquarters that evening described him as "not in good humor over the miscarriage of his plans and his orders" — although in his report he painted it over with a bright coat of optimism. "The result of this day's operations," he wrote of July 2, "induced the belief that, with proper concert of action, and with the increased support that the positions gained on the right would enable the artillery to render the assaulting columns, we should ultimately succeed, and it was accordingly determined to continue the attack."

Lee took that decision Thursday night before the guns had hardly cooled. In contrast to General Meade, he did so without consulting a single one of his lieutenants. In a display of sublime self-confidence he said simply, "The general plan was unchanged."[17]

It was James Longstreet's habit, after a hard day's fighting, to present himself at Lee's headquarters to report on the condition of his command and to discuss what ought to be done next. It was a hallmark of their relationship. After that bloody, terrible day at Sharpsburg, for example, Old Pete had ridden to Lee's headquarters and been greeted warmly — "Ah! here is Longstreet; here's my old war-horse!" After this bloody, terrible day at Gettysburg, however, Old Pete merely sent a courier with a brief report of his doings to army headquarters, and remained stolidly at his own headquarters behind the Emmitsburg Road. His mood was sour. When the Austrian observer FitzGerald Ross queried him about the day's events, he said shortly, "We have not been so successful as we wished," and blamed it on officer casualties, especially those of Hood and Barksdale.

Later, writing privately to General McLaws, Longstreet revealed what his true intentions had been for July 2. The offensive "went further than I intended that it should. . . . It was my intention not to pursue this attack, if it was likely to prove the enemy's position too strong for my two divisions." But instead of stepping in to halt the misguided operation the moment it ran into trouble, Longstreet had watched his inspired officers and men smash through the Yankee lines. "Then was fairly commenced," he wrote proudly, "what I do not hesitate to pronounce the best three hours' fighting ever done by any troops on any battle-field." In the end Old Pete had to pull back somewhat from his gains in the face of heavy Federal reinforcements, and his opinion that from the beginning this was a misguided operation was not changed in the least.[18]

General Lee, for his part, very likely did not care to listen to Longstreet's predictable opinions and objections, and so he did not visit him or summon him to headquarters. Lee's orders for July 3 reached Longstreet probably about 10 o'clock that Thursday night. The orders themselves are not on record — they were probably delivered verbally — but the best description of their content is artillerist Porter Alexander's. He visited Longstreet's headquarters that evening "to ask the news from other quarters & orders for the morning. . . . I was told that we would renew the attack early in the morning. That Pickett's division would arrive and would assault the enemy's line. My impression is the exact point for it was not designated, but I was told it would be to our left of the Peach Orchard."

James Longstreet could be a remarkably stubborn man, and the receipt of these attack orders did not dissuade him from again building a case against them. During the night he sent scouts off to his right, around Round Top, to investigate the possibility of seizing the Taneytown Road and turning Meade's southern flank. This was not the grand turning movement he had first proposed on July 1 — to impose the army to the south between Meade and Baltimore and Washington — but a repeat of his July 1 alternate plan: a close-in tactical turning movement designed simply to threaten the Yankees' flank and rear and pry them out of their imposing lines. As Longstreet later described it to McLaws, he proposed to "move Ewell's corps around my rear and right so as to command this other road, and that we then place our Army in a strong position for the day and await the enemy's attack." Referring to his pre-campaign "understanding" with Lee, he added that such a move "would give us just the kind of battle that we had agreed to seek and to fight." (It would also be the kind of battle the Yankee generals, then in council in the Leister house, were concerned about.)[19]

Lee's orders to Dick Ewell, also sent out that evening, called on the Second Corps "to assail the enemy's right" at daylight on July 3, in conjunction with Longstreet's attack. So far as the record shows, Ewell neither filed a protest nor offered an alternative plan. Like Longstreet, he was in a sour mood after the July 2 failures. He and his generals believed more than ever that a daylight assault against the ranked guns on Cemetery Hill would be suicidal — Harry Hays said such an attack would invite "nothing else than horrible slaughter" — so the morning's target would again be Culp's Hill. It was to be launched from the empty works captured by Allegheny Johnson the night before.

Ewell set about reinforcing Johnson. From Rodes's division, without an assignment for July 3, he took the brigades of Junius Daniel and Edward O'Neal. Now that Stuart's cavalry was finally on the scene to guard the army's rear, Extra Billy Smith's brigade from Early's division, and the

Stonewall Brigade from Johnson's, were available to add to the attacking force. This would give Johnson seven brigades, effectively doubling his force of the previous day. Ewell completed these arrangements during the night, and was poised, as ordered, to assail the Yankees at daylight.

Jeb Stuart was ordered to operate on Friday on Ewell's left and rear. Artillery chief William Pendleton was to prepare for a bombardment along the entire line "as early as possible on the morning of the 3d. . . ." It is not known what orders, if any, Lee gave Powell Hill that Thursday evening. For his attack scheme he presumably intended Hill's Third Corps, at the center of the Confederate line, to act as a general reserve, to apply the finishing touches to any breakthrough achieved by Longstreet or Ewell.

Perhaps the most noteworthy aspect of Lee's battle plan for Day Three, as he conceived it that Thursday evening, is how barren and uninformed it was. There is no knowing what Longstreet's and Ewell's couriers may have said to Lee about the July 2 fighting, but they were surely poor substitutes for personal accounts delivered by the two generals themselves. It is thus astonishing how little General Lee knew of his own army, of the enemy's army, and of the battlefield when he announced that his general battle plan was unchanged and that the attack would continue.

The contrast to General Meade's knowledge at that moment is striking. From the B.M.I. Meade had trustworthy intelligence on his enemy — about Lee's reserves (Pickett's division) and, since he was known to be part of Longstreet's corps, approximately where Pickett might be employed. Meade knew in detail, as did his generals, the condition of the Potomac army — that the Third Corps, for example, was pretty well "used up." He had his generals' best estimates of their effective strength. And, most important, army commander Meade and his corps commanders were in full and thoroughly discussed agreement about what they were going to do on July 3.

None of that could be said for Robert E. Lee. He knew little of Meade's forces, except that they seemed to be massed just where he had attacked. Presumably he realized, from the reports of prisoners taken, that by now he faced the whole of the Army of the Potomac. Yet he had gained no sense of the mettle displayed that day by the Yankee army (and by its commander), in contrast to Chancellorsville, where both had earned Lee's contempt. Whatever Lee had observed of the fighting was limited to what was visible with binoculars from his field headquarters on Seminary Ridge. That meant very little of Ewell's front, not much more of Longstreet's, and something of Hill's in the center. Any reports he received from these battlegrounds were sketchy and secondhand. Consequently, when that evening he ordered Longstreet and his two wounded divisions to renew their effort to strike the lower end of Cemetery Ridge and roll up the Yankee line toward Cemetery Hill — with no change from Thursday's effort except the addition of Pickett's division — Lee was taking a military decision utterly divorced from reality. Longstreet knew the reality all too well, and not surprisingly he sought out a different course.

That neither Lee nor Longstreet, before or after these orders were issued, made any effort that night to meet and to discuss the course of the battle thus far and the course to follow for tomorrow, reveals two strong-minded men engaged in a contest of wills. Neither would blink. Lee, without a serious examination of the case, intent on enforcing his will, was refusing to deviate from his original battle plan. His unhappy lieutenant, stretching a corps commander's discretion to its limit and beyond, was attempting to change a plan he was certain was misguided and doomed to fail.[20]

George Pickett's division had spent July 2 on the march from Chambersburg, reaching to within some three miles of the battlefield by late afternoon. Pickett sent Walter Harrison of his staff to report to General Lee, while he himself hastened toward the sound of the guns and reported to Longstreet. The two generals watched the fighting for a time, and Longstreet told Pickett that his division should go into bivouac until needed. Major Harrison then joined them, bringing a message from Lee: "Tell General Pickett I shall not want him this evening, to let his men rest, and I will send him word when I want him."

This message from the general commanding, delivered to Pickett in Longstreet's presence, proved to be the sole message Pickett received from his superiors in regard to his next day's duties. Therefore, being without further orders, General Pickett would rouse his men at the usual hour on July 3 and start them for the battlefield at daylight. According to General Lee's timetable, which was quite unknown to Pickett, he and the rest of Longstreet's corps, and Allegheny Johnson's division, were all supposed to go into action at daylight.

Here was yet another failure of the Confederates' high-command system, this one in so simple a thing as delivering orders. It appears that Longstreet, hearing Lee's message to Pickett ("I will send him word when I want him") — and remembering Lee earlier giving direct orders to another of Longstreet's generals, Lafayette McLaws — assumed that Lee would order up Pickett when he wanted him. Lee, having sent Longstreet orders Thursday night for a Friday attack that included Pickett, assumed Longstreet would order his subordinate to the front. Longstreet, of course, ought to have followed up on the matter, but in view of his strained relationship with Lee it is perhaps not surprising that he failed to do so.[21]

However that may be, Pickett's arrival from Chambersburg finally filled out the First Corps' order of battle. Yet his three brigades, after making good the corps' July 2 losses, represented a net gain of only about 1,100 in Longstreet's troop count. Hood and McLaws each had lost just under one-third of their men in the July 2 battle.

Hood himself was wounded and out of action, as were two of his brigadiers — Jerome Robertson, hit by a stray shot late in the fighting, and Tige Anderson. Of Hood's eighteen regimental commanders, nine were dead or wounded. McLaws suffered two of his brigadiers, Paul Semmes and William Barksdale, mortally wounded; six of his twenty regimental commanders were casualties. Of the half-dozen batteries overrun during Longstreet's offensive, all were recaptured by the Yankees except the three guns of James Smith's New York 4th Independent, above Devil's Den. During the night, Texans of Robertson's brigade crept up to the guns standing abandoned between the lines, wrapped the wheels in blankets, and silently dragged them off.

With the exception of what General Lee termed "the desired ground" of the Peach Orchard and along the Emmitsburg Road, that part of the battlefield gained by Hood's and McLaws's divisions was not of great value tactically. The two areas on the Federal left whose capture might have produced decisive consequences — Little Round Top, and the gap in the Union line on Cemetery Ridge behind the shattered Third Corps — eluded Longstreet primarily because of the absence of reserves to secure them. In this instance, specifically, it was the absence of Pickett's division. (Pickett, of course, was absent on July 2 because he was performing a guarding function that should have been the responsibility of Jeb Stuart.)

What Longstreet's attack did accomplish was to grievously damage the Army of the Potomac. Dan Sickles's Third Corps was wrecked beyond further use on this field, with a casualty rate of just under 40 percent and stragglers scattered to the Taneytown Road and the Baltimore Pike and beyond. The Fifth Corps, too, was heavily damaged, with the divisions of Barnes and Ayres each losing a quarter of their strength. Before Longstreet was finally subdued, he had attracted, in addition to the

Third and Fifth corps, substantial elements of the Second, Sixth, and Twelfth corps, and most of the reserve artillery.

Dick Anderson's division, of the Third Corps, had also threatened to break through the Federal line on Cemetery Ridge, but while the assaults of Wilcox, Lang, and Wright were bravely made, they were totally unsupported. Neither Anderson nor A. P. Hill (nor General Lee) thought to correct Anderson's dispositions so as to mount an assault in depth, as Hood and McLaws had done. And once the attack began, Anderson was neglectful in following it through. Posey's brigade fired hardly a shot in support; Mahone's brigade never budged off its starting line. Anderson's division did not even gain the satisfaction of a lodgment in the Union lines, ending up right back where it began. This was a particularly bitter pill for Rans Wright, for he lost very nearly half his men in this futile enterprise.[22]

FOR THE CITIZENS OF GETTYSBURG, it had been a long, nerve-racking day. They had awakened to see companies of Rebel soldiers bivouacking in the streets. At the southern end of town, facing Cemetery Hill, the streets were barricaded to block a Federal counterattack. Yard fences were demolished to permit the free movement of troops street to street. Although the authorities did not confine them to their houses, residents were wary of venturing out among their armed and dangerous occupiers. The lack of news added to their concerns. "It was an anxious time for us," remembered Gates Fahnestock. "We had no news of how the battle was going."

There were a few instances of thievery undertaken in the guise of searching houses for hiding Yankees, but most of what looting took place in Gettysburg was in houses abandoned by their owners. Sarah Broadhead watched such a house across the street from hers be plundered systematically by a party of Confederates who filled a wagon with their booty. But she, like most residents who remained in their homes, was not troubled by looters.

There was no avoiding requisitions, however. An officer claiming to be on the staff of General Ramseur, of Rodes's division, demanded food from the Moses McClean family. After emptying the McCleans's smokehouse of hams, he wrote out a receipt, saying, "Your government ought to pay you for that." Stores were ransacked and larders, root cellars, kitchen gardens, and barns stripped by hungry Rebels, and receipts were not always given. Every bakery in town was requisitioned to feed the troops and supply the field hospitals. Public buildings and many private

Artist Waud's sketch of Carlisle Street in Gettysburg looks northward past the railroad depot at right, showing a street barricade constructed of dirt, timber, and "old carts." (Library of Congress)

houses were filled with wounded, and townspeople volunteered or were commandeered to feed the casualties of both armies. A Confederate soldier, enjoying the fruits of his foraging, was heard to remark, "I think the people of this place are very kind considering we came here to kill off their husbands and sons."

At the Globe Inn a large party of Southern officers showed up calling for breakfast. Proprietor Charles Wills served them willingly enough, and when the meal was finished he presented the bill (raising his usual prices by half) and with some trepidation said he would not accept Confederate money. Without blinking an eye the diners paid in Union greenbacks. They were from Jubal Early's command and most likely their money supply came from the tribute Old Jube had recently levied on York. Mr. Wills kept his dining room open throughout the Confederate occupation and was one of the few in town to turn a profit in these days.

The southern end of the town was a danger zone, with sharpshooters taking over buildings and exchanging fire with the Yankees. John Rupp's house was squarely between the picket lines. "The Rebs occupied the whole of town out as far as the back end of my house ....," Mr. Rupp recalled. "Our men occupied my porch, and the Rebels the rear of the house, and I in the cellar, so you can see I was on neutral ground." This sharpshooter fire made it hazardous for anyone to venture outside. Businessman Jacob Hollinger spent the day in the cellar with his family, but he needed to visit the barn to feed the chickens and milk the cow. Federal riflemen nearly hit him between house and barn. When he remarked on this to a Confederate officer, he was told, "Why man, take off that gray suit. They think you are a Reb!"

The artillery duel in late afternoon, and the evening's fighting on Culp's and Cemetery hills, further raised fears among the townspeople. While the town was not in the direct line of fire, stray shells did hit here and there, and rifle fire peppered many buildings. There were no reported civilian casualties, but a number of near misses. According to Fannie Buehler, ". . . it was the most awful time of the awful battle . . . the ground trembled on which our house stood."[23]

Doctors at the field hospitals on both sides of the lines labored straight through the night by lantern light. Surgeon John Shaw Billings, Ayres's Fifth Corps division, set up in a stone house behind Little Round Top and "the wounded began to pour in. I performed a large number of operations of various kinds, received and fed 750 wounded, and worked all that night without cessation." The Fifth Corps' eighty-one ambulances had evacuated 1,300 casualties by 4:00 A.M. on July 3, reported the corps ambulance chief proudly. The last six wounded in his sector were beyond the picket line, "in which case we were unable to get them."

These hospitals, whether Union or Confederate, whether in tents or barns or houses or in the open, were aptly described by a Southerner as "miserable death Holes." The first sight to greet anyone approaching them was the growing piles of amputated hands and feet and whole limbs. A Pennsylvanian who witnessed this sight at a corps hospital in a stone barn likened it to a Philadelphia slaughterhouse. The bedlam of cries and screams emanating from these places became so loud that night that bands were paraded into the space between the field hospitals and the front lines and ordered to play with spirit, and loudly.[24]

Troops on the battle lines were not allowed fires, so they munched on whatever rations they had or could scrounge from any source, including the haversacks of the dead. At Spangler's Spring between the lines at Culp's Hill, men of both armies surreptitiously filled their canteens and (as one Yankee wrote) "backed out with the best grace he could command. . . ." Whether fed and watered or not, the two armies fell into exhausted sleep. Porter Alexander described his routine: "What with deep dust & blood, & filth of all kinds, the trampled & wrecked Peach Orchard was a very unattractive place, but I secured two good straight fence rails,

... placed about four inches apart under one of the trees, & with my saddle for a pillow & with the dead men & horses of the enemy all around, I got two hours of good sound & needed sleep."[25]

IN THE EARLY HOURS of July 3, after the war council had adjourned, a packet of high-profile intelligence arrived at General Meade's headquarters. Captain Ulric Dahlgren and a party of cavalry had intercepted a Confederate mail courier in Greencastle, some 30 miles to the southwest, and discovered dispatches addressed to General Lee from President Jefferson Davis and Adjutant General Samuel Cooper. The president and Cooper, in replying to Lee's queries, explained that no reinforcements would be forthcoming, and rejected Lee's proposal for at least a shadow army under Beauregard to assemble in northern Virginia to menace Washington while Lee menaced Pennsylvania. The captured letters served as a nice confirmation of the Bureau of Military Information's order of battle for Lee's army, and Meade no doubt took comfort knowing the enemy he was facing would get no stronger than it already was.[26]

During the night and into the morning Meade and his lieutenants hurriedly picked up the pieces from the July 2 fighting and arranged their troops as best they could calculate for what was to come. On the left, the Fifth Corps remained more or less where it was at the end of the fighting, digging in on Round Top and Little Round Top and extending north to the Millerstown Road. James Barnes's division had taken a beating, and late in the fighting Barnes himself was wounded by a shell fragment. Of Barnes's three brigades, Sweitzer's was the hardest hit. When the 9th Massachusetts rejoined Sweitzer after picket duty, wrote Colonel Patrick Guiney, "We could scarcely be said to *join* the Brigade; it seemed to me that it would be more appropriate to say that we *constituted* the Brigade. There were the flags of the regiments, & a remnant of a splendid regiment around each, & there were a few officers near their respective colors. . . ." Bracing the sagging Fifth Corps were two brigades from Sedgwick's Sixth Corps.

As part of Meade's process of rectifying his battle lines, two other brigades from the Sixth Corps were posted behind Round Top, facing south astraddle the Taneytown Road, to guard against a Confederate flanking movement. To the north of the Millerstown Road was a variegated command mostly patched together under John Newton of the First Corps. During the evening's crisis on Cemetery Ridge, Newton had come to Hancock's aid with Doubleday's First Corps division, and it was wedged into the center of the line. Into the gap between Doubleday and the Fifth

Corps was inserted Caldwell's battered Second Corps division, two fresh brigades from the Sixth Corps, and in reserve, what was left of the Third Corps.

Extending northward along Cemetery Ridge from Doubleday's position were the Second Corps divisions of John Gibbon — alerted by Meade to expect the brunt of a Confederate attack — and Alexander Hays. These carried the line to Cemetery and Culp's hills, where the remains of the First Corps supported Howard's Eleventh Corps and Slocum's Twelfth. The Twelfth's primary responsibility remained Culp's Hill.

The Sixth Corps, largest in the army, was parceled out in all directions — two brigades on the far left behind Round Top, two in support of the Fifth Corps, two in Newton's line, and the final two in support of the Twelfth Corps on the army's right. Being the last corps to arrive on the field, with all the others already in their places, this was perhaps inevitable, but it did not make Uncle John Sedgwick very happy. Richard Halsted of Sedgwick's staff wrote that "the General had not a man or a gun under his command, except a few orderlies. . . . The General himself said he thought he might as well go home."

Meanwhile Henry Hunt was tireless in organizing and reorganizing and refitting the artillery arm that night and morning. Broken batteries were consolidated, ammunition replenished, repairs made, teams replaced. Like its infantry, the Sixth Corps' artillery was parceled out to wherever the need appeared greatest. Hunt retained fourteen batteries as a tactical reserve behind the center of the line, along with the army's ammunition trains. His ace in the hole, however, was an extra, non-regulation, sixty-wagon supply of ammunition — twenty rounds per gun — that he had finagled in "a *sub-rosa* affair" with Rufus Ingalls, the Potomac army's chief quartermaster. By Hunt's account, "it stood us in hand at the pinch."

The decision in May to restore General Hunt to full and unfettered tactical command of the Army of the Potomac's artillery, taken grudgingly by Joe Hooker after the Chancellorsville debacle, paid off in full on this 3rd of July. Hunt testified to his role at Gettysburg: "ordered artillery from wherever I could find it, where I thought it could be spared, without any regard to the commands of others, except to inform them that it was necessary. . . ." Henry Hunt was certain that his guns would have to be at the core of the defense that day, and he vowed they would be ready.[27]

The often opportunistic, crisis-of-the-moment placement of troops had left the army's corps-command system in something of a tangle. On the left, Fifth and Sixth corps troops were intermixed. In the center, one of the Second Corps divisions was separated from the other two by a First Corps division, remnants of the Third Corps, and some Sixth Corps men. On Cemetery Hill was one First Corps division and the Eleventh Corps; on Culp's Hill, one First Corps division and the Twelfth Corps. For the defense of Culp's Hill the Twelfth was more or less autonomous, yet its nominal commander, Henry Slocum, continued to consider himself in command of the army's right wing. With the emergency over, David Birney reclaimed the remains of the Third Corps, and Winfield Hancock returned to his Second Corps command. It was not entirely clear, however, who commanded what in the tangle of units just north of the Fifth Corps.

With the army assuming a purely defensive stance on July 3, these tangled chains of command were not unduly alarming; generally, fighting defensively did not require the command timing and coordination of the offensive. When General Newton discovered a gap in the line that morning, for example, he got it filled by appealing separately to Meade and to Hancock, and July 2 had clearly demonstrated the willingness of one general to help another who was hard-pressed.

Yet on July 3 everything in the Army of the Potomac without exception was set up for defense; there was not a single preparation for taking the offense, either in forces or in command. Hancock would later testify that Meade told him — presumably this was on the morning of July 3 — "that if the enemy attacked me he intended to put the 5th and 6th corps on the enemy's flank." Meade, however, took no steps in that direction. The army's last reserve, the Sixth Corps, was now scattered literally from one end of the battleground to the other. The closest thing to a unified command — to launch a counterattack, say — were the two adjacent divisions of the Second Corps, under Hancock's lead. However, the two were squarely at the center of the line — just where Meade had predicted the Confederates' attack would fall.

General Meade seemed content with this untidy arrangement. On the right, in an emergency, he could still call on his trusted senior lieutenant, Henry Slocum. Having assumed the cloak of wing commander, Slocum would thereby act. At the center was the equally trusted Hancock, although Hancock's sphere of command was not exactly clear; still, during the heat of battle, officers tended to listen to and obey Winfield Hancock. Sykes led by default on the left. It is surprising that Meade made no use of his other trusted lieutenant, John Sedgwick, for the left. Uncle John may have been short on military imagination, but he was solid and dependable, especially on defense, and he was Sykes's senior. Perhaps Meade reasoned that Sykes knew the field and Sedgwick did not. However that may be, Meade had demonstrated on Thursday how active a commanding general he was, and no doubt he intended to replay that role on Friday.[28]

ON JULY 3 at about 4:30 A.M., daybreak, General Lee rode up to Longstreet's headquarters behind the Emmitsburg Road to watch the start of the day's renewed assault against "those people," as he often referred to the Federals. From the north came the crash of artillery, which he assumed signaled the start of Dick Ewell's part in the day's plan. Ewell was right on time, as ordered. At First Corps headquarters, however, Lee's orders appeared to have gone astray. He could see no preparations for an attack. Indeed, he found hardly any activity at all. Instead he was greeted by General Longstreet, who proceeded to expound on a quite different plan.

As Longstreet later explained it, he feared that General Lee "was still in his disposition to attack," and so he chose a preemptive course. "General," he said, "I have had my scouts out all night, and I find that you still have an excellent opportunity to move around to the right of Meade's army, and maneuver him into attacking us." He said he was just ordering his forces to prepare to move around Round Top and take a posting on the enemy's flank.

Lee was surely surprised by everything he saw and heard, and surely angry as well, but Longstreet only has him reacting "with some impatience" and pointing his fist at Cemetery Hill and saying that the enemy is there and he will strike him. Because it was the 15,000 men of his First Corps who were at risk, Longstreet said he felt it his duty "to express my convictions." He then did exactly that: "General, I have been a soldier all my life. I have been with soldiers engaged in fights by couples, by squads, companies, regiments, divisions, and armies, and should know, as well as any one, what soldiers can do. It is my opinion that no fifteen thousand men ever arrayed for battle can take that position." And then *he* pointed to Cemetery Hill.

In writing this some years later, Old Pete perhaps embellished his recollection somewhat, yet certainly these were his sincere convictions. But he had waited too long to express them. Perhaps the evening before, had he overridden his bruised sensibilities and gone to Lee with his firsthand evaluation of the day's fighting — something that Lee would undoubtedly have been bound to respect — he might have earned at least a look at his flanking plan, and his thought to bring Ewell or part of his corps, Early's division, say, around to the right. But now Lee was not to be swayed. He could hardly back down from his issued orders at this late hour. He could hardly — in public as it were — admit as general commanding that his battle plan was basically flawed. Longstreet saw that he was wasting his breath: "General Lee, in reply to this, ordered me to prepare Pickett's Division for the attack. . . . I said no more, however, but turned away." The contest of wills was over.

Pickett was not yet on the scene — which fact no doubt added to Lee's irritation — and so there was time for discussion of the attack plan. By now the party was enlarged — in addition to Lee and Longstreet, A. P. Hill, Harry Heth, various staff members, and Colonel Fremantle. Lee intended that the divisions of Hood (now under Evander Law) and McLaws, reinforced by Pickett, make the main attack, starting obliquely from the Peach Orchard foothold and rolling up the enemy line along Cemetery Ridge — a repeat of yesterday's original plan. Longstreet objected, pointing out that if Law and McLaws shifted north from their present positions to launch such an attack, they would be vulnerable to Yankee fire, and perhaps counterattacks, against their flank and rear.

Lee led the party on a careful reconnoiter from a point northwest of the Peach Orchard — his first look at Longstreet's July 2 battleground. "As we formed a pretty large party," wrote Fremantle, "we often drew upon ourselves the attention of the hostile sharpshooters, and were two or three times favored with a shell." After long study with his binoculars, Lee had to agree with his lieutenant. Law and McLaws must remain in place. The composition of the assault force would have to be changed.[29]

The manpower additions to Pickett's three brigades would of necessity come from A. P. Hill's Third Corps. The choices for the first line of attack fell on Hill's two divisions that had fought on the 1st of July but not on the 2nd — Harry Heth's and Dorsey Pender's. Heth's division, posted next to where Pickett deployed as he arrived, contributed all four of its brigades to the attack. Pender's contributed two. These six brigades were selected not because of their combat readiness — how much or little action they had seen — but because of their position on the field. It was a decision that would have greatly benefited from more thought.

Harry Heth was himself *hors de combat*. He had been clipped in the head by a bullet and although he remained on the field he was probably concussed. His place was taken by Johnston Pettigrew, new even to brigade command. Of the division's four brigades, on Wednesday Archer's and Joe Davis's had been routed, Brockenbrough's stopped cold, and only Pettigrew's brigade had made any gains — at the cost of a thousand casualties. "They were terribly mistaken about Heth's division in this planning," Colonel Charles Venable of Lee's staff would later observe.

Dorsey Pender, felled by a shell fragment on Thursday, was replaced by Major General Isaac Trimble. Trimble had earlier been scheduled for an army command, but a wound and illness sidelined him. He had come along on the campaign as a supernumerary. Trimble was a thorny and belligerent character, and brand-new to his command — he was appointed that morning. Of the two brigades he would lead, James Lane's had only skirmished on July 1, but Alfred Scales's had been very roughly handled. Even so, the division's overall condition seemed to make it a better choice for a main role in the attack than Heth's division. It appears that A. P. Hill had not informed himself about the condition of his command.

Since six of the nine brigades selected to lead the attack were from the Third Corps, a case could be made that Hill should have commanded them. That does not seem to have crossed General Lee's mind. As he originally planned it, Friday's assault was to be made solely by Longstreet's First Corps, and when the plan had to be changed and Hill's brigades substituted, Lee assigned them to Longstreet's command as a matter of course. To have replaced Old Pete would have demonstrated a lack of confidence, and that was very far from Lee's thinking. However he might doubt Longstreet's suggestions for fighting the battle, he had no doubts whatsoever about Longstreet's generalship.

By the same token, the July 3 assault would come to be universally known as Pickett's Charge rather than the Pickett-Pettigrew-Trimble Charge or some other coinage. Pickett's fresh division had been the core unit from the beginning, and later changes in the attack personnel did not change that logic. In this instance, logic (and brevity) triumphed over strict accuracy.

There was planning as well for a second wave of attackers, to exploit any triumph of the first wave. Two brigades from Dick Anderson's division — Cadmus Wilcox's and David Lang's — advancing on the right, were what might be called confirmed reinforcements. Others had a less formal status, with participation only on a contingency basis — "if opportunity offered," in the usual phrase. These included Pender's (Trimble's) other two brigades, under Abner Perrin and Edward Thomas, and the three other Anderson brigades of Rans Wright, Carnot Posey, and William Mahone. Promised even more vaguely were three of Robert Rodes's brigades from Ewell's Second Corps. In case of a wholesale triumph, McLaws's First Corps division would be called on to take a role as well.

The charge itself was to be preceded by a tremendous cannonade by batteries from all three corps. This was intended to overwhelm the defending artillery and soften up the defending infantry, clearing the path for the attackers.

All this represented, for the second day in a row, a major and quite unexpected change in the plan of attack. The night before, giving no real thought to the matter, making not a single inquiry, determined to enforce his will on his reluctant lieutenants, General Lee had ordered for Friday a repeat of Thursday's attack. In the light of day, however, he discovered that two-thirds of the attacking force had to be changed. More than that, the focus of the attack was thereby changed. Instead of resuming the original plan — Longstreet's corps launching an oblique assault on the Federals' flank, with intent to roll up their line on Cemetery Ridge and reach Cemetery Hill — the stark reality now was a straight-ahead frontal assault on the Federals' center. This meant a general shift to the north. Pickett's division, instead of forming the left wing of the attack, was now the right wing.

Taken as a purely military problem, this was hardly the best choice of targets. Porter Alexander later remarked that any military engineer studying the battlefield "will agree that the point selected for Pickett's attack was very badly chosen — almost as badly chosen as it was possible to be." Alexander thought Cemetery Hill, a salient subject to attack from three sides, would have been the wiser choice. Yet if General Lee wanted Pickett's fresh division to spearhead the assault, and his best general, Longstreet, to lead it, and as there was no time to spare, the choice of targets was strictly limited.

As finally arranged then, nine brigades would spearhead Pickett's Charge, with two brigades in immediate support and five more as possible reinforcements. And to finally seal the victory, there would be three brigades from the Second Corps and a further division from the First. Although General Longstreet would command, he did so with the greatest reluctance and only out of duty. "Never was I so depressed as on that day," he later wrote. "I felt that my men were to be sacrificed, and that I should have to order them to make a hopeless charge."[30]

AS SOON AS HE LEARNED that morning that Longstreet's attack would be a long time coming, General Lee sent a courier galloping to Dick Ewell to hold up Allegheny Johnson's assault on Culp's Hill. Ewell's terse verdict — "too late to recall" — signaled still another failure of Confederate forces to act in concert.

The sounds of battle Lee had heard from Ewell's front were actually the Yankees initiating the fighting there. The night before, when he discovered that the Rebels had seized a section of the Twelfth Corps' breastworks near the base of Culp's Hill, Alpheus Williams reported that fact to General Slocum. Slocum wasted no words: "Well! drive them out at daylight." All well and good for him to say, thought Williams, who expressed a more reasoned view of the matter: "An order that I then thought was more easily made than executed."[31]

It was General Williams's plan to open a sudden artillery bombardment on the Rebel lines at daybreak, and then attack with two brigades of John Geary's division, lost the previous evening but now found and primed for action. At 4:30 A.M. twenty-six guns, in five batteries, began to pour a converging fire into the captured breastworks now sheltering Maryland Steuart's brigade. A man in the 3rd Wisconsin, not in the initial attacking party, was awakened by this cannonade, "the shells going into the woods across the swale and screaming in a most frightful manner. These were followed by hundreds of other shots from our batteries, the shells crashing among the trees, splintering them and scattering the limbs over the ground." Major William Goldsborough of the 1st Maryland battalion, on the receiving end of this barrage, thought "the fire was awful, the whole hillside seemed enveloped in a blaze." Canister and shell fragments "could be heard to strike the breastworks like hailstones upon the roof tops."

Not all this fire fell on the enemy. Archibald McDougall's brigade lay under the line of fire of one of the batteries, and rounds began to fall short and dangerously close. McDougall sent back an alarm to the battery, but soon there was another short round, killing and wounding men in the 46th Pennsylvania. The aggrieved Pennsylvania colonel, James Selfridge, stormed back to the guns, waved his pistol under the nose of the battery commander, and said he would shoot him if one more round fell short. Adjustments were quickly made.

The guns ceased firing and Geary's men girded themselves to charge . . . and the Confederates beat them to it. During the barrage Steuart's brigade had used the captured breastworks for shelter and, comparatively undamaged, now burst forth with the Rebel yell. In company on the right came the brigades of Jesse Williams and Robert Dungan, who was replacing the wounded John M. Jones. This assault was basically a repetition of the previous evening's attacks. There was no change in tac-

Edward Johnson, left, led the July 3 attack against Alpheus Williams on Culp's Hill. (U.S. Army Military History Institute–Library of Congress)

tics or approach, just more men being thrown at the same targets — in daylight.

Dick Ewell had not inspected Johnson's front, and had simply accepted Lee's attack order as a mandate for Johnson to renew his Thursday evening offensive. Their hope was to capture Culp's Hill so as to dominate Cemetery Hill. In fact, the Federal works Steuart had captured, at the base of Culp's Hill, were only some 600 yards from the Baltimore Pike and the rear of the Army of the Potomac. This had been pointed out to Johnson the night before, but neither he nor anyone else in authority seems to have given further thought to the opportunity. To be sure, Thomas Ruger's division blocked the way, and two brigades from the Sixth Corps, as well as a brigade of cavalry, would soon be on the scene. Still, Allegheny Johnson had some 9,000 men under command on the morning of July 3, the way to the Baltimore Pike was considerably less rugged than the way to the crest of Culp's Hill, and the alternative was to butt heads against solid breastworks. That alternative was selected, however.[32]

The 66th Ohio, of Charles Candy's brigade, was sent during the night up to the summit of the hill to brace Pop Greene's extreme left. When the 66th's Lieutenant Colonel Eugene Powell reported his assignment, General Greene was appalled. "My God, young man, the enemy are right out there," he told Powell. "I am expecting an attack any moment. If you go out there with your Regiment they will simply swallow you." Powell was inclined to agree, but orders were orders, and Greene gave him a guide to help place his men.

They were able to form a downhill line at right angles to Greene's brigade, so that when Dungan's Virginians made their frontal attack, the 66th Ohio was perfectly positioned to deliver a devastating flanking fire. For the Rebels it was the same desperate scramble up the steep, rocky hillside as the previous night, except now it was daylight and the Yankee fire was thereby even deadlier. Morale was further tested by having to advance over their own dead from yesterday's fight. "You had better think we give them what they needed this time if they never got it before," an Ohioan wrote home. "Well I could not say that I killed one myself, but I can say that I shot enough at them. . . ." The Virginians soon realized the futility of it all and fell back down the hill and contented themselves with skirmishing fire. The Jones-Dungan brigade suffered 453 casualties in its July 2–3 attacks against the Culp's Hill summit; the 66th Ohio, which inflicted much of that damage that morning, suffered 17.

Jesse Williams's Louisianians attacked the center of Greene's line just as they had Thursday night, and with similar results. Their assault began, according to the 78th New York's Lieutenant Colonel Herbert von Hammerstein, "with the same energy which the rebels displayed on the evening before." Then he added, "Our men succeeded in repulsing them totally, with the same coolness and determination. . . ."

The Federals here kept up an extremely rapid and continuous fire from behind their breastworks by using the same tactic Greene had employed the previous evening — rotating regiments. Three regiments from Candy's brigade were posted in a hollow some 50 yards behind Greene's position, and as Greene's regiments ran low on ammunition, they exchanged places on the firing line. Pop Greene was pleased to report that "the fire was kept up constantly and efficiently over our whole line, and the men were always comparatively fresh and their arms in good order. . . ." As it happened, the men were more exposed to Rebel fire during the exchange than they were behind the sturdy breastworks.

There was an oddly parallel situation in the Confederate line. Williams's Louisianians had gone to ground to do battle, firing from behind the cover of boulders and trees and hillside ravines, and when Edward O'Neal's Alabama brigade, of Rodes's division, started forward to relieve them, the newcomers became exposed to a heavy fire. The Yankees aimed right over the heads of Williams's men to strike O'Neal's. As a man in the 12th Alabama wrote, "we were into it hot and heavy. I thought I had been in hot places before — I thought I had heard Minnie balls; but that day capped the climax." Once in position the Alabamians stubbornly kept up a steady fire of their own, but they could not advance any farther.[33]

It was at the lower part of the hill, where the Yankees did not have the advantage of being behind breastworks, that Allegheny Johnson believed he had the best hope of breaking through and turning in behind Culp's Hill defenders. The Federals posted here were the balance of Geary's division — the two right-hand regiments of Greene's brigade, the Pennsylvania brigade of Thomas L. Kane, and two regiments of Charles Candy's brigade. General Geary followed Greene's example and rotated regiments to keep his battle lines fresh and fast-firing. Over the morning his line would be reinforced by a miscellany — men from Henry Lockwood's brigade, a brigade from the Sixth Corps, even a pair of regiments from the First Corps. The latter were the 147th New York and the 84th New York (or 14th Brooklyn, as its men preferred being called), and their brief engagement gave them the distinction of being the only Union regiments to fight on all three days at Gettysburg.

The Federals on the lower portion of the hill may have lacked breastworks, but they were well posted with good cover at the edge of a woods overlooking a seven-acre meadow the Rebels would have to cross in their advance. Furthermore, artillery pounded at Steuart's men from the moment they left the shelter of the captured works. General Johnson's artillery battalion, by contrast, was under orders on July 3 to "await further orders" — which never came. As a consequence, Federal gunners were left free to pummel Johnson's infantry at will with a murderous flanking fire. As a man in the 1st Maryland battalion put it, "one could feel the earth tremble, so fearful was the cannonading."

There was a struggle for a stone wall crossing the meadow roughly parallel to the line of works. First to try the Rebels at the wall was the 1st Maryland Potomac Home Brigade, an untested regiment from Lockwood's newly arrived force. It got within perhaps 20 yards of the wall before Lockwood withdrew it, badly shot up and short of ammunition. General Geary then sent in the somewhat more experienced 147th Pennsylvania, of Charles Candy's brigade, which was successful enough in its charge that the meadow would be christened Pardee Field, after the Pennsylvanians' Lieutenant Colonel Ario Pardee.

By now it was becoming painfully clear to General Steuart that he

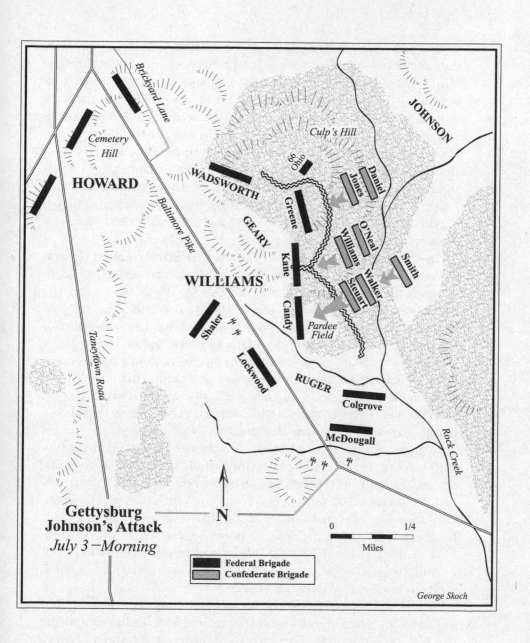

Brickyard Lane

Cemetery
Hill

HOWARD

WADSWORTH

Culp's Hill

JOHNSON

66
Ohio

Daniel

Jones

GEARY

Greene

O'Neal

Williams

Baltimore Pike

Taneytown Road

Kane

Smith

Walker

WILLIAMS

Stewart

Candy

Pardee
Field

Shaler

Lockwood

RUGER

Colgrove

McDougall

Rock Creek

Gettysburg
Johnson's Attack
July 3—Morning

N

0   1/4

Miles

Federal Brigade
Confederate Brigade

George Skoch

365

could make no headway against this Yankee line, just as his troops farther up the hill were discovering. The primary reason was the sheer intensity of the Federals' fire. Confederates spoke of being "exposed to a very heavy fire," of being "nearly annihilated." "So terrific was the strife that scarcely a leaf or limb was left on the surrounding trees," said a Marylander. A Virginian decided, "I think it was the hardest battle we ever had." All this was testimony to the efficiency of the Federals' rotation of forces. A regiment blazed away without restraint, then was replaced by a fresh regiment that in its turn blazed away without restraint. General Geary reported that on July 3 his infantry division alone expended 277,000 rifle rounds. That came to 70 rounds for each man — a full ammunition issue and more.[34]

The Confederates fell back and their fire slackened, leading General Slocum, viewing affairs from his distant headquarters on Power's Hill, to conclude that the enemy was "becoming shaky." He reached out to the nearest general, Thomas Ruger, and ordered him to retake the captured works. Ruger, on the scene and properly careful, wanted to reconnoiter the Rebel strength first before any attack, to which Slocum agreed. Ruger sent his aide to Silas Colgrove's brigade with the necessary instructions: Advance skirmishers, and if the enemy was "not found in too great force . . . advance two regiments, and dislodge him from the breastworks." In some fashion never explained, Colonel Colgrove misinterpreted this as a direct order for an immediate frontal attack by two regiments.

Colgrove selected the 2nd Massachusetts and his old regiment, the 27th Indiana. Their combined 650 men would encounter (as they discovered) perhaps 1,000 Rebels behind the works, and to reach them they had to cross some 100 yards of open meadow. When the 2nd Massachusetts' Lieutenant Colonel Charles Mudge heard the order, he insisted it be repeated. "Well," he declared, "it is murder, but it's the order." Dutifully Mudge ordered the charge. "They had scarcely gained the open ground," wrote Colonel Colgrove, "when they were met with one of the most terrible fires I have ever witnessed."

Within minutes five successive Massachusetts color bearers were shot down; Private James Murphy would be credited with finally rescuing the flag. Colonel Mudge was killed early in the charge and command fell to Major Charles Morse. As the veteran Morse remembered it, this battle in the meadow was "at the shortest range I have ever seen two lines engaged at. . . . I never saw men behave so splendidly. It was awful, yet grand. . . ." It was also hopeless, and he soon signaled a withdrawal. The 2nd Massachusetts, what was left of it, fell back without panic to a stone

The attack on Culp's Hill on the morning of July 3 by Edward Johnson's Confederate division, as pictured by Edwin Forbes. The defenders here were from George Sears Greene's brigade. (Library of Congress)

wall near its starting point. "I never saw a finer sight than to see that regiment, coming back over that terrible meadow, face about and form in line as steady as if on parade," wrote the regimental historian.

The 27th Indiana came up on the right of the 2nd Massachusetts. Colonel Colgrove, its old commander, sent it in personally: "Twenty-seventh, charge! Charge those works in your front!" As they started across the meadow the Hoosiers were harassed by Confederate skirmishers on the other side of Rock Creek. Then, halfway across the meadow, Extra Billy Smith's troops in their front unleashed a concerted volley. It was, as the 27th's regimental historian described it, "the scathing, fatal volley which all remember so well. . . . It was a terrific volley. It was one of those well-aimed, well-timed volleys which break up and retard a line, in spite of itself." The 27th's entire color guard was shot down. The Hoosiers halted to return fire, but this only made them stationary targets for the well-protected Virginians. At last Colgrove ordered retreat.

The ill-conceived venture cost the 2nd Massachusetts 43 percent of its numbers, and the 27th Indiana, 32 percent. Whether General Ruger's aide had misdelivered the order or Colonel Colgrove had misconstrued it would never be determined. Ruger called it "one of those unfortunate occurrences that will happen in the excitement of battle." It appears, however, that Colgrove might have confirmed any oral order that seemed so divorced from the reality of the moment. However that may be, Colgrove's charge stands as the only serious mistake committed by the defenders of Culp's Hill. General Slocum and his lieutenants were content thereafter to let their defenses carry the day.[35]

The contest was in its fourth hour now, and Allegheny Johnson's reserves were reinvigorating the attack. Against the upper reaches of Culp's Hill he had sent in Edward O'Neal's Alabama brigade, from Rodes's division, to assist Williams's Louisianians. Against the defenders on the lower hill, James Walker's Stonewall Brigade reinforced Maryland Steuart's efforts. From their positions on the respective flanks of the attackers, the 66th Ohio at the top of the hill and the 147th Pennsylvania at the bottom, behind the stone wall it had won in Pardee Field, continued to deliver deadly enfilading fire.

The result was repeated bloody repulse from one end of the line to the other. Colonel O'Neal summed it up with grim exactitude — his brigade, he wrote, "charged time and again up to their works but were every time compelled to retire. Many gallant men were lost. . . ." In some places on the hillside the Rebels found enough cover to keep up a fire at their tormentors, but they could not advance, and to retreat was to expose themselves to a galling fire. To resupply ammunition under fire, Johnson's staff hit on the idea of unloading boxes of cartridges into blankets, which were then slung from poles and hauled up the hill.

General Lee's revised directive to Ewell that morning had announced that Longstreet's assault would be delayed until 10:00 A.M. Apparently with that timetable in mind, Ewell ordered Johnson to continue his attacks so as to conform to Lee's stated intention for July 3 of striking both flanks of Meade's army simultaneously. As it happened, Longstreet was nowhere near ready to open his advance by 10 o'clock, but Lee did not notify Ewell of that fact. Presumably he wanted the Federals to continue to focus their attention on their right. Johnson's offensive, by now clearly seen to be senseless, was thereby rendered even more senseless.

Lieutenant Randolph McKim of Maryland Steuart's staff recorded in his diary that both General Steuart and General Daniel, from Rodes's division, "strongly disapproved of making the assault." Whether they made complaint to Johnson or to corps commander Ewell is not stated. In any event, Ewell did not visit Steuart's front, no minds were changed, and soon after 10 o'clock yet another attack was launched against Culp's Hill. When Major William Goldsborough of the 1st Maryland battalion received the order to charge yet again, he protested it as "nothing less than murder. . . . I moved slowly down the line to my position with feelings I had never before experienced on the battlefield. I felt that I had but a few minutes to live."[36]

Lieutenant Colonel Charles Randall, 149th New York, Greene's brigade, peering down the smoke-covered hill, suddenly shouted, "Here they come, boys! Give them hell, boys, give it to them right and left!" This newest attack was the strongest attempt yet to break past the Federal right at the foot of Culp's Hill. It was spearheaded by Steuart's brigade, supported by Junius Daniel's North Carolina brigade and the Virginians of the Stonewall Brigade. The tactics were unchanged — frontal assaults against the well-dug-in or well-secured positions of Geary's division, reinforced now with elements from Ruger's division and from the Sixth Corps.

Each advance along the line was met by a torrent of musketry. "It was the most fearful fire I ever encountered . . . ," Lieutenant McKim wrote of crossing Pardee Field. "The greatest confusion ensued — regiments were reduced to companies and everything mixed up. It came very near to being a rout." At the center of the line delivering this fire was the 29th Pennsylvania, Thomas Kane's brigade. Colonel William Rickards noticed that great numbers of leaves were fluttering down as the enemy advanced from the woods. He realized his men were firing too high, and shouted out a correction: Aim at the Rebels' knees. The effect, he said, "was noticeable at once." "It was truly awful how fast, how very fast, did our poor boys fall by our sides," wrote Private Louis Leon of Daniel's brigade. Leon's company began the fight with sixty men and ended it with sixteen.

The Federals continued rotating fresh regiments into their front-line positions. The Sixth Corps' 122nd New York, for example, was ordered as a replacement regiment to a ravine 50 yards behind the battle line. "A regt. in the 12th Corps had just fallen back from this place, they being out of ammunition," wrote Corporal Sanford Truesdell. "To reach it we had to cross a space of about ten rods, fully exposed to the fire of the enemy. We crawled on our hands and knees to the top of the bluff, and raising up, ran to our position as fast as our legs could carry us, but O! how the bullets whistled . . . and it seemed impossible for one of us to reach there alive. But when once there we had the advantage of the enemy. . . ." When the 122nd New York discovered it was posted next to the 149th New York, there was much neighborly cheering. Both regiments had been recruited from Onondaga County at the same time in the fall of 1862.

369

Virginia soldier Allen Redwood made this drawing of Confederates of the 1st Maryland Battalion, of George Steuart's brigade, storming Culp's Hill during the morning attack of July 3. (Century Collection)

In the Pardee Field fighting there was another meeting of neighbors, although not so pleasant a one. The 1st Maryland battalion of Steuart's Confederate brigade tangled with the 1st Maryland Eastern Shore Infantry of Lockwood's Union brigade. Both had been recruited in the same section of the state; each had relatives and friends, or former friends, in the other; cousins served in the opposing color guards. "The 1st Maryland Confederate Regiment met us & were cut to pieces," wrote Colonel James Wallace of the Eastern Shore Marylanders. "We sorrowfully gathered up many of our old friends & acquaintances & had them carefully & tenderly cared for."[37]

General Walker of the Stonewall Brigade had seen enough. The attack had met "with equally bad success as our former efforts," he wrote, "and the fire became so destructive that I suffered the brigade to fall back to a more secure position. . . ." Maryland Steuart did the same, and as his men streamed to the rear, the distraught Steuart cried, "My poor boys! My poor boys!" A good many attackers, trapped between the lines and unable to retreat without being hit, had no choice but surrender. The 7th Ohio took seventy-eight prisoners, the 122nd New York, seventy-five, the 137th New York, fifty-two.

By the final count, Allegheny Johnson lost 2,000 men, nearly a third of his division, trying to take Culp's Hill on those two days. Perhaps another 800 fell in the brigades of Daniel, O'Neal, and Extra Billy Smith on July 3. The defenders in the Twelfth Corps lost just over 1,000 men on July 2–3. The cost to Pop Greene, the primary defender, was 300 men, one-fifth of his brigade. Alpheus Williams was echoing many in Allegheny Johnson's division when he wrote, "The wonder is that the rebels persisted so long in an attempt that the first half hour must have told them was useless."

Gradually the smoke cleared and the slopes and fields and woods in front of the Yankee lines were found at last to be empty of Rebels, except for the dead and the helpless wounded. By 11:00 A.M. Culp's Hill fell silent but for the tendentious fire of opposing pickets. Pop Greene's brigade broke the silence with three rousing cheers.[38]

12   A Magnificent Display of Guns

GENERAL MEADE, who had gotten no rest at all Wednesday night, managed three or four hours' sleep early Friday morning, following his council of war, but he was up with the dawn on what he was confident would be a day of renewed battle. His first task was to ride the lines. He started where the morning's fighting was, at Culp's Hill, and called in help from Sedgwick's Sixth Corps to strengthen General Williams's hand. To further secure his right flank, he saw to it that the cavalry stood watch along the Hanover Road that entered Gettysburg from the east. The assignment there went to David Gregg's troopers.

In company with Winfield Hancock, he then inspected the center of the Cemetery Ridge line, the defense of which on July 3 would be primarily the responsibility of Hancock's Second Corps. Meade continued to think, as he had warned John Gibbon the night before, that this position would be critical in the day's events. In an 8:00 A.M. dispatch to John Sedgwick, he said it appeared to be the enemy's intention "to make the attempt to pierce our center." He wanted Sedgwick to mass forces "in a central position," where they might be "thrown to the right or left, as required."

Lieutenant Frank Haskell of John Gibbon's staff took note of the commanding general as he made his inspection: "He was early on horseback this morning, and rode along the whole line, looking to it himself, and with glass in hand sweeping the woods and fields in the direction of the enemy, to see if ought of him could be discovered. His manner was calm and serious, but earnest." Haskell listened in on Meade's conversation with Hancock. Meade seemed satisfied with the defenses on both right and left, and admitted, wrote Haskell, that an attack against the center, where "our artillery has such sweep . . . was not the favorite point of attack with the Rebel." Still, "should he attack the center, the General thought he could reinforce it in good season."

Completing his tour of the lines, Meade consulted with Generals Newton and Sedgwick, and on Little Round Top he and engineer Warren discussed the implications of the Confederate artillery beginning to be visible in front of Seminary Ridge. Back at headquarters, newspaper correspondent Whitelaw Reid described the commanding general as "Quick and nervous in his movements, but calm, and as it seemed to me, lit up with the glow of the occasion. . . ." Meade sent circulars to his corps commanders calling on them to keep the men alert and under arms at all times, and to make an effort to collect all stragglers and absentees and get them back to the firing line. Everything appeared to be pointing to an enemy attack — somewhere.

Yet Meade was thinking ahead as well. To General Darius Couch, commanding militia forces at Harrisburg, he explained that the sound of the guns at Gettysburg was all the signal "you need to come on. Should the enemy withdraw, by prompt co-operation we might destroy him." On the other hand, should the enemy gain the upper hand, Couch must turn back to the defense of Harrisburg and the Susquehanna line. To General William French, at Frederick, Maryland, with the Harper's Ferry garrison, Meade delivered similar contingency orders. If Lee fell back after being defeated at Gettysburg, French should "re-occupy Harper's Ferry and annoy and harass him in his retreat." If, however, "the result of today's operations should be our discomfiture and withdrawal," French must look to the defense of Washington.[1]

Another of Meade's conferees that 3rd of July was his chief of artillery, Henry Hunt. During these early-morning hours, General Hunt had been as tireless as the army commander in checking and adjusting and ordering his sphere of responsibility. His first concern had been the gunnery in the Culp's Hill clash, but he soon concluded there was nothing to worry about there. As he put it laconically in his report, "In this work the artillery rendered good service." He then examined, in close detail, the rest of the artillery postings on Cemetery Hill, Cemetery Ridge, and Little Round Top.

The Eleventh Corps' batteries on Cemetery Hill had put to rights any damage suffered in the previous afternoon's gun duel and, with twenty-nine guns, were prepared for whatever might now come their way. The artillery line that ran south from there along Cemetery Ridge was commanded by the Second Corps' John G. Hazard. Captain Hazard's brigade had been badly cut up during Longstreet's offensive the previous evening. In Lieutenant George Woodruff's Battery I, 1st U.S., for example, a third of the gun crewmen this morning were infantry volunteers

Ten o'clock on the morning of July 3, behind the Union lines looking north, sketched by Edwin Forbes. At left is the Taneytown Road, at right the Baltimore Pike, crowded with troops. Ziegler's Grove, on Cemetery Ridge, is at left rear, Culp's Hill (1) at far right. (Library of Congress)

from Alexander Hays's division. Battery B, 1st Rhode Island, overrun by Rans Wright's Georgians, had lost heavily, including battery commander Frederick Brown, seriously wounded. Captain James Rorty's Battery B, 1st New York Light, had also been badly damaged. The brigade's five batteries mounted twenty-seven guns now, but Captain Hazard had all his limbers and caissons filled and was ready to do battle once again. In due course, Hazard would be braced by two additional two-gun sections, one of them being all that remained of Bigelow's 9th Massachusetts battery after yesterday's fight.

At the next slot in the artillery line, Hunt ordered up two batteries to support Newton's orphaned First Corps division. Then, on lower Cemetery Ridge, came a grouping under the artillery reserve's Freeman McGilvery, who had performed so boldly in mustering the last-ditch gun line behind the shattered Third Corps on July 2. Colonel McGilvery's

patched-together assembly of Thursday was now a solid and substantial forty-one-gun line, thanks to additions from the reserve.

Hunt completed his inspection of the western front by visiting the two batteries on the far left, including the six 10-pounder Parrott rifles perched on Little Round Top. This had been the dead Charles Hazlett's battery; today it was commanded by Lieutenant Benjamin Rittenhouse. Hunt could count all told 119 guns facing west toward Seminary Ridge that morning.[2]

He saw that the positioning of support would be critical in the coming battle, and his last stop was the artillery reserve. The reserve and the ordnance trains were posted squarely behind the center of the line, within easy reach of any point on the front. Hunt's skilled deputy, Robert O. Tyler, was in the process of increasing the number of batteries in the reserve to eighteen through repairs and reconditioning. Hunt delivered his report to General Meade at army headquarters at the Leister house. In their discussion, Meade mentioned his continued concern about the center of the line, and asked Hunt to reappraise artillery coverage there. Since Meade took the center as beginning at Cemetery Hill,

Hunt rode there first, as it furnished a superior vantage point. It was about 11:00 A.M.

What he saw when he looked westward took his breath away. "Here a magnificent display greeted my eyes," he wrote. "Our whole front for two miles was covered by batteries already in line or going into position. They stretched — apparently in one unbroken mass — from opposite the town to the Peach Orchard, which bounded the view to the left, the ridges of which were planted thick with cannon. Never before had such a sight been witnessed on this continent, and rarely, if ever, abroad."

But what did it mean, Hunt wondered. It could be, he thought, merely a cover for shifting infantry to Ewell for a continued attack on that front. Or it could be simply for defense, or even to cover a general withdrawal. But Hunt's best guess — like most every Yankee witnessing the sight — was that it signaled a massive assault on the center of the Federal line.

Henry Hunt relished the challenge. Here was the moment he had been waiting for ever since his first artillery command at Bull Run in 1861. Hunt had long nurtured a vision of the proper use of artillery in battle, and he could not have ordered in advance a better scene or situation than what confronted him on this 3rd of July 1863. He was posted on the high ground (but not too high), with clear fields of fire. He had 119 guns of high quality massed in battery, with plentiful reserves and sufficient ammunition. He was positioned to catch an infantry attack in a deadly crossfire. His brigade commanders were chosen by him and trained by him, and all of them were conditioned (he hoped) to take their orders during battle from him. As he later put it, "it was evident that all the artillery on our west front, whether of the army corps or the reserve, must concur as a *unit,* under the chief of artillery, in the defense."

If there was going to be an infantry assault, it seemed all but certain that the Confederates would precede it with a bombardment by their massed artillery. Hunt immediately set out to ride his lines once again, this time to spell out to his artillery chiefs and battery commanders exactly what they should do in that event.

The message Henry Hunt preached that day was the "first importance" of the artillery primarily directing its fire against the enemy's advancing infantry. Counterbattery fire aimed at the enemy's guns must be only a secondary target. When the enemy batteries opened, he instructed his gunners not to reply for fifteen or twenty minutes, and then to fire slowly, not wasting ammunition, and only at "those batteries which were most destructive to us." In this manner, all his guns should have sufficient long-range ammunition — shell and case shot — for use, especially in crossfire, against the Rebel infantry right from the moment it started its advance, then canister to finish off the job at close range. Thus Henry Hunt's formula for destroying an attack by artillery alone.[3]

HENRY JACKSON HUNT'S counterpart in the Army of Northern Virginia was William Nelson Pendleton, but only in their respective titles was there any similarity. Brigadier General Pendleton was an 1830 West Point graduate who had spent most of the antebellum years in the ministry rather than the military. Pendleton understood the theory and administration of gunnery well enough, but he completely lacked any instinct for the battlefield. He had been appointed chief of artillery due to circumstance and his friendship with both Lee and Jefferson Davis, but in the field he repeatedly disappointed. His juniors called him "Old Mother Pendleton" and worked around him. "By the way Pendleton is Lee's weakness," an artilleryman had written after Sharpsburg. "P. is like the elephant, we have him & we don't know what on earth to do with him, and it costs a devil of a sight to feed him."

Over the past year there had been singular feats of brilliance by the Army of Northern Virginia's artillery arm, yet its overall management was all too often marked by failure. The closest parallel to the situation on this 3rd of July had been Malvern Hill on the Peninsula a year earlier. There the army's batteries were supposed to be massed to clear the way for an infantry assault, but at the crucial moment Pendleton and his artillery reserve were nowhere to be found. The charge was bloodily repulsed. A bitter D. H. Hill called the artillery's role at Malvern Hill "almost farcical." In the army's reorganization following Chancellorsville, the artillery reserve was divided up amongst the corps. Pendleton was given the inflated title General in Chief of Artillery, but his actual role was deflated to purely advisory. Yet in that role he remained the only supervisory figure in the artillery's chain of command, and when General Lee determined that a massive artillery bombardment precede Pickett's Charge, he issued the order through General Pendleton.[4]

The bombardment was the critical element of the plan. Lee was certainly aware of the inherent risks of a frontal attack — he could hardly have forgotten the lessons of Malvern Hill — but he intended this unprecedented volume of gunnery to pulverize the defending Federal batteries and overwhelm and demoralize the defending Federal infantry. The orders, said Porter Alexander, were to cripple the enemy, "to tear him limbless, as it were, if possible." In the wake of the cannonade, batteries would advance with the infantry to furnish close-in supporting fire, just

Brigadier General Henry J. Hunt, artillery chief of the Army of the Potomac, directed the Union batteries at Gettysburg. (Library of Congress)

as Alexander had advanced his guns to the Peach Orchard during Thursday's fighting.

The bombardment, in short, was designed to even the odds, or even to shorten them, and then what Lee firmly believed was the best infantry in the world would breach the center of the Union line. He was surely aware of a precedent. At Solferino in Italy in 1859, after a heavy preliminary bombardment, Napoleon III's frontal attack had broken the Austrian

Lee's artillery chief was William N. Pendleton, at left. E. Porter Alexander led Longstreet's artillery. (Cook Collection, Valentine Museum)

center. Lee's was potentially a workable plan, yet one that would require the perfect interlocking — and the perfect success — of each supporting element for it to work.

It became General Pendleton's task to design and execute the bombardment. It was an assignment larger than anything he or the Army of Northern Virginia had ever attempted before. It meant assigning or approving the best firing positions, specifying targets, ordering and coordinating the fire of a dozen battalions from three army corps, instructing battalion and battery commanders in firing discipline, detailing batteries to advance with the infantry, positioning replacement batteries and ordnance trains, and, of vital importance, appraising ammunition supply against anticipated demand. According to Pendleton, he gave his "earnest attention" to all these subjects. In point of fact, he fell far short in almost all of them.

Porter Alexander had begun the campaign in command of a battalion in the First Corps' artillery reserve, but upon reaching Gettysburg

Longstreet bypassed his chief of artillery, James Walton, to put Alexander in tactical command of the corps' artillery. Longstreet no doubt did so based on merit, for by report Alexander's handling of his battalion at Chancellorsville had been exceptional. On this Friday morning Longstreet worked closely with Alexander, whose guns in the coming fight would come nearest to achieving Lee's ideal for the bombardment. "Visiting the lines at a very early hour toward securing readiness for this great attempt, I found much (by Colonel Alexander's energy) already accomplished . . . ," General Pendleton wrote, and passed on.

Because Lee's initial plan specified an early-morning assault, Alexander had hurried to post his guns before dawn. At first light he discovered to his horror that a dozen of them were almost under the muzzles of enemy batteries. "It scared me awfully," he recalled, but by dint of fast, quiet work, he pulled them back to safer ground before the Yankees woke up. Through the morning hours he put in the rest of the First Corps' guns until he had seventy-five pieces massed in battery. His gun line ran some 1,300 yards from the Peach Orchard northward behind the Emmitsburg Road to Spangler's Woods. To his surprise and immense relief, the Federals made only scattered efforts to challenge this buildup. It was, he wrote, that day's policy "to save every possible round for the infantry fight," and he could hardly afford a gun-versus-gun duel beforehand.

In fact the same was true of the Federals. Henry Hunt's nearest artillery depot was at Westminster, in Maryland. To be sure, this was much closer than the Rebels' nearest depot, some 200 miles distant at Staunton in the Shenandoah Valley, yet on this day of battle Hunt, like Pendleton, would have to make his fight with whatever ammunition was in his ordnance trains.

Colonel Lindsay Walker, chief of artillery for A. P. Hill's Third Corps, deployed fifty-three of his cannon in front of Seminary Ridge for the bombardment. Well to the north, Walker posted two English-made Whitworth rifles, breechloaders of high accuracy that outranged everything on the field, and aimed them at Cemetery Hill. "To the Third Corps artillery attention was also given," reported General Pendleton, but it seems that little attention was paid to him in return. Walker's gunners would act that day with little restraint and expend substantial amounts of ammunition to little purpose.

Pendleton also reported issuing "specific instructions" to Dick Ewell's Second Corps' artillerists, who in the end would furnish just thirty-three guns to the bombardment. It was in his dealings with the Second Corps that Pendleton failed most dismally. "The great criticism I have to make on the artillery operations of the day is upon the inaction of the artillery of Ewell's corps," wrote Porter Alexander. The lengthy line manned by Lee's army — the exterior line condemned by all the military textbooks — did deliver one advantage on July 3: "It enabled us to enfilade any of the enemy's positions, near the centre of their line, with artillery fire. . . . No troops, infantry or artillery, can long submit to an enfilade fire." All that was required, Alexander went on, was decent aim; any shot sighted down the length of a line was bound to hit something. Ewell's guns were ideally positioned to deliver such a fire, yet only some two dozen shots were delivered by the one Second Corps battalion in that enfilade posting. That, said Alexander bluntly, was Pendleton's fault: "Gen. Lee's chief should have known, & given every possible energy to improve the rare & great chance to the very uttermost."[5]

In Lee's scheme, at the close of the bombardment the artillerists were to push batteries forward along with the advancing infantry to furnish close-in fire support during the charge. While in theory this seemed a sound tactic, in practice it posed certain difficulties. The problem was the often faulty Confederate ammunition. This might be due to poor powder, but mostly it was defective fuzes. As recently as Chancellorsville, wrote an observer, "An extraordinarily large percentage of Confederate shells failed to burst, and many were even more ineffective by reason of premature explosions." Porter Alexander remarked on the effect of this phenomenon during the heat of battle: "We were always liable to premature explosions of shell & shrapnel, & our infantry knew it by sad experience, & I have known of their threatening to fire back at our guns if we opened over their heads."

This became an important factor on July 3. A number of batteries, posted behind lines of infantry, were restricted to using solid shot in the bombardment, thereby cutting down the effectiveness of their fire. As for advancing in company with the infantry, shoddy ammunition affected that tactic as well. As Alexander put it, the risk of firing over the infantry meant that "each arm must have its own fighting front free, & they do not mix well in a fighting charge." Nevertheless, Colonel Alexander believed he had worked out a scheme for pushing his guns forward at the proper time.

General Pendleton had come to him with the offer of nine Third Corps guns, which apparently there was not room enough for in Hill's gun line. Alexander accepted them gratefully. His thought was to park them under cover behind his line and at the right moment bring them out, fresh and with full ammunition chests, to spring at the enemy. They would actually lead the charge, ahead of Pickett, go into battery just out of infantry range, and open fire to pave the way for the attack. This bold idea was entirely Alexander's. If Pendleton mentioned anything to the Second and Third corps about advancing their guns, it was only in the vaguest of terms. Ewell's artillery never moved at all. In the Third Corps Major William Poague understood that should the infantry gain Cemetery Ridge he was to bring his guns there. "Not a word was said about following the infantry as they advanced to the attack," Poague wrote.

As important a matter as the quality of the artillery ammunition was the supply of it. Like Meade, on this day Lee would have to make his fight with what was in the army's ordnance trains — with no possibility of refilling them except by capture. After three weeks on campaign (during which, among other expenditures, 400 artillery rounds were lost crossing the Shenandoah River), and after two days of exceedingly heavy artillery fighting, it seems obvious that artillery chief Pendleton would have kept a close count on what remained in the trains. If he did so, he did not inform anyone. He especially did not inform General Lee. There was no effort on anyone's part that morning to balance accounts between how much ammunition would be needed for an effective bombardment and follow-up, and how much was available. If there was any problem here, apparently Lee assumed Pendleton would announce it beforehand. What Pendleton assumed is impossible to say.

When General Lee wrote his final report on the Gettysburg campaign and made reference to the July 3 ammunition-supply situation, he remarked that the true case "was unknown to me when the assault took place. . . ." From this the inference could easily be drawn (as General McLaws, among others, noted) that had Lee been fully informed by General Pendleton, "the charge would not have been made."

Be that as it may, Porter Alexander recalled that on that hot July morning no one on the Confederate side was parsing the two armies' comparative strengths and weaponry and positions, or "I might not have felt as cheerful & sanguine as I did. But the fact is that like all the rest of the army I believed that it would all come out right, because Gen. Lee had planned it."[6]

PROFESSOR MICHAEL JACOBS of Pennsylvania College, as meticulous as a mathematician was expected to be, continued carefully recording the weather even amidst the greatest battle ever fought in America. The early-morning cloudiness on July 3 was typical of a Pennsylvania summer, but by midday the sky had cleared except for fleecy white cumulus clouds to the west. It was humid and still, and at 2:00 P.M. Professor Jacobs would record the temperature as 87 degrees. As it happened, that would be the highest temperature he recorded in Gettysburg all that month.[7]

As the Confederate artillery chiefs finally arranged it, 163 guns, the majority of them rifled pieces, formed a sweeping, irregular arc from the Peach Orchard northward to a point opposite the town, stretching more loosely beyond as far as Oak Hill. Nothing remotely like it had been seen before in this war. With their crews hidden from sight, the guns stood silent in their long ranks like deadly, solitary sentinels. Heat waves radiated off the black iron Parrott and Rodman rifles; the bronze Napoleons gleamed brightly in the sunlight. On Little Round Top an awed Major Thomas Hyde, viewing this array "seemingly directed toward the centre of our line," counted 100 guns visible just from his vantage point. When Meade reached the spot on his inspection tour, wrote Hyde, "I dodged back to tell the general that it looked like a cannonade pretty soon."[8]

Meanwhile Confederate infantry was filing into place, taking pains to keep concealed. Pickett's division, once the largest in the army before D. H. Hill expropriated two of its brigades in North Carolina, could put but 5,830 men on the battle line. This shortfall of manpower was one reason it became necessary to dip into Pender's Third Corps division for two brigades on July 3. Pickett formed as the left of Longstreet's corps. A shallow swale on the Henry Spangler farm, just in front of Mr. Spangler's woods and behind the artillery line, provided cover for James Kemper's and Richard Garnett's lead brigades. Kemper deployed to the right, Garnett to the left. Behind them, along the edge of the woods, Lewis Armistead's brigade formed a second, supporting line. The men were ordered to lie down, and the flags were lowered and out of sight.

These fifteen Virginia regiments of Pickett's were trustworthy veterans who had sat out the army's last two battles, at Fredericksburg and Chancellorsville. Even so, they had more combat experience than their commanding general. Pickett had been wounded at Gaines's Mill on the Peninsula and today would mark his first fighting command in more than a year.

George Pickett, of the flowing locks and the effervescent manner, was a protégé of Longstreet's, and Old Pete very carefully went over the day's attack plan with him. During his long hiatus Pickett had been promoted to major general and divisional commander, and he was eager to prove his worth. He saw July 3 as his opportunity. He met with Colonel Birkett Fry, commanding the brigade of Pettigrew's division on Pickett's imme-

Major General George E. Pickett's all-Virginia division formed a spearhead of Pickett's Charge. (Library of Congress)

diate left, to coordinate their advance. "He appeared to be in excellent spirits," Fry remembered, "and, after a cordial greeting and a pleasant reference to our having been together in work of that kind at Chapultepec, expressed great confidence in the ability of our troops to drive the enemy. . . ."[9]

While Pickett's division was receiving careful attention from the high command during the planning for the attack, rather less can be said for

384

Two of Pickett's brigade commanders, Brigadier Generals James L. Kemper, left, and Lewis A. Armistead. (Library of Congress–Valentine Museum)

the rest of the attacking force. A. P. Hill, contributing six of the nine brigades to the operation, remained that Friday the same elusive figure he had been on Wednesday and Thursday. Lee surely consulted with Hill on Friday morning about the availability of the troops in his command, yet the selection of Heth's (Pettigrew's) division for the main assault suggests that Hill had made no effort to evaluate its condition after Wednesday's fighting. In like fashion, Hill inexplicably approved of using Alfred Scales's wrecked brigade from Pender's (Trimble's) division.

The Third Corps contained four brigades that had seen only skirmishing action or no action at all on the 1st and 2nd of July — and just one of them would fight on the 3rd of July. The touchy Hill was not on good terms with Longstreet to begin with, and having to turn so much of his command over to Old Pete apparently did not sit well with him. After a stiff morning meeting between the two (they parted without shaking hands, it was noticed), Hill told his brigadiers to take their orders from Longstreet. It appears that Longstreet assumed Hill would at the least su-

perintend the Third Corps' deployment. Hill instead resumed his bystander role. (Hill had supposedly proposed to Lee that the entire Third
Corps be part of the assault, but was told that the uncommitted half of
his corps must serve as the army's reserve. Perhaps this contributed to
Hill's sulks.)

The order to Pettigrew, according to Lieutenant Lewis Young of his
staff, was "to place the division under the nearest cover to the left of
Pickett's Division, with which it would advance in line." The nearest
cover, at this point, was Seminary Ridge, and Pettigrew's four brigades
dutifully deployed behind the wooded crest of the ridge. This left Pettigrew's line some 200 yards behind that of Pickett and some 400 yards to
the left. The two divisions were further separated by a modest ridgeline
that ran eastward from Spangler's Woods. Thus to advance "in line" with
Pickett would require a certain amount of extra effort on Pettigrew's part
and a certain amount of shifting on Pickett's.

What on Wednesday had been Harry Heth's newly formed division
was on Friday a very different organization. Pettigrew commanded in
place of the wounded Heth, and Colonel James K. Marshall directed
Pettigrew's brigade. Colonel Birkett Fry now led the brigade of James Archer, captured on July 1. Joe Davis, the president's nephew, continued in
command of his brigade, but in John Brockenbrough's brigade there was
a decidedly odd change. Colonel Brockenbrough had been a tepid leader
in the July 1 fighting, and now, without explanation, he split the command of his brigade. He took charge of two regiments, turning the other
two over to Colonel Robert M. Mayo.

Pettigrew's division lined up with Fry's brigade (two Alabama and
three Tennessee regiments) on the right. Then came Marshall's brigade of
North Carolinians, Davis's brigade (one North Carolina and now three
Mississippi regiments, the veteran 11th Mississippi having returned
from guard duty), and on the far left Brockenbrough's Virginians. It was
a division with dubious leadership in two of its brigades (Davis's and
Brockenbrough's) and, overall, a division gravely wounded by its July 1
ordeal. In that battle Pettigrew's brigade had suffered almost 40 percent
casualties, and Archer's brigade lost 33 percent. Officer casualties were
high all through the division, and some regiments were decimated —
the 26th North Carolina, for example, had lost 624 of its 840 men on
Wednesday. Even the division's deployment was questionable, with
Brockenbrough's jointly led and no doubt confused Virginians forming
the left flank of the entire attacking force.[10]

If Powell Hill made no effort either to temper the selection of Pettigrew's division or to manage its deployment, he was even more derelict in regard to the selection of the two brigades from Pender's division. He simply told Pender's second-in-command, James H. Lane, to turn the division's "second line" over to Longstreet. That meant Lane's own comparatively fresh brigade and also the brigade of Alfred Scales, led now after Scales's wounding by Colonel William Lowrance. During Wednesday's fighting Scales's brigade had charged into a hornet's nest of Yankee artillery and been slaughtered. Its casualty rate was 63 percent, and it lost its commander and no fewer than fifty-five field and company officers. "In this depressed, dilapidated, and almost unorganized condition, I took command of the brigade . . . ," Colonel Lowrance reported.

By Jim Lane's account, "General Longstreet ordered me to form in rear of the right of Heth's division, commanded by General Pettigrew." Surely there was some misunderstanding or misdeployment here, on Pettigrew's part or Longstreet's. Lane's two brigades deployed in a considerably shorter line than Pettigrew's four, leaving no supporting troops at all behind Davis's and Brockenbrough's left-flank brigades — the two most suspect brigades on the battle line. Then Isaac Trimble arrived to take over the command from Lane. Apparently General Trimble was too busy acquainting himself with his new command to question its peculiar deployment. Nor, it seems, did anyone else. Generals Lee and Longstreet, for example, inspected the front twice and were not heard to comment. As Porter Alexander later noted, "The arrangement of all the troops *must* have been apparent to Gen Lee when he was going about the lines between 11 & 12, & his not interfering with it stamps it with his approval."[11]

The orders to Dick Anderson's division of the Third Corps were contingent. "I received orders to hold my division in readiness to move up in support, if it should become necessary," Anderson reported. Presumably that decision would be Longstreet's. After Thursday's fighting, Anderson's five brigades had bivouacked back where they began the day, and those positions dictated their July 3 role. The brigades of Wright, Posey, and Mahone to the left would support Pettigrew and Trimble — "if it should become necessary." Wilcox's Alabamians and Lang's Floridians, assigned to Pickett's right, were already well forward that morning in support of Alexander's batteries.

Wilcox and Lang, having attacked this same Yankee line on Thursday, were not optimistic on Friday. What should they do, Lang wondered, if they were ordered forward once the main attack was repulsed, "as we both felt confident it would be." Wilcox, who had lost 577 men in yester-

On July 3 Johnston Pettigrew, left, led the division of the wounded Henry Heth. Isaac Trimble led two brigades of the wounded Dorsey Pender. (Southern Historical Collection–U.S. Army Military History Institute)

day's bungled assault, said he "would not again lead his men into such a deathtrap." Should an order to advance be imperative and not discretionary, he said, he would protest it.[12]

As the infantry filed into place for the attack, attention became focused on the target. General Lee, having already attacked both enemy flanks, reasoned that the enemy's center must now be comparatively less well defended. With Longstreet still threatening their left and Ewell still threatening their right, the Federals would be unlikely to risk massing against the threat of an assault on their center. Apparently to sustain this pressure, Lee had allowed Allegheny Johnson to continue his assault on Culp's Hill that morning. Furthermore, so far as Lee could see, the Federals had not entrenched themselves along the ridge — all that was visible in the way of works was a low stone wall. Yesterday Lee had watched Rans Wright's Georgians aim their charge toward a little copse of scrub oaks — soon to be christened the Copse — atop Cemetery Ridge, and very nearly reach it. What one brigade almost accomplished on Thursday, he reasoned, nine brigades should be able to accomplish on Friday.

Some 500 yards north of the Copse was a second, more prominent feature silhouetted on the ridgeline, a woods known locally as Ziegler's Grove. Pickett and Pettigrew mutually agreed that the attack should guide on the center of the battle line, and Birkett Fry's brigade, on the right of Pettigrew's division, was chosen for the honor. As Fry and Pickett discussed the matter they were joined by Dick Garnett, whose brigade formed Pickett's left, and "it was agreed," wrote Fry, "that he would dress on my command. . . . It was then understood that my command should be considered the centre and that both divisions should align themselves by it." Marching straight ahead, due east, would take Fry's brigade right between Ziegler's Grove and the Copse — which therefore became the obvious and easily visible aiming points for the attack.

There was another, easily visible reason as well — that was where the Yankee guns were. Porter Alexander counted five batteries there, and promptly took them as *his* aiming point. From their vantage on Seminary Ridge the Confederates could see additional Yankee guns on Cemetery Hill and on Little Round Top, but a modest rise of ground between the two ridges occupied by the armies prevented them from seeing the defenses posted on the low section of Cemetery Ridge. This, as it happened, comprised a centerpiece of Henry Hunt's gunnery scheme — Freeman McGilvery's powerful gun line, forty-one pieces from the artillery reserve, positioned so as to take any infantry assault against the Federal center under a deadly enfilade fire. And because they were not seen, McGilvery's guns were not designated a target of the Rebel bombardment.[13]

AS THE ARMIES GATHERED THEMSELVES, the bloody feud over the Bliss farm heated up again. William Bliss's large brick barn stood like a citadel squarely between the lines, and sharpshooters from whichever side held it could harass the infantry and artillery of the other side. The fight for the Bliss barn was a sort of battle in miniature, with opportunity for individual derring-do. At one point Captain James Postles, 1st Delaware, volunteered to deliver a crucial order. On horseback he made a breakneck dash for the barn. The enemy's fire, he recalled, "grew hotter and hotter as I drew near . . . till it was a constant wonder and surprise to me that none of the bullets, which I heard whistling around and so close to me, had hit me. . . ." He delivered his message and somehow managed to return to Cemetery Ridge unscathed. An admiring Samuel Fiske watched Captain Postles's return: "On reaching our lines . . . he reined his horse round, waved his hat in the air and made a graceful bow to the unseen marksmen, who, I really don't believe were sorry to see him escape unharmed."

July 2 had ended with the 12th Mississippi, of Carnot Posey's brigade, holding the Bliss farm. Alexander Hays's division fronted the farm on the Union side, and on the morning of July 3 Hays dispatched the 12th New Jersey to drive the Mississippians out. In a column of companies the Jerseymen stormed the barn, rushing in one end while the outnumbered Mississippians escaped out the other. Mr. Bliss's house and orchard furnished good cover for a counterstroke, however, and soon enough it was the Jerseymen's turn to scramble back to their lines.

Called out next was the 14th Connecticut. Instead of charging in a tight, vulnerable formation, the men of the 14th rushed each man for himself, spreading out the enemy's fire and seizing the barn without great loss. The fight by now had reached the boiling point, drawing in artillery. Porter Alexander was appalled at the waste of hundreds of rounds of precious ammunition by Hill's Third Corps batteries, firing at an essentially worthless target. "I would not let one of my guns fire a shot," he wrote in righteous anger.

Recognizing that there was little prospect of a prompt ending to this scrap, General Hays ordered the Bliss house and barn burned. The volunteer this time was Sergeant Charles A. Hitchcock, 111th New York. Gathering paper and matches, Hitchcock "started on my mission at a double-quick, and kept it up till I reached the buildings. . . ." That, he said modestly, was the only hard part of the mission. After getting everyone out, including the dead and wounded, he fired the house and barn. For his effort, General Hays saw that Sergeant Hitchcock became Lieutenant Hitchcock. The ruins on the Bliss farm would smoke and smolder the rest of the day, as if marking the battlefield for distant travelers.[14]

In Gettysburg that morning the renewal of the fighting at Culp's Hill sent citizens scurrying to their cellars once more. Overshot artillery rounds flew into the town. On July 1 Catherine Foster had narrowly escaped an errant shell that hit her house on South Washington Street. Now, as she and her family were starting down their cellar steps during this new outburst of fighting, two shells in rapid succession plunged into the house and wrecked the kitchen and a bedroom. The three hits on the Foster house would prove to be the town record.

The southern end of town continued to be highly dangerous, especially for those in buildings that lay in the no man's land between the skirmish lines. One such was a house on Baltimore Street on the lower slope of Cemetery Hill occupied by Georgia Wade McClellan, whose husband was away in the Union army. Mrs. McClellan was confined to her bedroom with her newborn son, and her mother and her younger sister, Ginnie Wade, were there caring for her and the baby. Twenty-year-old Ginnie was in the kitchen kneading dough for biscuits that morning when a bullet ripped through two doors and into her back and through her heart and killed her instantly. Ginnie Wade would be the only civilian killed during the battle.[15]

In late morning, after the fighting on Culp's Hill died down, Dick Ewell and his engineer officer, Major Henry Richardson, rode into Gettysburg to reconnoiter. Sharpshooters on Cemetery Hill were keeping the Rebel troops off many of the streets, and Ewell was warned not to go any farther forward. He was reminded that he had already had his horse shot from under him two days earlier. Old Bald Head scoffed. A bystander noted him saying that the Yankee sharpshooters "were fully fifteen hundred yards distant — that they could not possibly shoot with accuracy at that distance & that he would run the risk of being hit." The two had not advanced twenty paces when Major Richardson was shot through the body and seriously wounded. Ewell announced that he too had been shot. When an anxious aide asked where he was hit, Ewell pointed to his wooden leg and said, "I'll trouble you to hand me my other leg." Thus refitted, he bantered with General John Gordon. Suppose it had been Gordon the ball struck, Ewell said; "we would have had the trouble of carrying you off the field, sir. You see how much better fixed for a fight I am than you are. It don't hurt a bit to be shot in a wooden leg!"[16]

Behind Ewell's Second Corps, Jeb Stuart was preparing, finally, to join the battle at Gettysburg. He and Lee had worked out a contingent part for the cavalry to play in Friday's offensive. Should Pickett's assault break into the Cemetery Ridge line, a simultaneous thrust into the Yankee rear by the cavalry ought to create havoc and net many prisoners. That would be at best; at the least Stuart could create a diversion, or perhaps threaten the Yankees' supply line. Therefore on Friday morning Stuart led four brigades out the York Pike east of Gettysburg. Two and a half miles beyond the town, the column turned off on a country road leading southward toward the Hanover Road. Reaching a long, commanding height called Cress Ridge, Stuart gained a sweeping view westward across the fields toward the Gettysburg battleground. At the moment it was empty of Yankee cavalry, but that was soon to change.

Stuart's column had been sighted on the York Pike and a warning sent out to the cavalry command. David Gregg was moved up to a blocking position along the Hanover Road with the brigades of John B. McIntosh and George Armstrong Custer. Stuart ordered his artillery to fire a four-shot salvo. This presumably was the signal to General Lee that the cavalry was in position. It also announced his presence to the Yankees. By all appearances the stage was set for a cavalry battle royal.

At the other extreme of the battleground, south of Round Top, Judson Kilpatrick, in command of the Union cavalry's Third Division, was looking to start a battle royal of his own. Kilpatrick had scrapped inconclusively with Wade Hampton's Rebel troopers the day before at the hamlet of Hunterstown, northeast of Gettysburg, and he was eager for something more decisive. Alfred Pleasonton had been managing the cavalry corps erratically, and when the day began he had only four of his eight brigades in the immediate vicinity of Gettysburg. One of Kilpatrick's two brigades, under Custer, had been sent on loan to David Gregg. With the other, under Elon Farnsworth, Kilpatrick sought some way to attack Longstreet's flank. "Kilpatrick's orders," wrote one of his officers, "were to press the enemy, to threaten him at every point, and to strike at the first opportunity. . . ." To replace Custer, Kilpatrick was promised the brigade of Wesley Merritt, then on the way up from Emmitsburg.

For cavalry to attack the lightly protected rear of an army, as Jeb Stuart was hoping to do that July 3, was one thing, but for cavalry to attack infantry defending a line of its own choosing was something very different — indeed something very reckless. Unfortunately for the men of his command, "reckless" perfectly described Kill-Cavalry Kilpatrick. While he waited for Merritt, Kilpatrick put dismounted troopers to skirmishing with Evander Law's Texans and pondered how he would launch his assault.[17]

Meanwhile, on the Confederate battle line on Seminary Ridge, the last guns were laid and the last infantry moved into position. Pickett's three fresh brigades furnished 5,830 men. Pettigrew's and Trimble's six brigades, after subtracting their losses in Wednesday's fighting, added some 7,200, bringing the total count of infantry in the first wave of attackers to just over 13,000. The brigades of Lang and Wilcox, firmly defined as support for Pickett's right, numbered perhaps 1,600 men. Anderson's remaining three brigades, rather more loosely designated as support for the left "if it should become necessary," might in due course add another 3,350 troops to the attack. Nine brigades would make the charge, and five others might (or might not) support them, according to circumstances. Thus an attack well started and promising success might involve as many as 17,980 men, with elements of Ewell's and Longstreet's forces presumably available to secure and exploit the gains.[18]

It was agreed that two guns fired by the Washington Artillery at the Peach Orchard would signal the bombardment. Porter Alexander was ordered by Longstreet to find the best position from which to view the effects of the gunnery. Then, not long after noon, Alexander was handed a message from Longstreet: "Colonel: If the artillery fire does not have the effect to drive off the enemy or greatly demoralize him, so as to make our effort pretty certain, I would prefer that you should not advise Pickett to make the charge. I shall rely a great deal upon your judgment to determine the matter and shall expect you to let Gen. Pickett know when the moment offers."

Knowing that he had exhausted all his own arguments against the attack, Longstreet with this note was now hoping that the most accomplished artillerist in the army might convince Lee that if the bombardment was failing, the infantry attack would surely fail as well — that, in effect, it would be Malvern Hill all over again.

Alexander was taken aback. General Lee had provided the inspiration for this massive attack, and Lieutenant General Longstreet was in charge of its execution — and now in their place a colonel of artillery was to decide whether the attack should or should not be made, based on "my cold judgment to be founded on what I was going to see." He talked this over with Rans Wright, who advised him to make his position very clear to Longstreet.

That thought was uppermost in Alexander's reply: "General: I will only be able to judge of the effect of our fire on the enemy by his return fire. . . . If, as I infer from your note, there is any alternative to this attack, it should be carefully considered before opening our fire, for it will take all the artillery ammunition we have left to test this one, and if result is unfavorable we will have none left for another effort. And even if this is entirely successful, it can only be so at a very bloody cost."

Longstreet's second note was a restatement of his first one, and still assigned to Alexander the final say: "Colonel: The intention is to advance the infantry if the artillery has the desired effect of driving the enemy's off, or having other effect such as to warrant us in making the attack. When that moment arrives advise Gen. Pickett and of course advance such artillery as you can use in aiding the attack."

"He has put the responsibility back upon you," Rans Wright said. Alexander asked Wright for his opinion of the planned assault. "Well, Alexander," said Wright, "it is mostly a question of supports. It is not as hard to get there as it looks. I was there yesterday with my brigade. The real difficulty is to stay there after you get there — for the whole infernal Yankee army is up there in a bunch!"

Alexander realized that nothing he would be able to see during the bombardment could possibly determine its effectiveness in the definitive way Longstreet required. The smoke of his firing and of the enemy's return fire would soon obscure his view of Cemetery Ridge. The basic question (he later wrote) "whether or not that attack was to be made, must be decided before the cannonade opened." Alexander also pondered the matter of supports that Rans Wright had insisted were necessary. He had seen several of Hill's brigades forming to support Pickett — and had heard a camp rumor that morning "that Gen. Lee had said he intended to march every man he had upon that cemetery hill that day." Alexander took that as encouraging.

Next he rode over to see Pickett: "I did not tell him my object, but just felt his pulse, as it were, about the assault. He was in excellent spirits & sanguine of success." There seemed nothing more to do or say, and Porter Alexander determined to limit his decision-making to just his own field and his own batteries. He sent Longstreet a brief note: "General: When our fire is at its best, I will advise Gen. Pickett to advance."[19]

On Cemetery Ridge, as the firing at Culp's Hill died away late in the morning, what General Carl Schurz described as a "perfect stillness" enveloped the field; "it settled down into a tranquillity like the peaceful and languid repose of a warm midsummer morning in which one might expect to hear the ringing of the village church-bells. . . ." To Schurz "there was something ominous, something uncanny, in these strange, unexpected hours of profound silence so sharply contrasting with the bloody horrors which had preceded, and which were sure to follow them."

Enough of the Confederate guns in their silent ranks could be seen aimed at the 500-yard section of Cemetery Ridge between Ziegler's Grove and the Copse that the Yankees manning the line there suspected that any attack that followed this midday pause would come right down their throats. They were not the sort to flinch. These were Winfield Scott Hancock's Second Corps men — the divisions of Alexander Hays and John Gibbon — and they were as good as the best in the Army of the Potomac.

In line south of Ziegler's Grove were two of Hays's three brigades, under Thomas A. Smyth and Eliakim Sherrill, who was commanding in place of George Willard, killed on July 2. Hays's third brigade, Samuel Carroll's, had gone to the rescue of Otis Howard's Eleventh Corps the evening before, and now the nervous Howard would not return his rescuers. Of Carroll's brigade, only the 8th Ohio, which had earlier been on picket duty, was with Hays on July 3.

Posted from Hays's left to beyond the Copse were Gibbon's three brigades, under Alexander S. Webb, Norman J. Hall, and William Harrow. Webb and Hall had already experienced a sharp taste of combat in repelling Rans Wright's Georgians the evening before. In Harrow's brigade, the 1st Minnesota had been thrown alone into the breach by Hancock on July 2 and suffered grievous casualties. To Gibbon's left was support from the First Corps, especially the large brigade of nine-month Vermonters led by George Stannard. The total number of defenders in this sector between Ziegler's Grove and south of the Copse — Hays's and Gibbon's divisions and their First Corps support — came to fewer than 8,000 men.

General Lee, in his binocular inspection of the Union line, had detected no fortifications except a stone wall below the crest of Cemetery Ridge. This wall was actually a stone boundary fence, low and not very substantial, crossing the farm of a free black named Abraham Bryan. Hancock's men were quick to improve on it, however, rebuilding its more derelict parts and piling fence rails atop it. For a man lying down or kneeling it furnished a fair protection, and it also furnished a handy line for the defenders to align on. The fence ran south from Ziegler's Grove to within 100 yards of the Copse, made a jog west for some 80 yards, and angled back south in front of the Copse for some 280 yards. Before the day was done, that jog would be known as the Angle. The first line of defenders followed this stone fence, and for much of its length there was a second line on ground high enough to fire over the first line. The lines had gaps to provide fields of fire for Captain John Hazard's five batteries that guarded the sector.[20]

John Gibbon's resourceful mess staff had with some effort scrounged the makings of a midday meal of stew whose principal ingredients were potatoes and what General Gibbon remembered as "an old and tough rooster." Gibbon persuaded Meade to join them, arguing that the commanding general must keep up his strength in these trying times. Also present at the feast were Generals Hancock, Newton, and Pleasonton. Afterward the generals lit up cigars and tried to relax in the ominous quiet — the quiet, they guessed, before the storm — "chatting over the battle and the probable events of the day." Presently Meade returned to his headquarters, and the generals and their staffs conversed quietly or dozed in the noontime heat, awaiting General Lee's next move.[21]

"LET THE BATTERIES OPEN," General Longstreet's note read; "order great care and precision in firing." The first signal gun of Merritt B. Miller's Third Company, Washington Artillery of New Orleans, shattered the battlefield stillness. A faulty friction primer momentarily delayed the second gun's firing, but that was soon put to rights and the "batteries open" signal completed. In Gettysburg the meticulous Professor Jacobs noted the time as 1:07 P.M.

From the Peach Orchard to the Chambersburg Pike, Confederate gunners ran to their pieces and unleashed a barrage such as no one on the field had ever before even imagined; or as Professor Jacobs put it, "producing such a continuous succession of crashing sounds as to make us feel as if the very heavens had been rent asunder. . . ." In their letters home Yankee soldiers groped for words to describe it. The effort of Alexander Biddle, 121st Pennsylvania, was typical. Major Biddle wrote his wife the next day, "there is no other expression but terrible to designate the character of their fire. . . ." Sergeant Ben Hirst, 14th Connecticut, told his wife, "Turn your eyes which way you will the whole Heavens were filled with Shot and Shell, Fire and Smoke."[22]

General Gibbon was in the orchard behind the Union center where he had hosted his luncheon gathering, when "the whole air above and around us was filled with bursting and screaming projectiles, and the continuous thunder of the guns. . . ." He called for his horse, but one of the first shells had killed his orderly. Too anxious to get to his command to wait for a mount, Gibbon ran to the crest of the ridge. "At last I reached the brow of the hill, to find myself in the most infernal pandemonium it has ever been my fortune to look upon." The infantry, he saw, had gone to ground, scrambling for any shelter, many crowding behind the stone fence running along the front. The Union batteries — at least those on the Second Corps front — were now beginning to return fire, adding to the indescribable din and shrouding the ridge in choking smoke.

Veteran artillerist that he was, Gibbon cast a professional eye on the enemy's gunnery. Smoothbore solid shot and shells could be plainly seen during their downward arc, he wrote, but the higher-velocity rifled shells "came with a rush and a scream and could only be seen in their rapid flight when they 'upset' and went tumbling through the air, creating the uncomfortable impression that, no matter whether you were in front of the gun from which they came or not, you were liable to be hit." Gibbon noticed, too, that many of the enemy's shells were not detonating over the lines — or not detonating at all — but were soaring over the ridge and landing in the rear areas.[23]

While some Confederate batteries had ranged in on today's targets during yesterday's fighting, most had not, and trying to do so under fire proved uncommonly difficult. The barrage and the return fire quickly blanketed Cemetery Ridge in smoke, which in the hot, still air did not disperse. It therefore became almost impossible for battery captains to gauge the fall of their shot. In any case, an infantry line, fired at head-on, presented a very shallow target. This was also true of a gun line, although a battery's caissons and limbers and their teams at the rear were vulnerable to overshot rounds. But the Confederate artillerists' gravest handicap on July 3 was the inferior quality of their fuzes. Colonel Wainwright of the First Corps entered in his diary that the Rebel barrage "was by no means as effective as it should have been, nine-tenths of their shot passing over our men." While this was surely an exaggeration, it did suggest that on this afternoon even the best-plotted shot was not likely to hit what it was aimed at.

(Henry Hunt, too, was professionally critical of the Confederate shooting, and at the Appomattox surrender he said so in conversation with Armistead Long, of Lee's staff. Long had been a gunnery student of Hunt's in the old army and was bemused by the criticism: "I remembered my lessons at the time, and when the fire became so scattered, wondered what you would think about it!")

In consequence, the entire reverse slope of Cemetery Ridge was inundated by an iron hail of shot and shell. As the Second Corps' historian put it, "The plain behind the ridge was almost immediately swept of all camp followers and the unordered attendants of an army." Teamsters and ambulance drivers scrambled for safety, and by no means did all of them or their vehicles escape. Field hospitals were hastily evacuated. Matthew Marvin of the 1st Minnesota, wounded on July 2, had thought "that if the rebs had a shell for me that it could not kill me any younger & that they cant do it but once," but now he began to wonder.

On the Taneytown Road a marching column of Henry Eustis's brigade of the Sixth Corps, returning from duty at Culp's Hill, was caught in the rain of shells. "Solid shot would strike the large rocks and split them as if exploded by gunpowder," wrote diarist Elisha Hunt Rhodes. "The flying iron and pieces of stone struck men down in every direction." The artillery reserve, posted behind the center, was squarely in the path of this fire, and General Tyler promptly ordered the ordnance trains to find a safer refuge. The reserve batteries went back too, but couriers were ordered to remain at their original posts to deliver orders for ammunition and replacement batteries when those on the gun line signaled for them. Tyler, like Hunt, intended to be prepared when the infantry came, as he was sure it would.[24]

One of the worst-hit sites was the Leister house, General Meade's headquarters. Located some 400 yards behind the center of the main line, the little farmhouse was directly in the path of much of the Confederates' misdirected fire. Shells hit the foundation and the front porch, went through the garret and through the front door, and one narrowly missed the general commanding. "They burst in the yard — burst next to the fence on both sides, garnished as usual with the hitched horses of aides and orderlies," reported *New York Times* correspondent Samuel Wilkeson. "The fastened animals reared and plunged with terror. Then one fell, then another — sixteen lay dead and mangled before the fire ceased."

General and staff soon evacuated to the back yard, where Meade noticed some of the staff sidling up to the dubious shelter of the back wall of the little house. "Gentlemen," he said with a sardonic smile, "are you trying to find a safe place?" He said they reminded him of an incident at the Palo Alto fight, back in '46. A teamster, he related, caught in the midst of a Mexican bombardment, was seen to tilt up his flimsy cart and crouch behind it. Just then General Zachary Taylor, old "Rough and Ready," rode by and shouted, "You damned fool, don't you know you are no safer there than anywhere else?" "I don't suppose I am, general," the man replied, "but it kind o' feels so."

Meade led the staff to a barn farther in the rear, "but which on reaching," he observed dryly, "was found as much exposed as the place I had left." That reality was confirmed when Chief of Staff Butterfield was wounded by a shell fragment.

Meade kept insisting he had to be where his lieutenants could find him, and his staff only persuaded him to move to Slocum's less exposed headquarters on Power's Hill on the promise that Slocum's signal officer would be able to communicate with Meade's signalman left at the Leister house. On reaching Power's Hill, however, Meade discovered that he was not linked with his old headquarters after all; the signalman there evacuated the place soon after he did. Waving off his staff's objections, Meade returned to the Leister house. Before the artillery fire finally tapered off,

The Leister house, General Meade's headquarters, was hit repeatedly in the Confederate artillery bombardment on July 3. (Library of Congress)

he was again on the move, now toward the front lines. Like Henry Hunt, George Meade expected an infantry attack, and he was going personally to meet it.[25]

The ranking generals of the Second Corps felt duty bound to show themselves to the troops, to hearten them amidst this maelstrom. Rough-and-ready Alexander Hays rode up and down the lines as the shells flew over and past him, shouting defiance to the enemy and encouragement to his troops. He told the men to round up all abandoned rifles, clean and load them, and have them at hand to greet the Rebels when they charged. "Some of the men were so energetic as to have four loaded muskets," recalled Hays's aide David Shields; "it was very common for men to have two."

Being without a mount, John Gibbon, with his aide Frank Haskell, toured the full length of his divisional line on foot, bantering with the men. Observing the Rebel guns generally overshooting, Gibbon concluded that he could just as easily boost morale by being seen out *ahead* of the lines, and coincidentally be much safer that way. They went forward some 75 yards to a little clump of trees — the men, Gibbon wrote, "peering at us curiously from behind the stone wall as we passed along" — and sat down in the shade to observe the scene. Theirs proved to be one of the better vantage points on the battlefield just then. According to Haskell, "On either crest we could see the great flaky streams of fire, and they seemed numberless, of the opposing guns, and their white banks of swift convolving smoke; but the sound of the discharges was drowned in the universal ocean of sound."

Winfield Scott Hancock, who on horseback presented a splendid martial image, not surprisingly chose to ride the lines rather than walk them. With an orderly bearing the corps flag behind him, he rode the length of the Second Corps front, to the cheers of his men. A staff man told him that an officer of his rank should not risk his life in such a manner, to which Hancock replied, "There are times when a corps commander's life does not count."[26]

When he saw the Federal batteries initially not engaging — they were obeying Henry Hunt's directive to hold their fire for fifteen minutes or so — Hancock's hair-trigger temper erupted. General John Geary once observed, "Hancock always swore at everybody, above all on the battlefield." That was certainly the case when he braced his chief of artillery, John Hazard, about the silent Second Corps guns, and was told of Hunt's orders to save the long-range ammunition to use against the enemy's infantry when it stepped out on the charge. Hancock's concern was his own infantry. As one of his disciples put it, "Every soldier knows how trying and often how demoralizing it is to endure artillery fire without reply." Captain Hazard was told in no uncertain terms who was in charge here, and that he must open his guns without a moment's delay. Poor Hazard had no choice. After all, his batteries were brigaded with the Second Corps, and he could hardly refuse a direct order from the Second Corps' commanding general.

Hunt had not informed Hancock of his plan to delay the return fire, or the reasoning behind it — perhaps there was no time, perhaps he thought its wisdom was self-evident — and that further raised Hancock's hackles. The next battery he came to was Patrick Hart's 15th New York Independent, of the artillery reserve. Why was he not firing, Hancock wanted to know, in language that Captain Hart described as "profane and Blasphemous such as a drunken Ruffian would use." Hart said he was under the chief of artillery's orders; Hancock said this battle line was under *his* orders. Hart's response was "that should he give me a written order that I would open fire under protest."

Just then Freeman McGilvery, commanding the large bloc of artillery reserve batteries in the battle line, rode up and confronted the seething major general. "Why in hell do you not fire with these batteries?" Hancock demanded. Because he was under special instructions from General Hunt not yet to do so, "and the time was not come," said Colonel McGilvery; this tough former Maine sea captain was not one to be intimidated. Hancock said Hunt had not anticipated the circumstances of the enemy's bombardment. On the contrary, said McGilvery, General Hunt's orders "were given to meet this very case." With that Hancock huffed away and went back to encourage his command.

McGilvery's stubborn stance importantly saved the ammunition of his forty-one guns to contest the Rebel charge when it came, but there was more to it even than that. McGilvery's batteries in their concealed position had thus far been neither seen nor targeted by the Confederate gunners; indeed, only one of his batteries would be hit all afternoon. By fighting off Hancock's demands, McGilvery did not reveal his position and so preserved a major weapon of surprise for use against Pickett's Charge.[27]

In contrast to the comparative peace and quiet on McGilvery's line, John Hazard's batteries on the Second Corps line were hit repeatedly. Ziegler's Grove and the Copse being the enemy's aiming points, the space between and around them was savaged. Here again the Rebel gunners were generally aiming too high, or perhaps it was their faulty ammunition, yet enough shells still struck their targets to create havoc among the Yankee gun crews. In Captain James Rorty's Battery B, 1st New York Light, two of its four guns were knocked out, and so many crewmen were down that some two dozen infantrymen from the 19th Massachusetts were detailed to carry ammunition and help man the guns. The explosion of a limber chest mortally wounded Captain Rorty; then his successor, Lieutenant Albert Sheldon, went down with a bad wound.

In Battery B, 1st Rhode Island, commanded today by Lieutenant Walter S. Perrin, the No. 4 Napoleon took three hits. One of them struck the gun's muzzle just as it was being loaded, killing two gunners and deforming the barrel so that it could not be fired. In due course, for want of men and ammunition, Perrin's battery was limbered up and withdrawn. The same was true, for the same reasons, for Captain William Arnold's Bat-

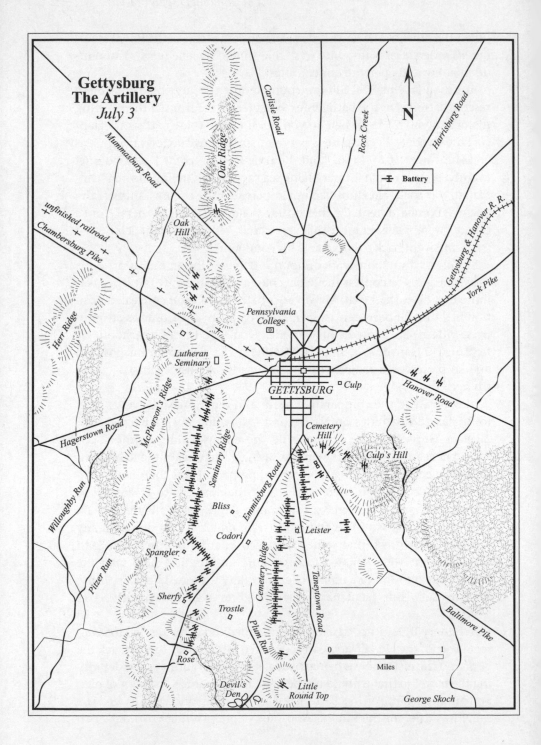

**Gettysburg
The Artillery**
July 3

N

Battery

Carlisle Road

Rock Creek

Harrisburg Road

Mummasburg Road

Oak Ridge

Gettysburg & Hanover R. R.

unfinished railroad

Chambersburg Pike

Oak
Hill

York Pike

Pennsylvania
College

Herr Ridge

Lutheran
Seminary

McPherson's Ridge

GETTYSBURG

Culp

Hanover Road

Hagerstown Road

Seminary Ridge

Cemetery
Hill

Culp's Hill

Willoughby Run

Bliss

Emmitsburg Road

Codori

Leister

Pitzer Run

Spangler

Cemetery Ridge

Sherfy

Taneytown Road

Baltimore Pike

Trostle

Plum Run

0   1

Rose

Miles

Devil's
Den

Little
Round Top

George Skoch

tery A, 1st Rhode Island. In Lieutenant George Woodruff's Battery I, 1st U.S., a shell ignited a caisson with a tremendous crash. To keep his guns firing, Woodruff had to call on the 108th New York for volunteers to replace his crew casualties. In his diary a surgeon recorded the scene on the ridgeline: "The horses rolled in heaps everywhere tangled in their harness with their dying struggles — wheels knocked off, guns capsized and artillerists going to the rear or lying on the ground bleeding in every direction."

Probably the most often hit of the Second Corps batteries was Lieutenant Alonzo Cushing's Battery A, 4th U.S. Young Cushing, graduated early from West Point in 1861 to meet the need for educated soldiers, kept his guns firing steadily despite grievous losses among the crews. "He was as cool and calm as I ever saw him," recalled one of his men, "talking to the boys between shots with the glass constantly to his eyes, watching the effect of our shots." But so many gunners were down that Cushing too had to call on infantrymen to help man the guns. John Gibbon saw three of Cushing's limber chests blow up at once, sending up a huge column of smoke and fire and triggering "triumphant yells of the enemy. . . ." Finally only two of Cushing's 3-inch Ordnance rifles were still serviceable. A shell fragment eviscerated one of the infantry volunteers, who pleaded for someone to put him out of his agony. When no one had nerve enough, he pulled out his pistol and ended the agony himself. Presently Cushing was painfully wounded in shoulder and groin but stayed at his post. His sergeant urged him to go to the rear. "No," Cushing said, "I stay right here and fight it out or die in the attempt."[28]

For a time, Dick Ewell's guns created concern on Cemetery Hill by delivering the enfilade fire that Porter Alexander predicted could be so effective. "From the first they had our range and elevation exactly, and the havoc among my guns, men, horses and ammunition chests was fearful," wrote Thomas Osborn, the Eleventh Corps' chief of artillery. Some of this havoc came from a pair of 20-pounder Parrott rifles near Benner's Hill, all the way around on the Confederate left. But Osborn's gunners also had the range and elevation, after yesterday's fight, and they put more guns into the effort than did the Confederates, and in short order this fire was beaten down. The two long-range English Whitworth rifles on Oak Hill remained an annoyance, however. A Yankee officer wrote of the "fiendish wailings" of the Whitworth's peculiar hexagonal projectiles, "sounding like the predatory howls of demons in search of their prey."[29]

Through all this the Federal infantry waited out the shelling with remarkable patience. "The men of the Infantry," wrote Frank Haskell, "have seized their arms, and behind their works, behind every rock, in every ditch, wherever there is any shelter, they hug the ground, silent, quiet, unterrified, little harmed." It was soon evident that with the enemy gunners overshooting, the safest place on the field was actually in the front lines, and anyone tempted to skedaddle realized the danger in trying it. Unfortunately the wounded faced danger too if they risked going to the rear for aid, and so most stayed and suffered, and some thereby bled to death.

One of the few who kept count of casualties from the bombardment was Alexander Webb. "This was awful, I lost fifty of my men lying down," General Webb wrote his wife, "and more excellent officers. . . ." Webb's brigade, at the Angle, was squarely in the middle of the target area and surely suffered the greatest loss among the six brigades defending the Federal center. It is probable that all told no more than 150 to 200 infantrymen were casualties of the shelling. The day's first officer of rank to fall was Thomas Smyth, commander of one of Alexander Hays's brigades, wounded in the face by a shell burst.

There was a randomness about these incidents that left men shaking their heads. A high, wild round through Ziegler's Grove clipped off a tree limb that fell and injured several men. A solid shot striking near an 80th New York soldier sent his cap high in the air and flipped him over, and he was found to be dead, without a mark on him, a victim of concussion. Frank Haskell noticed a soldier, sent to the rear for water, returning through the hail of fire with his canteens when a shell fragment neatly sliced the knapsack right off his back. "The soldier stopped, and turned about in puzzled surprise — put up one hand to his back to assure himself that the knapsack was not there, and then walked slowly on again unharmed. . . ."[30]

The return fire that Winfield Hancock had ordered was meanwhile taking a toll in the Confederate ranks on Seminary Ridge. Like his Union counterparts, General Longstreet felt obliged by this counterfire to show himself to his men to reassure them. "Longstreet rode slowly and alone immediately in front of our entire line . . . ," General James Kemper recalled. "His bearing was to me the grandest moral spectacle of the war. I expected him to fall every instant. Still he moved on, slowly and majestically, with an inspiring confidence, composure, self-possession and repressed power. . . ." Kemper joined him and Longstreet asked how his command was holding up. Kemper replied, "a man is cut to pieces here every second while we are talking." Longstreet said he was "greatly distressed at this; but let us hold our ground a while longer; we are hurting the enemy badly; and will charge him presently."

Kemper's brigade formed the right front of Pickett's line, behind Porter Alexander's guns, and Colonel Joseph Mayo, 3rd Virginia, found it an ugly place to be. In just the first minutes of the bombardment, Colonel Mayo counted 13 men killed or wounded among Kemper's regiments. Like the Confederates, the Yankee gunners were hampered by the smoke clouds in gauging their ranges, and tended to fire long — and long meant striking among the Rebel infantry. Because of the artillerists' restrictions on firing over their own men, due to faulty ammunition, most Southern infantry on July 3 was posted behind the guns. This was in contrast to the Yankees' postings on Cemetery Ridge. Consequences were therefore reversed. Among the Yankees, the artillery suffered more than the infantry; it was just the opposite on the Confederate side.

There were also casualties in the other front-rank brigade on Pickett's line, Dick Garnett's. A man in the 18th Virginia remembered that "shrill shot overhead or bounding madly across the field would alike dip through a line of prostrate men and rush on with a wail to the rear leaving a wide track of blood behind." Lewis Armistead's brigade, in Pickett's second line, was largely spared such losses. Armistead and Garnett, like Kemper, made a point of showing themselves to the troops for morale's sake. To several nervous men glancing about for a haven from the shelling, Armistead counseled, "Lie still boys, there is no safe place here." Confederate infantry losses during the bombardment very likely exceeded those of the Federals, but the Rebels' artillery losses were comparatively light.[31]

It had been Porter Alexander's first thought that a bombardment of 15 to 30 minutes would sufficiently prepare the way for the charge. The enemy's response was slow at first but then increased dramatically, and he was persuaded that it would be "madness" to send a storming force against a line "blazing like a volcano." Yet if he continued the bombardment long enough to beat down the Federal guns, he risked running out of ammunition. He decided he must make this clear, and 25 minutes after the guns opened he sent a note back to Pickett, with a copy to Pettigrew: "General: If you are to advance at all, you must come at once or we will not be able to support you as we ought. But the enemy's fire has not slackened materially and there are still 18 guns firing from the cemetery." (Alexander would later explain that at the time he misunderstood the location of the town's cemetery: "The 18 guns . . . occupied the point at which our charge was to be directed. I had been incorrectly told it was the cemetery.")

Just after sending off this note, Alexander began to "notice signs of some of the enemy's guns ceasing to fire." Batteries could be seen to limber up and retire. He waited to see if they would be replaced, "but there was not a single fresh gun replacing any that had withdrawn." He long remembered the moment: "I felt encouraged to believe that they had felt very severe punishment, & that my fire had been generally well aimed & as effective as could be hoped." Fifteen minutes after his previous note, he dispatched a second note to Pickett: "For God's sake come quick. The 18 guns are gone. Come quick or my ammunition will not let me support you properly."[32]

In fact there was method behind this slackening of the Federals' fire. Henry Hunt had been riding his artillery line, checking on its condition, and he ended his tour in Evergreen Cemetery on Cemetery Hill. There he met with the Eleventh Corps' artillery chief, Thomas Osborn, and Generals Howard and Schurz. It was now plain to all that Lee intended an infantry assault on the center, and Major Osborn thought that should be encouraged. So did the general commanding. General Meade had just visited Cemetery Hill, said Osborn, and "expressed the hope that the enemy would attack, and he had no fear of the result." Osborn suggested that the artillery cease fire all along the line, to lure Lee into thinking his bombardment was successful and thus be persuaded to send in his infantry.

Hunt was all for the plan — its other objective would be to save ammunition to meet the infantry attack, which had been his goal from the beginning — but he asked General Howard if his troops would hold their ground if the guns were not returning fire. Howard knew this was a veiled reference to the Eleventh Corps' shaky reputation, and he drew himself up: "I support Major Osborn's idea of stopping the artillery fire, and my men will stay!"

Hunt took the responsibility for the decision, and hastened to notify Meade. He was gratified to learn that Meade had been looking for him with the same proposal, "so I had only anticipated his wishes." (Meade had had a message from Gouverneur Warren, on Little Round Top, saying the guns were accomplishing little more than "filling the valley with smoke" and advising a pause.) Hunt passed the word to the battery commanders to cease firing. He then sent for four fresh batteries from the artillery reserve to reinforce the center of the line the moment the Rebel cannonade ended.

General Meade was meanwhile ordering up infantry reinforcements. John Robinson's First Corps division on Cemetery Hill was to shift over to support Alexander Hays's right. The Sixth Corps, still serving as a floating reserve for the whole army, was called on for two brigades to support Hancock's line. Elements of the Third Corps were shifted to their right. Henry Slocum was alerted to have the Twelfth Corps in position behind the battle front. With his customary forethought, George Meade thus had some 13,000 troops — as it happened, just about the same number as stepped off in Pickett's Charge — positioned and ready for any contingency.[33]

After he received Porter Alexander's first note, Pickett hurried to Longstreet for orders. He found Old Pete sitting on a snake-rail fence by Spangler's Woods near the center of the line, watching the gunnery. Longstreet read Alexander's note without comment. Pickett asked, "General, shall I advance?" Longstreet turned his face away and did not answer. He afterward admitted to Alexander that "he knew the charge must be made, but he could not bring himself to give the order." After a few awkward moments, Pickett said, "I am going to move forward, Sir," and he rode back to prepare his division. In due course, wrote Alexander, his "come quick" note reached Pickett, which "of course brought him some comfort & encouragement."

Longstreet now went to Alexander's advanced position for the latest observations and reports. He was surprised to learn from Alexander of the artillery's depleted ammunition status. Like the Federals, the Confederate fire had slackened, but in the latter's case it was unintentional. Up and down the line, ammunition chests were empty or nearly so, and crewmen sent back to the ordnance train had returned empty-handed and angry. The witless Pendleton had moved the trains back for safety but neglected to leave anyone at their former location to give directions for finding them. Alexander also explained that the nine-gun "bonus" he had been awarded by the Third Corps, and intended to send forward to support the attack, had also disappeared. General Pendleton, it turned out, had expropriated four of the guns, and the others had been pulled back to safer (and hidden) ground by their commander.

All this was enough to rouse Longstreet to one last effort to stifle the attack. As Alexander remembered it, "Gen. L. spoke at once, & decidedly, 'Go & halt Pickett right where he is, & replenish your ammunition.'"

"General, we can't do that . . . ," Alexander told him. "Even if we had it, it would take an hour or two, and meanwhile the enemy would recover from the pressure he is now under. Our only chance is to follow it up now — to strike while the iron is hot."

Longstreet stood silent for a time, focusing his glasses on the enemy line. As he scanned the scene he said quietly, pausing between phrases, as if he were talking to himself, "I don't want to make this attack . . . I believe it will fail . . . I do not see how it can succeed . . . I would not make it even now, but that General Lee has ordered and expects it."

Alexander was stunned. It appeared that with any encouragement from him, Longstreet might even now stop the attack. But the responsibility "in so grave a matter" was too great for a mere colonel of artillery. Alexander held his tongue, and as the silence between them stretched on he became almost embarrassed. Finally Pickett's legions came striding past, and the moment was gone.[34]

13   *The Grand Charge*

THE THUNDER AND CRASH of the cannonade died away, and seemingly on cue, as if the god of battles were stage-managing the scene, a light breeze sprang up and gradually carried away the clouds of smoke obscuring the battlefield. It was like a curtain rising, and the sheer magnitude of the sight revealed took breaths away. Involuntarily, all along the Yankee line, came the cry, "Here they come!" "Here comes the infantry!"

Lieutenant Frank Haskell, of General Gibbon's staff, was in the audience at front and center of the Union line. "None on that crest now need be told that *the enemy is advancing,*" he wrote. "Every eye could see his legions, an overwhelming, resistless tide of an ocean of armed men, sweeping upon us! . . . Right on they move, as with one soul, in perfect order, without impediment of ditch, or wall, or stream, over ridge and slope, through orchard, and meadow, and cornfield, magnificent, grim, irresistible." Haskell looked around him and took note that "All was orderly and still upon our crest — no noise, and no confusion." These Second Corps men of Hancock's were veterans, "survivors of a dozen battles," as Haskell put it, and they "knew well enough what this array in front portended. . . ."

For some among the Federal infantry, the impending charge was almost welcome. It finally meant relief from the deadly shelling, finally meant a chance to shoot back at their tormentors. For others, the charge was welcome for a different reason. The 20th Massachusetts, for example, in Norman Hall's brigade, had taken 163 casualties at Fredericksburg in December, most of them in a fruitless charge against the deadly stone wall at Marye's Heights. Now the positions were reversed, as the 20th's Captain Henry Abbott was quick to recognize. It was a "magnificent sight," Abbott wrote, yet . . . "The moment I saw them I knew we should give them Fredericksburg. So did every body."

However determined these Yankees might be, the mere sight of that great throng of attackers was intimidating. A man in the 125th New

York, posted on the Union right, confessed in his diary of his fear that "our line would give way as I noticed the uneasiness of some of the men." Tully McCrae, an artilleryman in Woodruff's battery, also on the right, remembered watching that approaching mass of men, "and knowing that we had but one thin line of infantry to oppose them, I thought that our chances for Kingdom Come, or Libby Prison were very good."[1]

Alexander Hays, whose division formed the right half of the Union center on Cemetery Ridge, continued to ride his lines exhorting his men. Pennsylvanian Hays thoroughly enjoyed a good fight, and for what was coming he was primed and in his element. His message was: Hold your fire until the Rebels reach the Emmitsburg Road — which, slanting across the valley between the two ridges, lay some 200 yards from the center of his line — and then aim low. "Now boys, look out; you will see some fun!" he promised. Hays made a particular point of urging the 12th New Jersey to hold fire until the range closed. The 12th's .69-caliber smoothbores firing buck-and-ball would be deadly in a short-range encounter.

Hays did not hold back any troops as a reserve. Instead he pushed his two brigades right up to the stone fence in their front, packing them together tightly until in places they were four ranks deep. Thomas Smyth's brigade comprised the 14th Connecticut, 1st Delaware, 12th New Jersey, and 108th New York. Eliakim Sherrill, replacing the slain George Willard, commanded the 39th, 111th, 125th, and 126th New York. But in intermingling the regiments along the front, Hays was directing what was in effect a single grand brigade. His idea was to mass fire to break the enemy's charge before it could reach him — before a reserve was needed. His front-line firepower, additionally strengthened by the numerous spare rifles he had the men collecting, was described by a 1st Delaware officer as "an embryo arsenal." Of his third brigade, Samuel Carroll's, expropriated by Otis Howard to reinforce the unsteady Eleventh Corps on Cemetery Hill, Hays retained only the 8th Ohio. He posted the Ohioans out front and to the right as a flank guard. The two brigades, plus the 8th Ohio, came to 2,580 men.[2]

John Gibbon's division was formed on Hays's left, holding the line from the Angle of the wall southward past the Copse for some 500 yards. All three of Gibbon's brigades had been engaged on Thursday defending the Union center and suffered accordingly, with the 1st Minnesota's 68 percent loss the most severe. Gibbon would thus face Pickett's Charge with perhaps 2,700 men.

The division of John Gibbon, left, met Pickett's Charge. The brigade of Alexander Webb was at the point of attack. (Library of Congress)

Defending the Angle — which would prove to be a central focus of the afternoon's struggle — was Alexander S. Webb's brigade, 69th, 71st, 72nd, and 106th Pennsylvania. This was the Philadelphia Brigade, a veteran outfit but led too long under a loose rein to be judged by Gibbon as entirely reliable. The evening before, for example, Colonel Richard Smith of the 71st had backed away from the fight when sent over to help out at Culp's Hill. July 3 marked only Webb's sixth day of command. Previously he had served the Potomac army in staff positions. "Webb has taken hold of his Brig. with a will," wrote a pleased General Gibbon, and "comes down on them with a heavy hand and will no doubt soon make a great improvement."

It promised to be a testing day for both Webb and his new command. The 106th Pennsylvania, except for two companies on the skirmish line, had earlier been commandeered by General Howard to brace the Eleventh Corps. (Surprisingly, Winfield Hancock seems to have made no effort to demand that Howard return these troops, as well as Carroll's, in time for the Day Three showdown.) This left Webb with barely 940 men. In contrast to Hays's front, Webb mounted a defense in depth. He had

411

The division under Alexander Hays defended the Union right
on July 3. (U.S. Army Military History Institute)

posted the 69th at the stone fence, leaving a gap right and left for the fire
of Cushing's and Brown's (now Perrin's) batteries. His other regiments
formed a second line to the rear.

To Webb's left was Colonel Norman Hall's brigade, forming the center of Gibbon's position. A twenty-six-year-old West Pointer, Hall had
headed the brigade since Antietam, quietly and efficiently and without
fuss, and his troops reflected his calm competence. In the front line Hall
put the 59th New York, 7th Michigan, and 20th Massachusetts. In a sec-

ond line, in support, were the 42nd New York and 19th Massachusetts. Hall's men had thrown up an entrenchment of sorts, one of the few man-made obstacles on the ridge. "The thin line of our division . . . ," Captain Abbott explained, "was very well shielded by a little rut they lay in & in front of our brigade by a little pit, just one foot deep & one foot high, thrown up hastily by one shovel. . . ." They had scraped out this shallow trench where the stone boundary fence ended, then piled up a parapet of dirt and fence rails in front of it. It was decidedly unimposing, but the men gratefully sheltered behind it during the bombardment and would find it handy in the fight to come.

The third of Gibbon's brigades, William Harrow's, formed the left of the divisional line. Harrow, like Webb, was commanding a brigade for the first time. Before the war he had been a lawyer in Illinois, where he rode the circuit with Abraham Lincoln, and he entered the war as a captain in the 14th Indiana. By the time of Gettysburg, however, due to ill health he had gained only limited combat experience. In the fighting on Thursday, Harrow tried to impress himself on his command by haranguing them. "He called upon all of us by all that was Good & Infernal to kill every son-of-a-bitch that runs without a cause," a man in the 15th Massachusetts wrote approvingly. Of Harrow's regiments, the 1st Minnesota, 82nd New York, and 15th Massachusetts had served together since the Peninsula; the 19th Maine joined in time for Fredericksburg. Thus these men had considerably more fighting time than their general, but after Thursday's casualties all except the 19th Maine were led by new commanders.[3]

Harrow positioned all four of his regiments in the front line. In support were two regiments from John Newton's First Corps that had come over to plug a hole in the Second Corps line late on July 2. The 80th New York and the nine-month 151st Pennsylvania, severely handled in the first day's fighting on Seminary Ridge, were about to be thrown again into the breach, this time on Cemetery Ridge. This demi-brigade was commanded by the 80th New York's Colonel Theodore B. Gates.

On Thursday Hancock's third division, John Caldwell's, had been ordered to the left to bail out the Third Corps, and there it remained. Guarding the Second Corps' left flank today was the Vermont brigade of George J. Stannard, the First Corps' reinforcement belatedly sent up from the Department of Washington. These nine-month Vermonters had served eight months or so of their enlistment peacefully enough in the Washington defenses, and General Stannard, for one, was doubtful about their motivation. On the march north from the capital he noted in his diary, "They count their time by days. Consequently they do not have any heart in the work. Officers as little as men." Two of Stannard's five regiments had been assigned to guard trains; that left the 13th, 14th, and 16th Vermont to demonstrate, on this July 3, whether or not their hearts were in the work. (The 13th, at least, had shown plenty of heart when thrown into the fight by Hancock on July 2.) However that might be, the First Corps troops of Stannard and Gates added some 2,700 much-needed men to the defenses of the Union center.[4]

If the Second Corps infantry had for the most part been spared by the enemy's bombardment, the case was very different for the corps artillery. John Hazard's five batteries began the day with a total of twenty-seven cannon, but in this sector at least, the Confederate gunners could claim a considerable success — the batteries of Walter Perrin and William Arnold badly knocked about and withdrawn, and two others, Alonzo Cushing's and James Rorty's, reduced to two serviceable guns each. George Woodruff's six-gun battery continued in action, but only with the aid of infantry volunteers. The two sections sent to Hazard as reinforcement from the artillery reserve now had but three pieces firing. Of thirty-one guns originally defending the Union center, then, the count was down to thirteen. But as the charge began and in response to General Webb's plea — the general was seen waving his hat and gesturing frantically — the Sixth Corps' Andrew Cowan rushed his 1st New York Independent Battery's six rifled pieces into Perrin's empty place in the line at just the right moment, raising the defenders' count to nineteen.

Henry Hunt had ordered up other replacements from the reserve, but with the reserve batteries driven to cover by the Rebel bombardment, their arrival was going to take time. Furthermore, due to Winfield Hancock's insistence that the corps artillery respond to the bombardment, its long-range ammunition stocks were depleted. At the very center of the Union line the guns now sat silent, and would remain silent until the Confederate infantry advanced to within canister range. As Captain Hazard phrased it, "half the valley had been passed over by them before the guns dared expend a round of the precious ammunition remaining on hand."[5]

ON JULY 1, from atop Oak Hill west of Gettysburg, an Alabama soldier had looked out over the fighting between A. P. Hill's corps and the Yankee legions and pronounced it "like some grand panorama with the sounds of conflict added." From atop Cemetery Hill the panorama presented on July 3 was equally grand. What Lieutenant Haskell described as an "ocean of armed men" was perhaps a mile and a half across. Nothing like it had been seen before in this war; indeed nothing like it had been seen since the wars of Napoleon. General Lee himself would term it a "grand charge." Rank after rank of fighting men in gray or butternut, under their red-slashed battle flags and the blue banners of Virginia, emerged from cover along the Seminary Ridge front. The Song of Solomon had a phrase for it: "terrible as an army with banners."[6]

When George Pickett left Longstreet and rode back to his command to give the order for the advance, he reined up first beside Dick Garnett and offered a bit of last-minute counsel. His advice was to "make the best kind of time in crossing the valley; it's a hell of an ugly looking place over yonder." For the rank and file Pickett assumed a more inspirational stance. "Up, men, and to your posts!" he shouted. "Don't forget today that you are from Old Virginia!" That produced cheers and the Rebel yell, and on cue Garnett took his place before his brigade, waved his hat, and shouted for the men to follow.

Rather surprisingly, James Kemper, former speaker in the Virginia legislature, did not take this opportunity to address his brigade beyond the usual forward-march orders. Perhaps he believed Pickett's injunction was inspiriting enough. On the other hand, the usually gruff, no-nonsense Lewis Armistead, whose brigade was the second line of the division and therefore beyond the reach of Pickett's voice, was moved by the moment to make a gesture. Drawing his sword, he called out, "Men, remember what you are fighting for! Your homes, your firesides, and your sweethearts! Follow me!" A man in the 9th Virginia remembered how the troops "caught his fire and determination. . . . It was his example, his coolness, his courage that led that brigade over that field of blood."[7]

Pickett's division, lying concealed in the swale in front of Spangler's Woods and well forward of both Pettigrew and Trimble, was first to advance in the grand charge. Exactly what time Pickett stepped off would become a matter of some debate. By taking Pennsylvania College's Professor Jacobs as the benchmark — Jacobs carefully noted the Confederate bombardment opening at 1:07 P.M., a fairly close confirmation of the 1 o'clock starting time Porter Alexander recorded for it — and then considering the times marked on Alexander's notes to Pickett, it appears that Pickett's Charge commenced about 2:30. Pettigrew started soon thereafter, and Trimble followed Pettigrew.[8]

Kemper's brigade formed the extreme right of the charge, and his five regiments — from right to left, 24th, 11th, 1st, 7th, and 3rd Virginia — deployed in a single line, two ranks deep. General Kemper ignored the order for line officers to advance on foot. Perhaps he was influenced by looking to his left and seeing Dick Garnett mounted at the head of his brigade.

Garnett's explanation was that a horse had kicked him and he could not walk. He apparently also hoped that this highly visible gesture of leading his men into battle on horseback — and dressed resplendently in a fine new uniform — would finally erase the stain of the charges Stonewall Jackson had preferred against him back in 1862 during Garnett's command of the Stonewall Brigade. Like Kemper, Garnett had his five regiments — from the right, 8th, 18th, 19th, 28th, and 56th Virginia — deployed in a single line, two ranks deep. That was also the formation employed in Armistead's brigade, marching some 80 yards to the rear. Armistead's regiments, right to left, were the 14th, 9th, 53rd, 57th, and 38th Virginia. Lew Armistead would lead his brigade on foot, as ordered. General Pickett and staff, all mounted, took their position at the center of the division between the two lines. Out ahead was the divisional skirmish line.

In Pickett's division there were some sunstroke victims and a few shirkers who hung back from the advance, but generally morale was reported good and confidence high. Sergeant David E. Johnston of the 7th Virginia looked back on the moment and thought that if anything the mood tended toward overconfidence. This was evident, he wrote, from General Lee down to the "shakiest private in the ranks." As Sergeant Johnston reckoned it, "Too much over-confidence was the bane of our battle."[9]

Right from the start, the left wing of the grand assault, under Pettigrew and Trimble, did not act in perfect concert with Pickett's wing. This was almost inevitable due to their initial positioning. By taking its concealment back in the woods on Seminary Ridge, Pettigrew's battle line started some 200 yards behind Pickett's and 400 yards to the north of it. Pettigrew deployed his division in a different fashion than did Pickett. All four of Pettigrew's brigades formed as a single front, but with each regiment in a so-called double line of battle — that is, five companies (in two ranks) in front and five companies (in two ranks) behind. In this more compact deployment, colonels could keep better control of their men in the din of battle, and could reinforce the front line with their own second line rather than having to depend on some other commander for support. This also left Pettigrew's four-brigade front roughly equal in length to Pickett's two-brigade front. Trimble's two brigades, formed up some 150 yards to the rear of Pettigrew, would be the last to advance.[10]

Although severely wounded in his first battle, at Seven Pines on the Peninsula, Johnston Pettigrew had lived up to his high promise in his second, on July 1. Heth's wounding that day moved Pettigrew, as senior brigade commander, into the divisional command. He confronted a challenge this Friday considerably greater than Pickett's. Pettigrew's brigade leaders were new (Fry and Marshall) or of doubtful ability (Davis and Brockenbrough), all his troops had been roughly hammered in Wednesday's fighting, and he was a stranger to most of them and they to him.

Although Pickett's wing set out in advance of the rest of the charge, it would be guiding on Birkett Fry's right-hand brigade of Pettigrew's division. These centrally posted Tennesseans and Alabamians — from right to left, 1st Tennessee, 13th Alabama, 14th and 7th Tennessee, and 5th Alabama Battalion — had been mauled by the Iron Brigade on July 1, losing about a third of their numbers and suffering General Archer captured. Still, Colonel Fry seemed to have the men well in hand and there was no hesitation. "After lying inactive under that deadly storm of hissing and exploding shells," Fry recalled, "it seemed a relief to go forward to the desperate assault."

Next to Fry in line came Pettigrew's old brigade, today under Colonel James Marshall. These North Carolinians (from the right, 47th, 26th, 52nd, and 11th regiments), transferred north from D. H. Hill's department in May, had undergone their first real test of battle on Wednesday. They passed the test, certainly, but at the staggering cost of more than a thousand casualties. Afterward General Pettigrew and his officers had labored to recruit and restore morale: "The cooks were given muskets, etc.; in fact everything was done to get as many fighting men in ranks as possible." When on Friday the advance was signaled, Pettigrew rode up to Colonel Marshall and said, "Now, Colonel, for the honor of the good old North State, Forward!" Of Fry's and Marshall's brigades a man wrote, "We all moved off in as magnificent a style as I ever saw, the lines perfectly formed."[11]

Such a glowing description could hardly be applied to the rest of Pettigrew's division that afternoon. Joe Davis's brigade, next in line, failed to see Marshall advance and so made a belated start. Apparently its command was still rattled from the battering the brigade had suffered on July 1. Finally the four regiments — 55th North Carolina and 2nd, 42nd, and

11th Mississippi — burst out of the woods at the double-quick in an effort to catch up with the rest of the line. The inexperienced Davis and his staff now seemed unable to control the ardor of their men, for in the attempt at alignment the line started and stopped and bunched up and was thereby a better target for the Yankee guns.

Of John Brockenbrough's brigade, forming the far left of the advance, nothing was to be seen initially either. Pettigrew had sent his aide Louis Young hurrying over to prod Joe Davis, but the general seemed indifferent to Brockenbrough's nonappearance. As Young recalled it, Pettigrew said Brockenbrough's brigade "might follow, and if it failed to do so it would not matter." It was a small brigade — after Wednesday's fight, perhaps 500 muskets — with poor morale and worse leadership, "and was not to be relied upon; it was virtually of no value in a fight." That had clearly been the case on July 1, when Brockenbrough's Virginians simply stopped in their tracks at the first enemy fire . . . and it was to be the case again on July 3.

The brigade's divided command imposed by Brockenbrough — he led the 40th Virginia and 22nd Virginia Battalion, while Colonel Robert M. Mayo took charge of the 47th and 55th Virginia — did not help matters at this point, especially when Colonel Mayo could not be found to give the order to advance. In due course these Virginians would lurch forward independently of everyone else. "We were a long ways behind, and had to run to catch up with the rest of the Brigade," explained Colonel William S. Christian of the 55th Virginia. And as it happened, Brockenbrough's brigade would suffer its fate independently of everyone else.[12]

Isaac Trimble, the new-that-morning commander of Lowrance's and Lane's brigades from Pender's division, would complain afterward that the entire left wing of the assault (his two brigades and Pettigrew's four) should have set out fifteen minutes ahead of Pickett, to close the gap between the two wings in a timely fashion. Yet neither Trimble nor anyone else seems to have brought up that idea during the morning's planning. Longstreet passed the start instructions to Pickett in effect through Alexander, and at least initially Pickett's sole concern was his own division. So each commander in the left wing would take his direction from the actions of the command immediately to his right, with inevitable delays. When it came his turn to advance, General Trimble keyed his movements on those of Fry and Marshall in front of him.

William Lowrance, commanding Alfred Scales's decimated brigade (16th, 22nd, 34th, 13th, and 38th North Carolina), was posted on the right in this second line behind Pettigrew. Trimble's second brigade next to him, under Jim Lane, was also an all–North Carolina command — 7th, 37th, 28th, 18th, and 33rd regiments. Trimble and his staff mounted and took position between the two brigades. Jim Lane explained the posting of this second line for the charge — Pettigrew's division "was much larger than Lowrance's brigade and my own, which were its only support, and there was consequently no second line in rear of its left." Thus Pettigrew's left — Davis's and Brockenbrough's ill-led brigades — was quite without support. This was symptomatic of the indifferent planning applied to the left wing of the attack, from Lee's lack of oversight through A. P. Hill's negligence to Longstreet's inattention.

Of the six brigades in the left wing, only Lane's 1,700 men could be considered fresh, having seen just minor skirmishing in Wednesday's fighting. And of the six, only Pettigrew's former brigade, now under James Marshall, was coming off a victorious (if costly) action on Wednesday. Four had experienced rout or been stopped cold by the Federals. Whether today they proved to be gun-shy or bent on revenge would very much depend on their leadership.

The 13,000 or so men of Pickett's Charge needed to cross three-quarters of a mile of open ground to reach their aiming points on Cemetery Ridge. To be sure, there were several shallow swales in that ground that might offer brief shelter, yet for most of the distance, especially when they reached the Emmitsburg Road, they would be completely exposed to a concerted fire by the Yankee defenders. Marching at "common time," with perhaps a pause or two for realignment on the way, would require some twenty minutes to half an hour to cover the distance.

On Day Three it had, it seemed, all come down to this.[13]

WHILE PICKETT'S CHARGE, as revamped that morning, was simply a direct frontal assault, its execution involved certain complexities. For one thing, the Confederates' starting line and their target line were not parallel, requiring continuous adjustments by the marchers, under fire, to square up the attacking force. These adjustments were further complicated by the fact that the two wings of the attack did not start off together, either in space or in time. Then there was the Emmitsburg Road, which acted as an artificial but unavoidable and deceptive dividing line in the advance. The road slanted southwest-to-northeast across the valley between Seminary and Cemetery ridges, so that upon reaching it, Pettigrew's northern wing would come within rifle (and canister) range of the Yankees. Pickett's southern wing, upon reaching the road, was merely catching up to its own skirmish line. But the largest of the complexities involved the funneling of the mile-and-a-half-wide assembled force into a far narrower striking force that was to storm the targeted area of Cemetery Ridge.

On most of Pickett's front the sturdy wood fences along the Emmitsburg Road had been pulled down by the Rebel skirmishers on Thursday or on Friday morning, but on Pettigrew's front the road lay within the Union skirmish line and so the fences were intact and a barrier to the attackers. The gently rolling, open ground between the two ridges was planted in wheat and corn and clover, and offered no hindrance to the marchers. Their lines would be broken, however, by the Nicholas Codori and William Bliss farmsteads, now unwitting landmarks in the middle of a battlefield.

Some of Pettigrew's men, as they crossed the artillery line and glimpsed what lay ahead, cast a jaundiced eye at their prospects. Captain Joseph Graham, commanding the Charlotte Artillery of North Carolina, wrote that as the infantry passed through his battery "I feared then I could see a want of resolution in our men. And I heard many say, 'that is worse than Malvern Hill,' and 'I don't hardly think that position can be carried,' etc., etc., enough to make me apprehensive about the result." (Cadmus Wilcox had earlier warned Dick Garnett that the enemy's line here was "twice as strong" as at Gaines's Mill, that other Federal stronghold on the Peninsula.) There was similar alarm among Pickett's troops. A man in Garnett's brigade who had viewed the scene from the artillery's position came back and told his comrades, "This is going to be a heller! Prepare for the worst!" In Wilcox's and Lang's reserve brigades, which had attacked Cemetery Ridge the day before, cautions were issued to Kemper's Virginians as they passed by — "Boys, that's a hot place. We were there yesterday."

To a veteran like Lieutenant John Dooley, 1st Virginia, the old homilies of a picture-book war had long since given way to stark reality. As Dooley put it, "when you rise to your feet as we did today, I tell you the enthusiasm of ardent breasts in many cases *ain't there,* and instead of burning to avenge the insults of our country, families and altars and firesides, the thought is most frequently, *Oh,* if I could just come out of this charge safely how thankful *would I be!*"[14]

For Pickett and his generals, their immediate preoccupation in directing the assault was to close the considerable gap between their men and Pettigrew's. The decision setting Pickett's target as the easily visible scrub oaks of the Copse meant that his division would be making what amounted to a left oblique advance — and for Kemper's brigade on the far right it would have to be a quite sharp oblique. Marching orders at first were simply to dress the lines to the left, but because for almost the first half of the advance Birkett Fry's guiding brigade lagged behind and was not even visible on the left, this produced only a modest sideling in that direction. The 3,600 men of Garnett's and Kemper's lead brigades, without specific orders for a left-oblique, tended instead to bunch up. In Kemper's brigade, for example, the 11th Virginia began overlapping the 1st Virginia to its left, causing a verbal skirmish between officers. When orders finally were given for a deliberate left oblique, most of Pickett's formations would abruptly be presenting their flank squarely to the enemy. All of this was accomplished — and accomplished with admirable discipline — under a rising storm of enemy fire.[15]

The first hostile shots no doubt came from Benjamin Rittenhouse's Battery D, 5th U.S., perched atop Little Round Top. Lieutenant Rittenhouse was, from an artillerist's perspective, in the best site on the battlefield. As he afterward put it succinctly, "I watched Pickett's men advance, and opened on them with an oblique fire, and ended with a terrible enfilading fire." His six 10-pounder Parrott rifles had the range and the elevation not only to hit Kemper's flank brigade but to reach into Garnett's and Armistead's brigades as well. Percussion shells, designed to explode on contact, were particularly deadly when fired from an elevated enfilading position. "Many times a single percussion shell would cut out several files, and then explode in their ranks," Rittenhouse explained; "several times almost a company would disappear, as the shell would rip from the right to the left among them."

There was so little space on Little Round Top's cramped, rocky western crest that when the Rebel advance reached halfway across the valley, four of Battery D's pieces could no longer be shifted to follow. The two guns still bearing were under a pair of Irish sergeants, Samuel Peeples and Timothy Grady — "both splendid shots," Rittenhouse remarked. "Almost every shot pointed by these two men seemed to go where it was intended." The massed reserve batteries of Freeman McGilvery would now take up the contest against Pickett's wing, but Sergeants Peeples and Grady continued their deadly fire throughout the charge.[16]

On the opposite flank the first Yankee guns to open were those posted on the opposite high ground, Cemetery Hill — all or parts of eight batteries under the general command of Thomas Osborn. Major Osborn's own Eleventh Corps batteries had been strongly reinforced from the First Corps and especially from the artillery reserve, and by the time

Union soldier Charles Reed sketched Confederates forming up for Pickett's Charge. The arrow at left rear marks the copse of trees, the focus of the attack. At far left is the Bryan house. (Library of Congress)

Pettigrew's wing stepped off on its advance, thirty-nine cannon would be trained on it.

This fire swept obliquely across the entire face of Pettigrew's four front-line brigades. "They were at once enveloped in a dense cloud of smoke and dust," wrote Lieutenant Colonel Franklin Sawyer of the 8th Ohio. "Arms, heads, blankets, guns and knapsacks were thrown and tossed in to the clear air. . . . A moan went up from the field, distinctly to be heard amid the storm of battle. . . ."

From atop Cemetery Hill General Schurz had a longer view: "Through our field-glasses we could distinctly see the gaps torn in their ranks, and the ground dotted with dark spots — their dead and wounded. . . . But the brave rebels promptly filled the gaps from behind or by closing up on their colors, and unshaken and unhesitatingly they continued their onward march." This was an accurate enough depiction of the brigades of Fry and Marshall and Joe Davis, but it was a different case with Brockenbrough's brigade making its disordered march on the Confederate far left flank.[17]

General Hays had posted the 8th Ohio along the Emmitsburg Road, out ahead and to the right of his battle line, to serve as a flank guard. Colonel Sawyer, in turn, aggressively pushed his skirmish line out ahead to a

fence at the far end of a cornfield in his front. He could see toward his left the main line of Rebels as it braved Osborn's artillery barrage, and in his left front a smaller force approaching — Brockenbrough's Virginians, as it proved. Seeing his opportunity and seizing the moment, Sawyer led his little force at the double-quick through the cornfield to the skirmishers' fence line, deployed in a single rank, and opened a raking fire at the Rebels some 100 yards distant.

There were barely 160 Ohioans in this firing line, but so sudden and so unexpected was their musketry that Brockenbrough's confused Virginians, already stunned by the artillery fire, panicked and (said Sawyer) "fled in the wildest confusion." Perhaps as much as half the brigade did not stop running until it had crossed Seminary Ridge. Colonel Lowrance, commanding one of Trimble's two trailing brigades, would complain that Brockenbrough's men "came tearing through our ranks, which caused many of our men to break." Pettigrew and even Pickett sent staff officers to try and rally the fugitives, but without success. In virtually the blink of an eye the left-flank brigade of the grand charge was driven from the field.

This coup did not satisfy the resourceful Colonel Sawyer. Sighting the approach of the Rebels' next-in-line brigade — it was Joe Davis's Mississippians and North Carolinians — Sawyer put his regiment in a left wheel so that it was facing due south and aligned behind a board fence. Resting their rifles on the fence, the Ohioans opened a close-in, deadly accurate fire straight into the enemy's flank. As Colonel Sawyer later phrased it, "our blood was up, and the men loaded and fired and yelled and howled at the passing column." Before they were done for the day, wrote the 8th Ohio's Thomas Galway, "We got three stands of colors and many prisoners."[18]

Thus far the 8th Ohio was the only infantry positioned to open on the attackers. The range for the infantry lines on Cemetery Ridge was still too great, and so for the next few minutes the killing continued to be the work of the artillery. First Osborn's thirty-nine guns on Cemetery Hill to the north and then McGilvery's forty-one on lower Cemetery Ridge to the south smothered the Rebel columns in an enfilading crossfire. And with each step of the advance, the range decreased, the enfilading angle increased, and the destruction mounted. It was all exactly as Henry Hunt had planned it, and almost all he had hoped for. All that was missing from his master scheme was cannon fire from the center. There the guns stood silent, their long-range ammunition exhausted, their gunners impatiently waiting for canister range.

The Yankee artillerists utilized three types of ammunition in this long-range fire. The smoothbore Napoleons fired solid shot with a deliberately low trajectory that, skipping and bounding into the flank of a column of marching men, was as demoralizing as it was destructive; in its random, very visible course one of these 12-pound iron balls might knock down an entire file of men. The rifled pieces fired primarily either percussion shells, exploding on contact, or fuzed case shot, exploding overhead and raining down shrapnel on the marchers. In enfilading fire all that was required was aim; against these long ranks of marching men a decently aimed shot simply could not miss. And unlike the Rebels' ammunition, exceedingly few Federal shots were misfires due to faulty fuzes.

Captain Elijah Taft, commanding three of the powerful 20-pounder Parrott rifles on Cemetery Hill, described this artillerists' dream — and this attackers' nightmare. "I could sight down the entire length of their line," he recalled, "which stretched as far south as the eye could see, a perfect enfilading shot for my gunners. . . . I watched my fire stop and break one column, all the men turning back in mass seeking cover in the woods." Taft and Major Osborn's other battery commanders had opened this long-range fire the moment Pettigrew's brigades emerged from the woods on Seminary Ridge, and they continued it as fast as the guns could be served for twenty minutes or more, until the attackers reached the Emmitsburg Road and came within canister range. Their fire reached deep into the marching columns, but the most immediate effect was relentlessly to peel away the now exposed left flank of the attack. Pettigrew's attacking wing was crippled before its men could fire a shot.

The sheer ferocity of the bombardment literally staggered Pettigrew's men. Frederick Edgell reported that his New Hampshire battery, posted on Cemetery Hill, fired 248 rounds of shell and case shot at the attackers. If Captain Edgell's expenditure was typical of Osborn's batteries, it meant that more than 1,600 rounds of long-range shot and shell were aimed at Pettigrew's brigades that afternoon. The crash of the guns and the blast of the exploding shells were indescribable. A man in the 7th Tennessee, in Fry's brigade, remembered it as "a deepening roar that no exaggeration of language can heighten."

The collapse of Brockenbrough's brigade left Joe Davis's Mississippians and North Carolinians as the flank brigade of Pettigrew's wing and consequently a primary target of these Yankee gunners. Already in some disorder as his men picked their way through the smoldering Bliss farmstead, Davis reported that "we were met by a heavy fire of grape, canister, and shell, which told sadly upon our ranks." Hardest hit was the left-hand regiment, the 11th Mississippi, a veteran outfit that had been guarding trains and missed the brigade's battering on Wednesday. The 11th paid its dues on Friday. The enemy's fire, said Davis, "commanded our front and left with fatal effect. . . ." The 11th Mississippi would lose 312 of its 592 men in Pickett's Charge, and easily a third to a half that number fell before the Yankee artillery.[19]

On the southern flank, meanwhile, the rise of ground that had largely shielded McGilvery's reserve artillery position from Confederate eyes during the opening bombardment now served in its turn — for a time at least — to shield Pickett's advancing infantry from McGilvery's guns. As Kemper's and Garnett's and Armistead's battle lines crested the rise, however, there was surely a moment of mutual surprise — 5,830 Confederate marchers abruptly confronting a massed array of cannon none of them had suspected was there; and McGilvery's gunners at last sighting the enemy's infantry, marching not toward them but at an oblique angle past them, ideal for enfilade fire. As Colonel McGilvery explained it, the Rebel battle lines "presented an oblique front to the guns under my command, and by training the whole line of guns obliquely to the right, we had a raking fire through all three of these lines." The reality behind that matter-of-fact recital was terrifying.

McGilvery's forty-one guns sent a torrent of fire raining down on the marchers. Like Osborn's guns, their missiles were primarily solid shot, percussion shells, and case shot. "The execution of the fire must have been terrible" was McGilvery's judgment. In the 53rd Virginia Captain Benjamin Farinholt watched as a single shell left a file of thirteen men "in a perfect mangled mass of flesh and blood indistinguishable one from the other." One strike in the midst of the 56th Virginia, Garnett's brigade, killed or wounded sixteen men. The color guard of the 11th Virginia in Kemper's brigade was smothered in shell fragments; three times the flag went down, and three times it was rescued. "I tell you, the gaps we made were simply terrible," wrote Yankee artillerist Edwin Dow. "But they closed up their lines, and closed up and closed them up. . . ." And they kept coming.[20]

Pickett's officers worked quickly to keep them coming. "Steady, men!" Dick Garnett called out in his commanding voice. "Close up! A little faster; not too fast! Save your strength!" Garnett, on horseback, was easily seen and widely obeyed. James Kemper, also mounted, calmly continued dressing his lines to the left as ordered. He would later admit that in the intensity of the moment he was oblivious of most everything except the needs of his own brigade. Lew Armistead, marching out ahead of his second line, ignoring the fire, continued to raise his sword high as a guide for the troops.

General Pickett, from his position behind the advance, ranged back and forth to the best observation sites left and right, so he might better direct events. According to his orderly, Thomas Friend, Pickett "went as far as any Major General, commanding a division, ought to have gone, and farther." As the division approached the Emmitsburg Road, staggering under the withering artillery fire, Pickett sent back to Longstreet for help. Pickett instructed his aide Robert Bright to say "that the position against which he had been sent would be taken, but he could not hold it unless reinforcements were sent to him."[21]

GENERAL PICKETT, in agreeing earlier in the day that the grand charge would guide on Birkett Fry's brigade of Pettigrew's command — the center brigade of the attacking force — seems not to have given much thought to the effect of that decision on the movements of his own brigades. Or perhaps Pickett simply misjudged the lay of the land he would have to cross to reach Cemetery Ridge. In any event, as his division neared the Emmitsburg Road it became obvious that its sideling movements "dressing left" would not be enough to close up on Pettigrew's division. There promised to be two separate assaults rather than one concerted one. Since only Pickett was in a command position to see and

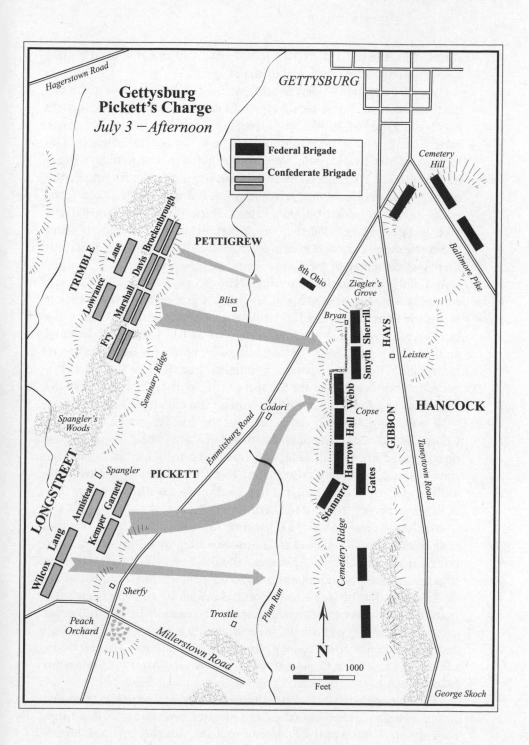

**Gettysburg
Pickett's Charge**

July 3 — Afternoon

Federal Brigade

Confederate Brigade

Hagerstown Road

GETTYSBURG

Cemetery
Hill

Baltimore Pike

TRIMBLE

Lowrance

Lane

Davis

Brockenbrough

Marshall

Fry

PETTIGREW

8th Ohio

Bliss

Ziegler's
Grove

Bryan

Smyth

Sherrill

HAYS

Leister

Seminary Ridge

Spangler's
Woods

Codori

Emmitsburg Road

Webb

Hall

Copse

HANCOCK

GIBBON

Taneytown Road

LONGSTREET

Spangler

PICKETT

Armistead

Kemper

Garnett

Harrow

Gates

Stannard

Wilcox

Lang

Sherfy

Trostle

Plum Run

Cemetery Ridge

Peach
Orchard

Millerstown Road

N

0   1000

Feet

George Skoch

427

correct this, the order to make a left oblique had to come from him —
but he waited dangerously long to give it.

The approximately 45-degree turn, setting the division on a north-by-
northeast course almost parallel to the Emmitsburg Road, was smartly
executed by the well-drilled Virginians, but it proved a very costly move.
Now Pickett's men were marching right past the Federal batteries. The
farthest of McGilvery's guns were within 800 yards of Kemper's rightmost regiment. The closest were within 400 yards. Furthermore, the
northward turn offered the Yankee gunners full enfilade fire. "Load canister!" came the order. Captain Patrick Hart, 15th New York Battery,
McGilvery's brigade, loaded his four Napoleons with double canister
when the range closed. "I continued this dreadful fire on this line until
there was not a man of them to be seen," he reported.

As it had been from the beginning of the charge, Kemper's flanking brigade was the most immediate victim of this fire. Its new course took it
across the Emmitsburg Road and onto the Codori farmstead. There was a
brief respite crossing a shallow swale, but as the Virginians detoured
around Mr. Codori's big barn they also came under fire from Yankee infantrymen. These three Vermont regiments, from George Stannard's brigade, had been posted on the Second Corps' southern flank to serve the
same guarding function as the 8th Ohio on the northern flank.

"It was a terribly costly movement for the enemy," wrote Lieutenant
George Benedict of General Stannard's staff. "The 14th regiment . . . at
once opened fire by battalion, and continued it by file, at about sixty
rods distance, with very great effect. The 13th joined its fire with the
14th, and a line of dead rebels at the close showed distinctly where they
marched across the front of the Vermonters."

With the course now set, for good or ill, toward the Copse, Kemper
rode back to find Armistead to coordinate support during the coming
critical minutes. "General," Kemper called out over the din, "I am going
to storm those works, and I want you to support me." Armistead acknowledged that he would, and pointed pridefully to his brigade's formation. "Did you ever see anything better on parade?" he asked. "I never
did," said Kemper, and threw him a salute. Pickett's men, trailing dead
and wounded at every step, doggedly closing the gaps torn in their ranks,
strode on toward the Copse and the wall. General Armistead raised his
black slouch hat on his sword's point to better show the way.[22]

This oblique march by Pickett's division finally closed the gap between
it and Pettigrew's division. The Confederates now had a united front,
roughly on the line of the Emmitsburg Road. But this by itself did not

produce a united result. The two wings of the grand charge would have very different tales to tell in these next hectic, hellish minutes.

Pettigrew's troops would founder at the Emmitsburg Road, which proved to be both literally and figuratively a barricade to their further advance. The fences along this northern section of the road were intact and too strongly built — post-and-rail on the west, post-and-plank on the east — and the enemy's fire too hot, for the men to stop long enough to pull them down. They had to climb over instead. To make matters worse, they had now come within musketry range. The command "Fire!" swept along Alexander Hays's Yankee line, triggered by the general himself. "The time it took to climb to the top of the fence seemed to me an age of suspense," wrote John H. Moore of the 7th Tennessee, of Fry's brigade. "It was not a leaping over; it was rather an insensible tumbling to the ground. . . ."

The roadbed here was some two feet below the road edges, and the first shelter of any sort these men had encountered since their march began on Seminary Ridge. Ahead of them was the second roadside fence to climb, then some 200 yards of open, rising ground, bisected by yet another rail fence, to the stone fence now wreathed in smoke and ablaze with what appeared to be one continuous sheet of flame. The artillery blasts from the left had subsided somewhat — a shoulder of Cemetery Hill now masked a number of Osborn's batteries from targets in the road — but in their place came a searing barrage of canister from the immediate front. The source of the canister was George Woodruff's Battery I, 1st U.S., six Napoleons posted in front of Ziegler's Grove with a clear field of fire toward the Emmitsburg Road.

Leadership in Pettigrew's division was being decimated. Pettigrew himself, painfully wounded in the left hand by shrapnel, was unhorsed and had to scurry about on foot to direct events. At about the time his brigade reached the Emmitsburg Road, Birkett Fry was shot through the thigh and had to turn over his command. As Fry remembered it, "I was so confident of victory that to some of my men, who ran up to carry me off, I shouted, 'Go on — it will not last five minutes longer!'" Moments later, James Marshall, today in charge of Pettigrew's North Carolina brigade, was shot dead off his horse by two bullets to the head. All four of Marshall's regimental commanders went down. Brockenbrough and his brigade had already been driven from the field, leaving Joe Davis as the only one of Pettigrew's brigade leaders still standing.

Whether because of the seeming shelter offered by the sunken road, or the excessive command casualties, or simply the terrific volume of the

Charles Reed pictured Pickett's men coming under fire from the Union batteries. The copse of trees is at right center, the Bryan house at left center. Reed's battery was posted at the far left. (Library of Congress)

enemy's fire, a sizable majority of Pettigrew's men did not, or could not, take the charge beyond the Emmitsburg Road. Lieutenant Moore of the 7th Tennessee thought perhaps two-thirds of the "front line" that reached the road never advanced beyond it. "I know when I reached the top of the second fence there seemed to remain a line of battle in the road," he recalled. The 7th Tennessee's colonel, John A. Fite, estimated that only half his regiment reached the road, and only half of those, some fifty men, advanced beyond it. As Fite put it, "what wasn't shot down of our crowd fell down."[23]

Alexander Hays's tactic of crowding every rifle in his two brigades right into the front line, holding no one back, proved to be murderously effective against Pettigrew's charge. The 260 yards of wall Hays was defending appeared to be one solid line of rifle barrels. Men were two, three, even four deep behind it. Within reach were scores of extra rifles gleaned from yesterday's battlefield. A Federal would fire, fall back to load, and his place on the firing line was immediately filled. Some just loaded and passed pieces forward to better shots. Like Pop Greene's earlier tactic of rotating the Culp's Hill defenders, the result was one massive, steady, continuous volley of musketry.

Employing the language of home, Yankee farm boys described the

430

enemy as falling before them like ripe grain before the sickle or the scythe — similes of unsparing accuracy. Afterward an industrious observer examined the board fence along the eastern edge of the Emmitsburg Road. One board, he wrote, "was indeed a curiosity. It was sixteen feet long, fourteen inches broad, and was perforated with eight hundred and thirty-six musket balls."

Sergeant Ben Hirst, 14th Connecticut, wrote his wife, "such a Volley of rifles we gave them you cannot imagine. Soon the first line was Shattered to pieces, and with shouts of Derision we awaited for the next, served them the same way. . . ." Two companies of the 14th Connecticut were armed with Sharps breechloaders, with a rate of fire about three times that of muzzleloaders. In these few critical moments they were fired so fast that water had to be poured on their barrels to cool them. The 12th New Jersey could also be said to have special armament. Equipped with obsolete .69-caliber smoothbores that fired buck-and-ball, the Jerseymen were determined to make the best of their handicap. A number of them spent the morning altering cartridges, taking out the ball and adding a handful of buckshot. So it happened that those Rebels who dared push on across the Emmitsburg Road and into the Jerseymen's range were greeted with blasts from these deadly shotguns.[24]

Isaac Trimble, bringing up his two brigades behind Pettigrew, watched as Fry's and Marshall's brigades directly ahead of him reached the Emmitsburg Road, when suddenly "they seemed to sink into the earth under the tempest of fire poured into them." The same image could have been applied to Joe Davis's brigade on the far left. After the flight of Brockenbrough's Virginians, Davis's Mississippians and North Carolinians absorbed the full weight of the Federals' oblique fire. At first this came from Osborn's guns on Cemetery Hill. Then came the canister blasts from Woodruff's battery at Ziegler's Grove. At the same time, the 8th Ohio, reinforced by a hundred or so adventuresome skirmishers from the 125th and 126th New York, continued to pour close-range fire squarely into the Rebels' flank. By now, according to the Ohioans' Colonel Sawyer, "the mass appeared more like a cloud of moving smoke and dust than a column of troops."

The veteran 11th Mississippi on the left struggled on doggedly through this gauntlet of fire. Led by its color bearer — the fifth of the afternoon, his flag now "dangling in graceless confusion from one corner" — a handful of the Mississippians made it across the Emmitsburg Road and rushed the Yankee line. Fourteen men somehow survived and managed to gain the shelter of Abraham Bryan's barn, near the northern end of the Yankee line. While they awaited reinforcements, they aimed an occasional shot around the corner of the barn.

"Thinking the line rather a long time coming up," said Lieutenant William Peel, "I looked to the rear. The state of my feelings may be imagined, but not described, upon seeing the line broken, & flying in full disorder. . . ." His little party certainly could not advance, and it could not retreat without becoming "the 'flying target' of a thousand muskets." In due course someone found a scrap of white cloth and waved it around the corner in token of surrender. Lieutenant Peel's party had come the closest to the Yankee line of any of Johnston Pettigrew's troops.

The rest of Davis's brigade was stymied at the Emmitsburg Road. Pummeled simultaneously from front and flank by musketry, its ranks torn by canister, it retained neither the strength nor the spirit for a further advance. A Mississippi soldier named Wiley Heflin wrote the epitaph for Joe Davis's brigade on July 3: "our line was so cut down and demoralized by the enemy's batteries before we got in gun shot distance that we could not carry the works." Lieutenant Louis Young of General Pettigrew's staff described the brigade at this point as "reduced to a line of skirmishers." There was nothing for it now but to turn back to Seminary Ridge.[25]

The brigades of Fry and Marshall, less damaged by the Cemetery Hill guns and the musketry from the flank than those of Brockenbrough and Davis, were able to reach the Emmitsburg Road in better order. They also pushed across the road in greater numbers, but this was merely a matter of degree. The final result, the final checkmate, was just the same.

A substantial number of these Confederates simply lay or crouched in the sunken roadbed, alongside the bloodied heaps of dead and wounded, and tried to return the enemy's fire. Possibly 300 of Fry's Tennesseans and Alabamians and perhaps another 600 or so of Marshall's North Carolinians succeeded in advancing beyond the road and its two fences. But far fewer of them penetrated beyond the rail fence — the *third* fence — that extended northward from the Angle in the stone wall. The range here at this fence closed to only some 80 yards, and there were two or three Federal riflemen for each Confederate who reached that far. There was also a major last-minute addition to Hays's battle line — the six Napoleons of Lieutenant Gulian Weir's Battery C, 5th U.S.

Weir's battery had been roughly handled by Rans Wright's Georgians during Thursday's fighting, losing (but later regaining) three of its guns. That morning it was refitted, and as the bombardment ended Weir was sent forward by one of Hunt's staff and directed to take the place of Arnold's wrecked Rhode Island battery near the Angle. "Go right up there," he was told, ". . . and you will come in on their flank, and mow them down." Unlimbering smartly under fire, loading with double canister, Weir literally blew away a line of Rebels who had reached the third fence.

As always in any attack, the color bearers, the focus of all eyes and the most visible of all targets, suffered staggering losses. The 14th Tennessee and the 5th Alabama battalion, of Fry's brigade, each reached the limit of its advance behind its fourth color bearer of the day. Private Boney Smith of the 14th planted his flag at the third fence and stood holding it there defiantly and then he too was shot down. The 26th North Carolina had lost fourteen color bearers on July 1; on July 3 it lost four more, and lost its flag as well.[26]

Here and there little groups of a few dozen men led by officers of driving force pressed on through the storm toward the wall. A Federal gunner watched as these officers, "with uplifted swords, rushed madly up and down, calling to their men to follow. One after another they fell." Probably the closest any of these parties came to the wall was 15 or 20 yards. An officer in the 12th New Jersey compared their brave efforts to "spray driven from a wave," marking the high-water mark of each desperate push against Hays's line. Surely the largest such effort was that of Lieutenant Colonel John Graves, taking command of the 47th North Carolina after its colonel fell wounded. Graves drove some 150 of his Tar Heels to within 40 yards of the fence, going to ground there and demanding the men hold on until their supports arrived. But there were no supports. Graves and his stranded survivors soon became prisoners.[27]

The story of these supports was a matter of too little, too late, and too hopeless. When he saw his left collapsing, first Brockenbrough's brigade and then Davis's, General Pettigrew sent back to ask Isaac Trimble to shore up the crumbling flank. Trimble's orders to Jim Lane's brigade were confusing, however, and only three and a half of Lane's five North Carolina regiments moved up to the Emmitsburg Road in Davis's place. The scene they found was chaotic. Dead and wounded literally carpeted the roadway, breaking up Lane's formations. Canister from Woodruff's guns came whistling into this mass of men, kicking up clouds of dust to add to the roils of battle smoke. The flanking force built around the 8th Ohio, further reinforced now, pounded mercilessly at Lane's flank. This fire, said Lane, was "murderous." Here again there were spurts of advance by these North Carolinians beyond the road, and even beyond the third fence, but without any power behind them they soon withered and shriveled under Hays's relentless musketry.

The second of Trimble's brigades, Scales's North Carolina brigade led today by William Lowrance, was a frail hope to begin with. It had lost almost two-thirds of its men on Wednesday and nearly all its field officers, and to have to advance once again straight into this maelstrom of enemy fire must have seemed a nightmare revisited. As Colonel Lowrance phrased it, without exaggeration, "Then we were ordered forward over a wide, hot, and already crimson plain."

Like Lane's men, the tangle of dead, wounded, and stymied men at the Emmitsburg Road formed an obstacle to Lowrance's command. At this point, wrote Lieutenant Henry C. Moore, 38th North Carolina, echoing several others in the charge that day, "The fire from the enemy's artillery and infantry was now terrible, and we were reduced to a mere skirmish line." In that state there was little they could do: "Our men kept up a weak fire through the plank fence." In his report, Colonel Lowrance, who was himself wounded, wrote plaintively that by now his brigade and Lane's "were the only line to be seen upon that vast field, and no support in view. The natural inquiry was, What shall we do? and none to answer." The decision was soon taken out of his hands: "The men answered for themselves, and, without orders, the brigade retreated. . . ."[28]

While Pettigrew's and Trimble's brigades did not finally have strength enough to break through the line at the stone fence, or even to seriously threaten it, their firepower was enough to damage the Yankees severely. Alexander Hays's tightly massed battle line might deliver great killing power, but it was thereby greatly vulnerable to return fire. In their spur-of-the-moment battle line in the Emmitsburg Road, the Rebels rested their rifles on the roadside fence for accurate counterfire. The 1st Delaware, at about the center of Hays's line, had two color bearers killed within two minutes. The 111th New York, on the right, suffered four color bearers killed during the assault, matching several Confederate regiments in that grim statistic.

Lieutenant George Woodruff was shot through the body while maneuvering a section of his guns at Ziegler's Grove, but waved off aid until the guns were posted properly. He would die the next day. Both of Hays's brigade commanders were also casualties. Colonel Smyth had been wounded during the bombardment, and now, at the peak of the attack, Colonel Eliakim Sherrill was shot in the stomach, a wound that proved mortal. In the fighting on July 3, said one of his men, Colonel Sherrill was being "too brave a man to live."

Eliakim Sherrill had assumed the command the day before when George Willard was killed, and he helped the brigade expunge the humiliation of its 1862 capture at Harper's Ferry. As the fighting wound down, however, the excitable Winfield Hancock took offense when Sherrill prudently withdrew his men to safer ground, and relieved him of the command. Alexander Hays later talked Hancock into rescinding the order and Sherrill got his brigade back, but today the colonel apparently went out of his way to regain the honor he believed he had lost. (Some months later, in a conversation with Hays, Hancock asked about that colonel he had put in arrest at Gettysburg. "I guess I ought to apologize to him," he said. "That's just like all your damned apologies, Hancock," said Hays shortly. "They come too late. He's dead.")[29]

From the bombardment all through the charge, General Hays was an indomitable force, riding back and forth just behind his battle line, shouting encouragement to his men. "Hurrah! Boys, we're giving them hell!" he assured them. Two horses were shot from under him, and fourteen of his twenty orderlies were hit. One of his men, writing home the next day, insisted that neither "Shell, shot, nor the bullets of the Rebel sharpshooters seemed to intimidate him in the least; in fact, he paid not the least attention to them. . . ." But Hays did more than simply cheer on the troops. When he saw the Rebel flank crumbling, for example, and realized that his own flank was thereby secure, he quickly added weight to the 8th Ohio's flanking force that was dealing out so destructive a fire. All in all, Alexander Hays's July 3 performance was inspired.[30]

AT ABOUT THE SAME TIME that Pettigrew's division engaged along the Emmitsburg Road, Pickett's three brigades were completing their oblique turn and swinging back eastward to storm John Gibbon's battle line. Pickett's Virginians did not have the barrier of roadside fences to contend with, nor did they encounter the solid wall of fire that Pettigrew did, and so their fight would reach its climax at closer quarters with the enemy.

General Gibbon had found his mount by now, and as he rode along behind the lines he encouraged his men. Where Alexander Hays was all loud exhortations, John Gibbon was all quiet practicality. "Gnl. Gibbon rode down the lines," Frank Haskell noted, "cool and calm, and in an unimpassioned voice he said to the men: 'Do not hurry, men, and fire too fast — let them come up close before you fire, and then aim low, and steadily.'" Haskell added, "The coolness of their General was reflected in the faces of his men."

Alexander Webb, whose Philadelphia Brigade held the center of the Union position, at the Angle, was also encouraging his troops. Webb's message was simple. If they did as well today as they had yesterday, he said, he would be well satisfied. One of his colonels even invoked the embattled colonists of yore and cautioned his men not to fire until they "could distinguish the whites of their eyes." A primary concern for Webb was his artillery support, and he spoke of this to Lieutenant Alonzo Cushing, whose Battery A, 4th U.S., was posted behind the Angle. Only two of Cushing's 3-inch Ordnance rifles were still operable after the bombardment, and Cushing himself was grievously wounded and could barely stand. When Webb said he expected the enemy would come straight at them, Cushing replied, "I had better run my guns right up to the stone fence and bring all my canister alongside of each piece." "All right," said Webb, "do so."[31]

Webb's sector of the battle line was awkward to defend. The jog in the stone fence here meant that his front line, running southward from the Angle, was some 80 yards in advance of Hays's battle line on his right. Furthermore, Webb was short-handed, with eight companies of the 106th Pennsylvania co-opted by Howard for his fragile Eleventh Corps. Initially Webb had posted just the 69th Pennsylvania at the fence, leaving the 71st, 72nd, and the two remaining companies of the 106th Pennsylvania to the rear, on the artillery line. But when Cushing pushed his two remaining guns right up to the fence, Webb ordered the 71st Pennsylvania forward into the Angle to support the guns. There was not room enough there for the whole regiment, however, so two companies of the 71st remained behind.

Thus when Pickett's troops came storming toward them, Webb's 940 men were divided roughly in half — the 69th Pennsylvania and eight companies of the 71st at the front behind the stone fence, and at the rear in support the 72nd Pennsylvania and two companies each of the 71st and 106th. Although the men of the 69th had, like Hays's men, picked up rifles left from yesterday's fighting for additional firepower, Webb's battle line by itself could not begin to match the massed fire being delivered against Pettigrew by Hays's command.

The forces to Webb's left — the Second Corps brigades of Norman Hall and William Harrow, and the First Corps troops of George Stannard's Vermont brigade and Theodore Gates's demi-brigade — were, most of them, not fated to be in the direct line of Pickett's attack. Indeed it happened in the next critical minutes that these defenders played more the role of the hunter than the hunted.[32]

The Vermonters, in their advanced position on the left, had been the first Federal infantry to engage Pickett's advance. Now, as the Rebels completed their oblique move and resumed their eastward course, General Stannard saw opportunity and jumped at it. At the moment his three regiments were facing west; a rapid pivot to the right, he realized, would put him facing northward and squarely on the Confederates' flank just as they were attacking.

This change of front would be somewhat tricky, however, especially for nine-month troops in their first battle and amidst a smoky, deadly bedlam. The 13th Vermont, on Stannard's far right, had the easier task. It was ordered to "Change front forward on first company!" — that is, to pivot 90 degrees on the rightmost company. Stannard determined to leave the 14th regiment where it was, facing west as a guard for the new position, and in a more complicated maneuver, to march the 16th regiment by the right flank behind the 14th for some 300 yards and then deploy it facing north alongside the 13th.

Just then Winfield Scott Hancock reined up in front of Stannard in a swirl of dust and demanded to know what was going on. As was his custom in a fight, Hancock was all over the field, urging men on, pushing in reinforcements ("Go in there pretty God damned quick!" he yelled to one of his colonels), gauging the action. Like Stannard, he had seen the opportunity to deliver a flanking fire into the attackers, but apparently he disagreed with or misunderstood the Vermonter on how to carry it out. As Stannard remembered it, Hancock "remarked that I was gone to Hell." George Stannard was not to be intimidated: "My answer was 'that

Pickett's Charge from the Confederates' perspective, looking east, with the opposing battle lines in the middle distance. Ziegler's Grove is at left center, rear. Painting by Edwin Forbes. (Library of Congress)

to Hell it was then,' as it was the only thing that could possibly save the day." The matter seems to have been settled quickly enough, for the maneuver continued without any alterations by Hancock.[33]

Moments later Lieutenant George Benedict, Stannard's aide, watched Hancock start to ride away "when he uttered an exclamation and I saw that he was reeling in his saddle." Staff men eased the general to the ground and (wrote Benedict) they "opened his clothing where he indicated by a movement of his hand that he was hurt, a ragged hole, an inch or more in diameter, from which the blood was pouring profusely, was disclosed in the upper part and on the side of his thigh." Hancock said urgently, "Don't let me bleed to death. Get something around it quick!" A tourniquet was applied and a doctor summoned. It was found that a bullet had gone through the pommel of Hancock's saddle and carried

with it into the wound splinters of wood and a saddle nail. It was a severe but not mortal injury. Said General Stannard, "I reported the condition of the fight to him from time to time while he laid there awaiting an ambulance."

John Gibbon was also ranging right along the battle line as he directed matters. At one point he even rode out ahead of a regiment to redirect its posting. "I was suddenly recalled to the absurd position I had assumed by the whole regiment opening fire!" he later wrote. "I got to the rear as soon as possible." Soon after, while prodding troops forward, a bullet slashed through his left arm and into his shoulder. He turned command over to the senior officer, William Harrow, and was helped to the rear.[34]

Observing the flanking move of the Vermonters from the opposite perspective was Henry T. Owen, 18th Virginia, Garnett's brigade. Looking off to his right, Captain Owen saw "A body of yankees 800 or 1000 yards away coming at a double quick . . . muskets glittering in the sunlight and battle flags fluttering. . . . Their line was perpendicular to our own and they were hastening to strike us before we reached the stone wall. I saw it was to be a race and as Genl. Garnett came along saying several times 'faster, faster men' I put my men to the double quick. . . ."[35]

Freeman McGilvery's batteries on the southern flank were in full voice now, driving shell and canister down the length of the Rebel lines. On Little Round Top the two guns of Rittenhouse's battery still bearing added percussion shells to the melee. Behind the Union center the surviving guns of John Hazard's Second Corps artillery prepared to join in as the range closed. Of the two still functioning pieces of James Rorty's battery (commanded now by Robert Rogers), one was manned by volunteers from the 15th Massachusetts, who enhanced their ammunition by jamming down the barrel rocks, bayonets, nails, tin cups, and any other battlefield debris they could find.

The strongest battery now defending the Union center was Andrew Cowan's just arrived 1st New York Independent, with its six 3-inch Ordnance rifles. These small-bore rifles fired a smaller-sized canister round than the Napoleons, but with double or even triple charges they were deadly enough at close range. Five of Cowan's guns were posted to the left of the Copse and one to the right, and when he saw how exposed he was, Cowan had the prolonge ropes laid out behind the pieces so they could be quickly hauled back to safer ground if it should come to that.

The moment he saw Pickett set the advance in motion, Porter Alexander had made a hurried survey of his batteries to get, as he later put it, "the best which was left most immediately to the front." He ordered any guns with intact teams and at least fifteen rounds of long-range ammunition remaining to move up on Pickett's right to support the charge. Close-in artillery support had been an integral part of Lee's attack plan from the beginning, yet in the end the only artillerist who made any effort to carry it out was Alexander. He pushed forward perhaps a dozen guns, but they were too few and too late to have any real effect on the outcome. Nevertheless, the Yankee gunners on Cemetery Ridge made short work of the attempt. In the case of one Rebel battery, noted the historian of the 5th Massachusetts Light, "in less than ten minutes not a cannoneer was left to work the guns: all were dead or had 'skedaddled.'"

By this time Pickett's infantry was fully engaged. "Then there was soon nothing to see but volumes of musketry smoke," Porter Alexander remembered, "& the crashing roar which went up — it seemed to me the heaviest I had ever heard — told that the matter was now being brought to the final test."[36]

The final test began as a swiftly paced running battle — Pickett's three brigades, following their distorted march route, coming first within range of Stannard's Vermont brigade, then Harrow's brigade and Gates's demi-brigade, then Hall's brigade, and finally a climactic struggle with Webb's brigade at the Angle. George Pickett, his troops already fearfully savaged by the Yankee artillery, watched appalled as they were progressively cut to pieces by a raking infantry and artillery fire until all that remained was a forlorn hope.

While Stannard's Vermonters were maneuvering into their new flanking position, Harrow's and Gates's men to the right took their turn against the Rebels marching invitingly across their front. "Command was given not to fire until ordered — and then to fire at their feet," explained Sergeant James Wright, 1st Minnesota. "This was to correct, as far as possible, the tendency to overshoot." Kemper's brigade, on Pickett's far flank, was once again the first to come within range. "Well," Minnesotan Edward Walker wrote home, "we *mowed* them down — twas Fredericksburg reversed — the first line went down in no time and the others broke. . . . Perhaps we didnt feel good when we saw them scatter?" Walker's elation was tempered somewhat when a bullet smashed through his canteen, "making the water fly a little."

Like the Minnesotans, the men in the 80th New York and 151st Pennsylvania, of Theodore Gates's demi-brigade, were more than ready to gain some revenge for their losses in the earlier fighting. These two First Corps regiments had been badly hurt in the losing struggle for Seminary Ridge on July 1, and so when Colonel Gates ordered them forward to the stone fence to engage, they went, he said, "cheering, and in gallant style, and poured a volley into the enemy at very short range. . . ."

Soon it was the turn of Norman Hall's brigade. The Confederates' 45-degree oblique was carrying them closer to the Yankee line with every step, and by the time Hall's men opened fire they were at a killing range. Captain Henry Abbott of the 20th Massachusetts wrote home that they took careful aim at the Rebel regiment in front of them "& then bowled them over like nine pins, picking out the colors first. In two minutes there were only groups of two or three men running round wildly, like chickens with their heads off. We were cheering like mad. . . . By jove, it was worth all our defeats." These Massachusetts men gained their own particular revenge that bloody afternoon, shouting out "Fredericksburg! Fredericksburg!"[37]

Except for skirmish-line exchanges, Pickett's men had obeyed orders not to stop to fire, and under the tight rein of command they held to that stricture through most of the oblique turn. A man in the 19th

Virginia noted the litany — "Steady, boys! . . . Don't fire! . . . Close up!"
— intoned repeatedly by the line officers. To this point their torment
was coming from artillery fire, which they knew they could do nothing
about. But as their slanting march brought them ever closer to Cemetery
Ridge and the blasts of infantry fire scorched their ranks, they pleaded for
permission to shoot back. Then, with permission or without it, they began to return fire. It was a matter of self-preservation — this was an enemy they could reply to.

As they turned eastward and pushed straight on toward the Angle and
the Copse, Pickett's brigades began to lose their carefully maintained order and to bunch together. This was due certainly to the terrible pressures
of the enemy's raking fire, but it was also due in part to the primal instinct to close as quickly as possible with their tormentors. Kemper's brigade, turning first, was perhaps slightly ahead, with Garnett close by on
the left and Armistead equally close by to the left and somewhat to the
rear. But the closer they came, the less the distinction there was between
units. Observers spoke of the Confederate troops in a "mass" as they
closed on the wall.

The sound of this final charge — "a kind of savage roar" was how General Gibbon described it — was audible even above the din of the guns.
Some would also remember a scattering of Rebel yells, but by now most
Rebels were too tired for that. To others the sound seemed more of an incoherent, animalistic shouting — and, as the two sides came to grips,
from Rebels and Yankees alike. The battle smoke swirled and coiled and
spread thickly across the slope, and nothing could be seen very clearly.
Nothing could be heard very clearly. Within the mass of Rebels, recalled
Virginian Randolph Shotwell, there was an impression of being in a sleet
storm, which "made one gasp for breath. . . . I noticed that many of the
men bent in a half stoop as they marched up the slope, as if to protect
their faces, and dodge the balls."[38]

By now General Stannard's 13th and 16th Vermont regiments were
coming into place on the Confederates' flank. They opened a devastating fire. The range here was only 80 to 100 yards, and there were some
900 Vermonters on this new firing line. As the 16th Vermont's Colonel
Wheelock Veazey put it, "those great masses of men seemed to disappear
in a moment."

Kemper's brigade was taking the bulk of this fire, and to meet the danger the two leftmost regiments, 24th and 11th Virginia, were directed to
refuse their line and face south. General Kemper wanted to add the 1st
Virginia, his center regiment, to this new defensive line. That, however,

proved beyond the powers of Lieutenant Edward Reeve, the officer immediately in command. As Reeve recalled it, "the few men left were shot down as fast as I placed them in position and turning to the adjutant, I told him it was too late and there was no 1st Regiment left to execute the movement."

As Kemper's brigade swiftly melted away under the concentrated musketry and artillery of the Federal left, Garnett's brigade was increasingly exposed to the killing fire. Henry Owen of the 18th Virginia, Garnett's command, remembered the confusion and the now tangled demands on his men: "I saw men turn deliberately and coolly commence upon this new enemy while others shot to the front. At one time I saw two men cross their muskets one fired to our right and the other to our front."

Garnett's and Armistead's brigades, and what was left of Kemper's, pushed straight on toward the center of the Union line. The parade-ground battle lines of the march were completely gone now, in their place crowding, ragged groupings around the flags, prodded ahead by gesturing officers. Men by dozens, by scores, by hundreds were being consumed by the fire. Those still standing would pause to fire back, then resolutely stride on into the storm.[39]

COLONEL FREMANTLE, the British observer, had spent the early-afternoon hours scrambling about in search of what he called a "commanding position" from which to view the battle. His first thought was the cupola of a church in Gettysburg, but he found getting there, amidst the rival cannonading, to be highly dangerous. He finally determined "to go into the thick of the thing" and join General Longstreet at his vantage point. Riding back through the woods on Seminary Ridge, Fremantle encountered wounded men trailing back from the attack. "The further I got," he noted in his diary, "the greater became the number of the wounded. At last I came to a perfect stream of them flocking through the woods in numbers as great as the crowd in Oxford-street in the middle of the day."

Fremantle found Longstreet perched on a snake-rail fence on the edge of the woods at the Confederate center. With him was Captain Robert Bright of Pickett's staff, who had just delivered Pickett's call for reinforcements to hold the lodgment he expected to seize in the enemy's line. From this perspective Fremantle had his first clear look at the panorama of the grand charge, and he was excited. "I wouldn't have missed this for anything!" he said to Longstreet.

Old Pete sat there calmly and outwardly unperturbed, and Fremantle reported that he gave his reply with a laugh. Surely it was a bitter laugh. "The devil you wouldn't!" Longstreet told him. "I would like to have missed it very much; we've attacked and been repulsed. Look there!"

On second look Fremantle could see in the valley Confederate troops "slowly and sulkily returning towards us in small broken parties. . . ." At this stage of the fighting these were most likely remnants of Brocken-brough's or Joe Davis's wrecked brigades, but Longstreet had already identified them as the outriders of a larger defeat. He told Captain Bright to return to Pickett "and tell him what you have heard me say to Colonel Fremantle." Bright started out, but then Longstreet called him back — he was also to tell Pickett "that Wilcox's brigade is in that peach orchard, and he can order him to his assistance."

There is a clear echo here of Longstreet's admission that on July 2 it was never his intention to press what he viewed as a misguided offensive, had the enemy initially appeared too strong for his divisions that day. As to July 3, Old Pete had argued from the first that Pickett's Charge was misguided. Now, while he could not defy Lee's orders and recall it, he could at least steer additional troops away from a forlorn hope. No doubt he assigned Wilcox's brigade (and Lang's, attached to it) to Pickett primarily to assist him in withdrawing when it came to that. Dick Anderson reported that he had Wright's and Posey's brigades ready to advance on the left, but that Longstreet "directed me to stop the movement, adding that it was useless, and would only involve unnecessary loss. . . ."

So the grand charge would play out, and most likely within a matter of minutes. It would not end, Longstreet wrote bitterly, until "the utmost measure of sacrifice demanded by honor was full. . . ."[40]

However the case may have looked to Longstreet, just then to Generals Kemper, Garnett, and Armistead at the front opportunity appeared to beckon. Unlike the solid wall of fire greeting Pettigrew's charge, Pickett's charge met a Union line that had two large gaps in it.

One of these gaps was right at the Angle itself. Colonel Richard Smith of the 71st Pennsylvania continued today, as he had yesterday, to be overly solicitous of his men. The evening before, on Culp's Hill, he had pulled them out of the battle line lest they be "murdered." Today, when General Webb ordered the 71st forward into the Angle, Smith put Lieutenant Colonel Charles Kochersperger in charge of the eight companies that squeezed into the space between the Angle and Cushing's guns. Smith remained safely to the rear with the other two companies. Then, saying nothing of his intentions to Webb, he cautioned Kochersperger to withdraw should the enemy come too close, especially too close to the regiment's flank at the Angle.

The Confederates promptly came too close. After a volley or two Kochersperger dutifully ordered the 71st Pennsylvania into retreat . . . and opened a gap of some 50 yards in Webb's line. Frank Haskell was an appalled witness: "Great Heaven! . . . There by the group of trees, and the angles of the wall, was breaking from the cover of their works, and without orders or reason, with no hand lifted to check them, was falling back a fear-stricken flock of confusion!"[41]

At about the same time, to the south, beyond the Copse, a second gap abruptly opened in the Federal line. This was at the position of the 59th New York, the rightmost regiment in Norman Hall's brigade. The 59th was in a bad way to begin with. By the time of Gettysburg it had been consolidated into just four companies, and in Thursday's fight it lost (among others) its commander, Lieutenant Colonel Max Thoman. Now, as Kemper's Virginians turned and came right toward it, the 59th suddenly and unaccountably bolted. Captain John H. Smith of the 11th Virginia remembered the moment: In the Yankee battle line directly in front of him he "could see first a few and then more and more and more — and presently to my surprise and delight, the whole line break away in flight."

Andrew Cowan, whose 1st New York Independent had just gone into battery in rear of the 59th New York, was equally surprised. "Our infantry," Cowan wrote, "which was a half dozen yards in front of my guns, lying down, all at once became panic stricken and broke in confusion. The enemy rushed forward with wild cheers. . . ." (The prospect of Cowan's guns blasting away just over their heads may have had something to do with the infantry's panic.) One of Cowan's infuriated gunners smashed a coffee pot down over the head of a fleeing New Yorker.

Calling for double rounds of canister to meet the charge, Captain Cowan was startled to see Henry Hunt at his side. Here was the army's chief of artillery rushing into the fray like some young subaltern. "The display of Secesh Battle flags was splendid and *scary*," Hunt told his wife. Cowan heard him shout, "See 'em! See 'em!" as he emptied his pistol at the oncoming Rebels. Then Hunt's horse was down, pinning him as it fell. Gunners pulled him to safety and found him a mount. "I have escaped as by a miracle," Hunt confessed to his wife, "when it appeared as if there could be no escape."[42]

There was no one in front of the battery now except a few score charg-

Forbes here pictures the charge from the Union perspective, looking west. The copse of trees and the fighting at the Angle are at left center. Forbes drew on his battlefield sketches for the scene. (Library of Congress)

ing Confederates, led by an officer waving his sword and shouting to his men to take the guns. Then Cowan gave the command to fire. Five guns, barrels depressed to give maximum play to the double rounds of canister, went off in one concerted roar. When the smoke cleared the entire Rebel line, and the officer, had simply disappeared. This was the last of Cowan's canister, and his gunners took up the prolonges and dragged the guns to safer ground in the rear. A man in the 7th Michigan wrote home, "I never saw such slaughter. Never saw men mowed so by canister as they was there."

Farther to the south, the two remaining guns of Robert Rogers's Battery B, 1st New York, added their fire to the repulse. One of these guns was manned by 15th Massachusetts volunteers, whose enthusiasm exceeded their knowledge of gunnery. While continuing to jam battlefield debris down the barrel of their piece, they failed to realize that double and triple rounds of canister were still fired with only one charge. The 10-pounder

Parrott rifle finally exploded so violently that it tipped over, crushing one of the substitute gunners. All the while, Hall's regiments elsewhere on the battle line held stubbornly to their places, additional artillery reinforcements arrived, and in the end the gap in Hall's line was not exploited.[43]

The gap at the Angle left by the departed 71st Pennsylvania was a different matter. It was a larger gap, for one thing, and there were a good many more Confederates poised close by to exploit it, and there were fewer Yankee guns to challenge them. The men of Garnett's and Armistead's brigades facing the Angle could focus without distraction solely on the enemy in front of them, for they had cover on both flanks — Kemper's brigade to the south, Fry's and Marshall's brigades, of Pettigrew's command, to the north. Finally, their leadership was inspired and inspiring. Dick Garnett, mounted and clearly visible to his followers, and Lew Armistead, marching resolutely twenty paces ahead of the line, hat on his upraised sword, were generals that men would follow to the death.

Perhaps most important, at their intended point of attack they outnumbered the defenders. The only infantry now in line at the Copse was a single regiment, the 258 men of the 69th Pennsylvania, Webb's Philadelphia Brigade. The only guns in the immediate vicinity were Alonzo Cushing's two 3-inch Ordnance rifles, at the stone fence to the Pennsylvanians' right. The closest supporting infantrymen, also Webb's, were posted 80 yards or so to the rear — the 72nd Pennsylvania, and two companies each of the 71st and 106th Pennsylvania. (The rest of the 71st regiment was farther to the rear, Colonel Smith regarding his fleeting role in the day's fighting as finished.)

The Rebels came on, hurrying now, seeing the gap and just the two guns in the Yankee line. "Onward they came, and it would seem as if no power could hold them in check," said a man in the 69th Pennsylvania. The 69th was solidly Irish, so much so that next to the national colors was displayed the emerald flag of Ireland rather than the usual regimental flag. Colonel Dennis O'Kane had sternly reminded his men that they were defending the soil of their native state, and should any man flinch in his duty, he expected "that the man next to him would kill him on the spot." It was also Colonel O'Kane who urged his men not to fire until they could see "the whites of their eyes."

His men obliged him. According to Corporal John Buckley, the Rebels were barely 50 yards away when the 69th opened fire. "The slaughter was terrible," said Buckley, a slaughter immediately multiplied by the spare rifles the Irishmen had gleaned from yesterday's battlefield. Major Charles Peyton of the 19th Virginia wrote that his command "recoiled under the terrific fire that poured into our ranks. . . ."

The Confederates' return fire, by contrast, was diluted by the growing disorder of their charge. Rather than advancing in line, where everyone had a clear shot, now they were bunched up many ranks deep, sharply limiting the number who could return fire. Still they drove on toward the wall through the coiling smoke and the crashing volleys, stumbling over the bodies of their dead and wounded.

By now, however, James Kemper's brigade, on Pickett's flank, was in ruins, torn to pieces first by artillery and then by the successive musketry of three and a half brigades of Yankee infantry. Half its survivors were facing south, trying to stem the deadly flanking fire from Stannard's Vermonters. The rest had pushed on toward Cemetery Ridge, but after their bloody repulse in front of Cowan's battery there was hardly any strength left in their efforts. Then General Kemper was down, knocked off his horse by a bullet that ranged through his body and lodged near his spine.

"I know that I was then near enough to the enemy's line," Kemper recalled, "to observe the features and expressions on the faces of the men in front of me, and I thought I observed and could identify the soldier who shot me." He lay there unable to move as the battle surged on around him.[44]

The cascade of enemy fire driving in against their right, and the inviting gap in the Federal line near the Angle, caused Garnett and Armistead to slide their brigades leftward, slanting across the 69th Pennsylvania's front and aiming toward Cushing's guns. As the battle approached its climax, Garnett and Armistead had between them perhaps 2,500 to 3,000 men remaining under command.

The moment the Rebels were within canister range, Cushing had begun working his two guns steadily. Private Anthony McDermott of the 69th Pennsylvania watched him. Despite his severe wounds, Cushing stood at the stone fence next to his guns, glass in hand, gauging the fall of his shot. "He would shout back to his men to elevate or depress their pieces so many degrees," McDermott wrote; ". . . his last command, that we heard was, 'that's excellent, keep that range.'" Then Cushing was felled, killed instantly by a bullet to the head.

Gunners Frederick Fuger and Christopher Smith loaded their last rounds of canister and ducked behind the stone fence and waited. When the Rebels were 20 yards away, Fuger yelled, "Let 'em have it!" and they jerked the lanyards. By Smith's account, two 50-foot-wide swaths were cut in the Rebel ranks. The battery crewmen raced for the rear.[45]

General Armistead, somehow spared in this bloody maelstrom, became the literal spearhead of the attack, rushing forward right to the wall and the abandoned guns. Lieutenant Colonel Rawley Martin, 53rd Virginia, came up with him. "Colonel, we can't stay here," Armistead said. "Then we'll go forward!" Martin said. With that Armistead turned to the men who had followed him this far and called out, "Come forward, Virginians! Come on, boys, we must give them the cold steel! Who will follow me?"

Over the wall they went. There were perhaps a hundred of them crowding resolutely behind Armistead and the 53rd Virginia's flag bearer — the fourth man to carry the regimental flag in those few minutes. Their rush forward impelled the command of the 69th Pennsylvania to order the three rightmost companies to swing back 90 degrees to counter the charge. Two companies did so, but the captain of the third was killed before he could give the order and nearly all his men were overrun and captured. Others of Armistead's men seized Cushing's abandoned guns

Alfred Waud portrayed the struggle for Cushing's Federal battery at the Angle, the high-water mark of Pickett's Charge. Waud's drawing was published in *Harper's Weekly* on August 8. (Library of Congress)

and swung one of them around to face the Yankees. But there was no ammunition for them to fire, and they were left with nothing more than a symbolic gesture.

Indeed, Armistead's captures, of these men and these guns, would come to symbolize the high-water mark of Pickett's Charge. Armistead and his little band could advance no farther. To their right, the stubborn Irishmen of the 69th Pennsylvania stood fast, so close in places that the fighting was hand-to-hand — clubbed muskets and fists and stabbing thrusts. To their front, but farther away, was the battle line of the 72nd Pennsylvania, a regiment that in its own way proved to be just as stubborn as the 69th.

General Webb was mortified by the 71st Pennsylvania's abrupt retreat from the wall. "When my men fell back," he wrote his wife, "I almost wished to get killed, I was almost disgraced. . . ." He rushed back to the 72nd Pennsylvania in the second line and called on it to go forward to fill the gap. The 72nd was one of those 1861 independent-minded regiments that had adopted the distinctive if impractical Zouave uniform, and almost two years later some of the men still wore the colorful jackets and white leggings. They were veterans with a good fighting record, and what this young general was yelling at them, with many gestures and much sword-waving, did not make much sense to them.

The 72nd had already shifted by the right flank so that it was directly opposite the Angle. With it were the two companies each of the 106th and 71st Pennsylvania. The men were nicely aligned there, some 80 or 90 yards from the enemy, with a clear shot at an easy range for everyone, and they could see no reason to endanger themselves any further by getting closer. What they were required to do, they could do best right where they were. Being new to the command, Webb was probably not recognized by most men in the ranks, but that could hardly be said of the officers; those who heard him in the clamor simply ignored him. Webb even tried to wrest the flag away from the color bearer to lead the advance himself, but the man would not give it up. Finally Webb stalked away and gave his attention to the 69th regiment at the wall. He would write home that a Rebel general he later learned was Armistead "came over my fence and passed me with four of his men."

Fired on now from front as well as flank, the Confederates' toehold beyond the wall quickly collapsed. Three bullets — fired, it was noted, from the 72nd Pennsylvania's line — severely wounded General Armistead. He fell close by one of Cushing's guns, and close to the spot where Cushing had fallen earlier. What remained of the general's little band was shot down or captured or retreated back over the wall. Their sortie had lasted perhaps ten minutes.[46]

The battle raged on now right at the wall, from the Angle to the Copse — Pickett's men who had reached that far unable to go farther but holding there stubbornly; Webb's men standing their ground on the other side of the wall with equal stubbornness; both sides firing point-blank at each other as fast as they could load. "The opposing lines were standing as if rooted, dealing death into each other," wrote a Northern regimental historian. "There they stood and would not move." Joseph McKeever of the 69th Pennsylvania was amazed: "How they fired without killing all our men I do not know. We thought we were all gone." The 69th's Colonel O'Kane went down with a mortal wound, and General Webb was nicked in the leg. On the Confederate side, Captain John H. Smith of the 11th Virginia remembered looking back and expecting to see the rest of

General Lee's army marching up to take over the fight. But he "could see nothing but dead and wounded men and horses on the field behind us. . . . It was a grievous disappointment."

Charles Wainwright, the First Corps artillerist, recorded in his diary the next day a conversation with General Webb about this critical moment in the battle. "Webb told me," Wainwright wrote, "that when the enemy reached the wall all his lines began to shake, and for a moment he thought they were gone; but most of the rebs stopped at the wall. . . . That halt at the wall was the ruin of the enemy, as such halts almost always are; yet so natural is it for men to seek cover that it is almost impossible to get them to pass it under such circumstances."

There was an additional factor contributing to the stalemate, had Webb known it — the destruction of the Rebel high command. Kemper was already down, badly wounded. Armistead's wounds would prove to be mortal. Now Dick Garnett's thus far miraculous survival came to an end. Still mounted, still at the head of his troops, he rode to within 20 yards of the wall. "Just as the General turned his horse's head slightly to the left," wrote Garnett's courier, "he was struck in the head by a rifle or musket ball and fell dead from his horse. . . ."[47]

What would finally tip the balance at the Angle was the arrival of reinforcing Union troops. First on the scene was the second line of Norman Hall's brigade, immediately to the south. Colonel Arthur Devereux, 19th Massachusetts, explained that he had been "watching the course of events unable to make use of my own men up to the time when I saw that Webb could not sustain the shock with his front line." Devereux already had Winfield Hancock's blessing to join the fight "God damned quick," so he did not hesitate. Along with Hall's other second-line regiment, the 42nd New York, the 19th Massachusetts hurried at a slanting run toward the Copse and the struggle along the stone fence.

At the same time, Lieutenant Frank Haskell of General Gibbon's staff was casting about for help for the embattled Webb. Haskell had been sent back to headquarters to report the attack, and on his return he could find neither Gibbon nor Hancock, both now wounded, so he took it upon himself to act. He rode first to Norman Hall, directing the three regiments of his brigade in the front line. Hall asked him how the battle was going. "Well, but Webb is hotly pressed, and must have support or he will be overpowered," Haskell replied. "Can you assist him?" Hall said he would. "You cannot be too quick," Haskell told him.

Hall could safely shift his troops to the right because by now Pickett's dwindling attack was focused entirely on the 100 or so yards between the

Angle and the Copse. With Hall supervising the movement, it was carried out (as Haskell put it) "in reasonable time, and in order that is serviceable, if not regular. . . ." Haskell rode on to Harrow's brigade, and soon those troops too were heading for the fighting at the double-quick. Haskell could now see the Rebel front beginning to crumble and men turning toward the rear, and he shouted encouragement to the reinforcing troops: "See the *'chivalry.'* See the gray-backs run!"

Lieutenant Haskell's characterization of the march order of these reinforcements as "serviceable" was perhaps overly generous. According to Colonel Francis Heath of the 19th Maine, Harrow's brigade, "it was impossible to get them in any order. Everyone wanted to be first there and we went up more like a mob than a disciplined force." The move took on the shape of a series of arrowheads, men crowding behind gesturing officers and color bearers.

These Yankees came up to the battle line very much like Garnett's and Armistead's Rebels came rushing in toward the wall from the west a few minutes before — all jammed together, many ranks deep, with only the few men at the head of the advance able to get a clear shot. It was, said one of Webb's staff, more a melee than a line of battle. Men pushed forward to fire, then fell back to reload. Others dodged around, looking for any opening to shoot. Major Edmund Rice of the 19th Massachusetts would remember rifles "exploding all around, flashing their fire almost in one's face and so close to the head as to make the ears ring." Directly in front of Rice was an incongruous tableau: one Rebel kneeling and aiming his rifle right at him, a second man lying on his back "coolly ramming home a cartridge," and a third on his knees nearby waving a white cloth in surrender. Frustrated Yankees at the rear of the melee threw rocks at the enemy.[48]

However unmilitary and chaotic it might look, the Yankee line now forming was rock-solid and unbreakable. Just to the north, Alexander Hays crushed out the last struggling efforts of Pettigrew's and Trimble's brigades. Isaac Trimble had suffered a severe leg wound but remained on the field, and when his aide Charles Grogan reported that the men of Trimble's two brigades were starting to fall back and asked if he should try to rally them, Trimble told him no. "Charlie, the best these brave fellows can do is to get out of this." Later, turning his command over to Jim Lane, Trimble added a footnote: "He also directs me to say," Grogan told Lane, "that if the troops he had the honor to command today for the first time, couldn't take that position, all hell can't take it."

It was now plain that Pickett's men could not take the position either.

Webb's brigade, especially the 69th Pennsylvania, had stymied them, and then the rest of the Second Corps stormed in to seal the bargain. "The rows of dead after the battle I found to be within 15 and 20 feet apart, as near hand to hand fighting as I ever care to see," wrote Captain Henry Abbott, 20th Massachusetts. "The rebels behaved with as much pluck as any men in the world could; they stood there, against the fence, until they were nearly all shot down."[49]

GENERAL CARL SCHURZ was watching from Cemetery Hill: "At last, looking again at the field which had been traversed by the splendid host of assailants, we saw, first, little dribblets, then larger numbers, and finally huge swarms of men in utter disorder hurrying back the way they had come, and then, soon after, in hot pursuit, clouds of blue-coated skirmishers from our front rushing in from both sides, firing and capturing prisoners." Pickett's Charge was collapsing, but there was one scene in the drama still to play out.

Pickett's call to Cadmus Wilcox and David Lang, on the Confederate right, had been no more specific than to come to his support. Longstreet's authorization merely mentioned "assistance." By the time Wilcox's Alabamians and Lang's Floridians assembled and started forward, there was no knowing even where Pickett might be in that great welter of smoke and gunfire. No one from Pickett came to serve as guide. Therefore Wilcox, with Lang on his left, some 1,600 men all told, simply advanced straight ahead.

General Wilcox had spoken earlier of his misgivings about the operation, recalling yesterday's trials, and his officers shared his view. Colonel Hilary Herbert of the 8th Alabama would write that when they looked at the prospect ahead, "every private at once saw the madness of the attempt." As the two brigades passed his batteries, Porter Alexander remembered "feeling a great pity for the useless loss of life they were incurring, for there was nothing left for them to support."[50]

The Yankee gunners spotted the new formation the moment it appeared. Starting with Rittenhouse's battery on Little Round Top, progressing through Freeman McGilvery's array, finally engaging batteries just up from the artillery reserve, they delivered a blistering fire that stopped the Confederates in their tracks. Within minutes, fifty-nine guns had opened on Wilcox and Lang, at first with shell and case shot, then with canister. In addition, Colonel Wheelock Veazey of the 16th Vermont deftly maneuvered his regiment to take the Rebels under an oblique fire. "To remain in this position, unsupported by either infantry or artillery, with infantry on both flanks and in front and artillery playing upon us with grape and canister, was certain annihilation" was how Colonel Lang appraised the situation. He ordered his Floridians to seek cover in some wooded ground along Plum Run and prepare to retreat.

Wilcox's brigade, directly fronting McGilvery's guns, was engulfed by the artillery fire. "I could hear their missiles," wrote the 8th Alabama's Colonel Herbert, "some of them grape shot, crashing through the bones of my men 'like hail-stones breaking through glass.'" Wilcox raced back to the artillery line to demand supporting fire, only to be told there was no long-range ammunition. With that, Wilcox reached the same conclusion as had Lang: "knowing that my small force could do nothing save to make a useless sacrifice of themselves, I ordered them back."

Most of his Alabamians did make it back, although having to run a bloody gauntlet of artillery fire. The retreat of the Floridians was a fiasco. There were fewer than 450 of them in the three small regiments, and their officers lost touch when the men scattered for cover in the woods. Before Lang's retreat order could reach them all, the 16th Vermont was on them. The Vermonters scooped up prisoners by the score, mostly from the 5th and 2nd Florida, which regiment also lost its flag. One of Lang's officers wrote home that the Florida brigade "was small before the fight, it is *very* much smaller now."

The price tag on this misguided assault came to some 360 dead, wounded, and captured. It commenced too late to affect the outcome of the main assault, and was carried out with no guidance from the command it was supposed to assist. One of Garnett's Virginians would later claim that Wilcox and Lang had "diverted the attention of the enemy from the stragglers of Pickett's division, and enabled a considerable number of them to escape." That 360 Virginians were thereby saved, to at least balance the account, seems doubtful.[51]

In Pickett's and Pettigrew's and Trimble's commands no one issued a general order to retreat, primarily because hardly anyone was left in command. In Pickett's division Garnett had been killed, Armistead left for dead at the Angle, and the wounded Kemper very nearly captured — Federals were carrying him away when his men rescued him at the last moment. All but two of Pickett's fifteen regimental commanders were dead or wounded. In Pettigrew's four brigades, Marshall was dead, Fry wounded, and Davis and Brockenbrough had already retreated. Pettigrew was wounded slightly, Trimble seriously. George Pickett had taken a central location just behind the lines on the Codori farm, but events had spun swiftly out of his control and well beyond his reach. The men in the ranks still at the front and still fighting simply realized the battle had turned against them and it was time, and past time, for them to go. Isaac Trimble put the matter succinctly in his diary: "here the men broke down from exhaustion & the fatal fire & went no further but walked sullenly back to their entrenchments."

Captain John H. Smith, 11th Virginia, Kemper's brigade, was bandaging his wounded leg when he saw the Yankees approaching and agreed with his comrade that it was "time to get away from here." The first stage of their retreat was the most dangerous, for they were still well within musketry range. "We ran out of range," Smith wrote, "shot after shot falling around us until we got over the Emmittsburg road toward our lines. . . . No organized body of troops did I meet in going back." Other men gauged the risk of retreating through this raging storm of musketry and artillery fire and decided that surrender was their best option to live. On the northern flank the 8th Ohio collected prisoners in greater numbers than its own. The Vermonters on the southern flank did almost as well.

Over much of the course of the retreat, Pickett's troops kept reasonably good order, especially at first when under fire; pride would not let them run. On reaching Seminary Ridge, officers tried to rally them and re-form the lines — there was concern about a Yankee counterattack — but a distraught General Pickett told his men to keep going, back to yesterday's bivouac behind the ridge.

This seemed to act as a release for all the pent-up emotions of the past hour. At a narrow crossing of Willoughby Run, wrote Henry Owen of the 18th Virginia, "the fugitives, without distinction of rank, officers and privates side by side, pushed, poured and rushed in a continuous stream, throwing away guns, blankets, and haversacks as they hurried on in confusion toward the rear." Before long there was another attempt to restore order, but again Pickett intervened. "Don't stop any of my men!" he cried. "Tell them to come to the camp we occupied last night." As he said this he was "weeping bitterly," and then he rode on alone toward the rear. That evening cartographer Jed Hotchkiss noted in his diary that he had encountered Pickett's division "scattered all along the road; no officers and all protesting that they had been completely cut up."[52]

On Cemetery Ridge the infantry reinforcements in their thousands that Meade had called for — from the First, Sixth, and Twelfth corps — were filing into place behind the front, but already the crisis was past. When one of Alexander Hays's aides announced that help was on the way, the general pointed to the swarms of retreating Rebels and said,

Edwin Forbes's sketch of a long column of Confederate prisoners from Pickett's Charge being escorted to the rear along the Baltimore Pike is labeled by the artist "July 3rd 5 P.M." (Library of Congress)

"Damn the reinforcements! Look there!" Hays was exuberant. He seized a captured flag and had two of his staff do the same, and the three of them rode slowly past their cheering men dragging the flags of rebellion in the "dust and blood of the battlefield."

General Meade reached the crest of the ridge too late to witness the final turn of events. Encountering Frank Haskell of Gibbon's staff, he asked, "How is it going here?"

"I believe, General, the enemy's attack is repulsed," Haskell said.

With that, Haskell wrote, a look of "gratified surprise" crossed Meade's face, and he exclaimed, "What! Is the assault entirely repulsed?"

"It is, Sir," said Haskell. For a moment Meade seemed about to take off his hat "as if to hurrah," but checked himself and said simply, "Thank God!" Captain George Meade, the general's son and aide, did take off his cap and hurrah. Then Meade and a growing entourage of officers rode right along the full length of the line of battle, the troops raising a continuous volley of cheers for their commanding general.[53]

Over on Seminary Ridge, Robert E. Lee heard this ovation for his opposite number, and asked a staff man to ride forward to "see what that cheering means." He was told it was some Union general riding the lines. "I can understand what they have to cheer for," said Lee, "but I thought it might be our people."

Colonel Fremantle now joined the commanding general. "If Longstreet's conduct was admirable," the Englishman entered in his diary, "that of General Lee was perfectly sublime. He was engaged in rallying and in encouraging the broken troops, and was riding about a little in front of the wood, quite alone. . . ." Lee turned to Fremantle and said, "This has been a sad day for us, Colonel — a sad day; but we can't expect always to gain victories."

Soon afterward, meeting a bitter Cadmus Wilcox, Lee took him by the hand and told him, "Never mind, General, all this has been my fault — it is I that have lost this fight, and you must help me out of it in the best way you can."[54]

14   *A Long Road Back*

A PENNSYLVANIA TROOPER named Charles Gardner, at his posting on the Low Dutch Road east of Cemetery Ridge, would always remember the surprise and shock of the Confederate bombardment that preceded Pickett's Charge. "The very ground shook and trembled," he wrote, "and the smoke of the guns rolled out of the valley as tho there were thousands of acres of timber on fire." It was this barrage that acted as a catalyst on the cavalry battle royal that had been smoldering and crackling since before noon.[1]

At about 11:00 A.M. Jeb Stuart had fired off his four-round artillery salvo to inform General Lee that he was behind the Yankee army. This of course also announced his presence to the Yankee army. Stuart's objective — "pursuant to instructions from the commanding general" — was apparently to push aside any cavalry screen he found and reach the Baltimore Pike and the Federals' vulnerable rear. He occupied the high ground of Cress Ridge some three miles southeast of Gettysburg, and set out the 34th Virginia battalion as a dismounted skirmish line.

Stuart had the three brigades — under Wade Hampton, Fitz Lee, and John Chambliss — that had ridden with him on their nine-day odyssey around the Army of the Potomac. By all accounts all three were much diminished in strength and perhaps even in spirit. The 2nd North Carolina, of Chambliss's brigade, was down to 35 men from 145. The 9th Virginia of the same brigade, according to one of its officers, "was not more than one hundred strong, and the brigade could have hardly exceeded three hundred." One of Chambliss's troopers wrote that "No man can stand more, and I never wish to be called on to stand this much again. I had one horse killed under me and rode three others down." The men were bone-weary and so were their horses, and neither were primed for a battle royal.

Possibly Chambliss's command was more cut down than either Hampton's or Fitz Lee's, yet of the 4,800 men supposed to be in the three brigades, it is likely that only 3,000 or fewer were engaged on July 3. Attached to Stuart for the day was the brigade of Albert Jenkins, which thus far in the campaign had mostly foraged for Dick Ewell's corps. Jenkins had been wounded on July 2, and Colonel Milton Ferguson now commanded. Some 430 of his men would see action this day.[2]

The Federals would bring some 3,250 troopers to the contest, their numbers in two brigades being about the same as in Stuart's attenuated four. Guarding this sector of the battlefield was the cavalry division of David Gregg. Gregg had been warned of Stuart's approach, and he led John McIntosh's brigade to a blocking position astride the Hanover Road that ran southeasterly out of Gettysburg. Already posted at the intersection of the Hanover and Low Dutch roads — which, as it happened, was Stuart's target — was the brigade of George Armstrong Custer. Custer was then on loan to Gregg from Judson Kilpatrick's division, but Gregg brought with him cavalry chief Pleasonton's order for Custer's return.

Custer greeted him, Gregg recalled, and "expressed the opinion that I soon would have a big fight on my hands" — the enemy was squarely in front of them in great force. Gregg decided that General Pleasonton, passing the day at army headquarters, was quite out of touch with what was happening in the field, and he had no qualms about ignoring his orders. He told Custer he would welcome the assistance of his brigade. "If you will give me an order to remain," said Custer, "I will only be too happy to do it." The matter was quickly arranged, and with Custer's and McIntosh's brigades in hand David Gregg prepared to do battle.

Custer had already set out his own skirmish line and his horse artillery was exchanging shots with the Confederate gunners. Twenty-three-year-old George Custer, West Point '61, youngest brigadier in the Potomac army, was dressed for battle in a sailor's blouse with silver stars on its wide collar points, red cravat, black velveteen hussar's jacket spangled with gold braid, olive corduroy pants, gleaming jackboots, and wide-brimmed felt hat. It was said he looked "like a circus rider gone mad." Yet for all the gaudy trappings, George Custer always led his Michigan troopers by example and always from out front.[3]

Gregg set about raising the stakes by reinforcing Custer's skirmish line and challenging the Rebels to an artillery duel. His gunners soon had the best of it. "The Federal Artillery seemed very effective," admitted one of Stuart's officers, "while ours seemed to be of little service." Yankee Alanson Randol, commanding a battery of horse artillery, would write dismissively, "As a rule their Horse Art'y was so badly handled in battle that we Art'y officers paid but little attention to it."

Stuart's plan had been to fix the Federals in place with aggressive dismounted skirmishers and then from the concealment of Cress Ridge swing around their left flank. But the Federal skirmishers pushed back so hard they disrupted his plan, so Stuart determined instead to launch a mounted charge to shake the Yankees loose. He selected his old command, the 1st Virginia cavalry, and took General Lee's 1 o'clock cannonade as the signal to open his own assault.

The Virginia troopers came pelting through the farmstead of John Rummel, sending the Yankee skirmishers scattering for their horses. Gregg countered by directing Custer to send in the 7th Michigan. Custer himself took the lead, crying out, "Come on, you Wolverines!" The two regiments collided along one of farmer Rummel's fence lines. An astonished Union skirmisher watched the 7th Michigan, "apparently without any attempt to change direction, dash itself upon a high staked and railed fence, squadron after squadron breaking upon the struggling mass in front, like the waves of the sea upon a rocky shore, until all were mixed in one confused and tangled mass." Troopers of both sides, many dismounted or unhorsed by the collision, struggled at point-blank range with carbines, pistols, and sabers. Custer's horse was hit and he took another from one of his men. Victor Comte on the skirmish line saw him "plunge his saber into the belly of a rebel who was trying to kill him. You can guess how bravely soldiers fight for such a general."

Enough Yankees managed to break down the fence and spur through to send the Virginians into retreat. Now Stuart countered. Elements from all three of his brigades, hastily thrown into the spreading fight, were enough to drive back the Yankee pursuit. Both sides were now back about where they began, and there was a pause. This was the first real fight for Lieutenant John Clark, 7th Michigan, and he had expressed himself curious "what it was to charge upon the enemy." Now he knew. "I had my curiosity fully gratified & have not harkened for a fight since. . . ."[4]

"Soon there appeared emerging from the woods a large force advancing in fine style," David Gregg wrote. "It was evident that a grand charge was intended." This proved to be the better part of Wade Hampton's brigade, and it promised to be Stuart's greatest effort yet to gain a breakthrough. According to a Union officer, these enemy squadrons advanced as if on review, and "the spectacle called forth a murmur of admiration." Their gait went from walk to trot to gallop. Hampton's officers could be heard calling out, "Keep to your sabers, men, keep to your sabers!"

The Federal horse batteries opened a sharp fire of shell and then canister, tearing gaps in the advance, but the Rebels closed swiftly before very many rounds could be fired. Confronting the attackers head-on was the 1st Michigan — with Custer riding alongside Colonel Charles Town in the lead. Buglers sounded the charge, and again Custer shouted, "Come on, you Wolverines!" From his posting on the flank Pennsylvania trooper William Miller was watching: "As the two columns approached each other the pace of each increased, when suddenly a crash, like the falling of timber, betokened the crisis. So sudden and violent was the collision that many of the horses were turned end over end and crushed their riders beneath them."

The tangle evolved into a wild melee of swinging sabers and blazing pistols and carbines, wreathed in smoke and clouds of dust. John McIntosh sent in every man he could find against the right flank of the attackers, leading them himself. At the same time, the 3rd Pennsylvania assailed their left. The Pennsylvanians cut right through the enemy column, driving off its trailing squadrons, then reversed course and repeated the maneuver. Custer's horse went down, but he soon found a riderless mount and continued the fight. Wade Hampton too plunged into the struggle, and suffered a bad saber wound. Sergeant William Harrison, the 13th Virginia's color bearer, employed his flagstaff as a lance to spear two Yankees and save the colors.

Finally the failing Southern troopers, on their failing horses, assailed it must have seemed from every direction, began to break off and turn back. The Yankees were too shattered themselves to mount a serious pursuit. Having played his last card, Stuart broke off the action.

In this cavalry battle royal the Federals would record a loss of 254 men, 219 of them in Custer's Michigan brigade. The Confederates' loss came to 181. The fighting had lasted perhaps forty minutes. Tactically it was a draw, but certainly Stuart, by being halted in all his ambitions for the day, was the loser. The victor, David Gregg, summed it up: "General Stuart had in view the accomplishment of certain purposes. . . . His was to do, ours to prevent. Could he have reached the rear of our army . . . disastrous consequences might have resulted."[5]

If there was purpose to Stuart's attack, there was no purpose whatever to the ill-conceived attack launched shortly afterward by Yankee cavalryman Judson Kilpatrick at the southern end of the battlefield.

Cavalry chief Pleasonton, without bothering to visit the field, had issued a vague directive to Kilpatrick to press the enemy on the left "and to strike at the first opportunity." What was to be gained by this exercise was not explained. The enemy here was not cavalry but the infantrymen of Hood's division, holding the position they had gained in front of Round Top on July 2. Looking back on what happened that July 3 afternoon, one of Hood's Texans wrote that any infantry "who will stand their ground and fight can always defeat cavalry without any trouble. . . . It was simply a picnic to fight cavalry under such conditions."

Evander Law, commanding in place of the wounded Hood, had posted his four brigades in the hard-won ground between the Emmitsburg Road and Round Top. At first Law had just the 1st Texas facing to the south when Kilpatrick appeared there at midday, but he soon reinforced the Texans with infantry and artillery. For the moment Kilpatrick had only Elon Farnsworth's brigade, and he awaited impatiently the arrival of Wesley Merritt's brigade from Emmitsburg. By the time Merritt took his place in the line, word had reached Kilpatrick of the repulse of Pickett's Charge, and that made him doubly eager to contribute something to the day's victory.

With his usual faint grasp of cavalry tactics, Kilpatrick put in his attacks piecemeal. Merritt went in first, west of the Emmitsburg Road. His 6th Pennsylvania troopers fought dismounted, and Tige Anderson's Georgians, assisted by Hart's South Carolina battery, drove them off with almost contemptuous ease.

Kilpatrick's orders to Elon Farnsworth left the young brigadier incredulous. Not only was he being told to launch a mounted charge against an obviously substantial force of infantry, backed by artillery, but the broken terrain he would have to cross was marked by stone walls and fences and woodlots. It was ground utterly unsuited to cavalry. Indeed, the day before, Confederate infantry had great difficulty maintaining order crossing it. Farnsworth protested the order, apparently with some heat, but Kilpatrick was adamant. "My God, Hammond," Farnsworth said to one of his officers, "Kil is going to have a cavalry charge. It is too awful to think of. . . ."

The first in Farnsworth's brigade to make its attack was the 1st West Virginia. "They rode down our skirmishers and charged us," wrote Thomas McCarty, 1st Texas; "they went through us cutting right and left, the firing for a few minutes was front, rear, and towards the flanks. In a few minutes, great numbers of riderless horses were galloping about, & others with riders were trying to surrender. . . ." Another Texan claimed that he killed a Yankee captain and wounded a lieutenant: "They were both trying to rally their men, who were in the greatest confusion."[6]

Then it was the turn of the 1st Vermont. To broaden the attack Farnsworth formed up the regiment in three battalions, one of which he led himself. They succeeded in breaking through the Texans' skirmish line, but then found themselves fired at from every side. The Vermont troopers dodged and veered and jumped walls and fences, firing and slashing with their sabers, but they could gain no respite from the incessant fire. "All of a sudden the Rebs in our front appeared by the thousands," so it appeared to one stunned Yankee. "They seemed to come out of the ground like bees and they gave us such a rattling fire we all gave way and retreated. . . ."

"Cavalry, boys, cavalry!" shouted an Alabamian. "This is no fight, only a frolic! Give it to them!" They did just that. There seemed to be a cavalryman target everywhere they looked. "Our boys really enjoyed that part of the battle," Turner Vaughan of the 4th Alabama remarked in his diary. At one point, a Rebel battle line neatly about-faced to fire at a band of Vermonters racing past behind them. In due course the troopers who survived managed to circle back to reach Union lines. Elon Farnsworth's little party had dwindled to perhaps ten men as he dashed this way and that until finally he was cornered. Ignoring calls to surrender, he was hit with five bullets and knocked off his horse. He was dead in moments.

"Why in hell and damnation don't you move those troops out," a now frantic Kilpatrick screamed at the last of Farnsworth's regiments, the 18th Pennsylvania. The Pennsylvanians dutifully went forward and were stopped in their tracks. With that, at last, there were no more troopers for Kill-Cavalry Kilpatrick to hurl into the battle.[7]

AS THE TIDE of Pickett's Charge receded, an ambulance arrived to carry off the wounded Winfield Hancock. When they were out of range of the enemy's parting shots, Hancock ordered the driver to stop so he could dictate a message to General Meade. "I repulsed a tremendous attack," he began, and went on to describe his actions in the fight and his arrangements for restoring the lines. As to what should be done next, Hancock was assertive: "I have never seen a more formidable attack, and if the Sixth and Fifth Corps have pressed up, the enemy will be destroyed."

Thoughts of an immediate counterattack — a classic ploy among military theorists — were already on Meade's mind. He soon recognized, however, that the Sixth and Fifth corps were not "pressed up" to launch an attack, nor could they be before dark. In Meade's commitment to the defensive on Day Three, he had allowed no provision for an offensive — or a counteroffensive. No substantial force was massed and ready to advance. Sedgwick's Sixth Corps, largest in the army, unengaged on the first two days, was scattered from one end of the battlefield to the other to patch holes from the earlier Confederate attacks. Sykes's Fifth Corps, spread along the army's left, had seen two of its three divisions severely battered on Day Two and was hardly prepared to spearhead an assault. Skirmishers were sent out "to feel the enemy," but, said Meade, events conspired to make it "so late in the evening as to induce me to abandon the assault which I had contemplated."

Beyond this reality was a question of where to aim a counterattack. On the left were McLaws's and Hood's (Law's) divisions of Longstreet's corps — which a reconnaissance by the Fifth Corps through the Wheatfield presently discovered were ready to fight. On the right were Ewell's corps and half of Hill's. The center of the Confederate line, whence the attack had come, was therefore the obvious target. It so happened, because an anguished General Pickett had taken his wrecked division far to the rear, the center just then was largely empty of infantry. This caused Lee and Longstreet considerable concern, but of course the Federals knew nothing of that. All they could detect from Cemetery Ridge was the menacing array of artillery, in an arc left and right as far as the eye could see. Of course the Federals knew nothing of the dearth of long-range ammunition for these guns. What they did know was the damage canister (of which there was a plentiful supply) would do to their charging men.

To be sure, had George Meade possessed the unerring prescience to know beyond any doubt that Lee would attack his center on July 3; and had he therefore massed the entire Sixth Corps under Sedgwick just behind Cemetery Ridge; and had he sent Sedgwick rushing forward right on the heels of Pickett's and Pettigrew's and Trimble's retreating troops; and had such doughty fighters as James Longstreet and A. P. Hill been too stunned to react — perhaps then Lee's army might have been split asunder. Yet neither Meade nor his generals would or could have advocated such a gamble. (When Hancock later said, "I think that our lines should have advanced immediately, and I believe we should have won a great victory," he conveniently forgot his July 2 vote for the army to stand on the defensive.) The fact of the matter was that Meade sensed Lee would welcome a counterattack, and he refused to oblige him. "I knew he was in a strong position, awaiting my attack," Meade told General William F. Smith on July 5, "which I declined to make, in consequence of the bad example he had set. . . ."[8]

Dusk brought a sense of great relief, wrote Colonel Charles Wainwright, First Corps artillery chief. "Not a certainty that the fight was done, or even that Lee might not try it again tonight or tomorrow, but a feeling that he had done his worst and failed." The task now on both sides of the field was to pick up the pieces from the day's fighting, to restore the battle lines and count the living and the dead and care for the wounded and bring up rations and ammunition, to generally try to get the two armies functioning and ready for whatever might come next. The most immediate problem was the wounded. That evening and through the night and into the next day the already overburdened field hospitals were swamped with casualties.

The first necessity was the exercise of what is now called triage — separating those who might be saved from those who could not be saved. The latter would be set off to the side somewhere in little groups rather like leper colonies, to die as peacefully as they might. These were the severely gut-shot or men with what looked to be fatal head wounds.

"The first sight that met our eyes," wrote a young Quaker woman who came to Gettysburg to help, "was a collection of semi-conscious but still living forms, all of whom had been shot through the head, and were considered hopeless. They were laid there to die and I hoped that they were indeed too near death to have consciousness. Yet many a groan came from them, and their limbs tossed and twitched." When the rush was past, a conscientious surgeon might inspect these moribund groups to see if perhaps a mistake had been made and one or another might still be saved, but that was a rare discovery. Mostly the original diagnosis was confirmed.

The stretcher cases — and the officers — were lined up and treated before the walking wounded. "Poor fellows lying wounded in every conceivable place and little or no attention paid them," a medical attendant with a North Carolina regiment wrote his father the night of July 3. "The doctors dont examine unless amputation is necessary or it is extraordinarily dangerous. In fact they come in so fast it is necessary." The walking wounded would wait patiently in their lines for their turn with the surgeons. Many waited through the night and into the next day.

With every barn and farmhouse and stable already filled with wounded from the first two days of fighting, this new flood of patients generally remained in the open. That evening there was a hard rain. The busy surgeons at their lamp-lit amputation tables had a canvas rigged overhead for shelter, but everyone else, the treated and the untreated alike, was drenched. Frank Haskell looked in at a Second Corps hospital that evening. "The Surgeons with coats off and sleeves rolled up . . . are about their work," he wrote; "and their faces and clothes are spattered with blood; and though they look weary and tired, their work goes systematically and steadily on — how much and how long they have worked, the piles of legs, arms, feet, hands, fingers . . . partially tell."[9]

The stricken Lewis Armistead was picked up by the Federals and borne to the rear. Captain Henry Bingham of Hancock's staff happened on the stretcher party and noticed Armistead's marks of rank and learned his identity. Bingham said he was on General Hancock's staff and could he do anything. Armistead asked if that was Winfield Scott Hancock. He and Hancock had been close friends in the old 6th Infantry in California before the war, and as Bingham remembered it, Armistead asked him to say to Hancock that he had done him "an injury which I shall regret" — he might have said "repent," Bingham thought — "the longest day I live." This would later be distorted into Armistead expressing regret "that he had been engaged in an unholy cause." It is far more likely that he merely regretted having to fight against his old friend and comrade. Whatever Armistead said, the longest day he lived was his last one; he died in a Union hospital on the morning of July 5.

Somehow Dick Garnett's body was never identified, and he was buried as an unknown with his men on the field. Birkett Fry, wounded leading one of Pettigrew's brigades, was left on the field for the Federals to capture. General Trimble's leg wound was serious enough to require amputation, and he had to be left behind for the Federals to care for. The same fate befell James Kemper. Of the leaders of Pickett's Charge, then, Garnett, Armistead, and Marshall were dead; Pettigrew and Lowrance wounded; and Trimble, Kemper, and Fry wounded and captured.[10]

The Federal provost marshals were flooded with prisoners. When General Meade rode up to Cemetery Ridge just after the repulse, he encountered a crowd of prisoners, who, seeing his general's stars, called out asking where they should go. With a laugh he pointed and told them, "Go along that way, you will be well taken care of." The 8th Ohio, being on the flank of the attack, was especially well placed for captures, and at the end of its day's work it marched back to the Union lines in a formation of 50 men in front with the color bearer and two captured flags, then some 200 prisoners, then the regiment's other 50 men. In all, an estimated 3,350 Rebels, wounded and unwounded, were taken captive from Pickett's Charge.

Another notable capture statistic was flags — twenty-eight of them. When Alexander Webb sent his aide to Alexander Hays to ask for the return of flags captured originally by the Philadelphia Brigade, Hays wondered, "How in hell did I get them if he captured them?" But he told one of his staff to pick out a half dozen Rebel flags and send them over to Webb with his compliments: "We have so many here we don't know what to do with them and Webb needs them."[11]

By the best estimate, better than half of the 13,000 Confederates who

One of Mathew Brady's cameramen took this portrait of three Confederate prisoners, posed on Seminary Ridge. (Library of Congress)

made Pickett's Charge were casualties — 6,600. And just over half *that* number, 3,350 (wounded and unwounded), became prisoners of the Yankees. The count of the dead came to some 1,190. Thus 35 percent of the men who made the charge were immediately removed from the Confederate rolls through death or capture.

The loss percentages in Fry's and Marshall's brigades of Pettigrew's division, on Pickett's immediate left, were about the same as those in Garnett's, Kemper's, and Armistead's brigades. This belies the postwar complaint by some of Pickett's veterans that Pettigrew's troops failed to support the Virginians and thereby the day was lost. In fact, Pettigrew and Trimble entirely occupied the attention of Hays's division in front of them. It was Gibbon's men and their First Corps supports — and the Yankee artillery — that stopped Pickett.[12]

Because the Federals did not record their Gettysburg casualties on a day-by-day basis, and because a number of the brigades and regiments had already fought on Day One or Day Two, their casualties in repelling Pickett's Charge can only be estimated. This calculation produces a figure

468

of some 2,300 dead, wounded, and missing — just over one-third that of the Rebels. The heaviest casualties were, of course, in Webb's Philadelphia Brigade, which lost 44 percent of its 940 men. The gallant Irishmen of the 69th Pennsylvania suffered a 47 percent loss in those few minutes at the Copse. The bombardment and the charge cost John Hazard's Second Corps artillery brigade almost 25 percent of its gunners.[13]

Colonel Wainwright made note in his diary that this was "the great battle of the war so far," and so the next morning he rode over to the Angle "to see what slaughter is." By way of preface, he observed that "historians draw largely on the imagination when they talk of heaps of slain, and rivers of blood." But imagination was not required today: "There was about an acre or so of ground here where you could not walk without stepping over the bodies, and I saw perhaps a dozen cases where they were *heaped* one on top of the other." The night's rain had left, if not rivers, at least large pools of red.[14]

THE TREMENDOUS CANNONADE on Friday afternoon sent Gettysburg's citizens once again hurrying to their cellars. "The vibrations could be felt and the atmosphere was so full of smoke that we could taste the saltpeter," remembered young Albertus McCreary. When the guns fell silent there was puzzlement over what it portended, but the observant Professor Jacobs guessed that an attack would follow. He hurried up to his garret with his glass and was just in time to see the Confederate infantry emerge from the woods on Seminary Ridge. He called down to his son, "Quick! Come! Come! You can see now what in your life you will never see again!"

By dusk the firing had died away and people emerged, being careful about the sharpshooters, trying to find out what had happened. It was noticed that the usually talkative Southerners suddenly had little to say. "Some think the Rebels have been defeated," Sarah Broadhead entered in her diary that evening, "as there has been no boasting . . . and they look uneasy and by no means exultant."

At first light the next morning, Saturday, July 4 — Independence Day — Henry Monath, 74th Pennsylvania, was at his picket post at the foot of Cemetery Hill when he was startled to see in the middle of Baltimore Street at the edge of town a group of citizens "waving their handkerchiefs for us to come." Sergeant Monath cautiously led his little party through the streets all the way to the town square, finding no enemy except about a hundred sleepy stragglers. During the night the Army of Northern Virginia had evacuated Gettysburg.[15]

As the Federals moved in force into the town, there emerged from their various hiding places any number of First and Eleventh corps soldiers who had managed to evade capture since Wednesday's retreat. One noteworthy fugitive was Brigadier General Alexander Schimmelfennig, who had been hiding behind the Henry Garlach family's woodpile these past days. Carl Schurz recorded the joyous reunion. As he rode down the street, wrote General Schurz, he saw his old friend standing in a doorway, waving his hat and calling to him. "'Halloh!' he shouted. 'I knew you would come. I have been preparing for you. You must be hungry.'" The lady of the house served them a "jolly repast" of fried eggs, and Schimmelfennig told his tale of derring-do and escape and how he survived on bread and water. Another discovery was Brigadier General Francis Barlow, wounded and captured on July 1 and found recuperating in a private home. All over town the mood that morning was elation. "How happy everyone felt," wrote Jennie McCreary. "None but smiling faces were to be seen. . . ."[16]

In the wake of the grand charge, after doing what he could to hearten and rally his beaten men, Robert E. Lee had wasted no time in deciding on a course of action. Unless he could somehow entice Meade into counterattacking him along his Seminary Ridge line, he must get the army back to Virginia with all speed. There was enough ammunition for only one battle, if that. It was obvious that the whole of Meade's army was at hand and might now threaten the Confederates' foraging efforts. His own army was grievously wounded in men and especially in officers. And Lee had to consider the possibility that Meade might aggressively seek to cut across the routes south to the Potomac. There was indeed no time to waste.

Lee's first move was to order the Second Corps to evacuate Gettysburg. Ewell's troops were shifted back to the Oak Hill area, thereby shortening and straightening the army's lines, and told to dig in. Then, so Jed Hotchkiss phrased it in his diary, "The Generals had a council at General A. P. Hill's headquarters on the Cashtown Road, about sun-down, and decided to fall back."

In an abrupt change from his familiar practice of hands-off management of his subordinates — a practice he must have recognized as wanting during the last few days — Lee stayed on for some time that evening with A. P. Hill, their tent lit by a single candle, studying the map and discussing how the retreat was to be conducted. The next day Lee would issue a general order spelling out the march routes and exactly who was to do what and where and when. In retreat, at least, every commander in the Army of Northern Virginia should have no doubt about his role.

General Lee did not return to his headquarters until 1 o'clock on the morning of July 4. Brigadier General John Imboden, commanding an irregular band of cavalry that had been liberally foraging the countryside to the west, was waiting there for him. Lee dismounted and, Imboden wrote, "threw his arm across the saddle to rest, and fixing his eyes upon the ground leaned in silence and almost motionless upon his equally weary horse." Imboden commiserated: "General, this has been a hard day for you."

"Yes, it has been a sad, sad day to us," Lee replied, and then (Imboden recalled) "relapsed into his thoughtful mood and attitude." But suddenly he roused himself to speak vigorously of the battle just fought. "I never saw troops behave more magnificently than Pickett's division of Virginians did today in that grand charge," he said. But, he went on, they were not supported as they were to have been — "for some reason not yet fully explained to me" — else "we would have held the position and the day would have been ours."

Thus, if General Imboden's account can be accepted, some nine hours after the event Robert E. Lee had convinced himself that his plan for Pickett's Charge was perfectly sound. Only its execution had been flawed.[17]

The task assigned to Imboden was to organize and lead a train of wagons and ambulances to carry the army's wounded to the Williamsport crossing of the Potomac. His route was to be westward through the Cashtown Gap in South Mountain, then a southward turning to reach Greencastle and the Williamsport Pike to the Potomac, some forty-two miles all told. In addition to the 2,100 troopers of his so-called Northwestern Brigade, Imboden was given two batteries of artillery and the assurance that the cavalry of Wade Hampton and Fitz Lee would protect his rear. As General Lee put it in his instructions, Imboden's watchwords must be secrecy, promptness, and energy. A citizen of Greencastle who watched this army of the wounded pass by put it more simply: "Hurry was the order of the day."

Beginning about 1:00 P.M. on the 4th a steady, pounding rain increased Imboden's problems manyfold, yet by 4 o'clock that afternoon he had the journey under way. He estimated this "vast procession of misery" stretched for seventeen miles. It bore between 8,000 and 8,500 wounded men, many in constant, almost unendurable agony as they jolted over the rough and rutted roads. One particularly bad stretch was known locally as the Pine Stump Road. The teamsters had strict orders: no halts for any cause whatsoever. "Of all the nights that I spent during the war I think this was the saddest," wrote one of the escorting cavalrymen. Another trooper remembered that "the cries of the wounded and dying were awful."[18]

The retreat decision that caused General Lee the most pain was the necessity of leaving behind wounded men too badly hurt to travel in Imboden's column. Generals Trimble and Kemper were the most prominent of these, but there were also some 4,500 others left to the mercies of the Yankees. (Left behind as well were numerous wounded prisoners. "Happiness was not our condition," wrote one of these reprieved Yankees; " — we were in seventh heaven.")

A second special wagon train was organized that day, this one by Ewell's corps and put under the direction of quartermaster John A. Harman. The feisty, famously profane Harman, who had served as Stonewall Jackson's quartermaster, was a hard driver, just the sort to manage a train that contained much of the booty Ewell had collected during his excursions across Pennsylvania. Colonel Fremantle termed it an "immense train of plunder." Ewell told Major Harman, according to Jed Hotchkiss, "to get that train safely across the Potomac or he wanted to see his face no more." Harman's train would cross South Mountain at the Fairfield Gap, southeasterly from Imboden's train, and reach Williamsport by way of Hagerstown. Behind Harman, the next day, would come the main army.

Otherwise the Confederates spent this rainy, depressing Independence Day caring for the wounded and burying the dead. "Every house, shed, barn and hut was filled with wounded, dying and dead men, both Yanks and Confederates," wrote diarist Henry Berkeley. "Blood everywhere. Dead and dying men everywhere. Can there be anything in this world more sad and gloomy than a battlefield. I think not."

The corpses, from the July 1 fighting, were described as "a horrid spectacle" by Campbell Brown of Ewell's staff: "Corpses so monstrously swollen that the buttons were broken from the loose blouses & shirts, & the baggy pantaloons fitted like a skin — so blackened that the head looked like an immense cannon ball, the features being nearly obliterated. . . ." In their new lines Ewell's men found themselves in the middle of Wednesday's battlefield, and artillerist Robert Stiles described the odors as nauseating: "in a short time we all sickened and were lying with our mouths close to the ground, most of us vomiting profusely."[19]

Timothy O'Sullivan photographed this unfinished Confederate grave, probably located on the Rose farm, on July 5. (Library of Congress)

After its many battles the Army of Northern Virginia had few illusions, and Campbell Brown's appraisal of the army's mood after the great three-day struggle reflected a common theme: "It would be rediculous to say that I did not feel whipped — or that there was a man in that Army who didn't appreciate the position just as plainly. But the 'fight' wasn't out of the troops by any means — they felt that the *position* & not the *enemy* had out done us. . . ." Everyone in the army knew they had won the first day's fight, and most took the same view of the second day; only on the third day had they failed. But on July 3 it was the enemy's superior position that had made all the difference. Just "compel the enemy to come out to a fair field," said Jed Hotchkiss, and see who would win. To be sure, there was some criticism of "our Genls making any attempt to storm" a position as strong as Cemetery Ridge. Indeed there was generalized commentary on the high command. One man was heard to say, "If Old Jack had been here, it wouldn't have been like this."[20]

THE 4TH OF JULY was passed by the Army of the Potomac in the mundane and frequently grim tasks of restoring its military health — aiding the wounded, burying the dead, bringing up rations and ammunition,

473

and, when possible, resting from the strains of the past few days. There were no sanctioned salutes to Independence Day, although some bands were heard to play patriotic airs. The rain was a damper on enthusiasms. The burial parties dug long trenches and, after separating Rebel from Yankee, without ceremony piled the bodies several layers deep and threw dirt over them. Charles Morgan of the Second Corps staff reported that all the Confederate corpses he saw had been plundered. The orders were to keep counts, but this was not always done, particularly for the enemy. Sometimes little markers were put up designating at least the units of the Federal dead, but for the most part these mass burials were classified as unknowns.[21]

That morning, under a flag of truce, General Lee proposed an exchange of prisoners, for their "comfort and convenience." Meade rejected the idea. Just now he would rather have the Confederates burdened with prisoners than reinforced with able-bodied soldiers. A second flag of truce crossed the lines that day, this one from the Union side. The bearer announced that General Longstreet had been wounded and captured, but offered the assurance that he "would be taken care of." (No doubt this stemmed from a persistent rumor misidentifying the wounded Lewis Armistead as Longstreet.) Old Pete chuckled and told the messenger he believed he could take care of himself quite well, thank you.[22]

During the day General Meade immersed himself in matters of military housekeeping and, unlike General Lee, seemed to devote little thought to his course of action. To be sure, he did not have to face his opponent's multiple crises. His only immediate concern was being attacked again, and after yesterday that was not a matter of great concern. Meade's telegrams to Washington on the 4th described the sketchy nature of his information about the enemy, and announced that he would "require some time to get up supplies, ammunition, &c., rest the army. . . ." He said in closing that he would order a reconnaissance for the next day, "to ascertain what the intention of the enemy is."

Meade appeared stunned by the magnitude of what had been accomplished by his army, but personally relieved (and satisfied) that he himself had risen to the occasion. When he found time to write his wife, he told her "it was a grand battle, and is in my judgment a most decided victory, tho I did not annihilate or *bag* the Confederate Army. . . . At one time things looked a little blue, but I managed to get up reinforcements in time to save the day." He then added something quite revealing of his state of mind. He assured Mrs. Meade that their son George, his aide, "is quite well & so am I, tho' at one time I feared I should be laid up with mental excitement."

On July 4 George Meade had been in command of the Army of the Potomac one week. Inheriting the command from the secretive Joe Hooker, he started with virtually no knowledge of either his own army or the enemy's. He was by nature careful and conservative, and from the start he thought defensively — defending Washington and Baltimore, defending the Pipe Creek line, and, finally, defending Cemetery Ridge. Defense, he believed, was the best posture for this recently twice-beaten army — and certainly the best posture for its new and untried commander. For Meade the strains of the past week must have been almost unendurable, the "mental excitement" almost too much to bear.

It was therefore asking a great deal of him to switch in one day from defense to offense, to take the aggressive, as Lee liked to say. Meade required time to take stock, to cope with the stress he admitted had almost prostrated him. Still, it should have been apparent to him that if he was to challenge Lee's retreat — if Lee *did* retreat — he dared not waste a moment. He must block or delay Lee's crossing of South Mountain, and he must reach the Potomac no later than the enemy if he was to have a favorable chance of bringing him to battle.

That Saturday, headquarters issued a congratulatory order to the army that was too rhetorical for plain George Meade to have written and was probably the work of Chief of Staff Butterfield (back at work despite his wound). But in it was a passage that Meade had surely approved, and in his state of mind just then probably agreed with: "Our task is not yet accomplished, and the commanding general looks to the army for greater efforts to drive from our soil every vestige of the presence of the invader."[23]

Mr. Lincoln, who was spending most of these tense days in the War Department telegraph office, was greatly troubled by Meade's declaration. "I left the telegraph office a good deal dissatisfied," the president told General Halleck. "You know I did not like the phrase, in Orders, No. 68, I believe, 'Drive the invaders from our soil.'" He went on to note several other dispatches from the army that he found disquieting. "These things all appear to me to be connected with a purpose to cover Baltimore and Washington, and to get the enemy across the river again without a further collision, and they do not appear connected with a purpose to prevent his crossing and to destroy him."

At an Independence Day fireworks display at the White House, Elizabeth Blair Lee encountered the president, and she recorded him telling her, "Meade would pursue Lee instantly but he has to stop to get food for his men!!" And at a Cabinet meeting, according to diarist Gideon Welles, "The President said this morning with a countenance indicating sadness and despondency, that Meade still lingered at Gettysburg, when he should have been at Hagerstown or near the Potomac to cut off the retreating army of Lee. . . . He feared the old idea of driving the rebels out of Pennsylvania and Maryland, instead of capturing them, was still prevalent among the officers."

George Meade was certainly not another George McClellan, as the president feared, nor indeed would he be content simply to see the enemy back across the Potomac. "For my part," Meade wrote his wife, "as I have to follow & fight him I would rather do it at once & in Maryland than to follow into Virginia." Nevertheless, right at the start Meade could not bring himself to gamble, to take a risk by sending out a strike force immediately to try and block the Confederates' primary escape route, or at least divert them to a longer passage through the mountains.

The Fairfield Gap in South Mountain, on the direct route from Gettysburg to Hagerstown and the Potomac, was well within the reach of, say, a mixed force of Federal cavalry and infantry — perhaps one or two brigades, or even a division, of John Sedgwick's fresh Sixth Corps. Before day's end on July 4 such a strike force might start south for Emmitsburg, then westerly toward the gap. Should Lee be forced to fight for the Fairfield Gap, the rest of the army might fall on his rear. Should the Confederates have to divert through the Cashtown Gap, Meade's chances of cutting them off at the Potomac would improve thereby.

To be sure, such a gamble meant moving before it was certain Lee would move. It meant anticipating Lee . . . which in the event Meade's native caution precluded him from doing. He told his wife, "The most difficult part of my task is acting without correct information on which to predicate action." To help him predicate action he called in his generals for a consultation — but only on the evening of July 4.[24]

Nine generals were invited to attend, according to Butterfield's notes — John Newton of the First Corps, replacing Reynolds; William Hays of the Second, replacing Hancock; David Birney of the Third, replacing Sickles; Sykes of the Fifth; Sedgwick of the Sixth; Howard of the Eleventh; Slocum of the Twelfth; Pleasonton of the cavalry; and Gouverneur Warren, the army's chief engineer. General Meade seems to have said little, beyond reminding them of his instructions to cover Washington and Baltimore. He said he "desired the earnest assistance and advice of every corps commander."

From his generals Meade extracted a rough count of 55,000 infantry effectives. Adding cavalry, artillery, and battle casualties to that figure still left perhaps 20,000 men unaccounted for. Most of these were stragglers or men knocked loose from their commands in the heat of the fighting, and in time the provost marshals would round them up, but for the moment Meade planned on the basis of 55,000 foot soldiers. The militia of Generals Couch and William F. Smith might (or might not) prove to be of use. Meade had assumed, on the eve of battle, the two sides to be about even; he probably now assumed their casualties to be about even. He knew, from the Bureau of Military Information, that Lee had committed his last reserves yesterday. He knew too, from the captured documents brought him by Captain Dahlgren, that Lee could expect no reinforcements from Richmond. The question remained: What would Lee do now?

After some rambling discussion, Meade posed four questions for his lieutenants. "Shall this army remain here?" was the first. No one wanted to appear to be giving up a victorious field, yet no one suggested promptly seizing the initiative from the Rebels. Warren's answer represented the consensus: The army should remain "until we see what they are doing."

The second question, "If we remain here, shall we assume the offensive?" brought a unanimous No. None had any interest in testing the Confederates' Seminary Ridge line. Question three, "Do you deem it expedient to move towards Williamsport, through Emmitsburg?" was also unanimous — this time, Yes. This route represented the so-called inside line, covering Washington and Baltimore, that the army had maintained since the start of the campaign.

The fourth question asked "Shall we pursue the enemy if he is retreating on his direct line of retreat?" Because of the answer to the previous question, this was merely a matter of degree. Howard's answer, "By a show of force," reflected the majority view. Some wanted to pursue with cavalry only, some with a mix of infantry and cavalry. Only Birney suggested no pursuit directly on the enemy's line of retreat.

There apparently was no discussion of one other pursuit scheme — dispatching a force to cross the Potomac at Harper's Ferry and turn upriver to try and thwart the Confederates from crossing at Williamsport. No doubt General Meade was reluctant to divide his understrength army for such a chancy venture. In any event, the idea lost force when, on July 7, Major General William F. French at Harper's Ferry destroyed the bridge there to prevent the Rebels from using it.

Since it appeared that there was little known definitively of the enemy's "position and designs," General Warren offered to take a division out the next morning simply to see if the Rebels were still there. And so the Federal high command adjourned, determined to wait until General Lee made the first move, and until they learned of it.

Writing at 6:00 A.M. on July 5, Yankee soldier-correspondent Samuel Fiske noted that Lee's skirmishers had "kept up a lively firing all along our left, but he would of course do that to cover the signs of his departure, and now this morning we learn that his artillery has been moving all night, and I suppose there is scarcely a shadow of doubt the old fox is gone."[25]

INDEFINITE STORIES of the first two days' fighting had been trickling into the Northern press, but by the 5th and 6th the battle's outcome was clear and a triumph was proclaimed. "A memorable day," wrote New York diarist George Templeton Strong on July 5. "Tidings from Gettysburg have been arriving in fragmentary instalments, but with a steady crescendo toward complete, overwhelming victory." By the 6th the *New York Herald* was running a standing headline, "The Great Victory," over its continuing coverage. The *Philadelphia Inquirer* trumpeted "Victory! Waterloo Eclipsed!!" At her Philadelphia home, Mrs. Meade was serenaded by a brass band, with the mayor offering complimentary remarks. There was "deafening applause" for her and her husband, "the victor of Gettysburg."

Now, to crown the celebration, came news from the West. On Independence Day, it was reported, Pemberton had surrendered the Vicksburg garrison to U. S. Grant. As soon as he heard the news, "his countenance beaming with joy," Mr. Lincoln addressed a note to General Halleck: "We have certain information that Vicksburg surrendered to General Grant on the 4th of July. Now, if General Meade can complete his work, so gloriously prosecuted thus far, by the literal or substantial destruction of Lee's army, the rebellion will be over." Halleck promptly telegraphed the president's note to Meade.

"Be assured I most earnestly desire to try the fortunes of war with the enemy on this side of the river," Meade told the general-in-chief, and added, with a touch of exasperation, ". . . but I should do wrong not to frankly tell you of the difficulties encountered. . . . I wish in advance to moderate the expectations of those who, in ignorance of the difficulties to be encountered, may expect too much."[26]

Once he was finally certain that Lee was retreating, Meade moved with commendable speed. He committed seven of his eight cavalry brigades to the pursuit. But his infantry started some twenty-four hours behind Lee's, and by staying east of the mountains he had half again as far to go as the Confederates. For the march he divided the army into three commands, under Sedgwick, Slocum, and Howard. They followed parallel routes to a scheduled rendezvous on July 7 at Middletown, on the old National Road that led westward across South Mountain toward Hagerstown and the Potomac crossing at Williamsport. After Sedgwick reported on the difficulties of breaking through the enemy's rear guard at Fairfield Gap, the force trailing the Rebels directly was reduced to a small mix of infantry and cavalry.

The difficulties the marchers encountered were (as Meade warned) substantial — rain, mud, supply shortages. Rufus Dawes of the Iron Brigade wrote that "the hurried pursuit of the enemy to this point has been by far the most trying campaign. . . . The men have become ragged and shoeless, thousands have marched for days barefooted over the flinty turnpikes." Often the pace fully qualified as a forced march. Meade reported to Washington on July 8 that one of his corps "marched yesterday and last night over 30 miles." That was the Eleventh Corps; the Twelfth marched 29 miles. "We are wanderers on the face of the earth, like the Israelites of old," Stephen Weld of the First Corps staff wrote home. "We don't stop 24 hours in the same place, but keep up this eternal marching all the time."[27]

The Confederates encountered the same problems, but at least their route was the shorter of the two, and they had a head start. A. P. Hill's corps led, followed by Longstreet, with Ewell acting as rear guard. General Lee, looking for any chance to retaliate, instructed Ewell, "If these people keep coming on, turn back and thresh them soundly." When he heard this, Dick Ewell, sounding very Jackson-like, said, "By the blessing of Providence I will do it!" In the end, however, nothing much came of the Yankees' direct pursuit.

"The march was very slow & tedious," Porter Alexander remembered. "Travel a little ways, & stopped by the thing in front of you stopping — it may be for a few seconds, it may be a half hour. Nothing is more wearying." Pickett's division, in the middle of the column, had the onerous task of guarding some 3,800 Union prisoners. Any earlier niceties about foraging were now forgotten by the hungry Rebels. "We encamped on a Dutchman's farm and went for his pigs, ducks and chickens," wrote

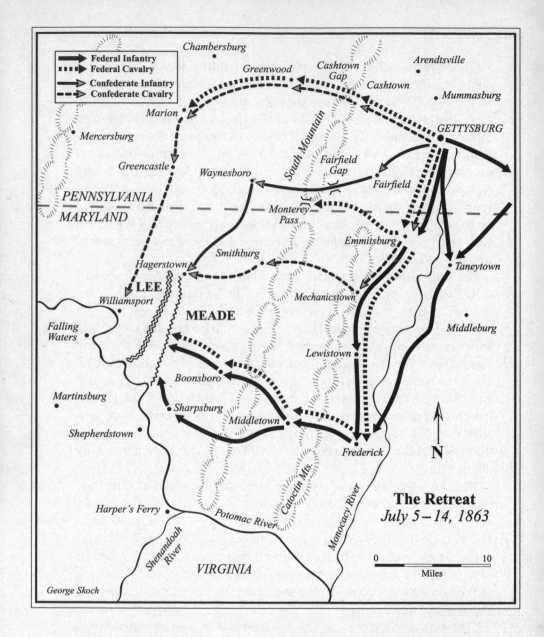

The Retreat
July 5–14, 1863

Legend:
- Federal Infantry
- Federal Cavalry
- Confederate Infantry
- Confederate Cavalry

George Skoch

artilleryman Henry Berkeley. "I don't think we left him a chick which was large enough to eat." By the time the Yankees reached Frederick and Middletown, the Confederates were at Hagerstown and Williamsport.[28]

Whatever action marked the retreat and pursuit was initiated by the Yankee cavalry. On the night of July 4, Judson Kilpatrick and two brigades of troopers — following the route that a preemptive strike force dispatched by a bold General Meade would have used — hit Ewell's train of plunder at a mountain summit called Monterey Pass. There was a wild scramble in the rainy darkness. When it was over, Kilpatrick extravagantly claimed the capture of 1,360 prisoners. The Confederates acknowledged the loss of thirty-eight wagons. Content with his swag, Kilpatrick made no effort to block the pass against the oncoming Confederate infantry.

John Imboden's train of wounded was meanwhile enduring its own trials. After it passed through Greencastle on July 4, a party of Union irregulars tore at the column. These were some 100 special-duty troopers of the 6th Pennsylvania, under the adventuresome Colonel Ulric Dahlgren, allied with a partisan band of 50 civilians led by a Greencastle Unionist named Thomas Pawling. Dahlgren and Pawling managed to wreck 130 wagons and take prisoners before the train guard countered. There followed a "severe fight," wrote a Yankee trooper, "in which we lost nearly all the prisoners we had previously taken, and a number of our own men captured." The next day Imboden's column was surprised by an attack from the west. These were some of "Milroy's weary boys," Union cavalry routed out of Winchester three weeks earlier by Dick Ewell, now rallied and looking for revenge. At the Maryland hamlet of Cunningham's Crossroads the rejuvenated weary boys took 134 wagons and 645 prisoners, most of them from among the wounded.

The dauntless Imboden pushed his battered train on to Williamsport on the Potomac, only to find the worst was not over. Something had gone very wrong. When General Lee called up the cavalry brigades of Beverly Robertson and Grumble Jones from Virginia, Jones was made responsible for guarding the army's pontoon bridge across the Potomac at Falling Waters, six miles downstream from Williamsport. With the Potomac at flood stage and rising, this bridge was the crucial link in the army's escape route. But in what was surely one of the major blunders of the campaign, the witless Jones left a guard of just fourteen cavalrymen at Falling Waters.

On July 4 General French displayed the initiative Grumble Jones so notably lacked. From his Harper's Ferry garrison French sent a party of Pennsylvania cavalrymen up the Potomac to Falling Waters. They swept up Jones's little guard and, French reported, "entirely destroyed the pontoon bridge." General Lee's escape to Virginia became suddenly very complicated. Now his only passage across the flooding Potomac was a small cable ferry at Williamsport that could carry at most two wagonloads of wounded in each transit.

On July 6 John Buford's Yankee troopers appeared in force in front of

A Federal 30-pounder fieldpiece, sketched by Edwin Forbes on a rainy day during the pursuit of Lee's army. (Library of Congress)

Williamsport, presenting Imboden with his greatest challenge yet. He posted his artillery, dismounted his cavalry, found arms for his teamsters, and prepared to hold to the last ditch. Every man of his command understood, wrote Imboden, "that if we did not repulse the enemy we should all be captured and General Lee's army be ruined. . . ."

Buford dismounted his men as well, and the fight of cavalry became a fight of infantry. The Federals had some 3,500 men to Imboden's 2,500, but they were considerably outgunned by the twenty-three pieces of Rebel artillery. At a critical moment two wagonloads of artillery ammunition from Winchester were run across the river on the cable ferry to supply Imboden's guns. Kilpatrick's arrival strengthened Buford's hand, then Hampton's and Fitz Lee's brigades arrived to support Imboden. Darkness finally ended the fighting, with the Confederates secure at Williamsport. One crisis was surmounted.[29]

By now Jeb Stuart had his troopers in place to screen the marching army and to fend off the Yankee cavalry. Just as important as Williamsport in the Confederates' scheme was Hagerstown, six miles to the northeast. Hagerstown lay at the center of a road network that Lee needed to control to bring his army safely to the river, and Stuart set

Allen Redwood's drawing of a Confederate column in retreat was intended to represent Imboden's train of wounded. (Century Collection)

about securing it. The battle for Hagerstown was fought at the same time as Imboden's battle for Williamsport, on July 6.

The opening clash saw the 18th Pennsylvania, of Farnsworth's brigade (led now by Colonel Nathaniel Richmond), dash down Potomac Street right into the town square, scattering the surprised troopers of John Chambliss's brigade. The Virginians gathered themselves and counterattacked, and there was a wild scramble of battling horsemen in the streets and byways. A civilian named W. W. Jacobs watched from the roof of the Eagle Hotel. "The discharge of pistols and carbines was terrific," Jacobs remembered, "and the smoke through which we now gazed down through and on the scene below, the screams and yells of the wounded and dying, mingled with cheers and commands, the crashing together of the horses and fiery flashes of the small arms presented a scene such as words cannot portray."

Civilians of both loyalties joined the battle. Mr. Jacobs came down from the rooftop and took up a rifle for the Union, sniping at the Rebels from behind an iron picket fence. The 18th Pennsylvania's historian told of an elderly civilian who came out of his house with musket in

Artist Forbes pictured Yankee scouts in a farmhouse attic observing the Rebel army near Williamsport on July 12. (Library of Congress)

hand "and fell in with our boys. . . . He was shot down before he had crossed the second block." By report, a young woman, the daughter of a Hagerstown doctor loyal to the South, took aim from her second-floor bedroom window and killed a sergeant of the 18th Pennsylvania.

Both sides reinforced, but the Rebels were additionally braced by infantry, and by day's end the Yankees had to fall back and concede Hagerstown to Stuart. By July 7 Lee was occupying the entire Hagerstown–Williamsport–Falling Waters area and the immediate danger was past. The next day Stuart boldly tried to extend his screen by driving the Federal cavalry out of Boonsboro, at the western foot of South Mountain, but this time it was the Yankee infantry that came up and saved the day.

While his army was catching up to the retreating Confederates, General Meade took the United States Hotel in Frederick for his headquarters. He enjoyed the luxury of a hot bath and a change into fresh clothes for the first time in ten days. "I think I have lived as much in this time as in the last 30 years," he complained to his wife. But his welcome in Frederick acted as a tonic: "The people in this place have made a great fuss with me. A few moments after my arrival I was visited by a deputation of ladies & showers of wreaths & bouquets presented to me." (Staff man Stephen Weld offered his own homely view of the scene: "Some ladies came in to see General Meade, giving him bouquets, and insisted on kissing him. I saw the performance through the window.") The general went on to remark that when he rode into town the street was crowded with people "staring at me & much to my astonishment I find myself a Lion."

He assured Mrs. Meade that his head was not turned by all this attention, and in fact he fully expected he would soon have to prove himself all over again: "I think we shall have another battle before Lee can cross the river tho from all accounts he is making great efforts to do so."[30]

AS SOON AS HE LEARNED that his pontoon bridge at Falling Waters had been destroyed, General Lee sent his engineers and artillerist Porter Alexander ahead to the Potomac to stake out a line to defend the Williamsport crossings. Right at Williamsport was a ford the army had easily marched across some three weeks before; just now it was under thirteen feet of rushing water. Falling Waters, six miles downstream around a sweeping bend, remained the best site for a replacement pontoon bridge. That task was assigned to the resourceful quartermaster John Harman.

As to the defensive line, in Colonel Alexander's words, "There was no very well defined & naturally strong line, & we had to pick & choose, & string together in some places by make-shifts & some little work." The high ground they chose, known locally as Salisbury Ridge, ran some nine miles from just west of Hagerstown southward to the Potomac, securing both the Williamsport and Falling Waters crossing sites. Federals attacking this line would encounter boggy ground in many places, then have to climb rocky slopes to reach the defenders. The double line of entrenchments was (as Alexander noted) largely makeshift, but no less imposing for that. Rocks, dirt, logs, fence rails, even wheat sheaves were incorporated into parapets and bastions. Artillery emplacements were made especially strong. Where the ground was weak defensively, Alexander massed batteries to deliver a crossfire. Behind the lines was a network of roads to enhance troop movements. All of this work was closely inspected and approved personally by no less than Generals Lee, Longstreet, Ewell, and Hill. Union officer Henry Abbott had to compliment the Rebels: "The same night that they arrived they made their defences, & their position became identically that of ours at Gettysburg, & theirs ours."

While it might have appeared to Yankee observers as the work of one night, this battle line was in fact the work of several nights and days. The troops as they arrived did most of the digging, and they did it enthusiastically; there was nothing they wanted more than to be attacked and to gain some revenge. In that event they could have shouted "Gettysburg! Gettysburg!" just as the Yankees had shouted "Fredericksburg! Fredericksburg!" a few days earlier. Alexander would write that the Yankees' pursuit reminded him of a mule chasing a grizzly bear — "as if catching up with us was the last thing he wanted to do." Of course Alexander, like his comrades, had desperately wanted them to catch up: "And, as we got things into shape, oh! how we all did wish that the enemy would come out in the open & attack us, as we had done them at Gettysburg."[31]

Major Harman, meanwhile, was tackling the bridge problem with his usual mixture of energy and profanity. According to the Prussian observer Justus Scheibert, who pitched in to help, seven of the original pontoons were found and repaired; the rest had to be fabricated out of materials at hand. Barns were dismantled and wharves and warehouses along the nearby Chesapeake & Ohio Canal taken down. Sawmills were appropriated and tools requisitioned. Within sixty-eight hours, by Captain Scheibert's count, fifteen rough pontoons were assembled, caulked with oakum and tar, floated downriver to Falling Waters, and there combined with crossbeams and planking to form an 800-foot floating bridge. On July 13 the bridge was pronounced ready for traffic. To the eye of staff officer Moxley Sorrel it was "a crazy affair," yet it was entirely serviceable and very much a credit to Rebel ingenuity.[32]

By July 7, the date on which the Army of the Potomac was supposed to rendezvous at Middletown, just east of South Mountain and 18 miles from Williamsport, only one corps had reached that far. Yet sometime over the next day or two, by means of a hellbent dash forward, one or likely two Federal corps might have broken through Stuart's cavalry screen to reach the Confederate works before they were completed. (Candidates for such a dash were the First and Second corps, which by July 8 had caught up with the advance — but of course neither John Reynolds nor Winfield Hancock was leading them.) Then it would be a question of holding there against Lee's oncoming infantry until the other corps came up. It would be a very bold gamble, to be sure, but one in which the risk would surely be balanced by the possible consequences.

In the event, George Meade once again demonstrated that he was not a gambling man. He was not yet altogether secure in his new command, and he was exceedingly respectful of Robert E. Lee. The army was only a few miles from the old Antietam battlefield, and the veterans (including General Meade) remembered all too well what it was like to attack Lee's Army of Northern Virginia when it was hunkered down in defense.

C.E.H. Bonwill's sketch, dated July 13, shows the Confederate army's cable ferry at Williamsport on the Potomac. (New York Public Library)

While Meade had clearly demonstrated at Gettysburg that he was not afraid to do battle with Lee, the habits of defeat were too deeply ingrained in him — and in the Potomac army's generals — to attempt it without favorable odds. The odds just then must have looked no better than even, and so he would not accept them.

Writing in his diary on July 11, Colonel Wainwright of the artillery offered a shrewd assessment of the general commanding: "It would nearly end the rebellion if we could actually bag this army, but on the other hand, a severe repulse of us would give them all the prestige at home and abroad which they lost at Gettysburg. . . . I trust therefore that General Meade will not attempt it, unless under circumstances which will make our chances of success at least four out of five. . . ."

By July 10 Meade acknowledged that he had finished second in the race to the Potomac. He reported to Washington that the whole of Lee's army was in front of him, taking up positions to cover the Williamsport crossings. "These positions they are said to be intrenching." He explained that he was now advancing on a line perpendicular to the enemy's. "I shall advance cautiously on the same line to-morrow until I can develop more fully the enemy's force and position, upon which my future operations will depend."

487

For these future operations Washington assured him that two brigades from the Department of West Virginia would soon be coming in from the west. There was as well the militia under Generals Couch and Smith coming down from the north, but these Sunday soldiers — Smith described them as "an incoherent mass" — hardly seemed the answer to the army's needs. (The president remarked that these militiamen "will, in my unprofessional opinion, be quite as likely to capture the Man-in-the-Moon, as any part of Lee's Army.")

True to his word, Meade proceeded cautiously. He wrote his wife on July 12 that he was in the immediate vicinity of the enemy, and "expect at any hour to be engaged with him. He appears to be getting into a strong position, where he can act on the defensive. I shall be prudent & not act rashly." That same day, heading a letter to his sister "In line of Battle," Lieutenant Charles Brewster of the Second Corps wrote, "I do not know what is going on, but we expected to have had another desparate battle before this, but we get on mighty slow, and I am afraid they will get away from us. . . ." But he added hopefully, "one more such thrashing as we gave them at Gettysburg could finish up their little excursion to the north."[33]

Some months afterward, when he reviewed the Gettysburg campaign with the historian John C. Ropes, General Meade said that he had made up his mind upon reaching the Potomac to attack Lee without consulting "any of them," meaning his corps commanders. But on second thought — and apparently on seeing Lee's defenses — he decided, just as he had decided on July 2 and July 4, to call in his generals for consultation. He scheduled the meeting for the evening of July 12, at his headquarters.

Attending were James Wadsworth of the First Corps, in place of Newton, who was ill; William Hays of the Second Corps; William French, successor to David Birney as head of the Third Corps; Sykes of the Fifth; Sedgwick of the Sixth; Howard of the Eleventh; and Slocum of the Twelfth. Pleasonton represented the cavalry and Warren the engineers. Andrew Humphreys was there as Meade's new chief of staff. (Meade, it seems, had run out of patience with Dan Butterfield and sent him away with the excuse that his wound needed treatment.)

Before the conference Meade revealed his plan to Humphreys — a reconnaissance in force the next day, to be converted into a full-blooded attack if a weak point was discovered. The problem was a lack of intelligence on the enemy positions. Little had been done by way of reconnaissance over the past two or three days, and Meade hoped his lieutenants would offer their thoughts. But (as he wrote his wife) he had his doubts: "I *want Corps Comdrs.*"

General Meade preferred to call these gatherings consultations rather than formal councils of war, but in this case at least a vote was going to decide the issue. "I left it to their judgment," he later testified, "and would not do it unless it met with their approval." He told his listeners that he could not "indicate any precise mode of attack or any precise point of attack." Nevertheless, he favored attacking the enemy the next day "and taking the consequences." What, he asked, was their opinion?

Warren the engineer argued in favor of Meade's scheme, but it was the infantry commanders' votes that would be counted. That fact also ruled out Humphreys's in-favor opinion. Pleasonton also wanted to attack, but since the cavalry would not be engaged his view was discounted. Otis Howard of the Eleventh Corps was in favor as well. "But General Howard's opinion did not carry much weight with the rest," said Warren, "because his troops did not behave well." James Wadsworth, too, called for an attack, but since it was known that Newton, for whom he was substituting, opposed attacking, his view was taken at a discount.

But all the other corps commanders — Sedgwick, Slocum, Sykes, Hays, and French — "strenuously opposed a fight," according to Wadsworth. Sedgwick seems to have spoken for the five of them when he said that General Meade had just won a great victory, "and he thought he ought not to jeopard all he had gained by another battle at that time." As Gouverneur Warren phrased it, "I do not think I ever saw the principal corps commanders so unanimous in favor of not fighting as on that occasion." It may be that John Reynolds turned over in his grave, and Winfield Hancock and John Gibbon in their hospital cots.[34]

With the vote of the infantry commanders standing at five to two against his plan for a next day's attack, Meade abandoned his aggressive stance. As Humphreys explained, "General Meade deferred to them so far as to delay until he could examine our own ground and that of the enemy. . . ." Then it took another day for Meade to gather his thoughts and to determine on a definite plan of action. Orders went out to the commanders of the Second, Fifth, Sixth, and Twelfth corps instructing each to conduct a reconnaissance in force — commencing at 7:00 A.M. on July 14. When Meade announced his decision to Halleck, the general-in-chief was sharply critical. "Act upon your own judgment and make your generals execute your orders," he telegraphed. "Call no council of war. It is proverbial that councils of war never fight." This telegram was sent the evening of July 13, and whatever it might have done to stiffen Meade's resolve, it came too late.[35]

AS SOON AS MAJOR HARMAN completed the pontoon bridge at Falling Waters, ambulances and wagonloads of wounded were hurried down from the cable ferry at Williamsport and started across to Virginia. The Potomac was meanwhile falling steadily, with predictions that it would fall to four feet at the Williamsport ford by July 13. This was a critical point. To complete the crossing in one night, at least one corps had to be able to wade the river at the ford. Then the rest of the infantry, the artillery, and the wagons should be able to cross over the bridge by daylight. General Lee therefore set the evacuation for the night of July 13.

Ewell's Second Corps, holding the lines on the far left, near Hagerstown, pulled out at dusk and took the road to Williamsport. It was rainy and foggy, and the march proceeded with much confusion, deepening mud, and many halts. The way was lighted by torches and bonfires of fence rails. Stuart's cavalry stayed behind to guard the battle lines, with instructions to cross after the infantry. At the ford the men were told to hang their cartridge boxes around their necks, for the water would be up as high as their armpits. A great bonfire was lit on the Virginia shore to mark their target. The tallest men were stationed as a guard line across the river, with rifles interlocked to prevent anyone from being swept away. While many shoes were lost in the mud and numerous cartridges wetted and ruined, it was said that no one drowned. General Robert Rodes even insisted that the men met their various hardships "with cheers and laughter." Perhaps they did, at least from a sense of gratitude at returning safely to Virginia.

At Falling Waters, Longstreet's First Corps, on the right of the lines, was first to pull out. There was considerable delay here until Ewell's artillery could cross, but finally the way was clear for Old Pete's men. Porter Alexander would remember it as an "awful night. . . . We were marching all night in awful roads, in mud & dark, & hard rain. . . ." Daylight found the last of Longstreet's divisions across and just the first of A. P. Hill's. Cloaked in a morning fog, the evacuation continued.[36]

On a ridgeline a mile and a half from the pontoon bridge the engineers had thrown up a defensive line for the rear guard, a task assigned to Harry Heth's division of Hill's corps. Assured that the cavalry would be picketing well out in front of them, Heth told his men to stack arms and rest while the crossing continued. Heth, recovered now from his

July 1 head wound, had assigned Johnston Pettigrew to command the remains of Archer's brigade as well as his own. With the abilities of John Brockenbrough and Joe Davis still suspect, Heth clearly was relying on Pettigrew to carry the burden of command this morning.

It so happened that in the confusion of the evacuation there was a mix-up in the cavalry, and Stuart's troopers were not picketing out front after all. Harry Heth was unaware that his division was, literally, the army's sole rear guard. It was misty and foggy, and when a body of cavalrymen was dimly seen out ahead of the lines, Heth was unconcerned and let his men sleep. These mysterious troopers were in fact Yankees, of George Armstrong Custer's brigade of Judson Kilpatrick's division.

Kilpatrick had begun his day in Hagerstown. When the scheduled reconnaissances reported the enemy's lines empty, he rushed toward Williamsport in hopes of catching the Confederates astride the river. Instead he found the streets empty except for deserters and the stragglers, the detritus in every army who never quite get the word. When citizens told him of the other Confederate crossing at Falling Waters, Kilpatrick sent his troopers southward at the gallop. Sighting the works held by Heth's men, he told Custer to launch an immediate attack. Custer selected two companies of the 6th Michigan under Major Peter Weber and had them dismount to feel out the enemy position. Kilpatrick countermanded the order and ordered the men to mount up and charge.

For a moment this reckless order seemed about to pay off, as Heth, assuming the horsemen to be Confederate, yelled at his men to hold their fire. On the Yankees came, jumping their horses right over the works and into the midst of Pettigrew's defenders. There was a swirling clash of horsemen and foot soldiers, sabers and bayonets. But as a man in the 6th Michigan described it, the Confederates quickly rallied "and seizing their arms, made short work of their daring assailants." Major Weber was killed and a third of his men shot down.

Johnston Pettigrew was squarely in the midst of this new battle, just as he had been on July 1 and again on July 3. Unhorsed early in the fight, he singled out a Yankee trooper for combat. But the Yankee fired first and hit him in the stomach. Borne to the rear, Pettigrew was told by a surgeon his only chance for survival was to remain behind, to be ministered to by the enemy. Pettigrew had been wounded and captured before, on the Peninsula, and he would have none of it; he said he would die before becoming a prisoner again. And so it was. After a jolting ride in an ambulance back into Virginia, he died there three days later.

During this scrap the Confederates completed their evacuation, with

In Alfred Waud's drawing, the 6th Michigan cavalry charges the Rebels' rear guard at Falling Waters on July 14. (Library of Congress)

the rear guard having to fight off John Buford's troopers who broke in from the east. True to his usual extravagant record-keeping, Judson Kilpatrick claimed the capture of 1,500 prisoners. His total was probably a third of that number, many of them stragglers. Buford recorded capturing 500. The prisoners included no fewer than 230 from John Brockenbrough's brigade of unfortunates. In the last act of the campaign, the 28th North Carolina boarded the bridge, cut loose its Maryland moorings, and drifted safely to the Virginia shore.[37]

Newspaperman Noah Brooks remembered looking across the Potomac that evening at the Rebel campfires in the Virginia woods. "It is impossible now to describe — almost impossible to recall — the feeling of bitterness with which we regarded the sight. Lee's Army was gone. . . ." The 14th Connecticut's soldier-correspondent Samuel Fiske, describing for his readers the five-day mini-campaign on the Potomac, offered a view from the ranks. Of that final day, July 14, he wrote, "Fifth day: At daybreak we give the word to advance along our whole line. We 'move upon the enemy's works.' Works are ours. Enemy, sitting on the other side of the river, performing various gyrations with his fingers, thumb on his nose. . . ."[38]

Epilogue: Great God! What Does It Mean?

AT ABOUT NOON that Tuesday, July 14, a telegram from General Meade reached Washington reporting that the Rebel army had escaped across the Potomac during the night. Mr. Lincoln, according to his secretary John Hay, was "deeply grieved" by the news. "We had them within our grasp," he told Hay. "We had only to stretch forth our hands and they were ours. And nothing I could say or do could make the army move." The news appeared to bear out the president's grim forecast: "This is a dreadful reminiscence of McClellan."

The midday Cabinet meeting that Tuesday was thinly attended, and when he came into the room Lincoln was obviously distressed. It was agreed that no one was in the right frame of mind for deliberations, and the meeting was adjourned. Afterward, as he made his way across the White House grounds toward his office, Navy Secretary Welles was overtaken by the president. Seldom had he seen Lincoln "so troubled, so dejected and discouraged," Welles would confide to his diary.

He said, wrote Welles, "that he had dreaded, yet expected this; that there has seemed to him for a full week a determination that Lee should escape with his force and plunder. . . . There is bad faith somewhere. Meade has been pressed and urged, but only one of his generals was for an immediate attack, was ready to pounce on Lee; the rest held back. What does it mean, Mr. Welles? Great God! what does it mean?"[1]

Lincoln must have made his views equally clear to General-in-Chief Halleck, for in his reply to Meade's telegram Halleck was blunt: "I need hardly say to you that the escape of Lee's army without another battle has created great dissatisfaction in the mind of the President, and it will require an active and energetic pursuit on your part to remove the impression that it has not been sufficiently active heretofore."

For General Meade this was the last straw. Over the past ten days it seemed that an unthinking, ungrateful Washington had done nothing but nag at him. After he read Halleck's telegram, he turned to Rufus

Ingalls, his quartermaster, and asked, "Ingalls, don't you want to take command of this army?" "No, I thank you," Ingalls replied. "It's too big an elephant for me." "Well, it's too big for me, too," said Meade. Without delay he telegraphed Halleck that "the censure of the President conveyed in your dispatch of 1 P.M. this day is, in my judgment, so undeserved that I feel compelled most respectfully to ask to be immediately relieved from the command of this army."

Joe Hooker, the last Army of the Potomac commander to tender his resignation, was promptly accommodated, but that would not be George Meade's fate. Still, Halleck's brusque response was hardly a ringing endorsement. The president's disappointment, he telegraphed, "was not intended as a censure, but as a stimulus to an active pursuit. It is not deemed a sufficient cause for your application to be relieved."

That evening, describing the events of this momentous day to his wife, Meade in the end could only shrug. "This is exactly what I expected," he wrote, "— unless I did impracticable things fault would be found with me. I have ignored the senseless adulation of the public & press & I am now just as indifferent to the censure bestowed without just cause. Still it is hard after working as I have done & accomplishing as much to be found fault with for not doing impossibilities."

The same evening, in the same mood, Meade acknowledged a letter of congratulations for Gettysburg from General McClellan. He took little credit for himself, he told his former commander, "and am perfectly prepared for a loss of all my rapidly acquired honors the first time the fortune of war fails to smile on me. Already I am beginning to feel the reaction, Lee having crossed the river last night without waiting for me to attack him in one of the strongest positions he has ever occupied."[2]

That evening, too, Mr. Lincoln sat down and wrote a letter. It was addressed to General Meade, and as with previous such letters, particularly those to McClellan and Hooker, he sought to reason with his general, and as commander-in-chief to explain without artifice his views on issues between them. "As you had learned that I was dissatisfied, I have thought it best to kindly tell you why," he wrote.

He began with praise: "I am very — *very* — grateful to you for the magnificent success you gave the cause of the country at Gettysburg; and I am sorry now to be the author of the slightest pain to you." He went on to review the enemy's retreat and Meade's pursuit, at least as they were seen by him from the War Department's telegraph office. He described his "deep distress" at what appeared to be evidences "that yourself, and Gen. Couch, and Gen. Smith, were not seeking a collision with the enemy, but were trying to get him across the river without another battle. . . .

"Again, my dear general, I do not believe you appreciate the magnitude of the misfortune involved in Lee's escape. He was within your easy grasp, and to have closed upon him would, in connection with our other late successes, have ended the war. As it is, the war will be prolonged indefinitely. . . . Your golden opportunity is gone, and I am distressed immeasureably because of it."

Then the president put the letter in an envelope that he endorsed, "To Gen. Meade, never sent, or signed," and tucked it away in his desk. It would not be seen in his lifetime, or in Meade's. Perhaps just the writing of it furnished relief from his sore disappointment. He clearly recognized that sending it to his army commander would have done only harm. A few days later, speaking to John Hay, he repeated his metaphor of Meade having the enemy in his grasp and failing to close his fist, but by now he had apparently come to terms with events: "Still, I am very grateful to Meade for the great service he did at Gettysburg."[3]

To be sure, it had all looked easier from the perspective of the telegraph office or when tracing the movements on a map. In truth, Meade was not alone in speaking of the "impossibilities" he had faced. Those lieutenants who afterward inspected Lee's Williamsport lines were strongly impressed; Howard and Warren both recanted their earlier support for an attack. Artillerists Hunt and Wainwright, who had the eyes for such things, expressed themselves relieved no assault had been attempted. After studying the Rebel works on his front, Wainwright wrote, "These were by far the strongest I have seen yet; evidently laid out by engineers and built as if they meant to stand a month's siege."

Another factor, quite unappreciated by Washington, had dampened Meade's enthusiasm for taking the offensive at Williamsport — the sadly diminished state of his officer corps. To his plaintive cry, "I *want Corps Comdrs,*" he added, "The loss of Reynolds & Hancock is most serious — their places are not to be supplied." Newton of the First Corps was a competent but conservative engineer and no John Reynolds. William Hays was a nonentity, an inexplicable choice to head the Second Corps when Alexander Hays in that post would at least have echoed Hancock's aggressiveness. William French was far beyond his depth commanding the Third Corps. Sykes of the Fifth Corps and Sedgwick of the Sixth were trustworthy enough but excruciatingly cautious. Howard had demonstrated (again) that neither he nor his Eleventh Corps could be trusted. Slocum of the Twelfth Corps had shown himself spiritless at Gettysburg.[4]

Finally, there were the casualties in the fighting forces to consider, and their implications. At Gettysburg the Army of the Potomac had suffered a total of 22,813 casualties, including 3,149 dead. This was about one-quarter of Meade's forces on the battlefield, but that statistic did not tell all the story.

The First and Third corps had been wounded in body and soul, so to speak, and were in need of resuscitation. In the First Corps, John Reynolds was dead and five of his seven brigade commanders were wounded. Seventeen out of thirty-seven regimental commanders in the Third Corps were casualties. The Second Corps had been gravely wounded in the fighting on the second and third days of the battle, losing Hancock, Gibbon, and six (three of them dead) of ten brigade commanders. No one (including General Howard) any longer had any faith in the Eleventh Corps. That left only the Fifth and Twelfth corps as reasonably battle-ready, plus of course the big Sixth Corps, virtually untouched at Gettysburg. The Sixth, however, was not in the van of the pursuit and therefore not readily available for action. (The additional losses — in the march north, in Milroy's debacle at Winchester, and in the pursuit after Gettysburg — came to perhaps 7,300, raising the total of Union casualties for the campaign to some 30,100.)[5]

Contrary to critics in the capital and in the press, it had been simply not possible for the Army of the Potomac, on July 3, to switch from defense to offense immediately following Pickett's Charge; and probably not possible for a mentally exhausted General Meade to have turned his mind abruptly to the aggressive the next day. Perhaps the Yankees' best chance offered on about July 8, when a bold dash by, say, the First and Second corps toward Williamsport might have caught the Rebels before they were firmly dug in. Yet this would have involved a considerable gamble for a general wary of gambling. Furthermore, Meade may be excused if he did not regard John Newton and William Hays as the right commanders to lead so daring a strike.

Presently the prospects for a successful offensive against the completed Williamsport lines grew decidedly dim. It may be, however, that Meade might have enhanced his reputation, so far as Washington was concerned, had he made an effort to at least test those lines — had he followed his initial instinct to ignore his generals and *order* a reconnaissance in force for July 13. Perhaps he was even right in suspecting there *was* a weak point to be found that day.

However that might be, Meade was prompt to get the army moving again, and on July 17 he started it across the Potomac, at Harper's Ferry and downstream at Berlin. While Lee moved slowly up the Shenandoah, Meade kept pace east of the Blue Ridge. On the 23rd he took the aggressive, sending William French and the Third Corps as a spearhead through Manassas Gap in the Blue Ridge to attempt to cut off a sizable portion of Dick Ewell's command. But it was too much of a challenge for the bumbling French. Ewell slipped away and followed the rest of the Army of Northern Virginia to safer ground.

"Of course I was again *disappointed*," Meade wrote his wife, "& I suppose the President will be again dis-satisfied. . . ." On the contrary, the general was presently shown a tribute to him from the president. "A few days having passed," Lincoln wrote, "I am now profoundly grateful for what was done, without criticism for what was not done. Gen. Meade has my confidence as a brave and skillful officer, and a true man."[6]

BY JULY 24 Robert E. Lee was back at Culpeper Court House, whence he had launched the Pennsylvania campaign just over six weeks earlier. In his reports to Richmond the general had consistently put the best possible face on the failed campaign. Writing to Mr. Davis, he explained that in the fighting on July 3 the enemy's "numbers were so great and his position so commanding, that our troops were compelled to relinquish their advantage and retire. . . . It is believed that the enemy suffered severely in these operations, but our own loss has not been light."

By July 7 he was writing, "Finding the position too strong to be carried, and being much hindered in collecting necessary supplies . . . I determined to withdraw to the west side of the mountains." The next day he assured the president that the army's "condition is good and its confidence unimpaired," and that he himself was neither discouraged nor was his faith in "the fortitude of this army . . . at all shaken." On July 12 he summed up his accomplishments: "The Army of the Potomac had been thrown north of that river, the forces invading the coasts of North Carolina and Virginia had been diminished, their plan of the present campaign broken up. . . ." Soon afterward, in a conversation with Secretary Seddon's brother, Lee was said to have claimed that his admittedly heavy losses at Gettysburg were no greater than would have occurred "from the series of battles I would have been compelled to fight had I remained in Virginia." And then he supposedly said, emphatically, "sir, we did whip them at Gettysburg. . . ."

By the time Lee was back at Culpeper, however, his list of claimed accomplishments was contracted. The Army of the Potomac was again south of the Potomac and confronting him directly. The Union's Atlan-

tic seaboard forces had not in fact been diminished to supply reinforcements to Meade (or Hooker). Virginia had been freed of Yankee occupation for only some three weeks. Remaining on the plus side of Lee's
ledger was the fact that his army was subsisted (and then some) by the
enemy for a month; and whatever plans the Yankees might have had for
a summer offensive were interrupted. But there was one very large debit.
The ultimate (although unstated) objective of the entire campaign — to
win a major victory on Northern soil that might have at least offset the
disaster at Vicksburg — had failed completely.[7]

There was one other very large debit, of course — the casualties. General Lee recrossed the Potomac on July 13–14 with just under two-thirds
of the men who had marched north across the river with him in June.
The Confederate toll for the three days of Gettysburg came to 22,625, including 4,536 dead. Casualties on the march north, and on the retreat to
Williamsport, added just over 4,500, raising the total for the campaign to
some 27,125 men. This substantially exceeded the Seven Days' record of
20,200 casualties among Lee's previous campaigns.

Fighting (and losing) the campaign on Union soil sharply increased
the severity of these losses. In addition to the estimated total of 5,000
dead and the 5,445 missing, the Federals recorded the capture of 6,802
Confederate wounded at Gettysburg — men found on the field, or left
behind as too badly injured to join the retreat. Thus some 17,250 of Lee's
men — almost two-thirds of his total casualties — had to be struck off
the Confederate rolls as a consequence of Gettysburg. When Vicksburg's
losses were added to those of Lee's campaign — the grand total came to
some 56,600 — it made July 1863 easily the worst month so far in the
Confederacy's short annals.[8]

Damage to the officer corps was severe. In Longstreet's First Corps,
Barksdale, Semmes, Garnett, and Armistead were dead, Hood, Robertson, and Tige Anderson wounded, and Kemper wounded and captured.
Of Longstreet's fourteen division and brigade commanders, only six escaped unhurt. The Second Corps suffered two brigade-commander casualties, Avery dead and John M. Jones wounded. Among Third Corps officers, Pender, Pettigrew, and Marshall were dead, Heth, Fry, Scales, and
Lowrance wounded, Trimble wounded and captured, and Archer captured. In the cavalry, Wade Hampton and Albert Jenkins were wounded.
Of the officers heading the army's forty-six divisional and brigade infantry commands at Gettysburg, nineteen were casualties.

Losses among the field officers were severe as well, and in the most
heavily engaged brigades, murderously so. Of Cadmus Wilcox's five reg-

imental commanders, three were wounded and one wounded and captured; of Rans Wright's four, two were dead and one wounded and captured; of Alfred Iverson's four, one was dead and two wounded; of William Barksdale's four, one was dead and two wounded; of Jerome Robertson's four, two were wounded and one wounded and captured. The four regiments in Pettigrew's brigade suffered eight command casualties, including four dead. Just two of Pickett's regimental commanders survived unhurt. All told, of 171 infantry regiments, 78 (46 percent) suffered command casualties.

Gettysburg exemplified a grim statistical anomaly of this war. A great battle, it seemed, invariably claimed the best and boldest officers . . . and spared the worst. Extra Billy Smith, Alfred Iverson, Edward O'Neal, Joe Davis, and John Brockenbrough all survived without a scratch. (Like the dead, the worst required replacement too; of these five, only Joe Davis, the president's nephew, continued with the army.) The same harsh arithmetic applied to the field officers. The shortage of capable officers had already become a problem, and Gettysburg turned the problem into a crisis. "I am gradually losing my best men," General Lee told the president. In command and capability, indeed in offensive power, the Army of Northern Virginia would never recover.

As Lee's soldiers reflected on what they had accomplished, and had not accomplished, in Pennsylvania, there was widespread agreement that invading the enemy's country was not a very good idea. Nothing had come of it the previous September, and this latest invasion proved to be no different. "We had a nice time going into Pa.," a Virginian wrote, "but comeing out was quite to the contrary." Even before he was back across the Potomac, Colonel David Aiken of the 7th South Carolina had reached the same conclusion. "I am sick of Maryland, and never want to come this side of the river again," Aiken wrote his wife on July 11. ". . . Genl. Lee can whip with this army double as many Yankees in Virg. as he can in Penn. Better prolong the war by defending then ruin ourselves by failures at invasion."[9]

That sentiment was reflected in scattered complaints in the Southern press, and these General Lee seems to have taken personally. In a widely reprinted dispatch, correspondent Peter W. Alexander questioned Lee's choice of battlegrounds at Gettysburg. Alexander concluded that the general "acted, probably, under the impression that his troops were able to carry any position however formidable. If such was the case, he committed an error, such however as the ablest commanders will sometimes fall into." A considerably more outspoken critic was the choleric

Charleston Mercury. It described the "ill-timed Northern campaign" as consuming resources better applied to the straitened western theater. Their gorge rising, the *Mercury*'s editors insisted that "It is impossible for an invasion to have been more foolish and disastrous."[10]

General Lee wanted Mr. Davis to understand that "No blame can be attached to the army for its failure to accomplish what was projected by me, nor should it be censured for the unreasonable expectations of the public — I am alone to blame, in perhaps expecting too much of its prowess & valour." In thus confessing his overconfidence in his troops he concurred with Peter Alexander's appraisal. Still, he was not prepared to admit any battlefield misjudgments of his own: "But with the knowledge I then had, & in the circumstances I was then placed, I do not know what better course I could have pursued."

The Pennsylvania campaign marked two major departures for Robert E. Lee. The first was the questioning and the outright opposition on the battlefield that he encountered from his chief lieutenants. The second was what he termed "the expression of discontent in the public journals at the result of the expedition." He had met the former by a stubborn and all-but-blind enforcement of his will. The latter caused him, on August 8, to offer his resignation as general commanding.

There was a pro forma quality about this resignation letter to the president, a routine offering to step down for the good of the country in consequence of "the result of the expedition." Whether the discontent expressed in the press extended into the army General Lee could not say; "My brother officers have been too kind to report it, & so far the troops have been too generous to exhibit it." He supposed it did exist, however, and a commander who lacked the confidence of his men should not be commanding.

Lee also raised the matter of his health. He was not recovered from the illness of the past spring, he said, and that hampered him in giving operations in the field his personal supervision. "I am so dull that in making use of the eyes of others I am frequently misled." (This may well refer to the botched reconnaissance by Captain Samuel Johnston on July 2, which led to the misdirection of Longstreet's attack that afternoon.) "I cannot even accomplish what I myself desire," said Lee; consequently, "I the more anxiously urge the matter upon your Excy from my belief that a younger & abler man than myself can readily be attained."

There was of course no younger and abler man waiting in the wings — as General Lee well knew. "But suppose, my dear friend, that I were to admit, with all their implications, the points which you present, where am I to find that new commander," Mr. Davis asked in reply. The answer was nowhere. "To ask me to substitute you by some one in my judgment more fit to command, or who would possess more of the confidence of the army, or of the reflecting men in the country is to demand an impossibility." A day or so later, Senator Louis Wigfall wrote to a friend that the president "was almost frantic with rage if the slightest doubt was expressed" regarding General Lee's "capacity & conduct."[11]

The search for explanations of the failed campaign began soon enough. The observant Colonel Fremantle, writing in the immediate aftermath of Pickett's Charge, spoke of the sin of overconfidence: "It is impossible to avoid seeing that the cause of this check to the Confederates lies in the utter contempt felt for the enemy by all ranks." Longstreet told him, Fremantle wrote, that "the mistake they had made was in not concentrating the army more"; they should have attacked with twice as many men on July 3. General Lee, for his part, would say that victory was within his reach on several occasions at Gettysburg "if he could have gotten one decided simultaneous attack on the whole line." So far as he was concerned, the decisions were sound; it was the execution that had failed.[12]

What Longstreet described as "a sly undercurrent of misrepresentation of my course" — no doubt a reference to newspaper reporting — caused Old Pete to explain his views in a letter to his uncle on July 24, when the army returned to Culpeper. "The battle was not made as I would have made it," he wrote. "My idea was to throw ourselves between the enemy and Washington, select a strong position, and force the enemy to attack us." But General Lee "chose the plans adopted," he went on. "I consider it a part of my duty to express my views to the commanding general. If he approves and adopts them, it is well; if he does not, it is my duty to adopt his views, and to execute his orders as faithfully as if they were my own. . . . As we failed, I must take my share of the responsibility." Indeed, he would shoulder *all* the responsibility if it would contribute to public support for General Lee: "If the blame, if there is any, can be shifted from him to me, I shall help him and our cause by taking it."

A few days later, Longstreet offered Senator Wigfall his view of the principal reason for the defeat. "Our failure in Pa.," Longstreet wrote, "was due I think to our being under the impression that the enemy had not been able to get all of his forces up." It was under this impression that Lee decided to attack at once. "And we did attack before our forces got up and it turned out that the enemy was ready with his whole force, and ours was not."[13]

This explanation, in obvious reference to the second day's fighting, suggested that a cause beyond General Lee's control contributed to the defeat — that is, a lack of intelligence about the Federal army. That, in turn, led to the matter of Jeb Stuart's culpability. As early as July 18, Charles M. Blackford of Longstreet's staff was writing his wife, "General Stuart is much criticized for his part in our late campaign. . . . In his anxiety to 'do some great thing' General Stuart carried his men beyond the range of usefulness and Lee was not thereafter kept fully informed as to the enemy's movements as he should have been. . . ." Lee in his report was uncharacteristically blunt: "The movements of the army preceding the battle of Gettysburg had been much embarrassed by the absence of the cavalry."

In going on to note that Stuart had exercised "the discretion given him," Lee appeared to accept a share of the blame for that embarrassment. Yet his serious misjudgment in permitting Stuart to go off on his improbable adventure in the first place largely escaped notice. Stuart's dereliction in many eyes (including Lee's) was his utter failure to communicate with the army during his long sweep around Hooker's (and then Meade's) army. When Major Andrew Venable found Lee on the July 1 battlefield, he brought with him the first news of the cavalry in a week. Apparently it never occurred to Stuart during that eventful week that cavalry scouting reports on the Yankee army would be a great deal more valuable to General Lee than the 125 captured Yankee wagons he was dragging along with his column.

If Stuart in fact expected the brigades of Beverly Robertson and Grumble Jones, left behind with the army, to do Lee's scouting for him, that was a point he and Lee failed to settle in advance. Lee ignored the two and just waited for Stuart to appear; he seemed only to trust Stuart to bring him usable intelligence. As a consequence, when the Confederates stumbled into battle on July 1, they not only knew nothing of the opposing army but nothing of the battlefield either. Lee was guilty of mishandling his cavalry during the campaign, but Jeb Stuart's failing was the more grave. His lack of reconnaissance deprived Lee of one of the cornerstones on which his campaign was based — the choice of battlefield.[14]

To be sure, Stuart was not alone among Lee's generals in falling short of the mark at Gettysburg. A. P. Hill was guilty of simply doing nothing. He failed to supervise his officers, especially Harry Heth on the first day of the battle. He did even less on July 2, when the Third Corps' attacks in support of Longstreet's offensive were made piecemeal (or not made at all). On July 3 Hill stood completely aloof from the planning and management of Pickett's Charge even though the majority of the attacking force was from his command. He gave no thought to the selection of the Third Corps troops, and he made no effort to direct their deployment. In his first exercise of corps command, A. P. Hill seemed always to be waiting for General Lee to tell him what to do.

Dick Ewell, too, had seemed to shrink back from his new role as corps commander. At the time of the appointment, Lee recalled, he spoke "long and earnestly" to Ewell about his "want of decision." It so happened that when he was in the heat of the fight — at Winchester in June, at Gettysburg on July 1 — Ewell acted decisively enough, but when the guns cooled his decisiveness cooled as well. He grasped the importance of seizing Culp's Hill on the evening of July 1, then grew inattentive and let the prize slip away. He thrice argued Lee out of shifting the Second Corps away from its tactically poor position on the far left, then proved unable to coordinate the subsequent attacks there. On July 2 and July 3 the Second Corps contributed little more than casualties to the Confederates' battle record.[15]

It was only in the postwar years (and only after Lee's death), when the old generals refought old battles, that James Longstreet's role at Gettysburg came to dominate the debate over the lost campaign. That exercise, from first to last, generated great heat and very little light. But through the course of the war and in the years left to him, General Lee gave not a hint of any dissatisfaction with Longstreet's conduct on the second and third days of the battle. Their parting at Appomattox was carried out with the same old affection. Lee turned to Longstreet's aide Thomas Goree and said, "Captain, I am going to put my old war horse under your charge. I want you to take good care of him."

There is no doubt that Longstreet, exercising what he thought of as the prerogative of a corps commander, argued strongly against Lee's attack plans on the 2nd and 3rd. There is no doubt either that he directed those attacks with a heavy heart. Yet there is also no doubt that when he struck, he struck as hard as he always did. He could justifiably speak with pride of the attack on July 2: "the best three hours' fighting ever done by any troops on any battle-field." In managing Pickett's Charge, Old Pete gave more attention to Pickett than to Pettigrew and Trimble, but in this regard he apparently (and properly) expected A. P. Hill to at least do his duty by his own troops. Then, by holding back reinforcements, Longstreet saved lives in what was clearly a misbegotten venture. Indeed, at Gettysburg James Longstreet was the only one of Lee's corps commanders who lived up to expectations.[16]

In the final analysis, it was Robert E. Lee's inability to manage his generals that went to the heart of the failed campaign. Right at the start, for example, he backed away from ordering a recalcitrant D. H. Hill, in North Carolina, to return the troops loaned him from the Army of Northern Virginia. These included two of Pickett's brigades, and their lack greatly influenced how Pickett's division would be employed at Gettysburg. Lee let Jeb Stuart talk him into an expedition that, considering all the risks inherent in invading the enemy's country, made no military sense. On July 1 Lee issued vague and contradictory directions to Dick Ewell, who of all his generals most needed positive directions. This pattern of indecision continued in his dealings with Ewell. On the evening of the first day Lee twice determined to bring the Second Corps, or a substantial part of it, around to the right where it might be put to better use, and twice he gave in to Ewell's pleadings to remain where he was. That exercise was repeated the next morning.

At the same time — perhaps in part because of his unsatisfactory dealings with Ewell — Lee *did* impose his will on Longstreet. Since there is only Longstreet's record of what occurred between the two of them on these days, it is not clear what arguments Lee may have countered with. What is clear is that theirs was a serious, extended dispute, and that by morning on July 2 Lee would have no more of it. The general commanding entertained no further argument; the battle would be fought his way. As Longstreet explained it soon afterward, Lee was convinced that Meade's army was scattered and so he must attack immediately.

Longstreet's offensive that afternoon was checked — narrowly, so it appeared to Lee — and he took what proved to be the final, fateful decision that evening: for July 3 "The general plan was unchanged." Lee chose this course reflexively, without consulting his lieutenants, without a survey of the battlefield, without an appraisal of the enemy, apparently without any consideration of alternatives. Robert E. Lee felt obliged to demonstrate to his lieutenants that his way was the right way, and the only way.

Porter Alexander is easily the most astute of Confederate soldier-historians, and in his published appraisals of Gettysburg he wrote critically but with proper deference concerning General Lee's conduct of the battle. In a private letter, however, Alexander was rather more blunt. "Never,

never, never," he wrote, "did Gen. Lee himself bollox a fight as he did this."[17]

THERE WAS A TIME, in the Army of the Potomac, when the men would raise a cheer and toss their caps every time commanding general George McClellan appeared. Two years and much hard, discouraging fighting later, they had lost that innocence and put aside that habit of cheering. They eyed their generals more coldly now, even (in this instance) after a victory. "About Meade, I hardly know enough to form an immediate opinion," wrote Captain Henry Abbott, 20th Massachusetts, on July 27. "I can hardly tell yet whether he *is* Wellingtonian or simply apes it. . . . I certainly feel great confidence in him, as do most others, though no enthusiasm. He hasn't had a cheer, so far as I can learn."

While General Lee sought to excuse his defeat at Gettysburg, General Meade was in the peculiar position of having to defend his victory there. It seemed that victory was not enough. Mr. Lincoln complained of the failure to finish the job, to finally crush the Rebel army that (so he thought) had exposed itself to destruction by the very act of invading Pennsylvania. General-in-Chief Halleck softened this interpretation in his later dealings with Meade, and then the president swallowed his disappointment and paid proper tribute to the victor of Gettysburg. Still, Meade did not rest secure. "My conscience is clear," he wrote his wife. "I feel I have done my duty, and that I could not have done more than I have done, and now I intend to await events in patient submission to God's will, prepared for any contingency." As to his continued command of the Potomac army, "I presume I am retained simply as a matter of necessity, and that my head will be cut off the first moment it can be done with security to themselves."

The general was of course wrong in his prediction, and at Appomattox he still commanded the Army of the Potomac. But in the months following Gettysburg Meade would be tormented by the testimony of hostile generals paraded before the hostile congressional Committee on the Conduct of the War. The generals were intent on avenging themselves on Meade. The committee's radical Republicans were intent on seeing Meade replaced by the more politically correct Joe Hooker.

The miscreant Dan Sickles, who had been dressed down by Meade for his July 2 blundering, and then (so Sickles thought) blocked by Meade from reclaiming his Third Corps command, led the attack. He was joined by Dan Butterfield, a Hooker loyalist pushed out of his chief of staff position; Abner Doubleday, who blamed Meade (wrongfully) for denying him command of the First Corps after the July 1 fighting; and David Birney, a disappointed suitor for the Third Corps command. Their message was that General Meade had mismanaged the battle at Gettysburg, afterward let the Rebel army escape, and would even have given up the field on July 2 and retreated but for his more warlike lieutenants. All this was fabricated and contrived, but all of it became public when the committee leaked the testimony to the press, and when Sickles enlisted "Historicus," one of his staff, to write poison-pen letters defaming Meade to the *New York Herald*.

Meade's supporters, including such authentic heroes of Gettysburg as Hancock, Gibbon, Warren, and Hunt, defended him in print, and in time the unpleasantness faded away, but it left George Meade embittered. It was, he wrote, a "hellish ingenuity to rob me of my reputation." Unfortunately Meade did not live long enough — he died in 1872, age fifty-seven — to see History overtake Historicus and refurbish his reputation. The fact of the matter is that George G. Meade, unexpectedly and against the odds, thoroughly outgeneraled Robert E. Lee at Gettysburg.[18]

Lee demonstrated weakness in managing his generals in this battle, while that skill proved to be Meade's especial strength. After consultation and instructions, he entrusted responsibility to his best generals, and was rewarded. Assigning three army corps to John Reynolds, he deputized him to select a battlefield if it should come to that. It did come to that, on July 1. For a time that day Meade hesitated over the choice of fields — perhaps momentarily borne down by the stresses of command — but he steeled himself and ratified Reynolds's choice. He called up his forces and, ignoring seniority, sent Winfield Hancock ahead to take over for the slain Reynolds.

When he reached Gettysburg himself, Meade carefully surveyed the position and personally assigned its defenders. On July 2 he anticipated needs and had reinforcements promptly on the way. In council that night, the plan for July 3 was made abundantly clear, and each general knew what was expected of him. In meeting Pickett's Charge, Meade mobilized 13,000 troops — as it happened, the same number making the charge — to support his center where he had surmised any attack would strike. Although they were not needed, they were there. The more he studied Gettysburg, Henry Hunt later observed, "Meade has grown and grown upon me. . . . Rarely has more skill, vigor, or wisdom been shown under such circumstances as he was placed in, and it would, I think, belittle his grand record of that campaign, by a formal defence against his detractors. . . ."[19]

Like Meade himself, his principal lieutenants — most of them at least — rose to the occasion at Gettysburg. Before his death, Reynolds acted decisively in selecting Gettysburg as a good place to make a fight. Abner Doubleday, leading the First Corps on July 1, had his best day of the war. Hancock of the Second Corps was a singular, inspirational fighting general on the second and third days. George Sykes of the Fifth Corps and Gouverneur Warren of the engineers responded nicely to crises on the second day. John Sedgwick, while not called on to fight, force-marched his Sixth Corps so as to be there if needed. Artillerist Henry Hunt, granted the command independence by Meade that Joe Hooker had earlier withheld, proved to be a dominating presence on this battlefield.

There were painful exceptions, however. Otis Howard failed the challenge when in command of the field on July 1, and failed at the task of restoring the Eleventh Corps' morale following its Chancellorsville debacle. Dan Sickles, in not obeying Meade's explicit orders, risked both his Third Corps and the army's defensive plan on July 2. Henry Slocum's strangely imperious command behavior left him a virtual cipher at Gettysburg, but at least in the interim the command of the Twelfth Corps was in good hands. Cavalryman Alfred Pleasonton, like Slocum a cipher-like figure, fortunately had subcommanders with initiative in the persons of John Buford, David Gregg, and George Armstrong Custer.

For the most part, then — and for the first time ever — the soldiers of the Army of the Potomac had received the leadership they deserved. The victory won as a result became of surpassing importance to the rank and file. On that account it had perhaps more lasting meaning to the army than to the country at large. "What do people think now of the demoralized Army of the Potomac," Lieutenant Charles Brewster, 10th Massachusetts, asked in a letter home on July 12. "If the growlers could have seen that desparate fighting on that battlefield at Gettysburg I think they would shut up their potato traps about this Army. . . ." This was a widespread view among those in the ranks long belabored for their losing ways, and their soldiers' pride was revived. "Again I thank God that the Army of the Potomac has at last gained a victory," Elisha Rhodes of the 2nd Rhode Island entered in his journal. "I wonder what the South thinks of us Yankees now. I think Gettysburg will cure the Rebels of any desire to invade the North again."[20]

There was a sense in the ranks, too, that *they* had won this battle. It was not after all won by clever maneuvering or by Napoleonic inspiration, but by thousands of Yankee foot soldiers standing firm and strong against the best the vaunted Lee could hurl at them. And this time, in the end, it was the Rebels who skedaddled. "I really believe that we are learning to outfight the rebels on even fields, in spite of their dash and fanatical desperation," wrote cavalryman Charles Francis Adams, Jr.

With the Army of the Potomac poised on the Potomac for a new campaign in Virginia, the 14th Connecticut's soldier-correspondent Samuel Fiske summed up the situation for the folks back home: "Our army is in good spirits, as you may well suppose, but *very tired* . . . having done an amount of labor in the past five weeks that must be shared and seen to be appreciated. I believe the country does, in some measure, appreciate, and is grateful for it. This army 'deserves well of the Republic' for the work of these few weeks especially."[21]

LATE ON JULY 5 the first photographers — Alexander Gardner, Timothy H. O'Sullivan, and James F. Gibson — reached Gettysburg, and over the next few days they composed their graven landscapes of the dead. They and other photographers recorded freshly scarred landmarks of the struggle — Devil's Den, Little Round Top, Culp's Hill, Evergreen Cemetery. Already working at the scene were artists Alfred Waud and Edwin Forbes, furiously sketching incidents and anecdotes of the fighting for *Harper's Weekly* and *Leslie's*. Well before the month was out, readers across the North would glimpse the great battle through the woodcuts in the illustrated papers.[22]

When the two armies marched south, they left behind a third army — an army of the wounded, some 20,350 in number, a third of them Confederates. With another battle pending, the Army of the Potomac spared just 106 medical officers to remain at Gettysburg; the Confederates left perhaps 80 or 90 attendants with their wounded. While the majority of the amputations and other surgeries had by that time been done, the comparatively few overburdened surgeons and attendants now on duty still labored every day to the point of exhaustion.

The same was true of the volunteer nurses of Gettysburg. Mary McAllister described the scene in one of the town's requisitioned churches. "I went to doing what they told me to do," she wrote, "wetting cloths and putting them on the wounds and helping. Every pew was full; some sitting, some lying, some leaning on others. They cut off the legs and arms and threw them out of the windows. Every morning the dead were laid on the platform in a sheet or blanket and carried away." Sarah Broadhead surprised herself at her growing ability to tolerate the terrible sights and sounds and smells among the patients she nursed at the Lu-

Gettysburg death studies, by Timothy O'Sullivan. Above: Confederate dead on the Rose farm. Below: Union dead in the area of the Emmitsburg Road. (Library of Congress–Chrysler Museum of Art)

Confederate dead of Hood's division in the Slaughter Pen, at the foot of Round Top, by Alexander Gardner. (Library of Congress)

theran Theological Seminary. Day after day, she noted in her diary, she had "done what I never expected to do or thought I could. I am becoming more used to the sights of misery."

But help was on the way. The U.S. Sanitary Commission and the Christian Commission and the Sisters of Charity and other civilian volunteers rushed to Gettysburg in their hundreds. They brought organization to the hospitals, relief to the medical staffs and the local volunteers, and immense comfort to the wounded, whether blue or butternut. Herman Haupt, the Union's expert railroader, got the York & Cumberland line from Gettysburg to Hanover Junction back in running order, and soon the wounded were being shipped off to established military hospitals. On July 9, for example, trains carrying more than 1,000 wounded arrived in Baltimore; on the 12th the day's total was 1,219, half of them Confederates. Three weeks after the battle, the remaining wounded in and about Gettysburg were being cared for at a new hospital two miles from town on the York Pike called Camp Letterman.

Indeed, so well were matters organized that on September 23 Camp

Letterman was the site of a banquet organized by the Christian Commission and the ladies of Gettysburg. Every patient, Rebel or Yankee, was welcomed. The camp streets and tents were decorated with evergreen boughs, and there were many good things to eat — hams, chicken, oysters, pies, even ice cream. Mrs. Anna Holstein, in charge of the Camp Letterman kitchen, reported, "When the hour came for the good dinner, hundreds moved upon crutches with feeble, tottering steps to the table, looking with unmistakable delight upon the display of luxuries."

What was slowest to go away was the indescribable stench of the battlefield. For weeks it hung like the breath of Hell in the hot, still summer air. The bodies had mostly been buried within the first few days, but the job was very imperfectly done and their presence was evident. There were at least 3,000 dead horses and mules to dispose of, and this was done by burning, a slow and malodorous process. People in Gettysburg kept their windows closed through the heat of July and August. Albertus McCreary remembered that "the stench from the battlefield after the fight was so bad that everyone went around with a bottle of pennyroyal or peppermint oil."[23]

What ultimately to do with all these bodies — indeed, what to do to properly commemorate this at-long-last Union *victory* — became a matter of concern in Gettysburg and in Harrisburg. David McConaughy, one of Gettysburg's leading lights, organizer of the ring of citizen-spies who had furnished General Meade with intelligence on the Rebels, was first to act on the question. In short order, reported a local paper, McConaughy "secured the purchase of the most striking portions of the battle ground," including ground around Evergreen Cemetery on Cemetery Hill. McConaughy was president of the Evergreen Cemetery Association and, as he wrote Pennsylvania's Governor Andrew Curtin, he proposed making "the most liberal arrangements . . . with our Cemetery, for the burial of our own dead" and also the dead of "all the loyal states, whose sons fell in the glorious strife. . . ."

This idea of a private cemetery soon gave way to the concept of a *national* cemetery for these honored dead — these Union honored dead. Theodore S. Dimon, sent to Gettysburg by New York to care for that state's wounded and dead, "presented a proposition that a portion of the ground occupied by our line of battle on Cemetery Hill should be purchased for a permanent burial place for the soldiers of our army who lost their lives. . . ." Judge David Wills, another of Gettysburg's leading citizens and Governor Curtin's agent in this matter, seized on the idea and made a crusade of it. Seventeen acres adjacent to Evergreen Cemetery that McConaughy had acquired were sold by him (at cost) to the state of Pennsylvania, and Wills set about turning the vision of a national soldiers' cemetery into a reality, and properly consecrating it.

David McConaughy's own vision assumed another direction. "The thought occurred to me," he said, "that there could be no more fitting and expressive memorial to the heroic valor ... of our army than the battlefield itself." McConaughy's extensive land purchases would in time form the core of the Gettysburg National Military Park.[24]

The landscape architect William Saunders designed the new cemetery in the form of a great semicircle, its curving ranks of graves equally accommodating the states from which the dead had come. The process of disinterment and reinterment was soon begun. Much care was taken to try and identify the bodies, at least by state, but these efforts met with only limited success. Of the 3,512 bodies eventually interred in the Soldiers' National Cemetery, some 1,600 had to be marked unknown. And surely among these unknowns are a number of Southerners inadvertently placed in this hallowed ground.

(It would be two decades before the South's Gettysburg dead found final resting places in hallowed ground of their own in the former Confederate states. The count of bodies disinterred and shipped south came to some 3,320. By the best estimate, then, some 1,200 of Lee's men lie in unmarked graves on the Gettysburg battlefield.)[25]

To properly dedicate the cemetery, David Wills invited what was generally acknowledged to be the greatest orator of the day, Edward Everett. A former president of Harvard, Everett was described by Ralph Waldo Emerson as a "master of elegance." Judge Wills had wanted the event to take place on October 23, but Everett said he could not compose such an important work by that date, and so it was rescheduled for November 19. Wills also sought an ode by a noted poet, and he sounded out three of the best known — Henry Wadsworth Longfellow, John Greenleaf Whittier, and William Cullen Bryant — but none could oblige him. Then, on November 2, Wills wrote to President Lincoln, inviting him to attend the ceremony and "formally set apart these grounds to their sacred use by a few appropriate remarks . . . and perform this last but solemn act to the soldier dead on this battlefield."

Another invitee was General Meade, but he could not attend the ceremonies, he said, because of his duties with the army in Virginia. Yet Meade's duties did not seem very clear, to him or to anyone else. The war in the East, despite the great victory in Pennsylvania, was stalled. "I am now waiting to know what they in Washington want done," Meade

The crowd around the speakers' stand during Lincoln's address at the Gettysburg ceremonies on November 19. (National Archives)

wrote disgustedly to his wife. That fall both armies were called on to send substantial reinforcements to the battle for Tennessee, and so in these weeks Lee and Meade, like two wounded, spent gladiators, sparred list-lessly along the Rapidan. It seemed to Northerners that the fruits of Get-tysburg had been thrown away. "What little war news we have is not star-spangled," the New York diarist George Templeton Strong complained on October 13. Indeed, the very meaning of that great battle had become clouded. The two armies together, on the three days of Gettysburg, had suffered 45,438 casualties; during the six-week Pennsylvania campaign their joint losses came to some 57,225. And yet nothing was changed — nothing except the loss of all those men.[26]

So it was left to Mr. Lincoln, on a pleasant November day, on the speaker's stand atop Cemetery Hill, to unveil the meaning inherent in this terrible battle and its terrible losses. Someone had to speak for all these silent dead, and by rights that someone ought to be the commander-in-chief.

The president of course rose to the occasion — just as General Meade and the men of the Army of the Potomac (Mr. Lincoln's army) had risen to the occasion on this hilltop four and a half months earlier. It was reported that the president's few appropriate remarks were welcomed by warm applause from the large crowd. In fact what he said required more than merely listening and applauding. John Hay, Lincoln's secretary, wrote in his diary that evening, "Mr Everett spoke as he always does perfectly — and the President in a firm free way, with more grace than is his wont said his half dozen lines of consecration and the music wailed and we went home through crowded and cheering streets. And all the particulars are in the daily papers."

Surely those particulars were worth a second thought. Edward Everett, who had a sense of these things, saw the transfiguring power of Lincoln's address perhaps before anyone else. "Permit me . . . ," Everett wrote the president the next day, "to express my great admiration of the thoughts expressed by you, with such eloquent simplicity & appropriateness, at the consecration of the Cemetery. I should be glad, if I could flatter myself that I came as near to the central idea of the occasion, in two hours, as you did in two minutes."[27]

Indeed those two minutes, those 272 words, would forever define and interpret all that had been done there. It is surely a matter worth pondering . . .

Opposite: The earliest known draft in Lincoln's hand of his Gettysburg Address, and possibly what he spoke from on November 19. (Library of Congress)

Four score and seven years ago our fathers brought
forth, upon this continent, a new nation, conceived
in liberty, and dedicated to the proposition that
"all men are created equal"

Now we are engaged in a great civil war, testing
whether that nation, or any nation so conceived,
and so dedicated, can long endure. We are met
on a great battle field of that war. We have
come to dedicate a portion of it, as a final resting place for those who died here, that the nation
might live. This we may, in all propriety do. But, in a
larger sense, we can not dedicate— we can not
consecrate— we can not hallow, this ground—
The brave men, living and dead, who struggled
here, have ha[llowed it, far above our poor power]
to add or det[ract. The world will little note, nor long]
remember what [we say here; but it can never]
forget what t[hey did here.]
It is rathe[r for us, the living, to stand here, we be dedica-]
ted to the great task remaining before us—
that, from these honored dead we take increased devotion to that cause for which
they here, gave the last full measure of devotion— that we here highly resolve these
dead shall not have died in vain; that
the nation, shall have a new birth of free-
dom, and that government of the people by
the people for the people, shall not perish from the earth.

The Armies at Gettysburg

This tabulation of the orders of battle for the two armies, July 1–14, 1863, is drawn primarily from the *Official Records,* with modifications from primary sources. In the notation of officer casualties, (k) stands for killed; (mw) for mortally wounded; (w) for wounded; and (c) for captured or missing.

ARMY OF THE POTOMAC
Maj. Gen. George G. Meade

Headquarters

Chief of Staff: Maj. Gen. Daniel Butterfield (w)
Chief of Artillery: Brig. Gen. Henry J. Hunt
Chief of Engineers: Brig. Gen. Gouverneur K. Warren (w)
Chief Quartermaster: Brig. Gen. Rufus Ingalls
Signal Corps: Capt. Lemuel B. Norton
Bur. of Military Information: Col. George H. Sharpe
Medical Director: Surg. Jonathan Letterman
Provost Marshal: Brig. Gen. Marsena R. Patrick

First Corps

Maj. Gen. John F. Reynolds (k)
Maj. Gen. Abner Doubleday
Maj. Gen. John Newton

First Division: Brig. Gen. James S. Wadsworth
  First Brigade: Brig. Gen. Solomon Meredith (w)
    Col. William W. Robinson
  19th Indiana: Col. Samuel J. Williams
  24th Michigan: Col. Henry A. Morrow (w)
    Capt. Albert M. Edwards

2nd Wisconsin: Col. Lucius Fairchild (w)

    Lt. Col. George Stevens (k)

    Maj. John Mansfield (w)

    Capt. George H. Otis

6th Wisconsin: Lt. Col. Rufus R. Dawes

7th Wisconsin: Col. William W. Robinson

    Maj. Mark Finnicum

Second Brigade: Brig. Gen. Lysander Cutler

7th Indiana: Col. Ira G. Grover

76th New York: Maj. Andrew J. Grover (k)

    Capt. John E. Cook

84th New York (14th Brooklyn): Col. Edward B. Fowler

95th New York: Col. George H. Biddle (w)

    Maj. Edward Pye

147th New York: Lt. Col. Francis C. Miller (w)

    Maj. George Harney

56th Pennsylvania: Col. J. William Hofmann

Second Division: Brig. Gen. John C. Robinson

First Brigade: Brig. Gen. Gabriel R. Paul (w)

    Col. Samuel H. Leonard (w)

    Col. Adrian R. Root (w-c)

    Col. Richard Coulter (w)

    Col. Peter Lyle

16th Maine: Col. Charles W. Tilden (c)

    Maj. Archibald D. Leavitt

13th Massachusetts: Col. Samuel H. Leonard (w)

    Lt. Col. N. Walter Batchelder

94th New York: Col. Adrian R. Root (w-c)

    Maj. Samuel A. Moffett

104th New York: Col. Gilbert C. Prey

107th Pennsylvania: Lt. Col. James MacThomson (w)

    Capt. Emanuel D. Roath

Second Brigade: Brig. Gen. Henry Baxter

12th Massachusetts: Col. James L. Bates (w)

    Lt. Col. David Allen, Jr.

83rd New York: Lt. Col. Joseph A. Moesch

97th New York: Col. Charles Wheelock (c)

    Maj. Charles Northrup

11th Pennsylvania: Col. Richard Coulter (w)

    Capt. Benjamin F. Haines (w)

    Capt. John B. Overmyer

88th Pennsylvania: Maj. Benezet F. Foust (w)

    Capt. Henry Whiteside

90th Pennsylvania: Col. Peter Lyle

Maj. Alfred J. Sellers

Third Division: Maj. Gen. Abner Doubleday

Brig. Gen. Thomas A. Rowley

Maj. Gen. Abner Doubleday

First Brigade: Col. Chapman Biddle (w)

Brig. Gen. Thomas A. Rowley

80th New York: Col. Theodore B. Gates

121st Pennsylvania: Maj. Alexander Biddle

142nd Pennsylvania: Col. Robert P. Cummins (k)

Lt. Col. A. B. McCalmont

151st Pennsylvania: Lt. Col. George F. McFarland (w)

Capt. Walter L. Owens

Col. Harrison Allen

Second Brigade: Col. Roy Stone (w)

Col. Langhorne Wister (w)

Col. Edmund L. Dana

143rd Pennsylvania: Col. Edmund L. Dana

Lt. Col. John D. Musser

149th Pennsylvania: Lt. Col. Walton Dwight (w)

Capt. James Glenn

150th Pennsylvania: Col. Langhorne Wister (w)

Lt. Col. H. S. Huidekoper (w)

Capt. Cornelius C. Widdis

Third Brigade: Brig. Gen. George J. Stannard (w)

Col. Francis V. Randall

12th Vermont: Col. Asa P. Blunt

13th Vermont: Col. Francis V. Randall

Maj. Joseph J. Boynton

Lt. Col. William D. Munson

14th Vermont: Col. William T. Nichols

15th Vermont: Col. Redfield Proctor

16th Vermont: Col. Wheelock G. Veasey

Artillery Brigade: Col. Charles S. Wainwright

2nd Maine Light: Capt. James A. Hall

5th Maine Light: Capt. Greenleaf T. Stevens (w)

Lt. Edward N. Whittier

1st New York Light, Batteries L–E: Capt. Gilbert H. Reynolds (w)

Lt. George Breck

1st Pennsylvania Light, Battery B: Capt. James H. Cooper

4th United States, Battery B: Lt. James Stewart (w)

Second Corps

Maj. Gen. Winfield S. Hancock (w)
Brig. Gen. John Gibbon (w)
Brig. Gen. William Hays

First Division: Brig. Gen. John C. Caldwell
  First Brigade: Col. Edward E. Cross (mw)
          Col. H. Boyd McKeen
    5th New Hampshire: Lt. Col. Charles E. Hapgood
    61st New York: Lt. Col. K. Oscar Broady
    81st Pennsylvania: Col. H. Boyd McKeen
              Lt. Col. Amos Stroh
    148th Pennsylvania: Lt. Col. Robert McFarlane
  Second Brigade: Col. Patrick Kelly
    28th Massachusetts: Col. R. Byrnes
    63rd New York: Lt. Col. Richard C. Bentley (w)
              Capt. Thomas Touhy
    69th New York: Capt. Richard Moroney (w)
              Lt. James J. Smith
    88th New York: Capt. Denis F. Burke
    116th Pennsylvania: Maj. St. Clair A. Mulholland
  Third Brigade: Brig. Gen. Samuel K. Zook (mw)
          Lt. Col. John Fraser
    52nd New York: Lt. Col. C. G. Freudenberg (w)
              Capt. William Scherrer
    57th New York: Lt. Col. Alford B. Chapman
    66th New York: Col. Orlando H. Morris (w)
              Lt. Col. John S. Hammell (w)
              Maj. Peter Nelson
    140th Pennsylvania: Col. Richard P. Roberts (k)
              Lt. Col. John Fraser
  Fourth Brigade: Col. John R. Brooke (w)
    27th Connecticut: Lt. Col. Henry C. Merwin (k)
              Maj. James H. Coburn
    2nd Delaware: Col. William P. Baily
              Capt. Charles H. Christman
    64th New York: Col. Daniel G. Bingham (w)
              Maj. Leman W. Bradley
    53rd Pennsylvania: Lt. Col. Richards McMichael
    145th Pennsylvania: Col. Hiram L. Brown (w)
              Capt. John W. Reynolds (w)
              Capt. Moses W. Oliver

Second Division: Brig. Gen. John Gibbon (w)
         Brig. Gen. William Harrow
First Brigade: Brig. Gen. William Harrow
         Col. Francis E. Heath
    19th Maine: Col. Francis E. Heath
         Lt. Col. Henry W. Cunningham
    15th Massachusetts: Col. George H. Ward (k)
         Lt. Col. George C. Joslin
    1st Minnesota: Col. William Colville, Jr. (w)
         Capt. Nathan S. Messick (k)
         Capt. Henry C. Coates
    2nd Co. Minnesota Sharpshooters
    82nd New York: Lt. Col. James Huston (k)
         Capt. John Darrow
Second Brigade: Brig. Gen. Alexander S. Webb (w)
    69th Pennsylvania: Col. Dennis O'Kane (mw)
         Capt. William Davis
    71st Pennsylvania: Col. Richard P. Smith
    72nd Pennsylvania: Col. DeWitt C. Baxter (w)
         Lt. Col. Theodore Hesser
    106th Pennsylvania: Lt. Col. William L. Curry
Third Brigade: Col. Norman J. Hall
    19th Massachusetts: Col. Arthur F. Devereux
    20th Massachusetts: Col. Paul J. Revere (mw)
         Lt. Col. George N. Macy (w)
         Capt. Henry L. Abbott
    7th Michigan: Lt. Col. Amos E. Steele, Jr. (k)
         Maj. Sylvanus W. Curtis
    42nd New York: Col. James E. Mallon
    59th New York: Lt. Col. Max A. Thoman (k)
         Capt. William McFadden
    1st Co. Massachusetts Sharpshooters
Third Division: Brig. Gen. Alexander Hays
First Brigade: Col. Samuel S. Carroll
    14th Indiana: Col. John Coons
    4th Ohio: Lt. Col. Leonard W. Carpenter
    8th Ohio: Lt. Col. Franklin Sawyer
    7th West Virginia: Lt. Col. Jonathan H. Lockwood
Second Brigade: Col. Thomas A. Smyth (w)
         Lt. Col. Francis E. Pierce
    14th Connecticut: Maj. Theodore G. Ellis
    1st Delaware: Lt. Col. Edward P. Harris
         Capt. Thomas B. Hizar (w)

Lt. William Smith (mw)

Lt. John T. Dent

12th New Jersey: Maj. John T. Hill

10th New York Battalion: Maj. George F. Hopper

108th New York: Lt. Col. Francis E. Pierce

Third Brigade: Col. George L. Willard (k)

Col. Eliakim Sherrill (mw)

Lt. Col. James M. Bull

39th New York: Maj. Hugo Hildebrandt (w)

111th New York: Col. Clinton D. MacDougall (w)

Lt. Col. Isaac M. Lusk

Capt. Aaron P. Seeley

125th New York: Lt. Col. Levin Crandell

126th New York: Col. Eliakim Sherrill (mw)

Lt. Col. James M. Bull

Artillery Brigade: Capt. John G. Hazard

1st New York Light, Battery B / New York 14th Independent:

Capt. James McKay Rorty (mw)

Lt. Albert S. Sheldon (w)

Lt. Robert E. Rogers

1st Rhode Island Light, Battery A: Capt. William A. Arnold

1st Rhode Island Light, Battery B: Lt. T. Fredrick Brown (w)

Lt. Walter S. Perrin

1st United States, Battery I: Lt. George A. Woodruff (mw)

Lt. Tully McCrea

4th United States, Battery A: Lt. Alonzo H. Cushing (k)

Sgt. Frederick Fuger

Third Corps

Maj. Gen. Daniel E. Sickles (w)

Maj. Gen. David B. Birney

Maj. Gen. William H. French

First Division: Maj. Gen. David B. Birney

Brig. Gen. J. H. Hobart Ward

First Brigade: Brig. Gen. Charles K. Graham (w-c)

Col. Andrew H. Tippin

57th Pennsylvania: Col. Peter Sides (w)

Capt. Alanson H. Nelson

63rd Pennsylvania: Maj. John A. Danks

68th Pennsylvania: Col. Andrew H. Tippin

Capt. Milton S. Davis

105th Pennsylvania: Col. Calvin A. Craig

114th Pennsylvania: Lt. Col. Frederick F. Cavada (c)

            Capt. Edward R. Bowen

141st Pennsylvania: Col. Henry J. Madill

Second Brigade: Brig. Gen. J. H. Hobart Ward

            Col. Hiram Berdan

20th Indiana: Col. John Wheeler (k)

            Lt. Col. William C. L. Taylor (w)

3rd Maine: Col. Moses B. Lakeman

4th Maine: Col. Elijah Walker (w)

            Capt. Edwin Libby

86th New York: Lt. Col. Benjamin L. Higgins (w)

124th New York: Col. A. Van Horne Ellis (k)

            Lt. Col. Francis M. Cummins (w)

            Maj. James Cromwell (k)

99th Pennsylvania: Maj. John W. Moore

1st U.S. Sharpshooters: Col. Hiram Berdan

            Lt. Col. Casper Trepp

2nd U.S. Sharpshooters: Maj. Homer R. Stoughton

Third Brigade: Col. Régis de Trobriand

17th Maine: Lt. Col. Charles B. Merrill

3rd Michigan: Col. Byron R. Pierce (w)

            Lt. Col. Edwin S. Pierce

5th Michigan: Lt. Col. John Pulford (w)

40th New York: Col. Thomas W. Egan

110th Pennsylvania: Lt. Col. David M. Jones (w)

            Maj. Isaac Rogers

Second Division: Brig. Gen. Andrew A. Humphreys

First Brigade: Brig. Gen. Joseph B. Carr

1st Massachusetts: Lt. Col. Clark B. Baldwin

11th Massachusetts: Lt. Col. Porter D. Tripp

16th Massachusetts: Lt. Col. Waldo Merriam (w)

            Capt. Matthew Donovan

12th New Hampshire: Capt. John F. Langley

11th New Jersey: Col. Robert McAllister (w)

            Capt. Luther Martin (w)

            Capt. William H. Lloyd (w)

            Lt. John Schoonover (w)

            Capt. Samuel T. Sleeper

26th Pennsylvania: Maj. Robert L. Bodine

84th Pennsylvania: Lt. Col. Milton Opp

Second Brigade: Col. William R. Brewster

70th New York: Col. J. Egbert Farnum

71st New York: Col. Henry L. Potter

72nd New York: Col. John S. Austin (w)
　　　　　Lt. Col. John Leonard
73rd New York: Maj. Michael W. Burns
74th New York: Lt. Col. Thomas Holt
120th New York: Lt. Col. Cornelius D. Westbrook (w)
　　　　　Maj. John R. Tappen
Third Brigade: Col. George C. Burling
　2nd New Hampshire: Col. Edward L. Bailey (w)
　5th New Jersey: Col. William J. Sewell (w)
　　　　　Capt. Thomas C. Godfrey
　　　　　Capt. Henry H. Woolsey
　6th New Jersey: Lt. Col. Stephen R. Gilkyson
　7th New Jersey: Col. Louis R. Francine (mw)
　　　　　Maj. Frederick Cooper
　8th New Jersey: Col. John Ramsey (w)
　　　　　Capt. John G. Langston
　115th Pennsylvania: Maj. John P. Dunne
Artillery Brigade: Capt. George E. Randolph (w)
　　　　　Capt. A. Judson Clark
　New Jersey Light, Battery B: Capt. A. Judson Clark
　　　　　Lt. Robert Sims
　1st New York Light, Battery D: Capt. George B. Winslow
　New York 4th Independent Battery: Capt. James E. Smith
　1st Rhode Island Light, Battery E: Lt. John K. Bucklyn (w)
　　　　　Lt. Benjamin Freeborn
　4th United States, Battery K: Lt. Francis W. Seeley (w)
　　　　　Lt. Robert James

Fifth Corps

Maj. Gen. George Sykes

First Division: Brig. Gen. James Barnes (w)
　　　　　Brig. Gen. Charles Griffin
First Brigade: Col. William S. Tilton
　18th Massachusetts: Col. Joseph Hayes
　22nd Massachusetts: Lt. Col. Thomas Sherwin, Jr.
　1st Michigan: Col. Ira C. Abbott (w)
　　　　　Lt. Col. William A. Throop
　118th Pennsylvania: Lt. Col. James Gwyn
Second Brigade: Col. Jacob B. Sweitzer
　9th Massachusetts: Col. Patrick R. Guiney
　32nd Massachusetts: Col. G. L. Prescott

4th Michigan: Col. Harrison H. Jeffords (k)

Lt. Col. George W. Lumbard

62nd Pennsylvania: Lt. Col. James C. Hull

Third Brigade: Col. Strong Vincent (mw)

Col. James C. Rice

20th Maine: Col. Joshua L. Chamberlain

16th Michigan: Lt. Col. Norval E. Welch

44th New York: Col. James C. Rice

Lt. Col. Freeman Connor

83rd Pennsylvania: Capt. Orpheus S. Woodward

Second Division: Brig. Gen. Romeyn B. Ayres

First Brigade: Col. Hannibal Day

3rd United States: Capt. Henry W. Freedley (w)

Capt. Richard G. Lay

4th United States: Capt. Julius W. Adams, Jr.

6th United States: Capt. Levi C. Bootes

12th United States: Capt. Thomas S. Dunn

14th United States: Maj. Grotius R. Giddings

Second Brigade: Col. Sidney Burbank

2nd United States: Maj. Arthur T. Lee (w)

Capt. Samuel A. McKee

7th United States: Capt. David P. Hancock

10th United States: Capt. William Clinton

11th United States: Maj. DeLancy Floyd-Jones

17th United States: Lt. Col. J. Durell Greene

Third Brigade: Brig. Gen. Stephen H. Weed (k)

Col. Kenner Garrard

140th New York: Col. Patrick H. O'Rorke (k)

Lt. Col. Louis Ernst

146th New York: Col. Kenner Garrard

Lt. Col. David T. Jenkins

91st Pennsylvania: Lt. Col. Joseph H. Sinex

155th Pennsylvania: Lt. Col. John H. Cain

Third Division: Brig. Gen. Samuel W. Crawford

First Brigade: Col. William McCandless

1st Pennsylvania Reserves: Col. William C. Talley

2nd Pennsylvania Reserves: Lt. Col. George A. Woodward

6th Pennsylvania Reserves: Lt. Col. Wellington H. Ent

13th Pennsylvania Reserves: Col. Charles F. Tayler (k)

Maj. William R. Hartshorne

Third Brigade: Col. Joseph W. Fisher

5th Pennsylvania Reserves: Lt. Col. George Dare

9th Pennsylvania Reserves: Lt. Col. James McK. Snodgrass

10th Pennsylvania Reserves: Col. Adoniram J. Warner
11th Pennsylvania Reserves: Col. Samuel M. Jackson
12th Pennsylvania Reserves: Col. Martin D. Hardin
Artillery Brigade: Capt. Augustus P. Martin
Massachusetts Light, Battery C: Lt. Aaron F. Walcott
1st New York Light, Battery C: Capt. Almont Barnes
1st Ohio Light, Battery L: Capt. Frank C. Gibbs
5th United States, Battery D: Lt. Charles E. Hazlett (k)
Lt. Benjamin F. Rittenhouse
5th United States, Battery I: Lt. Malbone F. Watson (w)
Lt. Charles C. MacConnell

Sixth Corps

Maj. Gen. John Sedgwick

First Division: Brig. Gen. Horatio G. Wright
First Brigade: Brig. Gen. A.T.A. Torbert
1st New Jersey: Lt. Col. William Henry, Jr.
2nd New Jersey: Lt. Col. Charles Wiebecke
3rd New Jersey: Lt. Col. Edward L. Campbell
15th New Jersey: Col. William H. Penrose
Second Brigade: Brig. Gen. Joseph J. Bartlett
5th Maine: Col. Clark S. Edwards
121st New York: Col. Emory Upton
95th Pennsylvania: Lt. Col. Edward Carroll
96th Pennsylvania: Maj. William H. Lessig
Third Brigade: Brig. Gen. David A. Russell
6th Maine: Col. Hiram Burnham
49th Pennsylvania: Lt. Col. Thomas M. Hulings
119th Pennsylvania: Col. Peter C. Ellmaker
5th Wisconsin: Col. Thomas S. Allen
Second Division: Brig. Gen. Albion P. Howe
Second Brigade: Col. Lewis A. Grant
2nd Vermont: Col. James H. Walbridge
3rd Vermont: Col. Thomas O. Seaver
4th Vermont: Col. Charles B. Stoughton
5th Vermont: Lt. Col. John R. Lewis
6th Vermont: Col. Elisha L. Barney
Third Brigade: Brig. Gen. Thomas H. Neill
7th Maine: Lt. Col. Selden Connor
33rd New York: Capt. Henry J. Gifford
43rd New York: Lt. Col. John Wilson
49th New York: Col. Daniel D. Bidwell

77th New York: Lt. Col. Winsor B. French

61st Pennsylvania: Lt. Col. George F. Smith

Third Division: Maj. Gen. John Newton

Brig. Gen. Frank Wheaton

First Brigade: Brig. Gen. Alexander Shaler

65th New York: Col. Joseph E. Hamblin

67th New York: Col. Nelson Cross

122nd New York: Col. Silas Titus

23rd Pennsylvania: Lt. Col. John F. Glenn

82nd Pennsylvania: Col. Isaac C. Bassett

Second Brigade: Col. Henry L. Eustis

7th Massachusetts: Lt. Col. Franklin P. Harlow

10th Massachusetts: Lt. Col. Joseph B. Parsons

37th Massachusetts: Col. Oliver Edwards

2nd Rhode Island: Col. Horatio Rogers, Jr.

Third Brigade: Brig. Gen. Frank Wheaton

Col. David J. Nevin

62nd New York: Col. David J. Nevin

Lt. Col. Theodore B. Hamilton

93rd Pennsylvania: Maj. John I. Nevin

98th Pennsylvania: Maj. John B. Kohler

102nd Pennsylvania: Col. John W. Patterson

139th Pennsylvania: Col. Frederick H. Collier

Lt. Col. William H. Moody

Artillery Brigade: Col. Charles H. Tomkins

Massachusetts Light, Battery A: Capt. William H. McCartney

New York 1st Independent Battery: Capt. Andrew Cowan

New York 3rd Independent Battery: Capt. William A. Harn

1st Rhode Island Light, Battery C: Capt. Richard Waterman

1st Rhode Island Light, Battery G: Capt. George W. Adams

2nd United States, Battery D: Lt. Edward B. Williston

2nd United States, Battery G: Lt. John H. Butler

5th United States, Battery F: Lt. Leonard Martin

Eleventh Corps

Maj. Gen. Oliver O. Howard

Maj. Gen. Carl Schurz

First Division: Brig. Gen. Francis C. Barlow (w)

Brig. Gen. Adelbert Ames

First Brigade: Col. Leopold von Gilsa

41st New York: Col. Detleo von Einsiedel

54th New York: Maj. Stephen Kovacs (c)
           Lt. Ernst Both
68th New York: Col. Gotthilf Bourry
153rd Pennsylvania: Maj. John F. Frueauff
Second Brigade: Brig. Gen. Adelbert Ames
           Col. Andrew L. Harris
  17th Connecticut: Lt. Col. Douglas Fowler (k)
           Maj. Allen G. Brady
  25th Ohio: Lt. Col. Jeremiah Williams (c)
           Capt. Nathaniel J. Manning
           Lt. William Maloney (w)
           Lt. Israel White
  75th Ohio: Col. Andrew L. Harris
           Capt. George B. Fox
  107th Ohio: Col. Seraphim Meyer
           Capt. John M. Lutz
Second Division: Brig. Gen. Adolph von Steinwehr
  First Brigade: Col. Charles R. Coster
  134th New York: Lt. Col. Allan H. Jackson
  154th New York: Lt. Col. D. B. Allen
  27th Pennsylvania: Lt. Col. Lorenz Cantador
  73rd Pennsylvania: Capt. D. F. Kelley
  Second Brigade: Col. Orland Smith
  33rd Massachusetts: Col. Adin B. Underwood
  136th New York: Col. James Wood, Jr.
  55th Ohio: Col. Charles B. Gambee
  73rd Ohio: Lt. Col. Richard Long
Third Division: Maj. Gen. Carl Schurz
           Brig. Gen. Alexander Schimmelfennig
  First Brigade: Brig. Gen. Alexander Schimmelfennig
           Col. George von Amsberg
  82nd Illinois: Lt. Col. Edward S. Salomon
  45th New York: Col. George von Amsberg
           Lt. Col. Adolphus Dobke
  157th New York: Col. Philip B. Brown, Jr.
  61st Ohio: Col. Stephen J. McGroarty
  74th Pennsylvania: Col. Adolph von Hartung (w)
           Lt. Col. Alexander von Mitzel (c)
           Capt. Gustav Schleiter
           Capt. Henry Krauseneck
Second Brigade: Col. Wladimir Krzyzanowski
  58th New York: Lt. Col. August Otto
           Capt. Emil Koenig

119th New York: Col. John T. Lockman (w)

Lt. Col. Edward F. Lloyd

82nd Ohio: Col. James S. Robinson (w)

Lt. Col. David Thomson

75th Pennsylvania: Col. Francis Mahler (w)

Maj. August Ledig

26th Wisconsin: Lt. Col. Hans Boebel (w)

Capt. John W. Fuchs

Artillery Brigade: Maj. Thomas W. Osborn

1st New York Light, Battery I: Capt. Michael Wiedrich

New York 13th Independent Battery: Lt. William Wheeler

1st Ohio Light, Battery I: Capt. Hubert Dilger

1st Ohio Light, Battery K: Capt. Lewis Heckman

4th United States, Battery G: Lt. Bayard Wilkeson (k)

Lt. Eugene A. Bancroft

Twelfth Corps

Maj. Gen. Henry W. Slocum

Brig. Gen. Alpheus S. Williams

First Division: Brig. Gen. Alpheus S. Williams

Brig. Gen. Thomas H. Ruger

First Brigade: Col. Archibald L. McDougall

5th Connecticut: Col. Warren W. Packer

20th Connecticut: Lt. Col. William B. Wooster

3rd Maryland: Col. Joseph M. Sudsburg

123rd New York: Lt. Col. James C. Rogers

Capt. Adolphus H. Tanner

145th New York: Col. E. L. Price

46th Pennsylvania: Col. James L. Selfridge

Second Brigade: Brig. Gen. Henry H. Lockwood

1st Maryland Potomac Home Brigade: Col. William P. Maulsby

1st Maryland Eastern Shore Infantry: Col. James Wallace

150th New York: Col. John H. Ketcham

Third Brigade: Brig. Gen. Thomas H. Ruger

Col. Silas Colgrove

27th Indiana: Col. Silas Colgrove

Lt. Col. John R. Fesler

2nd Massachusetts: Lt. Col. Charles R. Mudge (k)

Maj. Charles F. Morse

13th New Jersey: Col. Ezra A. Carman

107th New York: Col. Nirom M. Crane

3rd Wisconsin: Col. William Hawley

Second Division: Brig. Gen. John W. Geary
  First Brigade: Col. Charles Candy
    5th Ohio: Col. John H. Patrick
    7th Ohio: Col. William R. Creighton
    29th Ohio: Capt. Wilbur F. Stevens (w)
        Capt. Edward Hayes
    66th Ohio: Lt. Col. Eugene Powell
    28th Pennsylvania: Capt. John Flynn
    147th Pennsylvania: Lt. Col. Ario Pardee, Jr.
  Second Brigade: Col. George A. Cobham, Jr.
        Brig. Gen. Thomas L. Kane
        Col. George A. Cobham, Jr.
    29th Pennsylvania: Col. William Rickards, Jr.
    109th Pennsylvania: Capt. F. L. Gimber
    111th Pennsylvania: Col. George A. Cobham, Jr.
        Lt. Col. Thomas M. Walker
  Third Brigade: Brig. Gen. George Sears Greene
    60th New York: Col. Abel Godard
    78th New York: Lt. Col. Herbert von Hammerstein
    102nd New York: Col. James C. Lane (w)
        Capt. Lewis R. Stegman
    137th New York: Col. David Ireland
    149th New York: Col. Henry A. Barnum
        Lt. Col. Charles B. Randall (w)
  Artillery Brigade: Lt. Edward D. Muhlenberg
    1st New York Light, Battery M: Lt. Charles E. Winegar
    Pennsylvania Light, Battery E: Lt. Charles A. Atwell
    4th United States, Battery F: Lt. Sylvanus T. Rugg
    5th United States, Battery K: Lt. David H. Kinzie

Cavalry Corps

Maj. Gen. Alfred Pleasonton

First Division: Brig. Gen. John Buford
  First Brigade: Col. William Gamble
    8th Illinois: Maj. John L. Beveridge
    12th Illinois / 3rd Indiana: Col. George H. Chapman
    8th New York: Lt. Col. William L. Markell
  Second Brigade: Col. Thomas C. Devin
    6th New York: Maj. William E. Beardsley
    9th New York: Col. William Sackett
    17th Pennsylvania: Col. J. H. Kellogg
    3rd West Virginia: Capt. Seymour B. Conger

Reserve Brigade: Brig. Gen. Wesley Merritt
    6th Pennsylvania: Maj. James H. Haseltine
    1st United States: Capt. Richard S. C. Lord
    2nd United States: Capt. T. F. Rodenbough
    5th United States: Capt. Julius W. Mason
    6th United States: Maj. Samuel H. Starr (w-c)
             Lt. Louis H. Carpenter
             Lt. Nicholas Nolan
             Capt. Ira W. Claflin

Second Division: Brig. Gen. David McM. Gregg
First Brigade: Col. John B. McIntosh
    1st Maryland: Lt. Col. James M. Deems
    Purnell (Maryland) Legion, Co. A: Capt. Robert E. Duvall
    1st Massachusetts: Lt. Col. Greely S. Curtis
    1st New Jersey: Maj. M. H. Beaumont
    1st Pennsylvania: Col. John P. Taylor
    3rd Pennsylvania: Lt. Col. E. S. Jones
    3rd Pennsylvania Heavy, Battery H: Capt. W. D. Rank
Second Brigade: Col. Pennock Huey
    2nd New York: Lt. Col. Otto Harhaus
    4th New York: Lt. Col. Augustus Pruyn
    6th Ohio: Maj. William Stedman
    8th Pennsylvania: Capt. William A. Corrie
Third Brigade: Col. J. Irvin Gregg
    1st Maine: Lt. Col. Charles H. Smith
    10th New York: Maj. M. Henry Avery
    4th Pennsylvania: Lt. Col. William E. Doster
    16th Pennsylvania: Lt. Col. John K. Robison

Third Division: Brig. Gen. Judson Kilpatrick
First Brigade: Brig. Gen. Elon J. Farnsworth (k)
             Col. Nathaniel P. Richmond
    5th New York: Maj. John Hammond
    18th Pennsylvania: Lt. Col. William P. Brinton
    1st Vermont: Lt. Col. Addison W. Preston
    1st West Virginia: Col. Nathaniel P. Richmond
             Maj. Charles E. Capehart
Second Brigade: Brig. Gen. George A. Custer
    1st Michigan: Col. Charles H. Town
    5th Michigan: Col. Russell A. Alger
    6th Michigan: Col. George Gray
    7th Michigan: Col. William D. Mann

Horse Artillery
 First Brigade: Capt. James M. Robertson
  9th Michigan Battery: Capt. Jabez J. Daniels
  6th New York Battery: Capt. Joseph W. Martin
  2nd United States, Batteries B–L: Lt. Edward Heaton
  2nd United States, Battery M: Lt. A.C.M. Pennington, Jr.
  4th United States, Battery E: Lt. Samuel S. Elder
 Second Brigade: Capt. John Tidball
  1st United States, Batteries E–G: Capt. Alanson M. Randol
  1st United States, Battery K: Capt. William M. Graham
  2nd United States, Battery A: Lt. John H. Calef
  3rd United States, Battery C: Lt. William D. Fuller

Artillery Reserve

Brig. Gen. Robert O. Tyler
Capt. James M. Robertson

First Regular Brigade: Capt. Dunbar R. Ransom (w)
 1st United States: Battery H: Lt. Chandler P. Eakin (w)
           Lt. Philip D. Mason
 3rd United States: Batteries F–K: Lt. John G. Turnbull
 4th United States: Battery C: Lt. Evan Thomas
 5th United States: Battery C: Lt. Gulian V. Weir
First Volunteer Brigade: Lt. Col. Freeman McGilvery
 5th Massachusetts Light / New York 10th Independent:
        Capt. Charles A. Phillips
 9th Massachusetts Light: Capt. John Bigelow (w)
        Lt. Richard S. Milton
 New York 15th Independent Battery: Capt. Patrick Hart (w)
 Pennsylvania Light, Batteries C–F: Capt. James Thompson (w)
Second Volunteer Brigade: Capt. Elijah D. Taft
 1st Connecticut Heavy, Battery B: Capt. Albert F. Brooker
 1st Connecticut Heavy, Battery M: Capt. Franklin A. Pratt
 2nd Connecticut Light: Capt. John W. Sterling
 New York 5th Independent Battery: Capt. Elijah D. Taft
Third Independent Brigade: Capt. James F. Huntington
 1st New Hampshire Light: Capt. Frederick M. Edgell
 1st Ohio Light, Battery H: Lt. George W. Norton
 1st Pennsylvania Light, Batteries F–G: Capt. R. Bruce Ricketts
 West Virginia Light, Battery C: Capt. Wallace Hill
Fourth Independent Brigade: Capt. Robert H. Fitzhugh
 6th Maine Light: Lt. Edwin B. Dow
 Maryland Light, Battery A: Capt. James H. Rigby

New Jersey Light, Battery A: Lt. Augustin N. Parsons
1st New York Light, Battery G: Capt. Nelson Ames
1st New York Light, Battery K: Capt. Robert H. Fitzhugh
Train Guard: 4th New Jersey: Maj. Charles Ewing

ARMY OF NORTHERN VIRGINIA

Gen. Robert E. Lee

Headquarters

Chief of Staff: Col. R. H. Chilton
Chief of Artillery: Brig. Gen. William N. Pendleton
Chief of Ordnance: Lt. Col. Briscoe G. Baldwin
Chief Quartermaster: Lt. Col. James L. Corley
Chief of Commissary: Lt. Col. Robert C. Cole
Medical Director: Surg. Lafayette Guild

First Corps

Lt. Gen. James Longstreet

McLaws's Division: Maj. Gen. Lafayette McLaws
  Kershaw's Brigade: Brig. Gen. Joseph B. Kershaw
    2nd South Carolina: Col. John D. Kennedy (w)
               Lt. Col. F. Gaillard
    3rd South Carolina: Maj. Robert C. Maffett
               Col. J. D. Nance
    7th South Carolina: Col. David W. Aiken
    8th South Carolina: Col. John W. Henagan
    15th South Carolina: Col. William D. DeSaussure (k)
               Maj. William M. Gist
    3rd South Carolina Battalion: Lt. Col. William G. Rice
  Semmes's Brigade: Brig. Gen. Paul J. Semmes (mw)
               Col. Goode Bryan
    10th Georgia: Col. John B. Weems (w)
    50th Georgia: Col. William R. Manning
    51st Georgia: Col. Edward Ball
    53rd Georgia: Col. James P. Simms
  Wofford's Brigade: Brig. Gen. William T. Wofford
    16th Georgia: Col. Goode Bryan
    18th Georgia: Lt. Col. S. Z. Ruff
    24th Georgia: Col. Robert McMillan

Cobb's (Georgia) Legion: Lt. Col. Luther J. Glenn
Phillips (Georgia) Legion: Lt. Col. Elihu S. Barclay, Jr.
3rd Georgia Sharpshooters: Lt. Col. Nathan L. Hutchins, Jr.
Barksdale's Brigade: Brig. Gen. William Barksdale (mw)
                Col. Benjamin G. Humphreys
13th Mississippi: Col. J. W. Carter (k)
                Lt. Col. Kennon McElroy (w)
17th Mississippi: Col. W. D. Holder (w)
                Lt. Col. John C. Fiser
18th Mississippi: Col. T. M. Griffin (w)
                Lt. Col. W. H. Luse
21st Mississippi: Col. Benjamin G. Humphreys
Artillery Battalion: Col. Henry G. Cabell
Manly's North Carolina Battery: Capt. Basil C. Manly
Fraser's Pulaski (Georgia) Battery: Capt. John C. Fraser (mw)
                Lt. W. J. Furlong
McCarthy's Richmond Howitzers, 1st Co.: Capt. Edward S. McCarthy
Carleton's Troup (Georgia) Battery: Capt. Henry H. Carlton (w)
                Lt. C. W. Motes
Pickett's Division: Maj. Gen. George E. Pickett
  Garnett's Brigade: Brig. Gen. Richard B. Garnett (k)
                Maj. Charles S. Peyton
8th Virginia: Col. Eppa Hunton (w)
                Lt. Col. Norborne Berkeley (w-c)
                Maj. Edmund Berkeley (w)
18th Virginia: Lt. Col. H. A. Carrington (w-c)
19th Virginia: Col. Henry Gantt (w)
                Lt. Col. John T. Ellis (k)
28th Virginia: Col. Robert C. Allen (k)
                Maj. Nathaniel C. Wilson (k)
56th Virginia: Col. William D. Stuart (mw)
  Kemper's Brigade: Brig. Gen. James L. Kemper (w-c)
                Col. Joseph Mayo, Jr.
1st Virginia: Col. Lewis B. Williams, Jr. (k)
                Maj. Francis H. Langley (w)
3rd Virginia: Col. Joseph Mayo, Jr.
                Lt. Col. Alexander D. Callcote (k)
7th Virginia: Col. W. T. Patton (mw)
                Lt. Col. C. C. Flowerree
11th Virginia: Maj. Kirkwood Otey (w)
24th Virginia: Col. William R. Terry

Armistead's Brigade: Brig. Gen. Lewis A. Armistead (mw)

Col. W. R. Aylett (w)

9th Virginia: Maj. John C. Owens (mw)

14th Virginia: Col. James G. Hodges (k)

Lt. Col. William White (w)

Maj. Robert H. Poore (mw)

38th Virginia: Col. Edward C. Edmonds (k)

Lt. Col. P. B. Whittle (w)

53rd Virginia: Col. W. R. Aylett (w)

Lt. Col. Rawley W. Martin (w-c)

57th Virginia: Col. John Bowie Magruder (mw)

Lt. Col. Benjamin H. Wade (mw)

Maj. Clement R. Fontaine (w)

Artillery Battalion: Maj. James Dearing

Farquier (Virginia) Artillery: Capt. R. M. Stribling

Hampden (Virginia) Artillery: Capt. W. H. Caskie

Richmond Fayette Artillery: Capt. M. C. Macon

Blount's Virginia Artillery: Capt. Joseph G. Blount

Hood's Division: Maj. Gen. John B. Hood (w)

Brig. Gen. Evander M. Law

Law's Brigade: Brig. Gen. Evander M. Law

Col. James L. Sheffield

4th Alabama: Lt. Col. L. H. Scruggs

15th Alabama: Col. William C. Oates

Capt. Blanton A. Hill

44th Alabama: Col. William F. Perry

47th Alabama: Col. James W. Jackson (w)

Lt. Col. M. J. Bulger (w-c)

Maj. J. M. Campbell

48th Alabama: Col. James L. Sheffield

Capt. T. J. Eubanks

Anderson's Brigade: Brig. Gen. George T. Anderson (w)

Lt. Col. William Luffman (w)

7th Georgia: Col. W. W. White

8th Georgia: Col. John R. Towers (w)

9th Georgia: Lt. Col. John C. Mounger (k)

Maj. W. M. Jones (w)

Capt. George Hillyer

11th Georgia: Col. F. H. Little (w)

Lt. Col. William Luffman (w)

Maj. Henry D. McDaniel

59th Georgia: Col. Jack Brown (w)

Capt. M. G. Bass

Robertson's Brigade: Brig. Gen. Jerome B. Robertson (w)
    3rd Arkansas: Col. Van H. Manning (w)
        Lt. Col. R. S. Taylor
    1st Texas: Lt. Col. P. A. Work
    4th Texas: Col. J.C.G. Key (w)
        Maj. J. P. Bane
    5th Texas: Col. R. M. Powell (w-c)
        Lt. Col. King Bryan (w)
        Maj. J. C. Rogers
Benning's Brigade: Brig. Gen. Henry L. Benning
    2nd Georgia: Lt. Col. William T. Harris (k)
        Maj. W. S. Shepherd
    15th Georgia: Col. D. M. DuBose
    17th Georgia: Col. W. C. Hodges
    20th Georgia: Col. John A. Jones (k)
        Lt. Col. J. D. Waddell
Artillery Battalion: Maj. Mathis W. Henry
    Branch (North Carolina) Artillery: Capt. A. C. Latham
    Charleston German Artillery: Capt. William K. Bachman
    Palmetto (South Carolina) Artillery: Capt. Hugh R. Garden
    Rowan (North Carolina) Artillery: Capt. James Reilly
Corps Artillery Reserve: Col. James B. Walton
    Alexander's Battalion: Col. E. P. Alexander
        Woolfolk's Ashland (Virginia) Battery: Capt. P. Woolfolk, Jr. (w)
                Lt. James Woolfolk
        Jordan's Bedford (Virginia) Battery: Capt. Tyler C. Jordan
        Brooks (South Carolina) Battery: Capt. W. W. Fickling
        Moody's Madison (Louisiana) Battery: Capt. George V. Moody
        Parker's Richmond Battery: Capt. William W. Parker
        Eubank's Bath (Virginia) Battery: Lt. Osmond B. Taylor
    Washington (Louisiana) Battalion: Maj. Benjamin F. Eshleman
        Squires's First Company: Capt. Charles W. Squires
        Richardson's Second Company: Capt. John B. Richardson
        Miller's Third Company: Capt. Merritt B. Miller
        Eshleman's Fourth Company: Capt. Joe Norcom (w)
                Lt. H. A. Battles

Second Corps

Lt. Gen. Richard S. Ewell

Early's Division: Maj. Gen. Jubal A. Early
    Gordon's Brigade: Brig. Gen. John B. Gordon
        13th Georgia: Col. James M. Smith

26th Georgia: Col. Edmund N. Atkinson
31st Georgia: Col. Clement A. Evans
38th Georgia: Capt. William L. McLeod
60th Georgia: Capt. W. B. Jones
61st Georgia: Col. John H. Lamar
Hoke's Brigade: Col. Isaac E. Avery (mw)
    Col. A. C. Godwin
6th North Carolina: Maj. S. McD. Tate
21st North Carolina: Col. W. W. Kirkland
57th North Carolina: Col. A. C. Godwin
Smith's Brigade: Brig. Gen. William Smith
31st Virginia: Col. John S. Hoffman
49th Virginia: Lt. Col. J. Catlett Gibson
52nd Virginia: Lt. Col. James H. Skinner (w)
Hays's Brigade: Brig. Gen. Harry T. Hays
5th Louisiana: Maj. Alexander Hart (w)
    Capt. T. H. Biscoe
6th Louisiana: Lt. Col. Joseph Hanlon
7th Louisiana: Col. D. B. Penn
8th Louisiana: Col. T. D. Lewis (k)
    Lt. Col. A. de Blanc (w)
    Maj. G. A. Lester
9th Louisiana: Col. Leroy A. Stafford
Artillery Battalion: Lt. Col. Hilary P. Jones
Carrington's Charlottesville Battery: Capt. James McD. Carrington
Latimer's Courtney (Virginia) Battery: Capt. W. A. Tanner
Louisiana Guard Artillery: Capt. C. A. Green
Garber's Staunton (Virginia) Battery: Capt. A. W. Garber
Johnson's Division: Maj. Gen. Edward Johnson
Stonewall Brigade: Brig. Gen. James A. Walker
2nd Virginia: Col. J.Q.A. Nadenbousch
4th Virginia: Maj. William Terry
5th Virginia: Col. J.H.S. Funk
27th Virginia: Lt. Col. D. M. Shriver
33rd Virginia: Capt. J. B. Golladay
Jones's Brigade: Brig. Gen. John M. Jones (w)
    Lt. Col. Robert H. Dungan
21st Virginia: Capt. W. P. Moseley
25th Virginia: Col. J. C. Higginbotham (w)
    Lt. Col. J. A. Robinson
42nd Virginia: Lt. Col. R. W. Withers (w)
    Capt. S. H. Saunders

44th Virginia: Maj. Norval Cobb (w)

        Capt. T. R. Buckner

48th Virginia: Lt. Col. R. H. Dungan

        Maj. Oscar White

50th Virginia: Lt. Col. L.H.N. Salyer

Steuart's Brigade: Brig. Gen. George H. Steuart

    1st Maryland Battalion: Lt. Col. J. R. Herbert (w)

        Maj. W. W. Goldsborough (w)

        Capt. J. P. Crane

    1st North Carolina: Lt. Col. H. A. Brown

    3rd North Carolina: Maj. W. M. Parsley

    10th Virginia: Col. Edward T. H. Warren

    23rd Virginia: Lt. Col. S. T. Walton

    37th Virginia: Maj. H. C. Wood

Nicholls's Brigade: Col. J. M. Williams

    1st Louisiana: Lt. Col. Michael Nolan (k)

        Capt. E. D. Willett

    2nd Louisiana: Lt. Col. Ross E. Burke (w-c)

    10th Louisiana: Lt. Col. Henry D. Monier

    14th Louisiana: Lt. Col. David Zable

    15th Louisiana: Maj. Andrew Brady

Artillery Battalion: Maj. J. W. Latimer (mw)

        Capt. C. I. Raine

    Dement's 1st Maryland Battery: Capt. William F. Dement

    Carpenter's Alleghany (Virginia) Battery: Capt. J. C. Carpenter

    Brown's 4th Maryland Chesapeake Battery: Capt. W. D. Brown (w)

    Raine's Lee (Virginia) Battery: Capt. C. I. Raine

        Lt. William W. Hardwicke

Rodes's Division: Maj. Gen. Robert E. Rodes

  O'Neal's Brigade: Col. Edward A. O'Neal

    3rd Alabama: Col. Cullen A. Battle

    5th Alabama: Col. J. M. Hall

    6th Alabama: Col. J. N. Lightfoot (w)

        Capt. M. L. Bowie

    12th Alabama: Col. S. B. Pickens

    26th Alabama: Lt. Col. John C. Goodgame

  Doles's Brigade: Brig. Gen. George Doles

    4th Georgia: Lt. Col. D.R.E. Winn (k)

        Maj. W. H. Willis

    12th Georgia: Col. Edward Willis

    21st Georgia: Col. John T. Mercer

    44th Georgia: Col. S. P. Lumpkin (mw)

        Maj. W. H. Peebles

Iverson's Brigade: Brig. Gen. Alfred Iverson
    5th North Carolina: Capt. Speight B. West (w)
                    Capt. Benjamin Robinson (w)
    12th North Carolina: Lt. Col. W. S. Davis
    20th North Carolina: Lt. Col. Nelson Slough (w)
                    Capt. Lewis T. Hicks
    23rd North Carolina: Col. Daniel H. Christie (mw)
                    Capt. William H. Johnston
Daniel's Brigade: Brig. Gen. Junius Daniel
    32nd North Carolina: Col E. C. Brabble
    43rd North Carolina: Col. T. S. Kenan (w-c)
                    Lt. Col. W. G. Lewis
    45th North Carolina: Lt. Col. S. H. Boyd (w-c)
                    Maj. John R. Winston (w-c)
                    Capt. A. H. Gallaway (w)
                    Capt. J. A. Hopkins
    53rd North Carolina: Col. W. A. Owens
    2nd North Carolina Battalion: Lt. Col. H. L. Andrews (k)
                    Capt. Van Brown
Ramseur's Brigade: Brig. Gen. S. D. Ramseur
    2nd North Carolina: Maj. D. W. Hurtt (w)
                    Capt. James T. Scales
    4th North Carolina: Col. Bryan Grimes
    14th North Carolina: Col. R. Tyler Bennett (w)
                    Maj. Joseph H. Lambeth
    30th North Carolina: Col. Francis M. Parker (w)
                    Maj. W. W. Sellers
Artillery Battalion: Lt. Col. Thomas H. Carter
    Reese's Jeff Davis (Alabama) Battery: Capt. William J. Reese
    Carter's King William (Virginia) Battery: Capt. W. P. Carter
    Page's Morris Louisa (Virginia) Battery: Capt. R.C.M. Page (w)
    Fry's Orange (Virginia) Battery: Capt. C. W. Fry
Corps Artillery Reserve: Col. T. Thompson Brown
  First Virginia Artillery: Capt. Willis J. Dance
    Watson's Richmond Howitzers, 2nd Co.: Capt. David Watson
    Smith's Richmond Howitzers, 3rd Co.: Capt. B. H. Smith, Jr.
    Dance's Powhatan (Virginia) Battery: Lt. John M. Cunningham
    1st Rockbridge (Virginia) Battery: Capt. Archibald Graham
    Griffin's Salem (Virginia) Battery: Lt. C. B. Griffin
  Nelson's Battalion: Lt. Col. William Nelson
    Kirkpatrick's Amherst (Virginia) Battery: Capt. T. J. Kirkpatrick
    Massie's Fluvanna (Virginia) Battery: Capt. John L. Massie
    Millidge's Georgia Battery: Capt. John Millidge, Jr.

Third Corps
Lt. Gen. A. P. Hill

Anderson's Division: Maj. Gen. Richard H. Anderson
  Mahone's Brigade: Brig. Gen. William Mahone
    6th Virginia: Col. George T. Rogers
    12th Virginia: Col. D. A. Weisiger
    16th Virginia: Col. Joseph H. Ham
    41st Virginia: Col. William A. Parham
    61st Virginia: Col. V. D. Groner
  Posey's Brigade: Brig. Gen. Carnot Posey
    12th Mississippi: Col. W. H. Taylor
    16th Mississippi: Col. Samuel E. Baker
    19th Mississippi: Col. N. H. Harris
    48th Mississippi: Col. Joseph M. Jayne
  Perry's Brigade: Col. David Lang
    2nd Florida: Maj. W. R. Moore (w-c)
               Capt. William D. Ballentine (w-c)
               Capt. Alexander Mosely (c)
               Capt. C. Seton Fleming
    5th Florida: Capt. R. N. Gardner (w)
               Capt. Council A. Bryan
    8th Florida: Lt. Col. William Baya
  Wilcox's Brigade: Brig. Gen. Cadmus M. Wilcox
    8th Alabama: Lt. Col. Hilary A. Herbert
    9th Alabama: Capt. J. H. King (w)
    10th Alabama: Col. William H. Forney (w-c)
               Lt. Col. James E. Shelley
    11th Alabama: Col. J.C.C. Sanders (w)
               Lt. Col. George E. Tayloe
    14th Alabama: Col. L. Pinckard (w)
               Lt. Col. James A. Broome
  Wright's Brigade: Brig. Gen. Ambrose R. Wright
    3rd Georgia: Col. E. J. Walker
    22nd Georgia: Col. Joseph A. Wasden (k)
               Capt. B. C. McCurry
    48th Georgia: Col. William Gibson (w-c)
               Capt. M. R. Hall
    2nd Georgia Battalion: Maj. George W. Ross (mw)
               Capt. Charles J. Moffett
  Artillery Battalion: Maj. John Lane
    Sumter (Georgia) Artillery, Co. A: Capt. Hugh M. Ross

Sumter (Georgia) Artillery, Co. B: Capt. George M. Patterson

Sumter (Georgia) Artillery, Co. C: Capt. John T. Wingfield (w)

Heth's Division: Maj. Gen. Henry Heth (w)

Brig. Gen. J. Johnston Pettigrew (mw)

First Brigade: Brig. Gen. J. Johnston Pettigrew (mw)

Col. James K. Marshall (k)

Maj. John T. Jones

11th North Carolina: Col. Collett Leventhorpe (w)

Maj. Egbert A. Ross (k)

26th North Carolina: Col. Henry K. Burgwyn, Jr. (k)

Lt. Col. John R. Lane (w)

Capt. H. C. Albright

47th North Carolina: Col. George H. Faribault (w)

Lt. Col. John A. Graves (c)

52nd North Carolina: Col. James K. Marshall (k)

Lt. Col. Marcus A. Parks (w-c)

Maj. John Q. A. Richardson (k)

Second Brigade: Col. John M. Brockenbrough

40th Virginia: Capt. T. E. Betts

Capt. R. B. Davis

47th Virginia: Col. Robert M. Mayo

55th Virginia: Col. William S. Christian (c)

22nd Virginia Battalion: Maj. John S. Bowles

Third Brigade: Brig. Gen. James J. Archer (c)

Col. Birkett D. Fry (w-c)

Lt. Col. S. G. Shepard

13th Alabama: Col. Birkett D. Fry (w-c)

5th Alabama Battalion: Maj. A. S. Van de Graaff

1st Tennessee: Lt. Col. Newton J. George (c)

Maj. Felix G. Buchanan (w)

7th Tennessee: Col. John A. Fite (c)

Lt. Col. S. G. Shepard

14th Tennessee: Capt. B. L. Phillips

Fourth Brigade: Brig. Gen. Joseph R. Davis

2nd Mississippi: Col. John M. Stone (w)

Lt. Col. David W. Humphreys (k)

Maj. John A. Blair

11th Mississippi: Col. Francis M. Green

42nd Mississippi: Col. Hugh R. Miller (mw)

55th North Carolina: Col. John K. Connally (w)

Maj. Alfred H. Belo (w)

Artillery Battalion: Lt. Col. John J. Garnett

Maurin's Donaldsonville (Louisiana) Battery: Capt. Victor Maurin

Moore's Norfolk (Virginia) Battery: Capt. Joseph D. Moore
Lewis's Pittsylvania (Virginia) Battery: Capt. John R. Lewis
Grandy's Norfolk (Virginia) Blues Battery: Capt. C. R. Grandy
Pender's Division: Maj. Gen. William D. Pender (mw)
        Brig. Gen. James H. Lane
        Maj. Gen. Isaac R. Trimble (w-c)
        Brig. Gen. James H. Lane
First Brigade: Col. Abner Perrin
    1st South Carolina: Maj. C. W. McCreary
    1st South Carolina Rifles: Capt. William M. Hadden
    12th South Carolina: Col. John L. Miller
    13th South Carolina: Col. B. T. Brockman
    14th South Carolina: Lt. Col. Joseph N. Brown (w)
        Maj. Edward Croft (w)
Second Brigade: Brig. Gen. James H. Lane
        Col. Clark M. Avery
        Brig. Gen. James H. Lane
        Col. Clark M. Avery
    7th North Carolina: Capt. J. McLeod Turner (w-c)
        Capt. James G. Harris
    18th North Carolina: Col. John D. Barry
    28th North Carolina: Col. S. D. Lowe (w)
        Lt. Col. W.H.A. Speer
    33rd North Carolina: Col. Clark M. Avery
    37th North Carolina: Col. William M. Barbour
Third Brigade: Brig. Gen. Edward L. Thomas
    14th Georgia: Col. Robert W. Folsom
    35th Georgia: Col. Bolling H. Holt
    45th Georgia: Col. Thomas J. Simmons
    49th Georgia: Col. S. T. Player
Fourth Brigade: Brig. Gen. Alfred M. Scales (w)
        Col. William L. J. Lowrance (w)
    13th North Carolina: Col. J. H. Hyman (w)
        Lt. Col. H. A. Rogers
    16th North Carolina: Capt. Abel S. Cloud (c)
    22nd North Carolina: Maj. Thomas S. Galloway, Jr.
    34th North Carolina: Col. William L. J. Lowrance (w)
        Lt. Col. G. T. Gordon
    38th North Carolina: Col. W. J. Hoke (w)
        Lt. Col. John Ashford (w)
Artillery Battalion: Maj. William T. Poague
    Albemarle (Virginia) Light Artillery: Capt. James W. Wyatt
    Charlotte (North Carolina) Artillery: Capt. Joseph Graham

Madison (Mississippi) Light Artillery: Capt. George Ward
Brooke's Warrenton (Virginia) Battery: Capt. James V. Brooke
Corps Artillery Reserve: Col. R. Lindsay Walker
  McIntosh's Battalion: Maj. D. G. McIntosh
    Danville (Virginia) Light Artillery: Capt. R. S. Rice
    Hardaway's (Alabama) Artillery: Capt. W. B. Hurt
    2nd Rockbridge (Virginia) Battery: Lt. Samuel Wallace
    Johnson's Richmond Battery: Capt. Marmaduke Johnson
  Pegram's Battalion: Maj. W. J. Pegram
                        Capt. E. B. Brunson
    Crenshaw's Virginia Battery: Lt. John H. Chamberlayne (c)
    Fredericksburg (Virginia) Artillery: Capt. Edward A. Marye
    Letcher (Virginia) Artillery: Capt. T. A. Brander
    Pee Dee (South Carolina) Artillery: Lt. William E. Zimmerman
    Purcell (Virginia) Artillery: Capt. Joseph McGraw

Cavalry Division

Maj. Gen. J.E.B. Stuart

Hampton's Brigade: Brig. Gen. Wade Hampton (w)
                     Col. L. S. Baker
  1st North Carolina: Col. L. W. Baker
  1st South Carolina: Lt. Col. John D. Twiggs
  2nd South Carolina: Maj. Thomas J. Lipscomb
  Cobb's (Georgia) Legion: Col. Pierce B. L. Young
  Jeff Davis Legion: Lt. Col. Joseph F. Waring
  Phillips (Georgia) Legion: Lt. Col. W. W. Rich
Fitz Lee's Brigade: Brig. Gen. Fitzhugh Lee
  1st Maryland Battalion: Maj. Harry Gilmor
                          Maj. Ridgely Brown
  1st Virginia: Col. James H. Drake
  2nd Virginia: Col. Thomas T. Munford
  3rd Virginia: Col. Thomas H. Owen
  4th Virginia: Col. Williams C. Wickham
  5th Virginia: Col. Thomas L. Rosser
Robertson's Brigade: Brig. Gen. Beverly H. Robertson
  4th North Carolina: Col. Dennis D. Ferebee
  5th North Carolina: Lt. Col. James B. Gordon
Jenkins's Brigade: Brig. Gen. Albert G. Jenkins (w)
                     Col. Milton J. Ferguson
  14th Virginia: Maj. Benjamin F. Eakle (w)
  16th Virginia: Col. Milton J. Ferguson
  17th Virginia: Col. William H. Frenach

34th Virginia Battalion: Lt. Col. Vincent A. Witcher
36th Virginia Battalion: Maj. James W. Sweeney
Jackson's (Virginia) Battery: Capt. Thomas E. Jackson
Jones's Brigade: Brig. Gen. William E. Jones
6th Virginia: Maj. Cabel E. Flournoy
7th Virginia: Lt. Col. Thomas Marshall
11th Virginia: Col. Lunsford L. Lomax
35th Virginia Battalion: Lt. Col. Elijah V. White
W.H.F. Lee's Brigade: Col. John R. Chambliss, Jr.
2nd North Carolina: Lt. Col. William H. F. Payne
9th Virginia: Col. R.L.T. Beale
10th Virginia: Col. J. Lucius Davis
13th Virginia: Lt. Col. Jefferson C. Phillips
Imboden's Brigade: Brig. Gen. John D. Imboden
18th Virginia Cavalry: Col. George W. Imboden
62nd Virginia Mounted Infantry: Col. George H. Smith
Virginia Partisan Rangers: Capt. John H. McNeill
Staunton (Virginia) Artillery: Capt. John H. McClanahan
Stuart Horse Artillery: Maj. R. F. Beckham
Breathed's (Virginia) Battery: Capt. James Breathed
Chew's (Virginia) Battery: Capt. R. Preston Chew
Griffin's (Maryland) Battery: Capt. William H. Griffin
Hart's (South Carolina) Battery: Capt. James F. Hart
McGregor's (Virginia) Battery: Capt. William M. McGregor
Moorman's (Virginia) Battery: Capt. Marcellus N. Moorman

Notes

Works cited by author and short title in the Notes will be found in full citation in the Bibliography. The abbreviation *OR* stands for U.S. War Department, *The War of the Rebellion: A Compilation of the Official Records of the Union and Confederate Armies* (Series I unless otherwise noted). *SHSP* stands for *Southern Historical Society Papers, PMHSM* for the *Papers of the Military Historical Society of Massachusetts,* and MOLLUS for the Military Order of the Loyal Legion of the United States. Dates without a year are understood to be 1863. Generally, senders and addressees of dispatches are the principals rather than staff officers sending them "by order of."

1. We Should Assume the Aggressive

1. May 15, J. B. Jones, *A Rebel War Clerk's Diary,* 1:325; William Preston Johnston to his wife, May 15, Barret Collection, Tulane University.

2. Lee to Davis, May 7, Jefferson Davis, *The Papers of Jefferson Davis,* 9:170; Stephen W. Sears, *Chancellorsville,* 492, 501; Lee to G.W.C. Lee, May 11, Robert E. Lee, *The Wartime Papers of R. E. Lee,* 482.

3. A memoir by Postmaster General John H. Reagan, published forty-three years later, claimed attendance at this May 15 conference. In fact, however, Reagan confused it with a May 26 meeting (which Lee did not attend) when Davis briefed his Cabinet. It is inconceivable that Davis would have invited his postmaster general to join *any* strategy conference with Lee and Seddon. John H. Reagan, *Memoirs: With Special Reference to Secession and the Civil War* (New York: Neale, 1906), 120–22, 150–53.

4. Pettus to Davis, Apr. 16, cited in Davis, *Papers,* 9:148; Pemberton to Davis, May 1, 12, 13, *OR* 24.3:807, 859, 870; Seddon to Johnston, May 9, Johnston to Davis, May 13, *OR* 24.1:215.

5. Thomas Lawrence Connelly and Archer Jones, *The Politics of Command,* 118–23; Longstreet to Wigfall, Feb. 4, Wigfall Papers, Library of Congress; Longstreet to Lee, Apr. 3, *OR* 18:958–59; Seddon to Longstreet, May 3, 1875, Longstreet Papers, Emory University.

6. Lee to Seddon, Apr. 9, Lee, *Wartime Papers,* 429–30; Samuel Cooper to Lee, Apr. 14, *OR* 25.2:720; Lee to Cooper, Apr. 16, Lee, *Wartime Papers,* 433–34.

7. May 6, Jones, *Rebel War Clerk's Diary,* 1:311; Longstreet to Lafayette McLaws, July 25, 1873, McLaws Papers, Southern Historical Collection, University of North Carolina; Connelly and Jones, *Politics of Command,* 123. Seddon's May 9 telegram is not on

record, but its content can be inferred from Lee's responses (Note 8).

8. Lee to Seddon, May 10 (telegram), *OR* 25.2:790; Lee to Seddon, May 10, Lee, *Wartime Papers*, 482; Richard M. McMurry, "Marse Robert and the Fevers: A Note on the General as Strategist and on Medical Ideas as a Factor in Civil War Decision Making," *Civil War History*, 35:3 (1989), 197–207. For the Federal intelligence leak, in the *Washington Chronicle*, see Sears, *Chancellorsville*, 126–27.

9. The fullest discussion of Longstreet's postwar demonization in the South, and his intemperate response, is William Garrett Piston, *Lee's Tarnished Lieutenant: James Longstreet and His Place in Southern History* (Athens: University of Georgia Press, 1987).

10. Longstreet to Wigfall, May 13, Wigfall Papers, Library of Congress; Longstreet to McLaws, July 25, 1873, McLaws Papers, Southern Historical Collection. For the circumstances and significance of the McLaws letter, see Richard Rollins, "'The Ruling Ideas' of the Pennsylvania Campaign: James Longstreet's 1873 Letter to Lafayette McLaws," *Gettysburg Magazine*, 17 (1997), 7–16.

11. Longstreet to McLaws, July 25, 1873, McLaws Papers, Southern Historical Collection; Lee quoted by John Seddon, c. July 15, in *SHSP*, 4 (1877), 154.

12. Longstreet to Wigfall, May 13, Wigfall Papers, Library of Congress.

13. Lee to Davis, Apr. 16, Lee, *Wartime Papers*, 434–35; Longstreet to McLaws, July 25, 1873, McLaws Papers, Southern Historical Collection.

14. James Longstreet, "Lee in Pennsylvania," *Annals of the War*, 416–17; William Allan, conversation with Lee, Apr. 15, 1868, in Gary W. Gallagher, ed., *Lee the Soldier*, 15; Longstreet to McLaws, July 25, 1873, McLaws Papers, Southern Historical Collection. In 1866, after interviewing Longstreet, correspondent William Swinton wrote that Lee had "expressly promised" Longstreet he would not

assume the tactical offensive in the coming campaign: Swinton, *Campaigns of the Army of the Potomac* (New York: Charles B. Richardson, 1866), 340.

15. Davis, *Papers*, 9:xlii; May 6, Jones, *Rebel War Clerk's Diary*, 1:312; Pettus to Davis, May 8, *Jackson Mississippian* editors to Davis, May 8, *OR* 52.2:468, 468–69.

16. Beauregard to Seddon, May 3, 12, *OR* 14:924, 938; Lee to Seddon, Apr. 9, Lee to Cooper, Apr. 16, Lee to Seddon, May 10, Lee to Davis, May 11, Lee, *Wartime Papers*, 429–30, 433–34, 482, 483. In his dispatches to Seddon (May 10) and to Davis (May 11), Lee cited intelligence, gleaned from Northern newspapers and other sources, that Hooker was being reinforced by 30,000 men from Washington and by 18,000 from elsewhere, probably from North Carolina.

17. Richard M. McMurry, "The Pennsylvania Gambit and the Gettysburg Splash," Gabor S. Boritt, ed., *The Gettysburg Nobody Knows*, 181–99. Beauregard argued that Longstreet's two divisions ought to have been sent west in March or April, to cause whatever effect they might on the war there; Chancellorsville was fought and won without them anyway (Beauregard to Johnston, May 15, *OR* 23.2:837). Yet Hooker, knowing Longstreet was in Tennessee rather than hurrying toward the battlefield from southeastern Virginia, would likely have remained in his lines on May 6 and invited Lee to attack him there — and it is doubtful that Lee would have prevailed.

18. Lee to Seddon, Apr. 9, Lee, *Wartime Papers*, 429–30; John Bigelow, Jr., *The Campaign of Chancellorsville* (New Haven: Yale University Press, 1910), 460–72; Jeffry D. Wert, *General James Longstreet*, 237–38.

19. Allan, conversation with Lee, Apr. 15, 1868, in Gallagher, ed., *Lee the Soldier*, 14; Northrop to Seddon, June 4, *OR* ser. IV.2:574–75; Sears, *Chancellors-*

ville, 33; Robert K. Krick, "Why Lee Went North," *Morningside Notes,* 24 (Dayton: Morningside House, 1988), 10.

20. Marshall to D. H. Hill, Nov. 11, 1867, D. H. Hill Papers, Library of Virginia; McClellan testimony, *Report of the Joint Committee on the Conduct of the War,* 1 (1863), 439. See Stephen W. Sears, "The Twisted Tale of the Lost Order," *North & South,* 5:7 (2002), 54–65.

21. Lee to his wife, Feb. 23, Lee to Davis, Apr. 16, Lee, *Wartime Papers,* 407–8, 434–35.

22. Lee quoted by John Seddon, c. July 15, in *SHSP,* 4 (1877), 154; Lee to his wife, Apr. 19, Lee, *Wartime Papers,* 438; Lee report, July 31, *OR* 27.2:305.

23. Justus Scheibert, *Seven Months in the Rebel States During the North American War, 1863,* 98; Lee reports, July 31, 1863, Jan. 1864, *OR* 27.2:305, 313; Allan, conversation with Lee, Apr. 15, 1868, in Gallagher, ed., *Lee the Soldier,* 13; Lee to D. H. Hill, May 25, Lee, *Wartime Papers,* 493.

24. Lee to his wife, Apr. 19, Lee, *Wartime Papers,* 437–38; Allan, conversation with Lee, Feb. 19, 1870, in Gallagher, ed., *Lee the Soldier,* 17.

25. Davis to Lee, May 31, Davis, *Papers,* 9:201–2; Seddon to Lee, June 10, *OR* 27.3:882. Clerk Jones noted the cancellation of the Fredericksburg train on May 16 (*Rebel War Clerk's Diary,* 1:325–26). Dispatches datelined Richmond show Lee therefore remaining in the capital on the 16th transacting army business, then returning to Fredericksburg on the 17th.

2. High Command in Turmoil

1. Hooker to Lincoln, May 13, Lincoln to Hooker, May 13, *OR* 25.2:473, 474; Lincoln to Hooker, May 14, Abraham Lincoln, *The Collected Works of Abraham Lincoln,* 6:217.

2. See "The Revolt of the Generals," Stephen W. Sears, *Controversies & Commanders,* 131–66.

3. Darius Couch memoir, 1873, Old Colony Historical Society; Meade to his wife, May 10, 20, George Meade, *The Life and Letters of George Gordon Meade,* 1:373, 379; Samuel P. Heintzelman diary, May 13, Heintzelman Papers, Library of Congress; Alexander S. Webb to his brother, c. May 9, Webb Papers, Yale University Library.

4. Hooker G.O. 49, May 6, *OR* 25.1:171.

5. Sedgwick to his sister, May 15, John Sedgwick, *Correspondence of John Sedgwick,* 2:128; Meade to his wife, May 10, Meade, *Life and Letters,* 1:373–74; June 20, Gideon Welles, *Diary of Gideon Welles,* 1:336; Abbott to his mother, May 17, Henry L. Abbott, *Fallen Leaves: The Civil War Letters of Major Henry Livermore Abbott,* 181. For Hooker's injury, see "In Defense of Fighting Joe," Sears, *Controversies & Commanders,* 177, 186–89.

6. Bruce Tap, *Over Lincoln's Shoulder: The Committee on the Conduct of the War* (Lawrence: University Press of Kansas, 1998), 170; Chandler to his wife, May 20, Chandler Papers, Library of Congress.

7. Hooker testimony, *Report of Joint Committee,* 1 (1865), 151; Meade to his wife, May 15, Meade, *Life and Letters,* 1:376. Curtin probably heard from a third prominent Pennsylvanian in the Potomac army, General David B. Birney. Birney was identified by Washington insider Elizabeth Blair Lee as a member of the anti-Hooker cabal: Elizabeth Blair Lee, *Wartime Washington: The Civil War Letters of Elizabeth Blair Lee,* 269.

8. Heintzelman diary, May 13, Heintzelman Papers, Library of Congress; Meade to his wife, May 15, 19, Meade, *Life and Letters,* 1:376, 377; Gouverneur K. Warren to his fiancée, May 15, Warren Papers, New York State Li-

brary; Hooker to Samuel P. Bates, May 30, 1878, Bates Collection, Pennsylvania State Archives. Webb described Meade's outburst to Charles S. Wainwright, who recorded it June 12 in *A Diary of Battle: The Personal Journals of Colonel Charles S. Wainwright, 1861–1865*, 219.

9. George W. Smalley, *Anglo-American Memories* (New York: Putnam's, 1911), 159–60.

10. Hooker testimony, *Report of Joint Committee*, 1 (1865), 151, 176; Chase to Hooker, May 23, cited in Walter H. Hebert, *Fighting Joe Hooker*, 229.

11. Hooker testimony, *Report of Joint Committee*, 1 (1865), 151; May 25, John Gibbon, *Personal Recollections of the Civil War*, 120; Francis A. Walker, *History of the Second Army Corps*, 254; Sedgwick to his sister, Nov. 16, Sedgwick, *Correspondence*, 2:161–62; Hancock to his wife, [May 1863], Almira R. Hancock, *Reminiscences of Winfield Scott Hancock* (New York: Charles L. Webster, 1887), 94–95; *New York Herald*, May 16, June 1.

12. Heintzelman diary, May 15, 17, Heintzelman Papers, Library of Congress; May 18, Marsena R. Patrick, *Inside Lincoln's Army: The Diary of Marsena Rudolph Patrick*, 250.

13. Gibbon, *Personal Recollections*, 121–22; Lincoln to Hooker, May 14, Lincoln, *Works*, 6:217. Howard piously but unconvincingly professed his loyalty to Hooker: Howard in *Atlantic Monthly* (July 1876), in Peter Cozzens, ed., *Battles and Leaders of the Civil War: Volume 5*, 320–21.

14. Donaldson to his brother, May 14, Francis A. Donaldson, *Inside the Army of the Potomac: The Civil War Experience of Captain Francis Adams Donaldson*, 264; June 10, Stephen M. Weld, *War Diary and Letters of Stephen Minot Weld, 1861–1865*, 213; Schurz to Lincoln, Jan. 24, Lincoln Papers, Library of Congress; Edward H. Ketchum to his mother, May 12, cited in Annette Tapert, ed., *The Brothers' War: Civil War Letters to Their Loved Ones from the Blue and Gray* (New York: Times Books, 1988), 142.

15. May 7, Theodore A. Dodge, *On Campaign with the Army of the Potomac: The Civil War Journal of Theodore Ayrault Dodge*, 258; William W. Folwell to his wife, May 12, 13, Minnesota Historical Society; John Willard to his mother, May 15, Margaret Bradley Willard Papers, Duke University Library.

16. Hooker to Lincoln, May 13, *OR* 25.2:473. The number mustered out of the Army of the Potomac in spring 1863 is compiled from data in: *OR* 25.2:532; *OR* ser. III.3:760, 775; *Report of Joint Committee*, 1 (1865), 219. The April 30 return of 111,650 infantry "present for duty equipped" reflects the five two-year regiments mustered out during April: *OR* 25.2:320.

17. James W. Latta diary, May 24, Library of Congress; Sedgwick to his sister, May 15, Sedgwick, *Correspondence*, 2:128.

18. Hooker to Lincoln, May 13, *OR* 25.2:473; Sedgwick to his sister, April 20, Sedgwick, *Correspondence*, 2:91; Meade to his wife, May 19, Meade, *Life and Letters*, 1:378. Hooker's reference to a marching force of "about 80,000" referred to rank and file. By return, the number of infantrymen on May 31 was 81,792: *OR* 25.2:574.

19. Hooker testimony, *Report of Joint Committee*, 1 (1865), 112; Halleck to Stanton, May 18, *OR* 25.2:504–6.

20. Edward G. Longacre, *The Man Behind the Guns: A Biography of General Henry J. Hunt*, 138–41; May 3, Wainwright, *Diary of Battle*, 194.

21. Hooker S.O. 129, May 12, *OR* 25.2:471–72; Tully McCrae, "Light Artillery: Its Use and Misuse," in Catherine S. Crary, ed., *Dear Belle: Letters from a Cadet & Officer to his Sweetheart, 1845–1865* (Middletown, Conn.: Wesleyan University Press, 1965), 195.

22. Stephen Z. Starr, *The Union Cavalry in the Civil War*, 1:367–69; Frank A. Haskell, *Haskell of Gettysburg: His Life*

and Civil War Papers, 133–34; Charles Russell Lowell to Josephine Shaw, July 23, Edward W. Emerson, *Life and Letters of Charles Russell Lowell* (Boston: Houghton Mifflin, 1907), 279; Hooker to Bates, July 12, 1878, Bates Collection, Pennsylvania State Archives; return of May 31, *OR* 25.2:574; Hooker to Stoneman, Apr. 12, *OR* 25.1:1067.

23. Haskell, *Haskell of Gettysburg,* 133; Theodore Lyman, *Meade's Headquarters, 1863–1865: Letters of Colonel Theodore Lyman,* 103.

24. Williams to his daughter, May 23, Alpheus S. Williams, *From the Cannon's Mouth: The Civil War Letters of General Alpheus S. Williams,* 203; Carswell McClellan, *General Andrew A. Humphreys at Malvern Hill . . . and Fredericksburg . . . a Memoir* (St. Paul, 1888), 15.

25. Timothy J. Reese, *Sykes' Regular Infantry Division,* 1861–1864, 17.

26. Lyman, *Meade's Headquarters,* 108; return of Apr. 30, *OR* 25.2:320; John W. Busey and David G. Martin, *Regimental Strengths and Losses at Gettysburg,* 16.

27. Schurz to Hooker, May 17, Carl Schurz Papers, Library of Congress; Apr. 19, Wainwright, *Diary of Battle,* 183.

28. Sept. 27, John Hay, *Inside Lincoln's White House: The Complete Civil War Diary of John Hay,* 86. For a summary and evaluation of the command makeup of the Army of the Potomac, see Larry Tagg, *The Generals of Gettysburg.*

29. Hooker to Lincoln, May 7, *OR* 25.1:438; Hooker to Samuel Ross, Feb. 28, 1864, in *Battles and Leaders of the Civil War,* 3:223.

30. *Richmond Examiner,* May 22; Heintzelman diary, May 27, Heintzelman Papers, Library of Congress. For this intelligence, and its sources and handling, see Edwin C. Fishel, *The Secret War for the Union: The Untold Story of Military Intelligence in the Civil War,* 416–18.

31. Hooker to John A. Dix, May 25, Hooker to Stanton, May 27, Halleck to Stanton, May 18, Hooker to Chase, May 25, Stanton to Hooker, May 27, *OR* 25.2:523, 527, 505, 524, 528.

32. Edward J. Nichols, *Toward Gettysburg: A Biography of General John F. Reynolds,* 182–84, 220–23; Reynolds to his sisters, Jan. 23, John F. Reynolds Papers, Franklin and Marshall College; Meade to his wife, June 13, Meade, *Life and Letters,* 1:385; T. J. Barnett to S.L.M. Barlow, June 26, Barlow Papers, Huntington Library; June 29, Wainwright, *Diary of Battle,* 229; Weld, *War Diary and Letters,* 227n. Although Henry Slocum was next on the Potomac army seniority list after Couch, there was apparently no thought of him for the command.

3. The Risk of Action

1. Pender to his wife, May 18, William Dorsey Pender, *The General to His Lady: The Civil War Letters of William Dorsey Pender,* 238; Lee to Davis, May 20, Lee, *Wartime Papers,* 488–89.

2. Pendleton to his mother, June 4, William Nelson Pendleton Papers, Southern Historical Collection, University of North Carolina; John B. Gordon, *Reminiscences of the Civil War,* 158; Donald C. Pfanz, *Richard S. Ewell,* 273, 574; Evans to his wife, June 6, Clement A. Evans, *Intrepid Warrior: Clement Anselm Evans, Confederate General,* ed. Robert Grier Stephens (Dayton: Morningside House, 1992), 187. Donald Pfanz credits Jackson's physician, Dr. Hunter McGuire, with recording Jackson's wish that Ewell succeed him.

3. Lee to Davis, Oct. 2, 1862, *OR* 19.2:643; James I. Robertson, Jr., *Gen-*

eral *A. P. Hill,* 119–21, 160–61. Biographer Robertson discovered Hill's illness to be prostatitis.

4. Lee to Davis, May 25, Robert E. Lee, *Lee's Dispatches: Unpublished Letters of Robert E. Lee to Jefferson Davis,* 91–92; A. P. Hill to Lee, May 24, cited in Douglas Southall Freeman, *Lee's Lieutenants,* 2:698–99.

5. Return of Dec. 31, 1862, *OR* 21:1082; return of Jan. 31, 1863, *OR* 25.2:601; Sears, *Chancellorsville,* 112, 442.

6. Lee to Davis, May 7, June 7, Davis, *Papers,* 9:170, 209; Longstreet to McLaws, June 3, McLaws Papers, Southern Historical Collection. This correspondence makes it clear that Lee was not suggesting that Beauregard take command of the Army of Northern Virginia, as Douglas Southall Freeman surmised in *R. E. Lee,* 2:560.

7. Hal Bridges, *Lee's Maverick General: Daniel Harvey Hill* (New York: McGraw-Hill, 1961), 187; Lee to D. H. Hill, May 16, 25, Lee, *Wartime Papers,* 485–86, 494.

8. Davis to Lee, May 29, *OR* 18:1077; Lee to Davis, May 29, 30, Lee, *Wartime Papers,* 495, 495–96; Davis to Lee, May 31, Davis, *Papers,* 9:202.

9. Lee to D. H. Hill, May 25, Lee, *Wartime Papers,* 494; D. H. Hill to his wife, June 25, D. H. Hill Papers, North Carolina State Archives; Davis to Lee, May 31, Davis, *Papers,* 9:202.

10. Lee to Hood, May 21, Lee, *Wartime Papers,* 490; Lee S.O. 146, May 30, *OR* 25.2:840.

11. G. Moxley Sorrel, *Recollections of a Confederate Staff Officer,* 48.

12. Ewell to his wife, June 5, 1865, Polk-Brown-Ewell Papers, Southern Historical Collection; Allan, conversation with Lee, Mar. 3, 1868, in Gallagher, ed., *Lee the Soldier,* 11.

13. Robert Stiles, *Four Years under Marse Robert* (New York: Neale, 1903), 189; Henry C. Walker, May 9, in Mills Lane, ed., *"Dear Mother: Don't grieve about me . . .": Letters from Georgia Soldiers in the Civil War* (Savannah: Beehive Press, 1977), 234.

14. Lee to Davis, May 20, Lee, *Wartime Papers,* 487.

15. A. P. Hill to Lee, May 24, cited in Freeman, *Lee's Lieutenants,* 2:698.

16. Sorrel, *Recollections of a Confederate Staff Officer,* 264. The Army of Northern Virginia's infantry commanders are described and evaluated in Larry Tagg, *The Generals of Gettysburg.*

17. Richard Rollins, "The Failure of Confederate Artillery at Gettysburg: Ordnance and Logistics," *North & South,* 3:2 (2000), 44–54.

18. Lee to Davis, May 7, Davis, *Papers,* 9:169; D. H. Hill to Seddon, Feb. 23, *OR* 18:891.

19. Busey and Martin, *Regimental Strengths and Losses at Gettysburg,* 129, 16; Stephen W. Sears, *To the Gates of Richmond: The Peninsula Campaign* (Boston: Houghton Mifflin, 1992), 156, 416n11.

20. Davis to Lee, May 26, 31, Davis, *Papers,* 9:192, 202–3; Johnston to Seddon, June 15, *OR* 24.1:227.

21. Lee to Seddon, June 8, Lee, *Wartime Papers,* 504–5; Edward Porter Alexander, *Fighting for the Confederacy: The Personal Recollections of General Edward Porter Alexander,* 221.

4. Armies on the March

1. Charles M. Blackford to his father, June 15, Blackford Family Papers, Southern Historical Collection, University of North Carolina; Alexander, *Fighting for the Confederacy,* 222.

2. Lee to Davis, June 7, Davis, *Papers,* 9:208; Allan, conversation with Lee, Feb. 19, 1870, in Gallagher, ed., *Lee the Soldier,* 17.

3. Sharpe to John McEntee, June 4, B.M.I., RG 393, National Archives; Hooker to Lincoln, June 5, *OR*

27.1:32–33; Sedgwick to Hooker, June 6, *OR* 27.3:13; Lee to Davis, June 7, Davis, *Papers,* 9:208.

4. Fishel, *Secret War for the Union,* 426; William W. Averell report, *OR* 25.1:47; Sears, *Chancellorsville,* 83–92; Hooker to Lincoln, n.d., B.M.I., RG 393, National Archives; Hooker to Halleck, June 6, *OR* 27.1:33.

5. Hooker to Lincoln, June 5, *OR* 27.1:30; Hooker testimony, *Report of Joint Committee,* 1 (1865), 160–61; Lincoln to Hooker, June 5, Lincoln, *Works,* 6:249; Halleck to Hooker, June 5, *OR* 27.1:31–32. Hooker never fully developed his plan for moving against A. P. Hill's corps, beyond crossing above and below Fredericksburg, but it surely would not have included attacking the entrenchments there frontally, as Halleck implied.

6. Return of May 31, *OR* 25.2:846; Heros von Borcke, *Memoirs of the Confederate War for Independence* (New York: Peter Smith, 1938), 2:264–67; Freeman, *Lee's Lieutenants,* 3:2; W. W. Blackford, *War Years with Jeb Stuart,* 212; H. B. McClellan, *The Life and Campaigns of Major-General J.E.B. Stuart,* 261–62; Lee to his wife, June 9, Lee, *Wartime Papers,* 507.

7. McClellan, *Life and Campaigns of Stuart,* 262–63; Hooker to Pleasonton, June 7, *OR* 27.3:27–28. Although the course of the Rappahannock here is west by north, for clarity the left (Federal) bank is termed the north bank, and the right (Confederate) bank is termed the south bank.

8. Gary W. Gallagher, "Brandy Station: The Civil War's Bloodiest Arena of Mounted Combat," *Blue & Gray,* 8:1 (1990), 11–12, 20; Patrick Brennan, "Thunder on the Plains of Brandy," Part I, *North & South,* 5:3 (2002), 21–25.

9. Buford report, *OR Supplement* 5:227–28; McClellan, *Life and Campaigns of Stuart,* 264–66; Charles R. Phelps to his aunt, June 11, University of Virginia Library; R. F. Beckham report, *OR* 27.2:772.

10. Buford report, *OR Supplement* 5:228–29; Phelps to his aunt, June 11, University of Virginia Library; James F. Hart in *Philadelphia Weekly Times,* June 26, 1880; Henry C. Whelan, George C. Cram reports, *OR Supplement* 5:239, 246–47. Due to ill health, Fitz Lee had turned over his brigade that day to Col. Thomas Munford.

11. Frank S. Robertson memoir, Jedediah Hotchkiss Papers, Library of Congress; Frank M. Myers, *The Comanches: A History of White's Battalion, Virginia Cavalry* (Marietta, Ga.: Continental Book, 1956), 183; Hart in *Philadelphia Weekly Times,* June 26, 1880.

12. McClellan, *Life and Campaigns of Stuart,* 269–72; Starr, *Union Cavalry,* 1:383–85.

13. Taylor to Bettie Saunders, June 11, Walter H. Taylor, *Lee's Adjutant: The Wartime Letters of Colonel Walter Herron Taylor,* 55; Noble D. Preston, *History of the 10th Regiment of Cavalry, New York State Volunteers* (New York: Appleton, 1892), 85; Henry C. Meyer, *Civil War Experiences* (New York: Knickerbocker Press, 1911), 28; George W. Shreve reminiscence, Library of Virginia.

14. James Moore, *Kilpatrick and Our Cavalry* (New York: W. J. Widdleton, 1865), 59; Edward G. Longacre, *The Cavalry at Gettysburg: A Tactical Study,* 80–81; June 9, Jedediah Hotchkiss, *Make Me a Map of the Valley: The Civil War Journal of Stonewall Jackson's Topographer,* 150.

15. Patrick Brennan, "Thunder on the Plains of Brandy," Part II, *North & South,* 5:4 (2002), 46–48; Longacre, *Cavalry at Gettysburg,* 84; Brooke to his mother, June 12, Philadelphia Civil War Library and Museum. On June 27, while recuperating in a private home, Rooney Lee was captured by a Federal raiding party. He was not exchanged until March 1864.

16. Pleasonton to Hooker, June 9, *OR* 27.1:903; Pleasonton to Hooker, June 9, Hooker to Pleasonton, June 9, *OR*

27.3:38, 39; Lee to Stuart, June 9, *OR* 27.3:876.

17. *OR* 27.1:168–70; *OR* 27.2:719; McClellan, *Life and Campaigns of Stuart,* 292.

18. Pleasonton report, *OR* 27.1:1045. For Pleasonton's fictional inventions, see Fishel, *Secret War for the Union,* 433–34, 588–92.

19. Stuart G.O. 24, June 15, *OR* 27.2:719–20; *Charleston Mercury,* June 15, *Richmond Enquirer,* June 13, *Richmond Examiner,* June 12; Pender to his wife, June 12, Pender, *General to His Lady,* 246.

20. Henry D. McDaniel, *With Unabated Trust: Major Henry McDaniel's Love Letters from Confederate Battlefields . . . ,* ed. Anita B. Sams (Monroe, Ga.: Historical Society of Walton County, 1977), 171; McClellan, *Life and Campaigns of Stuart,* 294; Walter S. Newhall to his mother, June 25, Historical Society of Pennsylvania.

21. Lee to Davis, June 18, Lee, *Wartime Papers,* 519; June 11, Hotchkiss, *Make Me a Map,* 150; June 10, 11, 12, Louis Leon, *Diary of a Tar Heel Confederate Soldier* (Charlotte: Stone Publishing, 1913), 30, courtesy Greg Mast; Busey and Martin, *Regimental Strengths and Losses at Gettysburg,* 150, 199.

22. Lee to Davis, Sept. 8, 1862, June 10, 25, 1863, Lee, *Wartime Papers,* 301, 507–9; 530–31; Stephens to Davis, June 12, Dunbar Rowland, ed., *Jefferson Davis, Constitutionalist: His Letters, Papers, and Speeches* (Jackson: Mississippi Department of Archives and History, 1923), 5:513–15; Davis to Stephens, June 18, cited in Davis, *Papers,* 9:229; Thomas E. Schott, "The Stephens 'Peace' Mission," *North & South,* 1:6 (1998), 40.

23. William H. Beach, *The First New York (Lincoln) Cavalry* (New York: Lincoln Cavalry Assoc., 1902), 220; Margaretta Barton Colt, *Defend the Valley: A Shenandoah Family in the Civil War,* 217; Davis message to Congress, Jan. 12, *OR* ser. IV.2:345.

24. Halleck to Schenck, June 11, Milroy to

Schenck, June 11, Schenck to Milroy, June 12, Halleck to Schenck, June 14, *OR* 27.2:171, 161, 125, 167; Milroy report, *OR* 27.2:43; Lincoln to Schenck, June 14, Lincoln, *Works,* 6:274. The Federal intelligence failure at Winchester is examined in Fishel, *Secret War for the Union,* 444–53, 572–74.

25. Milroy report, *OR* 27.2:43; Wilbur Sturtevant Nye, *Here Come the Rebels!,* 97–98; *Richmond Enquirer,* June 22. The 1,800 of Milroy's men at Berryville were counted apart from the 6,900 at Winchester. The total of Milroy's casualties and his survivors, collected at Harper's Ferry and in Maryland and Pennsylvania, came to 8,702: *OR* 27.2:53, *OR* 27.3:220, 295–96.

26. Mark Chance, "Prelude to Invasion: Lee's Preparations and the Second Battle of Winchester," *Gettysburg Magazine,* 19 (1998), 20–21; Hays report, *OR* 27.2:477; Harry Gilmor, *Four Years in the Saddle* (New York: Harper & Brothers, 1866), 89–91.

27. Milroy report, testimony, *OR* 27.2:47, 93, 161; Nye, *Here Come the Rebels!,* 108–23; Chance, "Prelude to Invasion," *Gettysburg Magazine,* 19 (1998), 27–34; Monroe Nichols report, *OR Supplement* 5:70; June 15, Hotchkiss, *Make Me a Map,* 152.

28. *OR* 27.2:53; Ewell report, *OR* 27.2:442; J. Thompson Brown report, *OR* 27.2:456.

29. Blackford to his wife, June 16, Susan Leigh Blackford, ed., *Letters from Lee's Army* (New York: Scribner's, 1947), 177; June 16, Hotchkiss, *Make Me a Map,* 153; Campbell Brown memoir, Brown, *Campbell Brown's Civil War: With Ewell and the Army of Northern Virginia,* 194; Ann C. R. Jones to Lucy R. Parkhill, June 18, Colt, *Defend the Valley,* 260.

30. Nye, *Here Come the Rebels!,* 140; Curtin to Lincoln, June 14, *OR* 27.3:113; June 15, Welles, *Diary,* 1:329–30.

31. Nye, *Here Come the Rebels!,* 142–45; *Chambersburg Repository,* cited in Frank Moore, ed., *The Rebellion Record:*

A Diary of American Events, 7:Documents, 197.

32. Thompson to Lincoln, June 16, *OR* 27.3:168; June 17, Welles, *Diary,* 1:332; Grant to Halleck, May 24, *OR* 24.1:37.

33. Butterfield to Rufus Ingalls, June 17, *OR* 27.3:175; Fishel, *Secret War for the Union,* 454–60; Pleasonton to Seth Williams, June 10, *OR* 27.3:48.

34. Hooker to Lincoln, June 10, *OR* 27.1:34–35; Lincoln to Hooker, June 10, Lincoln, *Works,* 6:257; Halleck to Hooker, June 11, *OR* 27.1:35; Army of the Potomac circular, June 11, *OR* 27.3:67.

35. Fishel, *Secret War for the Union,* 437–40; McEntee to Sharpe, June 12 (two), 13, B.M.I., RG 393, National Archives; Hooker to Halleck, June 13, *OR* 27.1:38; Dawes to Mary Gates, June 7, State Historical Society of Wisconsin.

36. Hooker to Halleck, June 13, *OR* 27.1:38; Hooker to Reynolds, June 12, *OR* 27.3:72–73; Hooker to Samuel P. Bates, May 30, 1878, Bates Collection, Pennsylvania State Archives.

37. June 17, Wainwright, *Diary of Battle,* 221; Dawes to Mary Gates, June 15, State Historical Society of Wisconsin.

38. Halleck to Francis Lieber, Aug. 4, Lieber Papers, Huntington Library; return of June 20, *OR* 27.1:151; Pleasonton to Hooker, June 14, *OR* 27.3:107. Expiring enlistments data: *OR* 25.2: 532; *OR* ser. III.3:760, 775; *Report of Joint Committee* 1 (1865), 219. The overestimate of Lee's army was due primarily to lack of intelligence on the nature and number of his reinforcements from the south.

39. Hooker to Lincoln, June 5, Halleck to Hooker, June 5, *OR* 27.1:30, 32.

40. Halleck to Hooker, June 15, *OR* 27.1:42; Lincoln to Hooker, June 15, Lincoln, *Works,* 6:273; Herman Haupt, *Reminiscences of General Herman Haupt* (Milwaukee: Wright & Joys, 1901), 205; Hooker to Lincoln, June 15 (two), *OR* 27.1:43; June 14, Welles, *Diary,* 1:329; Hooker to Lincoln, June 16, *OR* 27.1:45.

41. Lincoln to Hooker, June 16, 16 (telegram), Lincoln, *Works,* 6:281, 282.

5. Into the Enemy's Country

1. Elizabeth Blair Lee to her husband, June 15, Lee, *Wartime Washington,* 275.

2. Couch report, *OR* 27.2:211–12; Nye, *Here Come the Rebels!,* 155–56, 212–21; Curtin proclamation, June 12, *OR* 27.3:79–80; Lincoln proclamation, June 15, Lincoln, *Works,* 6:277–78; Stanton to Horatio Seymour, June 15, *OR* 27.3:138; Charles W. Sandford report, *OR* 27.2:227–28.

3. June 16, 19, 14, Welles, *Diary,* 1:331–32, 335, 329.

4. Lee to Davis, June 10, Lee, *Wartime Papers,* 508; June 17, George Templeton Strong, *The Diary of George Templeton Strong: The Civil War, 1860–1865,* ed. Allan Nevins (New York: Macmillan, 1952), 324; Hooker to Lincoln, June 15, *OR* 27.1:43.

5. Hooker to Lincoln, June 15 (two), *OR* 27.1:43, 43–44; Hooker to Reynolds, June 13, *OR* 27.3:87; Sharpe to Jansen Hasbrouck, June 20, Sharpe Collection, Senate House Museum, Kingston, N.Y.; Julia Lorrilard Butterfield, ed., *A Biographical Memorial of General Daniel Butterfield* (New York: Grafton Press, 1894), 332n; Hooker testimony, *Report of Joint Committee,* 1 (1865), 177.

6. Marsena R. Patrick diary, June 17, Library of Congress.

7. Lee to Longstreet, June 15, *OR* 27.3:890; Lee report, July 31, *OR* 27.2:306.

8. Cooper to D. H. Hill, June 15, Lee to Cooper, June 23, *OR* 27.3:891–92, 925–26; Lee to Davis, June 23, 25, Lee, *Wartime Papers,* 527–28, 532–33; Cooper to Lee, June 29, *OR* 27.1:75. Cooper's June 29 dispatch rejecting the

Beauregard scheme was intercepted by the Federals and thus was not seen by Lee, but by then events had overtaken the idea: Davis, *Papers*, 9:247.

9. Lee's numbers are summarized from Busey and Martin, *Regimental Strengths and Losses at Gettysburg*. For Lee's Chancellorsville numbers, see Sears, *Chancellorsville*, 112, 526n6.

10. Jerome Yates to his mother, June 17, cited in Bell Irvin Wiley, *The Life of Johnny Reb* (Indianapolis: Bobbs-Merrill, 1943), 310; H. Christopher Kendrick to his father, n.d., to his mother, June 3, Kendrick Papers, Southern Historical Collection, University of North Carolina; Johnston to Seddon, June 15, 18, *OR* 24.1:227; McLaws to his wife, June 5, Lafayette McLaws, *A Soldier's General: The Civil War Letters of Major General Lafayette McLaws*, 187.

11. Lee G.O. 72, June 21, *OR* 27.3:912–13; Roger Long, "General Orders No. 72, 'By Command of Gen. R. E. Lee,'" *Gettysburg Magazine* 7 (1992), 13–14; Reuben V. Kidd, July 17, Alice V. D. Pierrepont, ed., *Reuben Vaughan Kidd: Soldier of the Confederacy* (Petersburg, Va., 1947), 329; June [27] statement, *OR* 27.1:65; Taliaferro N. Simpson, June 28, July 27, Simpson, *Far, Far from Home: The Wartime Letters of Dick and Tally Simpson, Third South Carolina Volunteers*, eds. Guy R. Everson and Edward W. Simpson, Jr. (New York: Oxford, 1994), 251, 261–62; Evans to his wife, June 4, Clement A. Evans, *Intrepid Warrior: Clement Anselm Evans, Confederate General* (Dayton: Morningside House, 1992), 184.

12. Hooker to Lincoln, June 16, Halleck to Hooker, June 15, *OR* 27.1:45, 42; Hooker to Pleasonton, June 17, *OR* 27.3:172.

13. Longacre, *Cavalry at Gettysburg*, 104–9; Nye, *Here Come the Rebels!*, 175–81; Adams, June 19, W. C. Ford, ed., *A Cycle of Adams Letters, 1861–1865* (Boston: Houghton Mifflin, 1920), 1:36–37; *OR* 27.1:171; Munford report, *OR* 27.2:741.

14. McClellan, *Life and Campaigns of Stuart*, 303–4; Nye, *Here Come the Rebels!*, 181–85; Duffié report, *OR* 27.1:962–64; Pleasonton to Hooker, June 18, *OR* 27.1:907; Hooker to Pleasonton, June 18, *OR* 27.3:195.

15. Nye, *Here Come the Rebels!*, 186–95; John S. Mosby, *Stuart's Cavalry in the Gettysburg Campaign*, 65–67; Hooker to Pleasonton, June 17, Pleasonton to Hooker, June 20, *OR* 27.3:176–77, 224.

16. Longacre, *Cavalry at Gettysburg*, 126–32; Nye, *Here Come the Rebels!*, 196–211; George Baylor, *Bull Run to Bull Run; or, Four Years in the Army of Northern Virginia* (Richmond: B. F. Johnson, 1900), 149; Francis A. Donaldson to his aunt, June 25, Donaldson, *Inside the Army of the Potomac*, 285; John P. Sheahan to his father, June 23, Maine Historical Society.

17. *OR* 27.1:193; *OR* 27.2:712–13; Pleasonton to Hooker, June 21, 22, *OR* 27.1:911–13.

18. Ewell report, *OR* 27.2:442–43; Pender to his wife, June 23, Pender, *General to His Lady*, 251; Lee to Ewell, June 19, [21], 22, *OR* 27.3:905, 914–15.

19. Mark Nesbitt, *Saber and Scapegoat: J.E.B. Stuart and the Gettysburg Controversy*, 57–73; Mosby, *Stuart's Cavalry in the Gettysburg Campaign*, 76; Jeffry D. Wert, *Mosby's Rangers*, 91; Lee to Stuart, June 22, Longstreet to Lee, June 22, Longstreet to Stuart, June 22, *OR* 27.3:913, 915; Lee to Stuart, June 23, *OR* 27.3:923. (In the latter dispatch, in the phrase, should the enemy "not appear to be moving northward," "not" may have been added by clerical error.) June 18 is the only date for the Lee-Stuart-Longstreet Paris, Va., meeting that fits their respective timetables. Mark Nesbitt posits a third Lee order to Stuart, written June 23, the distinctive contents of which are described by Henry McClellan in *Life and Campaigns of Stuart*, 316–18, but which is not now on record. By McClellan's description, this third order clarified Stuart's objectives and en-

dorsed his move around Hooker's army. Nesbitt, *Saber and Scapegoat*, 65–68.

20. Longstreet to Stuart, June 22, *OR* 27.3:915; Pender to his wife, June 23, Pender, *General to His Lady*, 251; Lee to his wife, Feb. 23, Lee, *Wartime Papers*, 408; Alexander, *Fighting for the Confederacy*, 228.

21. McClellan, *Life and Campaigns of Stuart*, 321–24; Longacre, *Cavalry at Gettysburg*, 152–54; David Powell, "Stuart's Ride: Lee, Stuart, and the Confederate Cavalry in the Gettysburg Campaign," *Gettysburg Magazine*, 20 (1998), 27, 32–33, 36–37.

22. Randolph A. Shotwell, *The Papers of Randolph Abbott Shotwell*, ed. J. G. de Roulhac Hamilton (Raleigh: North Carolina Historical Commission, 1929–36), 1:486–87; John H. Stone diary, June 19, Thomas G. Clemens, ed., *Maryland Historical Magazine*, 85:2 (1990), 131, courtesy Scott M. Sherlock; Francis W. Dawson, *Reminiscences of Confederate Service, 1861–1865* (Charleston, 1882), 90–91.

23. Arthur J. L. Fremantle, *Three Months in the Southern States: April–June, 1863*, 231–32, 226, 234, 239, 237–38.

24. Jacob Hoke, *The Great Invasion of 1863*, 134–35; *Lancaster Daily Express*, July 11, courtesy Jeff Burke. These summary figures are drawn from 1868 war-damage claims: Daniel Bauer, "Did a Food Shortage Force Lee to Fight?" *Columbiad*, 1:4 (1998), 57–74. Ewell's aide Campbell Brown noted in his diary on June 20 the passage of more than 1,100 cattle "from *Pa.*": Brown, *Campbell Brown's Civil War*, 385.

25. Jedediah Hotchkiss to his wife, June 25, Hotchkiss Papers, Library of Congress; Edward M. Burruss to his sister, July 27, Burruss Papers, Louisiana State University; Joseph Hilton to Lizzie Lachlison, July 18, Georgia Department of Archives and History; Benjamin L. Farinholt to his wife, July 1, Virginia Historical Society; Joseph W. Jackson, July 20, Boyd Civil War Papers, Louisiana State University; Louis Leon, *Diary of a Tar Heel Confederate Soldier* (Charlotte: Stone Publishing, 1913), 32, courtesy Greg Mast.

26. Florence McCarthy to his sister, July 10, Virginia Historical Society; Fremantle, *Three Months in the Southern States*, 246; George W. Fahnestock diary, June 27, Historical Society of Pennsylvania; Edwin B. Coddington, *The Gettysburg Campaign: A Study in Command*, 140–41.

27. Charles Carleton Coffin, *The Boys of '61; or, Four Years of Fighting* (Boston: Estes and Lauriat, 1885), 259; Coddington, *Gettysburg Campaign*, 150; Nye, *Here Come the Rebels!*, 260.

28. Philip Schaff diary, cited in Hoke, *The Great Invasion*, 96; Wert, *Mosby's Rangers*, 91; William S. Christian to his wife, June 28, Moore, *Rebellion Record*, 7:Documents, 325; G. M. Sorrel to Pickett, July 1, *OR* 51.2:732–33; Ted Alexander, "A Regular Slave Hunt," *North & South*, 4:7 (2001), 82–89.

29. Hoke, *The Great Invasion*, 124–26; Nye, *Here Come the Rebels!*, 245–46.

30. June 25, Hotchkiss, *Make Me a Map*, 154–55; Ewell, Early reports, Lee to Davis, June 20, *OR* 27.2:443, 464–65, 296–97.

31. Hoke, *The Great Invasion*, 170–71; Jubal A. Early, *Autobiographical Sketch and Narrative of the War Between the States*, 255–56.

32. Linda G. Black, "Gettysburg's Preview of War: Early's June 26, 1863, Raid," *Gettysburg Magazine* 3 (1990), 3–8; John M. Chapman, "Comanches on the Warpath: The 35th Battalion Virginia Cavalry in the Gettysburg Campaign," *Civil War Regiments*, 6:3 (1999), 16–21; S. W. Pennypacker, "Six Weeks in Uniform, 1863," *Historical and Biographical Sketches* (Philadelphia, 1883), 342–43; Michael Jacobs, *Notes on the Rebel Invasion of Maryland and Pennsylvania and the Battle of Gettysburg*, 15, 16–17; Fannie J. Buehler,

Recollections of the Rebel Invasion and One Woman's Experience During the Battle of Gettysburg (Gettysburg, 1900), 11.

33. Robert Stiles, *Four Years under Marse Robert* (New York: Neale, 1903), 203–5; *York Gazette,* June 29, cited in Moore, *Rebellion Record,* 7:Documents, 321–22; William J. Seymour, *The Civil War Memoirs of Captain William J. Seymour,* 67; Nye, *Here Come the Rebels!,* 285–96.

34. Nye, *Here Come the Rebels!,* 302–3; Ewell to his wife, June 24, Ewell Papers, Library of Congress; James W. Sullivan, *Boyhood Memories of the Civil War, 1861–'65* (Carlisle, Pa., 1933), 16; D. C. Pfanz, *Richard S. Ewell,* 300; Ewell report, *OR* 27.2:443.

35. Hoke (*The Great Invasion,* 162) is a day early for Lee's arrival in Chambersburg. Lee left his Williamsport camp on June 26, and could not have reached Chambersburg by 9:00 A.M. that day, as Hoke indicates. Anderson's report (*OR* 27.2:613) and other Third Corps reports give the correct date as the 27th. Also Fishel, *Secret War for the Union,* 679n11.

36. Thomas E. Schott, "The Stephens 'Peace' Mission," *North & South,* 1:6 (1998), 40; Davis to Stephens, July 2, Stephens to Davis, July 8, *OR* ser. II.6:74–75, 94–95; July 4–6, Welles, *Diary,* 1:358–63.

37. Lee to Davis, June 25 (two), Lee, *Wartime Papers,* 530–33; June 26, Hotchkiss, *Make Me a Map,* 155; J. B. Hood, *Advance and Retreat: Personal Experiences in the United States & Confederate States Armies,* 55; Lee to Davis, June 23, *OR* 27.2:297; Lee report, Jan. 1864, *OR* 27.2:316; Isaac R. Trimble, "The Battle and Campaign of Gettysburg," *SHSP,* 26 (1898), 121. Portions of Trimble's recollections appear enhanced by hindsight, yet Lee's mention to Trimble of Gettysburg as a possible battle site echoes Lee's dispatch to Ewell of the day before, as noted in Hotchkiss's diary.

38. Nesbitt, *Saber and Scapegoat,* 68–70; Fishel, *Secret War for the Union,* 471, 459, 470, 456–57, 495, 475; Sharpe to Hooker, June 23, *OR* 27.3:266.

39. Babcock to Sharpe, June 24 (two), *OR* 27.3:285–86, entry 34, RG 107, National Archives; Hooker to Howard, June 24, *OR* 27.3:290–91; Fishel, *Secret War for the Union,* 480–81.

40. June 23, 26, Welles, *Diary,* 1:340, 344; Elizabeth Blair Lee to her husband, June 23 (citing Cabinet officer Montgomery Blair), Lee, *Wartime Washington,* 276; Hooker testimony, *Report of Joint Committee,* 1 (1865), 173; June [27] statement, *OR* 27.1:65; June 20 return, *OR* 27.1:151; Butterfield to Hooker, June 24, 27, *OR* 27.3:301–3, 355–58.

41. Hooker, Butterfield testimony, *Report of Joint Committee,* 1 (1865), 173–74, 418; Hooker to French, June 25, Hooker to Reynolds, June 25, Hooker to Slocum, June 27, *OR* 27.3:317, 304–5, 354; Sept. 9, Hay, *Inside Lincoln's White House,* 79; Hooker to Halleck, June 26, *OR* 27.1:58.

42. Halleck to Hooker, June 27, Hooker to Halleck, June 27, *OR* 27.1:59, 60; Warren Gettysburg notes, c. 1875, Warren Papers, New York State Library; Hooker to Butterfield, June 27, *OR* 27.3:349; French, Generals' Reports, RG 94, National Archives; Hebert, *Fighting Joe Hooker,* 245; Hooker to Halleck, June 27, *OR* 27.1:60.

43. Halleck to Hooker, June 27, *OR* 27.1:60; June 28, Welles, *Diary,* 1:348; War Department G.O. 194, *OR* 27.3:369; Meade to his wife, June 29, Meade, *Life and Letters,* 2:11–12, George Meade narrative, ibid., 2:1–2. Charles F. Benjamin's account of Hooker's removal ("Hooker's Appointment and Removal," *Battles and Leaders,* 3:239–43) is as largely fictitious as his account of Hooker's appointment.

44. Sorrel, *Recollections of a Confederate Staff Officer,* 147, 153, 155; Charles Marshall, *An Aide-de-Camp of Lee,*

218–19; James Longstreet, "Lee's Invasion of Pennsylvania," *Battles and Leaders*, 3:244, 249–50; Fairfax to Custis Lee, 1896, cited in Freeman, *Lee's Lieutenants*, 3:49n; Fishel, *Secret War for the Union*, 499–501. Harrison's identity was revealed in James O. Hall, "The Spy Harrison," *Civil War Times Illustrated*, 24:10 (Feb. 1986), 18–25. While Sorrel and Marshall both said that Harrison brought the news of Hooker's replacement, the spy's last contact with the Federals was on June

27, the day before the command change.

45. Lee report, Jan. 1864, *OR* 27.2:316; Marshall, *Aide-de-Camp of Lee*, 220; Lee to Ewell, June [29], *OR* 27.3:943–44. This Lee dispatch to Ewell, written at 7:30 A.M. on the 29th (misdated June 28 in the *OR*), began "I wrote you last night . . . ," a dispatch not on the record. Hotchkiss's diary confirms that Ewell only took action on Lee's orders on the 29th: June 29, Hotchkiss, *Make Me a Map*, 156.

6. High Stakes in Pennsylvania

1. Meade to his wife, June 25, Meade, *Life and Letters*, 1:388–89.
2. Lyman, *Meade's Headquarters*, 188.
3. June 29, Gibbon, *Personal Recollections*, 128–29; Williams to his daughters, June 29, Williams, *From the Cannon's Mouth*, 220–21; June 28, Patrick, *Inside Lincoln's Army*, 265–66; June 28, Wainwright, *Diary of Battle*, 227; Hooker G.O. 66, June 28, *OR* 27.1:373–74; Charles Carleton Coffin, *The Boys of '61; or, Four Years of Fighting* (Boston: Estes and Lauriat, 1885), 261–62.
4. Adams diary, June 28, Massachusetts Historical Society; T. C. Grey to Sydney H. Gay, June 29, Gay Collection, Columbia University Library; June 28, Isaac L. Taylor, "Campaigning with the First Minnesota: A Civil War Diary," ed. Hazel C. Wolf, *Minnesota History*, 25 (Dec. 1944), 359.
5. Rufus R. Dawes, *Service with the Sixth Wisconsin Volunteers*, 157–58; Donaldson to his aunt, June 28, Donaldson, *Inside the Army of the Potomac*, 289; June 29, Whitelaw Reid, *A Radical View: The "Agate" Dispatches of Whitelaw Reid, 1861–1865*, ed. James G. Smart (Memphis: Memphis State University Press, 1976), 2:6.
6. Halleck to Meade, June 27, *OR* 27.1:61; Halleck to Grant, July 11, *OR* 24.3:498. General Halleck's chief of

staff, G. W. Cullum, boasted of his part in the general-in-chief's manipulations, writing on July 4, "I did my share in getting rid of Hooker. . . .": Coddington, *Gettysburg Campaign*, 634n108.

7. Meade to his wife, June 25, Meade, *Life and Letters*, 1:389; Meade to Halleck, June 28 (two), *OR* 27.1:61–62, 65; Meade testimony, *Report of Joint Committee* 1 (1865), 329; Fishel, *Secret War for the Union*, 493–94; Busey and Martin, *Regimental Strengths and Losses at Gettysburg*, 129.
8. Coddington, *Gettysburg Campaign*, 218–19; Hooker to Humphreys, June 28, *OR* 51.1:1064; Warren to his wife, June 28, Warren Papers, New York State Library; Longacre, *Cavalry at Gettysburg*, 166; Pleasonton S.O. 98, June 28, *OR* 27.3:376.
9. Halleck to Meade (two), Meade to Halleck, June 28, *OR* 27.1:62–64; Elizabeth Blair Lee to her husband, July 1, Lee, *Wartime Washington*, 279; Longacre, *Cavalry at Gettysburg*, 157; George Edgar Turner, *Victory Rode the Rails: The Strategic Place of the Railroads in the Civil War*, 278–79.
10. Meade circular, June 28, *OR* 27.3:375–76; June 29, Wainwright, *Diary of Battle*, 228.
11. Stuart report, *OR* 27.2:694; John Esten Cooke diary notes, University of Vir-

ginia Library; Blackford, *War Years with Stuart,* 224–25; Longacre, *Cavalry at Gettysburg,* 155–59.

12. Lee to Ewell, June 28, is missing, but its contents can be inferred from Lee to Ewell, June [29], *OR* 27.3:943–44; Charles Marshall, "Events Leading Up To the Battle of Gettysburg," *SHSP,* 23 (1895), 226; Lee report, Jan. 1864, *OR* 27.2:316; Sharpe to David McConaughy, June 29, McConaughy Collection, Gettysburg College.

13. Marshall, *Aide-de-Camp of Lee,* 218; A. P. Hill report, *OR* 27.2:606; Lee to Ewell, June [29], *OR* 27.3:943–44; Early, Johnson reports, *OR* 27.2:467, 503; June 29, Hotchkiss, *Make Me a Map,* 156; George Thomas in *SHSP,* 14 (1886), 444; Nye, *Here Come the Rebels!,* 358–59; John O. Casler, *Four Years in the Stonewall Brigade* (Girard, Kan., 1906), 173.

14. Lee report, Jan. 1864, *OR* 27.2:317; Alexander, *Fighting for the Confederacy,* 229.

15. Heth report, *OR* 27.2:637; George A. Bruce, "The Strategy of the Civil War," *PMHSM,* 13:455; Louis G. Young, "Pettigrew's Brigade at Gettysburg," Walter Clark, ed., *Histories of the Several Regiments and Battalions from North Carolina,* 5:115–17; Heth in *SHSP,* 4 (1877), 157; A. P. Hill report, *OR* 27.2:607. That this was indeed the spy Harrison is suggested by the July 1 entry in Fremantle's diary: "A spy who was with us insisted upon there being 'a pretty tidy bunch of *blue-bellies* in or near Gettysburg,' and he declared that he was in their society three days ago." Fremantle, *Three Months in the Southern States,* 252. As to shoes: Early had requisitioned shoes in Gettysburg on June 26, but certainly did not report any shoe factory there, as stated in Nye, *Here Come the Rebels!,* 275. The 1860 census listed twenty-two shoemakers in Gettysburg, but neither a shoe factory nor a shoe warehouse: J. Matthew Gallman with Susan Baker, "Gettysburg's

Gettysburg: What the Battle Did to the Borough," Boritt, ed., *The Gettysburg Nobody Knows,* 149.

16. Alexander, *Fighting for the Confederacy,* 230; Pender to his wife, June 28, Pender, *General to His Lady,* 253–54.

17. Fremantle, *Three Months in the Southern States,* 250; A. L. Long, *Memoirs of Robert E. Lee,* 274. George C. Eggleston has Lee saying of his new opponent, "General Meade will commit no blunder in my front, and if I commit one he will make haste to take advantage of it," but his account is secondhand and of weak provenance: Eggleston, *A Rebel's Recollections* (New York: Hurd and Houghton, 1875), 145–46.

18. Allan, conversation with Lee, Apr. 15, 1868, in Gallagher, ed., *Lee the Soldier,* 14; Ewell, A. P. Hill reports, *OR* 27.2:444, 607; McClellan, *Life and Campaigns of Stuart,* 336; Nesbitt, *Saber and Scapegoat,* 65; James Power Smith, "General Lee at Gettysburg," *PMHSM,* 5:384.

19. Busey and Martin, *Regimental Strengths and Losses at Gettysburg,* 194; Stuart to Robertson, June 24, *OR* 27.3:927–28; James Longstreet, *From Manassas to Appomattox,* 343; McClellan, *Life and Campaigns of Stuart,* 319; David Powell, "Stuart's Ride: Lee, Stuart, and the Confederate Cavalry in the Gettysburg Campaign," *Gettysburg Magazine,* 20 (1998), 39–41; Blackford, *War Years with Stuart,* 229; Wert, *Mosby's Rangers,* 91.

20. McClellan, *Life and Campaigns of Stuart,* 336–37; Lee to Davis, June 23, *OR* 27.2:297; Marsena R. Patrick diary, June 17, Library of Congress; David Powell, "Stuart's Ride: Lee, Stuart, and the Confederate Cavalry in the Gettysburg Campaign," *Gettysburg Magazine,* 20 (1998), 35; Brown, *Campbell Brown's Civil War,* 205.

21. Fishel, *Secret War for the Union,* 502–9, 513–14; Sharpe to McConaughy, June 29, McConaughy Collection, Gettysburg College.

22. Halleck to Meade, June 27, *OR*

27.1:61; Meade to his wife, June 29, Meade, *Life and Letters,* 2:13–14.

23. Meade to Reynolds, June 30, *OR* 27.3:414–15; Army of the Potomac itinerary, *OR* 27.1:144.

24. Hooker to Butterfield, June 27, *OR* 27.3:349; Pleasonton S.O. 99, June 29, *OR* 27.3:400; Buford to Pleasonton (two), June 30, Buford to Reynolds, June 30, *OR* 27.1:923–24; Meade circular, June 30, *OR* 27.3:416; Fishel, *Secret War for the Union,* 510–13.

25. June 30, Samuel W. Fiske, *Mr. Dunn Browne's Experiences in the Army: The Civil War Letters of Samuel W. Fiske,* 101; Abner R. Small, *The Road to Richmond: The Civil War Letters of Major Abner R. Small,* 97; Meade, *Life and Letters,* 2:12; June 30, Richard S. Thompson, *While My Country Is in Danger: The Life and Letters of Lieutenant Colonel Richard S. Thompson, Twelfth New Jersey Volunteers,* eds. Gerry Harder Poriss and Ralph G. Poriss (Hamilton, N.Y.: Edmonston Publishing, 1994), 64; Donaldson to his aunt, June 28, Donaldson, *Inside the Army of the Potomac,* 289.

26. E. R. Brown, *The Twenty-seventh Indiana Volunteer Infantry,* 362; Seth Williams to Sickles, June 30, *OR* 27.3:420.

27. Dawes to Mary Gates, June 30, State Historical Society of Wisconsin; Alexander Biddle to his wife, June 29, Rosenbach Museum and Library; Coddington, *Gettysburg Campaign,* 226–27; Lyman Holford diary, June 30, Library of Congress; June 29, Wainwright, *Diary of Battle,* 228–29; E. D. Burdick diary, July 1, Chicago Historical Society.

28. John I. Nevin diary, June 29, Dana B. Shoaf, ed., "The Gettysburg Diary of Major John I. Nevin, 93rd Pennsylvania Infantry," *Civil War Regiments,* 6:3

(1999), 123–24; Meade circular, June 30, *OR* 27.3:416–17; Brown, *Twenty-seventh Indiana,* 363.

29. Meade circular, June 30, *OR* 27.3:415.

30. June 29, Wainwright, *Diary of Battle,* 229; Parker to Lincoln, June 29, Lincoln to Parker, June 30, McClure to Lincoln, June 30, Lincoln to McClure, June 30, Lincoln, *Works,* 6:311–12; *New York Herald,* June 18.

31. June [27] statement, *OR* 27.1:65; Meade to Reynolds, July 1, Herman Haupt to Halleck, July 1, *OR* 27.3:460–61, 476–77. In the July 1 dispatch to Reynolds (which he never received), Meade would have used the June 20 return (*OR* 27.1:151), plus French's 10,000, for a total of 104,974.

32. June 30 return, *OR* 27.1:151. For the final total, see Busey and Martin, *Regimental Strengths and Losses at Gettysburg,* 6, 16.

33. Meade circular, June 30, Meade to Reynolds, June 30, *OR* 27.3:416, 417–18; Meade circular, July 1, *OR* 27.3:458–59; Weld, *War Diary and Letters,* 232.

34. Howard to M. Jacobs, Mar. 23, 1864, O. O. Howard Papers, Bowdoin College; Oliver Otis Howard, *Autobiography,* 1:403–4; Reynolds to Meade, June 30, *OR* 27.3:417–18; Buford to Reynolds, June 30, *OR* 27.1:923–24; Nichols, *Toward Gettysburg,* 195–96.

35. Meade to his wife, June 30, Meade, *Life and Letters,* 2:18.

36. Heth in *SHSP,* 4 (1877), 157.

37. Blackford, *War Years with Stuart,* 225–28.

38. A. B. Jerome, "Buford in the Battle of Oak Ridge" (1867), in Eric J. Wittenberg, "An Analysis of the Buford Manuscripts," *Gettysburg Magazine,* 15 (1996), 10.

7. A Meeting Engagement

A note on numbers: Statistical data on the two armies are derived primarily from John W. Busey and David G. Martin, *Regimental Strengths and Losses at Get-*

tysburg. Army strengths are expressed in "present for duty" figures. In-battle counts for units in both armies, however, are expressed in "engaged" or "effectives" figures.

1. William A. Frassanito, *Early Photography at Gettysburg,* 153; Gerald R. Bennett, *Days of "Uncertainty and Dread": The Ordeal Endured by the Citizens of Gettysburg,* 1–3.
2. John C. Ropes to John C. Gray, Oct. 19, John Chipman Gray and John Codman Ropes, *War Letters, 1862–1865,* 240. Notable for displaying the topography of the Gettysburg battlefield are maps in Earl B. McElfresh's "A Civil War Watercolor Map Series."
3. Pleasonton S.O. 99, June 29, *OR* 27.3:400–401; Busey and Martin, *Regimental Strengths and Losses at Gettysburg,* 99; Eric J. Wittenberg, "John Buford and the Gettysburg Campaign," *Gettysburg Magazine,* 11 (1994), 38–40; *Aurora Beacon,* Aug. 20, cited in Laurence D. Schiller, "Buford at Gettysburg," *North & South,* 2:2 (1999), 40; Richard S. Shue, *Morning at Willoughby Run: July 1, 1863,* 37, 51. Buford's third brigade was guarding trains at Mechanicstown in Maryland.
4. A. B. Jerome, "Buford in the Battle of Oak Ridge" (1867), in Wittenberg, "An Analysis of the Buford Manuscripts," *Gettysburg Magazine,* 15 (1996), 10; Meade circular, June 30, *OR* 27.3:416; Buford report, *OR* 27.1:927. Meade's circular reached Reynolds at 4:00 A.M. on July 1, and would have reached Buford at Gettysburg probably an hour or so later. The claim that Buford learned of Reynolds's orders by riding to his camp at Moritz's tavern early on July 1 (Shue, *Morning at Willoughby Run,* 52) lacks support in any contemporaneous accounts. It cannot be imagined that Buford, expecting the enemy to advance against him at any moment that morning, would have left his command.
5. Riddle to Le Bouvier, Aug. 4, John F. Reynolds Papers, Franklin and Marshall College; Meade circular, June 30, *OR* 27.3:416; Doubleday report, *OR* 27.1:244; Howard to Reynolds, July 1, Reynolds to Sickles, July 1, *OR* 27.3:457, 51.1:1066; July 1, Weld, *War Diary and Letters,* 229; Wadsworth testimony, *Report of Joint Committee,* 1 (1865), 413; July 1, Wainwright, *Diary of Battle,* 232; L. Patrick Nelson, "Reynolds and the Decision to Fight," *Gettysburg Magazine,* 23 (2000), 38–39.
6. Couch to Meade, June 30, Meade to Reynolds, July 1, *OR* 27.3:433, 460–61; Buford to Pleasonton, June 30, *OR* 27.1:924; Meade, *Life and Letters,* 2:33.
7. Charles H. Veil to David McConaughy, Apr. 7, 1864, McConaughy Collection, Gettysburg College; July 1, 1863, Weld, *War Diary and Letters,* 229.
8. Ewell report, *OR* 27.2:444; Isaac R. Trimble to John B. Bachelder, Feb. 8, 1883, David L. and Audrey J. Ladd, eds., *The Bachelder Papers: Gettysburg in Their Own Words,* 2:927.
9. Hill report, *OR* 27.2:607; Allan, conversation with Lee, Apr. 15, 1868, in Gallagher, ed., *Lee the Soldier,* 13; Fremantle, *Three Months in the Southern States,* 254; Ewell report, *OR* 27.2:444.
10. Heth report, *OR* 27.2:637; John L. Marye, "The First Gun at Gettysburg" (1895), in *Civil War Regiments* 1:1 (1990), 30; Walter Kempster, "The Cavalry at Gettysburg," Wisconsin MOLLUS, *War Papers* (4: 1914), 49:402.
11. Gary M. Kross, "General John Buford's Cavalry at Gettysburg on July 1, 1863," *Blue & Gray,* 12:3 (1995), 14; John L. Beveridge, "The First Gun at Gettysburg," Illinois MOLLUS, *Military Essays and Recollections* (2:1894), 11:91–92; H. O. Dodge, T. Benton Kelley in Richard A. Sauers, ed., *Fighting Them Over: How the Veterans Remembered Gettysburg in the Pages of*

the National Tribune, 451, 453; John L. Marye, "The First Gun at Gettysburg" (1895), *Civil War Regiments* 1:1 (1990), 31; E. B. Brunson report, *OR* 27.2:677. There were other claimants for first-shot honors, but Marcellus Jones's claim gained legitimacy after being approved by the leading nineteenth-century Gettysburg authority John Bachelder.

12. Heth report, *OR* 27.2:637; Wittenberg, "Buford and the Gettysburg Campaign," *Gettysburg Magazine,* 11 (1994), 40–41; Theodore W. Bean, "Who Fired the Opening Shots," *Philadelphia Weekly Times,* Feb. 2, 1878; Busey and Martin, *Regimental Strengths and Losses at Gettysburg,* 205–6. The arms listing for Buford's division (in the latter source) does not include Spencer repeaters, as once believed.

13. Laurence D. Schiller, "Buford at Gettysburg," *North & South,* 2:2 (1999), 42; Heth, A. P. Hill reports, *OR* 27.2:637, 607; James L. Morrison, Jr., ed., "Memoirs of Henry Heth," *Civil War History,* 8:3 (1962), 304; Heth in *SHSP,* 4 (1877), 149. Walter Taylor of Lee's staff wrote that instructions "had been" sent to Heth, but whether on July 1 as well as June 30 is unclear: Taylor in *SHSP,* 4 (1877), 126.

14. Jerome to Winfield S. Hancock, Oct. 18, 1865, Ladd and Ladd, eds., *Bachelder Papers,* 1:201; Buford to Meade, July 1, *OR* 27.1:924; Charles H. Veil to McConaughy, Apr. 7, 1864, McConaughy Collection, Gettysburg College; William Gamble to William L. Church, Mar. 10, 1864, Chicago Historical Society; July 1, Weld, *War Diary and Letters,* 229–32; Meade, *Life and Letters,* 2:35. Signalman Jerome's dramatized account of Reynolds and Buford meeting at the Lutheran Seminary and their exchange there (Jerome's letter to Hancock; and Jerome, "Buford in the Battle of Oak Ridge," *Gettysburg Magazine,* 15 [1996], 10–11) is filled with after-the-fact embellishments and cannot be

reconciled with the more contemporaneous accounts of Reynolds's aides Veil and Weld.

15. Veil to McConaughy, Apr. 7, 1864, McConaughy Collection, Gettysburg College; Henry E. Tremain, *Two Days of War: A Gettysburg Narrative,* 14; Abner Doubleday, *Chancellorsville and Gettysburg,* 122; Doubleday to Samuel P. Bates, Apr. 3, 1874, Bates Collection, Pennsylvania State Archives; Nichols, *Toward Gettysburg,* 203.

16. George H. Otis, *The Second Wisconsin Infantry* (Dayton: Morningside House, 1984), 83; Rufus R. Dawes to Bachelder, Mar. 18, 1868, James A. Hall to Bachelder, Feb. 27, 1867, Ladd and Ladd, eds., *Bachelder Papers,* 1:322–23, 306. The 7th Indiana of Cutler's brigade, on detached service, did not engage on July 1. The McClellan rumor was also reported in the Second and Fifth corps: *Battles and Leaders,* 3:301; Fitz John Porter to McClellan, July 22, McClellan Papers, Library of Congress.

17. Doubleday, *Chancellorsville and Gettysburg,* 132; Jeffry D. Wert, *A Brotherhood of Valor: The Common Soldiers of the Stonewall Brigade and the Iron Brigade* (New York: Simon & Schuster, 1999), 252, 100–101, 188–89; Dawes, *Service with the Sixth Wisconsin,* 131–32n.

18. Marc Storch and Beth Storch, "'What a Deadly Trap We Were In': Archer's Brigade on July 1, 1863," *Gettysburg Magazine,* 6 (1992), 21–22; Busey and Martin, *Regimental Strengths and Losses at Gettysburg,* 177, 23; Charles H. Veil to McConaughy, Apr. 7, 1864, McConaughy Collection, Gettysburg College; Cornelius Wheeler, "Reminiscences of the Battle of Gettysburg," Wisconsin MOLLUS, *War Papers* (2: 1896), 47:210; Wert, *Brotherhood of Valor,* 251; George H. Otis, *The Second Wisconsin Infantry* (Dayton: Morningside House, 1984), 84. The woodlot was actually on the property of John Herbst, but it was so widely known as McPherson's Woods at the time of the

battle and for long afterward that that usage is retained here.

19. Veil to McConaughy, Apr. 7, 1864, McConaughy Collection, Gettysburg College. Myths grew up about Reynolds's death — that he was killed by a sharpshooter, by a sharpshooter hiding in a tree, even by friendly fire. But orderly Veil was at the general's side, and there is every reason to accept his clear and straightforward account. Doubleday had been in temporary command of the First Corps while Reynolds commanded the left wing. Doubleday's command on the field lasted only until Howard arrived and superseded him.

20. Marc Storch and Beth Storch, "Archer's Brigade," *Gettysburg Magazine*, 6 (1992), 22–27; W. H. Bird, *Stories of the Civil War* (Columbiana, Ala., n.d.), 7; S. G. Shepard report, *OR* 27.2:646; John Mansfield report, *OR* 27.1:274; E. P. Halstead, "The First Day of the Battle of Gettysburg," District of Columbia MOLLUS, *War Papers* (1: 1887), 42:5.

21. Busey and Martin, *Regimental Strengths and Losses at Gettysburg*, 175.

22. Terrence J. Winchel, "Heavy Was Their Loss: Joe Davis's Brigade at Gettysburg," *Gettysburg Magazine*, 2 (1990), 10–11; Hall report, *OR* 27.1:359; D. Scott Hartwig, "Guts and Good Leadership: The Action at the Railroad Cut, July 1, 1863," *Gettysburg Magazine*, 1 (1989), 7–9; Davis report, *OR* 27.2:649; Leander G. Woollard diary, Memphis State University, cited in Roger Long, "A Mississippian in the Railroad Cut," *Gettysburg Magazine*, 4 (1991), 22–23; A. H. Belo in *Confederate Veteran*, 8 (1900), 165; Cutler report, *OR* 27.1:282.

23. Hartwig, "Action at the Railroad Cut," *Gettysburg Magazine*, 1 (1989), 10–11; Winchel, "Joe Davis's Brigade at Gettysburg," *Gettysburg Magazine*, 2 (1990), 10–11; Hall to Bachelder, Dec. 29, 1869, J. V. Pierce to Bachelder, Nov. 1, 1882, Ladd and Ladd, eds., *Bachelder Papers*, 1:385–86, 2:911;

Cutler report, *OR* 27.1:281–82; Busey and Martin, *Regimental Strengths and Losses at Gettysburg*, 239; Sidney G. Cooke, "The First Day of Gettysburg," Kansas MOLLUS, *War Talks in Kansas* (1: 1906), 15:280.

24. Hall report, *OR* 27.1:359–60; Hall to Bachelder, Feb. 27, 1867, Dec. 29, 1869, Ladd and Ladd, eds., *Bachelder Papers* 1:306–7, 386–87.

25. J. A. Blair, June 9, 1888, William F. Fox, *New York at Gettysburg*, 3:1006; Davis report, *OR* 27.2:649; Woollard diary, cited in Long, "A Mississippian in the Railroad Cut," *Gettysburg Magazine*, 1 (1989), 23; Dawes to Bachelder, Mar. 18, 1868, Ladd and Ladd, eds., *Bachelder Papers*, 1:323–24; Dawes, *Service with the Sixth Wisconsin*, 167. A 100-man brigade guard was assigned to the 6th Wisconsin in this operation.

26. Dawes to Bachelder, Mar. 18, 1868, Ladd and Ladd, eds., *Bachelder Papers*, 1:324–25; Dawes, *Service with the Sixth Wisconsin*, 168–69; W. B. Murphy, June 29, 1900, Bragg Papers, State Historical Society of Wisconsin; Dawes report, *OR* 27.1:276; Clayton E. Rogers in *Milwaukee Sunday Telegraph*, May 13, 1887; Dawes to Mary Gates, July 6, Dawes, *Service with the Sixth Wisconsin*, 161–62.

27. Heth report, *OR* 27.2:638.

28. Robert McClean, "A Boy in Gettysburg — 1863," *Gettysburg Compiler*, June 30, 1909; Doubleday report, *OR* 27.1:244.

29. July 1, Weld, *War Diary and Letters*, 229–30; Veil to McConaughy, Apr. 7, 1864, McConaughy Collection, Gettysburg College; Tremain, *Two Days of War*, 14; Joseph G. Rosengarten to Samuel P. Bates, Jan. 13, 1871, Doubleday to Bates, Oct. 18, 1875, Bates Collection, Pennsylvania State Archives; Doubleday, *Chancellorsville and Gettysburg*, 126–27; Charles H. Howard, "First Day at Gettysburg," Illinois MOLLUS, *Military Essays and Recollections* (4: 1907), 13:242. Apparently to revive his military reputation,

much bruised by Chancellorsville and Gettysburg, Howard claimed it was he who selected the key ground of Cemetery Hill for the army to defend; he received the Thanks of Congress for doing so (Howard report, *OR* 27.1:702; Howard to Bates, Sept. 14, 1875, Bates Collection, Pennsylvania State Archives). However, Joseph Rosengarten's testimony (cited above), affirmed by Doubleday, that he heard Reynolds charge Howard with that task is considerably more persuasive than Howard's aide Captain Hall claiming, nineteen years later, that he did not remember Reynolds saying any such thing: Hall to Howard, May 20, 1882, O. O. Howard Papers, Bowdoin College.

30. Shue, *Morning at Willoughby Run*, 193–94; Howard report, *OR* 27.1:702; Howard, "Reminiscences," in Sauers, ed., *Gettysburg in the National Tribune*, 162.

8. The God of Battles Smiles South

1. Longstreet, *Manassas to Appomattox*, 351–52; Lee report, Jan. 1864, *OR* 27.2:313; Marshall, *Aide-de-Camp of Lee*, 229; Lee to Imboden, July 1, *OR* 27.3:947–48.
2. Longstreet, "Lee in Pennsylvania," *Annals of the War*, 420; A. L. Long, *Memoirs of Robert E. Lee*, 275; Walter H. Taylor in *SHSP*, 4 (1877), 126.
3. Anderson to Longstreet, n.d., cited in Longstreet, *Manassas to Appomattox*, 357; Brown, *Campbell Brown's Civil War*, 204–5; Brown narrative, Henry J. Hunt Papers, Library of Congress.
4. Couch to Halleck, June 30, *OR* 27.3:434 (forwarded to Meade July 1: *OR* 27.1:70); Buford to Reynolds, June 30, Buford to Pleasonton, June 30 (forwarded to Meade), *OR* 27.1:923–24; Meade to Halleck, July 1, *OR* 27.1:70–71.
5. July 1, Salmon P. Chase, *The Salmon P. Chase Papers: Journals, 1829–1872*, ed. John Niven (Kent, Ohio: Kent State University Press, 1993), 1:426; Halleck to Meade, July 1, *OR* 27.1:71; June 30, Welles, *Diary*, 1:352.
6. July 1, Weld, *War Diary and Letters*, 230–32; Meade, Hancock testimony, *Report of Joint Committee*, 1 (1865), 348, 403–4; Meade circular, July 1, *OR* 27.3:458–59; Meade to Sedgwick, July 1, Meade to Slocum, July 1, Meade to Reynolds, July 1, *OR* 27.3:462, 460–61. Meade became reluctant to elaborate on his Pipe Creek circular after his

enemies later used it against him, but the phrase "holding them in check sufficiently long" clearly suggests a deception to lure the Confederates into pursuit. Without such a bait, Lee would have little reason to give battle at Pipe Creek.

7. Meade to Reynolds, June 30, Reynolds to Meade, June 30, Meade to Hancock, July 1, *OR* 27.3:419–20, 417–18, 461; Meade to Couch, July 1, Couch to Halleck, July 1, *OR* 27.3:458, 473.
8. Meade, *Life and Letters*, 2:36; Meade to Hancock, July 1, *OR* 27.3:461; Walker, *Second Army Corps*, 264–65; Halleck to Meade, June 27, *OR* 27.1:61; Meade to Sedgwick, July 1, *OR* 27.3:465.
9. Howard report, *OR* 27.1:702; Joseph G. Rosengarten to Samuel P. Bates, Jan. 13, 1871, Howard to T. H. Davis, Sept. 14, 1875, Bates Collection, Pennsylvania State Archives; Howard to Sickles and to Slocum, July 1, Howard to Meade, July 1, *OR* 27.3:463, 457–58; Buford to Pleasonton, July 1, *OR* 27.1:924–25. Howard's 1:30 messages to Sickles and Slocum are not on record, but their content can be inferred from Sickles to Howard, July 1, and Sickles to Meade, July 1, *OR* 27.3:463, 464. Slocum never acknowledged receipt of either of Howard's dispatches.
10. Tremain, *Two Days of War*, 14; Sickles to Howard, July 1, Sickles to Meade, July 1, Meade to Sickles, July 1, *OR* 27.3:463, 464, 466. Howard's messen-

ger did not immediately find Sickles, delaying the Third Corps' start to the battlefield: E. P. Pearson to Howard, Jan. 22, 1886, O. O. Howard Papers, Bowdoin College.

11. Geary report, *OR* 27.1:825; Julian W. Hinkley, *A Narrative of Service with the Third Wisconsin Infantry* (Madison: Wisconsin History Commission, 1912), 82; Brown, *Twenty-seventh Indiana,* 365–66; Slocum to T. H. Davis, Sept. 8, 1875, Bates Collection, Pennsylvania State Archives; Charles H. Howard to E. Whittlesey, July 9, C. H. Howard Papers, Bowdoin College.

12. Doubleday report, *OR* 27.1:247; July 1, Wainwright, *Diary of Battle,* 234–35; Stannard report, *OR* 27.1:348–49; Busey and Martin, *Regimental Strengths and Losses at Gettysburg,* 21, 80–86; Howard, Osborn reports, *OR* 27.1:702, 748; Howard manuscript, n.d., Gettysburg National Military Park.

13. Doubleday to Samuel P. Bates, Oct. 18, 1875, Bates Collection, Pennsylvania State Archives. The 37 Confederate infantry brigades averaged 2,162 present for duty, against the 51 Union brigades' average of 2,196: Busey and Martin, *Regimental Strengths and Losses at Gettysburg,* 16, 129.

14. Ewell, Rodes reports, *OR* 27.2:439, 552; James M. Thompson, *Reminiscences of Autauga Rifles* (1879), cited in Robert K. Krick, "Three Confederate Disasters on Oak Ridge: Failures of Brigade Leadership on the First Day at Gettysburg," Gary W. Gallagher, ed., *Three Days at Gettysburg,* 91.

15. July 1, Hotchkiss, *Make Me a Map,* 156; Howard, Doubleday reports, *OR* 27.1:702, 248.

16. Rodes report, *OR* 27.2:552; Brown narrative, Henry J. Hunt Papers, Library of Congress; Ewell report, *OR* 27.2:444.

17. Pendleton report, *OR* 27.2:348–49; Morrison, ed., "Memoirs of Henry Heth," *Civil War History,* 8:3 (1962), 305; Brown, *Campbell Brown's Civil War,* 206; Blackford, *War Years with Jeb*

Stuart, 228; McClellan, *Life and Campaigns of Stuart,* 330.

18. Ewell, Rodes, Lee (Jan. 1864) reports, *OR* 27.2:444, 552–53, 317; Busey and Martin, *Regimental Strengths and Losses at Gettysburg,* 166; Krick, "Three Confederate Disasters," Gallagher, ed., *Three Days at Gettysburg,* 96–97.

19. Gary G. Lash, "Brig. Gen. Henry Baxter's Brigade at Gettysburg, July 1," *Gettysburg Magazine,* 10 (1994), 9–14; George W. Grant, "The First Army Corps on the First Day at Gettysburg," Minnesota MOLLUS, *Glimpses of the Nation's Struggle* (5: 1903), 30:49; Rodes, Carter reports, *OR* 27.2:553, 603; D. Scott Hartwig, "The 11th Army Corps on July 1, 1863," *Gettysburg Magazine,* 2 (1990), 39; Robert E. Park in *SHSP,* 26 (1898), 13.

20. Robinson report, *OR* 27.1:289; Lash, "Baxter's Brigade," *Gettysburg Magazine,* 10 (1994), 16–17; Gerard A. Patterson, "The Death of Iverson's Brigade," *Gettysburg Magazine,* 5 (1991), 15; "Twenty-third Regiment," Clark, *North Carolina Regiments,* 2:235.

21. Paul Clark Cooksey, "They Died as if on Dress Parade: The Annihilation of Iverson's Brigade at Gettysburg and the Battle of Oak Ridge," *Gettysburg Magazine,* 20 (1998), 102–5; "Twenty-third Regiment," "Twentieth Regiment," Clark, *North Carolina Regiments,* 2:238, 119; Krick, "Three Confederate Disasters," Gallagher, ed., *Three Days at Gettysburg,* 102–4; Lash, "Baxter's Brigade," *Gettysburg Magazine,* 10 (1994), 19; Busey and Martin, *Regimental Strengths and Losses at Gettysburg,* 288; July 2, Henry R. Berkeley, *Four Years in the Confederate Artillery: The Diary of Private Henry Robinson Berkeley,* ed. William H. Runge (Chapel Hill: University of North Carolina Press, 1961), 50; Charles C. Blacknall memoir, North Carolina State Archives.

22. Morrison, ed., "Memoirs of Henry Heth," *Civil War History,* 8:3 (1962), 305; Brown narrative, Henry J. Hunt Papers, Library of Congress; Trimble,

"Battle and Campaign of Gettysburg," *SHSP,* 26 (1898), 121; June 26, Hotchkiss, *Make Me a Map,* 155.

23. Grant, "First Army Corps," Minnesota MOLLUS, *Glimpses of the Nation's Struggle* (5: 1903), 30:50; Baxter report, *OR* 27.1:307; J. H. Stine, *History of the Army of the Potomac* (Washington, 1893), 484; John C. Robinson, "The First Corps," in Sauers, ed., *Gettysburg in the National Tribune,* 114; Small, *Road to Richmond,* 100.

24. William F. Fox, *Regimental Losses in the American Civil War* (Dayton: Morningside House, 1974), 261, 303; J. H. Bassler in *SHSP,* 37 (1909), 268–69.

25. William H. Tipton memoir, cited in Frassanito, *Early Photography at Gettysburg,* 86; Doubleday report, *OR* 27.1:255. The John Burns story would be greatly embellished in later tellings, by Burns and others. The dimensions of the story as related here appear reliable. For the whole story, see Timothy H. Smith, *John Burns: "The Hero of Gettysburg"* (Gettysburg: Thomas Publications, 2000).

26. Warren W. Hassler, Jr., *Crisis at the Crossroads: The First Day at Gettysburg,* 102–4; "2nd Battalion," Clark, *North Carolina Regiments,* 4:256; James Stewart, "Battery B Fourth United States Artillery at Gettysburg," Ohio MOLLUS, *Sketches of War History* (4: 1896), 4:185; D. Massy Griffin, "Rodes on Oak Hill: A Study of Rodes' Division on the First Day of Gettysburg," *Gettysburg Magazine,* 4 (1991), 44–45; Walton Dwight report, *OR* 27.1:342.

27. Doubleday, Generals' Reports, RG 94, National Archives; E. P. Halstead, "The First Day of the Battle of Gettysburg," District of Columbia MOLLUS, *War Papers* (1: 1887), 42:5–6; Doubleday to Samuel P. Bates, Apr. 3, 1874, Bates Collection, Pennsylvania State Archives.

28. July 1, Wainwright, *Diary of Battle,* 235–37.

29. Edwin R. Gearhart memoir, cited in Kevin E. O'Brien, "'Give Them Another Volley, Boys': Biddle's Brigade Defends the Union Left on July 1, 1863," *Gettysburg Magazine,* 19 (1998), 44–45; Alexander Biddle reports, *OR* 27.1:323, *OR Supplement* 5:151; "Forty-seventh Regiment," Clark, *North Carolina Regiments,* 3:90.

30. Doubleday report, *OR Supplement* 5:101; McFarland report, *OR* 27.1:327; John T. Jones report, *OR* 27.2:643; Nathan Cooper to his wife, July 2, cited in Michael A. Dreese, "The 151st Pennsylvania Volunteers at Gettysburg: July 1, 1863," *Gettysburg Magazine,* 23 (2000), 60; Dudley report, Ladd and Ladd, eds., *Bachelder Papers,* 2:941–42.

31. Young, "Pettigrew's Brigade at Gettysburg," Clark, *North Carolina Regiments,* 5:120; R. M. Tuttle in *SHSP,* 28 (1900), 202–4; R. Lee Hadden, "The Deadly Embrace: The Meeting of the Twenty-fourth Regiment, Michigan Infantry, and the Twenty-sixth Regiment of North Carolina Troops . . . ," *Gettysburg Magazine,* 5 (1991), 28–33; Morrison, ed., "Memoirs of Henry Heth," *Civil War History,* 8:3 (1962), 304–5.

32. Sears, *Chancellorsville,* 286, 421.

33. Barlow to his mother, July 7, Francis C. Barlow Papers, Massachusetts Historical Society; Howard, *Autobiography,* 1:414; Carl Schurz, *The Reminiscences of Carl Schurz,* 3:10; Schurz report, *OR* 27.1:728.

34. Early, *Autobiographical Sketch,* 267–68; Robert Stiles, *Four Years under Marse Robert* (New York: Neale, 1903), 210–11; Hartwig, "11th Corps on July 1, 1863," *Gettysburg Magazine,* 2 (1990), 43–44; William R. Kiefer, *History of the One Hundred Fifty-third Regiment Pennsylvania Volunteer Infantry* (Easton, Pa., 1909), 214. The 41st New York of von Gilsa's brigade was on detached duty on July 1.

35. Barlow to his mother, July 7, Barlow to Robert Treat Paine, Aug. 12, Barlow Papers, Massachusetts Historical Society; G. W. Nichols, *A Soldier's Story of*

His Regiment (61st Georgia) (Jesup, Ga., 1898), 116; Hartwig, "11th Corps on July 1, 1863," *Gettysburg Magazine,* 2 (1990), 44–45; Harris to Bachelder, Mar. 14, 1881, Ladd and Ladd, eds., *Bachelder Papers,* 2:744; *New York Times,* July 6. The Barlow-Gordon "incident," much embellished by Gordon on the postwar lecture circuit, has a factual basis about as narrated here. In *Blue & Gray,* 19:3 (2002), 6–7, Gregory C. White details what is known of the case, including the fact that it was Barlow, not Gordon, who first related the incident, at an 1879 Washington gathering.

36. Hartwig, "11th Corps on July 1, 1863," *Gettysburg Magazine,* 2 (1990), 44–49; Alfred Lee, "Reminiscences of the Gettysburg Battle," *Lippincott Magazine,* 6 (1883), 56; Theodore A. Dodge, "Left Wounded on the Field," *Putnam's Magazine* (1869), in Dodge, *On Campaign with the Army of the Potomac,* 319–20; Philip P. Brown, in John S. Applegate, *Reminiscences and Letters of George Arrowsmith* (Red Bank, N.J., 1893), 217; C. D. Grace in *Confederate Veteran,* 5 (1897), 614.

37. Charles W. McKay, "'Three Years or During the War' with the Crescent and the Star," *National Tribune Scrap Book,* n.d., 131; Joseph W. Jackson, July 20, Boyd Civil War Papers, Louisiana State University; Lewis Heckman report, *OR* 27.1:755; July 1, Hotchkiss, *Make Me a Map,* 156; D. C. Pfanz, *Richard S. Ewell,* 307–8; Harry W. Pfanz, *Gettysburg — Culp's Hill and Cemetery Hill,* 44. The Gettysburg losses for Gordon and Doles totaled 756, nearly all incurred on July 1: Busey and Martin, *Regimental Strengths and Losses at Gettysburg,* 286, 289.

38. Hunt report, *OR* 27.1:230; July 1, Wainwright, *Diary of Battle,* 235–36; William W. Robinson report, *OR* 27.1:280; O'Brien, "Biddle's Brigade Defends the Union Left," *Gettysburg Magazine,* 19 (1998), 49–50. James Lane's brigade, on the far right of Pender's division, skirmished with Gamble's Federal cavalry and did not participate in the attack. Pender held Edward Thomas's brigade in reserve.

39. J. Michael Miller, "Perrin's Brigade on July 1, 1863," *Gettysburg Magazine,* 13 (1995), 25–28; A. A. Tompkins and A. S. Tompkins, "Fourteenth South Carolina Volunteers, Company K," *Recollections and Reminiscences, 1861–1865* (South Carolina Division, U.D.C., 1995), 6:424; J.F.J. Caldwell, *The History of [Gregg's] Brigade of South Carolinians* (Philadelphia: King & Baird, 1866), 97–98.

40. Dawes, *Service with the Sixth Wisconsin,* 176; W. G. Lewis report, *OR* 27.2:573; *History of the 121st Pennsylvania Volunteers* (Philadelphia, 1893), 56; July 1, Wainwright, *Diary of Battle,* 236–37.

41. Richard A. Sauers, "The 16th Maine Volunteer Infantry at Gettysburg," *Gettysburg Magazine,* 13 (1995), 37–41; Small, *Road to Richmond,* 101–2.

42. John C. Hall, July 2, cited in Dawes, *Service with the Sixth Wisconsin,* 176n; Frederick C. Winkler, *Letters of Frederick C. Winkler, 1862 to 1865* (William K. Winkler, 1963), 70–71; Mark H. Dunkelman and Michael J. Winey, "The Hardtack Regiment in the Brickyard Fight," *Gettysburg Magazine,* 2 (1993), 21–22; Thomas Chamberlain, *History of the One Hundred and Fiftieth Pennsylvania Volunteers* (Philadelphia: Lippincott, 1895), 136–39; John A. Leach to Bachelder, June 2, 1884, Ladd and Ladd, eds., *Bachelder Papers,* 2:1047.

43. Bennett, *Days of "Uncertainty and Dread,"* 26–34; Sarah M. Broadhead, *Diary of a Lady of Gettysburg, Pennsylvania* (Hershey, Pa.: Hawbaker, 1990); Albertus McCreary, "Gettysburg: A Boy's Experience of the Battle," *McClure's Magazine,* 33 (July 1909); Liberty Hollinger Glutz, *Some Personal Recollections of the Battle of Gettysburg* (1925), 3; Schurz, *Reminiscences,* 3:34–37; Anna Garlach Kitzmiller, "Mrs.

Kitzmiller's Story," *Gettysburg Compiler,* Aug. 9, 1905.

44. Perrin to Milledge L. Bonham, July 29, *Mississippi Valley Historical Review,* 24 (1938), 522; A. P. Hill report, *OR* 27.2:607.

45. Small, *Road to Richmond,* 102; Hartwell Osborn, *Trials and Triumphs: The Record of the Fifty-fifth Ohio Volunteer Infantry* (Chicago: A. C. McClurg, 1904), 97.

46. E. P. Halstead, "The First Day of the Battle of Gettysburg," District of Columbia MOLLUS, *War Papers* (1: 1877), 42:6–7; Charles H. Morgan statement, Ladd and Ladd, eds., *Bachelder Papers,* 3:1350–52; Schurz, *Reminiscences,* 3:15–16; Warren testimony, *Report of Joint Committee,* 1 (1865), 377; Hancock to Meade, July 1, *OR* 27.1:366. The later dispute between Howard and Hancock over their Cemetery Hill meeting can be traced in H. W. Pfanz, *Gettysburg — Culp's Hill and Cemetery Hill,* 379–81.

47. Howard to Meade, July 1, Hancock to Meade, July 1, *OR* 27.1:696, 366; Doubleday to Samuel P. Bates, Oct. 18, 1875, Bates Collection, Pennsylvania State Archives.

48. Schurz, *Reminiscences,* 3:15–16, 19–20; Harry W. Pfanz, *Gettysburg — The First Day,* 333–35, 430n7; David G. Martin, *Gettysburg, July 1,* 470, 472, 371.

9. We May As Well Fight It Out Here

1. Thomas T. Munford memoir, Munford Papers, Duke University Library.

2. Brown, *Campbell Brown's Civil War,* 210–11; Henry Kyd Douglas, *I Rode with Stonewall* (Chapel Hill: University of North Carolina Press, 1940), 247; Rodes report, *OR* 27.2:555; Early, *Autobiographical Sketch,* 269; Ewell report, *OR* 2.27:446; James Power Smith, "With Stonewall Jackson in the Army of Northern Virginia," *SHSP,* 43 (1920), 57; Lee report, Jan. 1864, *OR* 27.2:318.

3. Brown, *Campbell Brown's Civil War,* 211; H. W. Pfanz, *Gettysburg — Culp's Hill and Cemetery Hill,* 77–78; James Power Smith, "General Lee at Gettysburg," *SHSP,* 33 (1905), 145; Young, "Pettigrew's Brigade at Gettysburg," Clark, *North Carolina Regiments,* 5:121n.

4. H. W. Pfanz, *Gettysburg — The First Day,* 347–48; D. C. Pfanz, *Richard S. Ewell,* 311–12; Thomas T. Turner statement, Early Papers, Virginia Historical Society; J. W. Bruce in *Charlottesville Daily Progress,* Mar. 22, 1904, John W. Daniel Papers, University of Virginia.

5. H. W. Pfanz, *Gettysburg — The First Day,* 346–47; Jubal Early in *SHSP,* 4 (1877), 271–75. Early's veracity may be judged by his having Lee remark at this conference, "Longstreet is a very good fighter when he gets in position and gets everything ready, but he is *so slow.*" That is a discourtesy Robert E. Lee would never have uttered within the hearing of his lieutenants.

6. William Allan memoir, Southern Historical Collection, University of North Carolina; Marshall to Early, Mar. 23, 1870, Mar. 13, 1878, Early Papers, Library of Congress; Ewell report, *OR* 27.2:446; Thomas T. Turner statement, Early Papers, Virginia Historical Society; Ira G. Grover report, *OR* 27.1:284–85; Sykes to Slocum, July 2, *OR* 27.3:483. Johnson did not say what time that night he sent out his reconnoitering party, but if the party immediately afterward captured a Federal dispatch written at 12:30 A.M. four miles away, it cannot have been much before 1:00 or 1:30 — after Ewell returned from Lee's camp.

7. Alexander, *Fighting for the Confederacy,* 233; Brown, *Campbell Brown's Civil War,* 212; For the postwar criticism of Ewell's role on July 1, see Gary W. Gallagher, "Confederate Corps Lead-

ership on the First Day at Gettysburg: A. P. Hill and Richard S. Ewell in a Difficult Debut," Gallagher, ed., *Three Days at Gettysburg,* 25–43; and Harry W. Pfanz, "'Old Jack' Is Not Here," Boritt, ed., *The Gettysburg Nobody Knows,* 56–74.

8. Longstreet, *Manassas to Appomattox,* 358; Longstreet, "Lee in Pennsylvania," *Annals of the War,* 421; Longstreet, "Lee's Right Wing at Gettysburg," *Battles and Leaders,* 3:329–30; Longstreet to McLaws, July 25, 1873, McLaws Papers, Southern Historical Collection; Brown, *Campbell Brown's Civil War,* 218; Coddington, *Gettysburg Campaign,* 730n22. Longstreet's accounts of the evening of July 1 are not consistent, but the earliest one, in the *Philadelphia Weekly Times* in 1877 (*Annals of the War,* 1879), appears the most reliable.

9. Longstreet report, *OR* 27.2:358; Sorrel to Walton, July 1, *OR* 51.2:733; J.S.D. Cullen to Longstreet, May 18, 1875, in *Annals of the War,* 3:439; Raphael J. Moses, "Autobiography," Southern Historical Collection. In their postwar vendetta against Longstreet, William Pendleton and Jubal Early invented an order by Lee for a sunrise attack on July 2, which Longstreet then disloyally disobeyed. For a disavowal by Lee's staff of any such order, see Longstreet, "Lee in Pennsylvania," *Annals of the War,* 437–38.

10. Lee report, Jan. 1864, *OR* 27.2:318; Bauer, "Did a Food Shortage Force Lee to Fight?" *Columbiad,* 1:4 (1998), 65–70; Alexander, *Fighting for the Confederacy,* 234; Longstreet, "Lee in Pennsylvania," *Annals of the War,* 421; Justus Scheibert in *SHSP,* 5 (1878), 92; Francis Lawley in London *Times,* Aug. 18.

11. Lee report, Jan. 1864, *OR* 27.2:318; Longstreet to Wigfall, Aug. 2, Wigfall Papers, Library of Congress.

12. Fremantle, *Three Months in the Southern States,* 256, 254; H. W. Pfanz, *Gettysburg — The First Day,* 350–51.

13. Hancock report, *OR* 27.1:368; Howard to Meade, July 1, Sickles to Meade, July 1, *OR* 27.3:457–58, 464; Meade to Halleck, July 1, *OR* 27.1:71–72. In his report Hancock said he sent his aide to Meade at 4:00 P.M., but it is clear from Hancock's 5:25 dispatch to headquarters (*OR* 27.1:366) that he himself did not reach Gettysburg until close to 4:30.

14. Meade to Sickles, July 1, *OR* 27.3:466; Meade, *Life and Letters,* 2:41; A. G. Mason to Meade, Mar. 10, 1864 (march orders to Sykes and Slocum), *OR* 27.1:126; Meade to Sedgwick, July 1, *OR* 27.3:465, 467–68; Hancock testimony, *Report of Joint Committee,* 1 (1865), 405.

15. Charles H. Howard to E. Whittlesey, July 9, C. H. Howard Papers, Bowdoin College; Daniel Hall to O. O. Howard, Feb. 19, 1877, O. O. Howard Papers, Bowdoin College; Meade to Hancock and Doubleday, July 1, *OR* 27.3:466; Slocum report, *OR* 27.1:758–59; Williams to his daughters, July 6, Williams, *From the Cannon's Mouth,* 224–26.

16. Humphreys testimony, *Report of Joint Committee,* 1 (1865), 389–90; C. B. Baldwin to Bachelder, May 20, 1865, Ladd and Ladd, eds., *Bachelder Papers,* 1:191; Humphreys to Archibald Campbell, Aug. 6, Humphreys Papers, Historical Society of Pennsylvania.

17. Meade, *Life and Letters,* 2:62; Howard in *Atlantic Monthly* (July 1876), in Cozzens, ed., *Battles and Leaders of the Civil War: Volume 5,* 334; Schurz, *Reminiscences,* 3:20–21.

18. July 2, Isaac L. Taylor, "Campaigning with the First Minnesota: A Civil War Diary," Hazel C. Wolf, ed., *Minnesota History,* 25 (Dec. 1944), 360.

19. Busey and Martin, *Regimental Strengths and Losses at Gettysburg,* 239–41, 253–55; Lance J. Herdegen, "The Lieutenant Who Arrested a General," *Gettysburg Magazine* 4 (1991), 25–30; Charles H. Howard to E. Whittlesey, July 9, C. H. Howard Papers, Bowdoin College; Dodge, *On Campaign with the Army of the Potomac,* 320–21.

20. Meade, *Life and Letters,* 2:62–63; July 2, Wainwright, *Diary of Battle,* 246; Gibbon, *Personal Recollections,* 139; Frassanito, *Early Photography at Gettysburg,* 127–28. For Meade's gathering of forces on July 1–2, see Coddington, *Gettysburg Campaign,* 323–58.

21. Thomas W. Hyde, *Following the Greek Cross; or, Memories of the Sixth Army Corps* (Boston: Houghton Mifflin, 1895), 143; David A. Ward, "'Sedgwick's Foot Cavalry': The March of the Sixth Corps to Gettysburg," *Gettysburg Magazine,* 22 (2000), 59–65; George W. Bicknell, *History of the Fifth Regiment Maine Volunteers* (Portland: Hall L. Davis, 1871), 242; James L. Bowen, *History of the Thirty-seventh Regiment Massachusetts Volunteers* (Holyoke, Mass.: Clark W. Bryan, 1884), 172; James S. Anderson, "The March of the Sixth Corps to Gettysburg," Wisconsin MOLLUS, *War Papers* (4: 1914), 49:80; Robert L. Orr, in John P. Nicholson, ed., *Pennsylvania at Gettysburg,* 1:3,77.

22. Meade to Slocum, July 2, Slocum to Meade, July 2, *OR* 27.3:486–87; Turner, *Victory Rode the Rails,* 278–81; Warren testimony, *Report of Joint Committee,* 1 (1865), 377; Meade to Halleck, July 2, *OR* 27.1:72.

23. Coddington, *Gettysburg Campaign,* 351–52; Pleasonton testimony, *Report of Joint Committee,* 1 (1865), 359; Meade to Pleasonton, July 2, *OR* 27.3:490; Meade, *Life and Letters,* 2:71.

24. Richard A. Sauers, *A Caspian Sea of Ink: The Meade-Sickles Controversy,* 27–29; George Gordon Meade II, *With Meade at Gettysburg,* 101–2; Meade testimony, *Report of Joint Committee,* 1 (1865), 331–32; Meade to C. G. Benedict, Mar. 16, 1870, in Meade, *Life and Letters,* 2:353–54.

25. William Glenn Robertson, "The Peach Orchard Revisited: Daniel E. Sickles and the Third Corps on July 2, 1863," Gallagher, ed., *Three Days at Gettysburg,* 139–42; Henry J. Hunt, "The Second Day at Gettysburg," *Battles and Leaders,* 3:301–2; Gibbon, *Personal Recollections,* 136; Henry L. Abbott to John C. Ropes, Aug. 17, MOLLUS Collection, Houghton Library, Harvard University.

26. July 2, Fiske, *Mr. Dunn Browne's Experiences,* 103–4.

27. S. R. Johnston to Lafayette McLaws, June 27, 1892, Johnston to George Peterkin, n.d., Johnston Papers, Virginia Historical Society; David Powell, "A Reconnaissance Gone Awry: Capt. Samuel R. Johnston's Fateful Trip to Little Round Top," *Gettysburg Magazine,* 23 (2000), 88–99.

28. Venable to Longstreet, May 11, 1875, in *SHSP* 4 (1877), 289; Ewell, Pendleton reports, *OR* 27.2:446, 350; Long to Early, Apr. 5, 1876, in *SHSP,* 4 (1877), 67.

29. Fremantle, *Three Months in the Southern States,* 256–57; Sorrel, *Recollections of a Confederate Staff Officer,* 161, 157; Longstreet, "Lee in Pennsylvania," *Annals of the War,* 422.

30. Hood to Longstreet, June 28, 1875, in *SHSP,* 4 (1877), 147–48; Johnston to McLaws, June 27, 1892, Johnston to Peterkin, n.d., Johnston Papers, Virginia Historical Society; Roger J. Greezicki, "Humbugging the Historian: A Reappraisal of Longstreet at Gettysburg," *Gettysburg Magazine,* 6 (1992), 63–65.

31. McLaws, "Gettysburg," *SHSP,* 7 (1879), 68; Harry W. Pfanz, *Gettysburg — The Second Day,* 113–14.

32. Ewell report, *OR* 27.2:446; Alexander, *Fighting for the Confederacy,* 234–35; July 2, Hotchkiss, *Make Me a Map,* 157.

33. Long, *Memoirs of Lee,* 281; Longstreet, "Lee in Pennsylvania," *Annals of the War,* 422; Alexander, *Fighting for the Confederacy,* 235–36; E. M. Law, "The Struggle for 'Round Top,'" *Battles and Leaders,* 3:319.

34. Paul M. Shevchuk, "The Lost Hours of 'Jeb' Stuart," *Gettysburg Magazine,* 4 (1991), 70–71; E. P. Alexander, *Military Memoirs of a Confederate,* 376–77.

35. H. W. Pfanz, *Gettysburg — The Second Day,* 118–22; McLaws, "The Battle of Gettysburg," *Addresses Delivered Be-*

fore the Confederate Veterans Association of Savannah, Georgia (1896), 73; Alexander, *Fighting for the Confederacy,* 236; McLaws, "Gettysburg," *SHSP,* 7 (1879), 69; J. B. Kershaw, "Kershaw's Brigade at Gettysburg," *Battles and Leaders,* 3:331; Sorrel, *Recollections of a Confederate Staff Officer,* 157; Hall to Butterfield, July 2, *OR* 27.3:488.

36. McLaws to his wife, July 7, McLaws, *A Soldier's General,* 196; Kershaw report, *OR* 27.2:367; McLaws, "Gettysburg," *SHSP,* 7 (1879), 70, 76; H. W. Pfanz, *Gettysburg — The Second Day,* 152–55, 163–65; J. C. Haskell report, *OR Supplement* 5:352; Hood to Longstreet, June 28, 1875, *SHSP,* 4 (1877), 149; Fairfax to Longstreet, Nov. 12, 1877, Fairfax Papers, Virginia Historical Society.

37. Sauers, *A Caspian Sea of Ink,* 37–38; William H. Paine to George Meade, May 22, 1886, James C. Biddle to George Meade, Aug. 8, 1880, Meade Papers, Historical Society of Pennsylvania; Sykes report, *OR* 27.1:592; John C. Ropes to John C. Gray, Apr. 16, 1864, Gray and Ropes, *War Letters,* 318; Isaac R. Pennypacker, "Military Historians and History," *Pennsylvania Magazine of History and Biography,* 53:3 (1929), 40.

10. A Simile of Hell Broke Loose

1. Hunt, "Second Day at Gettysburg," *Battles and Leaders,* 3:295–96, 304; Frassanito, *Early Photography at Gettysburg,* 266–68; Meade, *Life and Letters,* 2:79.

2. H. W. Pfanz, *Gettysburg — The Second Day,* 168–72; Law, "Struggle for 'Round Top,'" *Battles and Leaders,* 3:323–24; Alexander, *Fighting for the Confederacy,* 239; D. U. Barziza, *The Adventures of a Prisoner of War, 1863–1864,* ed. R. Henderson Shuffler (Austin: University of Texas Press, 1964), 45–46; W. C. Ward in *Confederate Veteran,* 8 (1900), 347; F. B. Chilton, *Unveiling and Dedication of Monument to Hood's Texas Brigade* (Houston, 1911), 350.

3. Haskell, *Haskell of Gettysburg,* 119; Hunt, "Second Day at Gettysburg," *Battles and Leaders,* 3:305; Smith report, *OR* 27.1:588; Warren testimony, *Report of Joint Committee,* 1 (1865), 377; July 2, Wainwright, *Diary of Battle,* 244. Warren wrote nine years later that "at my suggestion" Meade sent him to Little Round Top, but Warren's 1864 testimony seems the more accurate: Warren to Peter Farley, July 13, 1872, Warren Papers, New York State Library.

4. Alexander W. Cameron, "The Saviors of Little Round Top," *Gettysburg Magazine,* 8 (1993), 33–35; Warren to Porter Farley, July 13, 1872, Warren to his wife, July 2, 1863, Warren Papers, New York State Library; Mackenzie to Meade, Mar. 22, 1864, *OR* 27.1:138; Oliver W. Norton, *The Attack and Defense of Little Round Top,* 263–64.

5. H. W. Pfanz, *Gettysburg — The Second Day,* 215–17; William C. Oates, *The War Between the Union and the Confederacy,* 210; William C. Oates in *SHSP,* 6 (1878), 174; Daniel M. Laney, "Wasted Gallantry: Hood's Texas Brigade at Gettysburg," *Gettysburg Magazine,* 16 (1997), 40–41; Robertson report, *OR* 27.2:405.

6. Kathleen Georg Harrison, "'Our Principal Loss Was in This Place': Action at the Slaughter Pen and at the South End of Houck's Ridge," *Gettysburg Magazine,* 1 (1989), 57–59; A. W. Tucker in *National Tribune,* Jan. 21, 1886; Fox, *New York at Gettysburg,* 2:869–71.

7. J. B. Polley, *Hood's Texas Brigade: Its Marches, Its Battles, Its Achievements* (New York: Neale, 1910), 170, 169; Anderson to Bachelder, Mar. 15, 1876, Ladd and Ladd, eds., *Bachelder Papers,* 1:449–50; de Trobriand to his daughter, July 4, Régis de Trobriand, *Our No-*

ble Blood: The Civil War Letters of Régis de Trobriand, Major-General U.S.V., ed. William B. Styple (Kearny, N.J.: Belle Grove, 1997), 116–17; George W. Verrill, "The Seventeenth Maine at Gettysburg," Maine MOLLUS, *War Papers* (1: 1898), 16:266.

8. J. E. Smith, *A Famous Battery and Its Campaigns, 1861–'64* (Washington: W. H. Lowdermilk, 1892), 138; Waddell, Egan reports, *OR* 27.2:426, 27.1:526–27; Mauriel P. Joslyn, "'For Ninety Nine Years or the War': The Story of the 3rd Arkansas at Gettysburg," *Gettysburg Magazine,* 14 (1996), 58; Porter Farley, "Bloody Round Top," in Sauers, ed., *Gettysburg in the National Tribune,* 249.

9. Norton, *Attack and Defense of Little Round Top,* 265–66; Joshua L. Chamberlain, "Through Blood and Fire at Gettysburg," *Hearst's Magazine* (June 1913), in *Gettysburg Magazine,* 6 (1992), 48; Maine Gettysburg Commission, *Maine at Gettysburg* (Portland: Lakeside Press, 1898), 254.

10. H. W. Pfanz, *Gettysburg — The Second Day,* 215–19; Elisha Coan memoir, Coan Papers, Bowdoin College; Chamberlain to Bachelder, Mar. 10, 1884, Ladd and Ladd, eds., *Bachelder Papers,* 3:1884.

11. Thomas A. Desjardin, *Stand Firm Ye Boys from Maine: The 20th Maine and the Gettysburg Campaign,* 50–57; Val C. Giles, *Rags and Hope: The Recollections of Val C. Giles, Four Years with Hood's Brigade, Fourth Texas Infantry, 1861–1865,* ed. Mary Lasswell (New York: Coward-McCann, 1961), 180; Oates, *War Between the Union and the Confederacy,* 213, 218; Chamberlain report, *OR* 27.1:623–24.

12. Martin report, *OR* 27.1:659; Warren to T. H. Davis (notes), Warren to Porter Farley, July 13, 1872, Warren Papers, New York State Library; Joseph M. Leeper statement, A. S. Marvin to Warren, Oct. 29, 1877, Ladd and Ladd, eds., *Bachelder Papers,* 2:896, 1:511; Emerson G. Taylor, *Gouverneur*

Kemble Warren: The Life and Letters of an American Soldier (Boston: Houghton Mifflin, 1932), 128. Later Warren would be vague about his knowledge of Vincent's presence on Little Round Top (Warren to Farley, 1872), but by the time of Hazlett's arrival Vincent's fight could hardly have been a secret.

13. Hunt, "Second Day at Gettysburg," *Battles and Leaders,* 3:303; Lee report, Jan. 1864, *OR* 27.2:318–19; H. W. Pfanz, *Gettysburg — Culp's Hill and Cemetery Hill,* 168–89; July 2, Wainwright, *Diary of Battle,* 243; Nicholson, ed., *Pennsylvania at Gettysburg,* 2:901.

14. John W. F. Hatton memoir, 454, Library of Congress; James Stewart, "Battery B, Fourth U.S. Artillery at Gettysburg," Ohio MOLLUS, *Sketches of War History* (4: 1896), 4:190–91; Ewell report, *OR* 27.2:447; Thomas W. Osborn, "The Artillery at Gettysburg," *Philadelphia Weekly Times,* May 31, 1879.

15. Kershaw to Bachelder, Apr. 3, Mar. 20, 1876, Ladd and Ladd, eds., *Bachelder Papers,* 1:474, 455; McLaws, "Gettysburg," SHSP, 7 (1879), 73; Joseph B. Kershaw, "Kershaw's Brigade at Gettysburg," *Battles and Leaders,* 3:334; David W. Aiken to his wife, July 11, South Caroliniana Library. The Millerstown Road would later come to be known as the Wheatfield Road.

16. H. W. Pfanz, *Gettysburg — The Second Day,* 254–56; John Coxe in *Confederate Veteran,* 21 (1913), 434; Kershaw, "Kershaw's Brigade at Gettysburg," *Battles and Leaders,* 3:335.

17. Robert G. Carter, *Four Brothers in Blue* (Washington: Gibson Press, 1913), 308; John L. Smith to his wife, July 9, Smith Papers, Historical Society of Pennsylvania; Régis de Trobriand, *Four Years with the Army of the Potomac,* 498; Sweitzer report, *OR Supplement* 5:191; George W. Verrill, "The Seventeenth Maine at Gettysburg," Maine MOLLUS, *War Papers* (1: 1898), 16:267.

18. Barnes, Winslow reports, *OR* 27.1:601, 587–88; de Trobriand, *Four Years with the Army of the Potomac*, 498–500; Winslow to Bachelder, May 17, 1878, Ladd and Ladd, eds., *Bachelder Papers*, 1:590.

19. Hancock, Caldwell reports, *OR* 27.1:369, 379; Nicholson, ed., *Pennsylvania at Gettysburg*, 1:623; Mike Pride and Mark Travis, *My Brave Boys: To War with Colonel Cross and the Fighting Fifth*, 234; Charles A. Hale, "With Colonel Cross in the Gettysburg Campaign," John R. Brooke Papers, Historical Society of Pennsylvania; Tremain, *Two Days of War*, 84.

20. Eric Campbell, "Caldwell Clears the Wheatfield," *Gettysburg Magazine*, 3 (1990), 33–34; D. Scott Hartwig, "'No Troops on the Field Had Done Better': John C. Caldwell's Division in the Wheatfield, July 2, 1863," Gallagher, ed., *Three Days at Gettysburg*, 212–14; Caldwell, N. H. Davis, Brooke reports, *OR* 27.1:379, 27.3:1087, 27.1:400; Hale, "With Colonel Cross," Brooke Papers, Historical Society of Pennsylvania.

21. Pride and Travis, *My Brave Boys*, 238–41; Charles A. Fuller, *Recollections of the War of 1861–1865* (Sherburne, N.Y., 1906), 94–95.

22. Thomas B. Rogers, in *St. Louis Globe Democrat*, Mar. 9, 1913; Josiah M. Favill, *The Diary of a Young Officer Serving with the Armies of the United States During the War of the Rebellion* (Chicago: Donnelley, 1909), 246; Theodore Bean, "Fall of General Zook," *Philadelphia Weekly Times*, Jan. 6, 1883.

23. Kershaw, "Kershaw's Brigade at Gettysburg," *Battles and Leaders*, 3:336–37; Robert L. Stewart, *History of the One Hundred and Fortieth Regiment, Pennsylvania Volunteers* (Philadelphia, 1912), 105; John M. Bigham, "Four Brothers at Gettysburg," *Military Images*, 12:1 (1990), 9; Nelson report, *OR* 27.1:398.

24. Campbell, "Caldwell Clears the Wheatfield," *Gettysburg Magazine*, 3 (1990), 41–43; Brooke report, *OR* 27.1:400; H. W. Pfanz, *Gettysburg — The Second Day*, 284–86.

25. John Michael Gibney, "A Shadow Passing: The Tragic Story of Norval Welch and the Sixteenth Michigan at Gettysburg," *Gettysburg Magazine*, 6 (1991), 33–42; Welch report, *OR* 27.1:627–28; Norton, *Attack and Defense of Little Round Top*, 242–44.

26. Brian A. Bennett, "The Supreme Event in Its Existence: The 140th New York on Little Round Top," *Gettysburg Magazine*, 3 (1990), 17–25; Porter Farley narrative, in Norton, *Attack and Defense of Little Round Top*, 134; James R. Campbell, July 3, in *Rochester Evening Express*, July 11, Samuel R. Hazen in *National Tribune*, Sept. 13, 1894, unknown writer, Aug. 12, in *Rochester Evening Express*, Aug. 20, all cited in Bennett, "The Supreme Event."

27. Desjardin, *Stand Firm Ye Boys from Maine*, 64–68; Oates in *SHSP*, 6 (1878), 176; Oates, *War Between the Union and the Confederacy*, 218–20; Chamberlain, "Through Blood and Fire," *Gettysburg Magazine*, 6 (1992), 51; Chamberlain report, *OR Supplement* 5:197.

28. Desjardin, *Stand Firm Ye Boys from Maine*, 68–76; Chamberlain, "Through Blood and Fire," *Gettysburg Magazine*, 6 (1992), 51–55; Ellis Spear memoir, Collection of Abbott and Marjorie Spear, cited in Desjardin, *passim*; Coan memoir, Coan Papers, Bowdoin College; Oates, *War Between the Union and the Confederacy*, 220; William T. Livermore diary, University of Maine.

29. Chamberlain report, *OR Supplement* 5:197; Busey and Martin, *Regimental Strengths and Losses at Gettysburg*, 280; Oates to F. A. Dearborn, Mar. 28, 1898, Collection of Mrs. Robert H. Charles, in Glenn W. LaFantasie, ed., "William C. Oates Remembers Little Round Top," *Gettysburg Magazine*, 21 (1999), 63. Joshua Chamberlain would, in effect, dine out on his Gettysburg ex-

ploits for the rest of his life. For his career, see Thomas Desjardin's *Stand Firm Ye Boys from Maine,* and Glenn LaFantasie, "Joshua Chamberlain and the American Dream," in Boritt, ed., *The Gettysburg Nobody Knows.*

30. B. F. Rittenhouse, "The Battle of Gettysburg as Seen from Little Round Top," District of Columbia MOLLUS, *War Papers* (1: 1897), 42:39–40; Porter Farley, "Bloody Round Top," in Sauers, ed., *Gettysburg in the National Tribune,* 252.

31. William H. Powell, *The Fifth Army Corps,* 534–35.

32. FitzGerald Ross, *A Visit to the Cities and Camps of the Confederate States,* 52; Alexander, *Fighting for the Confederacy,* 239–40; Kershaw to Bachelder, Mar. 20, 1876, Ladd and Ladd, eds., *Bachelder Papers,* 1:457; McLaws, "Gettysburg," *SHSP,* 7 (1879), 74; Haskell, *Haskell of Gettysburg,* 120.

33. John R. Bucklyn diary, July 2, Ladd and Ladd, eds., *Bachelder Papers,* 3:72–73; Bucklyn report, *OR Supplement* 5:188; Tippin report, *OR* 27.1:499; James M. Martin, *History of the Fifty-seventh Regiment, Pennsylvania Veteran Volunteer Infantry* (Meadville, Pa., 1904), 88–89; Benjamin H. Humphreys to Bachelder, May 1, 1876, Ladd and Ladd, eds., *Bachelder Papers,* 1:480–81; David Craft, *History of the One Hundred Forty-first Regiment, Pennsylvania Volunteers, 1862–1865* (Towanda, Pa., 1885), 123.

34. Nicholson, ed., *Pennsylvania at Gettysburg,* 1:173; Humphreys to his wife, July 4, Humphreys Papers, Historical Society of Pennsylvania; Tremain, *Two Days of War,* 89–90; Henry L. Abbott to John C. Ropes, Aug. 17, MOLLUS Collection, Houghton Library, Harvard University; Hancock report, *OR* 27.1:370.

35. Hartwig, "Caldwell's Division in the Wheatfield," Gallagher, ed., *Three Days at Gettysburg,* 223–26; Sykes, Sweitzer reports, *OR* 1.27:592, 611; Sweitzer report, *OR Supplement* 5:192;

Powell, *Fifth Army Corps,* 534–35, 535n.

36. Kershaw report, *OR* 27.2:369; John Coxe in *Confederate Veteran,* 21 (1913), 434; William H. Parker in *Richmond Sentinel,* July 27; Francis Lawley in London *Times,* Aug. 18.

37. Fox, *New York at Gettysburg,* 1:420; Donaldson to his aunt, July 21, Donaldson, *Inside the Army of the Potomac,* 305; Brooke report, *OR* 27.1:401; Stephen A. Osborn, "Recollections of the Civil War" (1915), U.S. Army Military History Institute; Brooke to Francis A. Walker, Mar. 18, 1886, Ladd and Ladd, eds., *Bachelder Papers,* 2:1234; Morgan statement, Ladd and Ladd, eds., *Bachelder Papers,* 3:1355–56.

38. Sweitzer report, *OR* 27.1:611–12; Sweitzer report, *OR Supplement* 5:193–94; James Houghton journal, Michigan Historical Collection, Bentley Historical Library, University of Michigan.

39. Reese, *Sykes' Regular Infantry,* 248–55; Frederick Coriette, July 17, U.S. Army Military History Institute; Count of Paris, *The Battle of Gettysburg* (Philadelphia: Porter & Coates, 1886), 177; Floyd-Jones report, *OR* 27.1:650; Powell, *Fifth Army Corps,* 535n.

40. Alexander, *Fighting for the Confederacy,* 240; Frederick M. Colston, "The Campaign of Gettysburg," Campbell-Colston Papers, Southern Historical Collection, University of North Carolina.

41. July 3, Fiske, *Mr. Dunn Browne's Experiences,* 105.

42. H. W. Pfanz, *Gettysburg — The Second Day,* 390–91; Fremantle, *Three Months in the Southern States,* 269; Scheibert in *SHSP,* 5 (1878), 91.

43. Hill, Anderson, Lang reports, *OR* 27.2:608, 614, 631; William Miller Owen, *In Camp and Battle with the Washington Artillery of New Orleans,* 246.

44. Humphreys to his wife, July 4, Humphreys Papers, Historical Society of Pennsylvania; Edmund D. Patter-

son, *Yankee Rebel: The Civil War Journal of Edmund DeWitt Patterson*, ed. John G. Barrett (Chapel Hill: University of North Carolina Press, 1966), 116; Gibbon, *Personal Recollections*, 137; Silas Adams, "The Nineteenth Maine at Gettysburg," Maine MOLLUS, *War Papers* (4: 1915), 19:253; Hancock to Humphreys, Oct. 10, Humphreys Papers, Historical Society of Pennsylvania; Henry N. Blake, *Three Years in the Army of the Potomac* (Boston: Lee and Shepard, 1865), 215.

45. John Bigelow, *The Peach Orchard, Gettysburg, July 2, 1863* (Minneapolis: Kimball-Storer, 1910), 55; Michael Hanifen, *History of Battery B, First New Jersey Artillery* (Ottawa, Ill., 1905), 76–77.

46. Eric Campbell, "Baptism of Fire: The Ninth Massachusetts Battery at Gettysburg, July 2, 1863," *Gettysburg Magazine,* 5 (1991), 65–77; Bigelow letter, Bigelow account, Ladd and Ladd, eds., *Bachelder Papers*, 1:173–74, 176–77; McGilvery report, *OR* 27.1:882; J. S. McNeily, "Barksdale's Mississippi Brigade at Gettysburg," *Publications of the Mississippi Historical Society*, 19 (1914), 249.

47. McGilvery report, *OR* 27.1:882–83; Benjamin G. Humphreys to Bachelder, May 1, 1876, Ladd and Ladd, eds., *Bachelder Papers*, 1:480–81.

48. A. Wilson Greene, "'A Step All-Important and Essential to Victory': Henry W. Slocum and the Twelfth Corps on July 1–2, 1863," Gallagher, ed., *Three Days at Gettysburg*, 182–84, 188–90; Williams to Bachelder, Apr. 21, 1864, Nov. 10, 1865, Ladd and Ladd, eds., *Bachelder Papers*, 1:163, 215; Slocum to T. H. Davis, Sept. 8, 1875, Bates Collection, Pennsylvania State Archives.

49. Lang to E. A. Perry, July 19, *SHSP*, 27 (1899), 195; Gibbon, *Personal Recollections*, 137; Abbott to John C. Ropes, Aug. 1, MOLLUS Collection, Houghton Library, Harvard University; F. E. Heath to Bachelder, Oct. 12, 1889, Ladd and Ladd, eds., *Bachelder Papers*,

3:1651; John D. Smith, *The History of the Nineteenth Regiment of Maine Volunteer Infantry, 1862–1865* (Minneapolis, 1909), 70.

50. Bradley M. Gottfried, "Wright's Charge on July 2, 1863: Piercing the Union Line or Inflated Glory?" *Gettysburg Magazine* 17 (1997), 71–75; Weir report, *OR* 27.1:880; Andrew E. Ford, *The Story of the Fifteenth Regiment, Massachusetts Volunteer Infantry in the Civil War* (Clinton, Mass., 1898), 267; Gregory A. Coco, ed., *From Ball's Bluff to Gettysburg . . . and Beyond: The Civil War Letters of Private Roland E. Bowen, 15th Massachusetts Infantry, 1861–1864* (Gettysburg: Thomas Publications, 1994), 202; John H. Rhodes, "The Gettysburg Gun," Rhode Island MOLLUS, *Personal Narratives of the Rebellion* (7: 1892), 38:385.

51. A. R. Wright to his wife, July 7, cited in Freeman, *Lee's Lieutenants,* 3:126; H. W. Pfanz, *Gettysburg — The Second Day,* 382–84; Wilcox report addendum, cited in Freeman, *R. E. Lee,* 3:555.

52. Eric Campbell, "'Remember Harper's Ferry': The Degradation, Humiliation, and Redemption of Col. George L. Willard's Brigade," Part 1, *Gettysburg Magazine,* 7 (1992), 51, 64–73; William Love, "Mississippi at Gettysburg," *Publications of the Mississippi Historical Society,* 9 (1906), 32; "Biographical Sketch of William Barksdale," J.F.H. Claiborne Papers, Southern Historical Collection; Hays report, *OR* 27.1:453.

53. Williams to his daughters, July 6, Williams, *From the Cannon's Mouth,* 228; Williams to Bachelder, Nov. 10, 1865, Ladd and Ladd, eds., *Bachelder Papers,* 1:215. Williams marched with Ruger's division to settle an awkward command problem. The newly arrived but inexperienced Lockwood outranked the veteran Ruger, and so Williams treated Lockwood's brigade as "unassigned" to the corps and directed affairs himself.

54. Richard Moe, *The Last Full Measure: The Life and Death of the First Minnesota Volunteers* (New York: Holt, 1993), 268–74; Colville to Bachelder, June 9, 1866, Ladd and Ladd, eds., *Bachelder Papers,* 1:257; William Lochren, "The First Minnesota at Gettysburg," Minnesota MOLLUS, *Glimpses of the Nation's Struggle* (3: 1892), 28:49–50; Wilcox in *SHSP,* 6 (1878), 103; Robert W. Meinhard, "The First Minnesota at Gettysburg," *Gettysburg Magazine,* 5 (1991), 83; Hancock report, *OR* 27.1:371. The 1st Minnesota's 68 percent loss ratio is taken from the researches of Robert Meinhard, correcting previous estimates of 82 percent for July 2.

55. H. W. Pfanz, *Gettysburg — The Second Day,* 396–400; Richard T. Auchmuty to his mother, July 6, Auchmuty, *Letters of Richard Tylden Auchmuty, Fifth Corps, Army of the Potomac* (New York, 1895), 98; Crawford to Peter F.

Rothermel, Mar. 8, 1870, Rothermel Papers, Pennsylvania State Archives; Lafayette McLaws to Braxton Bragg, June 18, 1892, Palmer Collection, Western Reserve Historical Society; Longstreet, "Lee in Pennsylvania," *Annals of the War,* 425.

56. Alexander S. Webb to his wife, July 6, Ladd and Ladd, eds., *Bachelder Papers,* 1:18; Anthony W. McDermott, *A Brief History of the 69th Regiment Pennsylvania Veteran Volunteers* (Philadelphia, 1889), 28; Wright report, *OR* 27.2: 623–24.

57. George H. Scott, "Vermont at Gettysburg," *Proceedings of the Vermont Historical Society,* 1 (1930), 65.

58. Meade, *Life and Letters,* 2:89; Paul A. Oliver to George Meade, May 16, 1882, Meade Papers, Historical Society of Pennsylvania.

59. Williams to his daughters, July 6, Williams, *From the Cannon's Mouth,* 228; Meade, *Life and Letters,* 2:89.

11. Determined to Do or Die

1. George K. Collins, *Memories of the 149th Regiment, New York Volunteer Infantry* (Syracuse, 1891), 137; Jesse H. Jones in *Battles and Leaders,* 3:316; Randolph H. McKim in *SHSP,* 5 (1878), 193.

2. Lee report, Jan. 1864, *OR* 27.2:318–19; D. C. Pfanz, *Richard S. Ewell,* 316–17; Greene, Schurz reports, *OR* 27.1:856, 731.

3. Jones, Buckner, Richardson, Williams reports, *OR* 27.2:532, 538, 537, 513; Redington report, *OR* 27.1:862; Jesse H. Jones in *Battles and Leaders,* 3:316. Casualties in the 78th and 102nd New York for July 2nd and 3rd were 30 and 29 respectively.

4. Thomas L. Elmore, "Courage Against the Trenches: The Attack and Repulse of Steuart's Brigade on Culp's Hill," *Gettysburg Magazine,* 7 (1992), 85–90; Warren report, *OR Supplement* 5:396; Ireland report, *OR* 27.1:866; Fox, *New*

York at Gettysburg, 3:943; Randolph H. McKim, *A Soldier's Recollections,* 195; William W. Goldsborough, *The Maryland Line in the Confederate States Army* (Baltimore, 1869), 104.

5. Dawes, *Service with the Sixth Wisconsin,* 182; Hancock to Joseph Hooker, July 27, 1876, Bates Collection, Pennsylvania State Archives; Horton to Bachelder, Jan. 23, 1867, Ladd and Ladd, eds., *Bachelder Papers,* 1:294–95; Smith report, *OR* 27.1:432.

6. July 6, Williams to his daughters, Williams, *From the Cannon's Mouth,* 229; Charles F. Morse, *Letters Written During the Civil War* (Boston: T. R. Marvin, 1898), 145.

7. Samuel S. Carroll to Hancock, July 23, 1876, Bates Collection, Pennsylvania State Archives; H. W. Pfanz, *Gettysburg — Culp's Hill and Cemetery Hill,* 242; John T. Butts, ed., *A Gallant Captain of the Civil War: . . . Friederich*

Otto Baron von Fritsch (New York, 1902), 80; Seymour, *Civil War Memoirs,* 75; Early, *Autobiographical Sketch,* 273.

8. Maine Gettysburg Commission, *Maine at Gettysburg* (Portland: Lakeside Press, 1898), 94; Edward N. Whittier, "The Left Attack (Ewell's), Gettysburg," *PMHSM,* 3:330; Whittier report, *OR* 27.1:361; Fox, *New York at Gettysburg,* 3:1247; Van R. Willard, *With the 3rd Wisconsin Badgers: The Journals of Van R. Willard,* ed. Steven S. Raab (Mechanicsburg, Pa.: Stackpole Books, 1999), 194.

9. Harris to Bachelder, Mar. 14, 1881, Peter F. Young to Bachelder, Aug. 12, 1867, Ladd and Ladd, eds., *Bachelder Papers,* 2:745, 1:311; Jacob Smith, *Camps and Campaigns of the 107th Ohio Volunteer Infantry* (1910), 226; Joseph W. Jackson, July 20, Boyd Civil War Papers, Louisiana State University; July 2, Wainwright, *Diary of Battle,* 245–46; Harry Gilmor, *Four Years in the Saddle* (Harper & Brothers, 1866), 98–99; Schurz, *Reminiscences,* 3:25; John M. Lutz, Hays reports, *OR* 27.1:720, 27.2:480–81.

10. H. W. Pfanz, *Gettysburg — Culp's Hill and Cemetery Hill,* 258–59; Adin B. Underwood, *The Three Years' Service of the Thirty-third Massachusetts Infantry Regiment* (Boston, 1881), 129; Underwood report, *OR Supplement* 5:218; William R. Kiefer, *History of the One Hundred and Fifty-third Regiment Pennsylvania Volunteer Infantry* (Easton, Pa., 1909), 87.

11. Ricketts to Bachelder, Mar. 2, 1866, Dec. 3, 1883, Ladd and Ladd, eds., *Bachelder Papers,* 1:236–37, 2:980; Brockway to David McConaughy, Mar. 5, 1864, Rothermel Papers, Pennsylvania State Archives.

12. Hancock to Joseph Hooker, July 27, 1876, Carroll to Hancock, July 23, 1876, Bates Collection, Pennsylvania State Archives; J. L. Dickelman, "Gen. Carroll's Gibraltar Brigade at Gettysburg," in Sauers, ed., *Gettysburg in the*

National Tribune, 333; July 2, Wainwright, *Diary of Battle,* 247.

13. Hays, Rodes, Ewell reports, *OR* 27.2:481, 556, 447; Early, *Autobiographical Sketch,* 274; Early in *SHSP,* 4 (1877), 281.

14. Rodes, Ramseur, Ewell reports, *OR* 27.2:556, 588, 447; Brown to Henry J. Hunt, May 7, 1885, Hunt Papers, Library of Congress.

15. Meade to Halleck, July 2, *OR* 27.1:72; Fishel, *Secret War for the Union,* 526–28; Sharpe to Butterfield, July 2, B.M.I., RG 393, National Archives; Sharpe in *Kingston* (N.Y.) *Daily Freeman,* Jan. 18, 1899, and Babcock in *Mount Vernon* (N.Y.) *Daily Argus,* Nov. 21, 1908, cited in Fishel, *Secret War for the Union,* 527–30.

16. Gibbon, *Personal Recollections,* 140–45; Williams to Bachelder, Nov. 10, 1865, Ladd and Ladd, eds., *Bachelder Papers,* 1:217; Newton to Gibbon, Jan. 5, 1876, in Gibbon, *Personal Recollections,* 197; Williams to his daughters, July 6, Williams, *From the Cannon's Mouth,* 229–30; Gibbon to Seth Williams, Mar. 14, 1864, Meade to his wife, July 3, 1863, Meade Papers, Historical Society of Pennsylvania. Butterfield's notes on the July 2 council are in the Meade Papers.

17. Walter H. Taylor, *Four Years with General Lee,* 99; Henry Kyd Douglas, *I Rode with Stonewall* (Chapel Hill: University of North Carolina Press, 1940), 249; Lee report, Jan. 1864, *OR* 27.2:320.

18. Owen, *In Camp and Battle with the Washington Artillery,* 157; Longstreet, "Lee in Pennsylvania," *Annals of the War,* 426, 424; Ross, *Visit to the Cities and Camps of the Confederate States,* 55; Longstreet to McLaws, July 25, 1873, McLaws Papers, Southern Historical Collection, University of North Carolina.

19. Alexander, *Fighting for the Confederacy,* 244; Longstreet, "Lee in Pennsylvania," *Annals of the War,* 429; Longstreet to McLaws, July 25, 1873,

McLaws Papers, Southern Historical Collection.

20. Lee, Ewell, Hays, Pendleton reports, *OR* 27.2:320, 447, 480, 351; William Garrett Piston, "Cross Purposes: Longstreet, Lee, and Confederate Attack Plans for July 3 at Gettysburg," Gary W. Gallagher, ed., *The Third Day at Gettysburg & Beyond,* 35–45.

21. Walter Harrison, *Pickett's Men: A Fragment of War History* (New York: D. Van Nostrand, 1870), 88; Wert, *General Longstreet,* 280–82.

22. P. A. Work, Lee reports, *OR* 27.2:409, 308. Casualty rates are from Busey and Martin, *Regimental Strengths and Losses at Gettysburg.*

23. Bennett, *Days of "Uncertainty and Dread,"* 42–57; Gates D. Fahnestock, 1934 speech, Adams County Historical Society; Sarah D. Broadhead, *Diary of a Lady of Gettysburg, Pennsylvania* (Hershey, Pa.: Hawbaker, 1990); Elizabeth McClean, "The Rebels Are Coming," *Gettysburg Compiler,* July 8, 1908; "Battle Days in 1863," *Gettysburg Compiler,* July 4, 1906; John C. Wills, "Reminiscences," John Rupp to his sister, July 19, Fannie Buehler, "Recollections," Adams County Historical Society; Liberty Hollinger Glutz, *Some Personal Recollections of the Battle of Gettysburg* (1925), 5–6.

24. Billings report, *OR Supplement* 5:53; James A. Bates report, *OR* 27.1:597; C. N. Bryan, Nov. 17, Florida State Archives; Wilfred McDonald diary, University of Texas.

25. H. W. Pfanz, *Gettysburg — Culp's Hill and Cemetery Hill,* 379–80; Alexander, *Fighting for the Confederacy,* 244.

26. Fishel, *Secret War for the Union,* 530–32; Davis, *Papers,* 9:247–50. Dahlgren's intelligence, comforting as it may have been, had no bearing on Meade's decision to stand and fight at Gettysburg.

27. Guiney to Joshua Chamberlain, Oct. 26, 1865, Chamberlain Papers, Library of Congress; Halsted to Emily Sedgwick, July 17, Sedgwick, *Corre-*

spondence, 2:134; Coddington, *Gettysburg Campaign,* 476–78; Hunt to Bachelder, July 27, 1880, Ladd and Ladd, eds., *Bachelder Papers,* 1:675; Hunt testimony, *Report of Joint Committee,* 1 (1865), 448.

28. Coddington, *Gettysburg Campaign,* 480–82; Hancock testimony, *Report of Joint Committee,* 1 (1865), 408.

29. Longstreet, "Lee in Pennsylvania," *Annals of the War,* 429; Longstreet report, *OR* 27.2:359; Long, *Memoirs of Robert E. Lee,* 288; Taylor, *Four Years with General Lee,* 102–3; Fremantle, *Three Months in the Southern States,* 262.

30. Jeffry D. Wert, *Gettysburg: Day Three,* 102–6; Charles Venable in Taylor, *Four Years with General Lee,* 103n; Richard Rollins, "The Second Wave of Pickett's Charge," *Gettysburg Magazine* 18 (1998), 102–13; Alexander, *Fighting for the Confederacy,* 252; Longstreet, "Lee in Pennsylvania," *Annals of the War,* 430.

31. Ewell report, *OR* 27.2:447; Williams to Bachelder, Nov. 10, 1865, Ladd and Ladd, eds., *Bachelder Papers,* 1:219.

32. Williams report, *OR* 27.1:775; Van R. Willard, *With the 3rd Wisconsin Badgers: The Journals of Van R. Willard,* ed. Steven S. Raab (Mechanicsburg, Pa.: Stackpole Books, 1999), 197; William W. Goldsborough, "With Lee at Gettysburg," *Philadelphia Record,* July 8, 1900; H. W. Pfanz, *Gettysburg — Culp's Hill and Cemetery Hill,* 291, 223.

33. Powell to Bachelder, Mar. 23, 1886, Ladd and Ladd, eds., *Bachelder Papers,* 2:1248; William Sayre to family, July 5, Sayre Papers, U.S. Army Military History Institute; Hammerstein, Greene reports, *OR* 27.1:863, 857; *Mobile Evening News,* July 24, cited in Wert, *Gettysburg: Day Three,* 61.

34. H. W. Pfanz, *Gettysburg — Culp's Hill and Cemetery Hill,* 305–6; R. S. Andrews report, *OR* 27.2:544; Thomas G. Clemens, ed., "The 'Diary' of John H. Stone . . . ," *Maryland Historical Magazine,* 85 (1990), 133; Lockwood report,

OR 27.1:804; Wert, *Gettysburg: Day Three,* 66; Geary report, *OR* 27.1:833.

35. Ruger to Bachelder, Aug. 12, 1869, Ladd and Ladd, eds., *Bachelder Papers,* 1:364–65; Ruger, Colgrove reports, *OR* 27.1:781, 814; Alonzo H. Quint, *The Record of the Second Massachusetts Infantry, 1861–1865* (Boston: James Walker, 1867), 180, 183; Morse to his mother, July 17, Morse Papers, Massachusetts Historical Society; Brown, *Twenty-seventh Indiana,* 380–82. In his 1869 letter to Bachelder, Ruger, relying "on my own memory," timed this action at about 10:00 A.M. More specific accounts, especially those of Morse and Colgrove, place it earlier.

36. O'Neal report, *OR Supplement* 5:403; Randolph H. McKim in *SHSP,* 5 (1878), 296–97; Ewell report, *OR* 27.2:447; William W. Goldsborough, *The Maryland Line in the Confederate States Army* (Baltimore, 1869), 106.

37. George K. Collins, *Memories of the 149th Regiment, New York Volunteer Infantry* (Syracuse, 1891), 141; McKim, *A Soldier's Recollections,* 188; Nicholson, ed., *Pennsylvania at Gettysburg,* 1:220; Louis Leon, *Diary of a Tar Heel Confederate Soldier* (Charlotte: Stone Publishing, 1913), 36, courtesy Greg Mast; Sanford Truesdell to his sister, July 11, University of Chicago Library; Wallace to Bachelder, July 4, 1878, Ladd and Ladd, eds., *Bachelder Papers,* 1:636.

38. Walker report, *OR* 27.2:519; William W. Goldsborough, *The Maryland Line in the Confederate States Army* (Baltimore, 1869), 109; H. W. Pfanz, *Gettysburg — Culp's Hill and Cemetery Hill,* 325; Williams to Bachelder, Nov. 10, 1865, Ladd and Ladd, eds., *Bachelder Papers,* 1:221.

12. A Magnificent Display of Guns

1. Meade, *Life and Letters,* 2:101–5; Pleasonton to Gregg, July 3, *OR* 27.3:502; Meade to Sedgwick, July 3, *OR* 51.1:1068; Haskell, *Haskell of Gettysburg,* 142–43; July 4, Whitelaw Reid, *A Radical View: The "Agate" Dispatches of Whitelaw Reid, 1861–1865,* ed. James G. Smart (Memphis: Memphis State University Press, 1976), 2:52; Meade to Couch, July 3, Meade to French, July 3, Meade circular, July 3, *OR* 27.3:499, 501–2, 503.

2. Hunt report, *OR* 27.1:238; David Shultz, *"Double Canister at Ten Yards": The Federal Artillery and the Repulse of Pickett's Charge,* 9–18; David Shultz and Richard Rollins, "'A Combined and Concentrated Fire': Deployment of the Federal Artillery at Gettysburg, July 3, 1863," *North & South,* 2:3 (1999), 54–56; Henry J. Hunt, "The Third Day at Gettysburg," *Battles and Leaders,* 3:371.

3. Hunt, "Third Day at Gettysburg," *Bat-* tles and Leaders, 3:371–72; Gary M. Kross, "'I Do Not Believe That Pickett's Division Would Have Reached Our Line': Henry J. Hunt and the Union Artillery on July 3, 1863," Gallagher, ed., *Three Days at Gettysburg,* 291–92.

4. Peter S. Carmichael, "'Every Map of the Field Cries Out about It': The Failure of Confederate Artillery at Pickett's Charge," Gallagher, ed., *Three Days at Gettysburg,* 271; John H. Chamberlayne to George W. Bagby, Oct. 25, 1862, Chamberlayne, *Ham Chamberlayne, Virginian: Letters and Papers of an Artillery Officer,* ed. C. D. Chamberlayne (Richmond, 1932), 134; Stephen W. Sears, *To the Gates of Richmond: The Peninsula Campaign* (Boston: Houghton Mifflin, 1992), 318.

5. Alexander, *Fighting for the Confederacy,* 244–51; Alexander, *Military Memoirs,* 418–19; Pendleton, Nelson reports, *OR* 27.2:351–52, 605–6; Richard

Rollins, "The Failure of Confederate Artillery in Pickett's Charge," *North & South,* 3:4 (2000), 30–39.

6. Jennings C. Wise, *The Long Army of Lee, or The History of the Artillery Arm of the Army of Northern Virginia* (Lynchburg, Va.: J. B. Bell, 1915), 2:509–10; Alexander, *Fighting for the Confederacy,* 248–49, 254; William T. Poague, *Gunner with Stonewall: Reminiscences of William Thomas Poague,* ed. Monroe F. Cockrell (Jackson, Tenn.: McCowat-Mercer, 1957), 74; Henry, Lee (Jan. 1864) reports, *OR* 27.2:428, 321; McLaws, "Gettysburg," *SHSP,* 7 (1879), 82.

7. Thomas L. Elmore, "A Meteorological and Astronomical Chronology of the Gettysburg Campaign," *Gettysburg Magazine,* 13 (1995), 13–15.

8. Rollins, "Failure of Confederate Artillery," *North & South,* 3:4 (2000), 32–33; Thomas W. Hyde, *Following the Greek Cross, or Memories of the Sixth Army Corps* (Boston: Houghton Mifflin, 1895), 152–53.

9. Kathleen Georg Harrison and John W. Busey, *Nothing But Glory: Pickett's Division at Gettysburg,* 170; Wert, *Gettysburg: Day Three,* 113–14; Birkett D. Fry in *SHSP,* 7 (1879), 92.

10. Robertson, *General A. P. Hill,* 221–22; William H. Palmer to T.M.R. Talcott, Apr. 11, 1916, SHSP, 41 (1916), 40; Young, "Pettigrew's Brigade at Gettysburg," Clark, *North Carolina Regiments,* 5:124; Wert, *Gettysburg: Day Three,* 114–16; R. Lee Hadden, "The Deadly Embrace," *Gettysburg Magazine,* 5 (1991), 32.

11. Lane, Lowrance reports, *OR* 27.2:666, 671; Wert, *Gettysburg: Day Three,* 114–19; Alexander to Frederick Colston, Jan. 14, 1895, Campbell-Colston Papers, Southern Historical Collection, University of North Carolina.

12. Anderson, Wilcox reports, *OR* 27.2:614, 619; Lang to Bachelder, Oct. 16, 1893, Lang Papers, Florida State Archives.

13. Richard Rollins, "Pickett's Charge and the Principles of War," *North & South,* 4:5 (2001), 21–22; Fry to Bachelder, Dec. 27, 1877, Ladd and Ladd, eds., *Bachelder Papers,* 1:518; Rollins, "Failure of Confederate Artillery," *North & South,* 3:4 (2000), 35–36. In his *Military Memoirs* (418), Porter Alexander clarified the intended point of attack: "A clump of trees in the enemy's line was pointed out to me as the proposed point of attack, which I was incorrectly told was the cemetery of the town...."

14. Elwood Christ, *The Struggle for the Bliss Farm at Gettysburg,* 67–75; July 20, Fiske, *Mr. Dunn Browne's Experiences,* 127; Alexander, *Fighting for the Confederacy,* 250–51; Hitchcock to Bachelder, Jan. 20, 1886, Ladd and Ladd, eds., *Bachelder Papers,* 2:1183–84.

15. Bennett, *Days of "Uncertainty and Dread,"* 24, 58–59. Although history knows her as Jennie Wade, "Ginnie" is how she signed her name: Frassanito, *Early Photography at Gettysburg,* 121.

16. D. C. Pfanz, *Richard S. Ewell,* 319–20, 523–24; Seymour, *Civil War Memoirs,* 79; Gordon, *Reminiscences,* 157.

17. Longacre, *Cavalry at Gettysburg,* 200–201, 220–22, 232–33; McClellan, *Life and Campaigns of Stuart,* 337; C. H. Parsons, "Farnsworth's Charge and Death," *Battles and Leaders,* 3:393.

18. Battle strength figures are from Busey and Martin, *Regimental Strengths and Losses at Gettysburg,* and (for Pickett) Harrison and Busey, *Nothing But Glory: Pickett's Division at Gettysburg,* 170. The Third Corps losses subtracted for July 1 are estimates, as Confederate losses were not broken down day by day.

19. Alexander, *Military Memoirs,* 420–22; Alexander, *Fighting for the Confederacy,* 253–55.

20. Schurz, *Reminiscences,* 3:27; William Frassanito, *Early Photography at Gettysburg,* 233. Battle strength figures are from Busey and Martin, *Regimental Strengths and Losses at Gettysburg,* with

subtractions (some estimated) for July 2 losses.

21. Gibbon, *Personal Recollections,* 146; Haskell, *Haskell of Gettysburg,* 145–47.

22. Owen, *In Camp and Battle with the Washington Artillery,* 248; Jacobs, *Notes on the Rebel Invasion,* 41; Biddle to his wife, July 4, Rosenbach Museum and Library; Hirst to his wife, Oct. 1863, in Gallagher, ed., *Third Day at Gettysburg,* 140.

23. Gibbon, *Personal Recollections,* 146–47.

24. July 3, Wainwright, *Diary of Battle,* 249; Hunt, "Third Day at Gettysburg," *Battles and Leaders,* 3:373–74; Walker, *History of the Second Army Corps,* 292; Matthew Marvin diary, July 3, Minnesota Historical Society; Elisha Hunt Rhodes, *All for the Union: A History of the 2nd Rhode Island Volunteer Infantry,* ed. Robert Hunt Rhodes (Lincoln, R.I.: Andrew Mowbray, 1985), 116; Tyler report, *OR* 27.1:874.

25. *New York Times,* July 6; Meade, *Life and Letters,* 2:106–7; Gen. Meade to Bachelder, Dec. 4, 1869, Capt. Meade to Bachelder, May 6, 1882, Ladd and Ladd, eds., *Bachelder Papers,* 1:379, 3:852–53.

26. Shields to Bachelder, Aug. 27, 1884, Ladd and Ladd, eds., *Bachelder Papers,* 2:1067–68; Gibbon, *Personal Recollections,* 149; Haskell, *Haskell of Gettysburg,* 154; Francis A. Walker, *General Hancock* (New York: Appleton, 1894), 97.

27. John Geary to Henry J. Hunt, July 17, 1879, Patrick Hart to Hunt, Aug. 27, 1879, Hunt Papers, Library of Congress; Francis A. Walker in *Battles and Leaders,* 3:386; Hart to Bachelder, Feb. 23, 1891, Hunt to Bachelder, Jan. 20, 1873, Ladd and Ladd, eds., *Bachelder Papers,* 3:1798, 1:432–33; Rollins, "Failure of Confederate Artillery," *North & South,* 3:4 (2000), 35–36.

28. Earl J. Hess, *Pickett's Charge — The Last Attack at Gettysburg,* 141–45; Devereux report, *OR* 27.1:443; John H. Rhodes, "The Gettysburg Gun,"

Rhode Island MOLLUS, *Personal Narratives of the Rebellion* (7: 1892), 38:394–98; Francis M. Wafer diary, July 3, Queens University Library, cited in Richard Rollins, ed., *Pickett's Charge: Eyewitness Accounts,* 134; Christopher Smith in *Buffalo Evening News,* May 29, 1894, cited in Hess, *Pickett's Charge,* 143; Gibbon, *Personal Recollections,* 149; Frederick Fuger recollections, Webb Papers, Yale University Library.

29. Thomas W. Osborn, *The Eleventh Corps Artillery at Gettysburg,* 32; Jesse Bowman Young, *The Battle of Gettysburg* (New York: Harper, 1913), 295–96.

30. Haskell, *Haskell of Gettysburg,* 149, 151; Webb to his wife, July 6, Ladd and Ladd, eds., *Bachelder Papers,* 1:18; John D. S. Cook, "Personal Reminiscences of Gettysburg," Kansas MOLLUS, *War Talks in Kansas* (1: 1906), 15:333–34.

31. Kemper to E. P. Alexander, Sept. 20, 1869, Dearborn Collection, Harvard University; Joseph C. Mayo, "Pickett's Charge at Gettysburg," *SHSP,* 34 (1906), 34:330; Henry T. Owen, "Pickett's Division," Owen Papers, Library of Virginia; Benjamin L. Farinholt to John W. Daniel, Apr. 15, 1905, Daniel Papers, University of Virginia.

32. Alexander, *Military Memoirs,* 422–24; Alexander, *Fighting for the Confederacy,* 258–61.

33. Osborn, "The Artillery at Gettysburg," *Philadelphia Weekly Times,* May 31, 1879; Osborn, *Eleventh Corps Artillery,* 39; Hunt, "Third Day at Gettysburg," *Battles and Leaders,* 3:374; John B. Bachelder in *Philadelphia Weekly Times,* Dec. 15, 1877; Richard A. Sauers, "'Rarely Has More Skill, Vigor, or Wisdom Been Shown': George G. Meade on July 3 at Gettysburg," Gallagher, ed., *Three Days at Gettysburg,* 239; Coddington, *Gettysburg Campaign,* 531.

34. Alexander, *Fighting for the Confederacy,* 260–61.

13. The Grand Charge

1. Edmund Rice in *Battles and Leaders*, 3:387; Haskell, *Haskell of Gettysburg*, 158; Abbott to his father, July 6, Abbott, *Fallen Leaves*, 188; Charles W. Belknap diary, July 3, Brake Collection, U.S. Army Military History Institute; McCrae to Bachelder, Mar. 30, 1904, Gettysburg National Military Park.

2. Capt. Winfield Scott, "Pickett's Charge as Seen from the Front Line," California MOLLUS, *Civil War Papers* (1888), 60:9; Hess, *Pickett's Charge*, 198; George R. Stewart, *Pickett's Charge*, 165–66; John L. Brady to Bachelder, May 24, 1886, Ladd and Ladd, eds., *Bachelder Papers*, 3:1398.

3. Gibbon to his wife, June 30, Gibbon Papers, Historical Society of Pennsylvania; W. L. Curry report, *OR* 27.1:434–35; Abbott to his father, July 6, Abbott, *Fallen Leaves*, 186; Roland E. Bowen, *From Ball's Bluff to Gettysburg . . . and Beyond: The Civil War Letters of Private Roland E. Bowen, 15th Massachusetts Infantry, 1861–1864*, ed. Gregory A. Coco (Gettysburg: Thomas Publications, 1994), 201.

4. Stannard diary, June 29, in Ladd and Ladd, eds., *Bachelder Papers*, 1:52.

5. Shultz, "*Double Canister at Ten Yards*," 24, 31–33, 37; Cowen to Bachelder, Aug. 26, 1866, Ladd and Ladd, eds., *Bachelder Papers*, 1:281–82; Hazard report, *OR* 27.1:480.

6. Krick, "Three Confederate Disasters," Gallagher, ed., *Three Days at Gettysburg*, 91; John D. Imboden, "The Confederate Retreat from Gettysburg," *Battles and Leaders*, 3:421. Distance measurements on the Gettysburg battlefield are derived primarily from David Shultz and Richard Rollins, "Measuring Pickett's Charge," *Gettysburg Magazine*, 17 (1997), 108–17.

7. Randolph A. Shotwell, "Virginia and North Carolina in the Battle of Gettysburg," *Our Living and Our Dead*, 4 (1876), 90; D. E. Johnston, *The Story of a Confederate Boy in the Civil War* (Portland, Ore., 1914), 205–6; Robert Tyler Jones in *Confederate Veteran*, 2 (1894), 271; John H. Lewis, *Recollections from 1860 to 1865* (Washington, 1895), 83.

8. Jacobs, *Notes on the Rebel Invasion*, 41; Alexander, *Military Memoirs*, 423–24. This timetable allows some 50 minutes for the back-and-forth of decision-making and for Pickett to get his troops in motion.

9. Wert, *Gettysburg: Day Three*, 189, 191; D. E. Johnston, *Story of a Confederate Boy in the Civil War* (Portland, Ore., 1914), 204–5.

10. Wert, *Gettysburg: Day Three*, 191–92; Longstreet report, *OR* 27.2:359. Hess (*Pickett's Charge*, 59) disputes Pettigrew's double-line formation, but in his report Longstreet seems clear on the point. He described Pickett's formation as "two brigades in the front line," but said Pettigrew's four-brigade command "was arranged in two lines," supported by Trimble's command.

11. Fry to Bachelder, Dec. 27, 1877, Ladd and Ladd, eds., *Bachelder Papers*, 1:518; Thomas J. Cureton to John R. Lane, June 22, 1890, *OR Supplement* 5:427, 429; John T. Jones report, *OR Supplement* 5:411.

12. Hess, *Pickett's Charge*, 183, 186; Young, "Pettigrew's Brigade at Gettysburg," Clark, *North Carolina Regiments*, 5:125; Christian to John W. Daniel, Oct. 24, 1904, Daniel Papers, University of Virginia.

13. Trimble in *SHSP*, 9 (1881), 31–32; Lane report, *OR* 27.2:666.

14. Joseph Graham to William A. Graham, June 30, Graham, *The Papers of William Alexander Graham*, eds. Max R. Williams and J. G. de Roulhac Hamilton (Raleigh: North Carolina Office of Archives and History, 1973), 5:514; Edmund Berkeley reminiscence, *OR Supplement* 5:311–12; James I. Robertson, Jr., *Eighteenth Virginia Infantry*

(Lynchburg, Va.: H. E. Howard, 1984), 21; E. H. Compton reminiscence, U.S. Army Military History Institute; John E. Dooley, *John Dooley, Confederate Soldier: His War Journal*, ed. Joseph T. Durkin (Washington: Georgetown University Press, 1945), 104.

15. Hess, *Pickett's Charge*, 175–76.
16. B. F. Rittenhouse, "The Battle of Gettysburg as Seen from Little Round Top," District of Columbia MOLLUS, *War Papers* (1: 1897), 42:43.
17. Shultz, *"Double Canister at Ten Yards,"* 37–40; Franklin Sawyer, *A Military History of the 8th Regiment Ohio Vol. Inf'y* (Cleveland, 1881), 131; Schurz, *Reminiscences*, 3:31.
18. Sawyer report, *OR* 27.1:461–62; Lowrance report, *OR* 27.2:671; Sawyer reminiscence, cited in D. H. Daggett, "Those Whom You Left Behind You," Minnesota MOLLUS, *Glimpses of the Nation's Struggle* (5: 1903), 30:360; Galway to Bachelder, May 19, 1882, Ladd and Ladd, eds., *Bachelder Papers*, 2:870.
19. Shultz, *"Double Canister at Ten Yards,"* 75–77; Elijah D. Taft letter, n.d., Gettysburg National Military Park; Edgell report, *OR* 27.1:893; A. H. Moore in *Southern Bivouac*, 3:9 (1885), 391; Davis report, *OR* 27.2:651.
20. McGilvery report, *OR* 27.1:884; B. L. Farinholt memoir, Virginia Historical Society; Hess, *Pickett's Charge*, 172; John H. Smith reminiscence, John W. Daniel Papers, University of Virginia; Edwin B. Dow letter, n.d., Gettysburg National Military Park.
21. R. H. Irvine in *Confederate Veteran*, 23 (1915), 391; Kemper to W. H. Swallow, Feb. 4, 1886, Ladd and Ladd, eds., *Bachelder Papers*, 2:1192; Thomas R. Friend to Charles Pickett, Dec. 10, 1894, Virginia Historical Society; Robert A. Bright in *SHSP*, 31 (1903), 231.
22. Shultz, *"Double Canister at Ten Yards,"* 43; Hart report, *OR* 27.1:888; George G. Benedict, *Vermont at Gettysburg* (Burlington: Free Press, 1870), 16; James T. Carter in *Confederate Veteran*, 10 (1902), 263.

23. Hess, *Pickett's Charge*, 78; John H. Moore in *Military Annals of Tennessee, Confederate*, ed. John Berrien Lindsley (Nashville, 1886), 250; Shultz, *"Double Canister at Ten Yards,"* 53–54; Fry to Bachelder, Dec. 27, 1877, Ladd and Ladd, eds., *Bachelder Papers*, 1:519; Fite memoir, Tennessee State Library and Archives.
24. Hess, *Pickett's Charge*, 210–11; W. H. Swallow in *Southern Bivouac*. 4:9 (1886), 572; Hirst to his wife, July 5, in Gallagher, ed., *Third Day at Gettysburg*, 137; Theodore G. Ellis to Bachelder, Nov. 3, 1870, Ladd and Ladd, eds., *Bachelder Papers*, 1:408; Richard S. Thompson, "A Scrap of Gettysburg," Illinois MOLLUS, *Military Essays and Recollections* (3: 1899), 12:105–6.
25. Trimble in *SHSP*, 9 (1881), 33; Sawyer, *A Military History of the 8th Regiment Ohio Vol. Inf'y* (Cleveland, 1881), 131; William Peel memoir, in Rollins, ed., *Pickett's Charge: Eyewitness Accounts*, 275; Wiley P. Heflin, *Blind Man "On the Warpath,"* cited in Hess, *Pickett's Charge*, 208; Young, "Pettigrew's Brigade at Gettysburg," Clark, *North Carolina Regiments*, 5:126.
26. Shultz, *"Double Canister at Ten Yards,"* 56–57; Hess, *Pickett's Charge*, 203–5; Weir, "Recollections of the 3rd Day at Gettysburg with Battery C," cited in Rollins, ed., *Pickett's Charge: Eyewitness Accounts*, 326; R. Lee Hadden, "The Deadly Embrace," *Gettysburg Magazine*, 5 (1991), 32n.
27. Thomas M. Aldrich, *The History of Battery A, First Rhode Island Light Artillery, in the War to Preserve the Union, 1861–1865* (Providence, 1904), 217; Samuel Toombs, *New Jersey Troops in the Gettysburg Campaign from June 5 to July 31, 1863* (Orange, N.J., 1888), 300; Louis G. Young to William J. Baker, Feb. 10, 1864, *OR Supplement* 5:421.
28. Young, "Pettigrew's Brigade at Gettysburg," Clark, *North Carolina Regiments*, 5:127–28; Lane report, *OR* 27.2:666; Lowrance report, *OR* 27.2:671–72; Moore letter, Nov. 6, 1877, *OR Supplement* 5:468–69.

29. Shultz, *"Double Canister at Ten Yards,"* 54; John L. Brady, Clinton D. MacDougall, S. C. Armstrong in Ladd and Ladd, eds., *Bachelder Papers,* 3:1398, 3:1762–63, 2:1002; Clinton D. MacDougall to Charles Richardson, June 30, 1886, cited in Eric Campbell, "Remember Harper's Ferry," Part 2, *Gettysburg Magazine,* 8 (1993), 110.

30. Anonymous, July 4, in George T. Fleming, ed., *Life and Letters of Alexander Hays* (Pittsburgh, 1919), 442–43.

31. Haskell, *Haskell of Gettysburg,* 159; D. Scott Hartwig, "It Struck Horror to Us All," *Gettysburg Magazine,* 4 (1991), 96; Frederick Fuger recollections, Webb Papers, Yale University Library.

32. Coddington, *Gettysburg Campaign,* 511.

33. George H. Scott, "Vermont at Gettysburg," *Proceedings of the Vermont Historical Society,* 1:2 (1930), 70–71; Stannard to Abner Doubleday, Sept. 3, 1865, Doubleday Papers, New-York Historical Society; Arthur F. Devereux, "Some Account of Pickett's Charge at Gettysburg," *Magazine of American History,* 18 (1887), 16. For the dispute over who originated the Vermont brigade's maneuver, see Hess, *Pickett's Charge,* 237–38.

34. George G. Benedict, July 14, in Benedict, *Army Life in Virginia: Letters from the Twelfth Vermont Regiment* (Burlington: Free Press, 1895), 182–84; Charles H. Morgan statement, George J. Stannard diary, Ladd and Ladd, eds., *Bachelder Papers,* 3:1363–64, 1:56; Gibbon, *Personal Recollections,* 152–53.

35. Henry T. Owen to H. A. Carrington, Jan. 27, 1878, Virginia State Library.

36. Shultz, *"Double Canister at Ten Yards,"* 48, 51–52; Alexander, *Fighting for the Confederacy,* 262–63; Alexander to Bachelder, May 3, 1876, Ladd and Ladd, eds., *Bachelder Papers,* 1:490; *History of the Fifth Massachusetts Battery* (Boston, 1902), 652.

37. James A. Wright memoir, Minnesota Historical Society; Edward Walker letter, July 29, cited in Richard Moe, *The Last Full Measure: The Life and Death of the First Minnesota Volunteers* (New York: Holt, 1993), 289; Gates report, *OR* 27.1:322; Abbott to his father, July 6, Abbott to Oliver Wendell Holmes, Jr., July 28, Abbott, *Fallen Leaves,* 188, 194; Abbott report, *OR* 27.1:445.

38. William Nathaniel Wood, *Reminiscences of Big I,* ed. Bell Irvin Wiley (Jackson, Tenn.: McCowat-Mercer, 1956), 46; Gibbon, Gettysburg sketch, Historical Society of Pennsylvania; Randolph A. Shotwell, *The Papers of Randolph Abbott Shotwell,* ed. J. G. de Roulhac Hamilton (Raleigh: North Carolina Historical Commission, 1929–36), 2:13.

39. Veazey to George G. Benedict, July 11, 1864, Vermont Historical Society; Edward P. Reeve reminiscence, Southern Historical Collection, University of North Carolina; Henry T. Owen to H. A. Carrington, Jan. 27, 1878, Virginia State Library.

40. Fremantle, *Three Months in the Southern States,* 265–66; Robert A. Bright in *SHSP,* 31 (1903), 231–32; Longstreet to McLaws, July 25, 1873, McLaws Papers, Southern Historical Collection; Anderson report, *OR* 27.2:614–15; Longstreet, "The Mistakes of Gettysburg," *Annals of the War,* 627.

41. Gary G. Lash, "The Philadelphia Brigade at Gettysburg," *Gettysburg Magazine,* 7 (1992), 104; Haskell, *Haskell of Gettysburg,* 162.

42. Hess, *Pickett's Charge,* 242; John H. Smith reminiscence, John W. Daniel Papers, University of Virginia; Andrew Cowan to Bachelder, Aug. 26, 1866, Ladd and Ladd, eds., *Bachelder Papers,* 1:282–83; Longacre, *The Man Behind the Guns,* 176–77; Hunt to his wife, July 4, Hunt Papers, Library of Congress.

43. Cowan to Bachelder, Aug. 26, 1866, Dec. 2, 1885, Ladd and Ladd, eds., *Bachelder Papers,* 1:282, 2:1156–57; Cyril Tyler to his father, July 7, Gettys-

burg National Military Park; Shultz, *"Double Canister at Ten Yards,"* 57.

44. D. Scott Hartwig, "It Struck Horror to Us All," *Gettysburg Magazine,* 4 (1991), 89, 97–99; William Davis report, *OR* 27.1:431; Buckley to Bachelder, n.d., Ladd and Ladd, eds., *Bachelder Papers,* 3:1403; Peyton report, *OR* 27.2:386; Kemper to W. H. Swallow, Feb. 4, 1886, Ladd and Ladd, eds., *Bachelder Papers,* 2:1192.

45. McDermott to Bachelder, June 2, 1886, Ladd and Ladd, eds., *Bachelder Papers,* 3:1410; Frederick Fuger recollections, Webb Papers, Yale University Library; Christopher Smith account, *Buffalo Evening News* (1894), cited in Hess, *Pickett's Charge,* 246. For an analysis of Confederate numbers at this point in the battle, see Hess, *Pickett's Charge,* 232–33. That Cushing's initial wounding occurred during the bombardment rather than the charge is evident from Andrew Cowan to Bachelder, Dec. 2, 1885, Ladd and Ladd, eds., *Bachelder Papers,* 2:1157.

46. James Carter in *Confederate Veteran,* 10 (1902), 263; W. H. Swallow in *Southern Bivouac,* 4:9 (1886), 569; Hess, *Pickett's Charge,* 261–63; Webb to his wife, July 6, Ladd and Ladd, eds., *Bachelder Papers,* 1:19; Webb testimony (1891), cited in Rollins, *Pickett's Charge: Eyewitness Accounts,* 317; D. B. Easley in *Confederate Veteran,* 20 (1912), 379.

47. Ernest L. Waitt, *History of the Nineteenth Regiment Massachusetts Volunteer Infantry, 1861–1865* (Salem, Mass., 1906), 242; Joseph McKeever testimony (1891), cited in Hartwig, "It Struck Horror to Us All," *Gettysburg Magazine,* 4 (1991), 98; John H. Smith reminiscence, John W. Daniel Papers, University of Virginia; July 4, Wainwright, *Diary of Battle,* 252; R. H. Irvine in *Confederate Veteran,* 23 (1915), 391.

48. Arthur F. Devereux to Bachelder, July 22, 1889, Ladd and Ladd, eds., *Bachelder Papers,* 3:1609–10; Haskell, *Haskell of Gettysburg,* 165–67; Francis Heath cited in Silas Adams, "The Nineteenth Maine at Gettysburg," Maine MOLLUS, *War Papers* (4: 1915), 19:262; Charles H. Banes testimony (1890) in Ladd and Ladd, eds., *Bachelder Papers,* 3:1709; Edmund Rice, Apr. 19, 1887, Doubleday Papers, New-York Historical Society; Rice in *Battles and Leaders,* 3:389.

49. Trimble to John W. Daniel, Nov. 24, 1875, *SHSP,* 9 (1881), 35; "Another Witness: Gettysburg," *Our Living and Our Dead,* 3 (1875), 463; Abbott to his father, July 6, Abbott, *Fallen Leaves,* 188.

50. Schurz, *Reminiscences,* 3:33; David Lang to Bachelder, Oct. 16, 1893, Lang Papers, Florida State Archives; Herbert to Porter Alexander, Aug. 18, 1903, Alexander Papers, Southern Historical Collection; Alexander, *Fighting for the Confederacy,* 265.

51. Shultz, *"Double Canister at Ten Yards,"* 59–60; Lang, Wilcox reports, *OR* 2:632, 620; E. H. Shore to his wife, Aug. 16, Shore Papers, Emory University; Randolph A. Shotwell, *The Papers of Randolph Abbott Shotwell,* ed. J. G. de Roulhac Hamilton (Raleigh: North Carolina Historical Commission, 1929–36), 2:15.

52. Trimble, "The Civil War Diary of General Isaac Ridgeway Trimble," *Maryland Historical Magazine,* 17 (1822), 2; John H. Smith reminiscence, John W. Daniel Papers, University of Virginia; Franklin Sawyer report, *OR* 27.1:462; Hess, *Pickett's Charge,* 308–9; Henry T. Owen, cited in Hoke, *The Great Invasion,* 426–27; July 3, Hotchkiss, *Make Me a Map,* 158.

53. George T. Fleming, ed., *Life and Letters of Alexander Hays* (Pittsburgh, 1919), 464–65; Haskell, *Haskell of Gettysburg,* 173–74; Charles H. Morgan statement, George Meade to Bachelder, May 6, 1882, Ladd and Ladd, eds., *Bachelder Papers,* 3:1364, 3:856. A letter by a gunner on Hays's front suggests Meade had already been told the Rebels "are just turning." However,

Meade may have concluded this referred only to the right of the line when he met Haskell at the center. John Egan to George Meade, Feb. 8, 1870, Ladd and Ladd, eds., *Bachelder Papers*, 1:389–90.

54. Frederick M. Colston, "The Campaign of Gettysburg," Campbell-Colston Papers, Southern Historical Collection; Fremantle, *Three Months in the Southern States*, 267–69.

14. A Long Road Back

1. Charles Gardner memoir, U.S. Army Military History Institute.
2. Stuart report, *OR* 27.2:697; William A. Graham to H. B. McClellan, n.d., Ladd and Ladd, eds., *Bachelder Papers*, 3:1337; G. W. Beale cited in McClellan, *Life and Campaigns of Stuart*, 346–47; Daniel B. Balfour, *13th Virginia Cavalry* (Lynchburg, Va.: H. E. Howard, 1986), 22; Busey and Martin, *Regimental Strengths and Losses at Gettysburg*, 194–99, 320–21.
3. David McM. Gregg, "The Second Cavalry Division of the Army of the Potomac in the Gettysburg Campaign," Pennsylvania MOLLUS, *Military Essays and Recollections* (1907), 59:124–25; Longacre, *Cavalry at Gettysburg*, 167; Lyman, *Meade's Headquarters*, 17.
4. Edwin E. Bouldin to Bachelder, July 20, 1886, Alanson M. Randol to Bachelder, Mar. 24, 1886, Ladd and Ladd, eds., *Bachelder Papers*, 3:1442, 2:1252; Stuart report, *OR* 27.2:698; Wert, *Gettysburg: Day Three*, 266–67; Luther S. Trowbridge, Feb. 19, 1886, Ladd and Ladd, eds., *Bachelder Papers*, 2:1207; Earl J. Hess, *The Union Soldier in Battle: Enduring the Ordeal of Combat* (Lawrence: University Press of Kansas, 1997), 121; John A. Clark, July 30, Clark Papers, Clements Library, University of Michigan.
5. Gregg, "Second Cavalry Division," Pennsylvania MOLLUS, *Military Essays and Recollections* (1907), 59:125–26; William Brooke-Rawle in *Annals of the War*, 481; William E. Miller in *Battles and Leaders*, 3:404; William E. Miller, June 8, 1878, Ladd and Ladd, eds., *Bachelder Papers*, 1:653; Longacre, *Cavalry at Gettysburg*, 238–39; Daniel

B. Balfour, *13th Virginia Cavalry* (Lynchburg, Va.: H. E. Howard, 1986), 22–24.
6. H. C. Parsons, "Farnsworth's Charge and Death," *Battles and Leaders*, 3:393; D. H. Hamilton, *History of Company M, First Texas Volunteer Infantry* (Waco: W. M. Morrison, 1962), 29; Longacre, *Cavalry at Gettysburg*, 241–42, 311–85; Thomas L. McCarty memoir, Gettysburg National Military Park; H. W. Berryman, July 9, Brake Collection, U.S. Army Military History Institute.
7. Henry C. Potter memoir, Gettysburg College; Eric Wittenberg, *Gettysburg's Forgotten Cavalry Actions* (Gettysburg: Thomas Publications, 1998), 32; Turner Vaughan, "Diary of Turner Vaughan, Co. C, 4th Alabama Regiment, C.S.A.," *Alabama Historical Quarterly* 18 (Winter 1956), 589; H. C. Parsons, "Farnsworth's Charge and Death," *Battles and Leaders*, 3:394–96. The assertion that Farnsworth killed himself to defy capture is contradicted by the nature of his wounds. See Longacre, *Cavalry at Gettysburg*, 311–89.
8. Hancock to Meade, July 3, *OR* 27.1:366; Meade testimony, *Report of Joint Committee*, 1 (1865), 333; Hancock quoted in Samuel P. Bates, *The Battle of Gettysburg*, 175; Meade to Smith, July 5, *OR* 27.3:539.
9. July 3, Wainwright, *Diary of Battle*, 249; Cornelia Hancock, *South after Gettysburg: Letters of Cornelia Hancock, 1863–1868*, ed. Henrietta Stratton Jaquette (New York: Crowell, 1956), 7; George P. Erwin to his father, July 3, Erwin Papers, Southern Historical

Collection, University of North Carolina; Haskell, *Haskell of Gettysburg,* 191.

10. Henry W. Bingham to Hancock, Jan. 5, 1869, Ladd and Ladd, eds., *Bachelder Papers,* 1:352; Doubleday, *Chancellorsville and Gettysburg,* 195.

11. George Meade to Bachelder, May 5, 1882, Ladd and Ladd, eds., *Bachelder Papers,* 2:854–55; Franklin Sawyer reminiscence, cited in D. H. Daggett, "Those Whom You Left Behind You," Minnesota MOLLUS, *Glimpses of the Nation's Struggle* (5: 1903), 30:362; Harrison and Busey, *Nothing But Glory: Pickett's Division at Gettysburg,* 169; Hess, *Pickett's Charge,* 333, 335; Bruce A. Trinque, "Confederate Battle Flags in the July 3rd Charge," *Gettysburg Magazine,* 21 (1999), 127; Richard Rollins, *"The Damned Red Flags of Rebellion": The Confederate Battle Flag at Gettysburg* (Redondo Beach, Calif.: Rank and File, 1997), 194–95. Estimates of wounded prisoners from Pettigrew's and Trimble's commands are extrapolated from that figure in Pickett's division.

12. Harrison and Busey, *Nothing But Glory: Pickett's Division at Gettysburg,* 169–70; Hess, *Pickett's Charge,* 333, 335.

13. Three-day Federal totals in Busey and Martin, *Regimental Strengths and Losses at Gettysburg,* less estimated losses on July 1 (Gates's demi-brigade) and July 2. For Webb's brigade, see Bradley M. Gottfried, *Stopping Pickett: The History of the Philadelphia Brigade* (Shippensburg, Pa.: White Mane Books, 1999), 178–79. For the 69th Pennsylvania, see D. Scott Hartwig, "It Struck Horror to Us All," *Gettysburg Magazine,* 4 (1991), 99.

14. July 4, Wainwright, *Diary of Battle,* 251–52.

15. Bennett, *Days of "Uncertainty and Dread,"* 63–67; Albertus McCreary, "Gettysburg: A Boy's Experience of the Battle," *McClure's Magazine,* 33 (July 1909); Henry E. Jacobs, "How an Eye-Witness Watched the Great Battle," *Philadelphia North American,* June 29, 1913; Sarah M. Broadhead, *Diary of a Lady of Gettysburg, Pennsylvania* (Hershey, Pa.: Hawbaker, 1990); Henry Monath memoir, *Gettysburg Compiler,* Dec. 28, 1897.

16. Schurz, *Reminiscences,* 3:34–35; Jennie McCreary to her sister, July 22, Adams County Historical Society.

17. July 3, Hotchkiss, *Make Me a Map,* 157–58; Lee G.O. 75, July 4, *OR* 27.2:311; Imboden, "The Confederate Retreat from Gettysburg," *Battles and Leaders,* 3:420–21.

18. Lee to Imboden, July 4, *OR* 27.3:966–67; Hoke, *The Great Invasion,* 500; Imboden, "The Confederate Retreat from Gettysburg," *Battles and Leaders,* 3:422–25; Steve French, "Hurry Was the Order of the Day," *North & South,* 2:6 (1999), 36–38. The approximation of wounded in Imboden's train takes into account the estimated number of wounded men captured by the Federals or left behind in the retreat.

19. Dodge, *On Campaign with the Army of the Potomac,* 329; Fremantle, *Three Months in the Southern States,* 274; July 4, Hotchkiss, *Make Me a Map,* 158; July 4, Henry R. Berkeley, *Four Years in the Confederate Artillery: The Diary of Private Henry Robinson Berkeley,* ed. William H. Runge (Chapel Hill: University of North Carolina Press, 1961), 52; Brown, *Campbell Brown's Civil War,* 225; Robert Stiles, *Four Years under Marse Robert* (New York: Neale, 1903), 220. The Federals counted 6,802 wounded Confederates taken prisoner (*OR* 27.2:346), some 2,300 of them in Pickett's Charge.

20. Brown, *Campbell Brown's Civil War,* 225; Hotchkiss to his wife, July 5, Hotchkiss Papers, Library of Congress; James M. Simpson to his mother, July 8, Allen-Simpson Papers, Southern Historical Collection; Wayland F. Dunaway, *Reminiscences of a Rebel* (New York: Neale, 1913), 93.

21. Hess, *Pickett's Charge,* 344–45; Morgan statement, Ladd and Ladd, eds., *Bachelder Papers,* 3:1367.

22. Lee to Meade, Meade to Lee, July 4, *OR*

27.3:514; Fremantle, *Three Months in the Southern States,* 272–73.

23. Meade to Halleck, July 4, *OR* 27.1:78; Meade to his wife, July 5, Meade Papers, Historical Society of Pennsylvania; Meade G.O. 68, July 4, *OR* 27.3:519.

24. Lincoln to Halleck, July 6, *OR* 27.3:567; Elizabeth Blair Lee to her husband, July 4, Lee, *Wartime Washington,* 283; July 7, Welles, *Diary,* 1:363; Herman Haupt, *Reminiscences of General Herman Haupt* (Milwaukee: Wright & Joys, 1901), 227; Meade to his wife, July 5, 8, Meade Papers, Historical Society of Pennsylvania.

25. Butterfield, Warren testimony, *Report of Joint Committee,* 1 (1865), 426–27, 379; Meade to Halleck, July 5, *OR* 27.1:79; Warren to Henry W. Benham, July 7, *OR* 27.3:585–86; July 5, Fiske, *Mr. Dunn Browne's Experiences,* 114.

26. George Templeton Strong, *The Diary of George Templeton Strong: The Civil War, 1860–1865,* ed. Allan Nevins (New York: Macmillan, 1952), 328; *New York Herald,* July 6; *Philadelphia Inquirer,* July 6; July 7, Welles, *Diary,* 1:364; Halleck to Meade, July 7, Meade to Halleck, July 8, *OR* 27.1:83, 84. According to the recollection of Lincoln's son Robert, the president sent a peremptory order to Meade to attack Lee immediately, "and that if he was successful in the attack he might destroy the order but if he was unsuccessful he might preserve it for his vindication." No text of such an order has survived; if Lincoln did write it, it is virtually certain he did not send it; Meade says nothing of it in his unstinting letters to his wife in the Meade Papers, Historical Society of Pennsylvania. See Gabor S. Boritt, "'Unfinished Work': Lincoln, Meade, and Gettysburg," in Boritt, ed., *Lincoln's Generals* (New York: Oxford University Press, 1994), 98–99, 212–14n32.

27. Army of the Potomac circular, July 5, *OR* 27.3:532–33; Dawes to Mary Gates, July 14, Dawes, *Service with the Sixth Wisconsin,* 187; Meade to Halleck, July 8, *OR* 27.1:85; Weld to his sister, July 16, Weld, *War Diary and Letters,* 243.

28. July 6, Hotchkiss, *Make Me a Map,* 159; Alexander, *Fighting for the Confederacy,* 267; Henry R. Berkeley, *Four Years in the Confederate Artillery: The Diary of Private Henry Robinson Berkeley,* ed. William H. Runge (Chapel Hill: University of North Carolina Press, 1961), 52–53. The number of Union prisoners is estimated by subtracting 1,300 paroled (*OR* 27.3:549) from the number captured at Gettysburg (Busey and Martin, *Regimental Strengths and Losses at Gettysburg,* 239). Lee gave conflicting figures. In his report of July 31 (*OR* 27.2:309) he claimed 6,000 Union prisoners, 2,000 of which he paroled. In his Jan. 1864 report (*OR* 27.2:325) he claimed 7,000 prisoners, including 1,500 he paroled.

29. Eric J. Wittenberg, "The Midnight Fight in the Monterey Pass, July 4–5, 1863," *North & South,* 2:6 (1999), 44–53; Kilpatrick report, *OR* 27.1:994; Fremantle, *Three Months in the Southern States,* 280; Ted Alexander, "Ten Days in July: The Pursuit to the Potomac," *North & South,* 2:6 (1999), 19–23; French to Halleck, July 4, *OR* 27.3:524; Imboden, "The Confederate Retreat from Gettysburg," *Battles and Leaders,* 3:426–28.

30. Alexander, "Ten Days in July," *North & South,* 2:6 (1999), 16–18; Meade to his wife, July 8, Meade Papers, Historical Society of Pennsylvania; July 7, Weld, *War Diary and Letters,* 238.

31. Alexander, *Fighting for the Confederacy,* 269–71; Kent Masterson Brown, "A Golden Bridge: Lee's Williamsport Defense Lines and His Escape Across the Potomac," *North & South,* 2:6 (1999), 56–58; July 8, 9, Hotchkiss, *Make Me a Map,* 159–60; Henry L. Abbott to John C. Ropes, Aug. 1, MOLLUS Collection, Houghton Library, Harvard University.

32. Scheibert, *Seven Months in the Rebel States,* 120; Brown, "A Golden

Bridge," *North & South,* 2:6 (1999), 58; July 13, Hotchkiss, *Make Me a Map,* 161; Sorrel, *Recollections of a Confederate Staff Officer,* 165.

33. Army of the Potomac itinerary, *OR* 27.1:146; July 11, Wainwright, *Diary of Battle,* 259; Meade to Halleck, July 10, *OR* 27.1:89; Smith to Meade, July 8, *OR* 27.3:611; Lincoln to Lorenzo Thomas, July 8, Lincoln, *Works,* 6:322; Meade to his wife, July 12, Meade Papers, Historical Society of Pennsylvania; Charles H. Brewster, *When This Cruel War Is Over: The Civil War Letters of Charles Harvey Brewster,* ed. David W. Blight (Amherst: University of Massachusetts Press, 1992), 244.

34. Ropes to John C. Gray, Apr. 19, 1864, Gray and Ropes, *War Letters,* 319; Meade to his wife, July 12, Meade Papers, Historical Society of Pennsylvania; Meade, Humphreys, Warren, Wadsworth testimony, *Report of Joint Committee,* 1 (1865), 336, 396–97, 381, 415; R. F. Halsted to Emily Sedgwick, July 17, Sedgwick, *Correspondence,* 2:135; July 16, Hay, *Inside Lincoln's White House,* 63.

35. Humphreys testimony, *Report of Joint Committee,* 1 (1865), 397; Meade circular, July 13, *OR* 27.3:675; Halleck to Meade, July 13, *OR* 27.1:92.

36. Brown, "A Golden Bridge," *North & South,* 2:6 (1999), 59–60; W. P. Conrad and Ted Alexander, *When War Passed This Way* (Greencastle, Pa., 1982), 203; Rodes report, *OR* 27.2:559; Alexander, *Fighting for the Confederacy,* 272.

37. Brown, "A Golden Bridge," *North & South,* 2:6 (1999), 60–64; Longacre, *Cavalry at Gettysburg,* 268–69; J. H. Kidd, *Personal Recollections of a Cavalryman* (Ionia, Iowa, 1908), 183–86; Louis G. Young, "Death of Brigadier General J. Johnston Pettigrew," *Our Living and Our Dead,* 1 (1874), 30–31; Alexander, "Ten Days in July," *North & South,* 2:6 (1999), 34–60; Kilpatrick, Buford reports, *OR* 27.1:990, 929; R. M. Mayo report, *OR Supplement* 5:415–16.

38. Noah Brooks, *Washington in Lincoln's Time,* ed. Herbert Mitgang (New York: Rinehart, 1958), 91; July 14, Fiske, *Mr. Dunn Browne's Experiences,* 122–23.

Epilogue: Great God! What Does It Mean?

1. Meade to Halleck, July 14, *OR* 27.1:92; July 14, Hay, *Inside Lincoln's White House,* 62; July 14, Welles, *Diary,* 1:370–71.

2. Halleck to Meade, Meade to Halleck, Halleck to Meade, July 14, *OR* 27.1:92, 93, 93–94; Evelyn Page, ed., "Frederick Law Olmsted on the Escape of Lee," *Pennsylvania Magazine of History and Biography,* 75 (Oct. 1951), 440–41; Meade to his wife, July 14, Meade Papers, Historical Society of Pennsylvania; Meade to McClellan, July 14, McClellan Papers, Library of Congress.

3. Lincoln to Meade, July 14 (not sent), Lincoln, *Works,* 6:327–28; July 19, Hay, *Inside Lincoln's White House,* 64–65.

4. Meade to Halleck, July 31, Howard to Lincoln, July 18, *OR* 27.1:109, 700; Hunt to A. S. Webb, Jan. 19, 1888, *PMHSM,* 3:239; July 14, Wainwright, *Diary of Battle,* 261; Meade to his wife, July 12, 14, 18, Meade Papers, Historical Society of Pennsylvania.

5. Union casualties at Gettysburg: Busey and Martin, *Regimental Strengths and Losses at Gettysburg,* 239. Additional Union campaign losses adapted from *OR* 27.1:193.

6. Meade to his wife, July 26, Meade Papers, Historical Society of Pennsylvania; Lincoln to O. O. Howard, July 21, Lincoln, *Papers,* 6:341. On July 31 Meade wrote his wife that he had "recently received" Lincoln's letter to Howard, and he sent it to her for safe-

keeping: Meade Papers, Historical Society of Pennsylvania.

7. Lee to Davis, July 4, 7, 8, 12, Lee, *Wartime Papers,* 539, 540–41, 543–44, 548; Lee quoted by John Seddon, c. July 15, in *SHSP,* 4 (1877), 154–55. It was Henry Heth who recorded and published Seddon's recollection of his conversation with Lee.

8. Confederate casualties at Gettysburg: Busey and Martin, *Regimental Strengths and Losses at Gettysburg,* 280, with modified figures for Pickett's division from Harrison and Busey, *Nothing But Glory: Pickett's Division at Gettysburg,* 169. Additional campaign losses: *OR* 27.2:442, 713–16, and adapted from table in *North & South,* 2:6 (1999), 21. Captured Confederate wounded: *OR* 27.2:346. Seven Days' casualties: Stephen W. Sears, *To the Gates of Richmond: The Peninsula Campaign* (Boston: Houghton Mifflin, 1992), 243. Vicksburg captures: *OR* 24.1:62.

9. Lee to Davis, Sept. 23, Lee, *Wartime Papers,* 603; unknown writer, Aug. 4, Bowles-Jordan Papers, University of Virginia; Aiken to his wife, July 11, South Caroliniana Library.

10. *Savannah Republican,* July 20; *Charleston Mercury,* July 22, 30.

11. Lee to Davis, July 31, Lee, *Lee's Dispatches,* 110; Lee to Davis, Aug. 8, Davis to Lee, Aug. 11, Davis, *Papers,* 9:326–27, 337–38; Wigfall to C. C. Clay, Aug. 13, Clay Papers, Duke University.

12. Fremantle, *Three Months in the Southern States,* 275, 274; Allen, conversation with Lee, Apr. 15, 1868, Gallagher, ed., *Lee the Soldier,* 14.

13. Longstreet to A. B. Longstreet, July 24, in Longstreet, "Lee in Pennsylvania," *Annals of the War,* 414–15; Longstreet to Wigfall, Aug. 2, Wigfall Papers, Library of Congress.

14. Blackford to his wife, July 18, Susan Leigh Blackford, ed., *Letters from Lee's Army* (New York: Scribner's, 1947), 195; Lee report, Jan. 1864, *OR* 27.2:321.

15. Allan, conversation with Lee, Feb. 15, 1868, in Gallagher, ed., *Lee the Soldier,* 11.

16. Goree to E. P. Alexander, Dec. 6, 1887, Thomas J. Goree, *Longstreet's Aide: The Civil War Letters of Major Thomas J. Goree,* ed. Thomas W. Cutrer (Charlottesville: University Press of Virginia, 1995), 167; Longstreet, "Lee in Pennsylvania," *Annals of the War,* 424.

17. Longstreet to Wigfall, Aug. 2, Wigfall Papers, Library of Congress; Lee report, Jan. 1864, *OR* 27.2:320; Alexander to Thomas L. Rosser, Apr. 19, 1901, Rosser Papers, University of Virginia.

18. Meade to his wife, July 26, 27, Meade Papers, Historical Society of Pennsylvania; Meade to John Gibbon, May 15, 1864, in Gibbon, *Personal Recollections,* 187. The chief contriver was Butterfield, who distorted Meade's contingency plan for an orderly retreat into an abject giving up of the field. For Sickles's campaign against Meade, see "Dan Sickles, Political General," Sears, *Controversies & Commanders,* 217–22; and Richard A. Sauers, *A Caspian Sea of Ink: The Meade-Sickles Controversy* (Baltimore: Butternut & Blue, 1989).

19. Abbott to his father, July 27, Abbott, *Fallen Leaves,* 192; Hunt to A. S. Webb, Jan. 19, 1888, *PMHSM,* 3:238–39.

20. Brewster to his sister, July 12, Charles H. Brewster, *When This Cruel War Is Over: The Civil War Letters of Charles Harvey Brewster,* ed. David W. Blight (Amherst: University of Massachusetts Press, 1992), 244; Elisha Hunt Rhodes, *All for the Union: A History of the 2nd Rhode Island Volunteer Infantry,* ed. Robert Hunt Rhodes (Lincoln, R.I.: Andrew Mowbray, 1985), 117.

21. July 22, Worthington Chauncey Ford, ed., *A Cycle of Adams Letters, 1861–1865* (Boston: Houghton Mifflin, 1920), 2:53; July 15, Fiske, *Mr. Dunn Browne's Experiences,* 124.

22. The definitive works on photography at Gettysburg are by William A. Frassanito: *Gettysburg: A Journey in*

Time (New York: Scribner's, 1975), and *Early Photography at Gettysburg* (Gettysburg: Thomas Publications, 1995). For the sketch artists, see W. Fletcher Thompson, Jr., *The Image of War: The Pictorial Reporting of the American Civil War* (New York: Yoseloff, 1959), 121–25.

23. Edward P. Villum, Jonathan Letterman reports, *OR* 27.1:27, 197; Gerald A. Patterson, *Debris of Battle: The Wounded of Gettysburg* (Mechanicsburg, Pa.: Stackpole Books, 1997), 57, 107–8, 171; Mary McAllister memoir, Adams County Historical Society; Sarah M. Broadhead, *Diary of a Lady of Gettysburg, Pennsylvania* (Hershey, Pa.: Hawbaker, 1990); Albertus McCreary, "Gettysburg: A Boy's Experience of the Battle," *McClure's Magazine,* 33 (July 1909).

24. Bennett, *Days of "Uncertainty and Dread,"* 87–90; Kathleen Georg Harrison, "This Grand National Enterprise," Gettysburg National Military Park.

25. *Revised Report of the Select Committee Relative to the Soldiers' National Cemetery* (1865; reprint Gettysburg: Thomas Publications, 1988), 149; Gregory A. Coco, *Wasted Valor: The Confederate Dead at Gettysburg* (Gettysburg: Thomas Publications, 1990), 41. The interment at Gettysburg was not completed until March 1864, and included dead from other phases of the campaign.

26. Garry Wills, *Lincoln at Gettysburg: The Words that Remade America,* 23–25; Wills to Lincoln, Nov. 2, Lincoln Papers, Library of Congress; Meade to his wife, Sept. 16, Meade, *Life and Letters,* 2:149.

27. Nov. 19, Hay, *Inside Lincoln's White House,* 113; Everett to Lincoln, Nov. 20, Lincoln Papers, Library of Congress.

Bibliography

This Bibliography selectively lists printed sources of general interest to the study of the Gettysburg campaign and what led up to it. Numerous additional sources of narrower focus, manuscript and printed, are cited in full in the Notes.

Abbott, Henry L. *Fallen Leaves: The Civil War Letters of Major Henry Livermore Abbott.* Robert Garth Scott, ed. Kent, Ohio: Kent State University Press, 1991.

Alexander, Edward Porter. *Fighting for the Confederacy: The Personal Recollections of General Edward Porter Alexander.* Gary W. Gallagher, ed. Chapel Hill: University of North Carolina Press, 1989.

Alexander, Edward Porter. *Military Memoirs of a Confederate: A Critical Narrative.* New York: Scribner's, 1907.

Alexander, Edward Porter. "The Great Charge and Artillery Fighting at Gettysburg," *Battles and Leaders of the Civil War,* 3:357–68.

Alexander, Ted. "'A Regular Slave Hunt': The Army of Northern Virginia and Black Civilians in the Gettysburg Campaign," *North & South,* 4:7 (2001), 82–89.

Alexander, Ted. "Ten Days in July: The Pursuit to the Potomac," *North & South,* 2:6 (1999), 10–34.

Annals of the War, Written by Leading Participants North and South. A. K. McClure, ed. Philadelphia: Times Publishing, 1879.

Bandy, Ken, and Florence Freeland, eds. *The Gettysburg Papers.* Dayton: Morningside House, 1986.

Bates, Samuel P. *The Battle of Gettysburg.* Philadelphia: T. H. Davis, 1875.

Battles and Leaders of the Civil War. Robert Underwood Johnson and Clarence Clough Buel, eds. 4 vols. New York: Century, 1887–88.

Bauer, Daniel. "Did a Food Shortage Force Lee to Fight?" *Columbiad,* 1:4 (1998), 57–74.

Bennett, Brian A. "The Supreme Event in Its Existence: The 140th New York on Little Round Top," *Gettysburg Magazine,* 3 (1990), 16–25.

Bennett, Gerald R. *Days of "Uncertainty and Dread": The Ordeal Endured by the Citizens at Gettysburg.* Littlestown, Pa., 1994.

Blackford, W. W. *War Years with Jeb Stuart.* New York: Scribner's, 1945.

Boritt, Gabor S., ed. *The Gettysburg Nobody Knows*. New York: Oxford University Press, 1997.

Bowden, Scott, and Bill Ward. *Last Chance for Victory: Robert E. Lee and the Gettysburg Campaign*. Conshohocken, Pa.: Savas Publishing, 2001.

Brennan, Patrick. "Thunder on the Plains of Brandy," Parts I and II, *North & South,* 5:3 (2002), 14–34; 5:4 (2002), 32–51.

Brown, Campbell. *Campbell Brown's Civil War: With Ewell and the Army of Northern Virginia*. Terry L. Jones, ed. Baton Rouge: Louisiana State University Press, 2001.

Brown, E. R. *The Twenty-seventh Indiana Volunteer Infantry in the War of the Rebellion, 1861 to 1865*. Monticello, Ind., 1899.

Brown, Kent Masterson. "A Golden Bridge: Lee's Williamsport Defense Lines and His Escape Across the Potomac," *North & South,* 2:6 (1999), 56–65.

Busey, John W., and David G. Martin. *Regimental Strengths and Losses at Gettysburg*. Hightstown, N.J.: Longstreet House, 1994.

Campbell, Eric. "Baptism of Fire: The Ninth Massachusetts Battery at Gettysburg, July 2, 1863," *Gettysburg Magazine,* 5 (1991), 47–77.

Campbell, Eric. "Caldwell Clears the Wheatfield," *Gettysburg Magazine,* 3 (1990), 27–50.

Carmichael, Peter S. "'Every Map of the Field Cries Out about It': The Failure of Confederate Artillery at Pickett's Charge," Gallagher, ed., *Three Days at Gettysburg,* 270–83.

Christ, Elwood W. *The Struggle for the Bliss Farm at Gettysburg, July 2nd and 3rd, 1863*. Baltimore: Butternut and Blue, 1994.

Clark, Walter, ed. *Histories of the Several Regiments and Battalions from North Carolina in the Great War of 1861–'65*. 5 vols. Raleigh: State of North Carolina, 1901.

Cleaves, Freeman. *Meade of Gettysburg*. Norman: University of Oklahoma Press, 1960.

Coddington, Edwin B. *The Gettysburg Campaign: A Study in Command*. Rev. ed. Dayton: Morningside House, 1979.

Colt, Margaretta Barton. *Defend the Valley: A Shenandoah Family in the Civil War*. New York: Orion Books, 1994.

Confederate Veteran. 40 vols. Nashville, 1893–1932.

Connelly, Thomas Lawrence, and Archer Jones. *The Politics of Command: Factions and Ideas in Confederate Strategy*. Baton Rouge: Louisiana State University Press, 1973.

Cooksey, Paul Clark. "They Died as if on Dress Parade: The Annihilation of Iverson's Brigade at Gettysburg and the Battle of Oak Ridge," *Gettysburg Magazine,* 20 (1998), 89–112.

Cozzens, Peter, ed. *Battles and Leaders of the Civil War: Volume 5*. Urbana: University of Illinois Press, 2002.

Davis, Jefferson. *The Papers of Jefferson Davis.* Lynda Lasswell Crist, Mary Seaton Dix, and Kenneth H. Williams, eds. Vol. 9. Baton Rouge: Louisiana State University Press, 1997.

Dawes, Rufus R. *Service with the Sixth Wisconsin Volunteers.* Marietta, Ohio, 1890.

De Trobriand, Régis. *Four Years with the Army of the Potomac.* Boston: Ticknor, 1889.

Desjardin, Thomas A. *Stand Firm Ye Boys from Maine: The 20th Maine and the Gettysburg Campaign.* Gettysburg: Thomas Publications, 1995.

Dodge, Theodore A. *On Campaign with the Army of the Potomac: The Civil War Journal of Theodore Ayrault Dodge.* Stephen W. Sears, ed. New York: Cooper Square Press, 2001.

Donaldson, Francis A. *Inside the Army of the Potomac: The Civil War Experience of Captain Francis Adams Donaldson.* J. Gregory Acken, ed. Mechanicsburg, Pa.: Stackpole Books, 1998.

Doubleday, Abner. *Chancellorsville and Gettysburg.* New York: Scribner's, 1882.

Early, Jubal A. *Autobiographical Sketch and Narrative of the War Between the States.* Philadelphia: Lippincott, 1912.

Fishel, Edwin C. *The Secret War for the Union: The Untold Story of Military Intelligence in the Civil War.* Boston: Houghton Mifflin, 1996.

Fiske, Samuel W. *Mr. Dunn Browne's Experiences in the War: The Civil War Letters of Samuel W. Fiske.* Stephen W. Sears, ed. New York: Fordham University Press, 1998.

Fox, William F., ed. *New York at Gettysburg.* 3 vols. Albany: J. B. Lyon, 1902.

Frassanito, William A. *Early Photography at Gettysburg.* Gettysburg: Thomas Publications, 1995.

Frassanito, William A. *Gettysburg: A Journey in Time.* New York: Scribner's, 1975.

Freeman, Douglas Southall. *Lee's Lieutenants: A Study in Command.* 3 vols. New York: Scribner's, 1942–44.

Freeman, Douglas Southall. *R. E. Lee: A Biography.* 4 vols. New York: Scribner's, 1934–35.

Fremantle, Arthur J. L. *Three Months in the Southern States: April–June 1863* (1864). Lincoln: University of Nebraska Press, 1991.

Gallagher, Gary W. "Confederate Corps Leadership on the First Day at Gettysburg: A. P. Hill and Richard S. Ewell in a Difficult Debut," Gallagher, ed., *Three Days at Gettysburg,* 25–43.

Gallagher, Gary W. "'If the Enemy Is There, We Must Attack Him': R. E. Lee and the Second Day at Gettysburg," Gallagher, ed., *Three Days at Gettysburg,* 109–29.

Gallagher, Gary W. "Lee's Army Has Not Lost Any of Its Prestige," Gallagher, ed., *The Third Day at Gettysburg & Beyond,* 1–22.

Gallagher, Gary W., ed. *Lee the Soldier.* Lincoln: University of Nebraska Press, 1996.

Gallagher, Gary W., ed. *The Third Day at Gettysburg & Beyond*. Chapel Hill: University of North Carolina Press, 1994.

Gallagher, Gary W., ed. *Three Days at Gettysburg: Essays on Confederate and Union Leadership*. Kent, Ohio: Kent State University Press, 1999.

Gallman, J. Matthew, with Susan Baker, "Gettysburg's Gettysburg: What the Battle Did to the Borough," Boritt, ed., *The Gettysburg Nobody Knows,* 144–74.

Gambone, A. M. *Hancock at Gettysburg . . . and Beyond*. Baltimore: Butternut and Blue, 1997.

Gettysburg Discussion Group: http://www.gdg.org

Gettysburg Magazine. Dayton: Morningside House, 1989– .

Gibbon, John. *Personal Recollections of the Civil War*. New York: Putnam's, 1928.

Gordon, John B. *Reminiscences of the Civil War*. New York: Scribner's, 1903.

Gottfried, Bradley M. *Roads to Gettysburg: Lee's Invasion of the North, 1863*. Shippensburg, Pa.: White Mane Books, 2001.

Gottfried, Bradley M. "Wright's Charge on July 2, 1863: Piercing the Union Line or Inflated Glory?" *Gettysburg Magazine,* 17 (1997), 70–82.

Gray, John Chipman, and John Codman Ropes. *War Letters, 1862–1865*. Boston: Houghton Mifflin, 1927.

Greene, A. Wilson. "'A Step All-Important and Essential to Victory': Henry W. Slocum and the Twelfth Corps on July 1–2, 1863," Gallagher, ed., *Three Days at Gettysburg,* 169–203.

Greene, A. Wilson. "From Gettysburg to Falling Waters: Meade's Pursuit of Lee," Gallagher, ed., *Third Day at Gettysburg & Beyond,* 161–94.

Griffin, D. Massy. "Rodes on Oak Hill: A Study of Rodes' Division on the First Day of Gettysburg," *Gettysburg Magazine,* 4 (1991), 33–48.

Harrison, Kathleen Georg. "'Our Principal Loss Was in This Place': Action at the Slaughter Pen and at the South End of Houck's Ridge," *Gettysburg Magazine,* 1 (1989), 45–69.

Harrison, Kathleen Georg, and John W. Busey. *Nothing But Glory: Pickett's Division at Gettysburg*. Gettysburg: Thomas Publications, 1993.

Hartwig, D. Scott. "The 11th Army Corps on July 1, 1863," *Gettysburg Magazine,* 2 (1990), 33–49.

Hartwig, D. Scott. "Guts and Good Leadership: The Action at the Railroad Cut, July 1, 1863," *Gettysburg Magazine,* 1 (1989), 5–14.

Hartwig, D. Scott. "It Struck Horror to Us All," *Gettysburg Magazine,* 4 (1991), 89–100.

Hartwig, D. Scott. "'No Troops on the Field Had Done Better': John C. Caldwell's Division in the Wheatfield, July 2, 1863," Gallagher, ed., *Three Days at Gettysburg,* 204–28.

Haskell, Frank A. *Haskell of Gettysburg: His Life and Civil War Papers*. Frank L. Byrne and Andrew T. Weaver, eds. Kent, Ohio: Kent State University Press, 1989.

Hassler, Warren W., Jr. *Crisis at the Crossroads: The First Day at Gettysburg.* Montgomery: University of Alabama Press, 1970.

Hay, John. *Inside Lincoln's White House: The Complete Civil War Diary of John Hay.* Michael Burlingame and John R. Turner Ettlinger, eds. Carbondale: Southern Illinois University Press, 1997.

Hebert, Walter H. *Fighting Joe Hooker.* Indianapolis: Bobbs-Merrill, 1944.

Herdegen, Lance J., and J. K. Beaudot. *In the Bloody Railroad Cut at Gettysburg.* Dayton: Morningside House, 1990.

Hess, Earl J. *Pickett's Charge — The Last Attack at Gettysburg.* Chapel Hill: University of North Carolina Press, 2001.

Hoke, Jacob. *The Great Invasion of 1863: or, General Lee in Pennsylvania.* Dayton: W. J. Shuey, 1887.

Hood, J. B. *Advance and Retreat: Personal Experiences in the United States and Confederate States Armies.* New Orleans, 1880.

Hotchkiss, Jedediah. *Make Me a Map of the Valley: The Civil War Journal of Stonewall Jackson's Topographer.* Archie P. McDonald, ed. Dallas: Southern Methodist University Press, 1973.

Howard, Oliver Otis. *Autobiography.* 2 vols. New York: Baker and Taylor, 1907.

Hunt, Henry J. "The First Day at Gettysburg," *Battles and Leaders of the Civil War,* 3:255–84.

Hunt, Henry J. "The Second Day at Gettysburg," *Battles and Leaders of the Civil War,* 3:290–313.

Hunt, Henry J. "The Third Day at Gettysburg," *Battles and Leaders of the Civil War,* 3:369–85.

Imboden, John D. "The Confederate Retreat from Gettysburg," *Battles and Leaders of the Civil War,* 3:420–29.

Imhof, John D. *Gettysburg: Day Two: A Study in Maps.* Baltimore: Butternut & Blue, 1999.

Jacobs, Michael. *Notes on the Rebel Invasion of Maryland and Pennsylvania and the Battle of Gettysburg.* Philadelphia: Lippincott, 1864.

Jones, J. B. *A Rebel War Clerk's Diary at the Confederate States Capital.* Howard Swiggett, ed. 2 vols. New York: Old Hickory Bookshop, 1935.

Krick, Robert K. *The Gettysburg Death Roster: The Confederate Dead at Gettysburg.* 3rd ed. rev. Dayton: Morningside House, 1993.

Krick, Robert K. "Three Confederate Disasters on Oak Ridge: Failures of Brigade Leadership on the First Day at Gettysburg," Gallagher, ed., *Three Days at Gettysburg,* 72–106.

Kross, Gary M. "'I Do Not Believe That Pickett's Division Would Have Reached Our Line': Henry J. Hunt and the Union Artillery on July 3, 1863," Gallagher, ed., *Three Days at Gettysburg,* 284–305.

Ladd, David L., and Audrey J. Ladd, eds. *The Bachelder Papers: Gettysburg in Their Own Words.* 3 vols. Dayton: Morningside House, 1994.

Lash, Gary G. "Brig. Gen. Henry Baxter's Brigade at Gettysburg, July 1," *Gettysburg Magazine,* 10 (1994), 6–27.

Lash, Gary G. "The Philadelphia Brigade at Gettysburg," *Gettysburg Magazine,* 7 (1992), 97–113.

Law, E. M. "The Struggle for 'Round Top,'" *Battles and Leaders of the Civil War,* 3:318–30.

Lee, Elizabeth Blair. *Wartime Washington: The Civil War Letters of Elizabeth Blair Lee.* Virginia Jeans Laas, ed. Urbana: University of Illinois Press, 1991.

Lee, Robert E. *Lee's Dispatches: Unpublished Letters of General Robert E. Lee, C.S.A., to Jefferson Davis and the War Department of the Confederate States of America, 1862–1865.* Douglas Southall Freeman and Grady McWhiney, eds. New York: Putnam's, 1957.

Lee, Robert E. *The Wartime Papers of R. E. Lee.* Clifford Dowdey and Louis H. Manarin, eds. New York: Bramhall House, 1961.

Lincoln, Abraham. *The Collected Works of Abraham Lincoln.* Roy P. Basler, ed. 9 vols. New Brunswick, N.J.: Rutgers University Press, 1953–55. *Supplement,* Westport, Conn.: Greenwood Press, 1974.

Long, A. L. *Memoirs of Robert E. Lee.* New York: J. M. Stoddart, 1886.

Long, Roger. "General Orders No. 72, 'By Command of Gen. R. E. Lee,'" *Gettysburg Magazine,* 7 (1992), 13–22.

Longacre, Edward G. *The Cavalry at Gettysburg: A Tactical Study of Mounted Operations During the Civil War's Pivotal Campaign, 9 June–14 July 1863.* Rutherford, N.J.: Fairleigh Dickinson University Press, 1986.

Longacre, Edward G. *The Man Behind the Guns: A Biography of General Henry J. Hunt, Commander of Artillery, Army of the Potomac.* New York: A. S. Barnes, 1977.

Longstreet, James. *From Manassas to Appomattox: Memoirs of the Civil War in America.* Philadelphia: Lippincott, 1896.

Longstreet, James. "Lee in Pennsylvania," *Annals of the War,* 414–46.

Longstreet, James. "Lee's Invasion of Pennsylvania," *Battles and Leaders of the Civil War,* 3:244–51.

Longstreet, James. "Lee's Right Wing at Gettysburg," *Battles and Leaders of the Civil War,* 3:339–54.

Longstreet, James. "The Mistakes of Gettysburg," *Annals of the War,* 619–33.

Lyman, Theodore. *Meade's Headquarters, 1863–1865: Letters of Colonel Theodore Lyman from the Wilderness to Appomattox.* George R. Agassiz, ed. Boston: Atlantic Monthly Press, 1922.

Marshall, Charles. *An Aide-de-Camp of Lee.* Frederick Maurice, ed. Boston: Little, Brown, 1927.

Martin, David G. *Gettysburg, July 1.* Rev. ed. Conshohocken, Pa.: Combined Books, 1996.

McClellan, H. B. *The Life and Campaigns of Major-General J.E.B. Stuart.* Boston: Houghton Mifflin, 1885.

McKim, Randolph H. *A Soldier's Recollections: Leaves from the Diary of a Young Confederate*. New York: Longmans, Green, 1910.

McLaws, Lafayette. *A Soldier's General: The Civil War Letters of Major General Lafayette McLaws*. John C. Oeffinger, ed. Chapel Hill: University of North Carolina Press, 2002.

McMurry, Richard M. "The Pennsylvania Gambit and the Gettysburg Splash," Boritt, ed., *The Gettysburg Nobody Knows*, 175–202.

Meade, George. *The Life and Letters of George Gordon Meade*. George Gordon Meade II, ed. 2 vols. New York: Scribner's, 1913.

Meade, George Gordon, II. *With Meade at Gettysburg*. Philadelphia: John C. Winston, 1930.

Military Order of the Loyal Legion of the United States (MOLLUS). *Papers*, 1887–1915. Reprint, 62 vols. (numbered serially) plus index. Wilmington, N.C.: Broadfoot Publishing, 1991–97.

Miller, J. Michael. "Perrin's Brigade on July 1, 1863," *Gettysburg Magazine*, 13 (1995), 22–32.

Moore, Frank, ed. *The Rebellion Record: A Diary of American Events*. Vol. 7. New York: Van Nostrand, 1864.

Morrison, James L., Jr., ed. "Memoirs of Henry Heth, Part II," *Civil War History*, 8:3 (1962), 300–326.

Mosby, John S. *Stuart's Cavalry in the Gettysburg Campaign*. New York: Moffat, Yard & Co., 1908.

Nelson, L. Patrick. "Reynolds and the Decision to Fight," *Gettysburg Magazine*, 23 (2000), 30–50.

Nesbitt, Mark. *Saber and Scapegoat: J.E.B. Stuart and the Gettysburg Controversy*. Mechanicsburg, Pa.: Stackpole Books, 1994.

Nichols, Edward J. *Toward Gettysburg: A Biography of General John F. Reynolds*. University Park: Pennsylvania State University Press, 1958.

Nicholson, John P., ed. *Pennsylvania at Gettysburg*. 2 vols. Harrisburg: W. S. Ray, 1904.

Nolan, Alan T. *The Iron Brigade: A Military History*. New York: Macmillan, 1961.

Norton, Oliver W. *The Attack and Defense of Little Round Top: Gettysburg, July 2, 1863*. New York: Neale, 1913.

Nye, Wilbur Sturtevant. *Here Come the Rebels!* Baton Rouge: Louisiana State University Press, 1965.

Oates, William C. *The War Between the Union and the Confederacy and Its Lost Opportunities*. New York: Neale, 1905.

O'Brien, Kevin E. "'Give Them Another Volley, Boys': Biddle's Brigade Defends the Union Left on July 1, 1863," *Gettysburg Magazine*, 19 (1998), 37–52.

Osborn, Thomas W. *The Eleventh Corps Artillery at Gettysburg: The Papers of Major Thomas Ward Osborn, Chief of Artillery*. Herb S. Crumb, ed. Hamilton, N.Y.: Edmonston, 1991.

Owen, William Miller. *In Camp and Battle with the Washington Artillery of New Orleans*. Boston: Ticknor, 1885.

Papers of the Military Historical Society of Massachusetts. 15 vols. Boston, 1895–1918.

Patrick, Marsena R. *Inside Lincoln's Army: The Diary of Marsena Rudolph Patrick, Provost Marshal, Army of the Potomac*. David S. Sparks, ed. New York: Yoseloff, 1964.

Pender, William Dorsey. *The General to His Lady: The Civil War Letters of William Dorsey Pender to Fanny Pender*. William W. Hassler, ed. Chapel Hill: University of North Carolina Press, 1962.

Pfanz, Donald C. *Richard S. Ewell: A Soldier's Life*. Chapel Hill: University of North Carolina Press, 1998.

Pfanz, Harry W. *Gettysburg — Culp's Hill and Cemetery Hill*. Chapel Hill: University of North Carolina Press, 1993.

Pfanz, Harry W. *Gettysburg — The First Day*. Chapel Hill: University of North Carolina Press, 2001.

Pfanz, Harry W. *Gettysburg — The Second Day*. Chapel Hill: University of North Carolina Press, 1987.

Pfanz, Harry W. "'Old Jack' Is Not Here," Boritt, ed., *The Gettysburg Nobody Knows*, 56–74.

Piston, William Garrett. "Cross Purposes: Longstreet, Lee and Confederate Attack Plans for July 3 at Gettysburg," Gallagher, ed., *Third Day at Gettysburg & Beyond*, 31–51.

Powell, David. "A Reconnaissance Gone Awry: Capt. Samuel R. Johnston's Fateful Trip to Little Round Top," *Gettysburg Magazine*, 23 (2000), 88–99.

Powell, David. "Stuart's Ride: Lee, Stuart, and the Confederate Cavalry in the Gettysburg Campaign," *Gettysburg Magazine*, 20 (1998), 27–43.

Powell, William H. *The Fifth Army Corps*. New York: Putnam's, 1896.

Pride, Mike, and Mark Travis. *My Brave Boys: To War with Colonel Cross and the Fighting Fifth*. Hanover, N.H.: University Press of New England, 2001.

Priest, John Michael. *Into the Fight: Pickett's Charge at Gettysburg*. Shippensburg, Pa.: White Mane Books, 1998.

Reese, Timothy J. *Sykes' Regular Infantry Division, 1861–1864: A History of Regular United States Infantry Operations in the Civil War's Eastern Theater*. Jefferson, N.C.: McFarland, 1990.

Report of the Joint Committee on the Conduct of the War. Vol. 1 (1863 series). Vol. 1 (1865 series). Washington: Government Printing Office.

Robertson, James I., Jr. *General A. P. Hill: The Story of a Confederate Warrior*. New York: Random House, 1987.

Robertson, William Glenn. "The Peach Orchard Revisited: Daniel E. Sickles and the Third Corps on July 2, 1863," Gallagher, ed., *Three Days at Gettysburg*, 130–46.

Rollins, Richard. "Confederate Artillery Prepares for Pickett's Charge," "The Failure of Confederate Artillery at Gettysburg: Ordnance and Logistics," "The Failure of Confederate Artillery in Pickett's Charge," *North & South,* 2:7 (1999), 41–55; 3:2 (2000), 44–54; 3:4 (2000), 26–42.

Rollins, Richard. "The Second Wave of Pickett's Charge," *Gettysburg Magazine,* 18 (1998), 96–113.

Rollins, Richard, ed. *Pickett's Charge: Eyewitness Accounts.* Redondo Beach, Calif.: Rank and File Publications, 1994.

Ross, FitzGerald. *A Visit to the Cities and Camps of the Confederate States* (1865). Richard B. Harwell, ed. Urbana: University of Illinois Press, 1958.

Sauers, Richard A. *A Caspian Sea of Ink: the Meade-Sickles Controversy.* Baltimore: Butternut and Blue, 1989.

Sauers, Richard A. "'Rarely Has More Skill, Vigor, or Wisdom Been Shown': George G. Meade on July 3 at Gettysburg," Gallagher, ed., *Three Days at Gettysburg,* 231–44.

Sauers, Richard A. "The 16th Maine Volunteer Infantry at Gettysburg," *Gettysburg Magazine,* 13 (1995), 33–42.

Sauers, Richard A., ed., *Fighting Them Over: How the Veterans Remembered Gettysburg in the Pages of the National Tribune.* Baltimore: Butternut and Blue, 1998.

Scheibert, Justus. *Seven Months in the Rebel States During the North American War, 1863.* Stanley Hoole, ed. Tuscaloosa, Ala.: Confederate Publishing, 1958.

Schurz, Carl. *The Reminiscences of Carl Schurz.* 3 vols. New York: McClure, 1907–8.

Sears, Stephen W. *Chancellorsville.* Boston: Houghton Mifflin, 1996.

Sears, Stephen W. *Controversies & Commanders: Dispatches from the Army of the Potomac.* Boston: Houghton Mifflin, 1999.

Sedgwick, John. *Correspondence of John Sedgwick, Major General.* 2 vols. New York, 1903.

Seymour, William J. *The Civil War Memoirs of Captain William J. Seymour: Reminiscences of a Louisiana Tiger.* Terry L. Jones, ed. Baton Rouge: Louisiana State University Press, 1991.

Shue, Richard S. *Morning at Willoughby Run: July 1, 1863.* Gettysburg: Thomas Publications, 1995.

Shultz, David. *"Double Canister at Ten Yards": The Federal Artillery and the Repulse of Pickett's Charge.* Redondo Beach, Calif.: Rank and File Publications, 1995.

Shultz, David, and Richard Rollins. "'A Combined and Concentrated Fire': Deployment of the Federal Artillery at Gettysburg, July 3, 1863," *North & South,* 2:3 (1999), 39–60.

Small, Abner R. *The Road to Richmond: The Civil War Letters of Major Abner R. Small of the Sixteenth Maine Volunteers.* Harold A. Small, ed. Berkeley: University of California Press, 1939.

Sorrel, G. Moxley. *Recollections of a Confederate Staff Officer.* New York: Neale, 1905.

Southern Historical Society Papers. 52 vols. Richmond, 1876–1959.

Starr, Stephen Z. *The Union Cavalry in the Civil War.* Vol. 1. Baton Rouge: Louisiana State University Press, 1979.

Stewart, George R. *Pickett's Charge: A Microhistory of the Final Attack at Gettysburg, July 3, 1863.* Boston: Houghton Mifflin, 1959.

Storch, Marc, and Beth Storch. "'What a Deadly Trap We Were In': Archer's Brigade on July 1, 1863," *Gettysburg Magazine,* 6 (1992), 13–27.

Tagg, Larry. *The Generals of Gettysburg: The Leaders of America's Greatest Battle.* Campbell, Calif.: Savas Publishing, 1998.

Taylor, Walter H. *Four Years with General Lee.* New York: Appleton, 1877.

Taylor, Walter H. *Lee's Adjutant: The Wartime Letters of Colonel Walter Herron Taylor, 1862–1865.* R. Lockwood Tower, ed. Columbia: University of South Carolina Press, 1995.

Thomas, Emory M. *Bold Dragoon: The Life of J.E.B. Stuart.* New York: Harper & Row, 1986.

Tremain, Henry E. *Two Days of War: A Gettysburg Narrative and Other Excursions.* New York: Bonnell, Silver and Bowers, 1905.

Trimble, Isaac R. "The Battle and Campaign of Gettysburg," *Southern Historical Society Papers,* 26 (1898), 116–28.

Trudeau, Noah Andre. *Gettysburg: A Testing of Courage.* New York: HarperCollins, 2002.

Tucker, Glenn. *High Tide at Gettysburg: The Campaign in Pennsylvania.* Rev. ed. Dayton: Morningside House, 1973.

Tucker, Glenn. *Lee and Longstreet at Gettysburg.* Indianapolis: Bobbs-Merrill, 1968.

Turner, George Edgar. *Victory Rode the Rails: The Strategic Place of the Railroads in the Civil War.* Indianapolis: Bobbs-Merrill, 1953.

U.S. War Department. *The War of the Rebellion: A Compilation of the Official Records of the Union and Confederate Armies.* 128 parts in 70 vols. and atlas. Washington: Government Printing Office, 1880–1901. *Supplement,* 100 vols. Wilmington, N.C.: Broadfoot Publishing, 1994–2000.

Wainwright, Charles S. *A Diary of Battle: The Personal Journals of Colonel Charles S. Wainwright, 1861–1865.* Allan Nevins, ed. New York: Harcourt, Brace & World, 1962.

Walker, Francis A. *History of the Second Army Corps in the Army of the Potomac.* New York: Scribner's, 1887.

Weld, Stephen M. *War Diary and Letters of Stephen Minot Weld, 1861–1865.* 2nd ed. Boston: Massachusetts Historical Society, 1979.

Welles, Gideon. *Diary of Gideon Welles.* Howard K. Beale, ed. 3 vols. New York: Norton, 1960.

Wert, Jeffry D. *General James Longstreet: The Confederacy's Most Controversial Soldier.* New York: Simon & Schuster, 1993.

Wert, Jeffry D. *Gettysburg: Day Three.* New York: Simon & Schuster, 2001.

Wert, Jeffry D. *Mosby's Rangers.* New York: Simon & Schuster, 1990.

Williams, Alpheus S. *From the Cannon's Mouth: The Civil War Letters of General Alpheus S. Williams.* Milo M. Quaife, ed. Detroit: Wayne State University Press, 1959.

Wills, Garry. *Lincoln at Gettysburg: The Words that Remade America.* New York: Simon & Schuster, 1992.

Winchel, Terrence J. "Heavy Was Their Loss: Joe Davis's Brigade at Gettysburg," *Gettysburg Magazine,* 2 (1990), 5–14.

Wittenberg, Eric J. "An Analysis of the Buford Manuscripts," *Gettysburg Magazine,* 15 (1996), 7–23.

Wittenberg, Eric J. "John Buford and the Gettysburg Campaign," *Gettysburg Magazine,* 11 (1994), 19–55.

Index

Abbott, Capt. Henry L., 21, 314, 409, 413, 441, 454, 485, 505

Adams County, 154

Adams, Capt. Charles Francis, Jr., 98, 128, 508

Aiken, Col. David W., 284, 499

Alabama, infantry: 3rd, 197; 4th, 268, 271, 278, 295; 5th, 197; 6th, 198; 12th, 198; 13th, 162, 170–71, 174, 417; 15th, 271, 278–79, 294, 296; 26th, 198; 44th, 271, 273; 47th, 271, 278, 294; 48th, 271, 273, 292, 294; 5th Battalion, 417, 433

Aldie Gap, 97, 98, 104

Aldie, Va., 97, 101; battle of, 97–98, 99, 118

Alexander, Col. Edward Porter, 58, 59, 106, 136, 138, 233, 237; July 2, 257, 258–59, 265–67, 298, 305, 319, 347, 353–54; July 3, 360, 377–82, 387, 389–90, 393–94, 403, 405–8, 415, 418, 440, 454, 578n13; retreat to Potomac, 479, 485–86, 490, 504–5

Alexander, Peter W., 499–500

Alexandria, Va., 85, 90

Allan, Col. William, 231

Allegheny Mountains, 84

Ames, Brig. Gen. Adelbert, 214; July 2, 331, 335, 340

Anderson, Brig. Gen. George T., 52, 498; July 2, 274–75, 285, 350

Anderson, Maj. Gen. Richard H., 43, 45, 55, 184–85, 228–29, 238; July 2, 265, 306–7, 313, 317–18, 321, 351; July 3, 392, 444

Andrews, Lt. Col. R. Snowden, 282

Angle, the, 395, 410–11, 433, 436, 441–55 *passim,* 469

Antietam (Sharpsburg), battle of, 6, 13, 17, 25, 34, 38, 45, 51, 76, 104, 123, 144, 229, 265, 346, 486

Aquia Landing, Va., 85, 90

Archer, Brig. Gen. James J., 54, 172, 498; July 1, 163, 165, 169–72, 179–80, 225, 386, 417

Arkansas, infantry: 3rd, 268, 271, 273

Armistead, Brig. Gen. Lewis A., 52, 498; July 3, 383, 405, 415–16, 425–26, 428, 444, 447, 449–52, 455, 466–67, 474

Army of Northern Virginia, 6, 7, 11, 16, 43, 84, 123–24, 183, 226; strength, 7, 13, 47, 57, 87, 95, 119, 129, 149, 499; reinforcements, 47–51, 95, 116, 354, 477; organization, 43, 45–47, 50–51; morale, 96, 107, 473; supplies, 12–13; supply requisitions, 96–97, 102–5, 107–9, 113–15, 134, 237, 470, 479–80

CORPS: First (Longstreet), 3–4, 9, 11, 13, 51–52, 94, 98, 101, 112, 116, 118, 133, 136, 141, 143, 183–84, 185, 228–29, 240, 255, 348, 350, 359–60, 490, 498; Second (Ewell), 3, 52–54, 60, 74, 94, 101, 102–3, 112, 118, 133–34, 141, 143–44, 149, 154, 155, 183–84, 185, 190, 192, 201, 211, 230–34, 236, 238, 240, 256, 282, 312, 333, 337, 347, 359–60, 380–81, 465, 470, 490, 498; Third (A. P. Hill), 45–47, 50, 54–55, 60, 74, 76, 94, 101, 102, 112, 116, 118, 133, 135–36, 141, 143, 155, 165, 166, 180, 183, 185, 190, 192, 205, 227,

CHANCELLORSVILLE

*"For scope, analysis, drama, and richness of detail,
there is no better book on the subject."* — **New York Times**

One of the most dramatic battles of the Civil War, Chancellorsville was Robert E. Lee's masterpiece. Drawing on a wealth of sources, including personal accounts, Sears has written the definitive book on the battle.

ISBN 0-395-87744-X

CONTROVERSIES AND COMMANDERS: Dispatches from the Army of the Potomac

*"There is drama and intrigue aplenty here, and Sears lays
it out with great skill."* — **Noah André Trudeau**

In this fascinating look at some of the most intriguing generals in the Union Army, Sears paints a remarkable picture of key incidents and personalities that influenced the outcome of our nation's greatest cataclysm.

ISBN 0-618-05706-4

GETTYSBURG

*"The finest and most provocative Civil War historian
writing today."* — **Chicago Tribune**

In this remarkable single-volume history of the greatest of all Civil War campaigns, every moment of the battle of Gettysburg is brought to life with vivid narrative skill and impeccable scholarship. ISBN 0-618-48538-4

LANDSCAPE TURNED RED: The Battle of Antietam

*"Authoritative and graceful . . . a first-rate work
of history."* — **Newsweek**

For his engrossing examination of the Civil War's bloodiest battle, Sears drew upon previously unpublished diaries, dispatches, and letters as well as a survey of the recollections of thousands of veterans on both sides.

ISBN 0-618-34419-5

TO THE GATES OF RICHMOND: The Peninsula Campaign

"Military history at its best." — **New York Times Book Review**

To the Gates of Richmond charts General George McClellan's grand scheme of 1862 to march up the Virginia peninsula and take the Confederate capital. The book vividly recounts one of the bloodiest battles of the Civil War.

ISBN 0-618-12713-5